ORTHO'S
HOME
IMPROVEMENT
ENCYCLOPEDIA

Meredith® Books
Des Moines, Iowa

Ortho® Books
An imprint of Meredith® Books

Home Improvement Encyclopedia
Editor: Larry Erickson
Writer: Charles G. Wing
Art Director: Tom Wegner
Contributing Designers: Mary Bendgen, Jeff Harrison
Copy Chief: Catherine Hamrick
Copy and Production Editor: Terri Fredrickson
Contributing Copy Editors: Martin Miller, John Riha
Technical Proofreaders: Raymond L. Kast, Ralph Selzer
Contributing Proofreaders: Mary Pas, Debra Morris Smith
Indexer: Donald Glassman
Electronic Production Coordinator: Paula Forest
Editorial and Design Assistants: Kathleen Stevens,
   Karen Schirm
Contributing Editorial Assistants: Colleen Johnson,
   Mary Irene Swartz
Production Director: Douglas M. Johnston
Book Production Managers: Pam Kvitne,
   Marjorie J. Schenkelberg

**Additional Editorial Contributions from
Art Rep Services**
Director: Chip Nadeau
Illustrator: Dave Brandon

Cover photographs: John Holtorf

Meredith® Books
Editor in Chief: James D. Blume
Design Director: Matt Strelecki
Managing Editor: Gregory H. Kayko

Director, Sales & Marketing, Retail: Michael A. Peterson
Director, Sales & Marketing, Special Markets:
   Rita McMullen
Director, Sales & Marketing, Home & Garden Center
   Channel: Ray Wolf
Director, Operations: George A. Susral

Vice President, General Manager: Jamie L. Martin

Meredith Publishing Group
President, Publishing Group: Christopher M. Little
Vice President, Consumer Marketing & Development:
   Hal Oringer

Meredith Corporation
Chairman and Chief Executive Officer: William T. Kerr

Chairman of the Executive Committee: E.T. Meredith III

Thanks to
Jeff Abugel, Janet Anderson, Steve Hallam, Doug Kouma,
   Barbara Stokes

All of us at Ortho® Books are dedicated to providing you
with the information and ideas you need to enhance your
home and garden. We welcome your comments and
suggestions about this book. Write to us at:
   Meredith Corporation
   Ortho Books
   1716 Locust St.
   Des Moines, IA 50309–3023

If you would like more information on other Ortho
products, call 800-225-2883 or visit us at www.ortho.com

Note to the Readers: Due to differing conditions, tools,
and individual skills, Meredith Corporation assumes no
responsibility for any damages, injuries suffered, or losses
incurred as a result of following the information published
in this book. Before beginning any project, review the
instructions carefully, and if any doubts or questions remain,
consult local experts or authorities. Because codes and
regulations vary greatly, you always should check with
authorities to ensure that your project complies with all
applicable local codes and regulations. Always read and
observe all of the safety precautions provided by
manufacturers of any tools, equipment, or supplies,
and follow all accepted safety procedures.

CONTENTS

ACCESS

AVOIDING OBSTACLES

ALSO SEE...
Bathroom Design:
Pages 22–23
Doors:
Pages 86–97
Kitchen Design:
Pages 208–211

Making homes safe and accessible for people with disabilities and for older people is an important consideration when building, adding on, or remodeling a home. According to the National Organization on Disabilities, more than 50 million Americans are disabled. And, with the rising life expectancy and the increasing cost of nursing home care, more and more Americans are choosing to remain in their homes.

When you're building or remodeling, the extra costs associated with making things accessible typically range from zero to just a few percent. If a small amount spent for wider doorways and levered door handles will allow you to remain in your home for a few extra years, it might prove to be the best retirement investment you ever made.

As a result of the Americans with Disabilities Act (ADA) of 1990, public facilities, such as hotels and restaurants, are required to follow federal accessibility guidelines. This requirement has created a large market for accessible hardware and fixtures. Numerous manufacturers recognize this market, and as a result, finding accessible hardware in home centers is easy. Follow the guidelines shown here to make your home accessible.

FLOOR LEVEL CHANGES

The basic rooms of a house (kitchen, eating area, laundry, living room, bedroom, and full-size bath) should be grouped together on one floor—preferably the one closest to ground level. Avoid abrupt changes in floor levels. Here are some guidelines for fixing sudden shifts in floor height.

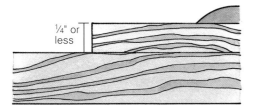

Abrupt changes in floor level must be less than ¼ inch. Modify larger changes by adding a solid piece of beveled flooring.

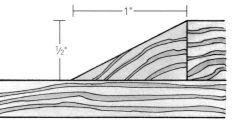

Beveled changes in floor level of less than ½ inch must have a slope of less than 1:2. Here a ½-inch change is spread over a 1-inch distance.

REACH LIMITS

Locate shelves, drawers, electrical switches, and outlets within easy reach of a person in a wheelchair.

A reach forward from a wheelchair should exceed 48 inches in height.

CLEARANCE AND TURNING

Make passageways a minimum 36 inches wide. You can get by with a 32-inch width, but for no more than 2 feet.

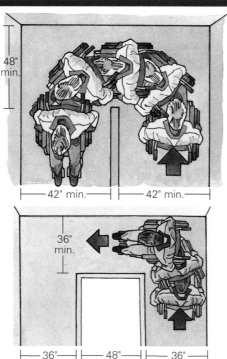

For U-turns around obstacles less than 48 inches wide, make the approaches 42 inches wide and the turning area 48 inches deep.

For U-turns around obstacles wider than 48 inches, make the approaches and the turns a minimum of 36 inches.

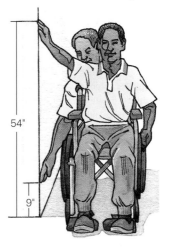

The vertical reach from the side of a wheelchair should extend from 9 to 54 inches.

The standard height for a kitchen countertop is 36 inches, assuming the base cabinet is 34½ inches high and the countertop is 1½ inches thick. To create a more accessible cabinet height, here are three solutions:

■ Install bathroom vanity cabinets in the kitchen. They are typically 29½ to 32 inches high.

■ Order custom cabinets in a height of your choice. Keep in mind, however, that dishwashers require 34 inches under the counter.

■ Install conventional cabinets, but add a vanity-based work center and cooktop.

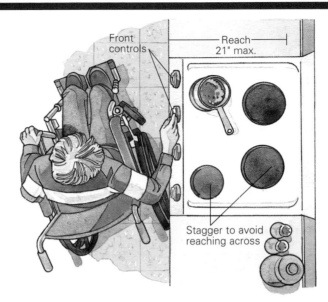

A kitchen range or cooktop should have burner controls located on the front face of the appliance. Burners should be staggered to eliminate the danger of reaching across them.

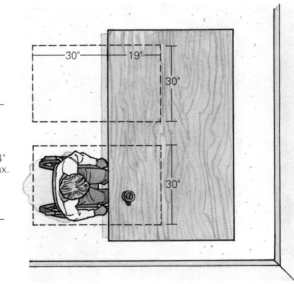

ADA requirements specify a maximum counter height of 34 inches and a clear undercounter space 36 inches wide and 27 inches high. Maximum reach to faucet controls must not exceed 21 inches.

An accessible table will have clear floor space at least 30 inches wide and 48 inches deep.

Knee space under the table must be at least 27 inches high and 19 inches deep. The tabletop or countertop should be no more than 28–34 inches above the floor.

CHOOSING FLOORING

Wheelchairs turn and maneuver more easily on hard, smooth flooring surfaces than on soft, cushioned ones. Wood strip, laminate plank, and vinyl are best. Avoid embossed vinyls and large ceramic tiles with wide grout lines. Tall-pile carpeting with thick foam pads are nice for walking, but can impede wheelchair progress. For carpet, try tough commercial varieties with short naps, and keep foam backing pads to a minimum thickness.

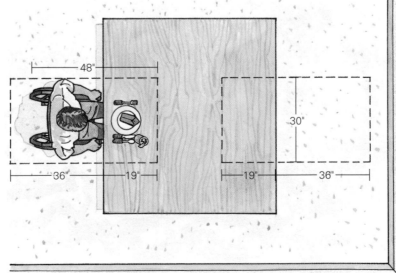

Provide space of at least 36 inches between tables and walls.

BATHS

The standard toilet seat is typically placed 15 inches above the floor, but accessible toilet seats must be at a height of 17 to 19 inches. Most people, particularly children, will find this taller height awkward and uncomfortable. Accessible-height toilets also are much more expensive than their common cousins. To solve both problems, install a regular toilet and add an inexpensive booster seat which can be used when necessary.

Grab bars of various widths are readily available at home centers.

TUB AND SHOWER FLOOR SPACE

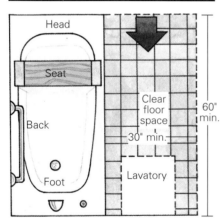

Next to the tub, provide clear floor space at least 30 inches wide and 60 inches long.

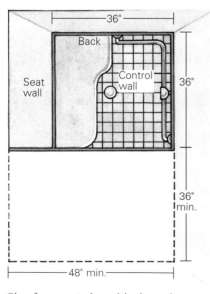

Clear floor space in front of the shower door must be at least 48 inches wide and 36 inches deep.

TOILETS

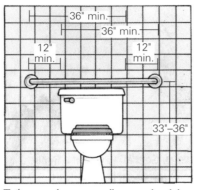

Toilets must have rear-wall-mounted grab bars 33–36 inches above the floor extending at least 12 inches on either side of the tank.

Toilets must have a side-wall-mounted grab bar 33–36 inches above the floor extending 12–54 inches from the wall behind the toilet.

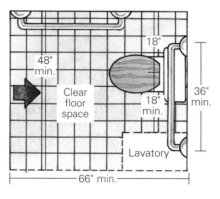

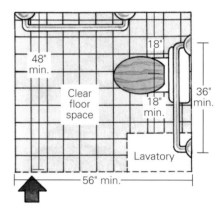

Toilets approached from the front must have a clear floor space at least 48 inches wide and 66 inches deep, including an 18-inch clear space from each side of the toilet's center line.

Toilets approached from the side must have a clear floor space at least 48 inches wide and 56 inches deep, including an 18-inch clear space from each side of the toilet's center line.

TUBS

A tub with a portable seat must have four grab bars 33–36 inches above the floor: one 24 inches long on the control wall, a 12-inch bar on the opposite wall, a side bar 24 inches long, and one 9 inches above the rim of the tub.

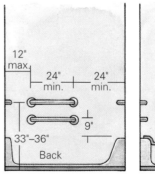

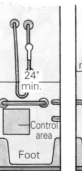

Seat wall

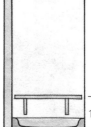

Back

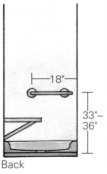

Control wall

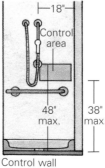

SHOWERS

A shower with a seat must have at least two grab bars, 33–36 inches above the floor—an 18-inch bar to the side and a full-width bar on the control wall. Controls must be 38–48 inches above the floor.

DOORS AND DOORWAYS

Wheelchairs and walkers generally require doorway widths of at least 32 inches, but a 36-inch width is more convenient. Since 36-inch doors cost little more than 32-inch doors, install 36-inch doors in new construction.

For people with limited mobility, lever-type door handles are much easier to operate than knobs. Levers are stylish and cost little more than knobs.

When doors are opened fully, the opening must be at least 32 inches wide. (Because of stops and hinges, a 32-inch door will generally have a clear opening of less than 32 inches.) Door handles must be operable with one hand with a force of less than 5 pounds and must not require tight grasping, pinching, or twisting of the wrist.

Doors in series must allow a 48-inch clearance with either or both doors open or closed.

DOORS IN SERIES—SAME SWING

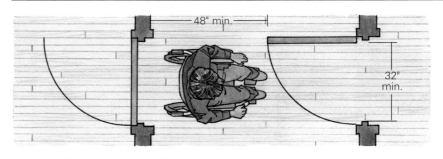

DOORS IN SERIES—OPPOSITE SWING

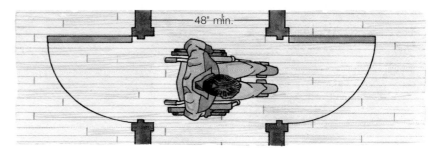

FRONT APPROACHES

Doors opening toward a frontal approach require spaces of 60 inches to the front and 18 inches to the side.

Doors opening away from a frontal approach require spaces of 48 inches to the front and 12 inches to the side if the door has both closer and latch.

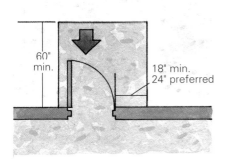

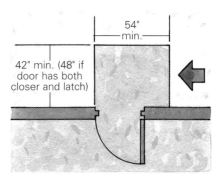

HINGE-SIDE APPROACHES

Doors approached from their hinge sides and opening toward the approach require a space in front of the doorway either 36 inches wide and 60 inches deep, or 42 inches wide and 54 inches deep.

Doors approached from their hinge sides and opening away from the approach require a space in front of the doorway 42 inches deep and 54 inches wide. A door with both closer and latch needs a depth of 48 inches.

LATCH-SIDE APPROACHES

Doors approached from their latch sides and opening toward the approach require spaces beside the doorway 24 inches wide and 48 inches deep. A door with both closer and latch needs a depth of 54 inches.

Doors approached from their latch sides and opening away from the approach require spaces beside the doorway 24 inches wide and 42 inches deep. A door with both closer and latch needs a depth of 48 inches.

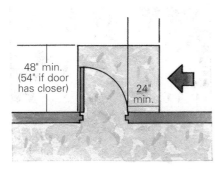

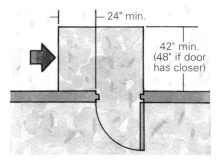

ADHESIVES

NO LONGER STUCK WITH THE SAME OLD GLUES

ALSO SEE...
Fasteners:
Pages 122–125
Tools:
Pages 374–383

An adhesive is any substance that bonds one thing to another. Although some adhesives are very versatile, no adhesive will work equally well in every situation. Consult the Adhesives Guide (below) to find the one that will bond best in your application.

■ **Construction adhesives** come in tubes and require a caulking gun for application. Use them to bond panels, tiles, wallboard, and flooring material. On walls and subfloors, they increase strength, reduce the number of fasteners needed, and deaden sound transmission. Typically, they are waterproof.

■ **Contact cement** bonds instantly and resists water and heat. It is widely used to apply plastic laminates to countertops. Apply the cement to both surfaces and let it dry; then press the surfaces together. Once the surfaces touch, there is no separating them, so you'll have no margin for error in alignment.

■ **Cyanoacrylates,** also known as "super" glues, are expensive, but only a drop or two bonds most plastics, ceramics, and metals. The fit of the pieces must be exact, however, because these glues will not bridge gaps. They clean up with acetone. Use caution: Cyanoacrylate glues bond very well to skin.

■ **Epoxy** consists of a resin and a hardener, each supplied in separate containers and mixed just before you're ready to use the glue. Epoxies generate heat and can make bonds with almost any material, even underwater. Often the bond is stronger than the joined materials. Epoxies resist heat, corrosion, shrinkage, and creep, but their bond to wood can deteriorate in water, because the wood deteriorates, not the adhesive.

■ **Glass and plastic cements** are limited to the repair of small glass, ceramic, metal, and plastic items and the assembly of craft items. They are waterproof and come in small, inexpensive quantities.

■ **Hot-melt glues** require an electric "gun" to melt solid glue sticks. Many have specialized uses. Hot glues have only moderate strength, and are used chiefly for their convenience in craft work. Their principal advantage is fast adhesion and a short bonding time, typically a minute or less.

ADHESIVES GUIDE

Adhesive	Strength	Water Resistance	Set Time	Cleanup	Uses
Construction adhesive	Medium	High	8 hours	Mineral spirits	Fastening paneling to studs, subfloor to joists, any sheet material to framing
Contact cement	Medium	High	1 hour	Acetone	Bonding plastic laminates to plywood, particleboard, etc.
Cyanoacrylate glue (Super/Krazy Glue)	High	High	Instant	Acetone	Any close-fitting materials; won't bridge gaps
Epoxy (two-part)	High	High	1–24 hours	Acetone	All materials; particularly good at filling and bridging gaps
Glass cement	High	Medium	30 minutes	Acetone	Repairing glass and ceramic china and crafts
Hot-melt glue	Varies	Medium	1 minute	Acetone	Wood, plastics, glass
Plastic cement (airplane cement)	High	Medium	30 minutes	Acetone	Assembling and repairing metal and plastic toys, jewelry, crafts
Polyurethane glue	High	High	8 hours	Acetone	All materials; particularly good at filling and bridging gaps
Resorcinol resin (mixed with water)	High	High	24 hours	Water	Wood, where moisture resistance is required
Silicone (also used as caulk)	Medium	High	8 hours	Nothing	Most materials; bridges gaps well
White glue	Medium	Low	30 minutes	Water	Interior craft projects; wood, paper, fabrics
Yellow glue (carpenter's glue)	Medium	Medium	30 minutes	Water	Interior wood projects; hard/soft woods, veneers, particleboard

TYPES OF CLAMPS

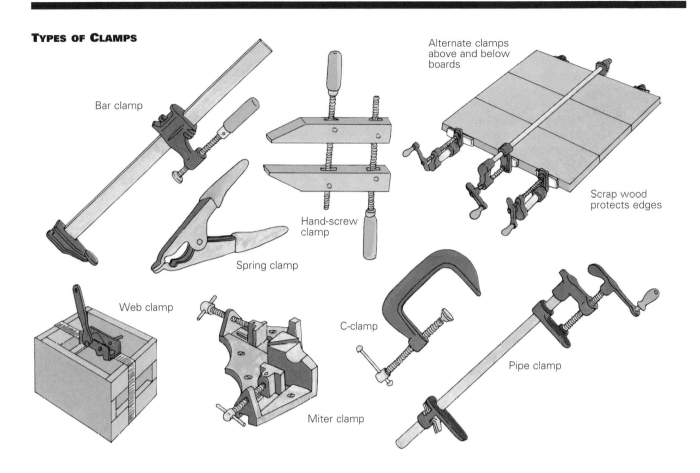

Bar clamp

Alternate clamps above and below boards

Hand-screw clamp

Spring clamp

Scrap wood protects edges

Web clamp

C-clamp

Miter clamp

Pipe clamp

■ **Polyurethane glue** has many of the properties of epoxy, but doesn't require mixing. It bonds nearly all materials, and because it expands slightly when curing, it is excellent for bridging gaps.

■ **Resorcinol,** a powdered glue you mix with water before each use, is strong and waterproof. Use it to bond wood when you want especially strong joints. The temperature must be at least 70°F, the wood must be dry, and the glue must be used within a few hours of mixing. Pressure, such as clamping, is mandatory for creating good bonds.

■ **White and yellow glues** (polyvinyl acetates) are the widely used, water-based glues that derive their names from their colors. Polyvinyl-acetate glues are inexpensive and widely available, but the white varieties are suitable for interior use only. Yellow glue (also known as carpenter's glue) has greater strength than white glue, and some manufacturers make yellow glues that are moisture resistant. However, both white and yellow glues soften above 110°F and allow creep (movement in a glued joint), so they are not considered structural adhesives.

TIPS FOR GLUING WOOD

■ Make sure the surfaces to be bonded are both dry and clean (no powdery or flaky residue of dirt, paint, or old glue).

■ Read the manufacturer's instructions carefully. Pay particular attention to the recommended temperatures and pressures to be applied.

■ Strong bonds require thin—not thick—layers of adhesive. Greater pressure is required to squeeze out the excess of a thick adhesive than of a thin, runny adhesive. Also, pressure is a measure of the amount of force applied to a unit of area, so large areas require proportionally greater force than small ones.

■ Rubber bands may exert enough pressure on small items, but use appropriate clamps for larger items.

■ Use scrap wood on both jaws of a clamp to distribute the pressure evenly and to prevent marring the workpiece. When gluing long pieces, such as a those in a tabletop, use at least three bar or pipe clamps. Clamp the ends across the top and in the middle under the workpiece in order to prevent buckling.

SEALING FOR REUSE

How many times have you discarded adhesive because you've misplaced the cap? Discard no longer. Simply insert a nail or wood wedge of the same thickness as the nozzle. The nail or wedge will usually seal the contents against the two most common curing agents, air and moisture—for a few months at least. When withdrawn, the "stopper" will create a fresh path for the remaining adhesive.

ASPHALT SHINGLE ROOFING

PREPARATION

ALSO SEE...
Flashing:
Pages 136–139
Roofs:
Pages 282–289

Asphalt shingles have little strength, so they must be supported by underlying roof sheathing that is solid and smooth. If there is any rot in the sheathing, replace it. Cover knotholes and wide cracks with sheet metal fastened with roofing nails. Nail a metal drip edge along the bottom eave, and starting at the bottom, cover the roof with 15-pound felt. Lap the edges about 2 inches (the felt is marked with a white line as a guide) if the roof slopes 3 inches or more each foot. If the slope is less than 3 in 12, overlap each course 19 inches.

Try to keep the white printed lines parallel to the edge of the roof so you can use them later to align the shingles.

YOU'LL NEED:

Ladder, tape measure, chalk line, utility knife, hammer, roofing nails, roof brackets and planks (if the roof is steep), shingle-ripping shovel or flat bar (if the old roof is to be removed).

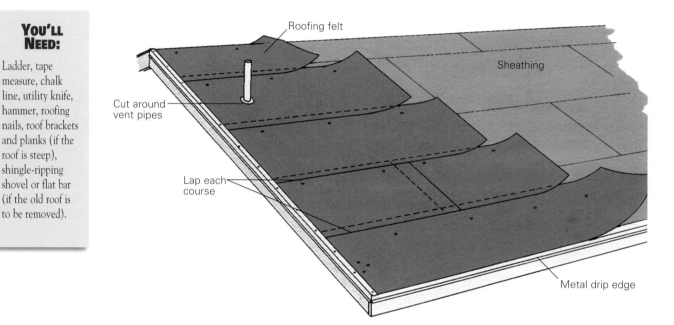

Roofing felt

Sheathing

Cut around vent pipes

Lap each course

Metal drip edge

THE FIRST COURSE

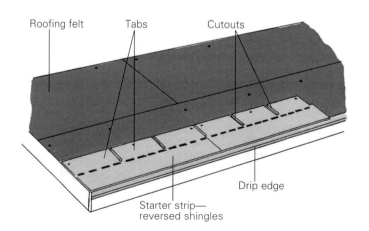

Roofing felt   Tabs   Cutouts

Drip edge

Starter strip—reversed shingles

The first or starter course is actually a double layer of roofing installed at the bottom edge (the eave) of the roof. Begin at the eave, using either starter-strip material or regular shingles turned upside down. Snap a chalk line along the length of the roof to keep the top edges perfectly straight.

ROOFTOP DELIVERY

Purchase your shingles from a supplier who has the equipment to deliver the shingles onto the roof.

Make sure the roof preparation is completed well before the delivery truck arrives. Definitely have a helper or two on hand at the time of delivery to distribute the shingle bundles along the length of the roof peak. The truck operator can't help because he will be busy on the loading end or operating the lift controls.

The starter course should overhang the drip edge by ⅜ inch. Apply the first course of shingles (tabs down) directly on top of the starter strip. Offset the first course so its ends do not line up directly on the ends of the starter strip.

Fasten each shingle with four nails or staples, each about one inch above the tab cutouts. Be sure to use 1¼-inch-long fasteners that penetrate completely into the roof sheathing below.
Important: Leave a slight gap between shingles so that they won't buckle in the heat.

PICKING YOUR PATTERN

The cutouts between shingle tabs create a strong pattern on the roof. Pick your shingle pattern before you start laying them. On 3-tab shingles each tab is 12 inches wide; if staggered evenly, the cutouts on each course would be offset by 6 inches. This "6-inch pattern" is the easiest to install but is the most demanding because it establishes strong vertical lines.

A 4-inch pattern creates diagonals. It wears better than the 6-inch pattern and is recommended for slopes less than 4 in 12. The most random-appearing pattern is 5 inch, which many professionals use. Save the cut-off ends for finishing courses.

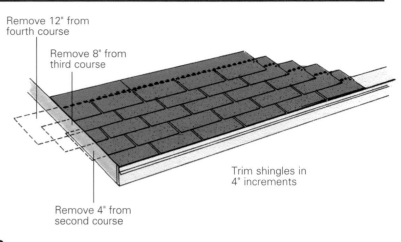

Remove 12" from fourth course

Remove 8" from third course

Trim shingles in 4" increments

Remove 4" from second course

APPLYING REMAINING COURSES

Always start a new course by cutting off new shingles; never use scraps. Work from the edge of the roof toward the center as far as you can reach, then start the next course without changing your position. Start as many courses as you can reach, then move over and repeat the process.

The exposure for composition shingles (the amount of each course that shows) is determined by the depth of the cutouts (nominally 5 inches). Keep the courses parallel by aligning the top edges with the white lines on the felt. If the felt is crooked, measure up from the eave at several points along the course you are applying and snap chalk lines, repeating the process every fourth or fifth course.

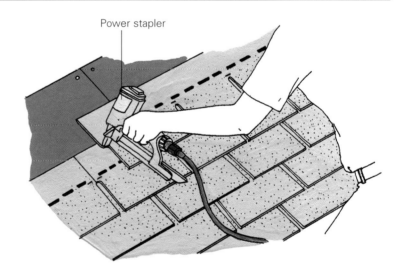

Power stapler

OPEN AND CLOSED VALLEYS

Shingled roof sections meet in open or closed valleys. Open valleys create a seam at the edges of the shingles along the length of the valley. A closed valley weaves shingles so there is no seam.

To create an open valley, coat the valley with roofing cement, then lay a half width (18 inches) of roll roofing, mineral-side down, into the valley. Nail one edge every 12 inches, press the roofing into the valley, and nail the opposite edge. Repeat the process with 36-inch roll roofing. Install all shingle courses to within 3 inches of the center of the valley, but do not nail the shingles within 6 inches of the valley.

Finally, shingle the valley. Begin at the bottom, and bond the shingle ends to each other and to the roll roofing with roofing cement.

To create a closed valley, flash the valley with a full-width sheet of roll roofing. Weave shingles of alternating courses so they cross over the valley and extend at least 1 foot up the opposite side. Don't nail within 6 inches of the valley center.

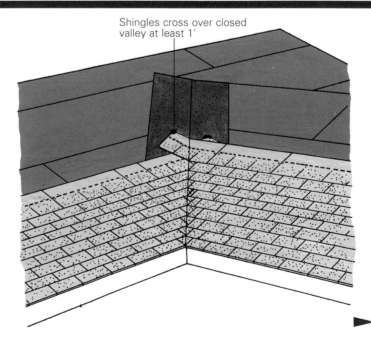

Shingles cross over closed valley at least 1'

SHINGLING A DORMER

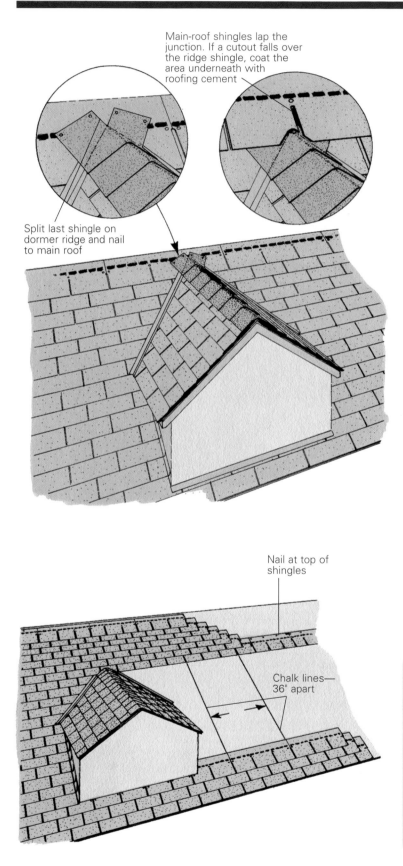

Main-roof shingles lap the junction. If a cutout falls over the ridge shingle, coat the area underneath with roofing cement

Split last shingle on dormer ridge and nail to main roof

Nail at top of shingles

Chalk lines— 36" apart

Shingle a dormer roof exactly as you would the main roof. Treat the intersections between the main and dormer roofs as either open valleys or closed valleys, as described on the previous pages. Make sure the courses on both roofs align with each other.

Apply ridge shingles to the dormer before nailing the main roof course that intersects with the dormer ridge. Begin at the outer end of the dormer and work toward the main roof. When you reach the main roof, split the last ridge shingle and carry it at least 4 inches onto the main roof.

How do you assure that the courses on either side of the dormer match when they join again above the dormer? As you shingle the roof toward the main ridge, extend the courses toward the dormer. Carry the courses below the dormer from one side to the other. When you reach the dormer roof, shingle it, then bring the main roof shingles over to it and complete the left valley.

Carry the course immediately in line with the top of the dormer roof at least 10 feet beyond the right side of the dormer roof. Nail only the tops of these shingles so you can later nail the course that comes up the other side and slips under this course.

Continue roofing above this line to the ridge. Now, using corresponding cutouts between the tabs of courses above and below the dormer as guides, snap a chalk line from the ridge back down to the eave near the right edge of the dormer. Snap a second line 3 feet further to the right, and so on. Then complete the shingling, sliding the last course under the tabs of the top course.

As you complete each course at the dormer, install step flashing (see Flashing, pages 136–139) along the side. Also, snap horizontal chalk lines on the right side of the dormer to keep the vertical spacing in line.

SAVE TIME: SAVE LABELS

Will you remember the manufacturer and exact name of the shingle color if you need to repair or extend your roof? Probably not. So do what smart roofers do—tuck the package label under either the first or last ridge shingle before nailing it down. Better yet, place it in your home management files for future reference.

Another foolproof method is to save scraps and leftover whole shingles along with a package label. That way, you'll have pieces for repairs and a record of the product you used.

Cut enough shingles into thirds (at their tabs) to cover the length of the hip, allowing 5 inches of exposure. Nail the bottom tab permanently and trim it to fit the eaves. Using another tab as a top guide, snap chalk lines on both sides of the hip to keep the hip shingles in line.

Nail each hip shingle 1 inch from its edges just below the adhesive strip. If two hips are joining at the top, trim the top hip shingles to meet neatly.

Finally, slit the first (or last) ridge shingle 4 inches, fold the split ends over each other, and fasten with a single long roofing nail.

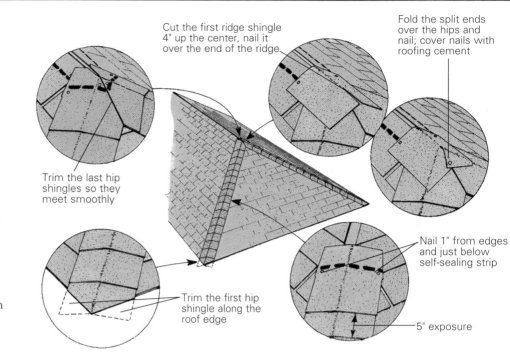

Cut the first ridge shingle 4" up the center, nail it over the end of the ridge

Fold the split ends over the hips and nail; cover nails with roofing cement

Trim the last hip shingles so they meet smoothly

Nail 1" from edges and just below self-sealing strip

Trim the first hip shingle along the roof edge

5" exposure

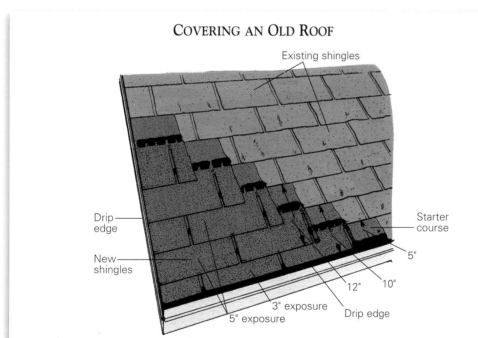

COVERING AN OLD ROOF

Existing shingles

Drip edge

New shingles

Starter course

5"

12" 10"

3" exposure

5" exposure

Drip edge

If you need a new roof and if your present roof has only a single layer of asphalt shingles, you can roof right over them. New roofing requires a sound foundation and will reveal all the bumps and dips of the underlying roof, so be sure to replace any protruding or damaged shingles, all ridge and hip shingles, and all flashing.

Begin by installing a new flashing strip at the eave. Make a new starter course by removing the tabs from new shingles and butt the solid strips up against the second course of the old shingles. Install the first full course of new shingles, trimming the width to 10 inches if necessary so they will butt up to the third course of existing shingles. Complete the roof in the same way you would a new roof, butting each course of new shingles up to an old course.

The roofing nails or staples should penetrate the wood deck by ¾ inch. Roofing over an existing asphalt shingle roof requires 1½-inch-long nails.

SPECIFY NO-CUTOUT

The common three-tab asphalt shingle is manufactured as a continuous sheet. Two notches are cut into the shingle later to make it more closely resemble wood shingles.

But where do you think the roofing will fail? You guessed it—at a cutout, because there the roof has only a single layer of protection.

For maximum protection against the weather, specify no-cutout (NCO) shingles. It may require a special order and a few extra days to obtain, but NCO shingles will add years to the life of your new roof.

FINDING ROOM AT THE TOP

ALSO SEE...
Dormers:
Pages 98–101
Framing:
Pages 152–159
Skylights:
Pages 316–319
Wallboard:
Pages 392–397

Remodeling an attic can be an efficient and cost-effective way to add living space to your home. But even if the attic already has stairs and is used for storage, converting it requires careful analysis.

Before proceeding, you'll need to answer two questions: (1) Does the attic have enough space and headroom (see Code Requirements, *below*). (2) Is conversion to living space structurally possible?

Read this section and the related cross-references, then consider whether the job is economically feasible and whether you need outside help on part or all of the project.

A finished attic does not have to look like the rest of the house. In fact, the unusual architectural lines of the roof create a unique appeal. An attic has boundless practical possibilities. For example, using the space behind kneewalls for built-in storage maximizes the floor space devoted to furnishings.

If there is enough floor space but not enough headroom, add dormers. Dormers are major projects, but they bring light, ventilation, and charm along with ceiling height.

A typical attic conversion creates a triangular room defined by the existing rafters and the ceiling joists of the lower floor. Collar ties—horizontal framing members that span between rafters to help stiffen them— may be raised to gain necessary headroom. Kneewalls with storage-access doors complete the room.

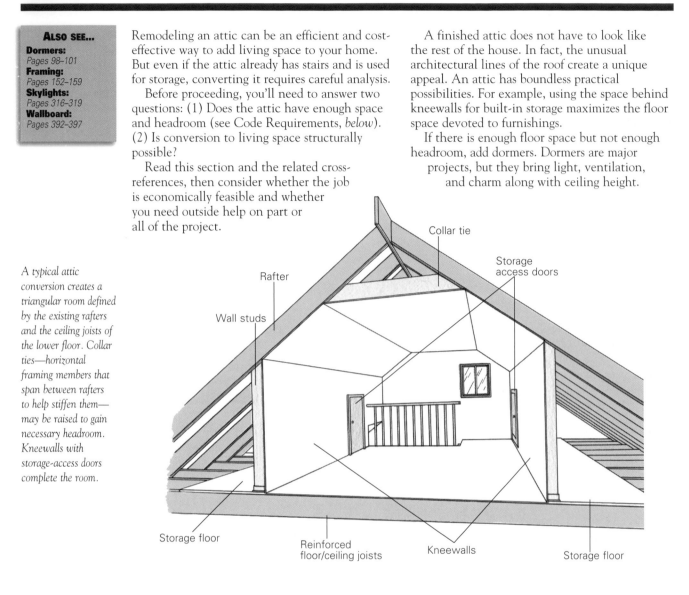

Collar tie

Storage access doors

Rafter

Wall studs

Storage floor

Reinforced floor/ceiling joists

Kneewalls

Storage floor

CODE REQUIREMENTS: HABITABLE ROOMS

A habitable room is one used for sleeping, living, cooking, or eating. Closets, hallways, utility rooms, bathrooms, laundries, and utility rooms are not subject to the requirements listed below.

Light and Ventilation: Window area in a habitable room must be at least 8 percent of the floor area. Unless mechanical ventilation is provided, 50 percent of the glazed area must be openable.

Egress: Sleeping rooms must have at least one exterior door or openable (egress) window. Egress windowsills must be no higher than

44 inches above the floor. They must have a minimum clear width of 20 inches, a minimum clear height of 22 inches, and a minimum clear opening of 5.7 square feet.

Room Size: Habitable rooms, except for kitchens, must have a floor area of at least 70 square feet (50 square feet for kitchens) and a minimum horizontal dimension of 7 feet.

Ceiling Height: Except for kitchens, habitable rooms must have ceiling heights of at least 7½ feet in 50 percent of their areas. No portion of the minimum room area may have a ceiling less than 5 feet tall.

Exception: Beams and girders spaced at least 4 feet on center may project downward as much as 6 inches. Non-habitable rooms and kitchens must have ceiling heights of 7 feet or more.

Stairs: Building codes specify stair requirements, such as minimum width and allowable angles. The requirements differ for stairs to attic storage areas and stairs serving living areas. If there are no existing stairs, allow for an opening at least 3 feet wide and 10 feet long. If stairs exist, consult with your local building code official about what changes may be necessary.

SPACE AND STRUCTURAL REQUIREMENTS

First determine whether you have to—or even want to—convert trusses to conventional rafters and joists. If you do, then determine how much ceiling height will be lost to the deeper rafters (see Span Tables, pages 326–331).

Next determine whether the existing attic floor joists are adequate. If the attic space will be used for sleeping, then the new floor live load will increase to 30 pounds per square foot (psf). If the space will be used for living, the load will increase to 40 psf. The Span Tables will give you a good idea of how strong the joists need to be. Bear in mind that as joists go up in size, the attic floor level goes up too, reducing headroom.

Now that you know the new rafter and floor joist heights, determine whether the space will meet the space and height requirements for its use. Don't forget to include the thicknesses of subfloor, finish floor, and ceiling wallboard in your calculation.

Begin by measuring how much total floor area will have the minimum ceiling height of 5 feet. Then calculate how much of the total area will have a finished-ceiling-to-finished-floor height of at least 7½ feet. If this second area accounts for more than half of the minimum-room-size requirement, you can proceed. If not, you may be able to move the kneewalls in to reduce the floor area where ceiling height is less than 7½ feet, and still exceed the minimum room size. Or, at greater cost, you can add one or more dormers.

SIDESTEPPING TRUSSES

Many houses are framed with trusses instead of rafters. Trusses are engineered to support the same roof loads, but with smaller lumber. If your attic is full of trusses, do not remove any of the truss members! In some cases, you may be able to strengthen the top and bottom members of the trusses and remove the intermediate truss members. However, you should consult an architect or registered engineer for advice before attempting to modify trusses.

INSTALLING FLOOR JOISTS

When the floor joists are inadequate, there are two simple solutions:
■ If the existing joists are 2×4s or 2×6s, you can leave the old joists in place, and install a new set of independent floor joists.
■ If the existing joists are 2×8s or larger, you can sister them (reinforce them by nailing the same size stock to the existing joists).

INDEPENDENT JOISTS

Installing an independent set of joists yields an additional benefit—increased sound isolation between floors. Space the new joists evenly between the old ones. Raise the new joists 1½ inches with wood blocks nailed to the top plates of the walls. For added insulation from unwanted sound, cut fiberglass batts to fit between the joists.

Toenail the new joists into the blocks with three 16-penny (16d) nails at each end. For long spans, lap two joists over the top plate of the center bearing wall and nail them together and to the cap plate with 16d nails. Or butt the ends together, sandwiching both sides with 2-foot lengths of ½-inch plywood.

If you plan to build partition walls in the attic, double the joists under them. Separate the doubled joists by 3½ inches if you plan to run plumbing or wiring into the new wall from below.

SISTER JOISTS

The simplest way to beef up the floor support is to nail reinforcing joists to the sides of the existing ceiling joists. The new joists rest on the same wall plates as the old joists. You will probably have to trim the joist ends to fit under the sloping roof sheathing. First remove any insulation between the old joists in order to make room for the new joists.

Toenail the ends of the new joists into the top plates below. If tight space limits your ability to swing a hammer, either drill starter holes or use a nail gun. When nailing the old and new joists together, stagger 16d nails every 12 inches. To ensure a tight fit, clamp the joists together as you nail.

If the ceiling below is lath and plaster, and you are concerned about damage to the plaster, use either a nail gun or a variable-speed drill with Phillips- or square-head screws.

If obstructions, such as wires running through the old joists, prevent you from setting the new joists directly on the cap plates, install blocks on the cap plates to elevate the new joists. These blocks can be made out of short lengths of 1×4 or 2×4.

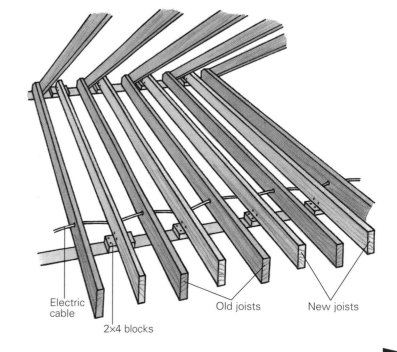

Electric cable

2×4 blocks

Old joists

New joists

INSTALLING A SUBFLOOR

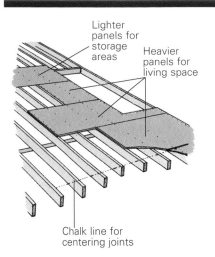

Lighter panels for storage areas

Heavier panels for living space

Chalk line for centering joists

INSTALLING CEILING JOISTS

If your joists and rafters meet load requirements specified by local building codes, you are ready to begin framing the interior. Choose a vaulted cathedral ceiling or a flat ceiling.

VAULTED CEILING

If you plan a cathedral ceiling, the rafters are the only framing you need. Any collar ties—the horizontal framing members that span the rafters near the roof peak—can be left in place as long as they are at least 4 feet on center and, when surfaced, will leave at least 7½ feet above the finished floor. If they are too low, raise them one at a time. If you plan to build kneewalls, you may be able to remove the collar ties entirely. (Check with your local building department.)

FLAT CEILING

If you plan a flat overhead ceiling, the distance from finished floor to finished ceiling must be at least 7½ feet. Allowing 3 inches for flooring and ceiling thickness, measure up from the floor joists 7 feet 9 inches and mark the rafters (that's where you'll fasten the bottom of your ceiling joists).

Consult the Span Tables, pages 326–331, to find the required joist size. Trim the ends of the joists at the angle of the roof to maximize the nailing surface. Position the new joists on the rafters and nail them with three 16d nails.

After the rough in is done and new wiring and plumbing are inspected, it is time to install the subfloor.

If you plan to use the space behind the kneewalls for storage, cover the joists with ½-inch plywood, or with ⅝-inch oriented strand board (OSB), the least expensive structural sheathing that will do the job. If the space will not be used, leave the joists uncovered.

In the living area use ¾-inch tongue-and-groove underlayment-rated plywood or OSB. Lay the sheets perpendicular to the joists, staggering the joints every 4 feet. Leave ¹⁄₁₆- to ⅛-inch gaps between sheets. To eliminate floor squeaks, apply construction adhesive to the joists as well as to the panel tongues before nailing them. Use 8d nails spaced every 6 inches around the panel perimeters and every 10 inches within the panels.

INSTALLING KNEEWALLS

If your local code allows it, install 4-foot kneewalls (4 feet allows you to use full panels of 4× wallboard). If building a 5-foot kneewall, use 4×10 wallboard panels cut in half.

A 4-foot kneewall is especially easy to lay out. The distance from the floor to the rafter should be 4 feet 2 inches to allow enough room for the ceiling wallboard and a finished floor.

Holding the level in a vertical position on a 2×4 shim, mark the room-facing side of the kneewall on the subfloor and rafter at each end of the kneewall. Snap chalk lines between the pairs of marks.

While the line is on the rafters, check for any that are out of plane more than ¼ inch. Low rafters will be jacked up by the kneewall, but high ones will need to be shimmed down before installation of the wallboard.

Cut two 2×4 plates the length of the wall and lay them doubled along the eave side of the layout line. Mark the center of an 8-foot stud (10-foot stud for a 5-foot kneewall) and make a diagonal cut at the angle of the roof slope.

Stand one stud on the doubled plates and align its inside edge with the upper chalk mark. Trace where the bottom of the rafter crosses the stud and cut the stud. Use this first stud as a template to mark the rest.

Assemble the kneewalls on the floor with one plate at the bottom of the studs and the second plate at the top. The studs need not align with the rafters, but keep them either 16 or 24 inches on center so the wallboard joints will rest on studs.

Tilt the kneewalls into place. Check for plumb with a level, and shim as required. Nail the soleplate into the floor joists and the top plate into the rafters with 16d nails.

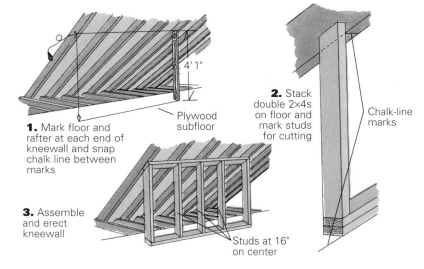

1. Mark floor and rafter at each end of kneewall and snap chalk line between marks

4' 1"

Plywood subfloor

3. Assemble and erect kneewall

Studs at 16" on center

2. Stack double 2×4s on floor and mark studs for cutting

Chalk-line marks

INSTALLING WALLS

Framing other walls is simplest when the wall falls directly under an existing rafter or ceiling joist. Drop a plumb line from that ceiling joist and mark the location of the wall on the subfloor. If, on the other hand, the wall falls between two rafters or joists, nail blocking between them and drop the plumb line from the desired spot on the blocking.

Next, cut a soleplate to fit between the two kneewalls and nail it in place at the location of the wall.

If there is to be a horizontal top plate, nail it to the ceiling joist or blocking between joists. Sloping top plates are nailed directly into rafters or to blocking installed between rafters.

Mark the stud locations every 16 inches on center along the soleplate. Holding a 4-foot level and the stud together with one hand, place the end of the stud on its mark on the soleplate, true it up with the level, and mark where it crosses the top plate. Cut the stud to length and nail it in place.

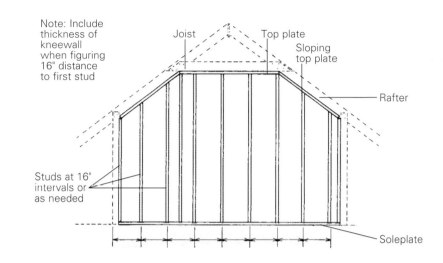

Note: Include thickness of kneewall when figuring 16" distance to first stud

Joist

Top plate

Sloping top plate

Rafter

Studs at 16" intervals or as needed

Soleplate

HEATING AND COOLING ATTIC ROOMS

One of the best ways to heat attic rooms is with supplemental heaters such as electric baseboard units or small gas heaters. Size your heater to the square footage of your attic room. Gas heaters should be vented to the outside. Although the vent pipe required is usually small, about 2 to 3 inches in diameter, you'll need to factor in the cost of installing a vent. In most instances, the vent will extend up through the attic roof. This will require cutting a hole in the roof and providing flashing for the pipe.

If your home has central forced-air heating or hot-water heating, it may be possible to extend the system to include attic rooms. You can hide new ductwork in the cavities behind knee walls or behind partition walls. Consult a qualified heating and cooling specialist before extending your existing system—it may not be capable of handling the extra load.

Use as many natural cooling sources in your design as possible. Windows, openable skylights, and ceiling fans all help improve air circulation. Deciduous trees—those that lose their leaves in winter—provide cooling shade during the warmest months, yet they let in sunlight during the coldest times of the year.

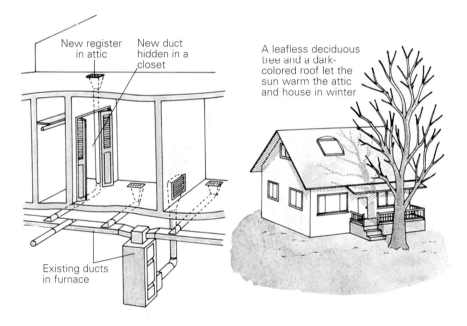

New register in attic

New duct hidden in a closet

Existing ducts in furnace

A leafless deciduous tree and a dark-colored roof let the sun warm the attic and house in winter

As with heating, you may be able to extend your existing central air-conditioning system by installing new duct work. Seek the advice of a qualified professional to make sure the system will handle the increased space. If extending the system is not feasible, add an independent, window-mounted air conditioner that uses normal household current.

It's natural for warm air to rise, making your attic rooms the warmest part of your house. While this may be fine in winter, in summer it can be a problem. You can help reverse this natural air flow by installing a vent system designed to redistribute warm air. The system uses an air intake located at the top portion of an attic wall. From there, warm air is moved by a thermostatically controlled fan to an outlet at the lowest rooms of your house.

BASEMENTS

COME ON DOWN!

With adequate height, light, and ventilation (see Code Requirements, pages 14 and 21), basements offer numerous possibilities for increased living space. They already have walls, ceiling joists, and a solid floor, and access is rarely a problem, since most basements have a legal stairway.

Beware, however, remodeling a basement can come with its own set of costly complications. Typical problems include excess moisture, rough walls and floors, insufficient ceiling height, and the necessity of rerouting an assortment of pipes and ducts. The message is: Be realistic about total costs before taking on a basement conversion, and fix moisture problems first.

ALSO SEE...
Ceilings:
Pages 52–53
Drainage
Pages 102–103
Floors:
Pages 140–141
Insulation:
Pages 186–193
Walls:
Pages 406–413

TESTING FOR MOISTURE

Concrete is far from waterproof. Water vapor passes through concrete readily without visible signs. This is not a problem unless you cover the concrete with a material that can be damaged by moisture.

To test for moisture, cut a 2-foot by 2-foot piece of clear plastic. Tape all four sides of the plastic to the concrete floors or walls with duct tape. After 24 hours you will have your answer. If there is a moisture problem, you'll see beads of water on the plastic.

The presence of moisture means you should place a vapor barrier (4-mil polyethylene sheeting) between the concrete and finish materials.

WHY IS MY BASEMENT DAMP IN SUMMER?

It is the middle of summer; there is a drought in your area; and your grass has turned brown. So why is your basement still damp?

For the same reason a cold drink "sweats" in summer, or dew forms on the grass at night. Cool air holds less water vapor than warm air. When warm summer air touches a cool object,

the air cools down, and some of its water content is forced out as liquid condensation.

Your basement—especially the floor—is cooler than the outdoor air in summer, so when outdoor air infiltrates the basement, some of its moisture content condenses on the cool surfaces.

SOLVING MOISTURE PROBLEMS

First analyze the problem. Is the basement merely damp and musty during the summer, does water appear during periods of heavy rain, or is there standing water for days at a time during the wet season?

DRYING A MUSTY BASEMENT

A damp summer basement means moisture-laden air is condensing on the walls and floor. A portable dehumidifier will remove excess moisture. Empty the collecting pan regularly for peak efficiency.

There are two permanent solutions for damp basements: (1) Excavate the basement walls and insulate them from the outside so that the wall heats to the same temperature as the inside air. (2) Insulate basement walls on the inside, preventing inside air from touching cold surfaces. Both solutions are described in detail under Insulation, pages 186–193.

IMPROVING DRAINAGE

Poor foundation drainage accounts for an overwhelming majority of leaky basements. Begin with an outside inspection, checking gutters and downspouts for clogs and leaks. Add splash blocks or downspout extensions to carry the water 8 to 10 feet away from the foundation. Check that the

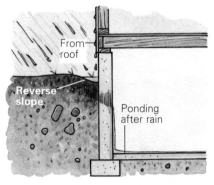

foundation grading slopes away from the house in every direction—at least ½ inch per foot for the first 3 feet. If you find spots where water accumulates, add soil to reestablish the proper slope.

Inside the basement, fill cracks and open joints with an expansive mortar, such as epoxy cement.

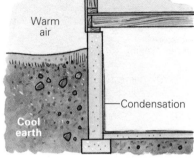

HIGH WATER TABLE

Water that appears during or immediately after a heavy rain means you have an inadequate or malfunctioning foundation drainage system—most likely a clogged perimeter footing drain (see Drainage, pages 102–103).

Long-term standing water indicates a seasonal water table that is higher than your basement floor.

Standing water due to a seasonal high water table requires either an extensive drainage system outside

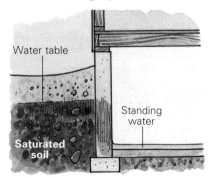

the foundation, draining to daylight or to a sewer lower than the basement floor (see Drainage, pages 102–103), or the installation of a basement sump pump (see Pumps, pages 264–265).

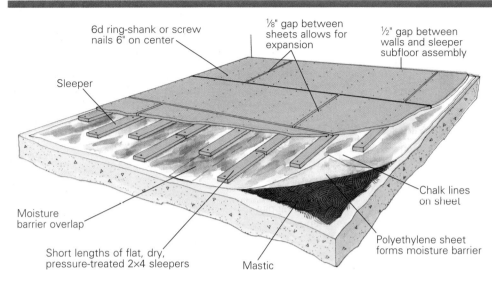

6d ring-shank or screw nails 6" on center

⅛" gap between sheets allows for expansion

½" gap between walls and sleeper subfloor assembly

Sleeper

Moisture barrier overlap

Short lengths of flat, dry, pressure-treated 2×4 sleepers

Mastic

Chalk lines on sheet

Polyethylene sheet forms moisture barrier

If the basement floor is concrete, dry, and reasonably smooth, you can install ceramic tile, carpet, and some types of resilient tile or sheet goods directly on it. First fill minor cracks and holes with patching cement and cover the entire floor with a waterproof sealer.

If the concrete is rough, uneven, sloped, or badly cracked, you'll need to take other steps:

■ Pour a leveling compound over old concrete after cleaning the surface according to the manufacturer's instructions. The compound forms a level surface that is smooth enough to use as a subfloor.

■ Replace the concrete slab with a new one to provide an opportunity to install inside drainage, insulate the slab, bury a fuel line, and solve a radon gas problem. (It also is the most expensive alternative.)

■ Install a wood subfloor.

INSTALLING A WOOD SUBFLOOR

Install a wood subfloor when the existing concrete slab is damp from condensation; when the concrete is rough, uneven, sloped, or badly cracked and you don't wish to use a leveling compound; or when you'd like to insulate the floor.

There are two basic methods for installing the subfloor.

Method 1: Vacuum the slab, scrub it with detergent and a stiff brush, rinse, and let it dry. Seal it with asphalt primer, and trowel an ⅛-inch layer of asphalt mastic on the entire surface. Lay 15-pound felt or sheets of 6-mil plastic polyethylene (poly) over the mastic, overlapping the edges by 6 inches. Press the felt or plastic into the asphalt to eliminate fishmouths (gaps) at the overlaps. Snap chalk lines every 16 inches on the poly across the width of the floor.

Next lay 4-foot lengths of pressure-treated 2×4 sleepers centered on the chalk lines. To allow for air circulation, leave about ½ inch between the ends of the sleepers and at the walls. Using a tightly-stretched string, make sure the sleepers are level with each other, and shim them with shingles if necessary. Fasten the sleepers to the slab with 8d concrete nails. If you're confident enough, rent a powder-actuated gun to drive the

nails. Wear eye and ear protection when using the gun and follow the directions carefully.

As an alternative, fasten the sleepers to the concrete with hardened screws. (They come with a masonry bit.) To use them, drill a pilot hole in the sleepers. At each hole in the moisture barrier, drill the concrete with the masonry bit and a hammer drill. Then install the hardened screws with a power screwdriver.

Apply construction adhesive to the sleepers, then nail ⅝-inch tongue-and-groove (T&G) underlayment-rated plywood over them, leaving ⅛-inch gaps between panels and a ½-inch gap at the walls. To prevent subfloor rot, cut holes along the two walls that are perpendicular to the sleepers. Size the holes for floor duct grills, and install the grills after installing the finished floor.

Method 2: Clean the floor by vacuuming, scrubbing, rinsing, and drying it. Then roll on a waterproofing sealer. After it dries, snap chalk lines 16 inches across the floor.

Along these marks, use a caulking gun to apply a construction adhesive made to bond wood to concrete. Lay lengths of pressure-treated 1×3 sleepers over the mastic lines, leaving a ½-inch gap between the ends. Fasten the sleepers by driving concrete nails or hardened screws into the floor every 24 inches.

Next, spread 6-mil polyethylene over the sleepers. Poly is available in rolls up to 40×100 feet, but interior support posts may limit the size you can use without cutting. If you have to use smaller sheets, overlap the joints 6 inches. Nail a second layer of untreated 1×3s to the sleepers below. Cover with an underlayment-rated T&G plywood subfloor, as described in Method 1.

WHAT ABOUT RADON?

Radon gas is odorless and colorless and occurs naturally in many types of soil. It is often present in negligible amounts in basements. Because it has been linked to lung cancer, high levels of radon should be considered a serious health threat. Most hardware stores or home improvement centers have do-it-yourself test kits that can give you an idea of radon levels in your basement. If your kit indicates high levels of radon, get advice from a trained technician. Look in the Yellow Pages of your telephone directory under "Radon Mitigation" or "Radon Testing."

THE WALLS

A finished wall is attractive and allows the installation of wiring, conventional wall switches, and receptacles. Support the wall with furring strips or build stud walls. Both can be insulated and finished with wallboard or paneling.

In all but the warmest climates, you should use at least R-10 of insulation. Particularly important to insulate are the high-heat-loss sections of walls above grade and the cavity along the rim joists above the mudsills.

If you are building a new home or will be excavating your existing foundation, add insulation to the outside of the foundation walls (see Insulation, pages 186–193).

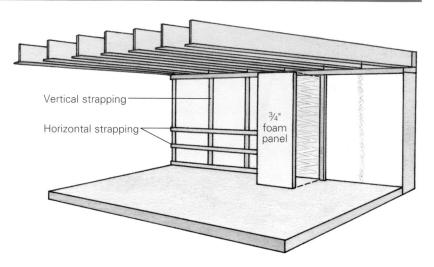

Vertical strapping
Horizontal strapping
¾" foam panel

INSTALLING FURRING STRIPS

Make sure the foundation walls are flat and plumb. Check them with a taut string and correct minor problems by putting shim stock behind the furring strips before they are attached. For walls with severe surface variations, a stud wall (described later) is more practical.

Measure the distance from the subfloor to the top of the wall. Cut pieces of 1×3 furring to this length. Starting at one end of the wall, snap vertical chalk lines every 16 or 24 inches. Apply construction adhesive along the chalk lines, press the furring strips into the adhesive, remove them for 10 minutes, then reapply. Don't install more strips than you can handle in 10 minutes. After all of the strips are installed, fill the spaces between

them (at the top and bottom) with horizontal 1×3s.

To add insulation, cut (on a table saw or with a utility knife) ¾-inch-thick closed-cell (either extruded polystyrene or urethane) foam sheets to fill the spaces between the furring. Apply the foam to the wall with construction adhesive.

To add wiring, nail a second layer of 1×3s horizontally on the first layer (spaced 16 inches on center). Shim this layer to make the wall flat. Run wiring in the spaces between the horizontal strips, protecting the cable where it crosses the vertical strips with metal plates (see Wire, pages 442–445). You can now apply the finish wall.

BUILDING INSULATED STUD WALLS

Before framing a stud wall, relocate any hot- and cold-water supply pipes that

run on the foundation wall. Pipes between the foundation wall and the new wall are likely to freeze in cold climates. If they are at least 1½ inches from the wall, you can slip insulation behind them.

Measure from the subfloor to the ceiling joists and subtract ½ inch. Build your stud wall to this length (assemble it on the subfloor). Raise the wall, plumb, and shim it tight to the joists using wood shims. Nail the plates to the joists and subfloor. If the floor is concrete, attach the sill plate with 2-inch concrete nails.

Install vapor-barrier-faced fiberglass insulation between the studs, overlapping and stapling the insulation flanges to the front of the studs. For unfaced fiberglass batts, staple a continuous 6-mil polyethylene sheet over the entire wall to hold the insulation in place.

THE FINISHED WALL

Cover the wall with wallboard or other finish material. All shutoff and drain valves, cleanout plugs, meters, and electrical junction boxes must remain accessible. Provide access panels by cutting openings in the finish material. Cover each opening with ¼-inch plywood or finish stock. Hold the cover in place over the opening and drill for expansion bolts at each corner; use wood screws if the corners are over studs. Secure the panel to the wall and paint it if necessary.

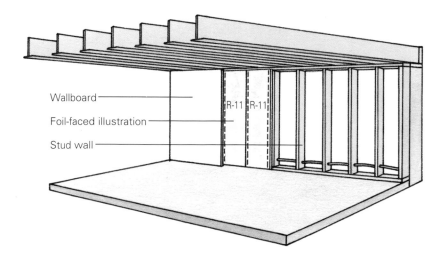

Wallboard
Foil-faced illustration
Stud wall
R-11 R-11

THE CEILING

HIDING DUCTWORK

In nonhabitable space, you can box in exposed plumbing and duct work, as long as you leave 76 inches of headroom beneath the box. However, for habitable spaces, the headroom requirement increases to 84 inches.

Construct two sides of the framework from 2×2s and attach them to the ceiling with nails or 3-inch drywall screws. Predrill screw holes through the framework but not into the ceiling. Once the framework is attached, nail or screw crosspieces between the bottom plates and cover the frame with wallboard or paneling.

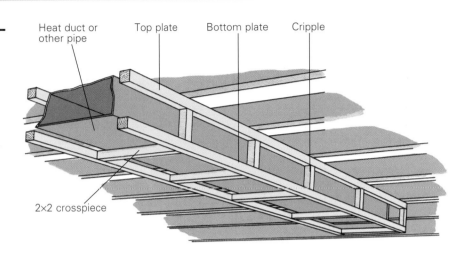

Heat duct or other pipe   Top plate   Bottom plate   Cripple

2×2 crosspiece

FURRING CEILINGS

Even if the ceiling is level, fur it to hide pipes and wires attached to the bottoms of the joists. A ceiling furred with resilient channel will increase sound isolation. Furring is also recommended when hanging a wallboard ceiling.

First, sight along the bottom of the joists. Jack up sagging joists and reinforce them with glued and nailed sister joists. The sister joists don't have to be as deep as the originals.

Then find the lowest point of the ceiling with a level. This is your baseline. Mark the ends of the ceiling at this height. Measure down from your baseline marks about 2 inches below the bottom of your furring stock, and at right angles to the joists, stretch a line—at this measurement from wall to wall. Install lines for every third furring piece (about every 4 feet).

Attach the furring with wallboard screws, shimming it as necessary to keep its bottom face at a consistent height above your lines. Screws allow for easy shimming; simply loosen them at the appropriate points, insert shims between the furring and joists, and tighten the screws.

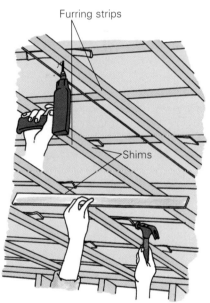

Furring strips

Shims

SUSPENDED CEILINGS

A suspended ceiling starts with a framework of metal channels hung from wires attached to the joists. The channels support lightweight acoustical panels that form a uniform, finished surface. It is unnecessary to move wires, pipes, or ducts, and joists do not have to be straight. Suspended ceilings are relatively inexpensive and easy to install.

You'll need adequate headroom to install a suspended ceiling. Building codes generally specify 90 inches of headroom from finished floor to finished ceiling in living areas.

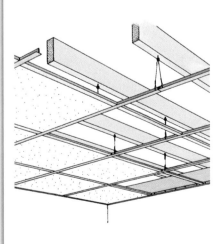

BATHROOM DESIGN

A successful bathroom design reflects the lifestyle of its users. A bathroom for adults with identical schedules needs to be laid out differently than one used by children or occasional guests.

Design your bath around family needs and schedules. Are people always waiting for someone to get out of the bathroom? Is there enough room for two people? How often is the tub used? Can guests get to the bathroom without going through someone's bedroom?

DESIGNER INSIGHTS

Here are some fine points to consider in your design:

■ All bathroom fixtures require vents (vertical pipes that connect the fixture to roof vents). Consult a plumber about the location of vent pipes before you commit to your layout.

■ Arrange the door swings, toilet, and partitions so that privacy is maintained.

■ Make sure you position the toilet paper holder conveniently.

■ Consider the possible future need for handicap access (see "Access," *page 4*).

■ Don't forget to include towel storage, towel bars, a wastebasket, and a clothes hamper in your design.

■ Place a wall vent where it can work most efficiently. An ideal location is directly behind the toilet.

■ Run the vent from a timer switch. That way you can leave the vent running when you leave the bathroom.

■ Always consider white. More white bathroom fixtures are sold than those in any other color, and if a manufacturer offers a loss-leader model, it will invariably be white. For these two reasons, white fixtures are your best buy. White offers the greatest compatibility with bathroom color schemes.

ENLARGING A BATHROOM

A bath with a tub, toilet, and two lavatories requires a minimum of about 50 square feet of floor space. But why settle for the minimum? In some respects the bathroom is the most important room in the house. To feel minimally luxurious, a bathroom requires 80 square feet—and 100 square feet is better. Even if you cannot move major walls, there are still ways to add space.

Annex an adjacent closet. There will be space for storage and the bathroom will feel larger if you convert closet space from an adjoining room into a bathroom cabinet with open shelves and a counter.

Change a hinged door into a sliding pocket door (not to a bearing wall, however). Even though it requires tearing out a portion of an existing wall, it may be worth the effort if you are remodeling extensively. Before proceeding, check to see if you will have to move any plumbing or wiring.

Install a bay (or greenhouse) window with a window seat. These additions add both space and light and don't need new foundations or major structural changes.

Eliminate interior walls. For instance, if the bathtub does not take up an entire wall and needs to be enclosed at one end, build a low divider, rather than a full-height wall. Before proceeding, check to make sure the existing wall isn't a bearing wall.

Let in the light. Natural daylight makes a bathroom appear larger and helps it stay drier. If there is a window above the tub or shower, use a transparent or translucent shower curtain or shower door to let in the light. Install a large mirror on one wall to reflect light, or flood the room with sunshine by installing a skylight overhead.

Put a bathtub (or a vanity) in the bedroom. You'll have to move and add plumbing and vents, but you'll free up space in the bathroom. You'll also take the burden off family bathroom schedules.

Finally, particularly if you live in a southern climate, consider incorporating outdoor space into a ground-level bathroom design. Install an outdoor shower and/or hot tub accessible through a patio door.

CODE REQUIREMENTS: BATHROOMS

Access to Connections: Fixtures having concealed traps must have access panels measuring at least 12 inches square.

Electrical: There must be at least one receptacle adjacent to each lavatory (wash basin), and it must be a ground fault circuit interrupter (GFCI) outlet. All other receptacles in a bathroom must be GFCI-protected. Ceiling lights in bathrooms must be of the sealed type (no hanging fixtures).

Light and Ventilation: Bathrooms must have a total glazed area of at least 3 square feet, one half of which must be openable. A common exception: No glazed area is required where there is mechanical ventilation direct to the outside of at least 5 air changes per hour.

Showers and Tubs: The minimum size of a shower base is 900 square inches, and it must contain a circular area 30 inches in diameter. Showerheads must be water conserving, with a maximum flow rate of 2.5 gallons per minute. Shower and bathtub control valves must limit water temperature to 120° F maximum.

Toilets: Toilets must be water conserving, rated at a maximum consumption of 1.6 gallons per flush.

There must be at least 15 inches of clear floor space to each side of the centerline of a toilet and 29 inches to the front of the toilet.

Washbasins: There must be a minimum clear area of 21 inches in front of a washbasin. Clearance between a washbasin and the centerline of a toilet must be 15 inches minimum.

USE YOUR IMAGINATION

These six plans show what you can do to a bathroom without moving the main structural walls or the toilet. The first five plans also manage to retain the original lavatory drains. The original bathroom was similar to Plan 1, except that it backed up to a deep hallway linen closet and had an in-swinging door. There was no shelving and only one washbasin.

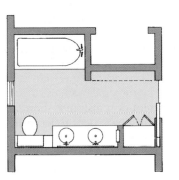

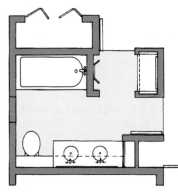

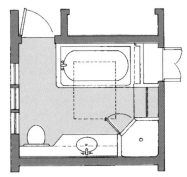

PLAN 1
Need: *Provide two washbasins, an enlarged floor area, and increased storage within the bathroom.*
Solution: *The hinged door is replaced by a pocket door. The hallway linen closet is replaced with a new storage unit within the bathroom. The original closet wall is moved to allow for a vanity with two basins. A narrow shelf unit on the back of the bedroom closet creates floor-to-ceiling storage. The original tub is still suitable and therefore remains.*

PLAN 2
Need: *Because the parents and children share this bathroom, there is a need for separate entrances and separate mirrors.*
Solution: *The original bedroom closet is converted into a dressing room with access to the bathroom. The dressing room includes a full-length, three-sided mirror and a dressing table. A new, enlarged bedroom closet replaces the old one. The door to the linen closet is moved around to the hallway side. The bathroom door now opens directly from the main hall. A shelf unit over the vanity provides towel storage in the bathroom while the shelf unit over the toilet provides storage for odds and ends.*

PLAN 3
Need: *Two separate washing areas and plenty of floor space are needed in order to clear up a traffic jam at the washbasin in the morning.*
Solution: *The existing linen closet is retained, but with a folding door. The bathroom door swings out to create more space. The bedroom closet is halved, and the bathtub is replaced with a shower to make space for a second lavatory. The custom vanity includes a basin, a lazy susan under the counter, and drawers underneath. A vanity in the opposite corner is set at the same angle as the shower front, with corner shelves above. A shelf unit is installed over the toilet.*

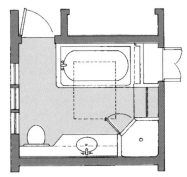

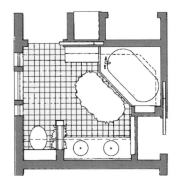

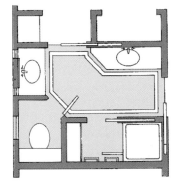

PLAN 4
Need: *The children have grown up, and the bathroom needs to be converted into a spacious, relaxing room off the master bedroom.*
Solution: *The original bedroom closet is replaced with a whirlpool tub and a utility closet that opens into the hall. A built-in, cushioned bench is added, with a storage unit above for towels and linen. The old linen closet is replaced with a corner shower. The spacious vanity has one basin and extends over a new low-line toilet. A skylight and an open wall with a large window make the room very bright and sunny.*

PLAN 5
Need: *Create a private and luxurious bathroom with access only from the master bedroom.*
Solution: *The bedroom closet is removed to make room for a sunken whirlpool bathtub. A new closet replaces the old one, and a built-in dresser unit is added. A pocket door leads to the bedroom. The original toilet is left in place, with storage above. A low divider between toilet and vanity creates privacy. The new vanity has two basins.*

PLAN 6
Need: *The bathroom is shared by the family and needs to be divided into private compartments.*
Solution: *A shower compartment is created by removing the linen closet and vanity. The compartment includes towel bars, a bench with storage beneath, and a pocket door. The toilet is placed in a compartment with a cabinet. A new window provides more light. The new vanity and basin have narrow windows on either side. The original bedroom closet is replaced by a second vanity. A new pocket door opens to the bedroom. A storage drawer unit is added in the entryway.*

BATHTUBS

NEW MODELS MAKE A CLEAN BREAK WITH THE PAST

ALSO SEE...
Bathroom design:
Pages 22–23
Plumbing:
Pages 256–263

Replacing or installing a new bathtub is a major project that usually involves framing, rough plumbing, fixtures, flooring, tiling, and accessories. Although bathtubs come in various sizes, shapes, and materials, the techniques of installation are similar for all models. Most manufacturers also include detailed instructions with the tub.

Old-style bathtubs, made of porcelainized cast iron or enameled steel, are still manufactured but due to their high price and difficulty of handling are losing ground to tubs made of acrylic and fiberglass-reinforced plastics. Not only are the new materials lighter and less expensive, they are also more comfortable and warmer to the skin. Standard-size plastic tubs, preplumbed with massage pumps and jets, are becoming quite common.

Although plastic tubs are not as durable as cast-iron or steel tubs (plastic is vulnerable to scratches and dulling), they hold up well enough under careful use and can be buffed and polished to their original luster with auto-body polishing compound.

CHOOSING A BATHTUB

When selecting a new bathtub, first consider the available space. If you are replacing an older tub, your new one should have the same dimensions and the same drain outlet (left or right side). Most tubs—old or new— are 30 inches wide and 60 inches long, so matching the size should not be difficult. The height of the new tub can be different, depending on the depth of water you prefer.

If you are installing a new tub, there is a great variety of sizes and shapes to choose from, ranging from little tubs, which can squeeze into a corner to giant tubs that could host a party.

If you are buying a tub that is larger than standard size, you may have to bring it into the space before you frame the last bathroom wall. Some tub-and-shower units come with separate tub and enclosure sections.

Also consider the weight of the tub and the location of its drain when framing the bathroom floor. Don't cut away joists to accommodate the drain under a tub that may weigh 1,000 pounds when full of water.

INSTALLING A TUB

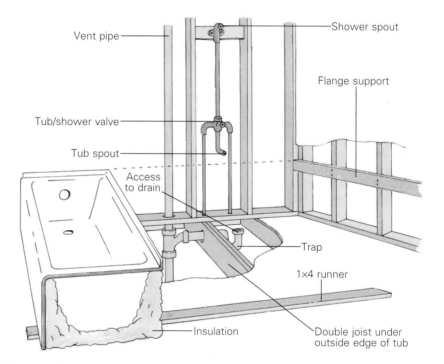

Vent pipe — Shower spout — Flange support — Tub/shower valve — Tub spout — Access to drain — Trap — 1×4 runner — Insulation — Double joist under outside edge of tub

ROUGHING-IN

First rough-in the supply plumbing. A typical supply consists of ½-inch cold-water and ½-inch hot-water pipes that connect to a mixing valve.

A short ½-inch nipple runs down from the valve to an elbow with a short stub, to which the spout will be attached. A second ½-inch pipe runs up from the mixing valve to the showerhead. By code, the mixing valve must protect against scalding by limiting the outflow to 120° F.

Make sure you don't install the mixing valve upside down! The flow to the showerhead is usually less than that to the tub spout. Connected upside down, you will find it takes forever to fill the tub! Since you won't get a chance to operate the shower until after the wallboard is in, you will be in big trouble if you find that you installed the valve upside down.

PROTECTIVE VINYL

If you plan to have sheet-vinyl flooring in your bathroom, install it before the tub or shower.

The vinyl will protect the wood subfloor from leaks or overflows. Even with the best of caulks, water will occasionally find its way under the edge of a tub or shower stall. With enough of these leaks over the years, you will have to replace the subfloor and floor joists, and that usually means removing the tub as well.

Your contractor may resist, being worried about damage to the vinyl during installation of the tub or shower. But a layer of builder's paper and plywood over the vinyl will protect it from scuffs and scrapes.

Next, rough-in the drain. Building codes require a 1½-inch drainpipe with a trap below floor level, with the inlet centered directly beneath the drain. It should have a slip nut or other means to connect to the waste-and-overflow pipe tailpiece coming from the tub. Many plumbers install a 2-inch drain because it clogs less often. If you use 2-inch waste pipe, you will have to adapt the 1½-inch tailpiece to the 2-inch trap. Install the waste pipe and trap so that the tailpiece from the tub drain and overflow (one piece to be installed later) is directly over the trap inlet.

INSTALLING AN ACCESS PANEL

Building codes require that bathtub drains with concealed trap joints be accessible through an access panel or other opening that measures at least a foot square. For tubs on the ground floor, the access can be from the basement or crawl space below. Just cut a 12×12-inch hole in the floor, under the drain location before you install the tub. If the bathroom is on a slab or an upper floor, build an access door or removable panel in the room behind the drain.

SETTING THE TUB

If the tub is acrylic or fiberglass, nail 2×4 flange-support cleats. Be sure these cleats are at exactly the right height and level. The manufacturer's instructions will provide the proper dimensions. Cast-iron tubs don't need these cleats.

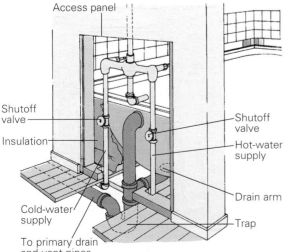

Access panel

Shutoff valve

Insulation

Shutoff valve

Hot-water supply

Cold-water supply

Drain arm

Trap

To primary drain and vent pipes

Next, stuff unfaced fiberglass batts into the tub's hollow cavities and between the wall and the tub. This will keep the bath water warm longer. Then slide the tub into place and screw the vertical flange to the studs.

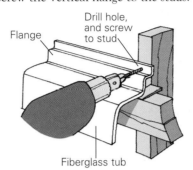

Flange

Drill hole, and screw to stud

Fiberglass tub

INSTALLING THE DRAIN

The tub itself does not come with any pipes, so you will have to purchase a tub drain assembly (drain arm, overflow pipe, connecting tee, and linkage). Spend the extra money for solid brass or Schedule 40 plastic rather than the bargain thin-walled plastic. The thin plastic unit won't seem such a bargain when your drain clogs and the auger breaks it.

Assemble the unit according to the manufacturer's directions and place it in position. You will need a helper to hold it from beneath. Put lots of plumber's putty around the drain hole in the tub and screw in the strainer. Tighten it with the plastic-coated handles of a pair of pliers inserted in the strainer. Do not overtighten.

Install the overflow cover with the screws supplied. Then, working under the tub, connect the overflow to the trap by tightening the compression nut with a spud wrench or spanner. Test the drain with a few buckets of water. Finally, install the stopper mechanism.

THE TUB ENCLOSURE

Insulate and finish the walls around the tub with panels appropriate to the amount of moisture exposure. If you don't have a showerhead, standard wallboard is fine, but moisture-resistant wallboard (green board) has a waterproof paper face and is better. For backing tile, use cement board, which is waterproof. Replace the stub-outs for the tub spout and showerhead with nipples of the right length, then screw on the fixtures.

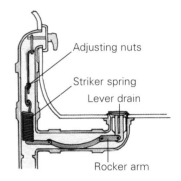

Adjusting nuts

Striker spring

Lever drain

Rocker arm

CAULKING

The last step in installing a tub is to caulk all the joints. To make a neat joint between the tub and tile, lay masking tape along the edge of the tub. Apply the caulk, smooth it with a wet finger, let the caulk set, then pull up the tape to reveal a straight, clean line.

A PLATFORM TUB

LOOK OUT BELOW!

We have all heard stories of tubs and their occupants crashing through a floor. Humorous and terrifying—but are they true?

Let's calculate how much a full tub weighs. The standard 30×60-inch tub holds approximately 50 gallons when filled to its overflow. A gallon of water weighs over 8 pounds, so 50 gallons weighs more than 400 pounds. A 250-pound person will displace about half of his or her body weight of water down the drain, so the net increase is 125 pounds. Finally, a fiberglass tub weighs

about 50 pounds. Therefore a full, occupied fiberglass tub weighs a total of about 575 pounds. That sounds like a lot, but when spread over the 30-inch by 60-inch area (12½ square feet), it amounts to only 46 pounds per square foot (psf)—not a lot more than the code allowance of 40 psf.

You will need to strengthen joists to accommodate a new tub, but the true problem is a floor that has rotted due to years of leaks and seepage under the tub/floor joint. That is why caulking tub joints is so important.

DROP-IN TUB PLATFORM

A drop-in tub set into a raised platform is an alternative to a sunken tub, and it is much easier to get in and out of—particularly for elderly bathers.

The platform exterior can be finished with a variety of materials, but tile is always a good, waterproof choice for bathrooms. Installed as a continuous surface that includes the floor, tub platform, and all or part of the walls, tile makes bathroom cleaning easy.

BUILDING THE FRAME

Make a frame of 2×4s with studs 16 inches on-center, one for each exposed side of the tub. The height of the frame plus the combined thicknesses of plywood and finish material must equal the height of the rim of the tub. Cut the studs to the inside dimensions of the frame—stud length is equal to the frame height less 3 inches. Construct the frames and attach them to the walls and floor with nails and construction adhesive.

EXTENDING THE SURROUND

To extend the horizontal ledge on any exposed side of tub, build a second frame identical to the first one. Set it parallel to and level with the first frame at the desired width of the ledge.

COVERING THE FRAME

Cover the tops and sides of the frames with ½-inch CDX plywood (¾-inch plywood for ledges wider than 12 inches). Paint the plywood with a moisture-resistant primer. If you're finishing with tile, install ½-inch cement board over the plywood. Finally, apply the tile, wood, or other finish material. To prevent water damage, seal the finish material.

CAULKING THE TUB

After the tile or other finish material is installed, caulk the joint between the rim of the tub and the ledge. To make a neat joint, apply masking tape to the edge of the tub. Cut the tip of the nozzle at an angle about ³⁄₁₆ inch. Hold the caulking gun at a 45-degree angle and push it forward. When you finish applying the caulk, smooth it with a soapy finger. After the caulk sets, pull up the tape to reveal a clean, straight line. (See Caulk, pages 50–51).

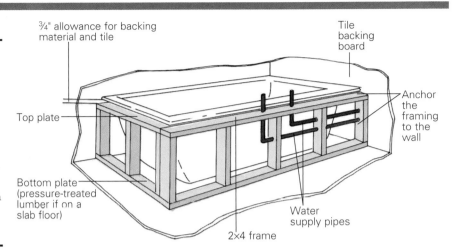

¾" allowance for backing material and tile

Tile backing board

Top plate

Anchor the framing to the wall

Bottom plate (pressure-treated lumber if on a slab floor)

Water supply pipes

2×4 frame

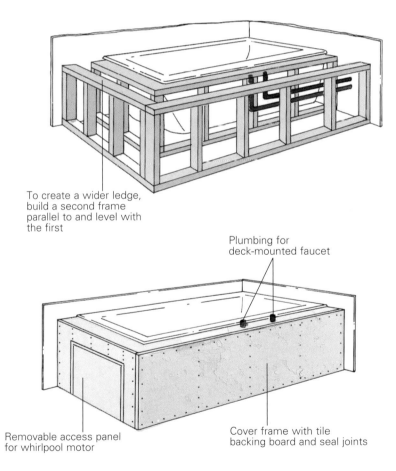

To create a wider ledge, build a second frame parallel to and level with the first

Plumbing for deck-mounted faucet

Removable access panel for whirlpool motor

Cover frame with tile backing board and seal joints

CODE REQUIREMENTS: TUBS AND SHOWERS

Drain Access: Slip-joint drains under tubs and showers must have minimum access of 12×12 inches.

Control Valves: Bathtub control valves limit water temperature to 120° F.

Tub Fill Spouts: Bathtub spout outlets must be 1½ inches minimum above the tub rim or be equipped with a vacuum breaker to avoid back-siphoning of bath water into the drinking-water supply.

Electrical Service: Whirlpool tubs and other tubs with pumps must be served by individual GFCI-protected circuits.

BOARD SIDING

THE STANDARD FOR EXTERIOR WALLS

ALSO SEE...
Fasteners:
Pages 122–125
Wood:
Pages 446–453

Board siding—siding made of wood—provides an excellent covering. It is reliable, durable, is easy to work with, and if maintained properly, will last for decades.

Synthetic sidings—vinyl, aluminum and pressed fiberboard—offer lower-cost and maintenance-free options and have captured a large share of the market. Which one you use will probably depend less on economics than on your preference for a natural or synthetic "look."

The price of board siding varies with the type and grade of lumber. If you are installing an interlocking pattern, make sure the wood is kiln dried. Green lumber shrinks and should be used only for shiplap or board-and-batten siding.

Durable species, such as cypress, redwood, and cedar, are superior for damp climates or for areas of the house that don't dry out thoroughly because they're in heavy shade. Pine, spruce, and Douglas fir are much less expensive and are suitable for exposure to direct sun.

Store board siding so that it is protected from the weather. Sort out the most attractive pieces for highly visible locations such as the front entrance or a patio.

PREPARATION

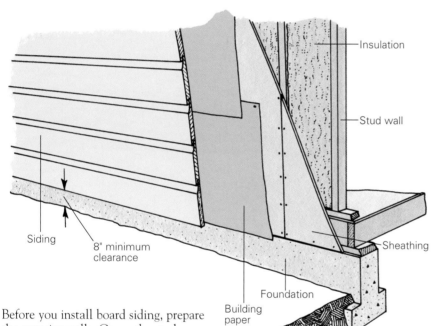

Siding

8" minimum clearance

Insulation

Stud wall

Sheathing

Foundation

Building paper

MAKE A STORY POLE

Marked story pole

Before you install board siding, prepare the exterior walls. Cover the studs with APA-rated sheathing whose size and physical properties are suited to the stud spacing. Traditionally, builders have installed exterior-grade (CDX) plywood as sheathing, but are now using oriented strand board (OSB) more frequently due to its much lower cost.

The grade stamp on the sheathing panel indicates maximum allowed framing spacing. For example, sheathing stamped at 24/16 can be installed on wall studs with a maximum 24-inch spacing and on floors with joists 16 inches on center.

On walls, apply the sheathing with its long side horizontal, using 6d galvanized nails every 6 inches at the edges and severy 12 inches throughout the field.

Next, apply a vapor barrier—building paper or sheets of spun polyolefin, popularly known as "house wrap." House wrap blocks water and wind, but passes water vapor in winter. Its use is subject to disagreement among building scientists who argue that plywood or OSB sheathing might need additional wind protection.

Regardless of your choice, staple the vapor barrier—house wrap—15-pound asphalt, or red rosin paper to the sheathing. Start at the bottom, lapping each successive course at least 2 inches over the one below it and the ends by at least 6 inches.

After the paper is up, snap vertical chalk lines over the center of each stud as a guide for nailing siding.

Save time when installing siding by making a "story pole"—a long stick with marks showing where each course begins.

Make a story pole by marking a 1×3 at the bottom course and the windowsills and drip caps above the windows. Measure between these marks, and divide by the nominal siding exposure to find the number of courses. Adjust the exposure to make the courses fall just right, then mark the story pole for each course.

Drive a long nail at the bottom mark. As you move around the house, align the nail with the top of the foundation wall. It is a simple matter to transfer the marks to the sheathing and keep the boards aligned.

TYPES OF HORIZONTAL SIDING

The table at right shows the four most popular board siding styles. Note that the sizes are standard, but board widths offered by individual manufacturers may deviate by as much as ½ inch.

The *area factor* is the nominal width divided by the exposure or the amount of board exposed after the next course is installed on top of it. Multiply the area factor by a waste factor of 1.05 to 1.10 to calculate the quantity of siding to order.

PLANNING AND GETTING STARTED

Plan your siding installation so that all joints meet at the corners and the exposures are aligned, if possible, with the tops of the doors and windows. If you are building new, frame the rough opening of the doors and windows so they are at the same height. On existing construction you probably won't have this "luxury" and will have to settle for lining up with the windows only.

Once you have decided on your coursing, construct your story pole and stick to it.

One way to start horizontal siding is to nail on a water-table board and water-table molding. It gives the building a real touch of class, but in the interest of shaving costs, this practice is falling out of favor.

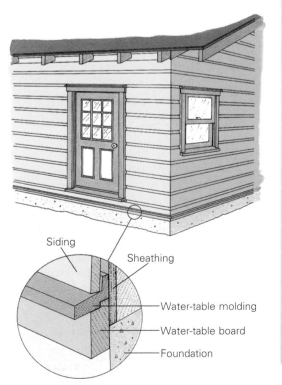

Siding
Sheathing
Water-table molding
Water-table board
Foundation

TYPES OF HORIZONTAL SIDING

Pattern	Nominal Size	Total Width	Face Width	Area Factor
Bevel (clapboard)	½×4	3½	3½	1.60
	½×6	5½	5½	1.33
	¾×8	7¼	7¼	1.28
	¾×10	9¼	9¼	1.21
Rabbeted Bevel (Dolly Varden)	¾×6	5½	5	1.20
	1×8	7¼	6¾	1.19
	1×10	9¼	8¾	1.18
	1×12	11¼	10¾	1.12
Tongue and Groove	1×4	3⅜	3⅛	1.28
	1×6	5⅜	5⅛	1.17
	1×8	7⅛	6⅞	1.16
	1×10	9⅛	8⅞	1.13
Drop Shiplap	1×6	5⅜	5⅛	1.17
	1×8	7⅛	6¾	1.16
	1×10	9⅛	8¾	1.13
	1×12	11⅛	10¾	1.10

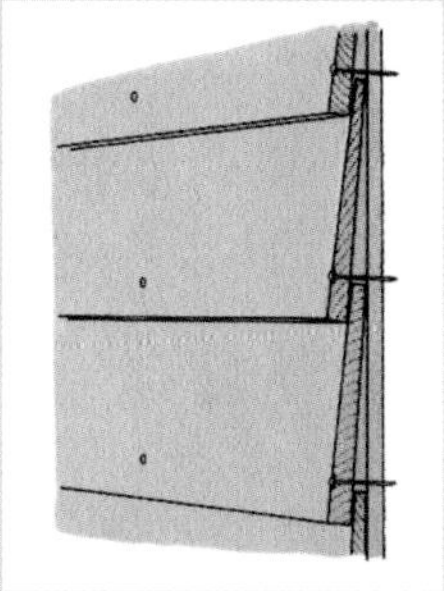

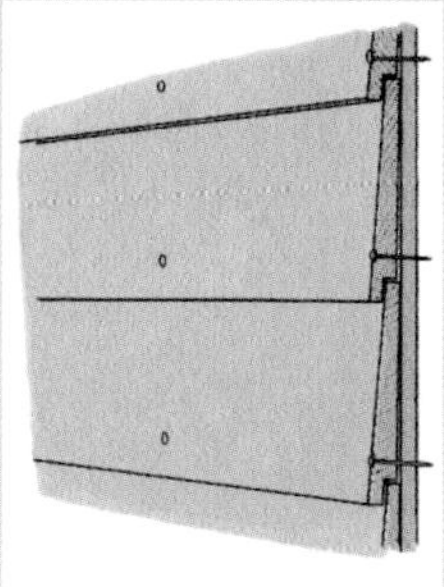

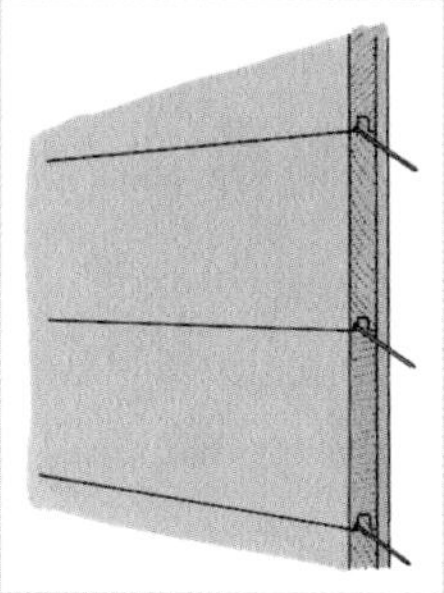

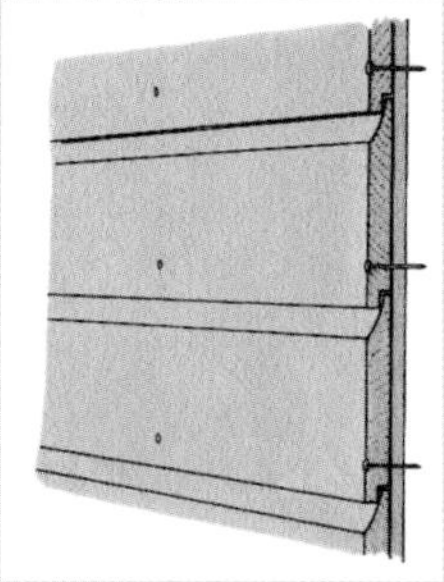

BOARD SIDING

continued

HORIZONTAL SIDING *continued*

INSTALLING THE BOARDS

Before you start nailing, hold the story pole at each corner with the wall at the top of the foundation. Transfer the marks to the corner boards. If you have installed a water table molding, the first course rests on it. If not, the first course actually starts about ½ inch below the bottom of the sheathing, so snap a chalk line to represent the top of the first course.

If the siding is beveled or lapped, rip a thin strip off the top edge of a piece of siding to shim the first course out at the proper angle.

Use only stainless steel or hot-dipped galvanized siding nails:

6d nails for siding up to ½ inch thick and 8d nails for all others.

Make sure all end joints fall on studs and preferably staggered throughout the surface of the wall. Except for beveled siding, miter both ends of a joint to create an overlapping scarf joint. Set the top board first, but don't nail the end. Position the lower board, predrill both boards to prevent splitting, and nail the joint to the stud.

If you are blind-nailing tongue-and-groove boards, use a nail set so the heads will not interfere with the fit of the next board. If a board is reluctant to fit, tap on a piece of tongue-and-groove scrap to protect the tongue.

TONGUE-AND-GROOVE BOARDS

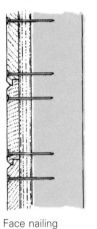

Face nailing   Blind nailing

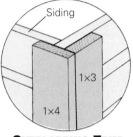

Blind nailing

GABLE ENDS

Set the angle of the rafter or roof sheathing on a bevel gauge and transfer the angle to the ends of siding boards for the gable. If you have one, a power miter saw makes accurate cuts.

Set the angle of the rafter on a bevel square and transfer the angle to gable board ends

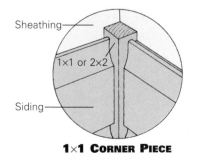

CORNER TREATMENTS

Horizontal siding requires special corner treatments to cover the exposed board ends.

Outside Corners: Install 1×3 trim, overlapped by 1×4 trim. On a very large or multi-story building use 1×5s and 1×6s. You can caulk the joints after all the siding is in place, but the preferred method is to caulk the butt of each course as you install it.

Siding

1×3

1×4

OVERLAPPING TRIM

A less common method is to use metal corner pieces. Nail opposing siding in place so that the ends just meet at the corners. Slip on the metal corner pieces and fasten with small brads.

METAL CORNERS

Inside Corners: At an inside corner nail a 1×1 (¾×¾ inch) or 2×2 (1½×1½ inches). Then butt the ends of the siding boards against it. Caulk the butts as you install them, or caulk the whole corner after it is complete.

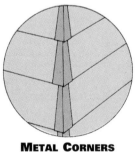

Sheathing

1×1 or 2×2

Siding

1×1 CORNER PIECE

REPAIRING HORIZONTAL SIDING

To repair to board siding, remove a damaged section and replace it with a matching piece. If you have only one or two pieces to repair but can't find replacement stock that matches, remove one from an inconspicuous location, such as under a porch, and replace it with the closest match you can find. For extensive repairs, take a sample of the original to a lumberyard or mill. They can duplicate it (at a substantial cost, however).

If you are patching a large section or splicing a new wall into an existing wall, do not make all the cuts over the same stud. Instead, cut alternating boards over the same stud, using a different stud for the rest. This will make the splice between the new and old siding less conspicuous. Caulk the butts ends of the new boards as you install them.

LAPPED SIDING

1 Cut the nails on both sides of the damaged section (and across the top, if necessary) by sliding a hacksaw blade between the boards. Inserting wooden wedges will make this easier.

2 Cut each side of the damaged area directly over the studs with a backsaw or circular saw. Don't damage the building paper. Finish the cut with the tip of the saw.

3 Remove the damaged piece and cut a new piece to replace it. Predrill holes at the ends, caulk the butts, and nail with 6d or 8d siding nails.

SPLIT BOARD

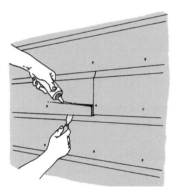

1 Carefully pry the split apart with a chisel and apply two-part epoxy to the gap.

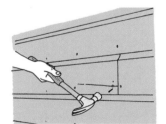

2 Predrill the split ends. Then, holding the split together, nail with siding nails.

DAMAGED TONGUE-AND-GROOVE BOARD

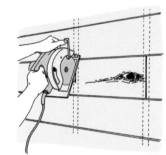

1 Cut through the damaged board at a point between studs or furring strips.

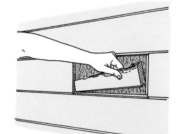

2 Split and pry out the damaged section.

3 Chisel off the back edge of the groove on a replacement board, caulk both butts and the half-groove at the bottom, and slip the new board into place.

4 Predrill and fasten at the bottom with small galvanized finish nails.

▶

31

BOARD SIDING
continued

VERTICAL SIDING

TYPES OF VERTICAL SIDING

When picking lumber for vertical siding, your choices will be influenced by both cost and aesthetics. Cypress, one of the best wood siding materials, has become too expensive for most budgets. Redwood and cedar are naturally weather resistant and, left unfinished, turn a silvery gray with age. Pine and Douglas fir are typically painted or stained.

Rough-sawn boards are usually an inch thick and an even number of inches wide. Surfaced or dressed (planed) boards are usually ¾ inch thick and range from 3½ inches to 11¼ inches wide. Some styles, such as channel shiplap, have rabbeted edges that make the joints weathertight.

Most boards cup, twist, or bow with moisture changes. The degree of change is somewhat dependent on the ratio of the board's width to its thickness. As a rule of thumb, limit this ratio to 8. For example, a 6-inch planed board ¾-inch thick has a width-to-thickness ratio of 8 (6 ÷ ¾ = 8). Painting or staining both front and back of siding reduces swelling and cupping.

PREPARING THE WALLS

To apply vertical siding to exposed studs, nail blocking between the studs at 24-inch intervals to provide a nailing surface. Next, cover the framing with 15-pound felt, starting at the bottom. Lap the top edges 2 to

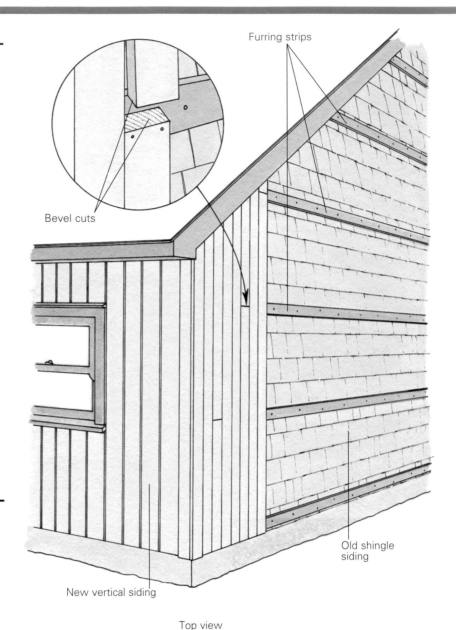

Furring strips

Bevel cuts

Old shingle siding

New vertical siding

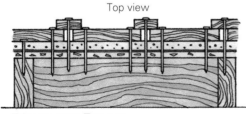

BOARD AND BATTEN

Top view

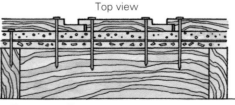

BOARD AND BOARD

Top view

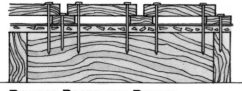

REVERSE BOARD AND BATTEN

Top view

CHANNEL SHIPLAP

4 inches and the ends by one stud space. Install Z-flashing over doors and windows and make sure the felt overlaps the flashing.

You can apply new siding over old without removing the old siding or applying building paper. Fasten 1×4 furring strips as nailers every 2 feet up the wall. The old siding and building paper will be weatherproof enough to prevent incursion of wind-driven rain.

Installing the Siding: Start at one corner, plumbing the first board with a 4-foot level. Don't worry if the building is out of plumb; a wide trim board will cover the discrepancy. Start tongue-and-groove siding with the groove edge to the corner. Install the rest of the boards the same way as horizontal siding. At a gable end you can run the siding all the way to the roof, or just to the bottom of the gable and finish the surface with horizontal siding (see Gable Ends, at right).

Board-and-Batten Sidings: Nail each board with one centered nail at each horizontal block or furring strip. Leave a ¼-inch gap between boards for expansion when the boards get wet. After nailing, let the boards dry a few weeks before applying the battens.

For the inverse pattern—batten-and-board—apply the battens first, then nail the boards over the battens with the board nails just missing the battens. Leave a gap of between ½ and 1 inch between boards.

Lapping End Joints: Cut all end joints at a 45-degrees so that the top pieces overlap to prevent leaks (see illustration, *opposite*). Make sure you caulk each joint before nailing the top board in place. If the building is exposed to driving rains, such as at an exposed coastal location, cut the ends square and apply a more effective continuous Z-flashing to the joint.

Corner Trim: Trim corners with 1×4s or 1×4s overlapping 1×3s. If you calculate right, you can make the corners come out just right by adjusting the spacing of the boards. If you find you have made a mistake, however, you can make things come out even by by trimming the widths of the last 3 or 4 courses.

You have a choice in finishing the gable ends. If the main siding is vertical, you can continue it all the way to the roof sheathing. Options include switching to horizontal siding or shingles on the gable section for more contrast, especially if the vertical siding consists of boards wider than 6 inches.

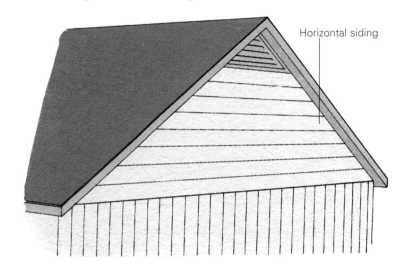

Horizontal siding

RAKES AND EAVES

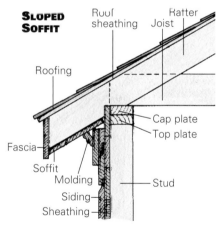

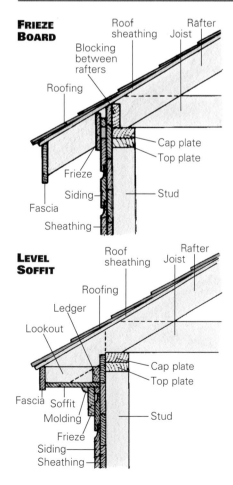

FRIEZE BOARD
Roof sheathing — Rafter — Joist
Blocking between rafters
Roofing
Cap plate
Top plate
Frieze
Siding
Stud
Fascia
Sheathing

SLOPED SOFFIT
Roof sheathing — Rafter — Joist
Roofing
Fascia
Cap plate
Top plate
Soffit
Molding
Siding
Stud
Sheathing

LEVEL SOFFIT
Roof sheathing — Rafter — Joist
Roofing
Ledger
Lookout
Cap plate
Top plate
Fascia
Soffit
Molding
Frieze
Siding
Stud
Sheathing

Finishing Options: Finish the underside of the rakes (the gable-end roof edges) the same way as the eaves (lower roof edges). If you do not cover them with a soffit, nail trim along the top edge of the siding where it meets the roof sheathing for a more finished appearance.

For a boxed look, build either a sloped or a level soffit. To build a level soffit, trim the bottoms of the rafters horizontally. For ventilation, drill 2-inch holes in the soffit and insert vent plugs or install a continuous vent strip.

33

BOILERS

SIMPLE PHYSICS

A boiler supplies hot water or steam—two of the oldest types of central heating systems. A boiler heats water in the same way as a tea kettle. Flame from a burner—fired by either gas or oil—heats water to 160 to 180°F (to 212°F in a steam system), then sends it through a loop of pipes. In a steam system, the steam condenses, giving up its heat, and flows back to the boiler as liquid water.

ALSO SEE...
Electrical Systems:
Pages 110–115
Energy:
Pages 116–117
Plumbing:
Pages 256–263

OPERATION

Boilers have elaborate gauges and controls that monitor and automatically regulate their operation:
■ The combination gauge shows water temperature, pressure, and a fixed minimum pressure. When the working pressure in a boiler drops below the minimum, the gauge calls for more water.
■ An aquastat controls the burner to maintain the boiler water temperature between high and low limits.
■ A low-water cutoff prevents the burner from firing when the level of the water in the boiler is too low.
■ A pressure-relief valve automatically opens to vent steam if the boiler pressure runs away.
■ On modern boilers a pressure-reducing valve automatically adds water to maintain the proper pressure.

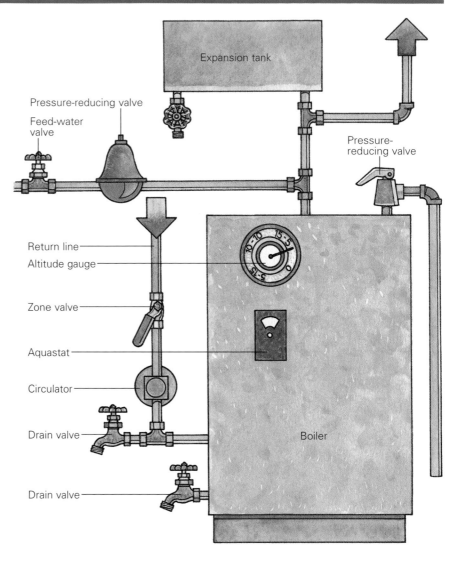

LOWER YOUR COST

"Turn down your aquastat."
  Say what?
  The aquastat controls the water temperature in the boiler. Normally the aquastat keeps the boiler between 160° and 180°F. If that temperature heats the house on the coldest day, then a much lower temperature would suffice for spring and fall. By manually turning the aquastat low and high limits down to 120° and 140°F, you should save 5 to 10 percent of your fuel bill.

TROUBLESHOOTING

Pipes that carry steam to radiators don't usually leak, even if they are old. However, shutoff valves do. They attach the pipe to the radiator, and over time they can develop leaks just like any faucet. Rust stains around the valve or water droplets condensing on the valve or pipes is a clue. You even may be able to hear steam escaping from a worn valve. Repair a worn valve like a compression-type faucet. First, let the valve cool off. Turn down the thermostat or switch off the system entirely. Disassemble the valve and install fresh packing around the packing nut.

Problems within the system are usually caused by corrosion. Naturally occurring minerals in domestic water supplies contribute to the problem, resulting in sediment buildup in the boiler. To minimize problems, drain the boiler twice each year and refill it with fresh water. When you refill, add a rust inhibitor to the water.

Over time, sediment will gather at the bottom of the boiler tank. You can reduce sediment levels by drawing off some of the water from the boiler drain. You'll need to let the system thoroughly cool beforehand. Then open the drain, remove a bucketful of sediment and water, and refill.

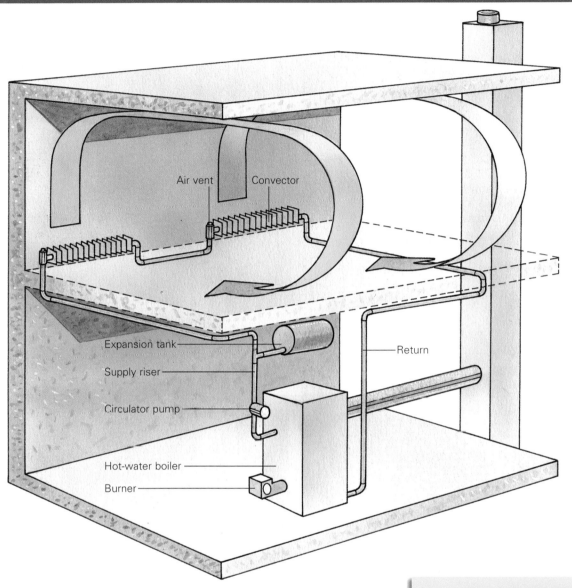

Air vent Convector

Expansion tank

Supply riser

Circulator pump

Return

Hot-water boiler

Burner

Heat from hot water or steam is distributed to the house through pipes. Usually, the house is divided into independent heating zones—each with its own thermostat and pump—allowing different temperatures for each area.

When the thermostat for a zone calls for heat, the circulator pump for that zone comes on, sending hot water or steam through the pipes.

Each zone also can be split into loops and the rate of heat supplied to each loop controlled by balance valves.

Domestic hot water can be supplied by treating a hot-water storage tank (boiler mate) as a heating zone. When the water in the storage tank cools, the hot-water thermostat turns on a circulator which sends hot water through a heat exchanger inside the hot water storage tank.

EASY EFFICIENCY

Boilers are like automobiles: The smaller the engine, the greater the efficiency. Your boiler might not be ready for a trade-in, but you can reduce the size of its "engine" to increase efficiency.

Oil burners are designed to run over a range of firing rates, say 0.6 to 1.0 gallons per hour. All you have to do to change the firing rate is change the nozzle—a $5 part.

To determine whether you can reduce your nozzle size, wait until a very cold night, go to the basement, and time the burner on/off times. If your burner fires just half the time, then it is firing at twice the required rate.

The next time you have the boiler cleaned, ask for a smaller nozzle.

CLEANER IS CHEAPER

Just a thin layer of soot on your boiler's heat-exchange surfaces can reduce its efficiency by 5 percent. If your annual oil bill is $1,000, then that 5 percent is costing you an extra $50 per year.

An oil system cleaning and checkup may cost $50. Get it done every other year and the annual cost is $25. That's $25 spent and $50 earned, a net gain of $25. What are you waiting for?

BRACING

STAND UP TO THE FORCES OF NATURE

Three powerful natural forces which can damage or even destroy your home are tornados, hurricanes, and earthquakes.

ALSO SEE...
Framing:
Pages 152–159
Framing Connectors:
Pages 160–161
Wood:
Pages 446–453

If you live in tornado country you should provide an in-the-ground or in-the-basement shelter to protect your family. Beyond that there is little you can do to reinforce your home sufficiently to withstand a tornado's 200-plus mile-per-hour winds.

Strict attention to detail about how a building is tied together and to its foundation is generally sufficient to protect it against 100-plus mile-per-hour hurricane-force winds.

In regions of high seismic risk, building codes are usually very specific, making new construction safe in moderate quakes.

HURRICANES

Hurricane damage comes from wind, wind-driven objects, waves, and flooding. The closer a building is to the coastline, the more susceptible it is to hurricane damage.

RAW POWER

Hurricanes can pulverize buildings with waves or blow them off their foundations. Their winds can lift off roofs, and falling trees can inflict structural damage.

Building code specifications for hurricane reinforcement vary widely from area to area. In general, the object of the codes is to tie a building securely to its foundation and to reinforce critical framing connections with metal framing ties.

SAFE DESIGN

Some roof designs are safer in hurricanes than others.

A roof-sized airplane wing can lift a 30,000-pound aircraft off the ground at hurricane wind speeds. Roofs that most resemble airplane wings (low-sloped shed and gable roofs) are the most susceptible to hurricane damage. Steeply pitched roofs spoil the airflow and actually reduce the lift. Hip roofs are the safest of all.

DAMAGE CONTROL

Danger from flying glass is easily prevented. Install real storm shutters of steel, vinyl, and wood—not to be confused with the fake decorative shutters.

Less expensive, but equally effective, are sheets of plywood cut to fit each window. Don't wait until 12 hours before the big storm to go to the home center, however. You'll probably find there isn't a sheet of plywood to be had in the county.

Steep hip roof less vulnerable to wind damage than low roof or gable roof

Composition-shingle roof in good condition

Gable roof

Low-sloped roof

Louvered steel storm shutters

Hurricane rafter ties

Framing securely tied to foundation with anchor bolts and hold-downs

EARTHQUAKES

Major earthquakes are not just a West Coast phenomenon. Scientists believe that during the past two centuries some of the biggest earthquakes in North America occurred in southern Missouri, South Carolina, and New England. These quakes today would affect more than a million structures.

The regions most likely to be affected by future quakes, however, are the coasts of California and Alaska. In these "seismic regions," building codes are very specific about earthquake protection for new construction.

How Buildings Fail

Earthquakes produce strong side-to-side and shaking motions that can tear a building apart and shake it off its foundation.

Unreinforced masonry structures are the most vulnerable because they are brittle, not elastic. The shaking causes the mortar joints to crack and the walls to move independently, pounding themselves to bits. Then the joints between the floors, walls, and roof separate, allowing the floors to fall and the walls to collapse.

Because wood is elastic, wood-frame houses generally fare better. Those which use plywood or other structural sheathing are even stronger.

There are three conditions, however, which make a wood-frame house vulnerable to earthquakes:
■ If the house is weakly attached to the foundation (or not attached at all) it may slide off. This will cause severe damage or complete destruction.
■ Kneewalls—short stud walls sometimes used between the foundation and the floor—may collapse unless they are braced.
■ Rot or insect damage can weaken structural connections so much that they fail in an earthquake.

Types of Reinforcement

Masonry construction requires that reinforcing rods (rebars) be embedded in the concrete during construction.

Wood-frame structures are reinforced with foundation anchor bolts, plywood wall sheathing, hold-downs, and metal ties across framing connections.

A brief inspection of the crawl space under a house will show whether the essential reinforcements are in place. Look for anchor bolts securing the sill to the foundation. If the house has kneewalls on the foundation (also called cripple walls), they should be sheathed with plywood.

The absence of either anchor bolts or plywood shear walls places a house at great risk during a quake. If there are no anchor bolts, installing them is your first priority.

Next reinforce the kneewalls with plywood.

The third step, installing hold-downs and metal framing connectors, is more complicated. Consult your local building code department for specific requirements and advice. You might even want to consult an architect, structural engineer, or contractor who specializes in seismic reinforcement of residential structures.

Low-Cost Steps

In addition to major structural reinforcement, there are a few more steps that can reduce earthquake losses.
■ Attach the water heater to the wall studs with plumber's strap (perforated steel strap that comes in a roll). If the water heater falls during an earthquake, it can cause a gas leak and fire. The water heater also is a source of drinking water if the quake is severe enough to disrupt the water supply.
■ Fasten tall furniture, such as bookcases, to the studs with lag screws.
■ Relocate heavy items, such as large cans of food, to the lowest shelves or the floor.
■ Put valuable breakable items such as glassware in secured cabinets with latching doors so they won't be tossed onto the floor.

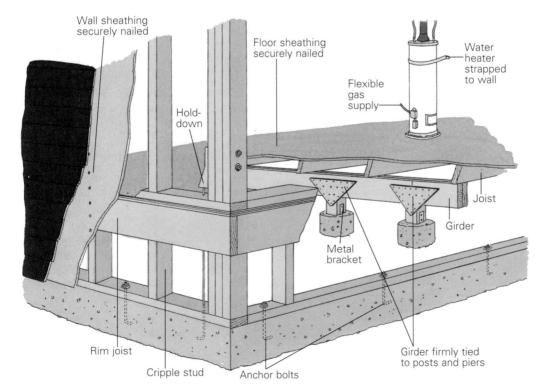

Wall sheathing securely nailed

Floor sheathing securely nailed

Water heater strapped to wall

Flexible gas supply

Hold-down

Joist

Girder

Metal bracket

Rim joist

Cripple stud

Anchor bolts

Girder firmly tied to posts and piers

BRICKS

DURABLE, CLASSIC, AND VERSATILE

Few building materials are as simple, and at the same time as elegant, as brick. Along with wood and stone, it's one of the three basic materials man has used since the beginnings of recorded history, and we still associate brick with the highest-quality construction.

ALSO SEE...
Chimneys & Stovepipes: Pages 54–55
Concrete: Pages 60–63
Fireplaces: Pages 134–135
Patios: Pages 246–249
Walks & Drives: Pages 414–415

Brick is found in traditional, contemporary, rustic, formal, and stately settings. It is ideal for walls, steps, paving, small structures, or decorative veneers. For these reasons, as well as the fact that it is easy to work with, brick is an ideal material for home-improvement projects.

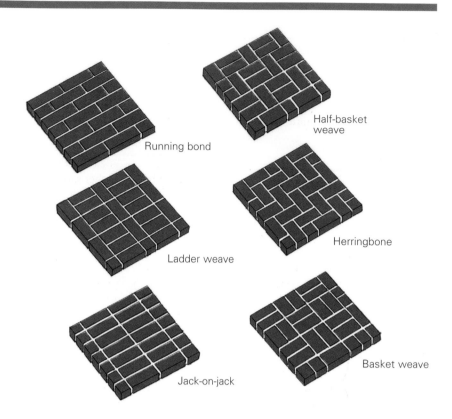

Running bond

Half-basket weave

Ladder weave

Herringbone

Jack-on-jack

Basket weave

TYPES AND SIZES

Although the basic proportions of all brick are similar, there are literally hundreds, if not thousands, of slight variations in brick size, texture, and color. For projects around the home, however, we can categorize brick into broad categories.

Common Brick: Common brick is the traditional building brick. It has a rough texture and is the least expensive. Most common brick is wire cut and has straight, rough sides. Sand-molded brick has a smoother texture and slightly tapered sides. Clinker brick is hard-baked and typically shows black oven burns.

Common brick is rated for how well it stands up to freezing and thawing. The three grades are: SW (severe weathering), MW (moderate weathering), and NW (nonweathering). Use only SW brick outdoors in northern areas; MW brick is suitable for southern areas; and NW brick should be restricted to indoor use.

Face Brick: Face brick is typically smooth or glazed on one face. It is used for commercial building and for a modern look in residential construction. Face brick doesn't come in as many sizes as common brick.

Specialty Brick: ■ Firebrick is used for fireplaces, barbecues, and other high-temperature locations. The mortar used to lay it must also have fireclay mixed in.

■ Pavers are slightly larger than common brick and they are harder, made to stand up to hard use in patios and driveways.

■ Split brick or half brick is used for veneers or paving where normal brick would be too thick; it is installed in the same way as tile.

■ Used brick is most often of the common variety. The most desirable used brick looks old, weathered, with rounded edges and an occasional patch of old mortar. The imperfections add to the charm. The ability of used brick to withstand the elements is always uncertain. If the brick will be subjected to freezing outdoor conditions, you should purchase manufactured "used" brick instead.

Size: Bricks are classified as either modular or nonmodular. Modular bricks have heights and lengths that, including the mortar joint, divide neatly into 4-foot intervals. Knowing this, you can plan a brick wall that will go up with a minimum of labor. With nonmodular brick, planning is a little more complicated.

Use the tables on page 42 to plan the composition and the heights of modular-brick walls.

PICKING THE PATTERN

The best way to decide on a pattern is to lay out bricks in different ways to see what you like. If you are not sure, stick with one of the basic patterns shown here.

Mixing patterns is usually not a good idea. A single pattern is busy enough. Multiple patterns clash with one another.

SEE THE FUTURE

Wouldn't it be nice if you could see what a finished wall or patio of all the different bricks would look like?

You can. Generally the largest brick distributors—those who sell only brick and block—have miniature walls on display. They also have samples of mortar dye.

LAYING PATIOS AND WALKS

CHOOSING THE BRICK

You can use common brick for walks and patios in mild climates and for low-traffic installations. In harsh winter climates, you'll need to set pavers in patios and walks. In any climate, pavers will minimize your maintenance.

CHOOSING THE BASE

There are three basic options from which to choose: sand, mortar (concrete), and sand and mortar.

Sand Base: A sand base is the simplest to install. You'll need two inches of sand laid, in harsh winter climates, over a 4-inch gravel base. Since you don't want weeds growing between the bricks, lay down landscape fabric. Hold the edges of the paving in place with a border of boards, concrete, or mortared brick.

Mortar Base: For this you'll need a concrete slab. You can utilize an existing concrete patio or you can pour a new one. After the slab has cured, the bricks are laid in a thin bed of mortar. Additional mortar grouts the joints between the bricks.

Sand and Mortar Base: Here, you lay bricks over a sand base and then mortar the joints. Grout the joints with wet mortar, or sweep dry mortar into the joints and then spray the patio or walk with water. This method is not suited to northern areas.

INSTALLING EDGING

The edging around a brick patio keeps the brick from shifting—especially important in a sand-base installation. Popular materials for edging include pressure-treated lumber, creosoted railroad ties, concrete, and brick.

Lumber: Pressure-treated lumber is very popular because it will not rot, is easy to cut and fasten, and comes in a range of sizes, from 2×4s to landscape timbers. Brace lumber edging every 4 feet with stakes nailed or screwed to the outside so that the tops of the stakes are about an inch below the edging.

Concrete: Build a 2×6 form as you would for the footing for a foundation (see Foundations, pages 144–151). To prevent the concrete from breaking up, suspend two rows of rebar inside the

form. Remove the form before laying the brick.

Brick: A brick edging works only when the bricks are mortared onto concrete. Pour a reinforced concrete strip and set the bricks in it while it's wet.

LAYING BRICKS IN DRY MORTAR

In this popular installation, the brick is laid on a base of either sand or concrete; but, rather than buttering the bricks with mortar, you merely sweep dry grout into the spaces and add water.

Set the bricks in the desired pattern, spacing them ¼ to ½ inch apart. Thoroughly mix 1 part masonry cement to 3 parts dry sand, and sweep the mixture over the bricks until all of the joints are filled. Sweep the bricks as clean as possible before continuing with the next step.

Adjust the spray from a garden hose to a fine mist. Spray the entire area uniformly, making sure that the water penetrates into the joints. Wait 15 minutes to let the wet grout settle, and spray the entire area again to thoroughly saturate the mortar.

Let the brick surface dry , then sweep in more dry mortar, filling all the joints. Repeat the misting process.

Board

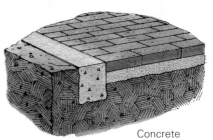

Concrete

Bricks laid flat

LAYING PATIOS AND WALKS *continued*

LAYING BRICKS ON SAND

Properly installed, a brick-in-sand installation will last for years. Its durability depends on a solid base and solid edging—lumber, concrete, or brick.

Brick edging can be set on edge or laid flat in a concrete footing at least 4 inches thick, and in areas subject to frost, 8 inches thick, reinforced with steel rebar.

When pouring the footings, slope them ¼ inch per foot so the patio drains properly.

Prepare the bed by excavating the soil deeply enough for adding a 4-inch gravel bed and 2 inches of sand, leveling and compacting each layer.

1 Excavate to a depth of 6 inches plus the paver thickness. Pour, level, and tamp 4 inches of gravel and spread a layer of damp, coarse sand. Level it with a screed board— a straight piece of lumber notched at both ends to the depth of one brick. Place the ends of the screed board on the border and drag it forward with a sawing motion. The bottom of the board will level the sand to the desired depth.

2 Starting at a corner, set the bricks in place, spaced about ⅛ inch apart. After placing several bricks, level them by laying a short 2×4 across them and tapping the board with a rubber mallet. If a brick is too low, lift it and add some sand; if too high, scoop some sand out.

3 Repeat Steps 1 and 2 for the remaining sections.

4 After all the bricks are in place, spread a layer of fine sand over the whole area and sweep it. Sweep, adding sand as necessary until the joints are filled. Wet the bricks with a fine spray. When they are dry, add more sand to the joints. Repeat the process until all the joints are full.

LAYING BRICKS IN MORTAR

Excavate, level, and compact the soil to allow for the concrete base. If drainage or freezing is a problem, excavate deeper and install 4 inches of gravel.

Build forms for a 4-inch concrete base (see Concrete, pages 60–63), allowing for a ¼-inch-per-foot slope for drainage. Then pour the slab. To level the concrete, use a screed board— a straight piece of lumber that spans across the tops of the forms. Move the screed with a sawing motion to level and smooth the concrete. Immediately after screeding, run a concrete float over the surface to level the surface. Do not smooth the surface further because you want the mortar to adhere to the concrete.

Let the slab cure for 3 days to a week. Mix a mortar of 1 part cement, 1 part hydrated lime, and 6 parts sand. Add only enough water for a buttery, firm consistency, and mix only as much as you can use in 1 hour.

Spread a 1-inch mortar base on the slab and set in the bricks. Let the bricks set overnight before grouting so you can walk on them. If you are paving a walk and you can reach all the bricks from the edges, you don't have to wait.

Mix grout in the same way as mortar, adding dye if you want the joints colored.

Either squeeze grout into the joints with a grout bag (like a bag for icing a cake) or sling the grout into the joints with a small brick trowel. Smooth the grout into an even concave shape with a jointing tool. Wipe fresh grout off the bricks with a wet sponge. If it dries on the bricks, wait for the mortar to cure. Then add 1 part muriatic acid to 10 parts water, wash the bricks, and rinse after one hour. When working with muriatic acid, be sure to wear rubber gloves and protect your eyes.

1 Before laying any bricks in the mortar, do a test layout to make sure your pattern will work.

2 When you are sure of your pattern, begin by laying the edging. Lay down a bed of mortar, then butter the brick edges and lay the entire frame.

3 After the edge frame is complete, start filling the interior area. Lay a base of mortar, then butter the end and side of each brick and push it into place.

4 Scrape off any excess mortar and, using an appropriate tool, smooth the grout.

ESTIMATING MATERIALS

To order your materials, you need to know the size of the brick you plan to use. Brick is sized two ways: actual size and nominal size. Actual size is what the brick measures without mortar; nominal size includes the mortar joints.

Once you know the brick size, you can determine how many you need for each square foot of surface. As a rule of thumb, estimate 5 bricks per square foot of patio or walkway pavers. For a single-thickness wall, consult the table, *right*.

Bricks are heavy! If you buy bricks at a lumberyard, chances are you will be unloading them one brick at a time. If you buy them instead from a brick supplier, they will come on a pallet and will be unloaded by a hoist.

BRICK AND MORTAR FOR SINGLE-THICKNESS RUNNING-BOND WALL

Nominal Size, Inches T×H×L	No. of Bricks Per 100 Sq.Ft.	Cubic Feet of Mortar			
		Per 100 Sq.Ft.		Per 1,000 Bricks	
		⅜" Joint	½" Joint	⅜" Joint	½" Joint
MODULAR BRICK					
4×2⅔×8	675	5.5	7.0	8.1	10.3
4×3⅓×8	563	4.8	6.1	8.6	10.9
4×4×8	450	4.2	5.3	9.2	11.7
NONMODULAR BRICK					
2¾×2¾×9¾	455 / 432*	3.2	4.5	7.1	10.4
2⅝×2¾×8¾	504 / 470*	3.4	4.1	6.8	8.7
3¾×2¼×8	655 / 616*	5.8	7.2	8.8	11.7
3¾×2¾×8	551 / 522*	5.0	6.4	9.1	12.2

Bricks for ⅜-inch joint / Bricks for ½-inch joint

BRICK WALLS

Brick walls are either bearing or non-bearing. Bearing walls support loads beyond their own weight. Uncommon in today's homes, they often are built as fences or as part of garden structures.

Nonbearing walls don't have any structural responsibilities and are often constructed for decorative purposes as a veneer or to define boundaries between garden or landscape areas. Typically, a brick veneer is applied on the outside of a regular stud wall. The veneer is held in place by thin metal straps positioned at regular intervals inside the mortar and held to the stud wall sheathing with screws.

Both bearing and nonbearing walls are subject to code requirements that specify the number and location of reinforcement rods and the location of veneer ties. Before you build, be sure to check your community's codes for all information pertaining to brick walls.

Solid brick walls are simple to construct. Wide brick walls can be fashioned with a hollow cavity or a concrete-block core. Wall footings are also governed by building codes.

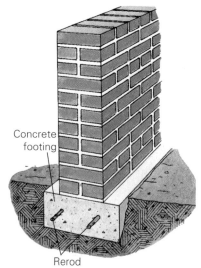

Concrete footing

Rerod

HEIGHTS OF MODULAR BRICK WALLS

Number of Courses	Nominal Thickness (Including Mortar)			
	2"	2⅔"	3⅕"	4"
1	2"	2¹¹⁄₁₆"	3³⁄₁₆"	4"
2	4"	5⁵⁄₁₆"	6⅜"	8"
3	6"	8"	9⅝"	1' 0"
4	8"	10¹¹⁄₁₆"	1' 1¹³⁄₁₆"	1' 4"
5	10"	1' 1¹⁵⁄₁₆"	1' 4"	1' 8"
6	1' 0"	1' 4"	1' 7³⁄₁₆"	2' 0"
7	1' 2"	1' 6¹¹⁄₁₆"	1' 10⅜"	2' 4"
8	1' 4"	1' 9⁵⁄₁₆"	2' 1⅝"	2' 8"
9	1' 6"	2' 0"	2' 4¹³⁄₁₆"	3' 0"
10	1' 8"	2' 2¹¹⁄₁₆"	2' 8"	3' 4"
11	1' 10"	2' 5⁵⁄₁₆"	2' 11¹³⁄₁₆"	3' 8"
12	2' 0"	2' 8"	3' 2⅜"	4' 0"
13	2' 2"	2' 10¹¹⁄₁₆"	3' 5⅝"	4' 4"
14	2' 4"	3' 1¹⁵⁄₁₆"	3' 8¹³⁄₁₆"	4' 8"
15	2' 6"	3' 4"	4' 0"	5' 0"
16	2' 8"	3' 6¹¹⁄₁₆"	4' 4³⁄₁₆"	5' 4"
17	2' 10"	3' 9⁵⁄₁₆"	4' 6⅜"	5' 8"
18	3' 0"	4' 0"	4' 9⅝"	6' 0"

BRICK REPAIRS

REPLACING A BRICK

Loose or cracked brick can be removed and easily replaced. If many bricks are loose or cracked, find out why before undertaking the repairs. There may be a structural problem that will thwart your efforts.

To remove a brick, use a cold chisel to chip away the surrounding mortar, and split the brick. Then pry it out. Clean the hole with a brush (or power washer if available), wet it, then smooth in a layer of mortar (1 part cement, 1 part hydrated lime, 3 parts sand) on the bottom.

Butter the sides and top of the new brick with mortar and slide it into place. Pack additional mortar in as needed. Finish the joints to match the rest of the wall or paving.

1 *Chip mortar and split the brick.*

2 *Mortar the bottom.*

3 *Butter and install the new brick.*

REPOINTING MORTAR JOINTS

Over time the mortar joints in most walls and chimneys may begin to crumble. Once the process starts, it accelerates, as rain water penetrates further into the joints. Unchecked, the process will reduce a structure to an orderly pile of bricks.

To increase the ability of joints to shed water, masons "point" (replace the mortar in) the joints. Shown below are common pointing styles.

If you find crumbling mortar joints, repoint promptly. A small masonry cutting disk on a power drill can quickly open up the joint. If necessary, finish the job with a narrow cold chisel and a hammer (wear gloves and goggles to protect yourself), then power-wash the joints or scour them with a wire brush. The opening should be at least ½ inch deep.

Wet the area to be repointed so the brick doesn't draw the water out of the mortar. Use a small trowel to pack the joint with mortar or hold a trowel just

below the joint and force mortar into it with a stick.

Tool (point) the renewed joints to match the old joints. Use a small trowel to point raked, weathered, or struck joints. Buy a raking tool

at home-improvement centers or masonry supply stores, or make one by driving a nail through a small block of wood. Concave and vee joints are produced with a pointing tool, available at most home centers.

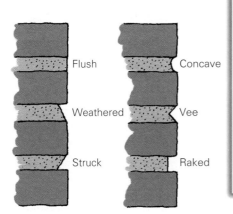

Flush — Concave

Weathered — Vee

Struck — Raked

POWDERY CLUES

Efflorescence, a powdery, white deposit that appears on bricks, consists of soluble salts that have been brought to the surface by migrating water. When caused by the evaporation of water left over from the construction, it is known as "new building bloom" and should disappear naturally within the first year.

Efflorescence that appears after the first year is evidence of a water problem within the brick wall. Check to find out how water is getting

into the wall (bad caulk at seams, bad rain cap, wicking from the ground) and why it isn't immediately escaping from the wall's weep holes.

Efflorescence is easily removed—at least temporarily—with a stiff wire brush. Do not wash it off with water since the water will dissolve a portion of the salt and put it back into the wall, from whence it will only reappear!

CARPET

COMFORT, WARMTH, COLOR, AND TEXTURE

ALSO SEE...
Floors:
Pages 140–141

Few things can so dramatically enhance the livability of a room as wall-to-wall carpet. It can hide an ugly floor, quiet a noisy room, warm a cold space, brighten a dark one—all for a reasonable cost when compared to other types of flooring.

The softness and resilience of carpet invite you to sit down or stretch out on it, and its broad expanse of color provides the perfect background for any decor.

Installing new carpet requires selection of the material, preparation of the floor to be carpeted, and installation of the perimeter tackless strip, the pad, and the carpeting.

Most homeowners leave the floor preparation and carpet installation to professionals, but a handy person can easily complete both the initial preparation for laying any type of carpet and the installation of cushion-backed carpeting. Stretching a thick wall-to-wall carpet is best left to professionals, although we will show you how it's done.

SELECTING A CARPET

In selecting a carpet ask yourself the following questions:

■ How much traffic will this carpet bear? If it's for the guest bedroom and you have guests only twice a year, save money here and spend it on an area that will see more wear, such as a hallway, stairs, or a family room.

■ Will food and drink be spilled? If it's for the kitchen or dining room, put stain resistance high on your list.

■ How even is the floor beneath? Floor boards—even joints between sheets of plywood—will show through a very thin carpet. A plush carpet on a thick pad, however, will hide nearly every defect underneath.

■ Will this carpet face direct sunlight? If so, make fade resistance important or pick a color, such as a dusty rose, that will look good even if it fades.

■ How damp is this location? If you are installing carpet in a damp, dark basement space, it must have high mildew resistance. Cushion-backed carpet should not be installed over basement floors.

For overall quality and traditional good looks, you'll want wool carpet. It has a luxurious feel and natural stain resistance, but it doesn't come without a price. Expect to pay $35 per square yard or more for wool carpet.

Carpets made of synthetic fibers continually improve in quality and endurance. Nylon is tough and stain-resistant, and it holds color well. A blend of wool and nylon fibers combines the best features of both—good looks and durability.

Carpets made of polyester fibers are usually soft to the touch. Although not

as durable as wool or nylon, polyester carpets are comfortable and are good choices for bedrooms. Acrylic fibers are generally not considered to be as soft or good-looking as other types, but their washability makes them good choices for bathroom and kitchen rugs.

VISUAL TRICKS

To make a room appear to be:
Bigger: use solid, light colors
Smaller: use busy, dark patterns
Longer: use linear patterns lengthwise
Wider: use linear patterns sideways

A GUIDE TO CARPETS

Material	Resilience	Staining	Abrasion	Fading	Mildew	Cost
Wool	Excellent. Feels springy	Very good, but may be difficult to clean	Very good	Damaged by long exposure to sunlight	Requires treatment	High
Nylon	Very good. Resists crushing	Very good. More easily cleaned than wool	Very good	Damaged by long exposure to sunlight	Excellent	Medium to high
Polyester	Fair. May crush	Fair. Cleans well	Excellent	Damaged by both heat and sunlight	Requires treatment	Low to medium
Acrylic	Nearly as good as wool	Good, but must be treated after deep cleaning	Poor	Good	Excellent	Low to medium
Polypropylene olefin	Varies	Very good. Doesn't retain dirt	Very good	Treated to resist fading	Excellent	Low

PREPARING THE FLOOR

Carpet installations usually require only minor floor preparation: Carpets require subfloors that are dry, free of debris, and smooth.

To replace an existing carpet, remove all metal edgings. Then pry one corner of the carpet loose from the tackless strip and pull up the carpet. Reuse the pad and tackless strip if they are in good condition.

To lay ordinary carpet over a wood floor or resilient flooring, sweep the floor clean and nail down any loose boards or tiles. Patch cracks or holes larger than ¼ inch with a quick-drying paste filler or nail down an underlayment-rated plywood.

Cushion-backed carpet must be glued to a very smooth surface. If the subfloor or finished floor surface is rough, install ¼- to ½-inch underlayment-grade plywood over it. Fill joints and surface depressions with a filler compound.

To lay conventional carpet over cushion-backed carpet, remove a strip around the edge of the room wide enough for the new tackless strips.

The remaining cushion-backed carpet becomes the pad for the new carpet.

When installing carpet on concrete, make sure the floor is perfectly dry and that there are no moisture problems (see Basements, pages 18–21). Don't apply carpet over floors with buried radiant heat. Not only might you drive a nail through the radiant heat pipe, but carpet is an excellent insulator and could cut the heat flow enough to make the room cold. If the radiant heat is no longer used, however, treat the slab like any other slab.

INSTALLING STRETCHED CARPET

1. INSTALLING TACKLESS STRIP

Tackless strip is readily available at home improvement stores. It is a thin strip of wood embedded with tiny teeth designed to grip carpet securely. All those teeth make tackless strips difficult to grasp without pricking a finger—you may want to use a pair of leather gloves while handling them.

Starting in a corner, nail tackless strip (teeth to the wall) around the perimeter of the room, with nails spaced 12 inches on center. Leave a gap between the strip and the wall of two thirds of the thickness of the carpet.

On concrete floors, use masonry nails and construction adhesive. Predrill a pilot hole in the strip to prevent the masonry nails from splitting it. If the strip-to-concrete adhesion does not appear secure, try adding a second row of strip in front of the first.

2. INSTALLING THE PAD

Cut a pad long enough to cover one end of the room. Butt the length and one end against the tackless strip. At the other end, cut the pad so it laps over the strip (you'll trim it later). On a wood floor, staple the pad every 6 to 12 inches around its edges. Continue cutting and stapling the pad until the entire floor is covered.

Butt the edges; don't overlap them. Trim the pad ¼-inch from the strip—to keep the pad from riding up on the strip when the carpet is stretched. Tape the pad seams with duct tape.

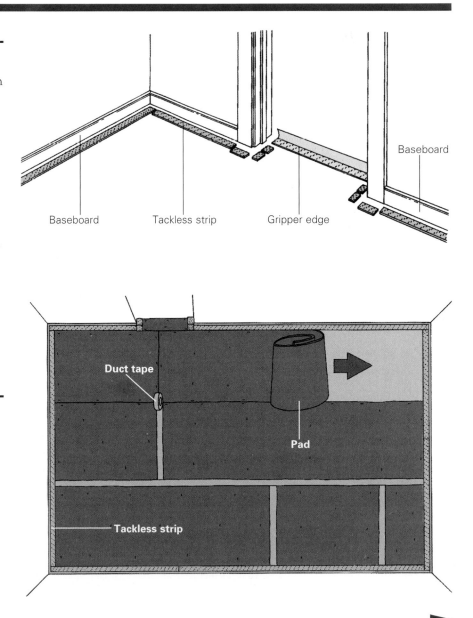

Baseboard

Baseboard   Tackless strip   Gripper edge

Duct tape

Pad

Tackless strip

INSTALLING STRETCHED CARPET *continued*

3. ROUGH-FITTING THE CARPET

Cut each section of carpet 4 to 6 inches larger than its finished dimensions (you will trim the carpet after it is stretched). Plan all cuts so that the pile of the fibers will lean in the same direction throughout the room.

To cut, snap a chalk line along the back of the carpet and cut from that side with a sharp utility knife. Only carpet having straight rows of loop pile is cut from the face side.

Unroll the pieces so that the pile faces in the proper direction. The excess along each side should curl up the walls slightly. At corners and obstructions, make vertical slits to allow the carpet to lie flat. The bottom of the slits should reach almost to the floor. Overlap pieces that will be seamed together by an inch or so.

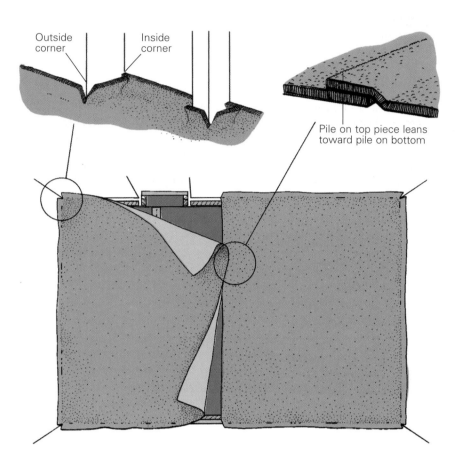

Outside corner

Inside corner

Pile on top piece leans toward pile on bottom

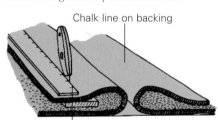

Chalk line on backing

Straightedge along chalk line

4. CUTTING SEAM EDGES

A good seam requires perfectly straight edges. Cut new edges on both pieces using a chalk line, straightedge, and utility knife.

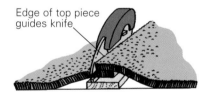

Edge of top piece guides knife

SAVED BITS SAVE THE DAY

Save your carpet scraps. What will you do when the dog chews up a corner, when the hall carpet wears, when a spark from the fireplace burns a hole?

Carpet is easily patched, provided the material you use is an exact match. When the time comes, however, you may find that your carpet pattern has been discontinued. Besides, why spend more money when you had the leftovers for free?

Since most carpet fades in strong sunlight, save some of the scrap in a dark location (closet, basement, etc.) and some in a location exposed to the sun.

If you can't find any scraps, take a piece from an inconspicuous location, such as a closet floor.

5. CUTTING SEAM EDGES OF LOOP PILE

Dress the edges of loop pile by cutting from the face with a "row cutter." Use the top piece as a guide for cutting the bottom piece.

6. POSITIONING SEAMING TAPE

Cut a length of hot-melt seaming tape the exact length of the seam. Center it under the seam, adhesive side up. Square the two pieces of carpet so that they butt against each other.

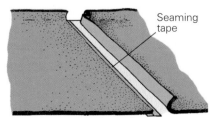

Seaming tape

Centerline

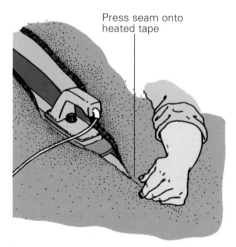

Press seam onto heated tape

7. MELTING THE ADHESIVE

Heat the tape with a seaming iron. As the iron passes slowly over the melted adhesive, pinch the carpet pieces together. Have an assistant place heavy objects on the bonded seam as you push the iron forward.

8. Stretching the Carpet

For short distances, such as across hallways or small bedrooms, it is possible to use a knee kicker. Start at one corner and dig the head of the knee kicker into the carpet about an inch from the wall. Lean on the handle to keep the head grip secure and swiftly kick the cushion with your knee. As you proceed, kick by kick, push the secured carpet down onto the strip so that it won't unhook.

In larger rooms, use a power stretcher with extension tubes that will stretch carpet across a room of any size. See the diagram for the kicking and stretching pattern.

To use a power stretcher, set the head 6 inches from the wall and adjust the extension tubes so that the foot rests against the opposite wall. Press down on the lever to stretch the carpet toward the front wall. The lever should lock easily. With the handle locked and the carpet stretched, fasten the section of carpet held by the head onto the tackless strip. Release the head, move the power stretcher 18 inches, and repeat the operation.

Protect the baseboard or a weak wall from damage by the stretcher foot with a piece of padded 2×4. Place it between the foot and the wall. The 2×4 should be long enough to span three or four studs.

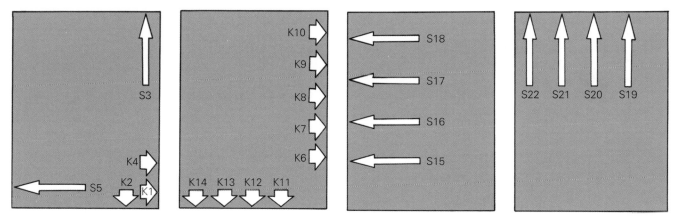

Use the knee kicker (K) at short-arrow positions and the power stretcher (S) on long-arrow points, following the numerical order indicated.

USING A KNEE KICKER

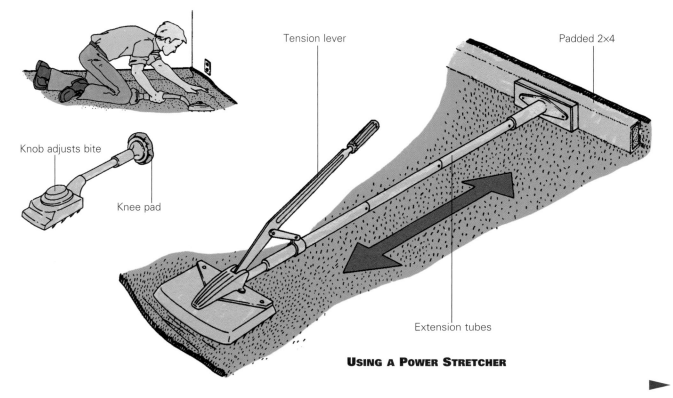

USING A POWER STRETCHER

INSTALLING STRETCHED CARPET *continued*

9. TRIMMING THE CARPET

Spend the money to buy or rent a wall trimmer. Adjust the trimmer to the thickness of the carpet. Starting at the lapped end, slice downward at an angle until the trimmer is flat against the floor. Then hold the trimmer against both the wall and the floor, and plow along the edge of the carpet. At the end, trim the last few inches with a utility knife.

10. TUCKING IN THE EDGES

Tuck the trimmed carpet edge into the gap between the tackless strip and the baseboard with a stair tool or a mason's chisel.

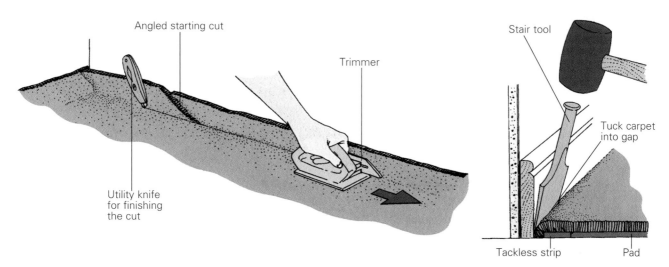

Angled starting cut

Trimmer

Utility knife for finishing the cut

Stair tool

Tuck carpet into gap

Tackless strip   Pad

11. FINISHING DOOR OPENINGS

At a doorway, trim the edge of the carpet so it falls under the closed door. Finish the edge with a metal strip suited to the type of subfloor.

If the subfloor is wood, tack the carpet to the floor and screw down a metal strip over the joint. Or, finish the edge with a binding strip that is concealed by the carpet and gives the finished carpet a folded edge.

If the subfloor is concrete, nail a gripper edge across the doorway (it's better to do this before the carpet is installed). Lay the carpet in the gripper and hammer down the curved metal flange, protecting the flange from hammer dents with a piece of scrap wood.

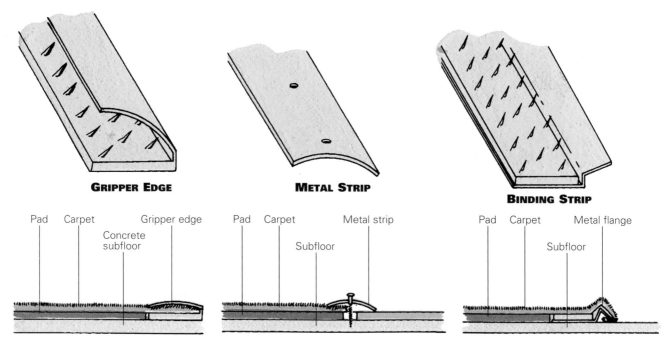

GRIPPER EDGE

Pad   Carpet   Gripper edge
      Concrete
      subfloor

METAL STRIP

Pad   Carpet   Metal strip
            Subfloor

BINDING STRIP

Pad   Carpet   Metal flange
            Subfloor

INSTALLING CUSHION-BACKED CARPET

Cushion-backed carpet is relatively thin and rigid and requires no stretching. Simply glue it to the subfloor floor with the appropriate adhesive. Prepare the subfloor carefully, however, because defects will show through the finished carpet.

In a wooden subfloor, fill and sand knotholes and other defects. Cover planks or tongue-and-groove floors with ¼-inch underlayment such as lauan plywood.

Patch defects in concrete floors and make sure the floor will always be free of moisture. Foam backing acts like a sponge. If moisture is minimal, try applying a coat of sealer to the subfloor. If the moisture persists, do not lay the carpet. (See Basements, pages 18–21, for testing concrete floors for moisture.)

You can lay cushion-backed carpet directly on a ceramic tile floor as long as the floor is flat and dry, but first, level the grout lines with a latex-type underlayment.

Before working with the carpet, install a toothless binder bar at door openings. If the carpet fits the room without having to be seamed, there is no need to glue it down. Simply rough-cut the carpet, place it in position, and go to step 5. Always cut cushion-backed carpet from its face side.

1. POSITIONING THE FIRST PIECE

Rough-cut the first piece of carpet and position it, allowing 3-inch excesses at the walls. Snap a chalk line on the floor where the seam will fall. Carefully align one edge of the carpet to this chalk line.

2. OVERLAPPING THE SEAM

Place the second piece of carpet so that its edge overlaps the first piece by ¼ inch.

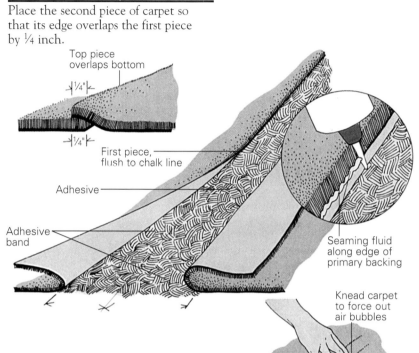

Top piece overlaps bottom

¼"

¼"

First piece, flush to chalk line

Adhesive

Adhesive band

Seaming fluid along edge of primary backing

Knead carpet to force out air bubbles

3. ADHERING THE SEAM EDGES

Fold both edges of the carpet back about 2 or 3 feet and trowel a thin, even coat of carpet adhesive onto the exposed floor. Roll the edge of the first piece into place; align the edge on the chalk line. Work the carpet to force out any bubbles of air.

Apply seaming fluid to the adhered edge of its primary backing material (the tough matrix that holds the carpet together). Cut the nozzle of the fluid dispenser at an angle so the bead of seaming fluid flows onto the carpet backing, not onto the foam or pile.

4. JOINING THE SEAM

Join the second piece of carpet to the first. Be sure that any pattern still lines up. Since you allowed a ¼-inch overlap, the edges should now press tightly against each other. Work any bulges away from the seam and let the seam adhesive dry completely before proceeding.

Glue the rest of the carpet down by folding the unglued edges back toward the center to expose the floor. Trowel adhesive onto the floor, then roll the carpet toward the wall so that it covers the glued area. Work out any wrinkles, creases, or bumps as you go. Repeat for the other half of the carpet.

5. FITTING, TRIMMING, AND TUCKING EDGES

Use a stair tool or mason's chisel to seat and crease the edge of the carpet against the wall. Trim the carpet with a sharp utility or carpet knife, leaving an excess margin just equal to the thickness of the carpet. Tuck this margin down at the wall with the stair tool or chisel.

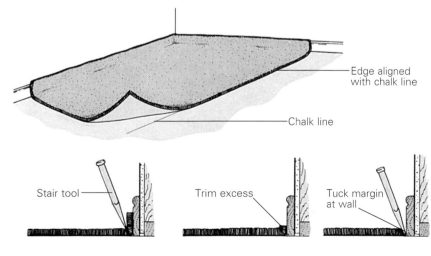

Edge aligned with chalk line

Chalk line

Stair tool

Trim excess

Tuck margin at wall

CAULK

RUNNING A TIGHT SHIP

Caulk serves two general purposes:
■ It helps prevent water damage by keeping moisture from reaching interior surfaces.
■ It also reduces air infiltration.

Caulk, properly applied, is the best way to seal leaks that occur where different components of the house join together, such as joints between the siding and the foundation, or cracks that have opened up from the natural settling and shifting of the house.

Caulk offers an easy and affordable way to make your home tighter—more energy efficient and less susceptible to moisture damage.

ALSO SEE...
Heat Leaks:
Pages 178–179
Insulation:
Pages 186–193
Siding:
Pages 308–309
Weather Stripping:
Pages 424–427

USING A CAULKING GUN

1 Turn the handle to disengage the ratchet. Pull the plunger all the way back and insert the cartridge, seating the bottom end first. Squeeze the trigger a few times until the plunger makes contact with the tube.

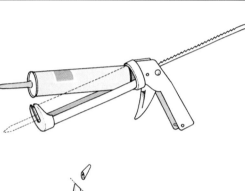

2 Cut the tip of the nozzle at an angle; the closer to the top, the finer the bead. Start with a fine bead and enlarge it if necessary. Puncture the seal inside the nozzle with a long nail.

45°

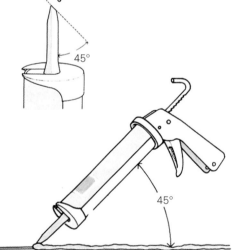

45°

3 Force caulk into the crack by pushing the gun forward at an angle and squeezing the trigger. The caulk should be as deep as the width of the crack and should adhere firmly to both sides. Release the trigger and the plunger just before you reach the end of the crack.

4 Moisten your finger with soapy water (for latex) or mineral oil to smooth the caulk and clean off adjacent surfaces.

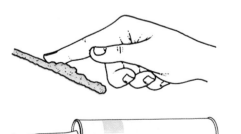

5 Release the plunger and insert a large nail into the nozzle. Wipe off any excess caulk and store in a freezeproof location.

WHERE TO CAULK

First, caulk all cracks and joints around the exterior of your home. The most likely spots are where building sections meet, such as joints between the chimney and house, between siding and door or window frames, between the roof and walls, or between a porch and the house.

Other prime targets for caulk are joints between dissimilar building materials, such as concrete and wood, or metal and brick. These joints are particularly vulnerable because materials expand and contract at different rates and under different weather conditions. Caulk remains flexible and expands and contracts with the joint.

Indoors, use caulk to seal cracks between walls and ceilings, between floors and walls, and around windows and doors. Also, caulk the entry of pipes and wires into the living area of the house. Finally, seal joints around bathtubs and sinks to prevent water damage to floors below.

CAULK IN A ROPE

The purpose of caulk is to seal cracks and joints in building surfaces. Since most joints "work" (open and close with the seasons), you need a caulk that is resilient—stretching and compressing to maintain the seal.

What if there were a "caulk" that looked like rope, was very inexpensive, had infinite shelf life, left no messy residue, and still did the job?

There is such a product. It's called "backer rod"—a flexible and compressible, extruded, closed-cell foam available in diameters from 1/8 inch to over 1 inch. Its purpose is to fill large joints in masonry construction behind a surface application of caulk.

Masonry supply companies sell it by the foot. Get some today! You will find no end to its uses in sealing up your house.

SEAL TUBES FOR LATER

Don't discard half-used tubes of caulk. Simply insert a nail of the same diameter as the nozzle hole. The nail will usually seal the contents against the two most common curing agents, air and moisture, for a few months at least. When withdrawn, the nail will create a fresh path for the remaining caulk.

HOW TO CAULK

PREPARATION

Clean out the crack or joint to be caulked. Use a putty knife to scrape away loose paint, old caulk, and other debris, and remove them with a brush. Use acetone or methyl ethyl ketone (MEK) solvent on greasy areas or metal surfaces. Read the caulk instructions to see if priming is necessary. Allow the crack to dry thoroughly before applying caulk.

FILLING CRACKS

Cracks over ¼-inch wide should be filled with foam backer rod (see Caulk in a Rope, opposite) before caulking. Using a screwdriver or putty knife, pack the material tightly into the crack so that the caulk will have a firm base.

APPLYING CAULK

After all joints are clean and dry, and you've packed large cracks with backer rod, apply caulk. Run a continuous bead of caulk along the entire length of the crack. To widen the bead, cut off as much of the nozzle tip as necessary.

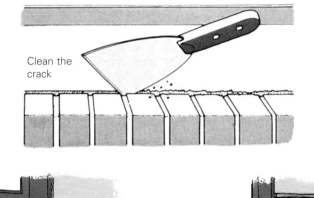

Clean the crack

Fill with backer rod

Apply caulk

CAULKING MATERIALS

Type	Cost	Life, in years	Ease to apply	Adhesion	Max. Gap	Max. Stretch	Problems
Oil	Low	1–3	Easy	Fair	¼"	1%	Harmed by direct sunlight. Porous surfaces require priming.
Vinyl latex	Low	3–5	Very easy	Fair	¼"	2%	Harmed by direct sunlight. Porous surfaces require priming. Interior use only.
Acrylic latex	Low	5–10	Very easy	Good	¼"	2%	Harmed by direct sunlight. Requires primer over metal.
Siliconized acrylic latex	Medium	10–20	Easy	Good	½"	10%	Doesn't adhere to plastics.
Butyl rubber	Medium	5–10	Fair	Good	½"	5%	Harmed by direct sunlight.
Polysulfide	Medium	20 +	Difficult	Very good	¾"	25%	Harmed by direct sunlight. Porous surfaces require priming. Requires temperature over 60°F.
Polyurethane	High	20 +	Difficult	Very good	¾"	25%	None.
Silicone	High	20–50	Easy	Good	1"	50%	Most cannot be painted. Doesn't adhere to plastics. Porous surfaces require priming.
Urethane foam	High	10–20	Difficult	Good	2"	1%	Requires temperature over 60°F. Harmed by direct sunlight.

CEILINGS

TRANSFORMING SPACE

ALSO SEE...
Attics:
Pages 14–17
Framing:
Pages 152–159
Lighting:
Pages 212–219
Moldings:
Pages 228–231
Wallboard:
Pages 392–397
Walls:
Pages 406–413

Ceilings have a strong impact on the look of a room. A low ceiling can make an area cozy and intimate—or oppressive. A high ceiling creates an atmosphere that can either inspire—or overwhelm. Although it's possible to create custom ceiling heights, there are limits—stud wall heights and building codes. A stud wall—typically made with 92½-inch studs, a 1½-inch bottom plate, and two 1½-inch bottom plates—will be 97 inches high. Subtracting for flooring and ceiling materials gives a finished height of about 8 feet. See Code Requirements (*below*) for ceiling limits in living space.

Color and pattern can play optical games. In general, a dark-colored or heavily patterned ceiling will look lower than the same ceiling finished with a simple texture and a light color.

Think about lighting when you plan your ceiling. Recessed fixtures usually require at least an 8-inch height for installation. Suspended or flush-mounted light fixtures should complement the style of the ceiling.

WALLBOARD

T brace made from 2×4s

Wallboard panel

Align brace under joists

CODE REQUIREMENTS: CEILINGS

Except for kitchens, habitable rooms must have ceiling heights of at least 7½ feet in at least 50 percent of their areas.

No portion of the required room area may have a ceiling height of less than 5 feet. One exception: beams and girders spaced at least 4 feet on center may project downward up to 6 inches.

As nonhabitable space, a basement can have a ceiling height of 6 feet 8 inches, except for under beams, girders, and ducts, where the clear height may be 6 feet 4 inches. However, when a basement is converted to a habitable space, the required ceiling height increases to 7 feet 6 inches (7 feet under beams and ducts).

Wallboard's smooth, paintable surface makes it ideal for ceilings. Some localities require it as a firebreak between floors. A sheet of wallboard weighs about 70 pounds and is heavy and awkward. Enlist a helper to hang it on ceilings or make a T-shape brace to hold up one end while you fasten it to joists (see Wallboard, pages 392–397). Hanging wallboard can also be easier from a scaffold of planks on strong boxes. Be careful—with your attention focused upwards, you won't want to step off your temporary scaffold.

ESTIMATING MATERIALS FOR WALLBOARD CEILINGS

Sheets Wallboard	Nails, Pounds		Screws, Pounds		Joint Compound, Gal.	Joint Tape, Feet
	1¼ Inch	1⅝ Inch	1¼ Inch	1⅝ Inch		
2	0.3	0.4	0.2	0.3	1	40
4	0.5	0.7	0.4	0.5	1	50
6	0.8	1.0	0.6	0.9	2	72
8	1.0	1.4	0.8	1.0	2	95
10	1.3	1.7	1.0	1.3	2	118
12	1.5	2.0	1.2	1.6	3	142
14	1.8	2.4	1.4	1.8	3	166
16	2.0	2.7	1.6	2.1	4	190
18	2.3	3.1	1.8	2.4	4	213
20	2.6	3.4	2.0	2.6	4	237

SUSPENDED CEILING

A suspended ceiling performs a number of functions. It lowers the ceiling (see Code Requirements, *opposite*), muffles sound, and conceals ductwork or uneven joists. Most varieties are insulating tiles. Some are smooth acrylic panels. The frames and panels are easy to install, and can be attached either before or after finishing the walls.

Start by fastening the outer support ledge (wall angles) all around the room. Use a level to position each piece, rather than measuring from the floor or ceiling.

Hang wires every 4 feet so the main tee supports will be perpendicular to the joists and spaced according to the size of the panels you are using. Let the wires hang 2 inches lower than the tees will be and use two wires where a tee will splice. After hanging all the wires, feed them through the holes in the tees and twist them, making sure all the tees are level.

Fill in the secondary cross-tees and lay in each panel. If necessary, trim the panels to fit.

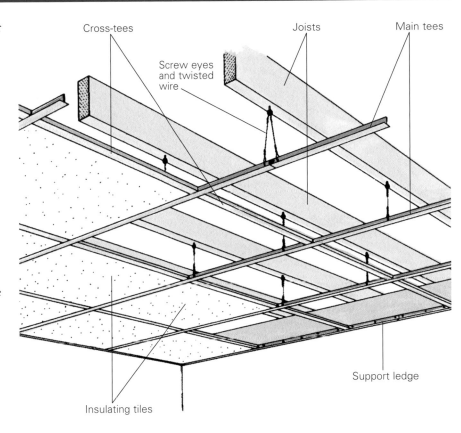

Cross-tees

Screw eyes and twisted wire

Joists

Main tees

Support ledge

Insulating tiles

TILED CEILING

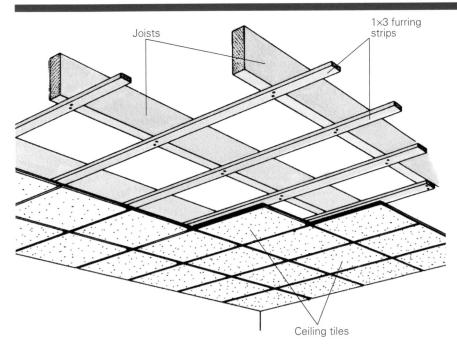

Joists

1×3 furring strips

Ceiling tiles

Ceiling tiles made from organic fibers are usually ½ inch thick. Those made from mineral fibers that won't burn are usually ¾ inch thick. Both are available in 12×12 and 12×24 sizes. Tiles can be applied with adhesive to an existing (and absolutely flat) ceiling, or they can be stapled to 1×3 furring, shimmed level if necessary.

Start by marking the exact center of the room. Measure from this point to the walls to determine the widths of the perimeter tiles. If you apply tiles with adhesive, install four tiles in the center and work out in all directions.

If you are applying the tiles with staples, fasten the first piece of furring across the joists and down the centerline of the room. Space the remaining furring on center the width of the tiles. Attach each tile with two staples, working so the stapling flange is always exposed.

CHIMNEYS AND STOVEPIPES

SAFETY FIRST

Although faulty stoves themselves are responsible for their share of unfortunate accidents, most household fires occur as a result of poorly installed or maintained chimneys and stovepipes.

If you are installing a new fireplace or wood-burning stove, the chimney or stovepipe must meet local code requirements, even if it's an existing chimney. Always have a fire or building official inspect your installation. Clean and inspect your chimney once each year—even a properly installed chimney or stovepipe can fail if not maintained, resulting ina disastrous fire.

The main cause of chimney and stovepipe fires is creosote buildup. Even the new generation of EPA-approved wood-burning stoves can produce large amounts of creosote in the vent systems if operated improperly.

If the creosote ignites, it can become a roaring inferno. Even if it doesn't ignite, creosote is caustic and will eat through materials. Always use materials that have been tested and approved, and install them according to local codes. High-quality materials cost more, but they are definitely worth it.

INSTALLING A RAIN CAP

You've heard of acid rain. A mixture of rain, soot, and fireplace gases can produce an acid rain—a caustic chemical mix that will attack the mortar joints inside your chimney as well as the cast-iron damper of a fireplace. To minimize both the entry of rain and down drafts, install a rain cap.

Chip away the concrete from each corner of the chimney top. Mortar a stack of bricks at each corner to a height of at least 12 inches. Place either a slate (flagstone) or concrete cap on top of the four corners. Rectangular concrete septic-tank covers are inexpensive and make nifty caps.

INSTALLING A SPARK ARRESTER

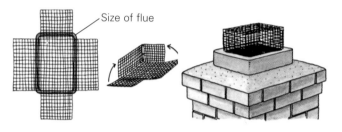

Size of flue

To protect your roof and neighboring houses, install a wire spark arrester. You can buy stainless steel models to fit all standard flue sizes, but they are expensive. An inexpensive one can be made from heavy galvanized mesh with a 1-inch grid. Cut the mesh large enough to fit over the opening. Fasten it to the flue wire.

CODE REQUIREMENTS: CHIMNEYS AND STOVEPIPES

Chimney/Roof Clearance: The chimney outlet must be at least 3 feet above the height of the roof where the chimney exits the roof. The outlet also must be at least 2 feet above the highest point of the roof 10 feet in any direction when measuring horizontally from the chimney.

Building Surface Penetrations: Chimney and vent-pipe connectors must not pass through floors, walls, or ceilings unless the connectors are UL-listed or are passed through listed devices.

Horizontal Runs: The horizontal length of an uninsulated stovepipe must be no more than 75 percent of the height of the chimney above the connection. The horizontal length of an insulated stovepipe must be no more than 100 percent of the height of the chimney above the connection.

Thimble Size: The size of the thimble connector must be at least as large as the flue collar of the appliance.

Fireplaces and Appliances: An appliance must not be connected to a fireplace flue unless the flue or fireplace opening is sealed below the connection.

Size of Masonry Chimneys: The effective area of a chimney flue must be at least as large as the appliance connector. The effective area of a chimney flue serving more than one appliance must be at least as large as the largest connector, plus half of the areas of the additional connectors.

Masonry Chimney Connectors: The connector must enter the chimney at least 6 inches above the chimney bottom or have a capped T for cleanout. The end of the connector must be flush with the chimney liner. Thimble connectors must be cemented into the masonry.

CLEANING A CHIMNEY

If you heat your home with wood, you should clean your chimney at the start of each heating season. Although chimney sweeps have specialized equipment that speeds things up, you can do the job yourself. Just measure the inside dimensions of your flue and its length and purchase the matching wire brush and extension handles at a wood-burning stove shop.

Start by removing the fireplace grate and opening or removing the damper. Block off the fireplace opening with a large piece of cardboard or plywood. Stuff rags around the edges.

Do the cleaning from the roof. Dress in old clothes and wear gloves and a dust mask. Screw one of the fiberglass handles into the cleaning brush and work the brush up and down vigorously inside the flue. Keep adding extensions and brushing until you have cleaned the entire length of the chimney. After retrieving the extension handles and the brush, remove the barrier from the fireplace opening and shovel up the soot. Use a brush or broom to knock soot down from the damper and shelf.

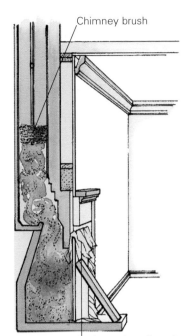

Chimney brush

Drape rags around edges of cardboard, then brace against fireplace opening

Place the soot in a double trash bag, seal it tightly, and dispose of it as you do your other trash.

RELINING A CHIMNEY

Unlined chimneys, or those with cracked tile liners, can allow the heat from a chimney fire to start a house fire. Provided the chimney is otherwise sound, it can probably be relined rather than replaced.

There are two principal relining methods. With both methods, the old liner is removed.

In the first method, a large diameter vinyl or rubber hose is inserted into the chimney and inflated. Lightweight concrete is poured around the hose, which is deflated and removed after the concrete sets.

In the second method, a stainless steel liner is inserted into the chimney. The liner is surrounded with lightweight concrete and either connected directly to a wood-burning stove or used as a fireplace chimney.

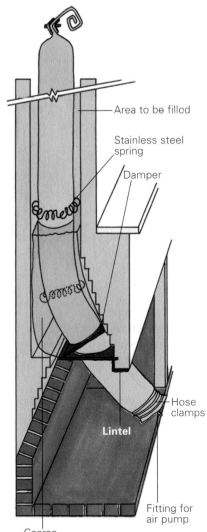

Area to be filled

Stainless steel spring

Damper

Hose clamps

Lintel

Fitting for air pump

Coarse vermiculite

GAS FIREPLACE ALTERNATIVES

Direct-vent gas fireplaces and stoves are ideal for retrofit situations. They are lightweight and can be installed virtually anywhere in your home without strengthening existing floor framing. They are simple to install, don't produce ash or creosote—messy by-products of burned wood—use either LP or natural gas, and are connected to existing gas lines with standard pipe fittings (see Plumbing, pages 256–263).

Although their exhaust gases must be vented to the outside, gas-burning units can use short lengths of narrow, 3-inch-diameter pipe.

Ventless gas fireplaces burn so efficiently that they don't require venting to the outside. Ventless fireplaces should include an oxygen depletion sensor (ODS), a safety device that warns if oxygen levels are low. Some states have banned these units as a possible health hazard.

CHIMNEY-BASE SHORTCUT

If you are building a small masonry chimney, ask your building code official about supporting it on an interior, beefed-up floor instead of the normal below-frost concrete footing. Some codes require only a sufficiently strong floor to carry the weight and 4 inches of noncombustible material (a 4-inch slab) between it and the wood floor.

DON'T VACUUM CREOSOTE

After cleaning your fireplace chimney, your first housekeeping impulse will be to reach for the vacuum cleaner. Unless you plan on buying a new vacuum right away, don't do it.

You will never get all of the traces of black, greasy creosote out of your vacuum.

Use a small whisk broom and a dustpan instead.

FINDING SPACE FOR STORAGE

ALSO SEE...
Doors:
Pages 86–97
Framing:
Pages 152–159
Shelving:
Pages 304–307
Storage:
Pages 338–347
Wallboard:
Pages 394–399

Closet space is near the top of any home-improvement wish list. If you never seem to have enough room for everything, it's probably time to make your life more convenient by building a new closet or adding shelving and other elements that will help to reorganize an existing one.

BUILDING A NEW CLOSET

DESIGNING THE CLOSET

For bedroom closets, allow at least 4 linear feet of hanging space and 8 square feet of storage shelf for each person. Hanging space should be at least 24 inches deep. Shelving should be at least 12 inches deep, and preferably 20 inches. If possible, doors should open the full width of the closet. Other closets can be smaller.

FRAMING THE WALLS

Plan your closet layout so that the closet walls can be fastened to existing wall studs. Assemble the front and side walls on the floor—½-inch shorter than the floor-to-ceiling height, so they will clear the ceiling when you raise them. Construct the corner post with two studs and blocking, as shown in the illustration, *right*.

Frame the door opening with a header only if the wall is to be load-bearing. Otherwise, use a single 2×4 for door openings up to 8 feet.

Do not cut out the section of the bottom plate within the doorway until the wall is in place; instead, before lifting the wall cut halfway through the underside of the bottom plate.

FINISHING THE WALLS

Raise the front wall in place. Square it plumb with a 4-foot level and nail through the bottom plate into the flooring and floor joists with 16d nails. Do not nail the door opening. Slide shims between the top plate and ceiling at all the ceiling joist locations. Nail through the plate, shims, and ceiling into the joists above. Nail the closet wall studs into the studs of the existing wall.

Install any side walls in the same way. Nail the front end into the corner post of the front wall and the back into a stud in the existing wall.

Cut the bottom plate of the door opening with a backsaw and remove the doorway section. Install wiring for an overhead light fixture. After attaching wallboard or other finish material, you are ready to install the doors.

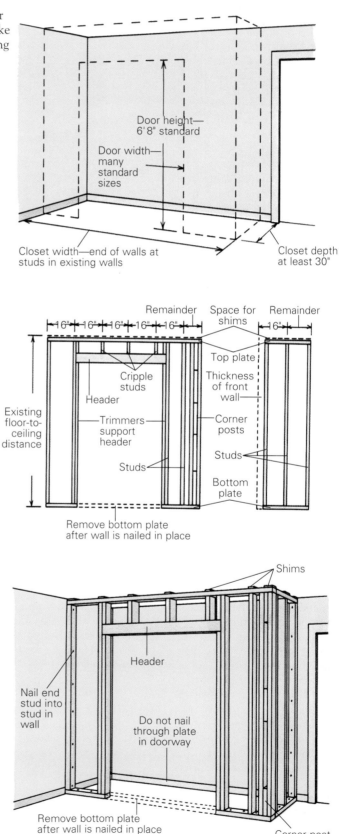

Door height— 6' 8" standard
Door width— many standard sizes
Closet width—end of walls at studs in existing walls
Closet depth at least 30"

Remainder · Space for shims · Remainder
16" · 16" · 16" · 16" · 16" · 16"
Top plate
Cripple studs
Thickness of front wall
Header
Corner posts
Existing floor-to-ceiling distance
Trimmers support header
Studs
Studs
Bottom plate
Remove bottom plate after wall is nailed in place

Shims
Nail end stud into stud in wall
Header
Do not nail through plate in doorway
Remove bottom plate after wall is nailed in place
Corner post

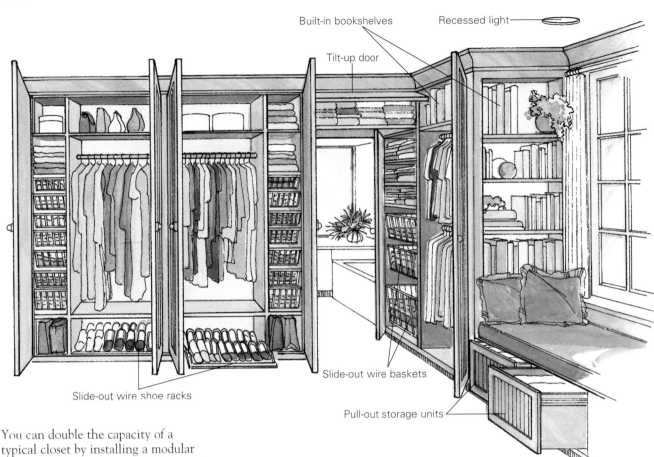

Built-in bookshelves

Recessed light

Tilt-up door

Slide-out wire shoe racks

Slide-out wire baskets

Pull-out storage units

You can double the capacity of a typical closet by installing a modular system of shelves, drawers, baskets, and poles. Home centers will typically carry two types of systems built around:
■ Particleboard panels and
■ Vinyl-coated wire frames
These systems are well-designed and complete, and you can completely reconfigure a walk-in closet in one day.

Designing Your System: Before you select a system, make a list of what you will store in the closet. Place the items in categories according to size, shape, and whether they will be on hangers, on hooks, on racks, or laid flat. Check the various systems to make sure your needs will be met by the various components.

Shelves: Replace single horizontal shelves at the top of the closet with vertical, floor-to-ceiling units. For maximum efficiency, make sure the shelves are adjustable. Place the highest shelf about 7 feet from the floor, leaving 12 inches of space above it. Be sure to leave clearance for any existing light fixture (see Code Requirements, *right*).

Drawers and Baskets: Pull-out vinyl-coated and plastic drawers, baskets, and bins provide ventilation and a view of the contents. They work best in the center third of the closet where they won't interfere with the doors or side compartments.

Hanger Poles: Increase hanging storage by replacing the typical single long poles with several short poles. Short poles installed at different levels allow you to devote a small section to the few really long garments and double the space in the rest of the closet. For instance, shirts and blouses can hang on a high pole, while skirts and jackets can hang on a pole directly below it.

Average clothing items require about 1 inch of lateral hanging space. Bulky winter clothing requires about 2–3 inches.

Doors: Doors will solve most shoe storage problems. Hang a shoe rack on the back of the closet door for dress shoes. Athletic shoes, slippers, and

other footwear that aren't prone to scratches and abrasions can be put into a wire basket or bin.

CLOTHES DRYERS

FEATURES TO CONSIDER

ALSO SEE...
Electrical Systems:
Pages 110–115
Receptacles:
Pages 272–273
Wire:
Pages 442–445

Clothes dryers are hard-working appliances that are expected to perform flawlessly for many years. When shopping for a dryer, select the highest quality appliance your budget will allow.

Here are a few things to look for:

Controls: Dryers with automatic and electronic controls sense moisture content and when the clothes are dry, they stop before they waste energy and possibly damage fabrics by overheating. This also reduces the buildup of static electricity. Dryers with timers (and without sensors) continue operation even if the clothes are dry.

Cycles: Most dryers have "regular," "permanent press," "knits," and "fluff" cycles. Some dryers also have an "extra care" cycle that continues tumbling, after the heat goes off. The "extra care" cycle keeps the clothes from wrinkling. Some models sound a periodic reminder when the clothes are dry.

Door Racks: The thumping of sneakers being dried is annoying. A stationary door rack will dry them quietly.

Newer models on the market include ventless dryers that channel moisture to a small holding tank. Ventless dryers are ideal for retrofit situations where installing a vent would be difficult or impossible.

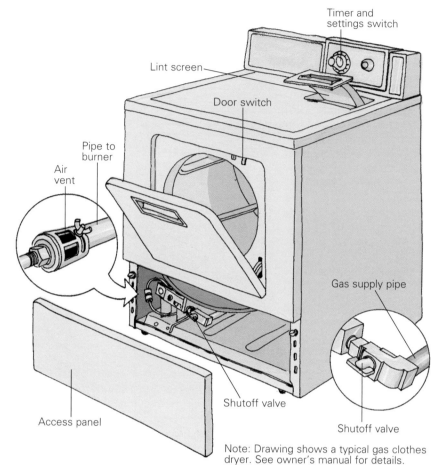

Note: Drawing shows a typical gas clothes dryer. See owner's manual for details.

VENT FLAPPER TUNE-UP

Clothes dryers are required to have backdraft dampers to prevent cold winter air from flowing back into the clothes dryer and house. That's the little flapper up inside the vent hood on your outside wall or up on the roof.

When was the last time you looked at your flapper? Dollars to doughnuts yours is no longer flapping, but is stuck in the open position due to lint. That means there is a 4-inch hole right through the side of your house!

An old toothbrush (it's time you got a new one, anyway) is the perfect tool to clean the flapper and its hinge.

INSTALLING A CLOTHES DRYER

Electric Clothes Dryer: An electric dryer requires a dedicated (with no other appliances on it) 240-volt circuit that terminates in a receptacle (if the dryer has a cord and plug), or a junction box next to the dryer (if it has a pigtail of flexible conduit). Both must meet the requirements of local codes. Place the outlet either on the side of the dryer or behind and above it so you can reach the plug.

If the dryer arrives without a cord, refer to the electrical schematic when you attach the cord wires to the corresponding color-coded dryer terminals. The schematic will be included in the product literature, or attached to the electrical access door of the dryer.

Connect 4-inch duct to the dryer vent. Make sure the circuit breaker is off, then plug the cord into the 240-volt receptacle. Slide the dryer into position and turn the breaker back on.

Gas Clothes Dryer: Have a licensed contractor install a gas line that ends with a gas cock at the dryer location. The size of the line will depend on the BTU per hour (BTUH) rating of the dryer and the length of the run. The run may include nipples, but cannot contain unions.

To hook up the dryer to the pipe, use a flexible gas line at least 3 feet long but no more than 6 feet long. Use pipe-joint compound at all joints and tighten the nuts with two wrenches.

Attach a 4-inch duct to the vent (see Code Requirements, *opposite*, for specifications), and plug the electrical cord into a grounded 120-volt laundry receptacle.

The first time you use the dryer, follow the manufacturer's instructions for bypassing the electric ignition to purge the air from the gas line. You will also need to adjust the air intake for the burner.

VENTING

Venting removes moisture-laden air from the dryer and allows it to run at peak efficiency. Most dryers use a galvanized, 4-inch diameter vent pipe. The shorter the vent, the more efficiently the dryer will remove old air, so locate your laundry facilities near an exterior wall. Keep bends and turns in the vent to a minimum and seal joints with duct tape. Make sure you have access to the outside vent hood so you can clean out lint periodically.

CODE REQUIREMENTS: DRYERS

Gas Supply Connection: The flexible gas connection line (part that connects to the dryer inlet) must not be longer than 6 feet and must not run through a wall or floor.

Dryer Vent: The dryer vent duct must be at least 4 inches in diameter, smooth on the inside (note—no sheet metal screws), and no longer than 25 feet. You must deduct 5 feet of allowable length for every 90-degree elbow. The outlet must have a backdraft damper, but no screen.

Electric Dryer: An electric dryer must be on its own 240-volt, 30-amp circuit.

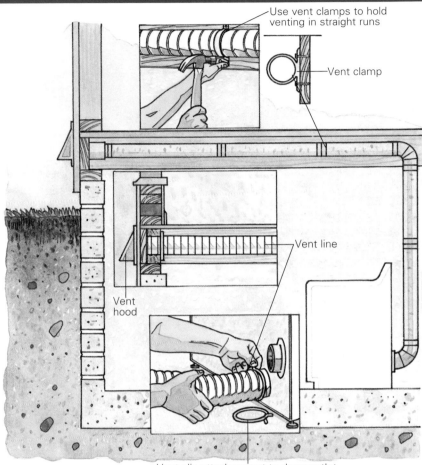

Use vent clamps to hold venting in straight runs

Vent clamp

Vent line

Vent hood

Vent clip attaches vent to dryer outlet

TROUBLESHOOTING: SOLUTIONS TO PROBLEMS

Some problems with dryers are a nuisance; others are potential hazards. This guide can help you respond to whatever trouble your dryer presents.

You Smell Gas: Close the gas shutoff valve immediately. In addition, turn off the main gas valve where the gas line enters the house. (For a propane system, turn off the valve on the tank.) Alert your local utility company that you smell gas.

Slow Drying: If the clothes are taking longer to dry than they should, the problem is not enough heat or not enough air flow through the vent.

In a gas clothes dryer the problem may lie in the fuel-air mixture. Pull out the bottom panel (you may have to depress a release spring first). With the dryer running, check the flame. If the flame has yellow tips, it is receiving too little air; if it is light blue and seems to be roaring, it is getting too much air.

To adjust the burner, turn the dryer off and let the burner cool. Loosen the thumb screw on the air vent and adjust it. Turn it to one extreme and then the other, and then settle for the place that gives a steady blue flame with no roaring sound.

If there is plenty of heat, but the clothes are still not drying, the venting system is clogged.

First check the pull-out lint filter in the top of the machine. It should be cleaned every time you use the dryer.

If that's clean, then the backdraft flapper or duct is clogged. Clean the flapper with a toothbrush. To clean the duct, tie string or wire to a hand towel, remove the dryer end of the duct, and pull the towel through the duct.

Drum Rotates, But No Heat: First check the temperature setting to make sure you are calling for heat.

If the controls are set correctly but

there is no heat, either the thermostat or the heating element (electric) is burned out, or the pilot light (gas) is out. For either of the electrical problems, call for service.

If the gas pilot light is out, follow instructions on the panel for relighting it, and try again. If it goes out again, clean the orifices with a fine wire and slide paper between the contacts to clean the thermostat. If it still goes out, replace the thermocouple.

Dryer Won't Run: The rotating drum, even on a gas clothes dryer, is powered by electricity, so make sure the dryer is plugged in.

There is a safety switch on the door that prevents the dryer from running unless the door is closed. Make sure the door is closed all the way.

If the dryer still won't run, check the fuse or circuit breaker.

CONCRETE

KEYS TO A SUCCESSFUL JOB

Concrete's unique properties make it indispensable in building. But because it's heavy and hardens so fast, the thought of working with concrete intimidates some people. Actually, the work is strenuous but simple. The keys to success are knowing how concrete behaves and being completely prepared before the mixer truck arrives.

MIXING YOUR OWN

Ready-mix trucks usually have a minimum quantity, below which you pay a stiff delivery charge. If you need only a small quantity of concrete— a cubic yard or less—mix it by hand or in a small cement mixer.

For really small batches, buy 80-pound bags of premixed cement and aggregate to which you merely add water. These bags typically make about 1 cubic foot of concrete.

For batches from 4 cubic feet up to a cubic yard (27 cubic feet), buy 94-pound bags of cement and mix the ingredients as shown in the table *below*.

If you're making your own, mix the dry ingredients first, then add water. For best results the machine should mix the entire batch for at least two minutes. When you are through, clean the mixer by throwing one or two shovelfuls of gravel and some water in it while it's running. Let it scour for a while, and then dump out the residue.

Cement | Wheelbarrow | Gravel | Water | Sand

CONCRETE MIXES

Concrete has three basic ingredients: portland cement, aggregate, and water. The proportions of these ingredients determine its workability and ultimate strength.

Portland Cement: Cement, the "glue" that holds the aggregate together, is a manufactured chemical product that solidifies and attains incredible strength when hydrated (combined with water).

Aggregate: Actually a combination of sand and gravel, aggregate constitutes the bulk of the mix. It provides great compressive strength and minimizes shrinkage as the concrete cures and dries. Aggregate must be clean so that the cement powder can adhere, and must include enough sand to fill the spaces between the larger gravel.

The size of aggregate refers to the largest stones in the mix. The size that is needed varies with the type of job. Typical aggregate sizes for residential use are ⅜ inch and ¾ inch. Use ⅜-inch aggregate for filling tight spaces, such as the cells of concrete blocks or when pumping concrete through a 3-inch-diameter hose. A ¾-inch aggregate mix is common for foundations, footings, and slabs. Aggregate size should not exceed one third the thickness of a slab or one fifth the narrowest dimension between wall forms.

Water: The third essential ingredient, water, brings about a chemical reaction in the cement. It's important to mix it in a proper water-cement ratio, approximately 1:2, by weight. Water in excess of the amount required to make the mix workable weakens the concrete by washing the cement off the aggregate and allowing the aggregate materials to segregate.

Admixtures: The qualities of concrete can be changed by ingredients called admixtures. The most common admixture is an air-entrainment agent, which makes the cement paste froth during mixing, creating microscopic air bubbles when the concrete hardens. The tiny air chambers provide space for water in the concrete to freeze and expand without fracturing the concrete— a useful quality in northern climates.

Other admixtures slow down or speed up the workability of the concrete under unusual conditions, such as extremely hot weather or when it is necessary to delay finishing time.

In very cold weather, when there is danger of freezing, calcium chloride is often added to speed up hydration so that the contractor can get the concrete under a protective blanket of insulation. It is not necessary to heat the insulated concrete because the hydration reaction produces heat within the concrete.

The "Mix": The proportions of the ingredients in a mix determine the final strength of concrete. In residential work it is customary to refer to the strength of a mix in terms of the number of 94-pound bags of cement per yard of concrete. For example, a 5-bag mix means the ready mix will contain 5 bags (470 pounds) of cement per cubic yard.

RECIPES FOR MAKING YOUR OWN CONCRETE

Application	Cement 94-Lb. Bags	Gravel Cu. Ft.	Sand Cu. Ft.	Gallons of Water Dry Sand	Gallons of Water Wet Sand	Concrete Cu. Ft.
Slabs less than 3" Severe freezing	1.0	2.0	2.2	5.0	4.0	3.5
Slabs more than 3" Sidewalks, patios	1.0	2.2	3.0	6.0	5.0	4.1
Footings, foundations, retaining walls	1.0	3.0	4.0	7.0	5.5	5.0

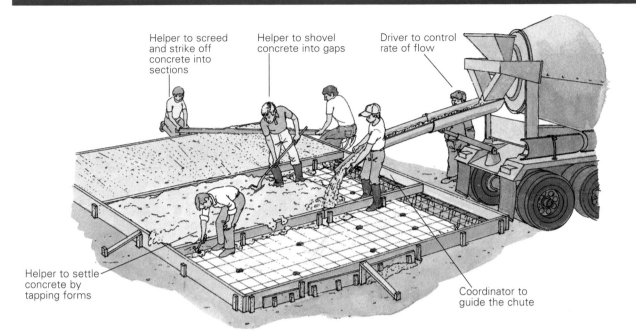

Helper to screed and strike off concrete into sections

Helper to shovel concrete into gaps

Driver to control rate of flow

Helper to settle concrete by tapping forms

Coordinator to guide the chute

If you need more than 1 yard (cubic yard), or if you want an admixture in the mix, order the concrete (in cubic yards) from a ready-mix company. Use the tables below to calculate the theoretical number, then add another 15 percent for normal waste, the typical uncertainty of the thickness,

and slight spreading of the forms.

The following are additional specifications that will help the ready-mix company match the concrete to your needs. Without them, the dispatcher will assume you are pouring a foundation and ask you only for the strength of the mix (bags per yard).

Cement Content: Specify 5-bag mix for footings and foundation walls; 6-bag mix for driveways, patios, walks, and slabs 3 or more inches thick; 7-bag mix for slabs less than 3 inches thick or for concrete that will be exposed to severe weather conditions.

Aggregate Size: For most jobs a ¾-inch aggregate is suitable, but if you are having the concrete pumped by a small cement truck that has only a 3-inch hose, or you are pouring walls with an intricate pattern built into the forms, for example, you will need to specify a ⅜-inch aggregate.

Water/Cement Ratio: Specify a ratio of .5 (point five).

Slump: This term is used to describe the consistency of fresh concrete. It refers to the number of inches a 12-inch-high core of concrete sags when it is fresh. A 1-inch slump is an extremely stiff mix (you wouldn't be able to work it by hand); a 10-inch slump is unacceptably soupy. For the best results specify about a 4-inch slump.

Air Entrainment: If you are in a cold, northern climate, specify 6 percent for concrete that will be exposed to water and freezing.

Calcium Chloride: If you absolutely can't wait for a time when temperatures will remain above freezing for several days and nights, specify no more than 2 percent.

CUBIC YARDS OF CONCRETE FOR WALKS, DRIVES, AND SLABS

Slab Area (Sq. Ft.)	Slab Thickness (Inches)						
	2	3	4	5	6	8	10
10	0.1	0.1	0.1	0.2	0.2	0.3	0.3
50	0.3	0.5	0.6	0.7	0.9	1.2	1.4
100	0.6	0.9	1.2	1.5	1.9	2.5	3.0
300	1.9	2.8	3.7	4.7	5.6	7.4	9.4
500	3.1	4.7	6.2	7.2	9.3	12.4	14.4

CUBIC YARDS PER LINEAR FOOT OF FOOTINGS AND WALLS

Depth/Height (Inches)	Width or Thickness (Inches)				
	6	8	12	18	24
8	0.012	0.017	0.025	0.037	0.049
12	0.019	0.025	0.037	0.056	0.074
24	0.037	0.049	0.074	0.111	0.148
72	0.111	0.148	0.222	0.333	0.444
96	0.148	0.198	0.296	0.444	0.593

POURING A SLAB

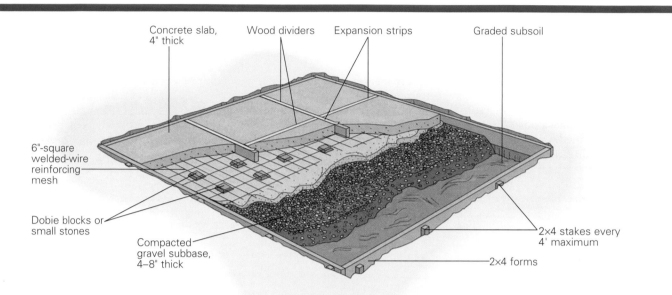

Concrete slab, 4" thick · Wood dividers · Expansion strips · Graded subsoil

6"-square welded-wire reinforcing mesh

Dobie blocks or small stones

Compacted gravel subbase, 4–8" thick

2×4 stakes every 4' maximum

2×4 forms

PREPARING THE SITE

Pouring concrete nearly always requires excavation and grading. You must always remove vegetation and loose soil. If you live in a cold climate, dig foundation footings to below the frost line, or pour on a well-drained gravel base that extends below the frost line. Walls and continuous footings need trenches excavated; for slabs and patios, dig deep enough for a gravel base, plus the concrete.

Dig carefully when you excavate. If you dig too deeply, you cannot throw the dirt back into the hole; you must use more concrete. The base of the excavation should be flat and level, especially on a sloping site.

FORMS

For slabs and most footings, make forms from boards held in place by stakes. Forms more than 12 inches high require a more sophisticated form system: either lumber held with metal ties or plywood with extensive 2×4 bracing. Beyond 3 feet, a pier or wall requires commercial concrete forms.

Most residential slabs, walks, and driveways are about 4 inches thick, so use 2×4s staked every 4 feet. Slope the forms ¼ inch per foot for drainage. On a large slab, place expansion strips of ¾-inch pressure-treated wood or felt (available at lumberyards) every 10 feet or "joint" the slab (groove the surface) to control cracks.

REINFORCEMENT

Patios and walks generally do not require reinforcing, but driveways, basement floors, and other structural slabs do. Your local code may require welded wire mesh, which comes in 6-foot-wide rolls. If so, you cut the wire with bolt cutters, and support the wire with "dobies" to hold it in the middle of the slab during the pour.

Ask your code official or the ready-mix company if fiberglass reinforcing is acceptable. If it is, the company will add chopped fiberglass to the mix—either at the plant or at the site, just prior to the pour.

FINISHING THE SURFACE

First, screed the surface using a straight piece of lumber that reaches all the way across the forms. Flatten and smooth the concrete by setting the screed board on edge and using a sawing motion to level the concrete. On large surfaces, you'll need two people for screeding—one on each end of the screed board.

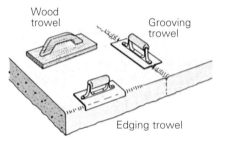

Wood trowel · Grooving trowel · Edging trowel

Immediately after screeding do a preliminary smoothing with a tool called a float. Some floats are made of wood; others are made of aluminum or magnesium (metal floats are required for air-entrained concrete). A bull float has a long handle for reaching to the center of large slabs. Run the float back and forth over the concrete, with the leading edge raised slightly, pushing the aggregate down and flattening the surface. Floating does not produce a perfectly smooth surface, but it does level it enough for finishing later. Clean up the perimeter edges by running a trowel between the forms and the fresh concrete.

After floating, wait for the surface water to evaporate before doing the final finish. This will take from a few minutes to several hours, depending on the weather, but there is usually enough time to clean the tools and take a well-deserved break. Begin finishing the concrete when troweling does not cause puddling.

Concrete lends itself to a variety of finishes. For a rustic, unstudied effect, leave the floated surface as it is. Refine the look with an edger and groover.

SAFETY PROVISIONS

The active ingredient in concrete is lime. When mixed with water, lime makes concrete highly alkaline. Wet concrete can be harmful to your skin, burning holes right through the outer layers and leaving painful sores.

Before any major concrete project, make sure you have on site: rubber gloves, rubber boots, a bottle of ordinary vinegar (a dilute acid that will neutralize the alkali), and a copious supply of water from a garden hose.

Run the edger back and forth against the side forms, and run the groover against a temporary straightedge (a straight 2×4 works well) held up off the concrete surface.

Scratching the surface with a stiff broom will produce a skid resistant surface with fine lines all running in the same direction. This is the preferred finish for walks.

Steel troweling produces the smoothest surface. An initial troweling can be done shortly after floating, but for smoother surfaces trowel again after the concrete stiffens and barely responds to light troweling activity. When working on the surface of a slab, be careful not to ruin your smooth surface. Use plywood knee boards to distribute your weight evenly.

Exposed aggregate is produced by "seeding" decorative stones into the surface after screeding. Wet the stones before spreading them over the slab. Then embed them below the surface with a float, level the surface, and wait for the concrete to set (not cure). When set, use a broom and a fine water spray from a hose to flush away the surface concrete and expose the top portion of the seeded stones.

CURING CONCRETE

A remarkable property of concrete is that it gains strength over time. While day-old concrete has a compressive strength of only a few hundred pounds per square inch (psi), that strength increases to 1,500 psi after 3 days, 2,000 psi after 7 days, and as much as 4,000 psi or more after 28 days. However, if the water evaporates too soon, the chemical reaction is arrested, and the concrete never reaches full strength. Freezing also disrupts the process and will ruin the concrete.

To ensure full strength, don't let water evaporate after the initial bleed water has disappeared. Leave the forms on walls and footings for at least seven days. If stripped sooner, the fresh concrete should be sprayed with a special curing compound.

Wet the surface constantly during the cure or slow the curing process by covering the concrete with plastic sheeting.

The most common repairs involve patching holes and filling cracks. To prevent repairs from failing, it's a good idea to select a mild, rainless day for the work.

For patches, enlarge the hole so all parts of it are at least 1 inch deep. Even better, try to undercut the sides with a small masonry chisel so that the patch is "keyed" (wider at the bottom than at the surface) and cannot fall out.

Clean out the keyed recess with a shop vacuum or a pressure washer. Next, etch the old concrete with diluted muriatic acid. Rinse again thoroughly and apply a liquid latex bonding agent (available through masonry-supply outlets) before filling the hole with new concrete.

Repair small cracks by using a masonry chisel to enlarge the cracks so that a cross section will be V-shaped. Clean the cracks thoroughly with a shop vacuum and fill with special expansive mortar.

FIXING BROKEN STEPS

First, undercut the broken area using a masonry chisel. Clean the broken area with a wire brush, then vacuum off any dust. Apply a latex bonding agent.

Mix the concrete patching material and apply it liberally to the broken area, using a trowel or wallboard knife. Immediately brace the front of the patch with a straight board and bricks. Trowel the top of the patch smooth, and use an edging tool to round off the front edge of the step. Leave the form board in place until the patch is thoroughly cured.

FIXING BROKEN STEPS

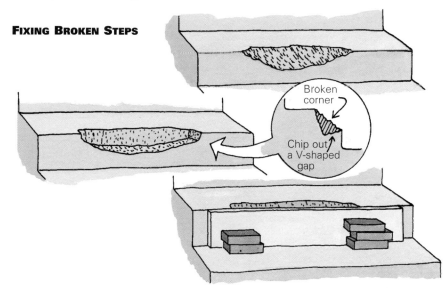

Broken corner

Chip out a V-shaped gap

WHEN GOOD CONCRETE GOES BAD

After about one hour in the truck, concrete begins to set up and requires the addition of water to keep it loose. But the extra water weakens the final product. As a rule of thumb, contractors consider concrete more than 90 minutes old to be unacceptable.

Be sure the ready-mix company knows how to get to your job site, and give them a telephone number (your number, your cell-phone number, or your neighbor's number) in case the driver gets lost. When you call for concrete, be sure forms are completely ready.

HOW TO AVOID WASTE

Estimating the amount of concrete for a job is difficult. The bottoms of footings and slabs are usually uneven, making it difficult to judge the thickness. Unfortunately, running short is worse than running over, because fresh concrete does not bond well to concrete that has set, resulting in structural weakness.

To play it safe and still not waste a cent, order 15 percent extra, but have forms set up for later projects, such as porch footings, patio blocks—even a walkway.

CONCRETE BLOCK

LAYING A BLOCK WALL

ALSO SEE...
Concrete:
Pages 60–63
Fireplaces:
Pages 134–135
Foundations:
Pages 144–151
Walls:
Pages 408–415

Concrete block makes walls that are incredibly strong and long-lasting. Working with block isn't complicated, but it does take patience and physical strength—a full day of laying block will give you a good workout.

The key to success is careful layout beforehand, and continually making sure that the block wall stays straight, level, and plumb as you build it. Start by excavating and laying a standard 8×16-inch concrete footing below the frost line (see Foundations, pages 144–151). Make sure the top of the footing is level.

While the footing concrete is still wet and pliable, embed vertical 4-foot lengths of ½-inch reinforcing rod (rebar) at 24 inches on center along the length of the wall. Make sure the

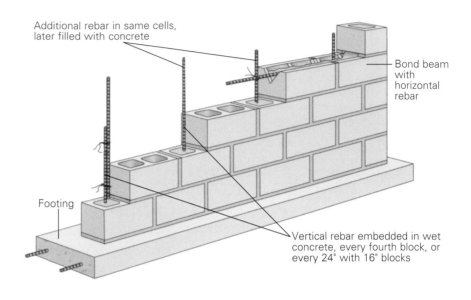

Additional rebar in same cells, later filled with concrete

Bond beam with horizontal rebar

Footing

Vertical rebar embedded in wet concrete, every fourth block, or every 24" with 16" blocks

rebar will fall into the cores of the blocks.

After the footing cures, chalk-line the perimeter of the walls on the concrete. Before mixing any mortar, lay out the proposed first course of blocks in a dry test run. Leave ⅜-inch spaces between each block. A good way to do this is to cut shims from ⅜-inch plywood—before you start the dry run. On the footing, mark where the joints fall.

When you are happy with the first-course layout, mix the first batch of mortar. Mortar consists of 1 part

portland cement and 3 parts clean sand, mixed with water to a fairly stiff consistency. The blocks should be perfectly dry.

Starting in a corner, lay down a 2-inch bed of mortar. Set an end block (a block with one square end) into the mortar, narrow face down, and tamp it down until the mortar joint is approximately ⅜ inch thick. Butter the end of the next block and place it next to the first block. Tamp it until both vertical and horizontal mortar joints are ⅜ inches wide. Any excess mortar squeezed out of the joints should be

CODE REQUIREMENTS: CONCRETE BLOCK

Minimum Thickness: The minimum thickness for solid or filled concrete block walls of a single story of height up to 9 feet is 6 inches, except that an additional 6 feet is allowed for gable end walls.

The minimum thickness of masonry walls of more than one story is 8 inches.

Lateral Support: Masonry walls must be supported either horizontally (by walls, pilasters, or structural frame members) or vertically (by floors or roof) at intervals equal to the wall's width multiplied by:

    20 for a solid bearing wall
    18 for a hollow bearing wall
    18 for a nonbearing exterior wall
    36 for a nonbearing interior wall

Reinforcing: Masonry walls must be reinforced at intervals and anchored to foundations and roofs as specified by an approved plan. Reinforcing steel must be completely covered by a minimum of ⅜ inch of mortar when placed in horizontal mortar joints, ¾ inch in all other locations, and 2 inches from the weather or soil.

Beam Pockets: Wood beams placed in pockets in a masonry wall must have an air gap of at least ¾ inch on three sides.

ESTIMATING

To order the correct amount of block, you'll need to do some simple math. As an example, we'll calculate the block needed to complete the three-course wall shown in the illustration *below*.

First, add the lengths of all sides of your project walls. In this case, one side 14 feet 8 inches plus one side 8 feet 8 inches totals 23 feet 4 inches.

Converting to inches equals 280 inches. Dividing by the length of one block, or 16 inches (remember that blocks are slightly short to allow for ⅜-inch mortar joints), gives 17.5 blocks per course. Multiplying by the number of courses (3) gives 52.5 blocks, or 53. Order six corner blocks, two half blocks, and a total of 47 stretchers.

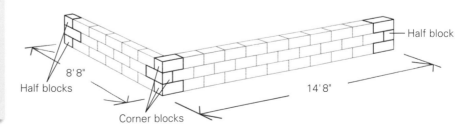

Half block

8'8"

Half blocks

Corner blocks

14'8"

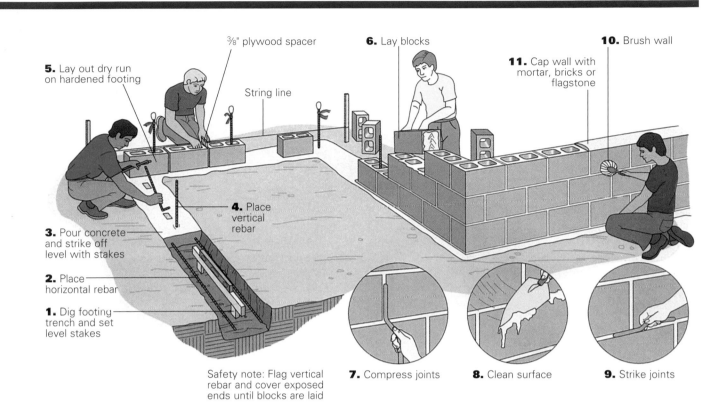

5. Lay out dry run on hardened footing

⅜" plywood spacer

String line

6. Lay blocks

10. Brush wall

11. Cap wall with mortar, bricks or flagstone

4. Place vertical rebar

3. Pour concrete and strike off level with stakes

2. Place horizontal rebar

1. Dig footing trench and set level stakes

Safety note: Flag vertical rebar and cover exposed ends until blocks are laid

7. Compress joints

8. Clean surface

9. Strike joints

immediately scraped off with a trowel and applied to the next block or put back in the mortar bucket. Continue laying block until you have completed the entire first course.

To keep each course straight and level, run mason's lines alongside the blocks for the length of the layout. Keep the lines 2 inches away from the blocks—a convenient distance for checking with a tape measure. Use these lines to keep the first course absolutely straight and level. That way, you greatly increase your chances that the project wall will end up being plumb and level. As you build, occasionally check the perpendicular level of the blocks across their width, from the outside face to the inside—using an 18-inch level.

Build the corners of the wall four courses high, then stretch mason's line between line blocks (available from masonry suppliers) as guides while you complete the central sections of each course. After completing the first four courses, build corners again and repeat the process until you've reached the planned height. Have frames for windows and doors handy to use as guides for constructing the openings.

As you go, extend the vertical rebar by wiring together overlapped lengths of at least 30 times the bar diameter.

When you reach the top course, you have three options:
■ Fill U-shape beam blocks with two rows of rebar and mortar.
■ Bed metal lath in the last layer of mortar, then fill the top blocks.
■ Cap the wall with solid cap blocks.

CELLS AND STANDARD SIZES

Note that concrete blocks have one face that is thicker than the other. Block is modular in size, making quantities easy to estimate and layouts that are simple to design and build.

■ Full blocks are 8×8×16 inches, including allowance for ⅜-inch joints.
■ Half blocks are 8×8×8 inches.
■ Half-high blocks are 4×8×16 inches.

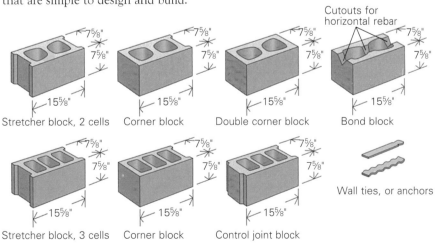

Cutouts for horizontal rebar

7⅝"
7⅝"
15⅝"
Stretcher block, 2 cells

7⅝"
7⅝"
15⅝"
Corner block

7⅝"
7⅝"
15⅝"
Double corner block

7⅝"
7⅝"
15⅝"
Bond block

7⅝"
7⅝"
15⅝"
Stretcher block, 3 cells

7⅝"
7⅝"
15⅝"
Corner block

7⅝"
7⅝"
15⅝"
Control joint block

Wall ties, or anchors

COOLING

COMFORT—THE BIG PICTURE

ALSO SEE...
Fans:
Pages 118–121
Insulation:
Pages 186–193
Ventilation:
Pages 386–387
Windows:
Pages 432–441

The goal of cooling is to create a home environment that is comfortable during the hottest months of the year. But comfort is a complex function that is affected by several variables. Some of these variables, such as the availability of seasonal breezes or the shading offered by nearby trees, are simple and cost virtually nothing. You should maximize the cooling available from natural sources before turning your attention to mechanical air conditioning.

Think about it: You are "comfortable" when you are not thinking about how to get warmer or cooler.

For example, on a sunny day, depending on whether you feel cool or warm, you might think of moving into the warmth of the sun or the cool of the shade. On a windy day, you might want to turn to face a cooling breeze or turn away from a bone-chilling wind. In other words, radiation and moving air can affect comfort as much as the temperature of the air.

THE HUMAN COMFORT ZONE

The chart, *above right*, demonstrates the effects of four variables on our perception of comfort. The majority of people, dressed in ordinary indoor clothing and doing sedentary tasks, feel comfortable within the boundaries of the central shaded zone—a distorted rectangle between 72° and 79°F, and between 20 and 70 percent relative humidity. Most of our effort to heat or

THE HUMAN COMFORT ZONE

Chart: Dry bulb temperature, °F (vertical axis, 40 to 100) vs. Relative humidity (horizontal axis, 0% to 100%)

- 400 ft/min (4.55 mph) breeze
- Air movement raises upper limit
- Typical human comfort zone
- Radiation depresses lower limit
- 150 Btuh/sq ft–hr

cool our homes is an attempt to create conditions within that zone of comfort.

RELATIVE HUMIDITY

Because evaporating perspiration has a cooling effect on the skin, and because evaporation is more rapid at lower levels of humidity, we can be comfortable at a higher air temperature when the humidity is low. This accounts for the old adage, "It's not the heat; it's the humidity," which actually sums up the condition accurately. Low humidities are characteristic of certain areas of the country, such as the American Southwest, where many people claim to be quite comfortable even when the temperature is well into the 90s and above.

RADIATION

Sunshine warms our skin and clothing. The chart shows that in the absence of wind, the radiation of the sun can help make us comfortable in cool air down to about to 45°F. Of course, the sun works against comfort during summer, making us avoid it by seeking shade.

MOVING AIR

Air moving against our bare skin removes heat, producing a cooling effect. A gentle 5 miles-per-hour breeze across bare skin allows the average person to feel comfortable at up to 87°F at 60 percent humidity and 93°F at 20 percent humidity. Thus, Miami

at 90°F and 90 percent humidity is intolerable, while Phoenix at 93°F and 20 percent humidity is quite comfortable.

We will show you how to take advantage of the effects of radiation and moving air in making your home a more comfortable environment—without the expense and complexity of mechanical air-conditioning.

Of course there are limits to these natural variables, so we will also show you how to maintain your air conditioner.

NATURAL COOLERS

Have you ever noticed how much cooler it is in the woods on a hot day? Deciduous trees are nature's evaporative coolers (see Evaporative Coolers, page 69). A mature maple tree evaporates thousands of gallons of water during a summer, dropping the temperature within its canopy by at least 10°F, and blocking 90 percent of the radiation from the sun.

TAKE ADVANTAGE OF TEMPERATURE SWINGS

We all have a sense of how a pump works: one or more valves opening and closing in sequence to push water in one direction. Have you ever tried operating your home as a cooling pump, using its doors and windows as flapper valves?

Whenever the outside air is cooler than the inside air, open all of your doors and windows. Then, when the outside temperature rises above the inside temperature, close them.

In most areas of the country the outdoor air temperature swings 20°F between day and night (in some areas as much as 40°F!). If your home is insulated, it is possible to pump its average operating temperature down 10°F for zero cost.

REDUCING HEAT GAIN

SHADING WINDOWS

Sunlight coming through a window heats any surface it touches. If the surface is light or shiny, some of the light is reflected onto another surface. Eventually, however, all of the light that comes through the window—with the exception of the small amount that is reflected back out—is absorbed by and warms room surfaces. The surfaces, in turn, radiate the stored heat and warm the air in the room.

Shading a window on the inside with curtains or drapes stops the direct radiation, but the drape itself is warmed, and it in turn warms the room air. It is much more effective to stop radiation before it gets into the house, with overhangs, awnings, trellised vines, or nearby trees.

A surprising amount of radiation is indirect. On a hazy day, for example, radiation comes almost equally from all parts of the sky. Even on clear days, hot surfaces such as streets and sidewalks reradiate the sun's heat in all directions. Thus, windows on all sides of the house benefit from overhangs.

The table, *below*, shows how much overhangs reduce heat gain through a 4-foot by 4-foot window in Florida. The numbers demonstrate that wider overhangs substantially reduce heat gain, regardless of orientation to the sun.

"Isn't a 6- to 10-foot overhang a little extreme?" you might ask. Not if it's a carport or a wraparound porch, which explains why so many older southern homes had porches.

Even better shading devices are foliage trees, shrubs, and vines. If you want to block the summer sun but invite the winter sun in, use deciduous trees and shrubs (they lose their leaves in autumn).

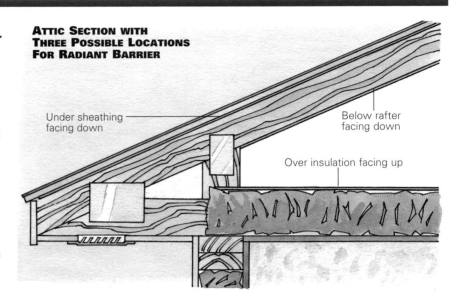

ATTIC SECTION WITH THREE POSSIBLE LOCATIONS FOR RADIANT BARRIER

Under sheathing facing down

Below rafter facing down

Over insulation facing up

Another way to shade windows is with shade screens and reflective films. Screens are made of clothlike woven material that you can hang on the outside of doors or windows. Reflective films generally attach to the inside of the window, where they are better protected. Both devices are designed for clear visibility but minimum heat gain.

REFLECTING HEAT FROM THE ROOF

Light-colored roofing materials reflect more of the sun's heat than dark materials, but an even greater savings is realized by installing "attic radiant barriers."

Install aluminum building foil (available in 36-inch-wide rolls) under the roof to reflect heat away from the attic. As the illustration shows, there are three possible locations:
1. For new construction—over the rafters and under the roof sheathing,
2. For existing homes—under the rafters, or
3. Over the insulation on the attic floor, after the attic has been insulated.

Either of the first two methods effectively reflects heat away from living areas while protecting the foil from gathering dirt and dust. The third method, with the foil installed flat and exposed to the attic space, permits dust to accumulate, reducing the efficiency of the reflective surface.

INSULATING CEILINGS AND ROOFS

Insulation is more cost-effective in cold climates than in hot ones because the temperature difference between indoors and outdoors is greater, and heat travels upward more readily than downward. Most areas of the country need insulation for the cold weather and benefit from it during the summer as well. In hot climates, after installing an attic radiant barrier, it may not be worth installing insulation unless you rely heavily on air-conditioning and need to increase its efficiency.

ELIMINATING HEAT SOURCES

Incandescent light bulbs are 97 percent efficient as heaters. That is, 97 percent of the electricity they consume is converted directly to heat, so turn them off when you leave a room.

Washing machines, clothes dryers, showers, and stoves all produce heat and moisture. In southern climates locate the washing machine and clothes dryer in a garage or other space outside of the living area. Make sure the clothes dryer as well as vent fans for bathrooms and the kitchen are vented to the outside.

Window Facing	Width of Overhang, Feet					
	1	2	3	4	6	10
South	1.0	2.0	2.2	5.0	4.0	3.5
North	1.0	2.2	3.0	6.0	5.0	4.1
East or West	1.0	3.0	4.0	7.0	5.5	5.0

PERCENTAGE REDUCTION IN WINDOW HEAT GAIN FROM OVERHANGS

MOVING AIR

Air movement not only produces a cooling effect on the skin, but it also helps remove heat from interior building furnishing surfaces that might otherwise radiate it to the occupants.

NATURAL VENTILATION

If you live where there are natural breezes, use them for most of your cooling needs. Open a door or window on opposite walls in every room. To give cross-breezes a buoyancy boost as they go through the house, open low windows where breezes enter and high windows where they leave.

Another way to enhance air circulation is with an open floor plan. It is not worth rearranging the walls of an existing home, but in a new design, keep interior walls and partitions to a minimum to facilitate air movement.

If your windows are not perpendicular to the prevailing breeze, use casement (side-opening) windows, or place fencing or other solid diverters outside the windows to direct the breeze into the windows.

A venting skylight will effectively exhaust household air whenever the inside is warmer than the outside. To take maximum advantage of this "chimney effect," install the skylight as high as possible and open only doors and windows on the lowest level.

AIR-CIRCULATING FANS

Every summer large piles of box, window, and oscillating fans appear in hardware stores and home centers across the country. It is no wonder that they are popular because all you have to do is plug them into a wall outlet. The breezes they create can easily let you raise a room air-conditioner's thermostat by 10°F or more, and save 40 to 80 percent off the cooling bill.

CEILING FANS

Ceiling fans circulate room air efficiently and are generally more attractive room features than window or box fans. Conversion of a ceiling light fixture to a ceiling fan is usually a simple matter (see Fans, pages 118–121). The table, *above right,* shows the proper size ceiling fan for various room sizes.

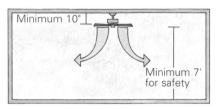

WINDOW FANS

Operated properly, a large window fan can cool a house nearly as well as a whole-house fan. However, you have to understand exactly what you are doing. Here are some rules of thumb:

■ Identify the areas you wish to receive the most cooling (such as the two rooms on the right in the illustration below).

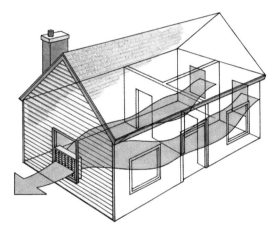

■ Set up the fan to blow out of a window located as far as possible from the rooms to be cooled. Make sure the fan fits snug and solid in the window.

■ Open only the windows that will let cool air flow directly across the occupants of the target rooms.

■ Open every door between the fan and the rooms to be cooled.

■ Close all other doors and windows in the house.

Now turn on the fan and enjoy a silent, natural cooling breeze through the open windows.

WHOLE-HOUSE FANS

A whole-house fan sucks air from every room of the house (and through

CEILING FAN SIZE	
Largest Dimension of Room	**Diameter of Fan**
under 12'	36"
12' to 14'	42"
14' to 16'	48"
16' to 18'	52"
over 18'	two fans

every open window). These fans are typically sized to exchange the entire volume of house air once every three minutes. Figuring the proper size fan is simple. For example, a 2,000 square-foot home with 8-foot ceilings has an interior volume of 2,000 × 8, or 16,000 cubic feet. To calculate the rating for a fan with a 3-minute exchange, divide 16,000 by 3 = 5,300 cubic feet per minute (cfm).

To achieve its rated flow, the combined areas of the attic vents and the open windows must be at least three times the area of the fan opening.

Like the cooling effects of a window fan, those of a whole-house fan can be concentrated in just the rooms with open windows.

Naturally, these fans are run only when the outdoor temperature is lower than the indoor temperature. Very often they are automatically controlled by thermostats that sense both indoor and outdoor temperatures.

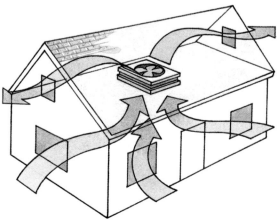

EVAPORATIVE COOLERS

We are all familiar with the cooling effect of a thunderstorm on a hot summer day. After the rain stops and the sun comes out, "steam" is seen rising from hot roads and rooftops. And it is suddenly dramatically cooler. What has happened?

The heat of those hot surfaces has been reduced as they evaporate the rain. Of course the air now contains more water vapor and is more humid, but the overall effect is greater comfort because the surfaces have less stored heat to radiate.

People who live in hot, dry climates, such as the southwestern states, can take advantage of this phenomenon and install evaporative coolers. The units are simple roof-top fans that pull hot dry air through wet pads to cool the air. Installation and operating costs are far less than for central air-conditioning.

Evaporative coolers are recommended wherever the summer air is dry enough to produce at least a 20°F temperature drop and the resulting moist indoor air will be below 79°F. They are not recommended for humid climates.

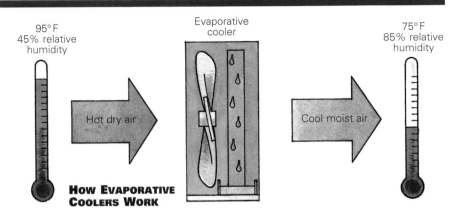

HOW EVAPORATIVE COOLERS WORK

95°F 45% relative humidity — Hot dry air — Evaporative cooler — Cool moist air — 75°F 85% relative humidity

The table *below left* lists cities in areas for which evaporative-cooling potential is great, the typical temperature drop which can be achieved, and the number of total-house-air-exchanges-per-hour required. The number of air changes assumes a home with normal insulation. For a highly insulated home, divide by 2; for an uninsulated home, multiply by 2.

MAINTAINING A HEAT PUMP OR ROOM AIR CONDITIONER

At the beginning of the cooling season and then as often as every few weeks, change or clean the filter on a room air conditioner or heat pump.

Unplug the unit, then remove the front panel and filter. Wash the filter in mild detergent, then rinse and replace it. Be careful not to tear it. Clean condenser coil fins with a vacuum cleaner with a soft brush attachment. If something bumps into the thin cooling fins, straighten them as best you can with needle-nose pliers or a toothpick.

POTENTIAL FOR EVAPORATIVE COOLING

City	Temperature Drop, °F.	Air Changes Per Hour
Albuquerque, NM	28	20
Bismarck, ND	22	20
Boise, ID	25	15
Casper, WY	27	15
Denver, CO	27	15
Great Falls, MT	25	20
Las Vegas, NV	34	20
Los Angeles, CA	18	30
North Platte, NE	22	20
Phoenix, AZ	30	30
Rapid City, SD	23	20
Salt Lake City, UT	28	15
Topeka, KS	20	30
Tulsa, OK	22	45

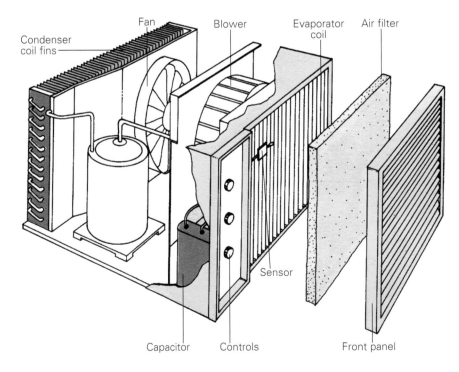

Condenser coil fins — Fan — Blower — Evaporator coil — Air filter — Sensor — Capacitor — Controls — Front panel

COUNTERTOPS

COUNTER INTELLIGENCE

ALSO SEE...
Sinks & Garbage Disposers:
Pages 314–315
Tile:
Pages 360–367
Vanities:
Pages 384–385
Washbasins:
Pages 416–417

Replacing old countertops adds fresh life to a room at a bargain price. Whether you buy a stock unit and install it yourself, order custom counters, or build them, keep these points in mind.

EDGES

Some materials are thick enough to have attractive edges without any modification. The edges of thinner materials need to be covered. You can also have a front edge that rolls up slightly to prevent spills from running onto the floor.

BACKSPLASHES

Counters can be made with or without backsplashes, a few inches high or extending up the wall, they can be made from the same or different materials, and can be joined to the countertop with a sloping curve or at a right angle.

MEASUREMENTS

The most important requirement of all, however, is to think through every detail and measure two or even three times before ordering a top. Talk with the design professionals at lumberyards and home centers. They may suggest options you haven't considered.

CUTOUTS

Be sure to locate cutouts for sinks or cooktops and allow for obstructions or insets. Measure where the backsplash needs to be lower for windowsills. Line up the countertop with the edges of wall cabinets. Plan finished edges around peninsulas and islands.

Above all, double-check dimensions of appliances to make sure they fit in the spaces of your design.

MATERIAL CHOICES

The material used for a countertop should harmonize with the other materials in a room.

LAMINATE

Plastic laminate is a very tough plastic sheet about $\frac{1}{16}$ inch thick with a decorative finish. It is easy to maintain and comes in hundreds of colors and patterns but is subject to scorches and cut marks.

Prelaminated countertops, with or without edging and back splashes, are stocked in a limited selection of colors in lumberyards and home centers as ready-made, 25-inch-wide sections that you cut to length. They also come with mitered ends for L-shaped corners that you join together with drawbolts.

The full selection of laminate colors, patterns, and widths is available when you order custom-made countertops.

STONE

Both marble and granite are used as countertops. Their cool, smooth surfaces are ideal for working with pastry and candy.

Marble is surprisingly vulnerable, however. A knife will scratch it, acid will etch it, and oil will stain it. Granite will neither scratch nor dissolve in acid, and it resists stains.

Both stones will crack with a heavy, sharp blow, but neither will burn, even at the highest heat.

Both are extremely heavy and difficult to cut, however, so consult a professional before undertaking a stone countertop project—even if you are an advanced do-it-yourselfer.

SOLID-SURFACE

Sold under such trade names as Corian®, Surrell®, and Avonite®, this material is cast acrylic resin, with a plain surface or made to resemble stone. It is not as hard as granite, but it is less likely to crack and is resistant to moisture, stains, and heat. One great advantage is that it can be worked with ordinary woodworking tools, and so is within the realm of do-it-yourselfer skills (although some manufacturers won't guarantee their products unless installed by a professional).

Solid-surface countertops come in thicknesses of $\frac{1}{8}$, $\frac{1}{4}$, $\frac{1}{2}$, and $\frac{3}{4}$ inch.

Materials thinner than $\frac{3}{4}$ inch should be glued to a supporting surface, such as $\frac{3}{4}$-inch plywood. Since the color permeates the materials, worn countertops can be sanded with very fine sandpaper.

TILE

Ceramic tiles come in a large variety of shapes, sizes, colors, and patterns. Bullnose (outside corner) and cove (inside corner) pieces are available to finish edges. Glazed tiles are impervious to heat, water, grease, and stains; unglazed tiles are porous and permeable and, for this reason, are not recommended for kitchen countertops.

WOODBLOCK

Genuine woodblock or "butcher block" is made of thick, laminated pieces of hardwood—usually maple—that are either oiled or untreated. It is generally used on only a portion of a countertop or as a separate chopping block. The porous surface is easily marred and stained, although burn and scratch marks can be eliminated by sanding. Woodblock countertops can be made to order from companies that specialize in making them.

After cutting, all you need to do is screw on a backsplash (if required), set the countertop in place, and screw it to the cabinets from underneath. Use a scroll saw and belt sander to round the corners of an island or peninsula.

INSTALLED COSTS	
Countertop Material	**Installed Cost Per Lin. Ft.**
Plastic laminate	$20–50
Ceramic tile	$10–50
Woodblock	$20–50
Solid surface	$100–200
Natural stone	$150–250

INSTALLING A LAMINATE COUNTERTOP

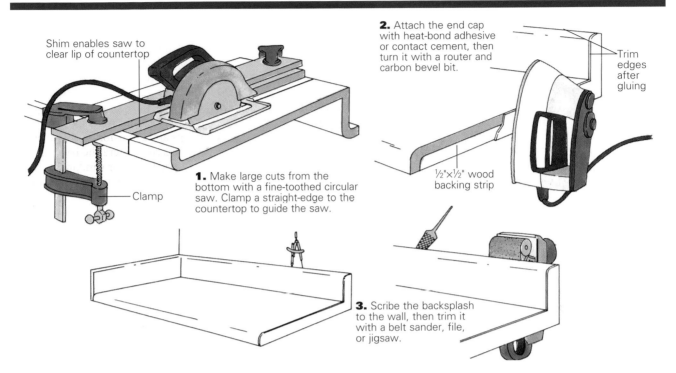

Shim enables saw to clear lip of countertop

Clamp

1. Make large cuts from the bottom with a fine-toothed circular saw. Clamp a straight-edge to the countertop to guide the saw.

2. Attach the end cap with heat-bond adhesive or contact cement, then turn it with a router and carbon bevel bit.

Trim edges after gluing

½"×½" wood backing strip

3. Scribe the backsplash to the wall, then trim it with a belt sander, file, or jigsaw.

The most common countertop, by far, is plastic laminate bonded to particleboard or plywood. Factory-made products usually have lipped or rolled front edges and coved corners between the top surface and the backsplash. Rolled edges and coved backsplashes are best left to the factory. If you make your own laminate countertop, don't attempt anything but square edges.

MEASUREMENTS

Most home centers stock 25-inch countertops in 2-foot increments in a limited number of colors and patterns. If you want a custom size or a nonstandard color, you will need to provide measurements for a special order. Check with the dealer first to find out exactly which dimensions are needed. For an extra charge, some dealers will send out an estimator, who will take measurements and plan for details such as windowsills, backsplashes, and corners.

SKETCH THE COUNTERTOP

Whether you're making your own countertop or having it made, sketch its layout. Double-check every measurement, and note the dimensions clearly on your drawing. Make measurements in inches (not inches and feet) to avoid confusion.

Be sure to note the depth of the base cabinets; cabinets built before countertops became standardized may be shallower or deeper than 24 inches.

For countertops fit between two walls, measure the width at the back as well as at the front. If the walls are not perfectly parallel, one of the measurements will be longer; use the longer measurement. Mark the centerline of the sink cutout and the measurements to the edges. Include a template of the cutout if you have one.

Generally, you'll want exposed edges, including those that butt refrigerators or ranges, to have finished ends. These are usually applied at the factory, as are the backsplashes.

The order taker at the lumberyard or home center will often make a detailed sketch of your order, showing exact lengths and widths and other details, such as miters, edging, and backsplash.

REMOVING OLD COUNTERTOPS

Laminate countertops usually are secured to cabinets with screws—very rarely with glue.

If necessary, remove drawers and doors to get at the screws. Remove the screws (a cordless screwdriver will save time and skinned knuckles).

Disconnect the sink plumbing. If the sink is clamped to the countertop, remove it after you

have turned the countertop over, and lift out the countertop.

If it is too heavy to lift, you can cut it into pieces, but be careful not to cut into the cabinet frames below.

PREPARATION

After you've removed the old countertop, check the base cabinets for level. If the cabinets are uneven, raise the low points on the countertop mounting surface with shims. Don't attempt to reposition the cabinets.

INSTALLATION

Cut the countertop to length and place it on the base cabinets. Laminate countertops with rolled backsplashes come with a back overhang of approximately ¼ inch.

Push the countertop up against the wall and find the widest gap between the backsplash and the wall. Set a compass to this width and use it to scribe the top of the backsplash for trimming.

Working from the top to avoid chipping the laminate, trim the backsplash with a file, belt sander (be careful, this tool removes material in a hurry), jigsaw, or circular saw. Tape the plate of the saw to prevent scratching the surface. Be sure the saw blade has fine teeth and is sharp. ►

INSTALLING A LAMINATE COUNTERTOP *continued*

Make the sink cutout before you join any miters because you may have to turn the countertop over to finish the cutout. Test-fit all of the pieces before you attach the countertop. Miter joints are usually secured with wood glue and specially designed clamps; test the fit of these as well.

Pull the countertop away from the wall if necessary to connect the joints. Push it back into position, make sure the mounting screws won't penetrate the countertop surface from below, and then secure it to the base cabinets.

DON'T GET BURNED

Plastic countertops can be burned (as you may have discovered). And once deeply scorched, there is little to do but to cover up the spot or replace the countertop.

Some homeowners are paranoid about burning their lovely counters. Actually, plastic laminate is not harmed by temperatures up to the boiling point of water, 212°F. What does scorch laminate are frying pans, which can easily reach temperatures of 500°F or more.

The solution? Keep inexpensive wood cutting boards on either side of the cooktop. The wood may scorch, but hardwood is easily scraped or sanded—and cutting boards are cheap.

INSTALLING A MARBLE COUNTERTOP INSERT

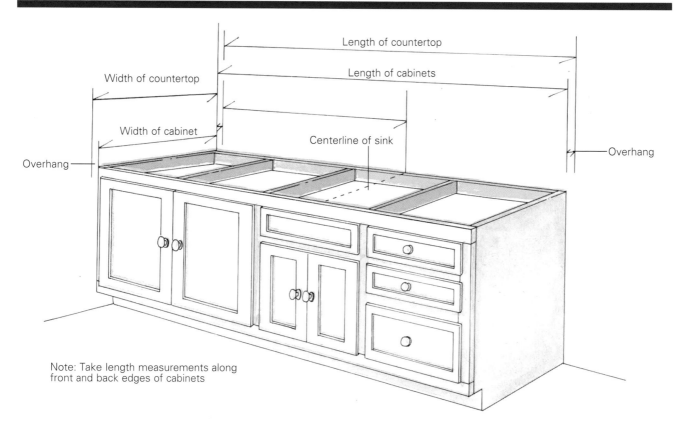

Note: Take length measurements along front and back edges of cabinets

Measure the area for the top and backsplash. If the insert will be lower than adjacent counter surfaces by more than the thickness of the adjacent countertop, measure for marble side pieces, too. Take your measurements to a marble dealer and have the pieces cut and edged.

■ Position the counter, back, and any side pieces to make sure they are even with the other counter surfaces and backsplashes. If not, raise the lower surface with shims glued and nailed to the top edges of the cabinet frame.

■ Gluing the slab in place may be unnecessary because marble is extremely heavy. To prevent shifting, however, apply adhesive to the cabinet edges before setting the slab in place. Use an adhesive recommended by the marble dealer to attach the sides and backsplash.

■ At edges and seams, place masking tape on both surfaces, leaving just ⅛ inch of counter and ⅛ inch of marble exposed. Run a bead of silicone sealant along the gap and smooth it with a dampened finger. Remove the masking tape, leaving a ¼-inch strip of sealant, and let it cure before using the countertop.

INSTALLING A CERAMIC TILE COUNTERTOP

For tiled countertops, use only glazed or semivitreous tiles, especially around sinks, food preparation areas, and any area that tends to get wet. Unglazed and vitreous tiles are not appropriate for these areas as they will absorb moisture and stain. For tile installations that will get wet, use latex additives in both the adhesive and grout.

Purchase tiles rated for use on horizontal surfaces; they are thicker than those made for walls. Polished dimensioned stone that is at least ⅜-inch thick can also be used.

Countertop tile installations require the same basic steps as any tile-setting job (see Tile, pages 360–367). Work from front to back on countertops backed by a wall, and from the center outward on island countertops. Set all full tiles first before measuring and cutting partial tiles.

Install tiles on the backsplash or the wall behind the counter after the counter tiles are set but before grouting the entire project. Tiles for backsplashes are installed in the same manner as wall tiles (see Tile, pages 360–367). Make sure that the vertical grout joints of the backsplash align with the grout lines on the countertop.

If your backsplash will stop short of the overhead cabinets, the installation will look neater with a final row of full tiles. Use either bullnose tiles or plan to finish the top edge of the backsplash with a trim piece. If the backsplash extends all the way to the lower edge of the upper cabinets, a final row of partial tiles will not be noticeable.

WHEN TO ORDER

Don't order your countertop until the cabinets have been installed and your appliance dimensions verified. Even custom countertops can be made and delivered within two weeks.

The reason you should wait is that cabinets have a way of "growing" as they are installed. First, no wall is perfectly square, so you start with a ⅟16-inch to ⅛-inch increase right at the beginning. By the time all the cabinets are in, it is not unusual to have gained ¼ inch. When you do measure, allow a ⅛-inch overhang wherever the countertop abuts an appliance.

ESTABLISHING THE LAYOUT

INSTALLING TILE

GROUTING

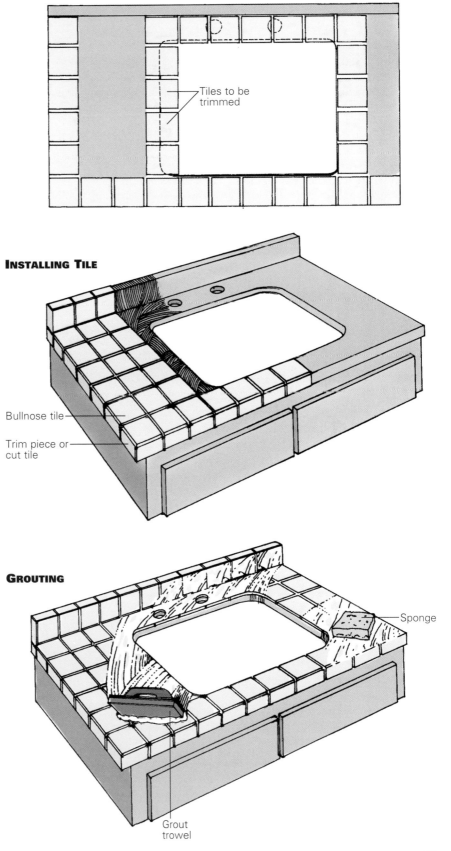

Tiles to be trimmed

Bullnose tile

Trim piece or cut tile

Sponge

Grout trowel

ROOM TO REACH OUT

For dramatic beauty and additional living space at a reasonable cost, few home improvements can rival a deck.

A successful deck should harmonize with the house and yard and be in scale—neither dwarfed by its setting nor overwhelming it. Consider how the deck looks from below as well as above, and choose details and a color that are in keeping with the character of the house.

Purpose: The start of a successful deck is careful planning, based on the uses of your yard. Do you want:
■ a quiet retreat?
■ a platform for sunbathing or displaying plants?
■ a children's play area?

The Elements: The size and location of the deck will also be affected by the forces of nature.

Are you building a deck to get you into the sun or out of it? Will a breeze be a welcome relief or an unwanted intruder? Study the patterns of sun, shade, and wind in your yard. Observe how these patterns change according to the season.

Access: Your deck should also be conveniently accessible from interior living spaces and, if possible, located where it capitalizes on dramatic vistas or intimate views.

The doorway should be at least 36 inches wide, easy to open with one hand, and ideally made of glass (tempered or safety) to reinforce the feeling of continuity with the indoor space.

Emotional Comforts: A deck that does not offer seclusion and a feeling of security is not comfortable. To prevent raised decks from putting people "on stage," locate the deck where the house, fences, or plantings shelter it. Add screens, extend fence heights, or lower sections of the deck to gain privacy. Add benches or perimeter plants around low decks—they'll give you a sense of enclosure.

Size and location may also be restricted by local zoning laws, as well as obstructions such as buried gas lines or water pipes. Check with your local building-code official before finalizing your design.

THE STRUCTURE OF A DECK

No matter how different they are, all decks are made with the same basic elements—posts, beams, joists, and decking. Every element is structural—that is, every element supports a load. The posts support the beams; the beams support the joists; the joists support the deck boards; and the deck boards finally support you.

Ledger and Joists: A ledger is bolted to the house. The ledger supports either a cleat on which all the joists rest or metal joist hangers for each joist. At the opposite end, joists are supported by beams that rest on posts.

Beams: Beams are solid timbers or built up from three or more thicknesses of 2-by members. Sometimes, 2×12 stringers are bolted to each side of the posts in place of the thicker beams that rest on top of the posts. This design allows the posts to extend up through the deck to become supports for the railing.

Base: The posts (normally 4×4s) are spaced according to the size and spacing of the beams. Each post rests on a concrete footing, or in some areas, is buried directly in the ground (suitable for pressure-treated lumber rated for ground contact; backfill with gravel or concrete).

Joists with spans longer than 10 feet must have blocking or bridging between them to prevent them from flopping over when under a load. Make blocking from solid pieces of joist material or 1×4 cross braces installed over beams or at the midpoint of the joist spans.

Decking: Decking is the most visible part of the deck. A popular decking material is pressure-treated 2×6s, which can span 2 to 4 feet. Other popular materials are ⅝×6 pressure-treated southern yellow pine and ⅝×6 cedar. A ⅝ board is actually a full inch thick and is strong enough for spans up to 24 inches.

Final Steps: Add stairs to a deck by doubling the end joist or providing a separate double header below it. Attach the stair stringers (they're what holds the treads) to the double header with joist hangers.

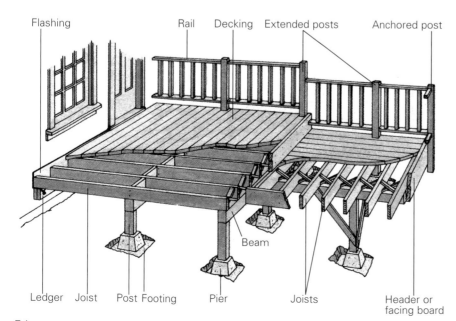

Flashing Rail Decking Extended posts Anchored post

Ledger Joist Post Footing Pier Joists Header or facing board

Beam

The charts on this and the next page will enable you to figure the size of posts, beams, joists, and decking. They will also tell you the maximum distances you can span with a board of a particular size. The figures take the varying strengths of different species and grades of lumber into account. If the span you have in mind is too great for a particular grade of lumber, choose a stronger species or better grade of the same size.

These charts assume a "live" load on the deck of 40 pounds per square foot. This includes furniture, people, planters—anything other than the deck itself. For a more substantial deck, or if you anticipate concentrated loads, like a large pile of firewood, use lumber one or two sizes larger than specified in the chart.

"Span" is a measure of the maximum distance a member can bridge between supports. "Spacing" refers to the center-to-center distance between identical members, such as joists or beams. Notice that the maximum spans for the same board increase as its spacing decreases.

These spans are also based on the assumption that more than one floor board is carrying the load. If concentrated loads are a rule, reduce the maximum span or increase the thickness of the decking.

ALLOWABLE SPANS FOR BEAMS

Species Group	Beam Size	Beam Spacing, feet								
		4	5	6	7	8	9	10	11	12
1	4×6	6	–	–	–	–	–	–	–	–
	3×8	8	7	7	6	–	–	–	–	–
	4×8	10	9	8	7	7	6	–	–	–
	3×10	11	10	9	8	7	7	6	6	–
	4×10	12	11	10	9	8	8	7	7	–
	3×12	12	12	11	10	9	8	8		
	4×12	12	12	12	11	11	10	9	9	–
	6×10	12	12	12	11	10	9	9		–
2	4×6	6	–	–	–	–	–	–	–	–
	3×8	7	6	6	–	–	–	–	–	–
	4×8	9	8	7	6	6	–	–	–	–
	3×10	10	9	8	7	6	6	–	–	–
	4×10	11	10	9	8	7	7	6	6	6
	3×12	12	11	10	9	8	7	7	–	–
	4×12	12	12	11	10	9	9	8	8	
	6×10	12	12	12	11	10	9	9		
3	4×6	6	–	–	–	–	–	–	–	–
	3×8	7	6	–	–	–	–	–	–	–
	4×8	8	7	6	–	–	–	–	–	–
	3×10	9	8	7	6	–	–	–	–	–
	4×10	10	9	8	7	7	6	6	–	–
	3×12	11	10	9	8	7	6	6	6	–
	4×12	12	11	10	9	8	8	7	7	–
	6×10	12	12	11	10	9	8	8	–	–

Beams are on edge. Spans are distances between posts or other supports. Grade is No. 2 or better. Group 1: Douglas fir, larch, and southern pine. Group 2: Hemlock and Douglas fir south. Group 3: Western pines and cedars, redwood, and spruces.

MAXIMUM POST HEIGHTS

Species Group	Nominal Post Size	Area Supported (Beam Spacing × Post Spacing), Sq. Ft.									
		36	48	60	72	84	96	108	120	132	144
1	4×4	to 12'				to 10'			to 8'		
	4×6					to 12'				to 10'	
	6×6								to 12'		
2	4×4	to 12'		to 10'			to 8'				
	4×6			to 12'			to 10'				
	6×6					to 12'					
3	4×4	to 12'	to 10'		to 8'			to 6'			
	4×6		to 12'		to 10'			to 8'			
	6×6			to 12'							

Grade is Standard and better for 4×4 posts and No.1 and better for larger posts. Group 1: Douglas fir, larch, and southern pine. Group 2: Hemlock and Douglas fir south. Group 3: Western pines and cedars, redwood, and spruces. Example: If the beam supports are 8' 6" on center, and the posts 11' 6" on center, then the area supported is 98 sq. ft. Use the next larger area: 108 sq. ft.

MAKE IT DURABLE

Not even pressure-treated lumber will last forever when exposed to the elements. There are three things you can do to make it last longer, however:

1. Select lumber with tight growth rings. Wood that has grown slowly contains a higher percentage of lignin—the chemical that makes the wood strong.

2. Regardless of appearance, always place decking with the heart side of the wood facing up. When it gets wet it will bow in the center, eliminating standing water.

3. Treat the deck annually with a water-repellent finish to keep water from penetrating the wood.

SIZING STRUCTURAL LUMBER *continued*

Species Group	Joist Size	Joist Spacing, Inches on Center		
		16	**24**	**32**
1	2×6	9' 11"	7' 11"	6' 2"
	2×8	12' 0"	10' 6"	8' 1"
	2×10	15' 3"	13' 4"	10' 4"
2	2×6	8' 7"	7' 0"	5' 8"
	2×8	11' 4"	9' 3"	7' 6"
	2×10	14' 6"	11' 10"	9' 6"
3	2×6	7' 9"	6' 2"	5' 0"
	2×8	10' 2"	8' 1"	6' 8"
	2×10	13' 0"	10' 4"	8' 6"

ALLOWABLE SPANS FOR JOISTS

Based on 40 psf live load and 10 psf dead load. Joists are on edge. Spans are distances between beams or other supports. Grade is No. 2 or better; No. 2 medium grain southern pine. Group 1: Douglas fir, larch, and southern pine. Group 2: Hem fir and Douglas fir south. Group 3: Western pines and cedars, redwood, and spruces.

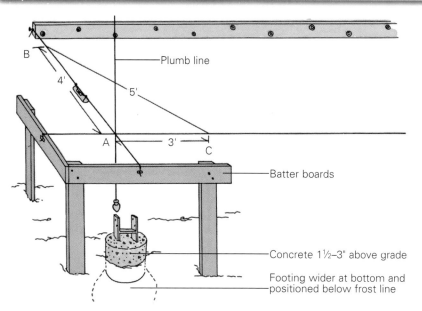

Plumb line

Batter boards

Concrete 1½–3" above grade

Footing wider at bottom and positioned below frost line

THE FOOTINGS

Check with your local building-code official for footing depths and dimensions. Codes generally require the bottoms of footings to be below the local maximum depth of frost. In the South this may be a matter of inches; in the North it can be 6 feet or more.

To locate the footings, lay out string lines between the ledger and batter boards (see illustration, *below left*). The strings can represent the centers of the posts, the outside corners of the posts, or the outside of the deck frame—just make sure you remember which!

Check Square: Use a 3'-4'-5' triangle to square the strings. From one corner, mark a point 3 feet along one side and a point 4 feet along the other side; the diagonal distance between those points will be 5 feet if the corner is square. Note that you can also use a multiple to increase your accuracy (6'-8'-10' or 9'-12'-15'). Then excavate the holes and build concrete footings.

Set Posts: In some regions pressure-treated posts can be buried directly in the ground. In other regions you will be required to extend the concrete in the form of a pier to above ground, using either concrete-filled and reinforced square concrete block or reinforced concrete-filled cardboard sono-tubes. If the wood/concrete connection will be made above ground, use metal post anchors (see Framing Connectors, pages 160–161) to anchor the post and deck in high wind and to keep the post base from contact with the concrete.

PRESSURE-TREATED WOOD

The Process: Pressure treatment consists of forcing chemical preservatives deep into the cell structure of lumber. The chemicals repel insects such as termites and decay-producing organisms. Some manufacturers guarantee the effectiveness of the treatment for 40 years or longer.

The Chemicals: There are three broad types of chemicals in use today. Water-borne arsenates are used to treat lumber likely to come in contact with people and animals. Arsenates are used to treat lumber intended for decks and other residential applications. Other treatments include pentachlorophenol (used for utility poles) and creosote (used for railroad ties, highway guardrails, and marine structures).

Maintenance: Though kiln-dried, pressure-treated lumber is still high in moisture content. To prevent excessive checking while the wood comes to moisture equilibrium with its environment (while lumber dries),

a water-repellent sealer should be applied immediately upon installation.

To maintain optimum appearance and protection, wood exposed to sun and rain should be cleaned and treated with a water repellent every year.

Painting: Do not paint pressure-treated lumber until you are sure it is completely dry. Do not use latex paint. Semitransparent, oil-based stains generally perform well with pressure-treated wood.

ATTACHING THE DECK TO A BUILDING WITH A LEDGER

Cut the ledger to length. Locate it so the surface of the deck will end up either 1 inch or 8 inches (one step) below the doorway—and mark a level line on the wall at that point. To protect the ledger from decay, use pressure-treated lumber. To protect the building from decay also, either cover the ledger with flashing after it is installed or use special metal stand-offs (available through lumberyards) to create an air gap.

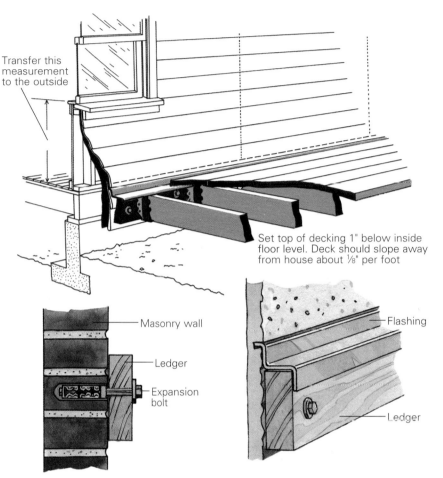

Transfer this measurement to the outside

Set top of decking 1" below inside floor level. Deck should slope away from house about ⅛" per foot

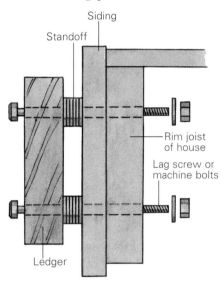

Siding

Standoff

Rim joist of house

Lag screw or machine bolts

Ledger

Masonry wall

Ledger

Expansion bolt

Flashing

Ledger

ATTACHING TO WOOD

Attach a ledger to a wood-framed house with ⅜- or ½-inch-diameter galvanized lag screws or machine bolts 16 to 24 inches apart. Drill pilot holes for bolts and squeeze caulk into the holes. Use metal standoffs for air circulation.

ATTACHING TO MASONRY

Use expansion bolts to attach a ledger to a masonry wall. Temporarily brace the ledger against the wall, then drill pilot holes through the ledger into the masonry, using a ³⁄₁₆-inch-diameter masonry bit. Use these holes as guides for drilling the ledger and masonry.

ATTACHING TO STUCCO

Use galvanized lag screws and the same method described for fastening on a wood-frame house. Install flashing by making a ⅜-inch-deep groove in the stucco, bending the top of the flashing to fit in the groove and sealing with butyl rubber.

POSTS AND BEAMS

ERECTING POSTS

Cut each post longer than needed and bolt it to the metal bracket on the pier. Use the layout strings to align the posts accurately. Plumb each post with a level, then temporarily brace it in both directions with scrap lumber and stakes driven in the ground.

If the posts are not going to extend through the deck to the deck railing, mark them for cutting by measuring down from the line the combined depth of both the joist and the beam. Scribe cutting lines and saw off the tops of the posts.

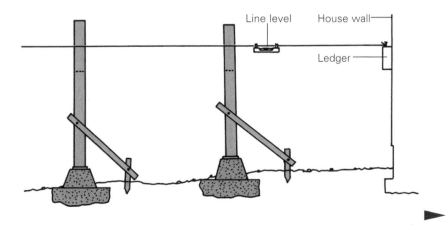

Line level   House wall

Ledger

POSTS AND BEAMS *continued*

CONNECTING BEAM TO POST

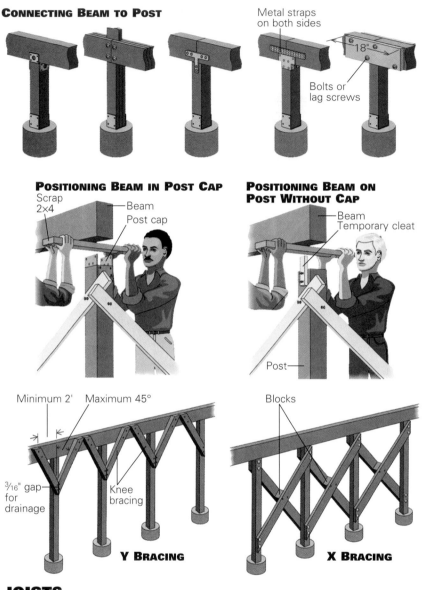

Metal straps on both sides

18"

Bolts or lag screws

POSITIONING BEAM IN POST CAP

Scrap 2×4

Beam
Post cap

POSITIONING BEAM ON POST WITHOUT CAP

Beam
Temporary cleat

Post

Minimum 2'   Maximum 45°

³⁄₁₆" gap for drainage

Knee bracing

Y BRACING

Blocks

X BRACING

INSTALLING BEAMS

Paint primer or sealer on the tops of the posts and lay the beams over them. Use metal post caps (see Framing Connectors, pages 160–161) to attach the beams to the posts. Splices between beams must be centered over the posts and must have a metal connector or cleats on both sides.

BRACING TALL POSTS

If the posts are taller than 5 feet, brace them diagonally with 2×4 knee braces, as shown, or with full diagonal braces between the bottoms of the posts and the beams. Each piece of bracing requires at least four fasteners— either galvanized nails or screws— two at each end where the bracing is attached to the framing members.

If the posts are taller than 5 feet, brace them diagonally with 2×4 knee braces, as shown, or with full diagonal braces between the bottoms of the posts and the beams.

ALLOW ROOM FOR SNOW

If you live in snow country, place the deck level one step (about 8 inches) below the level of the inside floor. That way it can snow up to 8 inches before the snow on the deck blocks the door to the deck.

JOISTS

ATTACHING JOISTS

To keep the joists evenly spaced at 16, 24, or 32 inches, mark a layout pattern on the ledger and beams, indicating at each mark on which side the joist goes. Be sure to start all layouts from the same end of the deck. Attach the joists using one of the methods shown.

If the joists rest on top of the beam, wait until they are all installed before cutting them to length. At that point, snap a chalk line across the tops, transfer the marks to the faces of the joists with a square, and trim them with a circular saw. Face-nail a rim joist to the ends of the cut joists.

BLOCKING

Install blocking between joists that rest on intermediate beams and joists that are more than 10 feet long. Stagger the blocks so that you can nail through the joists into the ends of the blocks.

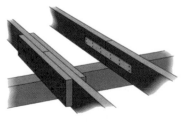

LAPPING

Joist layout on this side of beam shifts 1½"

END SPLICING

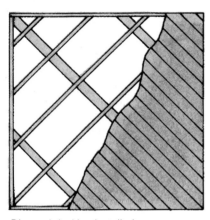

Diagonal decking installed across diagonal framing

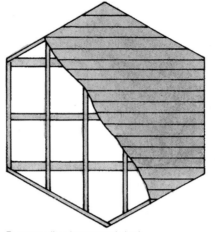

Freestanding hexagonal deck

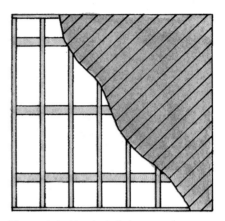

Diagonal decking installed across normal framing

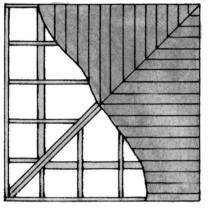

Bidirectional with mitered joints

Herringbone on normal framing

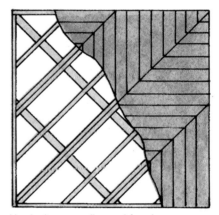

Herringbone on diagonal framing

DECKING PATTERNS

The simplest and most straightforward decking pattern is to lay all the boards perpendicular to the joists, but there are many ways to vary this layout. In some cases you can vary the decking pattern without altering the structure, such as laying boards diagonally across the joists or in a herringbone pattern. However, be sure the decking boards are strong enough for the increased distance they have to span. If you want to change the direction of the boards completely, or if you wish to lay out an elaborate design, you will have to plan the directions of the joists accordingly.

PLANNING STRUCTURAL FRAMING

When planning unusual decking patterns, remember to design structural framing members carefully. The cut ends of each piece of decking must always be centered on a joist. For simple patterns, such as perpendiculars and diagonals, install the joists and scatter the butted ends of decking randomly across the surface. For more complex styles, such as basket weaves and herringbones, support each modular decking unit with framing. Typically, this means installing blocking—short joist material cut to fit between the joists— at regular intervals, with joists often doubled to receive the edges of the decking pattern.

ALLOWABLE SPANS FOR DECKING

Species Group	Maximum Allowable Span, Inches					
	Decking Laid Flat			Decking on Edge		
	2×6	2×3	2×4	2×6	2×3	2×4
1	24	28	32	48	84	96
2	16	24	28	42	72	84
3	16	24	24	36	60	72

Spans are based on the assumption that more than one board carries normal loads. If concentrated loads are the rule, spans should be reduced. Group 1: Douglas fir, larch, and southern pine. Group 2: Hem fir and Douglas fir south. Group 3: Western pines and cedars, redwood, and spruces. Based on Construction grade or better (Select Structural Appearance No. 1, or No.2).

DECKING *continued*

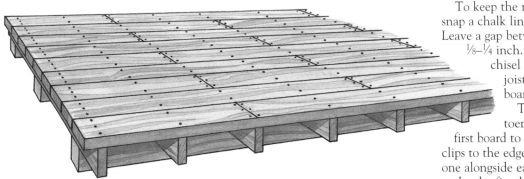

LAYING OUT THE DECK BOARDS

Natural wood decking has variations in color, grain, and knots. Before you start nailing boards, lay them loosely in place in order to coordinate their appearance. Plan where the joints will fall, staggering them and being careful not to place them or unattractive boards along the outer edges of the deck or in front of doorways or stairs. Place boards so that the grain pattern at the end of the board shows the heart side of the tree facing up.

INSTALLING DECK BOARDS

Decking can be glued with waterproof construction adhesive, nailed, screwed or secured with a combination of nails and deck clips. Adhesives and nails with deck clips result in a clean, nail-free surface; nails or screws work better if some of the boards are crooked.

Fasteners should be corrosion-resistant, such as stainless steel or high-quality HDG. Use 12d or 16d common nails for 2-inch lumber, 10d for 1-inch. Drive nails and screws at a slight angle toward each other, approximately ½ to ¾ inch from the edge of the board. Either drill holes at the ends of boards or blunt the nail tips to prevent splitting.

To keep the nailing lines straight, snap a chalk line along each row. Leave a gap between boards of ⅛–¼ inch. Use a pry bar or a chisel hammered into the joists to force crooked boards into alignment.

To install deck clips, toenail both sides of the first board to the joists. Nail the clips to the edge of the next board, one alongside each joist. Slip the clips under the first board, then toenail the exposed edge of the second board to the joists. Install the remaining boards in the same way.

OBSTRUCTIONS

Extra framing is needed when building a deck around a tree trunk or other obstruction. Cut the framing out of joist material and install headers and cripple joists on the edges that go around the construction.

TRIMMING DECK BOARDS

When all the decking is installed, snap a chalk line across the ends of the deck boards. Trim boards at this line with a circular saw. Leave the edges exposed or cap them with a fascia.

Strips of sealing material as option to prevent moisture penetration

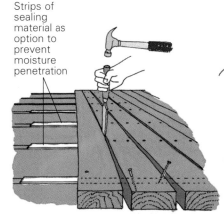

CODE REQUIREMENTS: DECKS

By definition, a deck is an exterior floor system supported on at least two opposing sides, i.e, as opposed to a balcony.

Load: A deck is treated the same as a living area in a house. It must be designed to carry 40 pounds per square foot (psf) of live load (furnishings and people), plus a dead load (its own weight) of 10 psf.

Foundation: Not all localities have codes that address deck foundations (posts or piers), but when they do they always specify that the footings be placed below frost lines.

Guardrails: Raised floor surfaces (decks) located more than 30 inches above grade (ground) must have guardrails at least 36 inches high. Stairs more than 30 inches high must have guardrails at least 34 inches high, measured from the nosing of the stairs.

Guardrail Openings: Required guardrails must have intermediate rails or posts or other ornamental fill which will not pass an object 4 inches in diameter (a 4-inch ball).

DECKING ON EDGE

Decking laid on edge creates a very refined and highly textured look, though it requires at least twice as much material as decking laid flat. The compensation is that the decking can span greater distances than normal, up to 8 feet for high-strength grades of 2×4. Decking laid on edge also has no visible nailheads, but does require spacers to stabilize the boards and prevent them from warping.

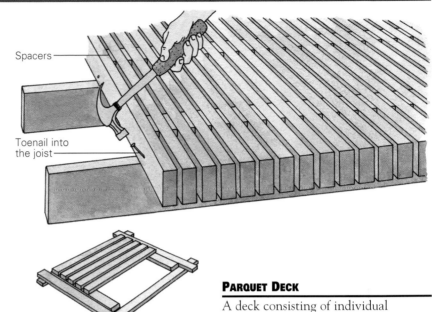

Spacers

Toenail into the joist

Framing jig

PARQUET DECK

A deck consisting of individual modules laid in crisscross fashion will create a parquet design. Typical modules are 3 feet square and made of 2×4s, although other configurations are possible. This type of decking can be laid over the same structure used for conventional decking, set directly onto a patio, a rooftop, or even laid on the ground if you use lumber suitable for ground contact and allow for drainage.

FINISH AND MAINTENANCE

FINISHING THE DECK

Completely finish railings, stairs, benches, and other features of your deck. If you don't apply the finish to all areas at the same time, you risk the deck looking piecemeal.

Make sure the wood is dry (if water soaks in quickly, it's dry) before attempting to apply any sort of finish except a water-repellent sealer. If you desire a weathered gray look, do nothing. The sun and rain will quickly turn it gray. If you later change your mind, the wood can be returned to an almost new look by pressure washing (use a fan tip—pressure washers with a straight tip can tip up the surface of a deck). You can then apply a finish.

Bleaching Oil: Accelerate the weathering process with bleaching oil. Wait until you are sure the wood is dry, then apply the bleach with a brush or roller, wait the specified period of time, and hose off the deck.

Clear Sealer: Applying a clear sealer prolongs the look of new wood and slows down (but does not stop) the weathering process. Use a sealer that penetrates the wood, rather than one that remains on the surface. Any finish that forms a hard skin on the surface is guaranteed to fail quickly and spectacularly.

Stain: The hands-down best way to retain the color of new wood is to stain the deck with a color that approximates it. There are two types of stain: semitransparent (light-bodied) and solid (full-bodied).

Semitransparent stains are preferable for two reasons:
■ They look more natural because they have less pigment and reveal the grain of the wood better.
■ They do not show wear as dramatically.

On the other hand, solid stains are more durable, hide defects better, and have to be renewed less frequently.

Use an oil-based instead of a water-based stain. Before staining, wait at least 60 days for the wood to season. Most stains are applied by brushing or rolling, one coat for solid and two coats for semitransparent varieties.

Paint: You can, of course, paint your deck—either all of it or just the railings and understructure. Again, the wood must be completely dry, although you can prime it at the time of construction and then wait 60 days. For best results, apply a water-repellent sealer before priming. The primer should be zinc free, preferably oil-based, and chemically compatible with whatever finish coat you'll apply.

Manufacturers of pressure-treated lumber advise against painting their products with latex.

DISHWASHERS

IT'S ONLY CIVILIZED

Once you have owned a dishwasher, it's hard to imagine a kitchen without one. Even if you don't have room under the counter, you can get a portable unit with a butcher-block top that can serve as a cutting board. The unit can be adapted for undercounter installation if you remodel.

A built-in dishwasher is easy to plan for; except for an occasional 18-inch version, virtually all models are 24 inches wide. Your main decisions involve design, performance, and available features, such as preheating units and energy-saving cycles.

ALSO SEE...
Electrical Systems:
Pages 110–115
Kitchen Design:
Pages 208–211
Plumbing:
Pages 256–263

WHERE SHOULD IT GO?

Locate the dishwasher as close to the sink as possible to make it easy to connect the drain and garbage disposer. Loading will be easier.
Space: Allow at least 24 inches in front of the dishwasher so you can open the door fully and slide the loading tray out. If you can't install the unit next to the sink, locate it so that the door swing will not interfere with the use of the sink. If dishwasher and sink have to be at right angles, locate the dishwasher at least 18 inches from the corner so that you don't have to back away from the sink to open the dishwasher door.
Side Cover: If you locate a dishwasher at the end of a run of cabinets, there are two ways to cover its exposed side. One is a thin, finished end panel that you can order with your cabinets. The other is a side panel that attaches to the dishwasher. If you are installing the dishwasher in a corner, allow at least 2 inches of clearance from the corner so the door will not hit drawers or cabinet doors that are ajar.
Utilities: Once you have decided on a location for the dishwasher, you'll need to measure the machine and follow the installation instructions. You will be running both electricity and hot water to the machine, as well as a waste line from it, so be sure there is sufficient space behind and under the machine where you plan to bring in services.

INSTALLATION

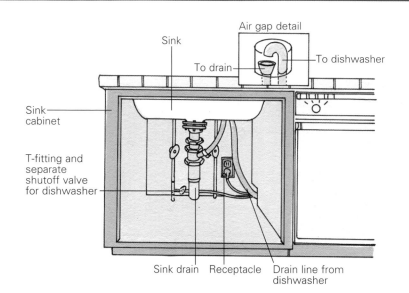

Air gap detail
Sink
To drain
To dishwasher
Sink cabinet
T-fitting and separate shutoff valve for dishwasher
Sink drain   Receptacle   Drain line from dishwasher

1. PREPARING THE OPENING

The kitchen flooring should extend under the dishwasher so leaking water will flow out and not be trapped. Vinyl floors are especially suitable because they are water-resistant and can be tightly sealed.

Before installing a dishwasher, check the manufacturer's specifications for all clearances and rough-in dimensions. If your unit hasn't arrived yet, measure the distributor floor model or ask the supplier for installation specifications. The specifications will indicate where pipes and wires can run without interfering with the mechanisms.

2. ROUGHING IN THE DRAIN

A ⅝-inch inside-diameter drain hose (usually 6 to 7 feet long) comes with the dishwasher. If it is not long enough, buy more hose and join it by slipping a short piece of ½-inch copper pipe inside both hose ends and clamping the hoses.

Some plumbing codes require that the drain hose have an air gap to prevent overflow from a clogged sink drain from siphoning back into the dishwasher. This device is mounted in a hole in the sink deck or countertop. The drain hose is connected to the air-gap inlet under the counter, and another short hose connects the outlet to the disposer or sink drain. Water can flow only one way through the air gap. If your code doesn't require an air gap, you should still loop the drain

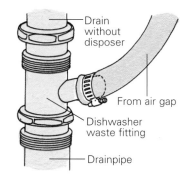

Drain without disposer
From air gap
Dishwasher waste fitting
Drainpipe

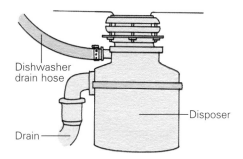

Dishwasher drain hose
Drain
Disposer

hose up over the top of the dishwasher or clamp it to the bottom of the countertop. Then run the hose into the disposer or sink drain.

3. ROUGHING IN THE HOT-WATER SUPPLY

The dishwasher should have its own supply stop valve. Install a tee in the sink faucet hot-water supply pipe or run a new hot-water line under the floor and stub it into the dishwasher space.

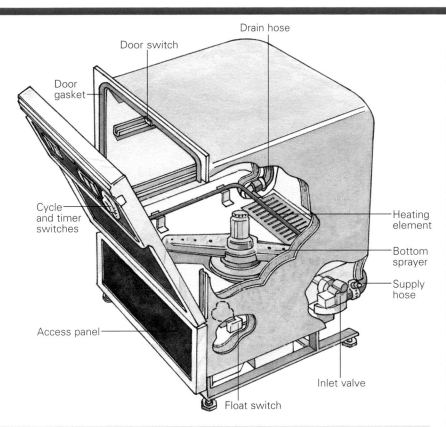

Drain hose

Door switch

Door gasket

Cycle and timer switches

Access panel

Float switch

Heating element

Bottom sprayer

Supply hose

Inlet valve

TROUBLESHOOTING

Problem	Cause	What to Do
Won't start	No electricity	Check the plug or the circuit breaker.
	Dial or latch in wrong position	Turn to "Start" or until you hear a click. If nothing happens, call repair.
Won't fill	Dial turned too far	Turn dial to "Start" or until you hear a click. Wait a minute because of delay between start and fill.
	Supply valve turned off	Check stop valve under machine or under sink.
	Float switch stuck	Open door, remove cylindrical float switch cover, and jiggle float.
	Float switch broken	Replace switch (under the front of machine) or call repair.
Won't drain	Air gap clogged	Replace air gap (at hardware store).
Water on floor	Door gasket worn	Happens only if machine is old. Replace gasket with authorized replacement.
	Leaking hose or valve	Tighten valve, tighten hose clamps, or replace hose.
	Float switch stuck	Open door, remove cylindrical float switch cover, and jiggle float.
	Float switch broken	Replace switch (under the front of machine) or call repair.
Unusual noise	Improper loading	Make sure nothing is hitting the spray arm. Pack the utensils more securely.
	Motor striking floor	Raise the dishwasher on leveling legs. Check motor mount to see if loose.
Rusty stain	Iron in water	Install an iron filter or softener in water supply.

Check the dishwasher specifications for the size of flexible supply tubing (usually ⅜ inch) and be sure the stop valve has a compression fitting outlet that matches the tubing.

4. ROUGHING IN THE WIRING

Dishwashers require a separate 110-volt circuit protected by a 15-amp breaker. If the dishwasher requires a junction box or outlet, check the manufacturer's specifications for locating it. Some units have a standard 3- to 4-foot appliance cord for plugging into a wall receptacle, located either low on the back wall of the dishwasher space or in the sink cabinet. Others have a short cable for wiring directly to the junction box. Still others include their own junction box to which you run a cable.

5. INSTALLING THE DISHWASHER

Slide the dishwasher into place and level it on its leveling feet. Make connections, usually underneath the unit, according to the manufacturer's instructions. Turn on the circuit breaker and the hot-water supply and run the machine through a test cycle. If everything checks out, secure it under the front of the countertop and install the base panel.

BACK OFF ON THE SOAP

Liquid dishwashing detergents are more concentrated than ever before. Because we want our dishes to be squeaky clean, we fill the dishwasher's soap dispenser to the brim.

This is not a good idea. The machine may fill with suds producing undesirable results:
- Dishes won't be sprayed with full force.
- Suds may overflow onto the floor.
- The machine may never get rid of all the detergent, leaving a film on the dishes.

Instead, cut the amount of detergent by half each time and inspect the results. Until the dishes come out less than perfectly clean, you have been wasting detergent.

DOORBELLS

HOW DOORBELLS WORK

ALSO SEE...
Switches:
Pages 352–355
Wire:
Pages 442–445

Although they come in many sounds, shapes, and designs, all electrical doorbells except the wireless variety operate in basically the same way.

The bell, chimes, buzzer, or recorded sound track are activated by low-voltage current from a transformer that steps normal 120-volt household current down to between 6 and 24 volts. Low-voltage wiring is perfect for the novice do-it-yourselfer because it will not cause a severe shock.

Plastic-coated "bell wire," usually 18 or 20 gauge, connects the transformer to the doorbell and a push-button switch. An electrical circuit is created by connecting one wire between the transformer and the button, a second wire between the button and the doorbell, and a third wire between the doorbell and the transformer. Pushing the button completes the circuit, allowing current to flow, actuating a solenoid that strikes the bell.

Additional bells and push buttons can be added so that you can distinguish between the bells for the front door and the back door.

THE TRANSFORMER

A transformer steps 120-volt household current down to low voltage for the doorbell. You'll find it wired into one of the house circuits at a junction box in the basement, or in the attic or a closet.

You can test the transformer very simply. If you are knowledgeable about electricity and have a voltmeter, simply measure the voltage across the output, or low-voltage terminals. These are the screws to which is attached the thinner bell wire. The voltage should read between 6 and 24 volts AC. If not, check the voltage at the input terminals. If this reads between 110 and 130 volts AC, then the transformer is bad. Take the old one with you to buy a replacement at an electrical- or radio-supply store.

Wire to bell or chimes   Low-voltage terminals   Junction box   House current

Wires to push button(s)

BELLS

Doorbells, chimes, and buzzers all have an electromagnet that is activated when the circuit is completed when the door button is pushed. When the current flows to a bell, the electromagnet pulls on the armature, causing the hammer to strike the bell. This also causes a contact breaker to open up, momentarily turning off the current and letting the armature spring back to remake the circuit. The whole process is repeated several times a second.

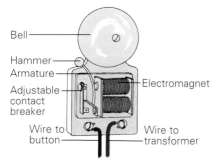

Bell

Hammer
Armature

Adjustable contact breaker

Electromagnet

Wire to button

Wire to transformer

CHIMES

When the bell button is pressed, current energizes the top electromagnet, causing the top striker to hit the high-note chime. Releasing the button breaks the circuit, and the spring pulls the striker back to strike the low-note chime.

When the back-door button is pressed, the lower magnet responds in the same sequence, except that the lower striker is not allowed to ring the low-note chime when it springs back. Either a padded screw blocks the backstroke, or the end of the striker is padded so that it makes no noise when it does hit the chime.

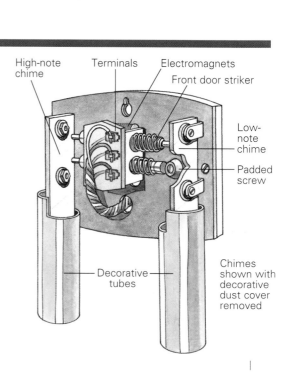

High-note chime   Terminals   Electromagnets

Front door striker

Low-note chime

Padded screw

Decorative tubes

Chimes shown with decorative dust cover removed

TROUBLESHOOTING A DOORBELL

The following steps will help you fix a doorbell that doesn't ring or rings very faintly.

1. Make sure that none of the circuit breakers in the house wiring are off or fuses are blown. The problem may simply be no power.

2. Check the push-button unit. This is most often where the trouble lies because it is a delicate switch exposed to wind-driven rain and dirt. Unscrew the unit from the wall and check the wire connections. If they have worked loose, tighten them, and test the button again. If the bell still doesn't ring, unscrew the two wires from the button and touch them to each other, holding them by the insulation. If the bell rings, it means the switch is defective. Straighten, clean, and sand the contacts, spray them with contact cleaner or lubricating and penetrating oil, and try it again. If it still doesn't work, replace the push-button unit.

3. If holding the button wires together produced only a buzzing or nothing audible at all, the problem could be in the bell. Clean off any dust or grease that may have accumulated on the striker, the bell, or any of the contacts.

4. Locate the transformer. If you have a voltmeter, measure the voltage at the screws to which is attached the thin bell wire. The voltage should read between 6 and 24 volts AC.

You can test the transformer by touching the ends of a jumper wire to both of the output terminals. If there is no spark (look closely, because it will be faint), then the transformer is not performing adequately. Check the voltage at the input terminals with a meter (do not check the input terminals with a jumper wire—you risk a dangerous shock or burn). If this reads between 110 and 130 volts AC, then the transformer is bad. Take the old one with you to an electrical- or radio-supply store.

5. If the transformer is good, but the bell still doesn't ring, it can be one of two things: a broken wire or the bell. If you have enough wire, you can test the bell by running wires directly from the two transformer output terminals to the two bell terminals. If the bell rings, you need to replace the wiring; if not, replace the bell.

CIRCUITS

REMOTE RINGER

This device, which plugs into a standard wall outlet, sounds when the doorbell rings. It can be located anywhere in the house.

TWO BELLS

Wire the circuit as if there were only one bell. Then connect the second bell to the first one in parallel.

TWO BUTTONS

Connect the bell to the transformer with one wire and run a separate switch loop for each button.

ONE BUTTON

The circuit between the bell and transformer is completed when you push on the switch button.

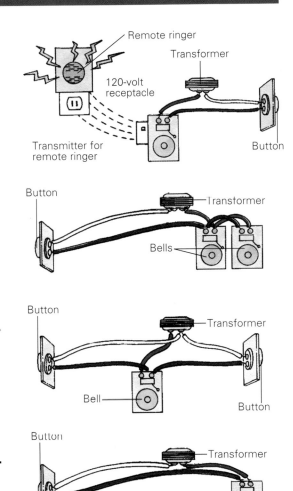

INSTALLING A NEW DOORBELL

1. Remove the old bell and connect the old wires to the terminals of the new unit. If you have both front-door and back-door buttons and you reverse the connections, you will hear the wrong bell. Test before mounting the bell unit to the wall.

2. Remove the old button and attach the new button to the old wires.

3. If you are installing a new system, you will have to wire a transformer to one of the house circuits, as well as run bell wire behind walls or under floors to connect the transformer to the button and bell unit.

Plan your installation for the most convenient wiring, locating the transformer where an accessible junction box already exists (a ceiling-light box in the basement is perfect) and locating the bell where wires can easily be fished through walls.

Be sure to turn off the circuit breaker or unscrew the fuse when you hook up the transformer. Transformers have a threaded sleeve around the high-voltage wires that you insert into a knockout hole in the junction box. The sleeve includes a nut that is used to secure the sleeve to the box.

WIRELESS MAGIC

If you are building new, or if the old bell fails, consider purchasing a wireless unit. Installing a wireless bell is no more difficult than hanging a picture on the wall.

DOORS

TYPES OF DOORS

ALSO SEE...
Hardware:
Pages 174–175
Locks:
Pages 220–221
Painting Trim:
Page 239
Security:
Pages 294–297
Weather Stripping:
Pages 424–427

EXTERIOR DOORS

The front door presents a first impression of your home and is an important architectural detail. When buying a new or replacement front door, take care to select a high-quality unit that harmonizes with the architectural style of your house.

Sizes: Standard-size entrance doors are 1¾ inches thick, 80 inches high, and 36 inches wide. Side and back exterior passage doors usually have the same dimensions as entrance doors but here codes permit narrower widths, typically require only one 36-inch exterior door.

Codes: Doors made for exterior use have solid panels or solid cores. "Solid" means the space between the front and back veneers is filled with solid wood, foam, or particleboard. A solid-core door generally offers better security, has better insulating properties, and is less likely to warp than a door without a solid core.

Hinging: Hinged exterior doors usually are hung on three pairs of 4-inch butt hinges made of solid brass or a corrosion-resistant alloy. The jambs on prehung doors usually are 4⁹⁄₁₆ inches wide, but it is possible to order wider jambs to accommodate 2×6 framed walls.

Materials: Exterior doors made entirely of wood are beautiful and expensive. They come either unfinished or stained and finished with protective coats of polyurethane. Real wood doors typically are paneled—that is, they feature a framework of vertical stiles and horizontal rails pinned together with dowels. These frames hold decorative wood panels, panes of glass, or a combination of both.

Steel doors are popular because they are strong, stable, and warp-resistant. They are made by encasing a rigid core of extruded foam with a thin steel "skin"—often given a slight texture to resemble real wood grain and thin enough to allow drilling for deadbolts and other security devices. Steel doors are available prefinished in a variety colors or primed and ready for you to paint in a color of your choice.

Because they feature a foam core, steel doors have excellent insulating capabilities. Thin wood strips along each edge can be trimmed and precisely fitted to door jambs. Steel doors are moderately priced and their many styles will match most architectural designs.

In another type of exterior door a fiberglass skin (often wood-textured) is molded over a solid foam core. Like a steel door, a fiberglass door is tough and weather-resistant. Fiberglass doors come in many styles with permanent, maintenance-free colors. They are, however, considerably more expensive than steel doors.

INTERIOR DOORS

Standard interior doors are 1⅜ inches thick and either 78 or 80 inches high. They are generally hung with two 3½-inch-tall butt hinges. Since interior walls are thinner than exterior ones, door jambs are only 4⅝ inches wide. Prehung interior doors are also available with "split jambs" which can be adjusted to fit finished walls from 4⅛ to 4¹¹⁄₁₆ inches thick.

Interior doors are either panel type or flush. Panel-type doors typically are found on houses that are at least 50 years old. If you are replacing an old paneled door, match its style unless you are changing the architectural character of the rooms as well.

Flush doors are made by covering a solid core of lumber or compressed wood fibers with thin sheets of plywood. The surface is either smooth or decorated with wood moldings.

Interior doors are lightweight and often feature a core that is made of honeycombed cardboard. Other styles of interior doors include sliding closet doors, bifold doors, and pocket doors.

LEFT- OR RIGHT-HANDED?

When you order a prehung door, you will have to specify its "handedness" or direction it opens. Here's how to know:

Stand in the doorway, with your back to the hinge, and imagine the door opening. If it opens toward your right hand, the door is "right-handed."

CODE REQUIREMENTS: DOORS

Glazing in Doors: Glazing in a door is considered to be glazing in a "hazardous location" and must be tempered glass or another type of safety glass. Locations specified in the code include:

■ Ingress and egress (entrance) doors, except jalousies
■ Patio doors
■ Swinging (revolving) doors
■ Unframed swinging doors

■ Doors and enclosures for tubs, showers, hot tubs, saunas, steam rooms, and whirlpools where the bottom of the glazing is less than 60 inches above the drain.

Exceptions to the above include:

■ Door openings (windows) less than 3 inches in diameter
■ Leaded-glass panels
■ Faceted and decorative glass

Exit Door: Every dwelling must have at least one exit door. The required exit door must be hinged at its side, at least 3 feet in width, and at least 6 feet 8 inches in height.

Patio-Door Air Infiltration: Patio doors must be tested in accordance with ASTME283 to have air infiltration no greater than 0.5 cubic feet of air per minute per square foot of door area at a pressure differential of 1.56 pounds per square foot.

Entry door with half-circle window

Entry door with sidelights

Dutch door

Double-sliding French doors with transom

Double entry doors with transom and sidelights

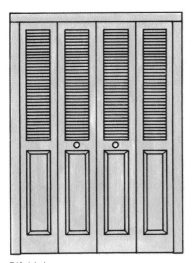

Bifold doors

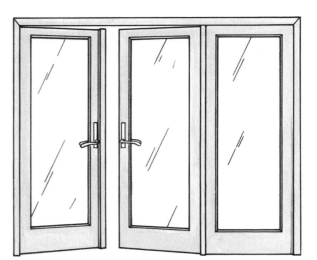

Three-piece patio door with double door and fixed panel

DOORS
continued

DESIGN CONSIDERATIONS

LOCATION

When a room has two doors, their locations will determine the traffic pattern through the room, as illustrated below. The most effective patterns channel traffic away from the center of the room to allow for groupings of furnishings.

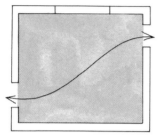
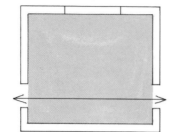
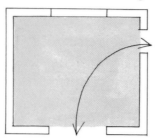
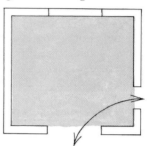

Doors at Diagonal Corners: Traffic from one door to the other naturally takes the shortest route, effectively splitting the room diagonally.

Doors Close to Both Corners of One Wall: Traffic eliminates any seating along one wall, but leaves most of the room unaffected.

Doors at Center of One Wall and an Opposite Corner: Traffic splits room into ⅓ and ⅔ seating areas.

Doors Close to Corner of Wall: Minimal disruption of room.

SWING

Plan your door installation carefully. Two doors in proximity should not be able to touch each other at any point along the arc of their swing. Occasionally, such problems can be solved be rehanging one of the doors on its opposite jamb. Another more drastic solution is to install a pocket door, eliminating problems caused by door swing.

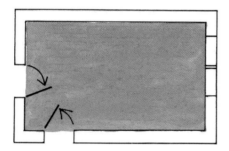

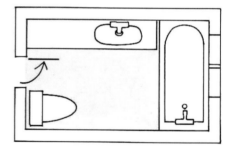

Conflicting Doors:
Corner doors can bang into each other, causing conflict and dinging.

Nonconflicting Doors:
Reversing the swing of one of the doors solves the conflict.

Door Opens to View of Toilet:
Person at toilet has no protection or privacy unless door is locked.

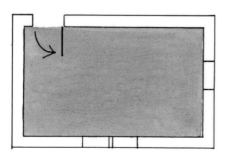
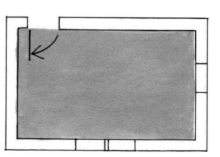
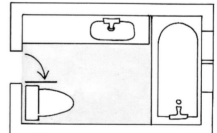

Single Door Hinged Wrong:
Door opening toward center of room restricts traffic flow and wastes space. It also limits the vision of a person entering the room, creating a safety hazard.

Single Door Hinged Correctly:
Door opening against wall allows unhindered flow and saves space. It allows an unrestricted view of the area around the door immediately upon entering the room.

Door Opens Against Toilet:
Even open door provides a measure of privacy for person on toilet.

88

INSTALLING POCKET DOORS

PREPARING THE OPENING

Frame a rough opening ½ inch wider and taller than the dimensions of the completed pocket frame. If you are cutting into an existing wall, plan the installation so that the latch jamb will be against an existing (but not recessed) stud. Then lay out the rough opening dimensions and cut back to the stud closest to the pocket. Install new trimmer studs and a properly sized header across the entire opening.

INSTALLING A READY-MADE UNIT

Set the pocket frame into the rough opening. Using a 4-foot level and shims, plumb the pocket end of the frame. Nail it through the shims to the opening studs.

Install the side jamb and head jamb, making sure they are plumb and level before nailing. Then screw the overhead track to the center of the head jamb.

After mounting the wheels onto the top of the door, lift the door in place and hook the wheels into the track. Adjust the wheels until the door hangs straight. Finish the walls and trim the opening.

INSTALLING AN ADJUSTABLE UNIT

Metal pocket-door kits are available and include everything but the door. To install one, first place and adjust the overhead track in the rough opening so that both ends butt against the trimmer studs. Center and level it, and screw or nail it to the studs.

Snap chalk lines on the floor between the outside edges of the trimmer studs. Then place the split jamb at the edge of the door opening and screw the top of the jamb to the track. Screw the bottom flange of the jamb to the floor at the chalk lines. Repeat the process with the split stud.

Mount the wheels to the door and hang it on the track, adjusting the wheel mechanisms to make the door the proper height.

Install door guides at the base of the split jamb, allowing about ⅛-inch clearance from the door. Then install the bumper halfway up the pocket trimmer stud. Adjust the bumper with shims or washers so that the door will remain ⅜ inch outside the split jamb when it is fully in the pocket.

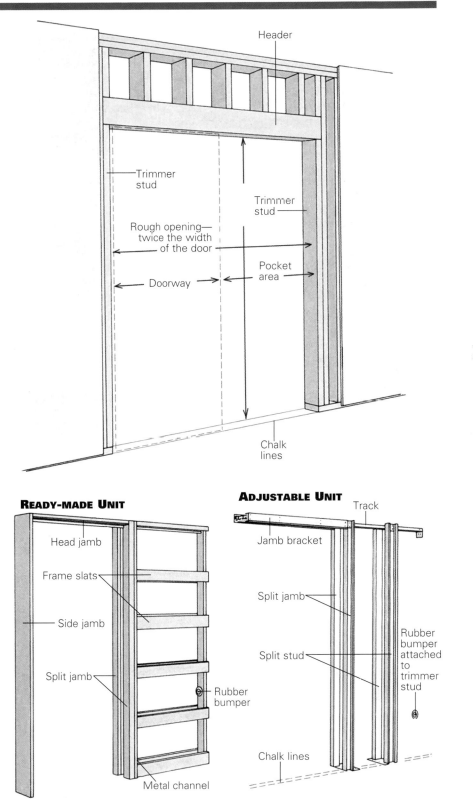

Cover the exposed trimmer stud with jamb stock and the framing with wallboard. Use 1⅛-inch doorstop molding to conceal the track and split jambs. Leave a ⅛-inch clearance for the door on both sides, then trim the opening with casing. ▶

HANGING A DOOR

If you are replacing a door or installing one that is not a prehung unit, you will have to work in stages. Here's your parts list: the door, a jamb set (two side and one top jamb), three hinges (two for an interior door), door stops, a lockset, and trim. For an exterior door, you will also need a sill and a threshold. The techniques described here for exterior doors are the same for interior doors, except that you won't install a sill.

1. Constructing the Jambs

The jambs must be of high-quality, knot-free finish lumber. You won't save much money milling your own, so buy a jamb set at a home center. Assemble the head and side jambs, using yellow carpenter's glue and three 8d nails driven from the outside of the rabbet in the side jambs. To prevent splitting, predrill holes for the nails.

2. Installing a Sill

Sill stock is beveled to slope away from the door to drain water. A drip groove on the underside prevents water from migrating back beneath the sill.

Occasionally, you'll run into a floor joist that must be trimmed to accept the sill so its back edge will be flush with the finished floor. A threshold covers the joint between the sill and the floor.

If you are installing a new door in an existing house, cut away the flooring to expose the joists. Make the cut directly under the inside edge of the closed door.

3. Adding a Sill Support

If the joists run parallel to the sill, you must add a support member for the edge of the subflooring that was cut, as well as for the back of the sill. Nail two blocks, of the same depth as the joists, between the joists on either side of the door opening. Cut two support joists to

length and nail them with 12d common nails through the blocks. One joist supports the edge of the subfloor and the other catches the inner edge of the sill.

Notch the tops of the joists at the edge of the house 2 inches deep, then fit the sill into this trimmed area. Shim as necessary to level the sill.

Predrill the nail holes through the hardwood sill, then nail it in place. Fill the joint at the sill bottom and siding with caulk and cover it with a strip of quarter round.

4. Installing the Jambs

Prepare the rough opening the same as for a prehung door (see Installing a Prehung Door, pages 92–93). Set the jamb assembly into the opening, and place a pair of shingle shims behind each hinge location. Plumb the hinge jamb with a 4-foot level and nail it through the shims with 12d finishing

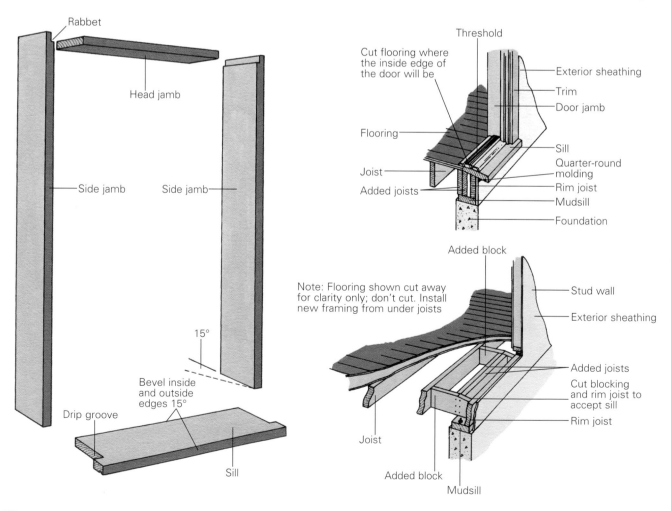

nails. Next, shim the top jamb, check it with a carpenter's square to make sure it is square to the hinge jamb and nail it. Square the latch jamb with the opening so the door will shut freely, and nail the latch jamb.

5. TRIMMING THE SHIMS

After checking for plumb and square and nailing the frame in position, cut the shims flush with the edges of the jambs using a handsaw.

6. INSTALL HARDWARE AND FINISHING TOUCHES

Before you start, be sure that the door is approximately ¼ inch narrower than the jamb opening and will clear the carpet, threshold, or weather stripping when hung. If the door is too large, trim the hinge and bottom edges with a table saw or jointer.

Then set the door into the jamb opening and temporarily shim it with ⅛-inch clearance on both sides and the bottom. Mark the hinge positions on both the jamb and the door. The top of the top hinge should be 7 inches from the top of the door and the bottom of the bottom hinge 11 inches from the bottom of the door. Center the middle hinge of an exterior door between the top and bottom hinges (interior doors need only two hinges).

Remove the door and trace the outlines of the hinges on the edge of the door. Extend each hinge leaf ¼ inch beyond the edge of the door so the hinge knuckle will clear the casing. Make sure the knuckle is inside, not outside the house so an intruder cannot remove the hinge pin. Using a router or a sharp chisel, cut mortises the thickness of the hinges. Screw the hinges to the door, predrilling for each screw. Be sure to drill straight holes—a crooked screw can pull the hinge out of alignment.

Cut similar mortises in the hinge jamb. A good trick is to attach the top hinge first, then mark and cut the other hinges.

After the door is up, check that it closes without binding. Make adjustments by placing a thin cardboard shim behind a hinge or by deepening the mortise.

Exterior jambs have integral door stops. If yours don't, use doorstop molding. Measure and cut the stops. Close the door, hold the stops loosely against the door, and nail them in place.

Install the threshold, lockset, weather stripping, and trim, using techniques described in other sections of this book.

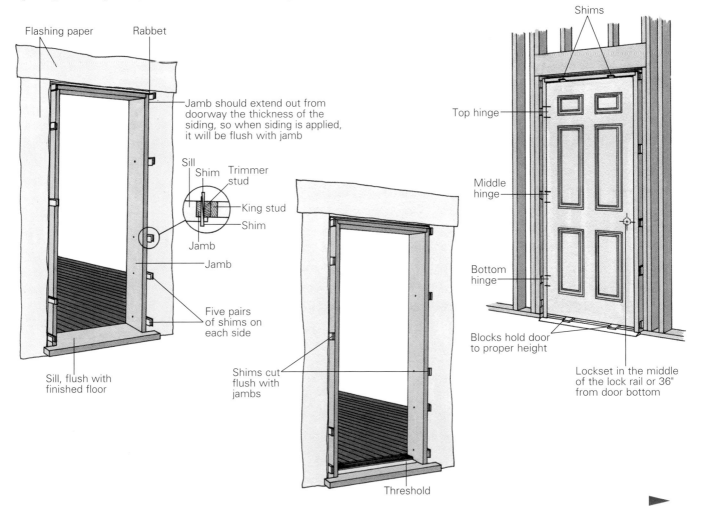

Flashing paper   Rabbet

Jamb should extend out from doorway the thickness of the siding, so when siding is applied, it will be flush with jamb

Sill
Shim   Trimmer stud
King stud
Shim
Jamb

Jamb

Five pairs of shims on each side

Sill, flush with finished floor

Shims cut flush with jambs

Threshold

Shims

Top hinge

Middle hinge

Bottom hinge

Blocks hold door to proper height

Lockset in the middle of the lock rail or 36" from door bottom

INSTALLING A PREHUNG DOOR

Both exterior and interior doors are available in prehung packages. In fact, it is rare to hang your own door today. A prehung door includes the jambs, the stops, and the door already hung on hinges. In addition, the door is usually predrilled for a lockset. Although prehung units are slightly more expensive than components purchased separately, they save hours of painstaking work.

Prehung doors come in two basic styles. In one, the door is mounted inside fully assembled jambs. In the other, called a split jamb, adjustable tongue-and-groove jambs are fitted together from opposite sides of the opening, and the door is already hung from the hinge jamb.

Before ordering a prehung door, determine its "handedness"—the way it will open. Stand in the doorway with your back to the hinge side of the door. If the door opens to your right, it's a right-handed door.

Installing a door used to require a finish carpenter, but the prehung door has changed that. Now you just set it into the rough opening and nail—almost.

Both interior and exterior doors are installed in the same manner. However, a sill must be installed with exterior doors. Techniques for installing the sill are covered in Hanging a Door, page 90.

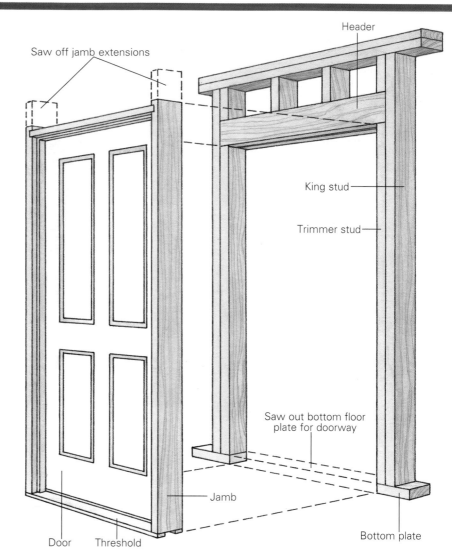

Header

Saw off jamb extensions

King stud

Trimmer stud

Saw out bottom floor
plate for doorway

Jamb

Bottom plate

Door   Threshold

PREPARING THE OPENING

Frame a rough opening with a king and trimmer stud on each side and a header across the top, heavy enough to carry the load above it. This rough opening should be ½–1 inch wider and 1 inch higher than the prehung unit. Install the wallcoverings on both sides of the framing and trim them flush with the opening. The combined thickness of the stud and finished wall material will determine the width of the jamb stock—usually 4⅝ inches for interior jambs and 5⅛ inches for exterior ones.

Tack strips of flashing paper or 15-pound felt building paper around the rough opening before hanging the door. First, with staples or roofing nails, install a strip across the bottom of the door opening. This bottom strip should overlap the building paper

below it. Then install strips on the sides, overlapping the bottom strip. The strips on the side of the opening should run up under the building paper above the opening. Place a strip of flashing paper on the top of the opening. It should overlap the side strips and nailing fin.

If you're framing the opening for an exterior door in a brick wall, lay out the dimensions carefully, so that as much of the cutting as possible will follow the mortar joints. Break a hole through the center of the opening with a hammer and chisel or a hammer drill, and remove bricks individually with a hammer and pry bar or masonry chisel. Remove whole bricks around the edges of the opening, leaving a sawtooth pattern, then fill in alternating courses with half bricks to trim the opening to a single edge. If the opening is wider

than 4 feet or the wall bears heavy loads, shore up the wall with bracing before cutting a hole in it. To complete the preparation for the door, head off the top of the opening with a lintel of concrete or angle iron.

PREPARING THE DOOR

Prehung packages come in different stages of assembly. Most are fully assembled, with the jambs, hinges, and door in place. Even if they're not assembled, all contain all the materials. The jambs are already cut to length; all you have to do is nail the side jambs to the frame with 12d finishing nails. If the package you buy already has the hinges attached to the jamb and door, pull the pins and detach the door while you nail the jambs together. Leave the door off until you fasten the jamb assembly in the frame. If necessary, trim off extensions above the jamb so they fit in the rough opening with ½- to 1-inch clearance.

If the prehung package is fully assembled, do not remove any temporary straps or braces that are attached to the unit until the door is in place. With many exterior doors the hinges are attached with long, heavy screws. If they penetrate through the side jamb far enough to interfere with clearances between the jamb and studs, saw off the excess.

INSTALLING THE DOOR

Set the door in the rough opening, centering it between the jambs. If the unit has split jambs, pull the two jamb pieces apart until the width of the jamb matches the wall thickness.

Use pairs of shims (one from the inside, one from the outside of the frame) to fill the gap between the jambs and studs. Adjust the thickness of the shims by sliding them toward or away from each other.

The first place to nail the jambs to the studs is through the shims behind the top hinge. Drive a 12d finishing nail at this point to hold the unit in place. Then use a 4-foot level to check the hinge jamb for plumb, adjusting shims in or out until the jamb is straight and plumb along its entire length. When it is, nail a 12d finishing nail through the center of the jamb at each shim location.

Next, level the head jamb by adjusting the shims above it and nailing it into the header. Then measure the width of the jambs at the top of the door, making sure the door can shut between them. Adjust the upper shims behind the latch jamb and nail. Use the same measurement to adjust the remaining shims, and nail the jamb to the stud. As you continue nailing, check from time to time to make sure the door shuts freely.

To complete the installation, saw or snap off the exposed ends of the shims by scoring them with a utility knife and tapping them with a hammer. Then install the lockset and striker plate. Finally, install casings or other trim to match existing doors and windows. If the door is an exterior door, fill the gaps between jambs and framing with insulation before installing the trim.

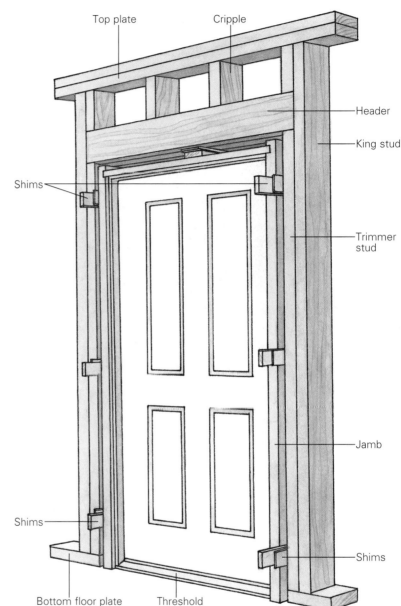

Top plate
Cripple
Header
King stud
Shims
Trimmer stud
Shims
Jamb
Shims
Shims
Bottom floor plate
Threshold

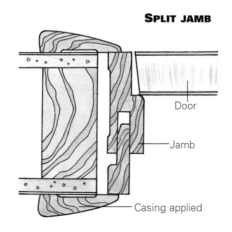

SPLIT JAMB

Door
Jamb
Casing applied

GET BIGGER DOORS

If you are designing a house or remodeling one, you probably have a choice in how wide to make many of the doors.

If money were no object, wouldn't you rather have 36-inch-wide doors? They look classy, they make moving a snap (well, easier anyway), and are the preferred size for wheelchair access.

Well, money *is* no object! A 36-inch door costs no more—*nada*—than a 30-inch door.

INSTALLING PATIO DOORS

To instantly transform a house, nothing succeeds quite like a sliding patio door. Standard sizes are 80 inches high by 5, 6, or 8 feet wide. Most building codes require the glass to be tempered or laminated safety plate. If you live in a cold climate, buy double-glazed or low-E doors to conserve energy.

Patio doors usually have wood or aluminum frames. If you choose the less expensive aluminum, make sure it has a "thermal break" that prevents the aluminum from conducting cold directly into the house.

For security choose a door with a good lock. Most patio doors come with a screw in the jamb that prevents it from being pried out of the lower track.

PREPARING THE OPENING

Frame the opening with king studs, trimmer studs, and a header sized to carry the load above the opening (see Preparing the Opening, page 92). The rough opening should be ½ inch larger than the door unit on both sides and on the top. Be sure that the header is level and the studs plumb. Use shims to correct variations. Make sure the subfloor is sound.

ATTACHING THE FRAMING

Remove the doors from the frame and set them aside. Before setting the frame in place, lay two thick beads of caulk along the floor near the edge of the

opening to provide a weathertight seal. Also caulk around the outside of the opening if the unit has nailing flanges or integral casings.

From the outside, have someone help you place the frame in the opening and align it so that there is an equal gap on both sides.

Level the sill with a 4-foot level, shimming with pairs of shingles, if necessary, and fasten the sill to the floor with screws. Do not drive them all the way in until the rest of the frame is set properly, however. Use a 4-foot level to plumb the side jambs. Even if the jambs are straight, use five pairs of shims on each side to keep them solidly in place. Check the corners with a carpenter's square and measure the opening at several places to make sure the doors will fit. If all seems in order, attach the jambs to the sides of the opening. Styles differ: Some have metal or plastic flanges on the exterior side of the jambs for nailing to the sheathing, others have wood casings, still others have predrilled jambs for screws.

If the sill overhangs the opening and seems to need additional support, nail a strip of pressure-treated wood to the sheathing under the lip of the sill for extra support. Some manufacturers also offer an optional sill support. Add more caulk to the bottom of the sill if necessary.

POSITIONING THE DOORS

Tilt the stationary door into one of the channels. You may have to use a hacksaw to complete a cut started along the top of a metal door before it will fit. Force the door firmly against the side jamb, and secure it to the frame with the supplied brackets.

Now tilt the sliding door into the other track. On wood-framed doors, put the security screws into the jambs, then remove the stop at the top

Casing

of the frame. Position the bottom of the door with the rollers resting on the rail in the sill, then press the top firmly against the weather stripping. Screw the stop back in place.

On metal doors, remove the security screw. Slip the top of the door up into the jamb channel, then lift the door and set the rollers on the rail. Slide the door open, and reinstall the security screw in the jamb.

Slide the door back and forth to check the movement. If it does not glide or close smoothly, adjust the heights of the rollers at the bottom corners.

FINISHING TOUCHES

Patch the wall, and install trim on the outside and inside, as needed. Be sure to install Z-flashing along the top edge if the unit doesn't come with an integral nailing flange.

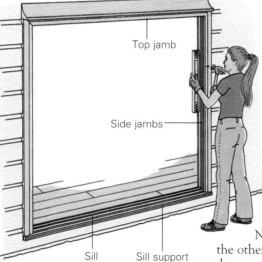

Top jamb

Side jambs

Sill   Sill support

Stationary door in the outside track

Sliding door secured according to manufacturer's instructions

Insulation

INSTALLING BIFOLD DOORS

Bifold doors are useful where there is not room for either a conventional door or a pocket door. When open they fold out of the way against the door jambs. Available in louvered, paneled, or flush versions, they provide architectural interest, as well as privacy, when closed.

Bifold pairs are generally 2 inches thick and come in widths from 2 feet to 3 feet. Two pairs can be combined to extend the range to between 4 feet and 6 feet.

Bifold doors can be installed inside an existing door frame. If the pair does not fit the opening exactly, trim both of the doors equally or build up the sides of the opening to create a narrower space.

Hardware includes an overhead track, a bottom pivot for each pair of doors, a slide guide, and an adjustable bolt that goes in the bottom corner of each pivot door to adjust its height. The hardware is available separately or as part of a complete package that includes two or four doors.

INSTALLING THE TRACK

Cut the overhead track with a hacksaw so it fits into the opening. Insert the rubber- or spring-cushioned bumper into the track, locating it where the slide guides will hit it. Slip the pivot guides into each end of the track, and screw the track along the centerline of the head jamb.

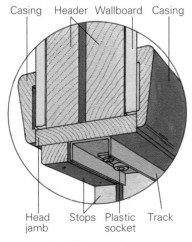

Casing   Header Wallboard   Casing

Head jamb   Stops   Plastic socket   Track

INSTALLING THE BRACKETS

Mark the location of the bottom pivot brackets on the floor by dropping a plumb bob from each pivot guide in the top track. Screw the bottom

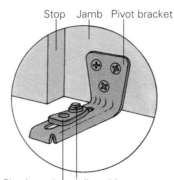

Stop   Jamb   Pivot bracket

Plastic socket   Adjustable screw

bracket to the side jamb, leaving the adjusting screws loose for the moment. If you plan to install carpeting later, allow for the carpet thickness by nailing plywood shims under the floor bracket.

INSTALLING THE DOORS

Measure the height and width of the opening carefully and trim the doors equally to allow a total clearance of $\frac{1}{2}$ inch at the sides and top. Join each pair of doors with three hinges. Then install the top and bottom pivots and the slide guides.

Set the bottom pivot into the bottom bracket first. Tilt the door toward the center of the opening and slide the top pivot guide to the center of the track so that you can insert the top pivot of the door into it.

Finally, tilt the door to vertical, inserting the slide guide into the track as you push on the door.

Top pivot in socket   Door

Bottom pivot in socket

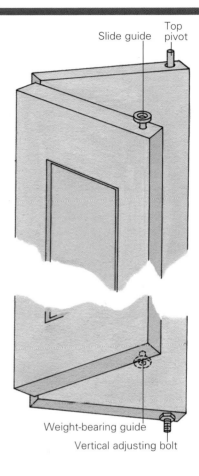

Slide guide   Top pivot

Weight-bearing guide
Vertical adjusting bolt

ADJUSTING THE GUIDES

When the door is vertical, tighten the top and bottom adjusting screws. Open the door to test it for clearance. If it binds on the top track or rubs against the floor, adjust the height by turning the adjusting nut located on the bottom pivot bracket. Repeat the same process for the second pair of doors.

WEATHER-STRIP DOORS

Open a window on the street just a crack and notice how much street noise comes in. You have just verified the fact that most sound transmission occurs through cracks and holes rather than through solid walls, windows, and doors.

If you really want to soundproof a bathroom, band-practice room, or bedroom, weather-strip its doors!

▶

95

INSTALLING SLIDING DOORS

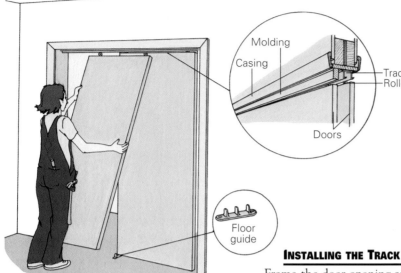

Molding
Casing
Track
Rollers
Doors
Floor guide

Sliding doors are often used for closets because they are inexpensive, take up no interior room space, and are easy to install. You can use any type of door: paneled, louvered—even used interior doors you find at a yard sale, and there is no limit to the number of doors you can use. Mount lightweight mirrors on the doors, giving you a place to look at yourself and to make the room seem like it's larger than it is.

The hardware basic for sliding closet doors includes an overhead track, a pair of wheels that attaches to the top of each door, and door guides that are fastened to the floor to keep the doors from swinging out. More expensive hardware packages will have a floor track with rollers to guide the doors smoothly and keep them from rattling. You can buy the hardware separately, or buy the doors and hardware in a kit.

The doors should be 1½ inches shorter than the height of the opening to allow 1¼ inches for the track and ¼-inch clearance above the floor or carpet. Each door should be ½ inch wider than half of the width of the opening so that they overlap by 1 inch when closed. The doors don't necessarily have to be the same width, as long as their total width is 1 inch greater than the width of the opening.

If you cannot find doors of the proper width, either trim the edges with a power saw or add trim to the inside of the doorway.

INSTALLING THE TRACK

Frame the door opening and install side and head jambs. Cut the overhead track to length with a hacksaw. Center the track on the overhead jamb, and mark it for predrilled screw holes. Remove the track and drill pilot holes in the top jamb. Then install the track with the open channels facing the inside of the closet. (If you wish, you can conceal the track from view with an extrawide top casing or a separate wood strip nailed to the head jamb.)

HANGING THE DOORS

Mount a pair of wheels on the top of each door about 2 inches in from each edge.

Hang the inside door on the innermost channel first, then hang the outside door. Slide the doors against a side jamb, and check the gaps between the doors and the jambs. If a door hangs unevenly, loosen the adjusting screws on the wheel mounts and raise or lower one corner of the door until it hangs straight.

If the hardware includes a bottom track, remove the doors and set the guide track on the floor between the jambs. Replace the doors, center the track under them (a level will help

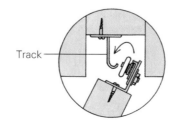

Track

plumb them), and raise or lower the doors by turning the adjusting screw until the rollers ride on the track. Screw the track to the floor.

ATTACH FLOOR GUIDES

If the hardware kit did not include a bottom track, it will certainly include a metal or plastic floor guide to keep the doors from swinging and banging into each other. Screw the guide to the floor between the doors in the center of the opening where they meet.
If the guide is adjustable, move the side pieces until there is a ⅛-inch clearance from the doors. If the guide is too low, nail a plywood shim to the floor before installing it.

Finish the installation by trimming around the doors. Install casings around the opening and a strip of molding across the head jamb to hide the overhead track.

ADJUSTING A NUT MECHANISM

Some wheel hangers have an adjusting nut that is turned with a small wrench. Turning the nut will move the door up and down or will loosen the door so that you can move it manually. If the latter, hold the door steady while you tighten the nut.

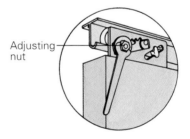

Adjusting nut

ADJUSTING THE DIAL

Other wheel hangers have a dial mechanism that raises or lowers the door. Loosen the set screw, turn the dial to adjust the door, then retighten the set screw.

Set screw

DOOR REPAIRS

REPLACING A THRESHOLD

Using a backsaw, cut the existing threshold into three pieces. As you approach the end of the cut, pry the threshold up so that the saw doesn't damage the finished floor.

After removing the center section, knock out the ends with a hammer and chisel.

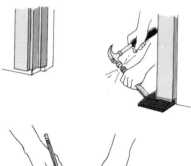

Reassemble the three pieces as a pattern on the new threshold and trace the outline. Don't forget to allow for the width of the saw blade.

After sawing out the new piece, and after removing any projecting nails from the floor, tap the new threshold in place from the outdoor side.

Predrill nail holes

Caulk underneath

Drill pairs of $\frac{1}{16}$-inch pilot holes at the ends and center of the threshold. Nail the threshold to the subfloor with 10d finish nails.

TRIMMING A DOOR

Mark the door while it is on its hinges. Then take it down and place it on sawhorses. Use a pencil and a straightedge to mark the cut line. To prevent the saw from splintering the surface, scribe the line with a knife.

Clamp a thin, straight piece of plywood to the door to use as a guide or fence for the circular saw. Check and double-check that the saw blade is on the cutting line, then make your cut.

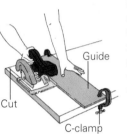

Guide

Cut

C-clamp

STRAIGHTENING A WARPED DOOR

This operation is done with the door open but still on its hinges. If you take the door off, you risk warping it along its hinge edge as well.

Attach wires to screw eyes in the corners (diagonal to the warp) and to a turnbuckle. If you object to seeing screw holes in the door face, screw the eyes into the top edge and the hinge edge, where they will not be seen later. Stretch the wire over a scrap of 2×4 and tighten the turnbuckle. Increase the tension daily for three or four days. To monitor your progress, loosen the turnbuckle and close the door.

BINDING DOORS

Before you start cutting or shimming, try two simple things that cure the problem 90 percent of the time:
1. Tighten all of the hinge screws. If a screw won't stay tightened, try one $\frac{1}{2}$ inch longer.

2. Probably neither the door nor the rough framing has moved since the door was installed, but the hinge jamb, attached only with finish nails, may have pulled out. To put it back where it belongs, drive a single 16d common nail just above or below each hinge.

If this doesn't solve the problem:
3. Slide paper between the door and jamb—it will bind where the door is sticking. If the door sticks at the top of the latch side, chisel the top hinge mortise more deeply, or shim the bottom hinge out (see Shimming Hinges, *below*).
4. To correct sticking at the bottom of the latch side, deepen the mortise of the bottom hinge, or shim the top hinge. If the door binds on the hinge side, shim one or both hinges, as needed. If these methods fail, plane off the edge and repaint.

SHIMMING HINGES

Shim stock for hinges should be dense and thin so it won't compress and you can use more than one layer if need be. Business cards, index cards, and notepad backs are ideal.

SETTING HINGES

Make sure you have a very sharp chisel. Otherwise you will really butcher the door.
1. Chisel the hinge outline slightly deeper than the desired mortise depth.
2. Make feather cuts to the required depth about $\frac{1}{8}$ inch apart.
3. Shave off the feather cuts and level the mortise so that the hinge lies flat.

MOVING A DOORSTOP

When a door won't close tightly on its stops, you may be able to move the stops to conform to the door. Assuming the stop is a separate piece fastened to the jamb, pry it from the jamb. Close the door, then place the stop against the jamb and flush with the door. Nail the stop in its new position.

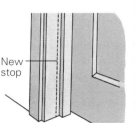

New stop

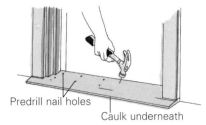

DORMERS

BRINGING LIGHT AND PURPOSE TO ATTIC SPACE

ALSO SEE...

Attics:
Pages 14–17
Flashing:
Pages 136–139
Framing:
Pages 152–159
Roofs:
Pages 282–289
Wallboard:
Pages 392–397
Windows:
Pages 432–441

A dormer can transform a small, dark attic into a bright and spacious living area. Adding one or more windowed dormers improves light and ventilation and can increase the usable floor space by as much as 30 to 40 percent. If you compare the cost of building a dormer to the cost of adding a room, a new dormer is an appealing project indeed.

Adding a dormer requires skilled carpentry. If you have only a little building experience, hire a professional for at least part of the job. Working alongside the contractor will give you an opportunity to learn as you go. Or have the contractor handle the more difficult aspects, such as cutting into the roof and framing the shell, then finish the job yourself. Remember that building a dormer will require building permits and regular inspections.

Plan the size and shape of a dormer carefully. Its style should match the existing architecture, with the same type of windows, siding, and roofing. Details, such as overhangs and fascia, should also be repeated. The dormer should blend smoothly with the rest of the house, complementing its overall design. In fact, it should look like part of the original structure.

DORMER STYLES

There are two basic shapes for a dormer. The shed shape is easier to build, but constructing it exposes your home to the elements longer than the much smaller gable dormer. Your choice, however, should depend more on how much raised-ceiling area you need and how well the dormer will blend in with the architecture of your home.

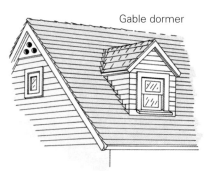

Gable dormer

Shed dormer

GABLE DORMER

A gable dormer has an appealing charm, but typically is not large. Because a single gable dormer is small and adds light but little floor space, several are usually required to balance the exterior proportions of a house.

Gable dormers work best with steeply pitched roofs.

SHED DORMER

A shed dormer adds more living space than a gable dormer, and can even extend across the entire length of the roof. The front can be built directly over an exterior wall, but in most cases a shed dormer looks better when set back on the roof with a foot or more of space in front of it.

DETERMINING THE SECTION

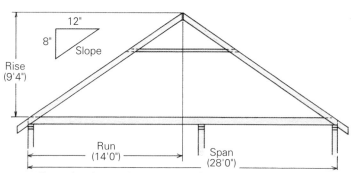

12"
8"
Slope

Rise
(9'4")

Run
(14'0")

Span
(28'0")

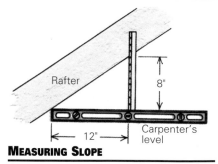

Rafter

8"

12"

Carpenter's level

MEASURING SLOPE

To begin, you'll need to know the slope of your roof. The slope of a roof is measured as the number of inches of vertical rise per 12 inches of horizontal run.

In the figure *above*, the width of the house is 28 feet, so the run of a single rafter is half, or 14 feet. The rise of the rafter, from the point where the plane of the outside wall cuts the top of the rafter to the very top of the rafter at the ridge, is 9 feet and 4 inches.

If you were to convert both dimensions into inches, you would find that the ratio (the slope) is 8 inches of vertical rise per 12 inches of horizontal run, or an "8 in 12 pitch."

An easy way to measure the slope of a roof is to hold a carpenter's level against the bottom of a rafter, as shown *above*. Mark the level 12 inches from the end that will touch the rafter. Then, with a square at the mark, measure the vertical distance between the top of the joist to the top edge of the rafter. That figure is the number of inches of rise in 12 inches of run.

DRAWING THE SECTION PLAN

Start by drawing to scale an accurate end view of the existing roof, showing the rafters and attic joists. Also determine the minimum slope of the dormer roof and the minimum ceiling height of the new space, as described in Code Requirements, *below*. These dimensions, as well as aesthetic considerations, such as the best place to connect the dormer to the roof and the best location for the front wall, will determine your plan.

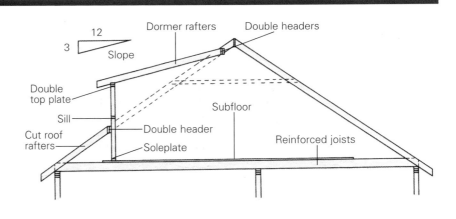

BUILDING A SHED DORMER

LAYING OUT THE OPENING

Make sure the attic floor is adequately supported for the new space and covered with subflooring (see Attics, pages 14–17). Lay out the dormer location on the attic floor. Holding a plumb bob over each corner, mark where the line hits the roof. These marks will be the corners of the roof opening.

To make the marks visible from the outside, drive nails up through the roof from the attic. You'll need to strengthen the rafters on either side of the proposed opening according to local building codes.

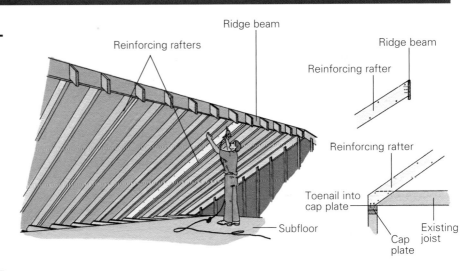

CODE REQUIREMENTS: DORMERS

Dormers added to make an attic habitable must satisfy the following requirements:

Light and Ventilation: Habitable rooms must have a total glazed area of at least 8 percent of their floor areas. Unless mechanical ventilation is provided, 50 percent of that area must be openable.

Egress: Sleeping rooms must have at least one exterior door or egress window. Egress windows must have a maximum sill height of 44 inches, minimum clear width of 20 inches, minimum clear height of 22 inches, and minimum net clear opening of 5.7 square feet.

Ceiling Height: Except for kitchens, habitable rooms must have ceiling heights of at least 7½ feet for at least 50 percent of their areas.

Roof Slope: Dormer roof coverings must have the following minimum slopes:

■ Wood shingles: 3/12 (3-inch rise every foot)
■ Asphalt shingles: 2/12 (2 inches per foot)
■ Roll roofing: 1/12 (an inch rise per foot)

CUTTING THE ROOF OPENING

Snap chalk lines on the roof surface between the four nails. Strip off the roofing to one foot beyond the lines. Resnap the chalk lines on the

sheathing. Cut through the sheathing along the chalk lines and remove it. Mark the rafters for cutting, as shown, but do not cut them yet.

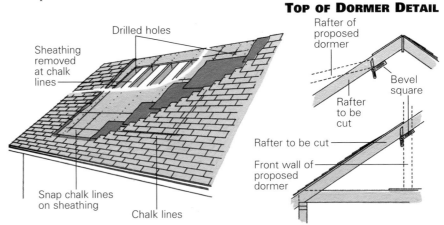

BUILDING A SHED DORMER *continued*

CUTTING THE RAFTERS

Brace the rafters before cutting them by building temporary support walls. Nail 2×4 top and side plates to the rafters and the joists, just above and below the opening. Wedge and tack studs between the two plates under each rafter. Have a helper support each rafter as you cut it, so that it doesn't fall and jar the ceiling.

INSTALLING THE HEADERS

To install double headers across the cut ends of the rafters, nail double 2×8 joist hangers (see Framing, pages 152–159) to the doubled rafters at each corner of the opening. Then cut a header from rafter stock, set it into the joist hangers, and nail it into all the rafter ends. Cut the second header piece, slide it into the same joist hangers, and nail it to the first. Repeat for the double top header.

FRAMING THE FRONT WALL

Now that the double headers are supporting the rafters, you can remove the temporary walls. Next, frame the front wall, using the attic floor as a work surface. The length of the wall is the distance between the double rafters, but extend the double top plate 3½ inches beyond the end studs. Use standard framing techniques (see Framing, pages 152–159) for the studs and the rough opening for the window(s).

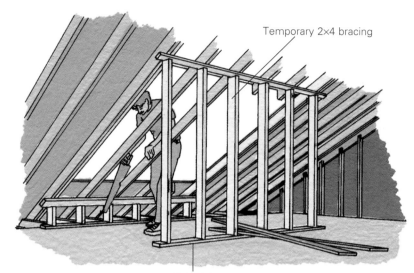

Temporary 2×4 bracing

Soleplate

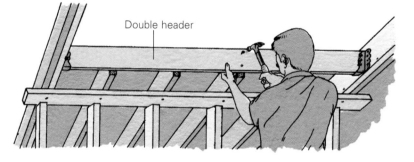

Double header

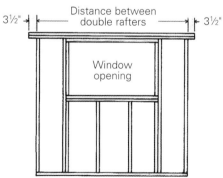

3½" · Distance between double rafters · 3½"

Window opening

ERECTING THE FRONT WALL

Stand the wall up. Nail a diagonal brace to it, plumb the wall, and secure the brace to a block nailed into the floor. Nail the soleplate to the floor, toenail the studs to the rafter header, and face-nail the end studs into the double rafters.

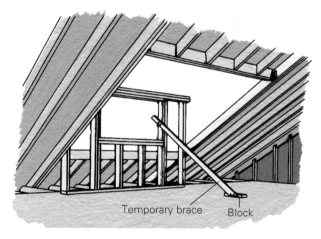

Temporary brace   Block

Corner posts

INSTALLING CORNER POSTS

Build corner posts for the wall with two 2×4s and scraps of ⅜- or ½-inch plywood. Measure them to fit between the top plate of the new wall and the roof sheathing, cutting the bottoms at the slope of the roof. Nail the corner posts to the end studs and top plate, toenailing them to the rafters under the sheathing.

MARKING FOR RAFTER CUTS

Cut rafters from lumber sized for the span of the opening (see Wood, pages 446–453). Mark the plumb cut for the top of the rafter with a framing square, as shown. Mark the bottom of the square at 12 inches. Mark the other area with the slope you computed for the dormer roof (see Drawing the Section Plan, page 99). Mark the cut along the vertical arm of the square. Cut one rafter and test the fit before cutting the rest.

ALTERNATIVE MARKING METHOD

If you do not know the slope of the dormer roof, you can still mark the plumb cut. Tack a piece of scrap to the top of the rafter and rest the rafter on the upper header. Align the bottom of the rafter with its inner edge flush with the inner edge of the cap plate, as shown. Position a straightedge against the rafter next to the header. Mark the plumb cut, cut the rafter, and check it for fit.

MAKING THE BIRD'S MOUTH CUT

Position the rafter so that the plumb cut rests flush against the upper header and the lower edge intersects the inside edge of the cap plate of the wall. Trace a mark on the rafter against the top and outside edge of the cap plate. Cut out the notch, called the bird's mouth, and test the fit of the rafter. Make any necessary adjustments, use this rafter as a pattern to cut all of the other rafters, except for the outside two.

INSTALLING THE RAFTERS

Lay out the rafter locations along the cap plate and header, 16 or 24 inches on center. Fasten the top ends to the header with metal hangers intended for sloping rafters. If you can't find any, use regular joist hangers, but notch the rafter where it rests in the hanger.

Toenail the bottom ends into the cap plate of the wall. The tops of the two end rafters should be angled to fit against the roof sheathing.

Finish the dormer by framing the end walls and installing sheathing, roofing, siding, and windows.

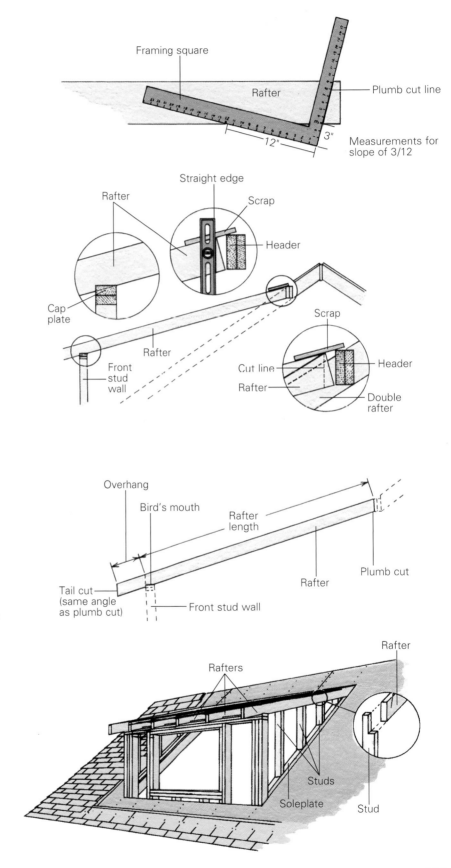

101

DRAINAGE

AVOID WATER HAZARDS

Improving drainage ranks at the top of the list of ways to make your home last longer. That's because water is the major cause of structural problems, such as decay, fungus, wood-destroying insects, and settling or upheaval of the foundation.

You first line of defense is to make sure you have adequate slope in the soil next to your foundation. Proper slope sheds water away from your house.

You also can provide drainage with surface ditches or underground pipes.

Most underground drainage systems consist of continuous lengths of corrugated, flexible plastic pipe or sections of rigid polyethylene pipe joined by fittings. Perforated pipe collects subsurface water in the uphill portions of the system. Solid pipes connect to the perforated pipes and carry water to the discharge point.

DRY WELLS AND TRENCHES

CONSTRUCTING A DRY WELL

If you can't discharge your drainpipes into a city system (some localities don't allow it), and if your slope is too flat to allow downslope discharge elsewhere in your yard, terminate the drainpipes in a rock-filled dry well.

You might want to hire an excavation contractor with a backhoe and a truck for hauling stone. No closer than 10 feet from the house, dig a hole at least 4 feet across and 4 to 6 feet deep (let him judge the size from the characteristics of your soil and the amount of runoff).

Fill the hole with rock. Run the drain line so the runoff will spill into the top of the well. Backfill the drain line trench with coarse gravel (covered with landscape fabric), sand, and garden soil.

DRAINAGE TRENCH

A typical drainage trench is 12 inches wide and as deep as needed to maintain a uniform slope of $\frac{1}{8}$ inch per foot. Fill half of the trench with gravel, install perforated drainpipe (holes

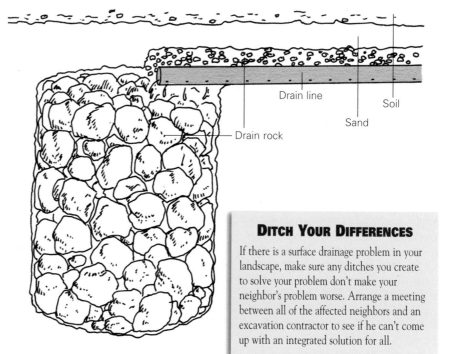

Drain line

Soil

Sand

Drain rock

down), and then add more gravel. Cover the gravel with landscape fabric, soil and sod.

DITCH YOUR DIFFERENCES

If there is a surface drainage problem in your landscape, make sure any ditches you create to solve your problem don't make your neighbor's problem worse. Arrange a meeting between all of the affected neighbors and an excavation contractor to see if he can't come up with an integrated solution for all.

DIVERSION DITCHES

The whole point to drainage is to keep water as far from your home's foundation as possible. If you have a sloping site, the simplest way to keep the surface runoff of a heavy rain away from the house is to intercept it upslope and divert it around your home until it is safely downslope.

Excavation contractors have keen eyes for drainage. With a backhoe or small bulldozer, they can totally change the drainage of your property in less than a day. When the work is finished, however, it will probably be your job to reseed or sod the area.

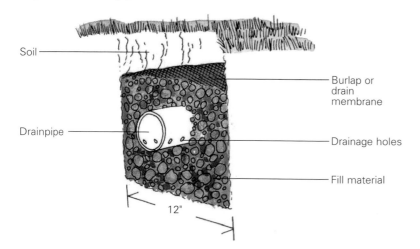

Soil

Drainpipe

Burlap or drain membrane

Drainage holes

Fill material

12"

MEASURING SLOPE

Here's a portable gauge to help you measure slope. On the side of a straight 8-foot 2×4, tack a piece of string as tight as you can with one end an inch below the top of the board and the other end 2 inches below the top. Hang a line level at the center of the string. When one end of the board is raised so the string is level, the board is at the proper slope for the drain line, ⅛ inch per foot (approximately 1 foot drop per 100 linear feet).

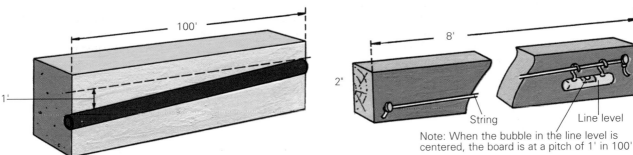

100'

1'

8'

2"

String

Line level

Note: When the bubble in the line level is centered, the board is at a pitch of 1' in 100'

FOUNDATION DRAINS

Install foundation drain lines whenever you build a new foundation. If an existing foundation has moisture problems, first increase the slope of the soil next to your foundation walls.

If the moisture appears mostly along an upslope wall, a diversion ditch or drain farther up the yard may save the trouble and cost of excavating the foundation. Measure the effectiveness of the new line by taping squares of plastic on the wall in several places. If moisture accumulates behind most of them, it will still be necessary to dig around the foundation and apply waterproofing as well as installing the drainage system.

Excavate to the base of the footing, but not below it. Slope the trench 1 inch per 8 to 10 feet. Make sure you have a place to discharge the drainpipe

so that the collected water will not find its way back to your house.

Place 1 inch of crushed stone or pea gravel in the bottom of the trench before you lay the pipe. Lay 4-inch perforated pipe all the way around the foundation, then solid pipe to carry the water away. Wrap the perforated pipe with drain fabric to prevent it from being clogged with mud.

Next, waterproof the exterior of the masonry walls. There are many new brush-on coatings that work better than the old standby, asphalt.

If you have a severe moisture problem, invest in a special waterproofing membranes, such as plastic backed with clay. This is much better than surface coatings. Protect the membrane from cuts from the gravel and other backfill with a

layer of rigid insulating foam or fiberglass panels.

Cover the pipe with 2 to 3 inches of crushed stone, then place drain fabric over the rock. Fill the trench with topsoil graded to slope away from the foundation.

AREA DRAINS

If surface drainage is inadequate and the source of the water is uphill, first try digging a surface diversion ditch to carry the water around and away from the house.

If the water is concentrated in one spot, such as a low area in the yard, install a small catch basin or dry well and run a drain line away from it.

To plan a drain line, first determine where you want to discharge the water. A street gutter, a drainage ditch, and a swale are potential discharge sites. If you cannot divert it from your property, dig a dry well to percolate

water beneath the clay or hardpan that prevents natural seepage.

Lay the drain lines back from the outfall. If you have only one low spot, one line will do. If the drain line is longer than 100 feet, install a clean-out at the high end of the system so you can clean a clogged pipe from both ends.

If you need to drain a very large area, place perforated 4-inch pipes in a herringbone pattern and connect them to a main trunk line. Space the branch lines 10 to 20 feet apart and

slope them toward the main trunk at a rate of 1 foot per 100 feet. Single or double Y-shaped connectors for either rigid or corrugated pipe are readily available. Construct the out-fall section using solid, unperforated pipe.

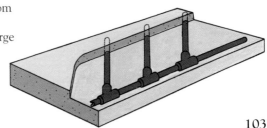

BUILDERS' SECRETS CONCEALED IN DRAWERS

A drawer is nothing more than a box: front, back, two sides, and bottom. Construction can be simple, with butt joints and a laminated face, or if you have a table saw, rabbet and dado the sides. For a tight fit, follow these guidelines:

■ Measure and cut precisely; the drawer fits into a restricted opening, so there is little room for error.

■ Glue all joints, including where the bottom meets the sides.

■ Make sure the drawer slides easily; it should not wobble or bind. If you use drawer slides or roller guides, align them very carefully.

Although drawer design is extremely simple, it requires precise measuring and cutting. Don't attempt construction without a table, radial, or chop saw.

Choose a design that you can build with confidence. The plans on this page show two designs that are easy to build. The construction sequence for both is the same:

1. Determine the size of the drawer by measuring the opening carefully. As a rule of thumb, drawers should not be wider than 24 inches nor deeper than 12 inches. If the opening is wider, divide it for two drawers.

2. Allow for any additional space needed for the sliding mechanism. Some are located on the top or bottom of the drawer and do not take up drawer space. Slides on the sides of the drawer usually require a narrower box to allow room for the slide.

3. Measure and cut the sides to equal length and the front and back to equal length. The front and back should fit between the sides to resist pushing and pulling forces.

4. Make the drawer face large enough to cover the gaps around the opening. It can be simple paint-grade plywood or a sanded and finished piece of dimension lumber. Glue it to the drawer front and screw it from the back with four short screws. This method is called paste-a-face.

5. Attach drawer guide hardware.

BASIC DRAWER CONSTRUCTION

The butt-joint design requires the fewest cuts and the simplest assembly, but drawers made with rabbet joints are much stronger.

BUTT-JOINT CONSTRUCTION

1. Cut the front, back and sides out of 1× lumber or ¾-inch plywood.

2. Working on a flat surface to keep all edges even, glue and screw the front and back between the sides.

3. Make the bottom of ⁷⁄₃₂-inch lauan plywood. Glue and nail it to the frame.

4. Cut the face from a piece of ½-inch plywood or other material 1 inch larger than the drawer front all around. Glue and screw in place.

5. Attach the drawer pull and drawer glide hardware.

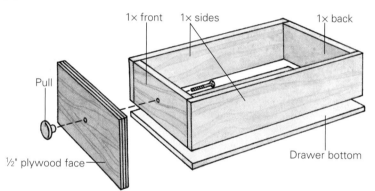

Pull
1× front   1× sides   1× back
½" plywood face
Drawer bottom

RABBET-JOINT CONSTRUCTION

1. Cut the sides to length. Rabbet both ends, removing two thirds of the stock. Cut the front and back pieces. Do a dry-fit assembly and make any necessary adjustments.

2. Cut ⁷⁄₃₂-inch-wide dadoes, ⅜ inch deep, that are ½ inch up from the bottom on all four pieces.

3. Cut the base from ⁷⁄₃₂-inch lauan plywood, allowing for the depth of the grooves. Check for fit.

4. Assemble the front and sides with finishing nails. Slide the bottom in place, and secure the back.

5. Attach the drawer face, a pull, and all of the glide hardware.

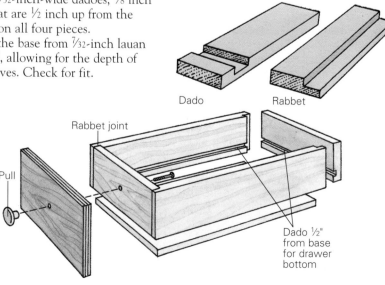

Dado   Rabbet

Rabbet joint
Pull
Dado ½" from base for drawer bottom

DRAWER FRONTS

Unless you paint, it is impossible to hide the edges of a plywood drawer face. Since the face is the only part of the drawer you ever see, invest a little extra in solid wood.

GUIDES

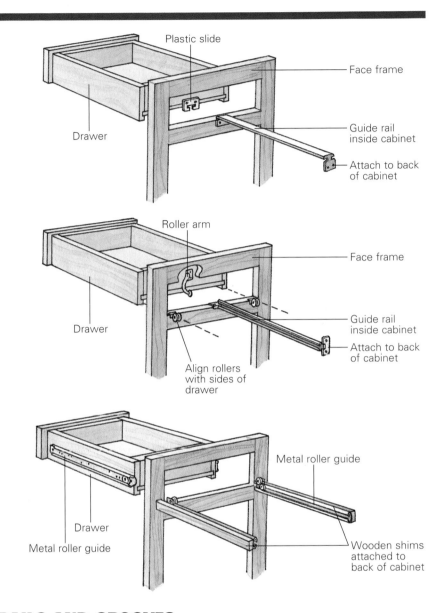

CENTER SLIDE GUIDE

This simple guide is used on the least expensive cabinets. The drawer actually slides on the cabinet frame, but side-to-side movement is restricted by a plastic slide that fits over a metal rail. Center the plastic slide on the back of the drawer and attach it with screws. Screw the guide and brackets into the face frame and into the back of the cabinet, making sure it is centered and level.

Plastic slide · Face frame · Drawer · Guide rail inside cabinet · Attach to back of cabinet

CENTER GUIDE AND ROLLERS

This guide allows the drawer to glide more smoothly because it rests on three rollers. Two of the rollers support the sides of the drawer, while the third roller engages the center roller arm.

Center the roller arm on the drawer back and fasten it with screws. Attach the two side rollers to the face frame so that the tops barely stick up. Attach the guide to the front and back of the cabinet, making sure it is both centered and level.

Roller arm · Face frame · Drawer · Guide rail inside cabinet · Attach to back of cabinet · Align rollers with sides of drawer

SIDE ROLLER GUIDES

This high-end mechanism utilizes telescoping guides attached to both the drawer sides and the sides of the cabinet opening.

Attach 1×2 strips inside the cabinet with the tops at the specified distance above the bottom rail of the face frame and the inside faces flush with the sides of the opening. Attach the metal roller guides, then set the drawer into the opening and mark where the bottom of its guides line up with the cabinet's. Remove the drawer and attach the guides to the sides.

Metal roller guide · Drawer · Metal roller guide · Wooden shims attached to back of cabinet

MAKE DRAWERS GLIDE

Sticking drawer? A little canning wax will make your drawers slide like new. Canning wax is more convenient (and cheaper) than candles because it comes in bar form.

Rub the wax on those surfaces that contact each other (they will be shiny from rubbing). While you are at it, pull out and wax all of your drawers so you won't have to try to find the wax again for years.

Also, look for signs of wear that indicate the drawer may be out of alignment. Adjust the hardware to make it operate smoothly.

RAILS AND GROOVES

This all-wood approach requires both the mindset and the tools of a cabinetmaker. The drawer sides are dadoed to slide over hardwood rails attached to the inside of the cabinet. The drawer fronts fit flush inside the opening, so all gaps must be narrow enough to look clean but wide enough to allow the drawers to slide.

This style does not have a separate face. The front is the finished face, and it must be sized so the gap around it is no thicker than a matchbook cover. After the side pieces are cut and rabbeted, cut a dado, centered along the outside of each piece. Then assemble the drawers.

Cut and tack the rails inside the cabinet. Test each drawer and make adjustments to the rails. Then glue and nail or screw them in place.

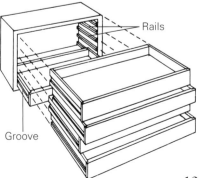

Rails · Groove

ELECTRICAL BOXES

CHOOSING BOXES

ALSO SEE...
Fans:
Pages 118–121
Lighting:
Pages 212–219
Receptacles:
Pages 272–273
Switches:
Pages 352–355
Wire:
Pages 442–445

Electrical boxes are either metal or plastic. Local building codes will dictate which type is acceptable in your area. Metal boxes can be ganged together, and cutting wallboard to fit around them is easier. Metal boxes must always be grounded. Plastic boxes are much less expensive—a major consideration for large wiring projects. Both have various brackets to make mounting simple.

Note: Always turn off power at the main service panel before attempting repairs or installations.

SWITCH BOXES

The type of box you choose depends on what you will be using it for. Switch boxes, also called utility boxes or handy boxes when used for surface mounting, are the most common and are used for wall switches and receptacles. For multiple fixtures, use large sizes or gang smaller ones.

TYPES OF METAL BOXES

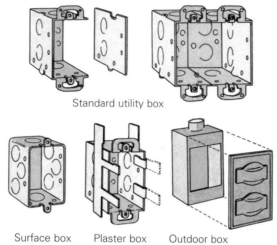

Standard utility box

Surface box   Plaster box   Outdoor box

CEILING BOXES

Boxes for most ceiling fixtures are octagonal and are usually (but not always) located in the center of the room. Various mounting brackets allow you to position them next to a joist, under a joist, or in a cavity between two joists.

Don't suspend a ceiling fan from the ears of a regular ceiling box unless the box is UL-listed for that purpose. Most ceiling-fan installations require a wood base or a bracket designed specifically for fan mounting.

CODE REQUIREMENTS: ELECTRICAL BOXES

■ Make all connections and splices inside the box.
■ Boxes must be accessible.
■ Cable must be secured to the box where it enters, except NM (nonmetallic sheathed) cable whose sheathing continues into a plastic box by at least ¼ inch and is stapled to secure framing within 8 inches of the box.
■ Ceiling outlet boxes must not be used to support ceiling fans unless they are UL-listed for that purpose.
■ Boxes in wallboard or wood ceilings or walls must fit flush with the finish surface.
■ Gaps around boxes in wallboard must not exceed ⅛ inch.
■ Unused openings in boxes must be plugged.
■ The number of conductors in a box must not exceed that shown in the table Conductors Allowed in Box on page 107.

CEILING BOXES

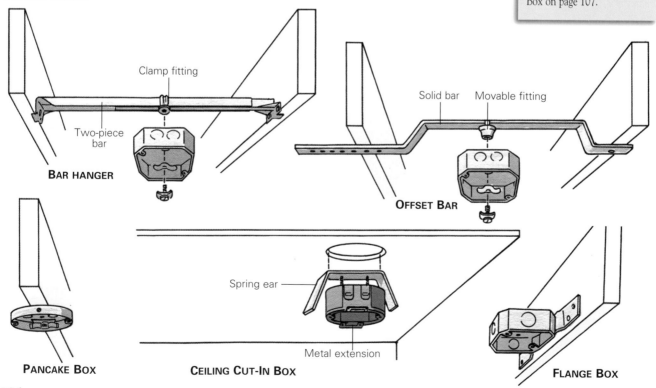

Clamp fitting
Two-piece bar
BAR HANGER

Solid bar   Movable fitting
OFFSET BAR

PANCAKE BOX

Spring ear
Metal extension
CEILING CUT-IN BOX

FLANGE BOX

CONNECTING CABLE

Connect cables to boxes with internal clamps or with connectors inserted through knockout holes. Nonmetalic sheathed "NM" cable used with plastic boxes does not require connectors, provided the cable sheathing continues a minimum of ¼-inch into the box and the cable is stapled to framing within 8 inches of the box.

KNOCKOUT CLOSURES

If a knockout is removed from a metal box and the hole is not used, it must be closed with an approved metal cover.

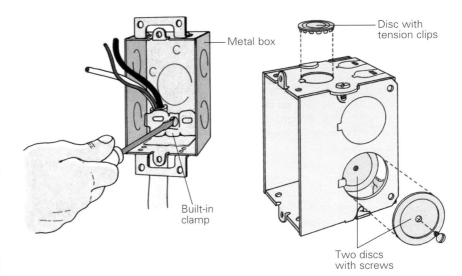

Metal box

Built-in clamp

Disc with tension clips

Two discs with screws

NUMBER OF CONDUCTORS

The National Electric Code specifies how many conductors are allowed in a box. By conductor, the code means anything that takes up space.

To count the number of conductors in a box add:
- Any wire ending or spliced inside the box
- Any wire running unbroken through the box
- Any cable clamp
- All grounding wires, lumped as one
- Any device, such as a switch or receptacle

The volume of a box is usually stamped on the box. If it is not, calculate the volume, in cubic inches, from the inside dimensions.

CONDUCTORS ALLOWED IN BOX

Box Shape	Dimensions in Inches	#6	#8	#10	#12	#14
Square	4×1¼	0	6	7	8	9
	4×1½	4	7	8	9	10
	4×2⅛	6	10	12	13	15
	4¹¹⁄₁₆×1¼	5	8	10	11	12
	4¹¹⁄₁₆×1½	5	9	11	13	14
Round/Octagon	4×1¼	0	4	5	5	6
	4×1½	0	5	6	6	7
	4×2⅛	4	7	8	9	10
Rectangular	2×3×2¼	0	3	4	4	5
	2×3×2½	0	4	5	5	6
	2×3×2¾	0	4	5	6	7
	2×3×3½	3	6	7	8	9

ELECTRICAL BOXES

continued

BOXES IN WALLBOARD WALLS

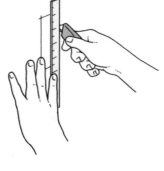

1 Measure the height of the box above the floor. Using the box as a template, draw its outline on the wallboard.

2 Cut through the wallboard paper along the outline with a utility knife, then cut out the hole with a wallboard saw.

3 From inside the wall, pull the cable into the box. Holding the cable, fit the box into the opening, then tighten the cable clamp.

4 The box shown is a remodeling box and uses brackets inserted beside the box and bent over its edges. Other remodeling boxes use toggles and side flanges.

BOXES IN LATH AND PLASTER WALLS

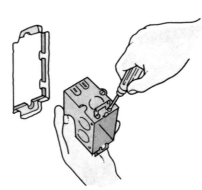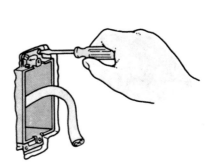

1 Locate the lath by chiseling away some plaster. Tape the outline of the box, centering it on the center of the lath. Cut through the lath and plaster with a keyhole saw, pushing hard but pulling back very gently to avoid cracking the plaster.

2 Move the ears of the box so its front edge is flush or slightly out from the wall surface. Reset the screws. Chip away enough plaster for the ears to fit against the lath.

3 Pull the cable into the box and attach it to the wall by screwing the ears to the lath with wood screws. Tighten the cable clamp.

BOXES IN BASEBOARDS

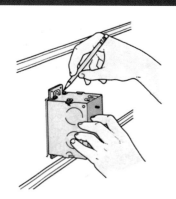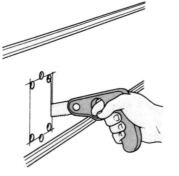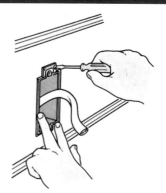

1 Trace an outline of the box on the baseboard—horizontally if the baseboard is too short for vertical mounting.

2 Drill holes in the four corners and at the top and bottom; cut out the baseboard by sawing between the drilled holes.

3 Pull cable through the box and set the box in place. Screw the ears of the box directly into the baseboard with small wood screws.

BOXES IN CEILING FROM ABOVE

1 To mark the location of the box on the attic floor, drill a pilot hole up through the ceiling below. Remove just enough of the floor to enable you to install the box.

2 From above, trace an outline of the box onto the top of the ceiling wallboard and drill holes in the corners.

3 From below, cut an opening for the box by sawing from hole to hole.

4 Install the box from above, using a bar hanger or a piece of 2×4 blocking to suspend it between joists. Attach nailing cleats and replace the attic floor boards.

BOXES IN CEILING FROM BELOW

1 Saw out a square of wallboard where the box will be located. Widen the hole enough to expose two joists.

2 Install the box by screwing each end of the hanger into a joist. Run the cable into the box. Make a wallboard patch and cut the hole for the box. Nail the patch to the joists.

3 Tape the joints and texture the patch to match the ceiling.

BOXES IN PLASTER CEILING

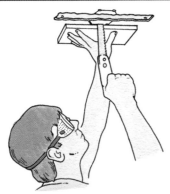  

1 Chip out a channel the width of a lath between two joists. Hold a piece of wood next to the outline of the ceiling box as you cut from marker hole to marker hole.

2 Cut the exposed lath on the outside of the two joists. Remove lath and nails.

3 Once the box is installed, fill the channel with patching plaster, allow to dry, and smooth in a layer of spackling compound.

ELECTRICAL SYSTEMS

THE PHYSICS OF CURRENT EVENTS

Before you attempt any wiring in your home, you should have a basic understanding of its electrical system. The following pages show how electricity enters your home, how it is distributed to the lights, switches, outlets, and appliances, and how its safety systems—the circuit breakers and ground wires—work.

Electricity deserves respect. Take safety precautions when you work with electrical installations; obtain proper permits; follow the code; and shut off the power.

Understanding your electrical system starts with the simple idea that electrical current travels in circles. It enters the home at the main service panel, runs in wires to outlets, switches, fixtures, and appliances, then returns "home." The entire path is called a circuit. The three basic terms associated with household current are volts, amps, and watts.

Voltage: Voltage is a measurement of electrical force or pressure. House wiring is a constant 120 or 240 volts. Amperage is a measure of the rate of current flowing in a circuit. Think of it as the number of electrons commuting "to work." When the workload is heavy (large appliances or many small ones), it is rush hour (high amperage); when there is little demand, traffic is slow (low amperage). Sometimes the highway gets overcrowded (a wire overheats). This can have dangerous results unless a traffic cop stops the flow of traffic (circuit breaker opens).

Amperage: The amperage rating of a circuit specifies how much amperage a wire can handle before the protective system (circuit breaker or fuse) opens. If the whole house circuit is rated at 125 amps, the main wires entering the meter are large enough to handle that much amperage. If the total usage in the house is higher than its rating, the wires will overheat unless protected by a main breaker or fuse. If a circuit is rated at 20 amps, the wires can handle that much amperage before the breaker

automatically shuts off the current to it.

Wattage: Wattage is a measurement of energy consumption (power). It is what your meter measures and what you get billed for. Somewhere on every electrical appliance you will find a label showing the watts the device will consume when on.

The three attributes of electricity are related in the following formula:

$$Watts = volts \times amps$$

With this formula, given any two quantities, you can always figure the third. For example, you can tell how many amps a 240-volt clothes dryer will need if it is rated at 7,200 watts.

$$7,200 = 240 \times amps, or$$
$$amps = 7,200/240 = 30$$

Given the label on the clothes dryer, we have found that the wire sizes in the dryer circuit should be rated at 30 amps and protected by a 30-amp circuit breaker.

Note: Always turn off electrical power at the main service panel before attempting repairs or installations anywhere in the house or outside.

HOW ELECTRICAL CURRENT ENTERS THE HOME

Electricity enters your home through wires hung from a power pole or buried underground. Most homes are served by three wires: two "hot" rubber-coated wires of 120 volts each and one "neutral" bare wire that provides a return path to complete the electrical circuit. Such a system has 120 volts for most household circuits and the capability of 240 volts for heavy-duty appliances.

The first instrument the current runs into is the meter. The two hot wires run through it so it can measure how much electricity you have consumed. Next in the circuit is the main disconnect, which allows you to turn off the entire electrical system. It might be a pull-down lever, a pull-out fuse block, or a large circuit breaker; it is located either in a box near the meter or atop the service panel.

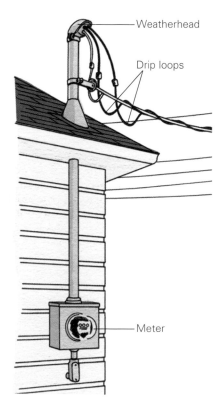

Weatherhead

Drip loops

Meter

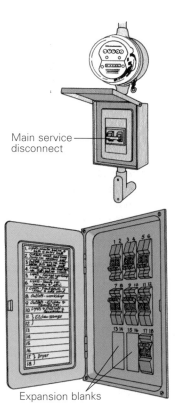

Main service disconnect

Expansion blanks

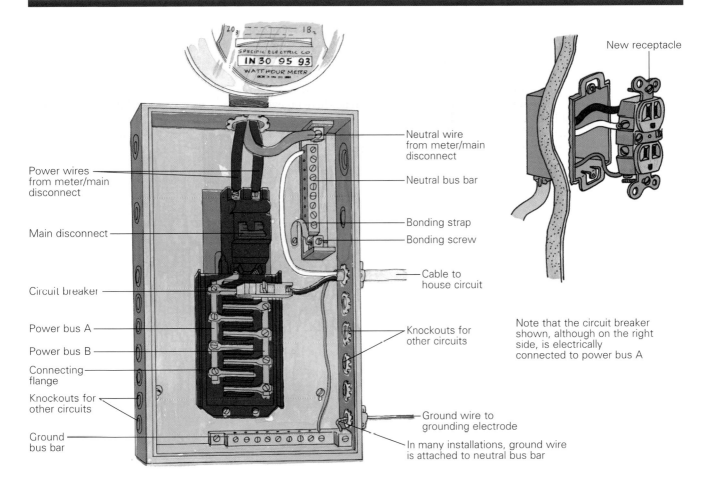

New receptacle

Neutral wire from meter/main disconnect

Neutral bus bar

Bonding strap

Bonding screw

Cable to house circuit

Power wires from meter/main disconnect

Main disconnect

Circuit breaker

Power bus A

Power bus B

Connecting flange

Knockouts for other circuits

Ground bus bar

Knockouts for other circuits

Ground wire to grounding electrode

In many installations, ground wire is attached to neutral bus bar

Note that the circuit breaker shown, although on the right side, is electrically connected to power bus A

After the main disconnect, the electricity is distributed within the service panel to branch circuits. In older homes the panel is a fuse box; in newer homes it is a circuit-breaker panel. You also may have a subpanel or two, such as for a workshop or for a major addition to the house. But even subpanels are fed from their own circuit breakers in the main service panel.

Power Buses: The illustration shows the inside of a typical service panel. For clarity, only one of the circuit breakers is shown. If the main disconnect is located outside the panel, three very thick wires will still come into the service panel from the disconnect. In either case the two black hot wires carry 120 volts each and are connected to two metal bars in the middle of the panel. The bars are insulated from each other and from the rest of the panel by a heavy plastic shield. These are the power buses and are controlled by the main disconnect switch.

Neutral and Ground Buses: The neutral wire (usually bare) bypasses the main disconnect and attaches to the neutral bus bar— a heavy metal bar with lots of screws for attaching the neutral wires of the branch circuits.

There is also a ground bus bar for attaching the bare ground wires of the individual circuits.

Neutral and ground come together at a single point—in the box that contains the main disconnect switch. If this is in the service panel (the usual case), the ground bus and the neutral bus are bonded. In this case, neutral (white) and ground (bare) wires can share the neutral bus.

Branch Circuits: Each circuit that is up to code has its own hot wire and neutral wire and is grounded. (Older circuits may not have a ground wire.) The hot wire, which provides electricity to appliances or fixtures, comes from the circuit breaker. The breaker, which is snapped onto a flange on the plastic shield, has contacts that

grip one of the two power buses. When the breaker is switched on, power flows from the bus through the breaker into the hot wire. It completes its path by returning along the neutral wire to the neutral bus bar. The backup grounding wire or conduit is connected to the ground bus.

Circuit breakers are arrayed along both sides of the plastic shield, drawing 120 volts from one power bus or the other. An individual circuit can be shut off by tripping its circuit breaker. Circuits that require 240 volts have two hot wires connected to a double breaker. The double breaker has contacts that grip both power buses, so that each of its hot wires (a black wire and a red wire) carries 120 volts. (No single wire ever carries 240 volts.)

The size of a panel determines the number of circuit breakers it can contain. If you're installing a new panel, allow blank spaces so you can add breakers. If you run out of space, you can buy half-size breakers, two in the space normally used for one.

CODE-REQUIRED CIRCUITS

Although it would be theoretically possible to have all of the lights and appliances in a house on a single circuit, the National Electrical Code (NEC)® forbids it. First, the system would have to have very large wires to handle the electrical demand. Second, if a fuse blew or a breaker tripped, everything in the house would shut down. In new homes the electrical load must be separated into several types of circuits: general-purpose/lighting, small appliance, and individual appliance.

GENERAL-PURPOSE/LIGHTING CIRCUITS

The NEC requires at least one general-purpose circuit, sometimes called a lighting circuit, for every 600 square feet of floor space—or 3 watts of power for every square foot. The NEC also specifies that there be a minimum of three such circuits, no matter how small the house. If there is any chance you will add living space in the basement or attic, include these areas when computing the number of lighting circuits you should have.

These circuits may be wired with No. 14 wire and 15-amp breakers, but if they include receptacles as well as lights, you should (not must) use No. 12 wire with 20-amp breakers. By using No. 12 wire, it is possible to accommodate an additional 600 watts per circuit.

SMALL-APPLIANCE CIRCUITS

Certain rooms of the house are required to have 20-amp circuits separate from general-lighting or individual-appliance circuits. Originally, the kitchen was the only room with this requirement, but with increasing use of high-wattage appliances throughout the house, the NEC continually changes to require 20-amp circuits in more rooms. The code now requires two such circuits for the kitchen, and one each for a dining room, a laundry room, a family room, and a breakfast nook. In some localities, all of the outlets in a house must be on 20-amp circuits that are separate from the lighting circuits.

INDIVIDUAL-APPLIANCE CIRCUITS

All 240-volt appliances require their own circuits. So does any 120-volt appliance or motor that is permanently installed. No outlets, fixtures, or other appliances may share the circuit. Each single-appliance 120-volt circuit must be wired with No. 12 wire and protected by a 20-amp breaker. The 240-volt circuits must have wire and breakers sized for the wattage of the particular appliance. The box, *right,* lists typical voltage, wire, and breaker size of appliances that require their own circuits.

APPLIANCES REQUIRING INDIVIDUAL CIRCUITS

Appliance or Device	Typical Voltage	Wire/ Breaker
Central AC	240	8/40
Clothes Dryer	240	10/30
Cooktop	240	8/40
Range	240	6/50
Water Heater	240	10/30
Well Pump	240	12/20
Compacter	120	12/20
Dishwasher	120	12/20
Disposer	120	12/20
Furnace	120	12/20
Freezer	120	12/20

CALCULATING THE ELECTRIC SERVICE (SIZE OF MAIN BREAKERS)

If you are sizing a service panel, the number of circuits will tell you only how large a panel to buy for it to have enough blanks for all the breakers. You also will need to know how large the main breaker entrance conductors should be. Here is the NEC-specified procedure, along with an example.

Load	Method	Calculation	Watts
General Purpose/ Lighting	3 watts × total square feet of living area, including full-height basement and attic	3 × 1,800	5,400
Small Appliance	1,500 watts × number of 15-amp circuits	2 × 1,500	3,000
	2,000 watts × number of 20-amp circuits	2 × 2,000	4,000
Water Heater	Nameplate wattage	5,000	5,000
Clothes Dryer	Nameplate wattage	5,000	5,000
Dishwasher	Nameplate wattage	1,500	1,500
Garbage Disposer	Nameplate wattage	1,000	1,000
Oven/range	Nameplate wattage	12,000	12,000
Other Appliance	Nameplate wattage (chest freezer)	400	500
Other Appliance	Nameplate wattage		
Other Appliance	Nameplate wattage		
Other Appliance	Nameplate wattage		
Motor over ½ hp	1.25 × nameplate wattage (table saw)	1.25 × 2,000	2,500
Motor over ½ hp	1.25 × nameplate wattage (sump pump)	1.25 × 1,000	1,250
A. Subtotal of all lines above			41,150
B. Line A minus 10,000			31,150
C. Line B times 0.4			12,460
D. Line C plus 10,000			22,460
E. HVAC	65% of electric resistance wattage, or 100% of air conditioning wattage, whichever is larger		9,500
F. Line D plus Line E		Total Watts	31,960
Line F divided by 240		Breaker Size	133A

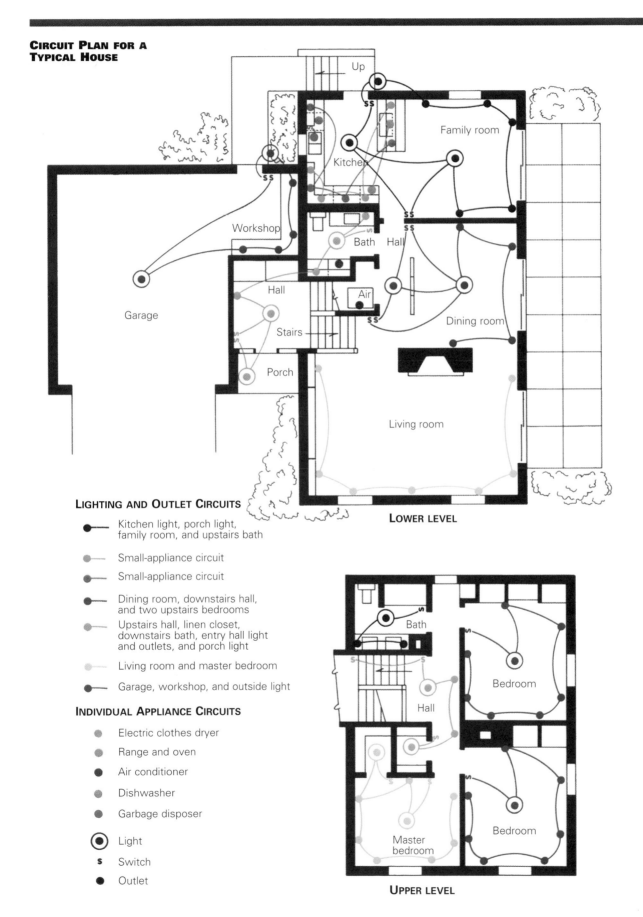

CIRCUIT PLAN FOR A TYPICAL HOUSE

LOWER LEVEL

Up

Family room

Kitchen

Workshop

Bath

Hall

Garage

Hall

Air

Stairs

Dining room

Porch

Living room

LIGHTING AND OUTLET CIRCUITS

- Kitchen light, porch light, family room, and upstairs bath
- Small-appliance circuit
- Small-appliance circuit
- Dining room, downstairs hall, and two upstairs bedrooms
- Upstairs hall, linen closet, downstairs bath, entry hall light and outlets, and porch light
- Living room and master bedroom
- Garage, workshop, and outside light

INDIVIDUAL APPLIANCE CIRCUITS

- Electric clothes dryer
- Range and oven
- Air conditioner
- Dishwasher
- Garbage disposer

- ⊙ Light
- s Switch
- ● Outlet

UPPER LEVEL

Bath

Bedroom

Hall

Bedroom

Master bedroom

THE GROUNDING SYSTEM

Electricity follows the path of least resistance, usually out from the hot and back through the neutral wires. When a neutral wire is broken or something else (you, for instance) provides a low-resistance path for the return "home," the electricity in the hot wire will follow that alternate path. Because earth provides a "home" for an electrical charge, the charge will jump through anything that touches the ground. This is dangerous.

The job of the grounding system is to provide a backup path, so the charge will go to ground instead of through a person who inadvertently touches a "hot" surface. The grounding system, in effect, neutralizes the grounding capacity of the human body. Ground wires, under current codes, must be connected to every receptacle, switch, fixture, and appliance.

These wires converge at the ground bus bar, which is connected to the ground by a No. 6 or larger copper wire. The critical link in the entire grounding system is the connection of this wire to the ground itself. An underground water pipe would be sufficient, and this was the standard residential grounding method for many years. But plastic plumbing materials now make it necessary to augment this connection with at least one of the "grounding electrodes" shown here.

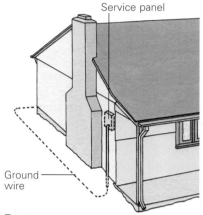

BURIED

Connect the ground wire from the service panel to a minimum of 20 feet of No. 2 or larger copper wire buried 2½ feet in the earth.

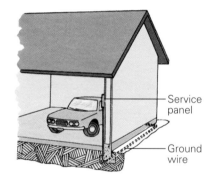

ATTACHED TO REBAR

Connect the ground wire from the service panel to a minimum of 20 feet of ½-inch steel rebar or No. 4 or larger solid copper wire enclosed in concrete (usually the foundation).

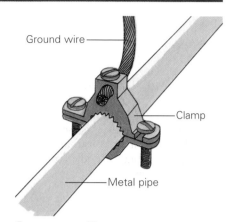

ATTACHED TO PIPE

Connect the ground wire from the service panel to a clamp connected to a metal (never plastic) cold-water pipe. Where the water pipe is interrupted by the water meter, use a bonding jumper from entrance to exit pipe.

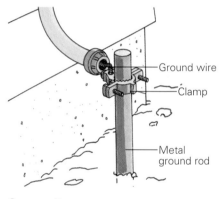

GROUND ROD

Connect the ground wire to an approved 8-foot copper or copper-clad ground rod driven into the ground.

WORKING SAFETY RULES

Never assume the grounding system will protect you against electrical hazards. The best safety system combines caution with common sense.

The Circuit: Always disconnect the circuit you are working on by tripping its breaker or removing its fuse. Confirm that you have the right circuit breaker by first plugging in a light or radio and seeing or hearing the device turn off when you trip the switch.
The Wires: Unless you are sure the circuit is dead, make sure any wires you are working on are dead by checking with a voltage tester.

Tools: When working with electricity, use plastic- or rubber-handled tools.
Damp Floors: Never stand on a wet or damp concrete or earthen floor while working with electricity. Instead, stand on a dry rubber mat or dry piece of plywood.
Touching Pipes: Never touch any metal plumbing or gas pipes when working with electricity.
Ladders: Avoid using or carrying aluminum ladders near overhead entrance wires.
Fuses: Never substitute a fuse with an amperage rating higher than that specified for the circuit.

Extension Cords: Avoid running extension cords across doorways or other traffic corridors or under rugs.
Grounded Fixtures: Never touch faucets or other grounded fixtures while holding an electric razor, hair dryer, or other appliance.
GFCI Outlets: When using power tools outdoors, on concrete floors, or where water is present, make sure the electrical outlet is GFCI protected.
Voltage Tester: After completing any electrical work, turn on the power and use a simple voltage tester to check your work. Buy two or three of the $5 devices so there will always be one at hand.

114

A GFCI is a special circuit breaker that protects against both circuit overloads and dangerous leaks to ground. The device compares the current flowing in the hot wire to the current returning on the neutral wire. If it senses the most minute difference, it assumes that some of the current is escaping to ground through a dangerous alternate path, such as a human body, and shuts the circuit down.

You can test and reset a GFCI by pushing a button on the device. There are three types of GFCI: a portable device that plugs into an ordinary receptacle, a GFCI receptacle that protects all receptacles farther along in the circuit, and a GFCI circuit breaker in the service panel that protects the entire circuit.

The National Electrical Code now requires this lifesaving circuit breaker for all circuits:

- Outdoors
- In a bathroom
- Within 6 feet of kitchen sink
- In a garage
- In an unfinished basement
- Near a pool
- Serving a whirlpool tub

The list is constantly growing, so check with your code official before you make any additions.

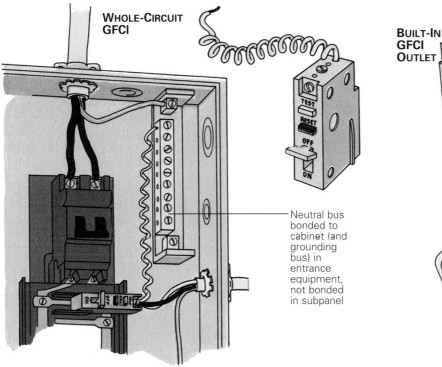

WHOLE-CIRCUIT GFCI

Neutral bus bonded to cabinet (and grounding bus) in entrance equipment, not bonded in subpanel

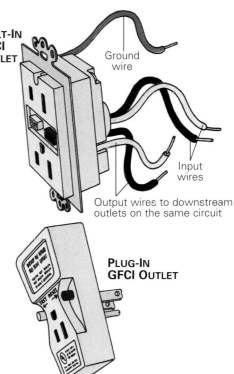

BUILT-IN GFCI OUTLET

Ground wire

Input wires

Output wires to downstream outlets on the same circuit

PLUG-IN GFCI OUTLET

COMPUTER POWER

If you use a home computer, you have probably experienced a momentary power outage and loss of data. In some areas this phenomenon occurs almost daily. The solution is an Uninterruptible Power Supply (UPS), consisting of a DC to AC inverter, running on an internal rechargeable battery. The computer runs on the output of the inverter, totally isolating it from the power line.

When the power goes down, the UPS continues to supply power from its internal battery and beeps to let you know you have 5 to 15 minutes to finish what you were doing and safely shut your computer down. The UPS also provides isolation from voltage spikes and lightning surges. At $100 to $200, you can't afford not to have one.

GENERAL CODE REQUIREMENTS: ELECTRICAL SYSTEMS

Service Disconnect: This must be installed in an accessible location either outside or inside at the point nearest the entrance of the service conductors.

Service Panel: The main disconnect and each branch circuit are to be labeled at their point of origin to indicate their purpose, except when it is obvious. The working space around the service panel must:
- Be at least 30 inches wide, 36 inches deep, and 78 inches high
- Lighted if inside

- Not be in a bathroom or clothes closet
- Not be used for storage

GFCI Protection: required for all circuits:
- Outdoors, if grade accessible
- In a bathroom
- Within 6 feet of kitchen sink
- In a garage
- In an unfinished basement
- Near a pool
- Serving a whirlpool tub

Required Receptacles: See Code-Required Circuits, Page 112.

ENERGY

ENROLLING FOR A COURSE AT BTU

ALSO SEE...
Boilers:
Pages 34–35
Cooling:
Pages 66–69
Heat Pumps:
Pages 180–181
Insulation:
Pages 186–193
Radiant Heat:
Pages 266–267
Wood-burning Stoves:
Pages 454–455

Every day energy plays a vital role in our homes, providing us with heat, air-conditioning, and our many conveniences—everything from refrigerators to video equipment. In recent years an increased awareness of energy costs has helped create new generations of appliances, insulation products, and high-performance windows and doors, and has made energy efficiency an increasingly important part of home ownership.

Not all energy-efficient upgrades are worth the investment, however. That's why payback figures are important. Payback figures, as demonstrated by the Fuel Savings chart on the opposite page, allow you to calculate whether or not an upgrade can save money in the long run. In a cold-winter region such as the upper Midwest, installing a new, efficient gas furnace might save enough in energy costs to justify the investment. In Houston, however, where a furnace runs hardly at all, the savings may never balance the added cost.

Most of us really don't care what type of fuel we burn to heat our homes and hot water. What really matters is the cost per British Thermal Unit (BTU) of useful heat.

To calculate cost comparisons for different fuels, we need three pieces of information for each type of fuel:
■ Energy content of the fuel, in BTU per unit of fuel
■ Cost of the fuel, in dollars per unit
■ Efficiency of the heating appliance expressed as a percentage
We will show you how to use these figures to choose your most economical source of energy.

In remodeling, however, there is often one further factor. In deciding whether to switch fuels or whether to simply purchase a more efficient appliance, we need to be able to figure the return on our investment. It may turn out that the cost of switching is greater than the potential savings.

ENERGY CONTENT OF FUELS

Fuel	Unit	BTU/ Unit
Coal		
Anthracite	ton	30M
Bituminous	ton	26M
Cannel	ton	22M
Lignite	ton	22M
Electricity	kWh	3,412
Gas		
Natural	ccf	103K
Propane	gal	91.6K
Oil		
Kerosene (#1)	gal	134K
Fuel Oil (#2)	gal	139K
Wood		
Ash	cord	25.0M
Birch, White	cord	23.4M
Douglas Fir	cord	21.4M
Hemlock	cord	18.5M
Hickory	cord	30.6M
Maple, Red	cord	24.0M
Maple, Sugar	cord	29.0M
Oak, Red	cord	24.0M
Pine, Pitch	cord	22.8M
Pine, White	cord	15.8M
Poplar	cord	17.4M
Spruce	cord	17.5M

Key:
K = 1,000
M = 1,000,000
ccf = 100 cubic feet
ton = 2,000 pounds
cord = 128 cubic feet, stacked

WHAT IS A BTU?

Technically, the British Thermal Unit (BTU) is the amount of energy required to raise the temperature of one pound (one pint) of water one degree Fahrenheit. In simple terms, it is approximately the amount of heat released when you burn a wooden match.

EFFICIENCIES OF HEATING APPLIANCES

The efficiency of a heating appliance (furnace, boiler, woodstove, etc.) is measured by the amount of useful heat it delivers, not the amount of total heat (some of which vents up the flue).

As with automotive efficiency (measured in miles per gallon), the efficiency of a heater depends on its pattern of use. The instantaneous efficiency of a furnace may be 90 percent, but its average efficiency over the entire heating season may be reduced to 75 percent by standby losses that occur when the thermostat is not calling for heat.

For this reason the U.S. Department of Energy (DOE) requires Annual Fuel Utilization Efficiency (AFUE) ratings for all new gas- and oil-fired furnaces and boilers sold in the U.S. All heating equipment comes with a label showing the AFUE, but you would be wise to compare numbers before you put your money down and the 500-pound unit arrives at your door.

Ask your heating contractor for comparative figures so you can make a wise choice.

Although AFUE varies (mostly with price), here are average figures:
■ Woodstove   70%
■ Gas furnace   75%
■ Gas boiler   80%
■ Oil furnace   80%
■ Oil boiler   85%

HEATING DEGREE DAYS

Heating degree days (HDD) measure how cold an area of the country is. HDD is based on the number of days the average temperature is below 65°F. If the maximum temperature for a 24-hour day was 40 degrees and the minimum was 20, then the average was ½(40+20), or 30 degrees, for that day. Adding up all the degree days gives the degree days in a year. In southern Florida the HDD might total 200. The upper Midwest, on the other hand, is likely to have more than 9,000 HDD.

PAYBACK AND RETURN ON INVESTMENT

Is it worth trading in that old pre-energy-crisis oil boiler for the super-energy-efficient model you just read about in your home-improvement magazine? Before you buy, calculate your payback.

Not all investments in energy-saving heating devices will prove wise and, to some degree, your usage will be a function of your climate. The method below will take usage into account.

Let's put the numbers to the test.

The table *at right* simplifies the calculations. Find the AFUE of your current heater and follow the line across until you find the new AFUE. The number in the column below the new AFUE is your savings.

Example: Your old boiler has an estimated AFUE of 65 percent. The new super-energy-efficient replacement has an AFUE of 90 percent (it says so on the label). Your fuel bill last year was $1,200, and the installed cost of the new boiler would be $3,500. So when will the new boiler pay for itself?

Answer: By increasing the AFUE from 65 to 90 percent, you will save 27.8 percent of your fuel bill, or $333.60 each year. The simple payback would be $3,500/$333.60 = 10.5 years. That sounds like an awfully long time.

But hold on! What are you currently getting for interest on your savings—merely 4 percent? If you invested in the boiler, your return would be $333.60/$3,500 or 9.5 percent at simple interest.

PERCENTAGE FUEL SAVINGS FROM INCREASED AFUE (ANNUAL FUEL UTILIZATION EFFICIENCY)

Present AFUE	New AFUE, % of Savings								
	55	60	65	70	75	80	85	90	95
40	27.3	33.3	38.5	42.9	46.7	50.0	52.9	55.6	57.9
45	18.2	25.0	30.8	35.7	40.0	43.8	47.1	50.0	52.6
50	9.1	16.7	23.1	28.6	33.3	37.5	41.2	44.4	47.4
55	0.0	8.3	15.4	21.4	26.7	31.3	35.3	38.9	42.1
60		0.0	7.7	14.3	20.0	25.0	29.4	33.3	36.8
65			0.0	7.1	13.3	18.8	23.5	27.8	31.6
70				0.0	6.7	12.5	17.6	22.2	26.3
75					0.0	6.3	11.8	16.7	21.1
80						0.0	5.9	11.1	15.8
85							0.0	5.6	10.5
90								0.0	5.3

FUEL COSTS PER BTU

You can calculate the "bottom line"—the average cost per BTU of heat—if you know the energy content of a fuel, the annual fuel utilization efficiency (AFUE) of the heating appliance, and the price of the fuel. Refer to the chart Energy Content of Fuels, *opposite*, and the chart showing the Annual Fuel Utilization Efficiency, *above*, to make sample calculations.

$$\text{Cost/BTU} = \frac{100 \times P}{F \times \text{AFUE}}$$

P = price per fuel unit
F = energy content per fuel unit
AFUE = annual fuel utilization efficiency percentage

Example 1: What is the cost per million BTU of heat from an oil furnace with an AFUE of 75 percent if the average price of fuel oil is $.90 per gallon?

Answer 1: Looking at the table Energy Content of Fuels, we find that F = 139K BTU/gal.

Therefore,

$$\text{Cost/BTU} = \frac{100 \times P}{F \times \text{AFUE}}$$

$$= \frac{100 \times \$.90}{139K \times 75}$$

$$= .00000863$$

Cost/MBTU = $8.63

Example 2: What is the cost per million BTU of useful heat from a wood-burning stove with an AFUE of 65 percent if the average price of red oak is $110 per cord?

Answer 2: Looking at the table Energy Content of Fuels, we find that F = 24M BTU/cord.

Therefore,

$$\text{Cost/BTU} = \frac{100 \times \$110}{24M \times 65}$$

$$= .00000705$$

Cost/MBTU = $7.05

WEIGHING RELATIVE COSTS

Fuels are pretty much fixed-price commodities. The price per unit varies little whether you order 100 or 1,000 gallons of fuel oil, one or 10 cords of wood, 100 or 1,000 kWh of electricity. Propane, or bottled gas, is the notable exception. Delivery of the gas in tanks is a costly, labor-intensive job, and the effort is largely independent of the size of the container. The delivered price per unit of propane gas, therefore, varies greatly with quantity.

So before you compare propane as a fuel, make sure you have the correct price for the quantity you expect to consume. The gas supplier will base his price on the type and number of gas appliances in your home.

FANS

COMFORT AND AIR MOVEMENT

ALSO SEE...
Cooling:
Pages 66–69
Electrical Boxes:
Pages 106–109
Switches:
Pages 352–355
Ventilation:
Pages 386–387

You're feeling comfortable when you are thinking neither of how to get warm or of how to get cool.

On a cold but sunny day, we instinctively move to the sunny side of the street to receive the warmth of the sun's radiation. On a hot but windy day, we seek out cooling breezes. In other words, both radiation and moving air can affect comfort as much as the temperature of the air.

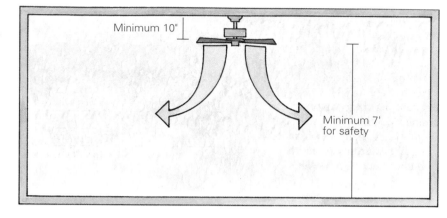

Minimum 10"

Minimum 7' for safety

THE EFFECT OF MOVING AIR

The human comfort zone (our perception of comfort) is determined by the effects of four variables: temperature, humidity, air movement, and radiation. The majority of people, dressed in ordinary indoor clothing and doing sedentary tasks, feel comfortable with the temperature between 72° and 79°F and the relative humidity between 20 and 70 percent.

Air flowing across our bare skin removes heat, producing a sensation of cooling—the wind-chill effect. A 5 mph breeze across bare skin allows the average person to feel comfortable at up to 87°F at 60 percent relative humidity and 93°F at 20 percent relative humidity.

We will show you how to use moving air to make your home more comfortable without the expense and complexity of mechanical air conditioning.

PROPER USE OF WINDOW FANS

Window fans come in a variety of sizes, made to cool anything from a single room to an entire house. Before incurring the cost of installing a whole-house fan in the attic, invest one-tenth as much in the most powerful multispeed window fan you can find and try the following experiment:

1. Identify the areas you wish most to cool. Be very specific. For example, while sleeping you may need to cool only the area of your bed. If so, then specify just the bed area.

2. Identify a window, suitable for fan installation, far from the areas to be cooled. This can be in a room at the opposite end of the house; it can even be on a different floor of the house.

3. Install the fan securely (so it won't rattle) and set it up to blow out, not in.

4. Close every exterior door and window throughout the house. If you have a fireplace, make sure its damper is closed. You are trying to make the house as airtight as possible.

5. Now open just the windows in the areas identified in Step 1.

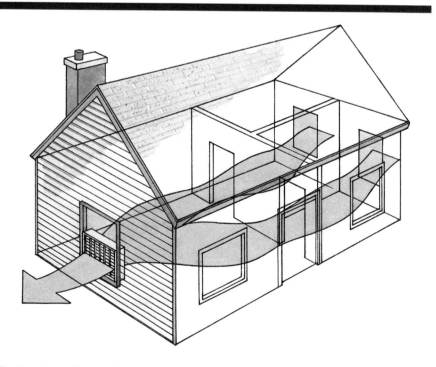

6. Provide a clear path for air flow between the fan and the windows you opened in Step 5. You may have to secure doors in the open position to avoid the "wind" slamming them shut.

7. Turn the fan on high. The fan pulls air out of the house, creating negative pressure. The result is a strong, silent, natural breeze flowing in through the open windows.

CHOOSING A CEILING FAN

Ceiling fans are made in styles, shapes, and colors to match virtually any decor—from traditional to contemporary. There are even models with fan blades fashioned to resemble baseball bats for kids' rooms. Besides looks, consider these factors when choosing a ceiling fan:

■ Number and diameter of blades
■ Length of warranty on motor
■ Whether the ceiling is sloped or flat

BLADES

The number of blades has little to do with the amount of air a fan moves. Blade diameter, however, has a significant effect. The amount of air passing through the circle of the blades is proportional to the square of the diameter (diameter × diameter) of the fan. A 48-inch fan would move roughly four times as much air as a 24-inch fan. The table, *above right,* shows recommended fan size for various floor areas.

MOTOR

Why do some fans cost twice as much as others of the same size? Probably because they have motor bearings which are bathed in oil. Such fans typically carry lifetime motor warranties. Of course, if you plan to operate your fan only on a half-dozen hot summer nights, you won't wear out the less expensive, oil-less fan in your lifetime, so save your money.

SLOPED VS. LEVEL CEILING

If the fan is to be mounted on a sloped ceiling, make sure the fan mount will accommodate the slope. You don't want the blades running into the ceiling. Most fans come with a ball-and-socket mount that allows the fan to hang like a pendulum. The range of slope accommodated, however, is generally quite small—typically only up to 5 in 12, or about 22 degrees.

If your ceiling has a greater slope, buy a fan with a greater range or one for which a high-slope hanger accessory is available. Of course you can also attach a wood or metal wedge to the ceiling to provide a flat mounting surface that will bring the blades down far enough that they won't touch the ceiling.

RECOMMENDED FAN SIZE

Maximum Room Size	Fan Blade Diameter
64 sq. ft.	32 inches
144 sq. ft.	42 inches
225 sq. ft.	44 inches
400 sq. ft.	52 inches
400+ sq. ft.	more than 1 fan

CODE REQUIREMENTS: CEILING FANS

Ventilation: Habitable rooms, including bathrooms, require either an openable window area of at least 5 percent of the floor area, or mechanical ventilation equivalent to 0.35 room air exchanges per hour.

Ceiling Fans: Ceiling fans may not be suspended on ordinary ceiling-fixture boxes unless the box is UL-listed for that purpose.

INSTALLING A CEILING FAN

Most rooms in which you would like to install a ceiling fan have an existing light fixture in the center of the ceiling. The ceiling fan can utilize the existing wiring, saving you the onerous task of running new wiring from a wall switch to the ceiling. However, be aware of two possible limitations:

■ Most codes prohibit hanging a ceiling fan from an existing ceiling box unless that box is UL-listed for the purpose.

■ To separately control the fan and light, you will need two wall switches and two hot conductors. The unit has separate on-off switches for the fan and light so that it can run off a single hot wire, but you will not be able to control the light with a dimmer switch.

Note that different fans may have slightly different configurations, so read the assembly instructions carefully.

1 *Turn off the circuit breaker for the light at the service panel. Remove the light fixture and the old metal box.*

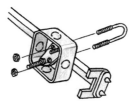

2 *Purchase a brace bar and 1½-inch drop-fixture box (some come already attached). Attach the fan-adapter plate inside the box with bolts. Remove a box knockout and install a connector for the cable.*

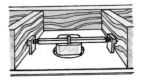

3 *Loosen the U-bar and adjust the position of the box along the bar to fit the existing ceiling hole. Tighten the U-bar. Then position the box in the ceiling hole with its edge flush with the ceiling, and tighten the bar.*

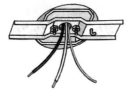

4 *Pull the old circuit wires through the knockout and tighten the clamp. Attach the fan ceiling plate to the projecting bolts of the fan adapter plate with locknuts.*

5 *Hang the fan motor from one of the hooks on the fan ceiling plate and connect the wires as directed in the instructions.*

6 *Unhook the fan motor and attach it permanently to the hanging bracket. Install the ceiling canopy to cover the ceiling hole and attach the fan blades.*

▶

INSTALLING A WHOLE-HOUSE FAN

HOW WHOLE-HOUSE FANS WORK

Whole-house fans are large units that exhaust hot, stale attic air out through attic vents, drawing fresher, cooler air from the interior of the house. This is an exceptionally efficient technique for lowering the overall inside temperature, especially when you consider that during the summer, attic air temperatures can exceed 150°F, and these temperatures radiate into the rooms below. Replacing this very hot air with air in the 85° F range will dramatically improve the comfort level of a house. Operated in the evening to bring in cooler night air, a whole-house fan can reduce air-conditioning costs, saving the air conditioner for the heat of the daytime.

LOCATIONS

Install your whole-house fan where it will have access to the air in the house—either in the ceiling of an upper room or in an attic wall. The ceiling location has the advantage of protecting the fan from the elements, but the attic wall location results in quieter operation. The manufacturer will provide detailed instructions for installation in either area. Be sure to read the instructions carefully, as the process shown for ceiling installation on the page *opposite* is intentionally generic.

Whole-house fans must be vented—through large gable or continuous soffit and ridge vents. You can estimate the air movement capacity of the fan you'll need by multiplying the square footage of your home's living areas by 3. Therefore, a 2,500 square-foot house requires a fan rated at least 7,500 CFM (cubic feet of air per minute). In very warm, humid regions, multiply by 4. Expect to pay $750 to $1,000 for a whole-house fan, plus $500 for installation.

To get the most from a whole-house fan, close all windows except for those on the lowest, shaded side of your house. Basement windows, if you have them, are ideal. Cooler air will be pulled in through these locations, creating air flows that help reduce heat throughout the home. This air movement can lower ambient temperatures by 5 to 10 degrees.

WALL MOUNT IN GABLE

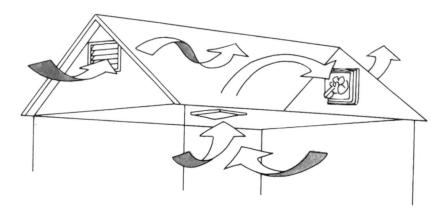

CEILING MOUNT

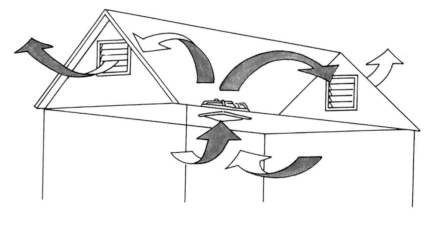

VENT INSTALLATION

If you prefer to do the work yourself, installing a whole-house fan is not a difficult project. You will need to run a separate electrical circuit for the fan because most building codes require individual circuits for fixed motors.

To install a continuous ridge vent, you'll need to make a long slit in your roof at its peak. Measure down about 3 inches on both sides of the roof peak and snap chalk lines the length of the roof. Using a power saw with a carbide-tipped blade made for cutting nails, cut through the roofing and roof sheathing, being careful not to cut the rafters. Remove the roofing and sheathing. Apply a bead of caulk under the ridge vent flanges and nail the vent along the ridge using galvanized roofing nails equipped with neoprene gaskets.

Gable-end vents should have slats pitched about 45 degrees to shed water away from the opening. Hold the vent on the inside of the gable and mark its outline on the wall sheathing. You can cut the outline from inside using a reciprocating saw, but you may prefer cutting from the outside to prevent the waste material from falling and damaging your house's siding. Transfer the marks to the outside of the house by drilling completely through the corners, using a small-diameter bit.

Once the hole has been cut, box in a rough opening with 2×4s. Slip flashing between the siding and the sheathing over the top of the vent unit, then fasten the siding and sheathing to the framework, using galvanized casing nails or screws. Caulk the inside edge of the vent and secure it in place.

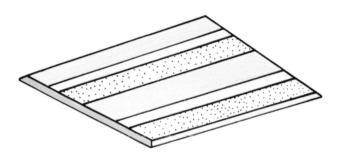

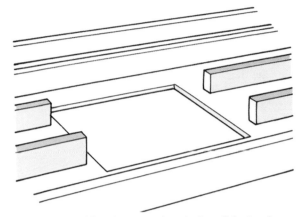

1 Cut an opening in the ceiling the same size as the fan shutter. If the attic is insulated, use plastic sheeting or pieces of plywood to make dams to hold the insulation back. If the insulation is loose fill, you may have to staple down building wrap to keep the insulation from blowing about.

2 Cut sections out of the ceiling joists where the fan will fit. Cut the joists so there will be 1½ inches of clearance around the opening.

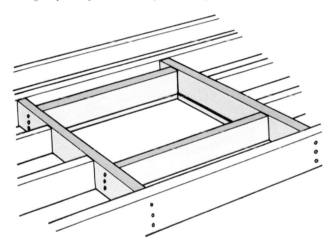

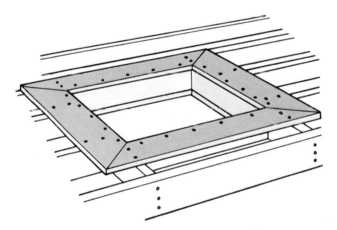

3 Support the cut joists with headers nailed between the full-length joists. Double up any headers that span more than 4 feet. Frame the other two sides of the opening by installing blocking between the headers.

4 Build a platform of 1×6s to fit over the framing. Miter the corners so that the available framing will support the platform.

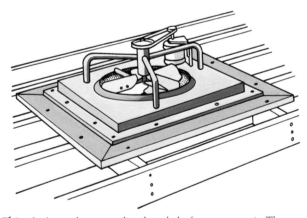

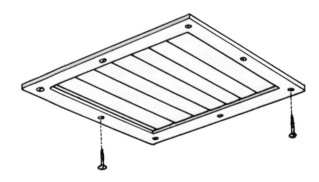

5 Set the fan in place, toenailing through the frame to secure it. Then run wiring for the fan. If you use NM (nonmetallic sheathed) cable, run the cable through holes drilled in the centers of the joists or staple cable beside the joists. If you run cable over the tops of the joists, you must nail 1×4s next to the cable to form a shield from foot traffic.

6 Install the shutter from below, driving wood screws through the ceiling up into the frame.

Fasteners

FINDING THE RIGHT HARDWARE FOR THE JOB

ALSO SEE...
Most entries

Fasteners are an essential part of any project, but they are often last-minute additions to a materials list and may not even appear on it. On this and the next three pages, we list the major types you will find at a hardware store so you can choose the right ones.

This selection is by no means complete, but you can augment it with common sense and attention to these guidelines:

■ Use your tape measure to determine sizes if you aren't familiar with the antique classification systems that some fasteners use.

■ Sort nails by pennyweight and screws by gauge or number.

■ Longer nails have larger numbers—a 16d nail is longer than an 8d nail. For screws, larger numbers mean thicker diameters.

The best fastener is the strongest, most attractive, and easiest to install. In many cases a substitute fastener will do, although it usually lacks one of the above attributes.

If you intend to do many projects, buy more fasteners than you need for one job. You will build up an inventory that could save you many trips to the store. When you buy in bulk you may also save money.

Any nails, bolts, or screws that you use outdoors should be galvanized.

Adhesives make excellent fasteners. Many are stronger and more convenient than the metal fasteners they replace, and some have become indispensable. Use adhesives to attach paneling, wallboard, subflooring, decking, furring strips, molding, countertops, and rigid insulation.

NAILS

HOW NAILS WORK

The holding power of a common nail is a function of friction, shank configuration, and the direction driven relative to the wood fibers.

Withdrawal resistance (the force required to pull a nail straight out) depends on the friction between the nail and the wood fibers surrounding it. When a nail is driven, the body of the nail displaces wood fibers, compressing them to either side. This pressure, multiplied by the coefficient of friction between the nail and the wood, equals withdrawal force. Because the withdrawal force tries to overcome sidewards pressure, splitting the wood reduces holding power to virtually zero. Some nails, such as glue-, spiral-, and ring-shank nails, increase their holding power with configurations that "grab" more wood surface—some at right angles to withdrawal force.

Lateral resistance (force to remove the nail sideways) is more complex, and involves the hardness of the nail as well as the strength of the wood species. If the nail doesn't bend, the resistance is that of the wood to splitting. Once the nail begins to bend, however, the lateral force translates into a withdrawal force.

NAIL CHARACTERISTICS

Nail sizes are designated by length, using the term penny, or "d" (for the origin of the term, see the box, *below*

left). The illustration *opposite* shows the lengths of nails.

The least expensive nails are bright (uncoated steel that rusts easily); better quality ones are coated with zinc to prevent corrosion; the best are hot dipped rather than electroplated. Nails also come in copper, bronze, aluminum, and stainless steel.

BUYING NAILS

Nails are sold by the pound, in small boxed quantities, or in 25- and 50-pound boxes. If planning a large project, buy 6d, 8d, 12d, and 16d nails by the 50-pound box—you will find

WHAT "D" MEANS IN NAILS

Have you ever wondered what the "d" in nail sizes meant? It comes from the Roman coin, the *denarius*. Originally, a 10d nail cost 10 denaria per 100; a 6d nail, 6 denaria per 100; etc.

Of course, with inflation and the shortage of denaria, this definition no longer holds. The "d" now refers to the length of a nail. For example, a 6d nail is 2" long; an 8d nail 2½", a 10d nail 3"; etc. You can calculate the length of a nail up to 10d by dividing its d size by 4, then adding ½ inch. A 4d nail, for example, is 1½ inches long.

NAILS PER POUND

Length, Inches	Penny-weight	Nail Type						
		Box	Casing	Common	Drywall	Finish	Roofing	Siding
1	2d			875		1350	255	
1¼	3d	635		570	375	805	210	
1½	4d	475	475	315	330	585	180	
1¾	5d	405	405	270	290	500	150	
2	6d	235	235	180	250	310	140	235
2¼	7d	210		160		240		240
2½	8d	145	145	105		190	120	210
3	10d	95	95	70		120		95
3¼	12d	85		65				
3½	16d	70	70	50		90		
4	20d	50		30		60		
4½	30d			25				
5	40d			20				
6	60d			15				

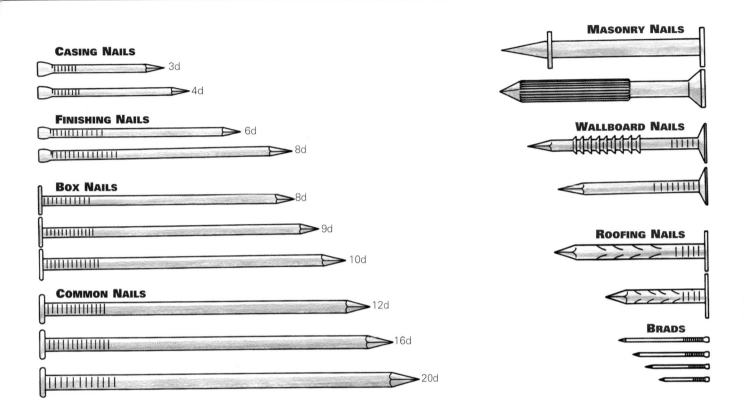

CASING NAILS
- 3d
- 4d

FINISHING NAILS
- 6d
- 8d

BOX NAILS
- 8d
- 9d
- 10d

COMMON NAILS
- 12d
- 16d
- 20d

MASONRY NAILS

WALLBOARD NAILS

ROOFING NAILS

BRADS

many uses for these basic sheathing and framing nails. The table, *opposite*, shows the approximate numbers of nails you can figure per pound.

NAIL TYPES

The nails shown are commonly used for the following purposes:

Casing nails are typically used in situations similar to those calling for a finishing nail, but requiring more strength. For this reason their heads are larger than finishing nails, yet they are ovoid and designed to slip easily into the wood surface. This makes them ideal for exterior trim and siding.

Finishing nails are intended to be countersunk below the surrounding surfaces and the resulting depression filled in with putty or filler. Finishing nails are ideal for interior trim and fine woodworking projects.

Box nails bear resemblance to their hardworking counterparts, common nails, but box nails are thinner, which helps prevent splitting of thin materials. They are often used in projects requiring ¾-inch wood.

Masonry nails are hardened and designed to penetrate concrete, stucco, and brick. Driving a masonry nail requires hard, straight hammer blows and absolute accuracy—one slip and the nail is likely to bend or fracture the masonry.

Wallboard or drywall nails feature slightly cupped heads designed to produce a depression (not a break) in the surrounding wallboard. The depression is then filled with wallboard compound, allowed to dry, and sanded smooth and flush with the wall surface.

Roofing nails are galvanized to resist corrosion. They have exceptionally large heads that grab more surface of soft roofing materials.

Aluminum roofing nails are used to fasten aluminum skylight trim and flashing where a galvanized nail would corrode the aluminum.

Brads are exceptionally thin, delicate nails for use on fine moldings, paneling, and parquet floors. Being small they can be difficult to start, and special "tack hammers" are made that feature magnetic heads to hold a brad during the first hammer stroke.

Common nails are used for framing, sheathing, and general construction. They are tough, and their large heads result in holding power.

Duplex nails are manufactured with two heads, one above the other. This gives the nail full holding power but leaves the second head protruding so it can be easily gripped with a hammer claw or nail puller and removed. Duplex nails often are used to build temporary bracing, scaffolds, and foundation forms.

Ring-shank nails have ridges along their shanks to give them superior holding power. They are commonly used to install plywood subflooring and for floor repairs. Removing ring-shank nails is virtually impossible without damaging surrounding surfaces.

Spiral-shank nails are similar to ring-shank nails, but their ridges travel in spirals around the nail shank.

Corrugated fasteners are rectangular and feature a wavy cross-section. They are used to secure the corners of picture frames.

SCREWS

HOW SCREWS WORK

A screw holds because its threads work their way between wood fibers without destroying their integrity. To pull the screw out (without unscrewing it) you literally have to tear the wood fibers apart. This type of pulling force exerted along the shaft of the screw is called tension. Screws have incredible holding power because of it.

TYPES OF SCREWS

The three basic types of screws are wood screws, sheet-metal screws, and drive screws, but different sizes, gauges, heads, points, and materials result in dozens of variations. You should keep an assortment on hand.

Wood Screws: Among wood-screw varieties, slotted-head are the most common. Phillips-head screws are easier to drive and do not damage as easily. Robertson, or square-drive, screws offer the surest grip for driving and are increasing in popularity.

Sheet-Metal Screws: Some sheet-metal screws have hex heads for driving with a nut driver. Self-tapping screws have a sharply grooved cutting point that enables them to cut their way through sheet metal without requiring a pilot hole.

Drive Screws: Drive screws, also called wallboard screws or bugle-head screws, were developed for use with power screwdrivers and have taken the place of nails for many carpentry and woodworking applications. Drive screws are available for driving into wood or sheet metal, have Phillips or Robertson heads, and come in many different sizes, coatings, and strengths. The screw shank is threaded and tapered all the way to the tip and has a very sharp point for easy starting. The head flares into a bugle shape for countersinking without drilling. Trim screws are small-sized drive screws, small enough to be hidden in the wood when countersunk. Because they have thin shanks, drive screws do not offer the same shear strength as other screws. Shear strength is the ability of a fastener to support weight at right angles to its shank. For example, a screw used to hold up a picture frame by a wire is demonstrating shear strength.

PILOT HOLES

Unlike a nail, the holding power of a screw in wood is due almost entirely to the grip of the screw's threads biting into the wood. If you don't drill a pilot hole into hardwood or at the edges and ends of any species, the screw shank will wedge the wood fibers apart, causing the wood to split. Splitting the wood spreads the fibers away from the threads, and the screw won't hold.

For pilot holes select a drill bit with a diameter slightly smaller ($\frac{1}{64}$ to $\frac{1}{32}$ inch) than the diameter of the solid shank of the screw. This will prevent the screw from splitting the wood. Smaller holes risk splitting; larger ones prevent the threads from holding.

The table *below* shows the recommended sizes for pilot holes in both hard and soft woods.

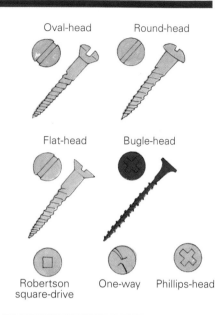

Oval-head   Round-head

Flat-head   Bugle-head

Robertson
square-drive   One-way   Phillips-head

BARGAIN FASTENER

Wallboard screws (also called bugle-head screws), now sold by the pound like nails, are a technological marvel, and a bargain to boot. Made of hardened steel, with a thin, straight shank and deep threads, the wallboard screw was designed to penetrate wallboard and hold it firmly to wall studs. Its bugle-shaped head was designed to countersink easily. Over the years consumers discovered that they could drive a wallboard screw into most softwoods and many hardwoods without a pilot hole and without splitting the wood. A galvanized version of the wallboard screw, the "decking screw," is made with a slightly thicker shank and is intended for fastening decking boards to joists, greatly reducing the time it takes to install decking material.

PILOT-HOLE SPECIFICATIONS FOR WOOD SCREWS

| Hole | Screw Size | | | | | | | | | |
	2	3	4	5	6	8	10	12	14	16
Body diameter, inches	$\frac{5}{64}$	$\frac{3}{32}$	$\frac{7}{64}$	$\frac{1}{8}$	$\frac{9}{64}$	$\frac{5}{32}$	$\frac{3}{16}$	$\frac{7}{32}$	$\frac{15}{64}$	$\frac{17}{64}$
Pilot drill										
softwood	#65	#58	$\frac{1}{16}$	$\frac{5}{64}$	$\frac{5}{64}$	$\frac{3}{32}$	$\frac{7}{64}$	$\frac{1}{8}$	$\frac{11}{64}$	$\frac{3}{16}$
hardwood	#56	#54	$\frac{5}{64}$	$\frac{3}{32}$	$\frac{3}{32}$	$\frac{7}{64}$	$\frac{1}{8}$	$\frac{5}{32}$	$\frac{7}{32}$	$\frac{15}{64}$
Body drill	#42	#37	$\frac{1}{8}$	$\frac{9}{64}$	$\frac{9}{64}$	$\frac{11}{64}$	$\frac{3}{16}$	$\frac{7}{32}$	$\frac{1}{4}$	$\frac{9}{32}$
Countersink diameter, inches	$\frac{5}{32}$	$\frac{3}{16}$	$\frac{7}{32}$	$\frac{1}{4}$	$\frac{9}{32}$	$\frac{11}{32}$	$\frac{3}{8}$	$\frac{7}{16}$	$\frac{15}{32}$	$\frac{11}{16}$

LAG SCREWS

Lag screws are larger than conventional screws and are used to fasten large framing members together. They make incredibly tight, strong connections and are tightened with lots of torque, with a wrench or a ratchet driver. They do not require nuts, but usually require washers to increase holding power and to prevent the heads from crushing or pulling through the surrounding surfaces.

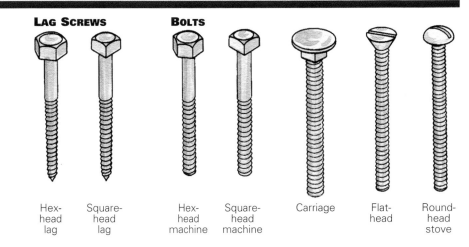

LAG SCREWS

Hex-head lag | Square-head lag

BOLTS

Hex-head machine | Square-head machine | Carriage | Flat-head | Round-head stove

ANCHORS

Anchor is a generic term for a variety of fasteners that attach objects to materials other than wood.

Anchor Bolts: These are used with concrete or masonry. Drill a hole into the surface the same diameter as the anchor and at least ½ inch longer than the distance the anchor will penetrate. Blow the dust from the hole, and drive the anchor with a nut and washer. Tighten the nut to expand the base. The anchor must expand without rotating to develop maximum withdrawal resistance.

Expansion Shields: The most common method of attaching to concrete uses an expansion shield and a lag screw. Drill a hole into the concrete with a hammer drill. Place the shield in the hole, insert the lag screw through the material to be fastened, and then tighten the screw into the shield.

Anchor bolt

Expansion shield

Hollow-Wall Anchors: Drill a hole the same diameter as the anchor. Insert the anchor with the screw and tighten the screw to draw the anchor

Hollow-wall anchor

flanges tight against the rear surface of the wall. Remove the screw, insert it through the material being attached, and reinstall the screw in the anchor.

Toggle Bolts: Also known as butterfly bolts, these use a spring-loaded folding nut that unfolds and grips the backside of the wall after you push it through a hole. Insert the bolt through the piece being fastened before pushing the nut into the hole.

Toggle bolt

Plastic Wall Anchors: Drill a hole and insert the anchor. Install the screw through the piece being attached. Tightening the screw expands and secures the anchor.

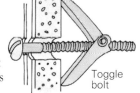

Plastic wall anchor

Screw Anchors: These metal or hard plastic devices have a threaded shell and a hollow central shaft and are intended as receptacles for ordinary screws. Use them with wallboard only. Screw the anchor directly into the wallboard without drilling, then drive the screw.

Drive Anchors: These also are used with wallboard only. Drive the anchor as you would a nail. Its legs will expand and secure it when a screw is driven into it.

BOLTS

HOW BOLTS WORK

Bolts hold things together in two ways. First, the bolt acts as a pin, preventing lateral or side-to-side movement. Second, the bolt squeezes the objects together like a mini-clamp, bringing enormous tension forces to bear on the bolted objects, preventing them from coming apart. A bolted connection develops its maximum strength only when the bolt and nut are tight enough to bring both forces into play.

Nuts and washers are used with the bolt to create pressure. The washer effectively increases the size of the nut, allowing greater force without crushing the wood fibers.

Bolts are sized by diameter, length, and the number of threads per inch. Galvanized bolts prevent the fastener from corroding.

Carriage bolts have a round head for a more attractive appearance and are used for finish applications where the bolt head is visible. At the base of the head, a square collar bites into the wood and prevents the bolt from turning.

Faucets and Valves

PLUMBING 101: THE INTRO COURSE

Also see...
Pipe:
Pages 250–255
Plumbing:
Pages 256–263
Sinks & Garbage Disposers:
Pages 314–315
Washbasins:
Pages 416–417

Installing or repairing a faucet gives you instant verification of the quality of your work—as soon as you turn the water on.

Some faucets (such as outside hose bibbs, laundry faucets, and most tub or shower valves) attach directly to the water pipes. To install or repair them, you have to shut off the main valve—where the water comes into the house. Other faucets have a stop close to the fixture. Turn it off, and you're ready to go to work.

TYPES OF FAUCETS

All faucets fall into two categories, distinguished by how they control the water flow.

Compression Faucets:

A compression faucet has a revolving handle that loosens and tightens a threaded stem. The stem has a washer at its end that fits tightly against a valve seat when the faucet is closed. When the washer wears from age and use, it no longer fits tightly, and the faucet leaks. Compression faucets are used for hose bibbs, washing-machine hookups, and dual-handled sink faucets.

Mixing Faucets:

A mixing faucet has a single lever or knob that adjusts both temperature and flow of the water through the spout. Though several variations are available, all mixing faucets open and close hot- and cold-water ports with a sliding mechanism rather than a stem with a washer that compresses against a seat.

Because the sliding mechanism is simple and not subject to the grinding action found in a compression fixture, a washerless mixing faucet typically lasts much longer without repair. Most homes now use mixing faucets for sinks, bathtubs, showers, and washbasins.

SUPPLY STOPS

The most difficult part of installing a supply stop is deciding which configuration to buy. There are three variables to consider:

1. Direction of Flow: On some stops the inlet and outlet are in a straight line. On angle stops, the inlet and outlet are at a right angle. Angle stops are the most common for sinks and toilets.

2. Inlet: The size of the inlet must match the size of the supply pipe, which is usually ½ inch. Some inlets are threaded to screw onto iron pipe (IP) or a male adapter (copper, sweated to IP). Others have a compression fitting that slides over copper pipe.

3. Outlet: The outlet must match the size of the supply tube to the faucet. Most supply tubes are ⅜ inch. Outlets have either slip-joint or compression fittings, depending on the type of supply tube. They are not interchangeable.

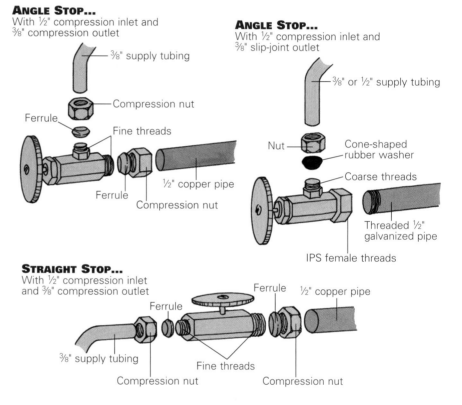

ANGLE STOP...
With ½" compression inlet and ⅜" compression outlet

⅜" supply tubing
Compression nut
Ferrule
Fine threads
Ferrule
½" copper pipe
Compression nut

ANGLE STOP...
With ½" compression inlet and ⅜" slip-joint outlet

⅜" or ½" supply tubing
Nut
Cone-shaped rubber washer
Coarse threads
Threaded ½" galvanized pipe
IPS female threads

STRAIGHT STOP...
With ½" compression inlet and ⅜" compression outlet

Ferrule
Ferrule
½" copper pipe
⅜" supply tubing
Fine threads
Compression nut
Compression nut

INSTALLING A SUPPLY STOP ON COPPER PIPE

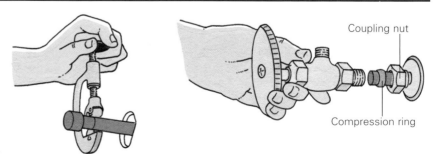

Coupling nut
Compression ring

1 *Turn off the water and cut off the capped end of the copper pipe with a tubing cutter. Polish the exposed end of the pipe with emery cloth.*

2 *Slip on the escutcheon (wall cover plate), coupling nut, and brass compression ring. Then slip the stop over the tubing. Screw the nut onto the stop, using two wrenches to tighten.*

SINK FAUCETS

Sink faucets have bottom inlet fittings that extend down through the rear surface of the sink. Holes in lavatories are usually 4 inches apart; in kitchen sinks they are usually 8 inches apart. Make sure the faucet you select matches the hole spacing of your sink.

REMOVING OLD FAUCETS

Turn off the supply stops. Then, using a basin wrench, disconnect the supply tubes from the faucet and remove the faucet body.

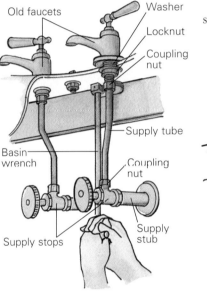

Old faucets
Washer
Locknut
Coupling nut
Supply tube
Basin wrench
Coupling nut
Supply stops
Supply stub

ATTACHING THE NEW FAUCET

If you are also putting in a new sink, it is much easier to install the faucet before placing the sink. In any case, proceed as follows:

Slide the rubber sealing gasket over the fittings and insert them through the holes in the sink. Some faucets come with long supply tubes instead of threaded fittings; guide the tubes through the center hole. To make the seal more watertight, apply a bead of plumber's putty around the bottom edge of the faucet before positioning it.

Secure the faucet to the sink by screwing the locknuts to the fittings

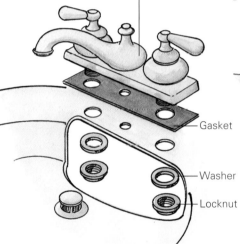

New faucet
Gasket
Washer
Locknut

from below. Some models have separate mounting bolts that are not part of the plumbing fittings.

If the sink is already in place, use a basin wrench—it enables you to reach up into the narrow space behind the sink—to tighten the locknuts and compression nuts.

CONNECTING THE SUPPLY TUBES

Attach the supply tubes to the fittings with coupling nuts. Connect the faucet fittings to the supply tubes from the hot- and cold-water stops, using the compression nuts supplied with the faucet. Bend the tubes gently so that they are in alignment with the fittings. Tighten the nuts until secure.

Stopper lift arm

CODE REQUIREMENTS: FAUCETS

Tub and Shower Control Valves:
All showers must be equipped with one of the following control valves: pressure-balance, thermostatic mixing, or combination pressure-balance/thermostatic mixing. The high limit temperature setting must not exceed 120° F.
Sink Faucets: Sink faucets must be of the water-conserving type, with a maximum flow rate of 2.2 gallons per minute (gpm) at a pressure of 60 pounds per square inch (psi).
Hot Water Heaters: Equipment used for heating or storing hot water must be protected by:
■ A pressure-relief valve and a separate temperature-relief valve, or
■ A combination pressure- and temperature-relief valve.

Water Pressure Tanks: Water pressure tanks must be protected by a pressure-relief valve set no higher than the tank working pressure. Exceptions include:
■ Water systems with an integral pressure-reducing valve
■ Systems with a water heater pressure-relief valve, provided there is no valve between the pressure tank and the water heater and the water heater valve is not set higher than the working pressure of the tank
Service Valve: Every dwelling must have an accessible main shutoff valve near the entrance of the water service, and the valve must have provision for drainage (sometimes called a bleed orifice).

HOSE BIBBS

If you run a new pipe to the bibb, terminate it with a threaded nipple or male adapter. If the bibb has male threads instead, attach a coupling or a female adapter to the pipe. Apply joint compound to the threads and screw on the bibb.

Some localities require hose bibbs to be of the siphon-breaker type. This prevents contaminants from being sucked into the water system from the hose if pressure drops.

Freezeproof hose bibbs are recommended for cold climates.

REPAIRING FAUCETS

You can improve the flow of water from a faucet just by cleaning its aerator. Simply unscrew the aerator, disassemble it (remember the sequence of parts so that you can put them back together correctly), and clean out the holes in the screen with a pin or by blowing through them.

If a faucet leaks around the handle or does not shut off completely, the repair is a bit more involved. For compression faucets, a leak around the handle indicates a loose packing nut or worn packing. A faucet that drips with the faucet completely shut off indicates a worn washer or valve seat. On a combination faucet with two handles and one spout, you can determine which side needs repair by turning off the stops below the sink one at a time.

If you have a washerless faucet, the model of the fixture will determine the repair. Examples are illustrated *below*. Some have replaceable cartridges. Repair others with new seals and gaskets. Disassemble the faucet and take the old parts to the store when you look for replacements.

COMPRESSION FAUCETS

To fix a leaking compression faucet, turn off the water at the stop and remove the faucet handle and packing nut. If the handle is stubborn, pry gently on both sides with two screwdrivers, being careful not to damage the sink. Protect the packing nut with masking tape and unscrew it with pliers or wrench. Back the stem out by turning it counterclockwise all the way. At the bottom of the stem, the old washer is held by a brass screw. Replace the washer with one of the same size. If the screw is missing or damaged, replace it with a brass screw of the same size. Because washers come in so many shapes and sizes, it is advisable to take the valve to the store so you can try the new washer.

Check the valve seat for damage. It must be smooth. You can dress the seat with an inexpensive refacing tool. Or, if an allen wrench fits into the seat opening, remove the seat and replace it.

If the faucet leaks around the handle or if the packing washer looks worn, replace the washer as well. If you can't find a replacement, wind a few coils of packing string around the washer.

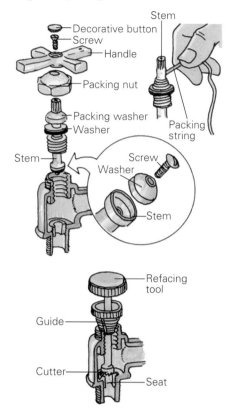

WASHERLESS FAUCETS

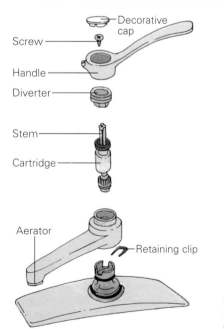

Cartridge Faucet: Cartridge faucets usually leak when the cartridge fittings become worn. To fix leaks, replace the cartridge.

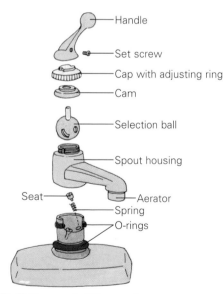

Ball Faucet: Worn gaskets cause most leaks in this type of faucet. The culprit is usually the large O-ring around the base or one of the small grommets inside. Use needle-nose pliers to remove the smaller rings; be sure to keep track of and replace the tiny springs and seats.

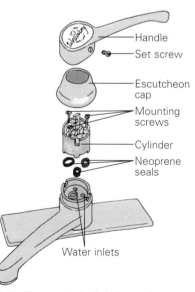

Disk Faucet: A disk faucet has two plastic or ceramic disks, an upper one that rotates with the handle and a lower stationary one that is part of the faucet body. Disk faucets depend on replaceable rubber seals, usually set into the fixed disk, for a positive seal.

VALVES

Valves are required in several places in the home. For example, the main valve allows you to turn off all the water entering your home. A valve in the inlet pipe of a water heater allows you to isolate the water heater from the rest of the plumbing system so you can drain the tank, replace the heater electrodes, thermostat, temperature-pressure relief valve, or the tank itself.

Some valves serve special functions. The bleeder valve on a main shutoff valve has an outlet on the side that allows you to backdrain the system when it is blocked or when the pipes are subject to freezing during your absence in the winter.

A check valve is a one-way valve that prevents water from flowing back through it. In a nonmunicipal household water system, use a check valve between the well and pump to keep water from draining back into the well.

A TPRV (temperature-pressure relief valve) is required on all water heaters to release excessive pressure.

A PRV (pressure relief valve) is required on solar collectors and is located at the topmost point of the system. Pressure tanks in well-water systems also require PRVs.

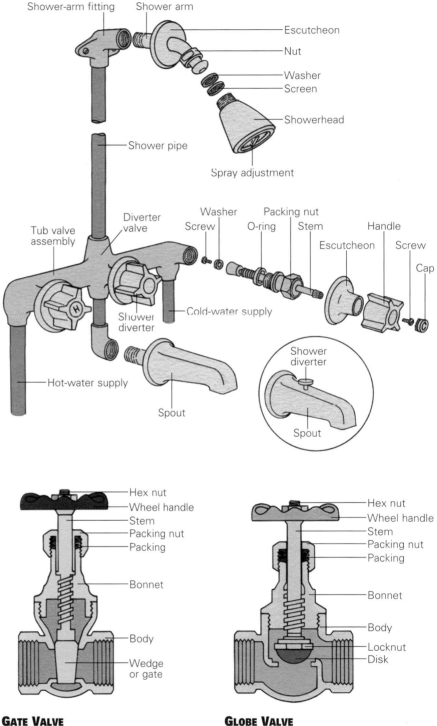

TUB AND SHOWER VALVES

Tub and shower faucets (called *valves* by plumbers because pipe attaches to both inlet and outlet) are installed at the same time as the rough plumbing. They come in several styles. Your selection will depend on whether you want to control the spout and shower functions with one, two, or three handles. The plumbing for all three arrangements is basically the same. Connect the inlets to the hot and cold supply pipes and outlets to the tub spout, shower, or both.

When you buy a tub and shower valve, specify whether the fittings should be IP (for threaded iron pipe) or CU (for copper tubing). Run pipes for the shower and spout as part of the rough plumbing. Then attach short nipples to the elbows. When the walls are finished, replace the nipples with the spout and showerhead.

GATE VALVE

Turning the handle of this valve causes a gate in the supply pipe to open or close. The gate valve does not have a baffle that distinguishes the inlet from the outlet. Because the water travels straight through, use gate valves where pressure is low, as a main valve, or to connect a water heater.

GLOBE VALVE

A globe valve works like a compression faucet, with a hard washer that seats into an opening inside the valve. It regulates the rate of flow by varying the effective size of the opening, and closes more tightly than a gate valve. The inlet and outlet sides are different, so an arrow on the outside of the valve indicates the direction of flow.

129

FENCES AND GATES

WHY BUILD A FENCE?

ALSO SEE...
Concrete:
Pages 60–63
Footings:
Pages 142–143
Hardware:
Pages 174–175
Wood:
Pages 446–453

There are plenty of reasons for erecting fences: defining space or marking boundaries, security from prowlers, establishing privacy, screening out undesirable views, protection from the wind, and creating outdoor limits for small children and animals. Before you fence something, clarify its purpose—sometimes a seemingly obvious solution is not the best. For example, a low, open fence may make the home more secure than a tall fence because neighbors can spot intruders.

Protection from the wind provides another example. A high, solid fence will not, in fact, screen the wind from a patio 20 feet away, because the wind just swirls over the top and continues on to the patio unabated.

Screening out objectionable views is a good reason for a fence, but you may find that you don't need a high fence to do so. A fence with staggered heights may work better because it blocks out some views while preserving others that are desirable.

Fencing also can provide shade, reflect light into dark rooms, and block noise. Each of these needs affects the shape, color, and size of a fence.

MAINTAINING A FENCE

Don't base your fence design on cost alone. Nothing can make a property look more run-down than a rotting, sagging fence. Think of your fence as a long-term investment, not just as a weekend project. When you eventually need to replace that cheap fence, you may not have the time or your current enthusiasm for home-improvement projects.

CONSIDERING THE NEIGHBORS

Your new fence will affect your neighbors, just as their fences affect you. A dispute always has two sides, and so does a fence. Even though you may pay for and erect it entirely on your own, your fence becomes your neighbor's fence too.

So before you start to build, talk with your neighbors. See if you can make it a joint effort. Letting them share in the design—or even the decision whether to erect a fence at all—may lead to splitting costs, as well as labor and future maintenance.

CHECKING HEIGHT REQUIREMENTS

For boundary fences, the first thing you must do is to verify your property lines. The local building codes may say little about fence construction, but your plans may be affected by zoning ordinances or the restrictive covenants of your neighborhood.

If there are any restrictions, they usually involve height. Normally, fences on the front property line are limited to 42 inches high; side and back fences, up to 6 feet. A higher fence may be allowed under certain conditions. To be sure, check with your local building department about any restrictions that apply to new fences.

AESTHETICS

A successful fence will harmonize with its surroundings. It should be level if the ground is fairly level, and it should either step down or follow the contour of any slopes. Its size should be in proportion to the site, neither dominating nor being dwarfed by its setting. Its materials should be in keeping with your home, whether rustic or formal, lively or subdued.

DEALING WITH SLOPES

There are two ways to deal with sloping terrain:
- Build the fence parallel with the ground, framing each bay so it follows the slope. All posts and infill materials are the same length. This approach suits almost any terrain, whether it is steep, gentle, or irregular. Post-and-rail, narrow boards, pickets, stakes, or slats work best.
- Step the fence. This method looks

best on gentle, even slopes. Posts are all the same length, but each bay is built with level top and bottom rails rather than with rails parallel to the slope. Any kind of fencing material works, including infill materials that are set between the framing rather than nailed to it.

Both styles are attractive. The sloped design looks more natural and flowing; the stepped design, more

architectural and crisp. A good way to judge which style will work best is to draw the slope to scale on paper and sketch each type of fence on it. To measure slope, purchase an inexpensive line level and hang it at the center of a taut nylon string. From the highest point, stretch the string to other points. When the bubble shows level, you can measure the height difference.

PARALLEL WITH GROUND

STEPPED

A Low Picket Fence

This is a classic American design and fits nearly any setting, whether formal or informal. Set the posts 6 to 8 feet apart. Cut them about 6 inches shorter than the fence height. Nail the top rail on top of the posts and the bottom rail flat between the posts, and about 6 inches above the ground. Buy precut pickets or cut your own. Cut simple pointed stakes with a circular saw, fancy shapes with a jigsaw. Use the first picket as a template for the others.

Stacked Rails

The rails can be 4×4s, 2×6s, or any other large-scale timbers. Stack them on top of each other, either spiked together or threaded onto rebar driven into the ground. The advantage is simplicity; the disadvantage, cost.

For more stability, pour a concrete foundation, set rebar into the concrete, and attach the rails by threading them over the rebar. The length of the rails can vary from 6 to 12 feet, depending on thickness.

Post-and-Rail

Build this traditional fence from split or dimensional lumber. One style has double posts with the rails wired between them, as shown. Others use mortise-and-tenon joints, which saves on lumber and allows the fence to move with changes in ground temperature without breaking apart.

Stack rails between the posts, setting the bottom rails on stones or nailing them level with the posts. When all rails are in place, wire the tops of the posts together with galvanized wire.

Vertical Boards

Vertical boards offer surprising design flexibility. They can be butted together, spaced like slats, slanted as louvers, or staggered on both sides of the framing. Any size lumber can be used, though larger sizes are stronger, more economical, and easier to install.

Set 4×4 posts 8 feet apart with a top rail on top of them and a bottom rail installed between them. Nail the fencing to one side of the framing or the other.

Board-and-Batten

Vertical boards with battens over the joints create a solid screen that is also a sound barrier. When the battens are the same size as the boards, the design is called board-on-board.

Rough-sawn boards are less expensive and hide defects better. Build the framework as you would for a vertical board fence and mount the boards with gaps between them. Cover the gaps with battens, overlapping the boards on each side by at least ¾ inch.

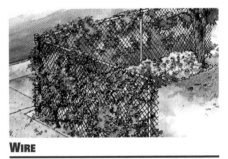

Wire

A chain link fence is strong and provides great security, but looks industrial and is better camouflaged with vines or other plantings.

Another type of wire fence is welded wire (also called sheep fencing), with rectangular openings in various sizes, such as 1×2, 2×4, or larger.

Both chain link and welded wire are available with vinyl coatings, the most popular being green. The green color renders it nearly invisible against a grass or shrubbery background.

Grapestake

Make grapestake fence from split redwood or cedar. Extend the grapestakes above the framing for a ragged effect or top them off with a cap rail for a more finished appearance.

Use 4×4 posts on 6-foot centers. Cut posts 3 to 4 inches shorter than the fence, and cap them with a 2×4 rail. For a bottom rail, nail 2×4s between the posts, 6 to 18 inches above the ground. The top and bottom rails should be level, unless the fence follows a sloping contour.

▶

FENCE STYLES *continued*

LATTICE

Prefabricated lattice is available in 4×8 foot sheets. Set posts in the ground, allowing 8 feet between them. Nail rails flat between the posts, on top and bottom. Then nail a 1×2 frame around the inside of each bay. Attach the lattice to the frame and cover the edges with another frame. Lattice is available in wood and white PVC that eliminates painting for life.

Install a kickboard beneath the bottom rail.

WOVEN BOARDS

Also called basket weave, the woven fence admits some breeze, but affords privacy. To build this type of fence, set posts 8 feet on center and weave 6- or 8-inch benderboards horizontally around the posts. Sandwich the ends between 1×1s and a center 1×2 nailed to the posts. Place vertical 1×3s at regular intervals and interweave the benderboards around them. Nail the benderboards at the ends and to the spacers. A 2×4 cap rail and vertical benderboard nailed onto the posts give the fence a finished look.

CLAPBOARD

Clapboard fences (one of the least expensive) look like finished siding and are most attractive when installed near houses with the same siding.

Set posts at 8-foot intervals. Attach 2×4 top and bottom rails, with intermediate vertical studs placed every 2 feet between them. Cover the framing with the clapboard siding, starting from the bottom and working up. Finish off the fence with a 2×8 cap to give it a trim appearance and to reduce moisture infiltration. Paint to match the house.

LAYING OUT POSTS

Lay out the fence with string lines and batter boards. The lines should represent the outsides of the posts, rather than their centers, so they can remain in place while posts are set. Locate posts 8 to 10 feet apart.

Dig the holes with an auger or clamshell digger—shovels make the holes too large. Check your local building codes for the depth of the holes. Most codes specify they must be dug below the frost line, or at least 24 inches for 6-foot-high fences and 18 inches for 4-foot fences.

Use pressure-treated lumber rated for direct ground contact. Usually, 4×4s are large enough, but unsupported corners and posts for heavy gates should be 6×6s, set 3 feet deep.

Fill the bottom of each hole with 4 inches of gravel. Set the corner posts first, aligning them to the string line and bracing them diagonally in both directions after plumbing them on two adjacent sides with a 4-foot level. Stretch an upper string line between the tops of the corner posts.

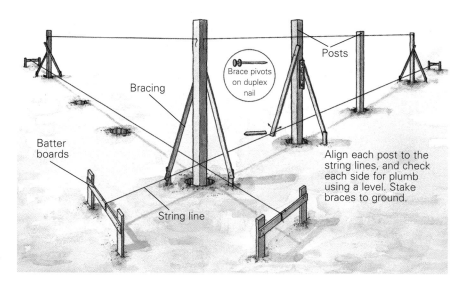

Brace pivots on duplex nail

Posts

Bracing

Batter boards

String line

Align each post to the string lines, and check each side for plumb using a level. Stake braces to ground.

Align the intermediate posts with the top and bottom string lines, bracing each in two directions. Fill the holes with concrete, mounding them at the top for water runoff.

In deep-frost areas, nail galvanized 16d nails around the bottoms of the posts and pour a foot-thick concrete "necklace." Add a layer of gravel and fill the top 6 inches with concrete. Then slide a tapered shingle between each side of the post and the concrete to create an expansion gap. After the concrete sets, remove the shingles and fill the gaps with asphalt roofing cement.

INSTALLING RAILS

Once the posts are set, wait at least 24 hours for the concrete to cure. Then, mark the posts and cut off the tops. Their height depends on the design. You can cut them so that the:
■ Top rails are flush with the tops of the boards
■ Posts are 6 to 12 inches shorter than the finished height of the fence, and the boards extend above the top rails
■ Tops are higher than the boards and beveled or capped with a 2×8 rail

Attach the top rails first, usually directly on top of the posts and face-nailed with two 16d nails at each post. Use 2×4s long enough to span at least two bays, and center all of the butt joints on the posts.

Cut the bottom rails to fit between the posts. There are several ways to attach them. The strongest and most convenient is with galvanized steel fence clips which are nailed to the posts—either angle brackets hidden

below the rails, or pockets the rails slip into. You can also toenail the ends of the rails into the posts, using 8d nails and predrilling the holes to prevent splitting. For a more elegant look use dado or mortise-and-tenon joints. Make sure both posts and rails are pressure-treated, however, because their joints can trap moisture and lead to decay.

GATES AND LATCHES

HARDWARE

Latches come in many styles. Dead bolts are the most secure, requiring a key to open from the outside. A thumb latch is good for entry gates because it has an inviting handle that can be operated with one hand. Another type

of latch has the same closing mechanism, but opens from the outside with a small wire or string instead of a prominent handle. The horizontal slide bolt is also simple and secure.

Gate hinge styles are as varied as gate latches. Gates less than 4 feet tall

can hang on two hinges, but taller gates should have three. Butt hinges work for light gates and can be mounted so that only the hinge knuckles show. Heavy gates need longer hinges, such as tees or straps.

GATE CONSTRUCTION

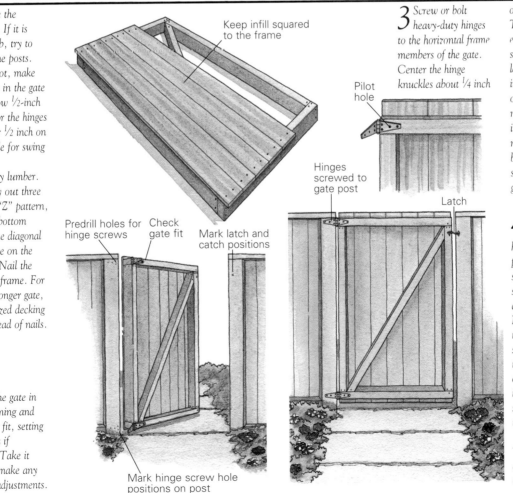

1 Measure the opening. If it is out of plumb, try to straighten the posts. If you cannot, make adjustments in the gate design. Allow ½-inch clearance for the hinges and another ½ inch on the latch side for swing clearance.

Select dry lumber. Cut and lay out three 2×4s in a "Z" pattern, so that the bottom corner of the diagonal brace will be on the hinge side. Nail the infill to the frame. For an even stronger gate, use galvanized decking screws instead of nails.

2 Place the gate in the opening and check it for fit, setting it on blocks if necessary. Take it down and make any necessary adjustments.

Keep infill squared to the frame

Predrill holes for hinge screws   Check gate fit   Mark latch and catch positions

Mark hinge screw hole positions on post

3 Screw or bolt heavy-duty hinges to the horizontal frame members of the gate. Center the hinge knuckles about ¼ inch

Pilot hole

Hinges screwed to gate post

Latch

outside the gate. To conceal the hinges entirely, use the butt style and screw the leaves into the ends instead of the faces of the horizontal members. This method is not as strong as face-mounting, however, because you are screwing into the end grain of the wood.

4 Set the gate in the opening so the hinges are against the post. Use shims to steady the gate, making sure it has equal clearance all around. Mount the hinges to the post with heavy screws or lag bolts, testing it for swing after one or two screws are in each hinge. When it swings properly, install the rest of the screws.

Install the latch. To save wear and tear on the latch, nail a wood stop to the post.

FIREPLACES

CONVENTIONAL DESIGN

ALSO SEE...
Chimneys & Stovepipes:
Pages 54–55
Concrete:
Pages 60–63
Mantels:
Pages 222–223

Not too long ago, when homes were heated exclusively by fireplaces, the rooms clustered around a massive center chimney, rising from the cellar all the way through the roof. With its central location, this massive masonry structure radiated stored heat back into the living spaces, rather than to outdoors.

With the advent of central heating, fireplace efficiency became secondary to the efficient use of space, and the fireplace found itself relegated to the outside wall. The result is a terribly inefficient fireplace that, depending on the location of the furnace thermostat, operates at a net heat loss and chokes up with condensed creosote.

How can a fireplace operate at a net loss? While the fireplace is operating, the flue damper is wide open to allow the smoke to escape up the chimney. Cold air flows in around doors and windows and through cracks and joints to replace the air flowing up the chimney. The furnace thermostat senses only the cold air, so works to heat that air. The furnace actually runs

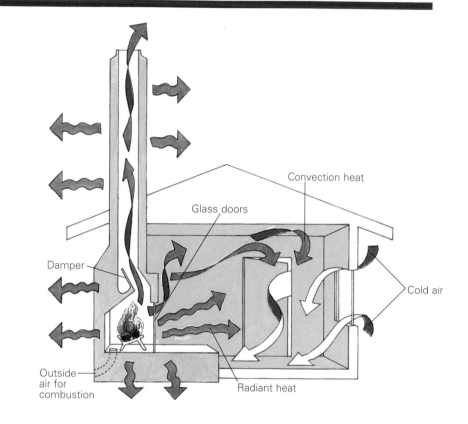

Convection heat

Glass doors

Damper

Cold air

Outside air for combustion

Radiant heat

more than it would, were there no fireplace at all! And of course, if the damper is accidentally left open after the fire is out, warm air continues to escape up the chimney until someone

remembers to close it. Fortunately, fireplace design has made significant strides toward higher efficiency, while still maintaining the elegance and ambience only a fireplace can offer.

EFFICIENT FIREPLACE DESIGN AND OPERATION

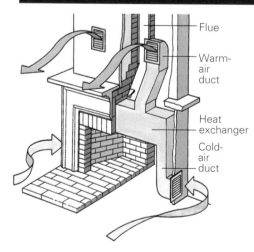

Flue

Warm-air duct

Heat exchanger

Cold-air duct

If you were purposely building the most efficient fireplace you could, here is what you should include:

RUMFORD DESIGN

Count Rumford—actually Benjamin Thompson, an American born in 1753—spent his life researching heat. One of his most notable accomplishments was increasing the efficiency of what was then the main source of heat in buildings, the fireplace. His design, now known as the Rumford fireplace, incorporated the following changes:
■ Reduced the firebox to a size that would just accommodate the logs

■ Made the firebox shallower, forcing the fire further out into the room to radiate heat more efficiently
■ Angled the firebox sides to allow more heat to radiate into the room
■ Streamlined the chimney throat, which reduced the required size of the opening and subsequent heat loss up the chimney

FIREPLACE DAMPER

By incorporating a damper (hinged metal plate) in the throat of the chimney, air flow up the chimney (and resulting heat loss) can be regulated. After the fire is out, closing the damper completely prevents further heat loss.

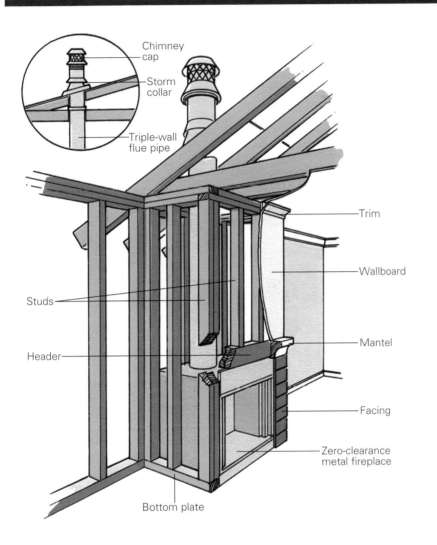

Chimney cap

Storm collar

Triple-wall flue pipe

Trim

Wallboard

Studs

Header

Mantel

Facing

Zero-clearance metal fireplace

Bottom plate

A zero-clearance fireplace can be installed on an interior wall with the chimney running straight up through the attic, or on an exterior wall with the chimney running up the outside of the house and boxed in with siding materials to match the house. Manufacturers provide complete installation instructions.

Begin by setting the unit directly on the subfloor in front of the wall. Cut a hole in the wall or ceiling for the chimney pipe to pass through, insert a metal collar in the hole, and run the pipe from the fireplace outlet through the collar. Build a frame of 2×4s around the fireplace, cover it with wallboard, and finish it. For exterior-wall installations, build a frame of 2×4s to box in the chimney. Add sections to the pipe where it comes through the wall until the chimney reaches the required height. Strap the sections to the frame. Cover the frame with siding, cap it with a flashing collar, and install a spark arrester. If you are running the chimney pipe straight up through the roof, build a box on top of the roof as you would for an exterior wall. Cover all roof connections with metal flashing.

GLASS DOORS

Glass doors across the fireplace opening allow you to shut off air flow when you want to go to bed, so you don't have to wait until the fire is out. You should normally operate the fireplace with the doors open, however, since the glass blocks much of the radiant heat from the fire.

OUTSIDE AIR DUCT

Another improvement, even more effective when combined with glass doors, is to duct air into the fireplace from outdoors. With an outdoor air source feeding the fire, the chimney draws less air from the other rooms, which, in turn, reduces the heating demand on the furnace.

WARM-AIR DUCTS

If you are building a new fireplace, consider installing ducts around it so that cool air is drawn in, heated in the firebox, and expelled back into the room. These warm-air ducts are completely self-contained; the warm air never mixes with the chimney smoke. If you want to have the warmed air blown out at floor level, install a fan in the duct system.

HEAT EXCHANGERS

If you have an existing fireplace and are not able to build a duct system around it, install a heat exchanger in the firebox. A heat exchanger consists of ducts or tubes shaped to fit around the fire. Cool air from the floor is

sucked into the bottom of the unit, heated by the fire, and expelled back into the room. The system works best if the intake air is from an outside source rather than from the room. It takes some fiddling and fine-tuning to position the exchanger so that the vents or tubes release the maximum amount of hot air without accumulating soot. The best heat-exchanger units come equipped with glass doors.

FLASHING

A DRY SUBJECT, IF ALL GOES WELL

Flashing is any sheet material used on the outside of a house to prevent rain from penetrating joints. It works with roofing and siding materials, covering joints such as the holes around vent pipes, the intersection of roofs with vertical walls, horizontal gaps between plywood siding panels, and joints around skylights and chimneys.

High-quality flashing is more permanent than caulk and should outlast roofing and siding materials (which you have to replace every 10 to 25 years). The best flashing materials are copper, lead, stainless steel, and terne metal, but aluminum and galvanized steel hold up well, provided they are installed properly, and they are much less expensive. Preformed shapes, such as roof vents, step flashing, and angled lengths, will satisfy most of your flashing needs. If a ready-made shape is not available, fabricate your own from roll or sheet material.

ROOF RAKES AND EAVES

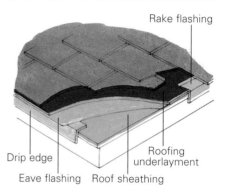

Rake flashing
Drip edge
Eave flashing
Roofing underlayment
Roof sheathing

A variety of flashing is used on eaves. A metal drip edge prevents rainwater from soaking back up under the roofing material. In cold climates, wider eave flashing protects against moisture damage from ice dams. Rake flashing is a similar material that runs along the edges of a gable to prevent rain and snow from being blown under the roofing paper underlayment.

Where the roof sheathing is plywood or composition board, flashing protects the vulnerable edges of the sheathing from weathering.

Nail drip edges to the roof decking beneath the underlayment. Nail rake flashing on top of the underlayment.

DOORS AND WINDOWS

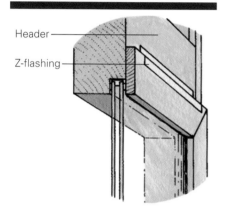

Header
Z-flashing

Water can penetrate the joints between doors and windows and siding, causing invisible damage behind the siding. Most prehung windows include an integral flashing system (the nailing flange) that prevents this problem. However, windows and doors installed before these systems were available—and many custom installations today—must have external flashing to cover the joint above the trim. Cut a length of Z-flashing, tuck the top edge under the siding, and lap the bottom over the window trim, nailing it in place.

PLYWOOD SIDING

Panel
¼" gap
Z-flashing

The horizontal joints between plywood panels are vulnerable to moisture because they interrupt the natural downward course of the water. Water tends to soak into the joint and wick upward behind it. To prevent the incursion of water, install Z-flashing along horizontal joints in the manner shown *above*. Flashing is available in different bent sizes to match the thicknesses (⅜, ½, or ⅝ inch) of the plywood. Always leave a ¼-inch gap between the bottom of an upper panel and the flashing.

MAKING FLASHINGS ON THE JOB

If you are planing a project that requires large amounts of flashing, consider buying it by the roll at a lumberyard or home-improvement center and making flashings yourself.

Galvanized steel has great strength and longevity, but it is extremely stiff and tough and requires that you rent a metal-bending "brake" to bend it properly. Aluminum flashing is a good compromise of strength and workability, and can be cut with ordinary tin snips. To bend it crisply, you can fashion a simple brake. You'll need a long, straight, stable edge—the edge of a table, workbench, or deck will do. Mark the material where you'd like to bend it and place the mark along the edge of your work surface. Clamp a long, straight piece of wood on top of the flashing at the mark. A newly sawn edge works much better than a 2×4, which has a factory-rolled edge. Lightly score along the mark with a utility knife. Bend the flashing, using a rubber mallet. Bend only a portion at a time, working along the length of the flashing.

STEP FLASHING

Where a sloping roof intersects a vertical wall—for example, at the sides of skylight curbs and chimneys—the only flashing that works is step flashing. Never use a continuous piece of angle flashing along such joints; if water gets underneath the shingles, it will never get back out again. With step flashing, any water that gets into the joint and finds its way under a shingle will exit on the surface of the next shingle down.

Step flashing is available in several different sizes, but the most common is made in 10-inch squares bent in half at a right angle. You can even fabricate your own. As you start each new course of shingles, install a piece of step flashing over the shingle below and cover it with the first shingle of the next course. On the wall, each succeeding piece of flashing laps the previous one. Install or replace the siding when the roof is finished.

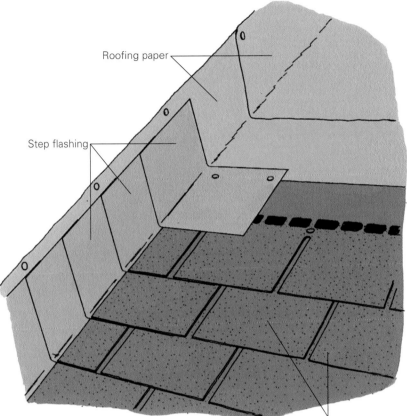

Roofing paper

Step flashing

Shingles

ROOF/WALL INTERSECTION

For installations in which a roof intersects a wall at a horizontal (not sloped) joint, use a continuous piece of metal, at least 10 inches wide and bent at an angle that corresponds to the roof slope. The top edge should tuck up under the siding and the bottom edge should lap over the roofing. You may have to tack the bottom flap down with a few roofing nails so that it lies flat.

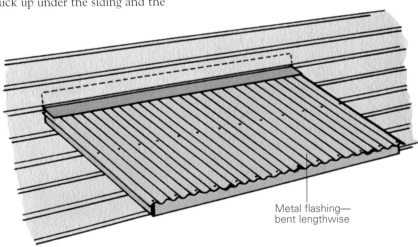

Metal flashing—
bent lengthwise

DON'T MIX METALS!

Do not mix metals when you are flashing. Some metals will corrode when touching each other. This is called galvanic action. Water, a natural electrolyte, speeds up galvanic action.

For example, galvanized roofing nails will chemically react with aluminum flashing, literally eating a hole through the flashing. If you are installing aluminum flashing, use only all-aluminum nails; if you are using galvanized steel flashing, use galvanized nails.

When nailing, keep the nails as far from the flashing crease as possible. Plan nail heads so they will be covered by subsequent layers of roofing material. In situations where flashing nails will be exposed to the elements, cover the heads with a dab of roofing cement. As an alternative, purchase roofing nails that include neoprene collars—rubber gaskets that seal the nail head tight to the flashing.

▶

VALLEYS

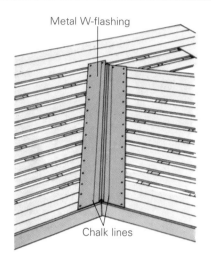

Metal W-flashing

Chalk lines

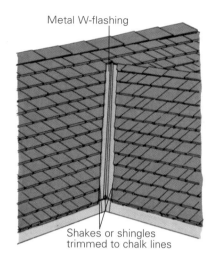

Metal W-flashing

Shakes or shingles trimmed to chalk lines

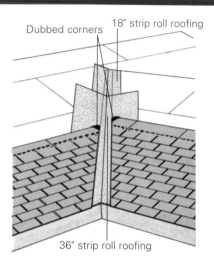

Dubbed corners

18" strip roll roofing

36" strip roll roofing

You must install flashing along the entire length of a valley before roofing over it. Most codes require a double layer of roll roofing or a continuous length of metal flashing.

Metal W-flashing is recommended for wood-shingle roofs. The preformed rib down the center of W-flashing prevents water on one side of the roof valley from crossing over and running under the shingles on the other side. For wood shingles and composition shingles that are not woven across the valley, snap chalk lines on the flashing so that the distance between the shingles widens 1/8 inch per foot, from top to bottom, to accommodate the increasing volume of water downslope.

VENT PIPES

Use vent flashing wherever a plumbing vent or other cylindrical object penetrates a roof. Install the flashing as if it were a shingle, with the top tucked under the shingles above it and the bottom lapped over the shingles below.

The three styles illustrated work well for both composition or wood-shingle roofs. For roll roofing, embed the flashing in roofing cement and nail it all around.

Use special lead flashing on tile roofs. Buy flashing collars that match the diameter of the pipe. If the bright metal is objectionable, paint it before installation.

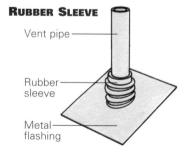

RUBBER SLEEVE

Vent pipe

Rubber sleeve

Metal flashing

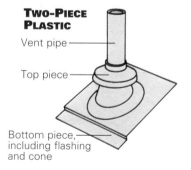

TWO-PIECE PLASTIC

Vent pipe

Top piece

Bottom piece, including flashing and cone

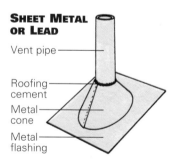

SHEET METAL OR LEAD

Vent pipe

Roofing cement

Metal cone

Metal flashing

SKYLIGHTS

If you're installing a new skylight, purchase the appropriate flashing kit and install it according to the manufacturer's directions. If you are reflashing an existing skylight, use step flashing on the sides and for the top and bottom have special collars custom-made at a sheet-metal shop. Give the supplier both the height and the outside dimensions of the skylight

curb. Don't worry about the angles—they're all 90 degrees.

After the curb is in place, install roofing up to the bottom edge and cover the roofing with the bottom collar. Continue roofing up both sides of the skylight, using step flashing against the curb. Before installing shingles across the top of the skylight, nail the top collar in place.

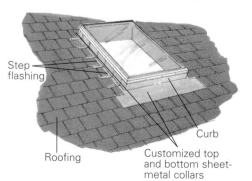

Step flashing

Curb

Roofing

Customized top and bottom sheet-metal collars

CHIMNEYS

Leaks around a chimney can be a major source of damage to the roof structure, and they're often undetected until expensive repairs must be made. Prevent them with proper flashing, but take into account the likelihood that snow and water will build up behind the chimney, as well as the fact that the chimney and house usually settle at slightly different rates, creating a moving joint.

APPLYING BASE FLASHING

Using sheet aluminum, fashion a base flashing large enough to lap around the sides by about 10 inches. Coat the bottom of the chimney bricks and the roof shingles just below them with asphalt roofing cement. Put the base flashing in place, pressing it into the sealant. Drive nails into the mortar to hold it in place. Install step flashing up both sides, embedding each piece into sealant.

BUILDING A CRICKET

In heavy-snow areas, or if the chimney is wider than 2 feet, build a cricket on the upslope side. Cut two pieces of ½-inch CDX plywood and nail them to the roof. Cover them with a large sheet of aluminum flashing bent to the shape of the cricket and extending about 6 inches up the chimney. Cut slits at each end of the main crease so that the flashing lies flat. Cover these slits with smaller pieces of flashing. Drive all nails into the chimney mortar or into the top side of the the flashing. Do not nail into the cricket.

APPLYING CAP FLASHING

Install cap flashing over all step and base flashings. Starting at the bottom, install the first piece in a mortar joint 2 bricks above the top of the base flashing. (Chisel mortar out from between the bricks to a depth of 1½ inches.) Cut and bend a piece of flashing so it will extend down to within 1 inch of the roof. Fit it into the cut mortar and pack in fresh mortar. Repeat the process on both sides of the chimney, overlapping the previous piece by 3 inches and wrapping the last pieces around the corner.

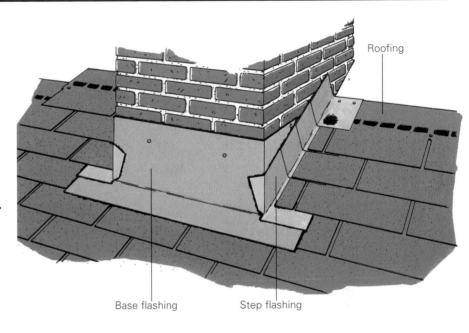

Roofing

Base flashing

Step flashing

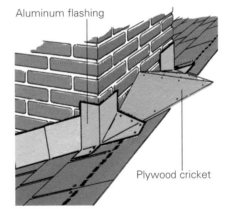

Aluminum flashing

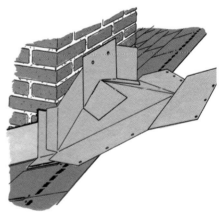

Plywood cricket

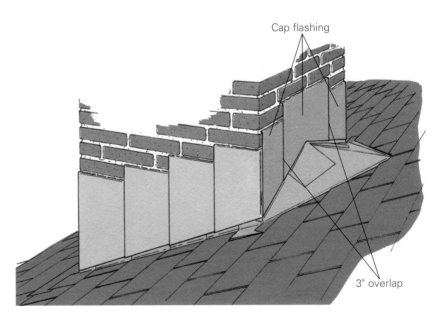

Cap flashing

3" overlap

FLOORS

ANATOMY OF A FLOOR

Floor systems are usually a series of layers. The part of the floor we are most familiar with is the finish floor, which is usually just a membrane over the real floor—the structural floor that holds everything up and keeps out moisture and drafts.

Not all floors have all the layers, but it is important to understand how they relate to each other. This knowledge is necessary whether you are repairing a damaged floor, installing new floor coverings, or building a new floor.

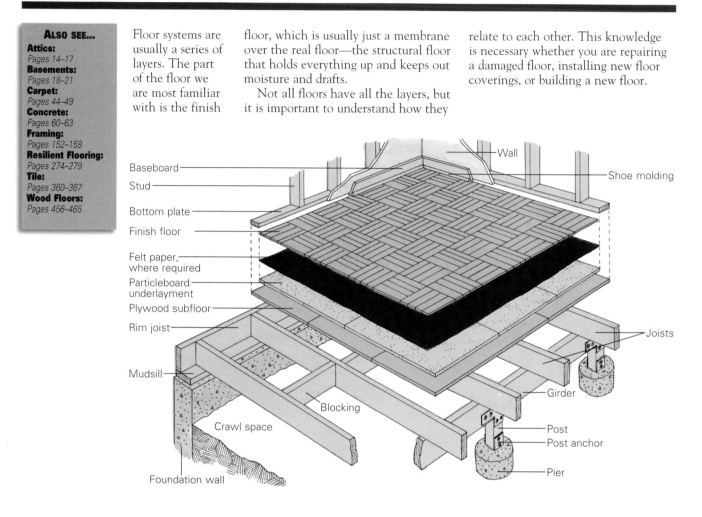

Baseboard
Stud
Bottom plate
Finish floor
Felt paper, where required
Particleboard underlayment
Plywood subfloor
Rim joist
Mudsill
Crawl space
Foundation wall
Blocking
Wall
Shoe molding
Joists
Girder
Post
Post anchor
Pier

SUBFLOOR, UNDERLAYMENT, AND FINISH FLOORING

ANATOMY OF A WOOD-FRAME FLOOR

Most floors are framed with wood members that span a crawl space, a basement, or habitable space below. The main framing members, called joists, are supported by heavier structural components, such as foundation sills, girders, and bearing walls. The size and spacing of the joists depend on the distance they have to span (see Span Tables, pages 326–331).

The subfloor is the main structural surface; it can be made of plywood, structural composition board, dimensional lumber, or tongue-and-groove boards. An underlayment of smooth particleboard or solid-core plywood, sometimes called lauan plywood, is installed over the subfloor if the finish flooring needs it. Some subfloor materials, such as

¾-inch tongue-and-groove wood or painted ¾-inch plywood, also double as a finished floor, but most are covered by a separate layer of finish material.

UNDERLAYMENT

Finish floors require stable, smooth surfaces beneath them. Though old-fashioned, ¾-inch-thick hardwood flooring can be attached to subfloors or even directly to the joists, new hardwood materials are thinner types and require underlayment. So do sheet vinyl, vinyl tiles, ceramic tiles, and some carpets. Sheet vinyl must be installed over a blemish-free surface.

Cement-based tile backing board is the best underlayment for ceramic tile. The combined backing board and subfloor must be at least 1⅛ inches thick to be stiff enough to prevent the tile grout from cracking.

INSTALLING UNDERLAYMENT ON AN EXISTING FLOOR

Remove the baseboard and cut back any casing with a backsaw.

Cut the underlayment to maintain a ⅜-inch gap at the walls. Mark cutouts for pipes or door openings with a compass or create a paper template. Cut them with a jigsaw. Install the sheets of underlayment with the joints staggered. If the subfloor is plywood, place the new underlayment at right angles to the plywood sheets.

Attach the underlayment with construction adhesive and 8d ring-shank nails spaced 8 inches apart throughout the field. Nail into the floor joists. At the edges use 1¼-inch ring-shank nails or wallboard screws spaced every 6 inches.

If the finish floor is vinyl, fill all seams and nail holes with a crack filler.

Some homes have concrete slabs as floors. Concrete is hard and unyielding, but can be covered with carpeting or with a wood subfloor.

A slab makes an excellent surface for thin or brittle floor coverings, such as tile and resilient flooring, which is glued directly to the concrete.

Concrete is not waterproof; it can wick moisture up from the ground and must have a vapor barrier under it or be adequately sealed before flooring is installed.

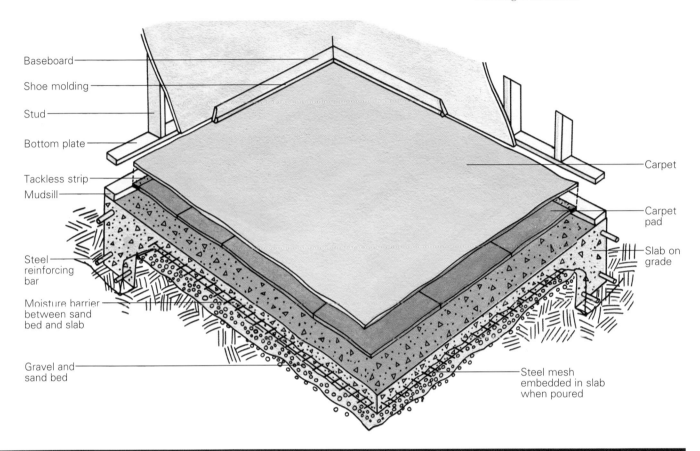

Baseboard
Shoe molding
Stud
Bottom plate
Tackless strip
Mudsill
Steel reinforcing bar
Moisture barrier between sand bed and slab
Gravel and sand bed
Carpet
Carpet pad
Slab on grade
Steel mesh embedded in slab when poured

CHOOSING A FINISH FLOORING

Because a floor is so important to the appearance and feel of a room, select new flooring carefully. In general, the simpler the floor treatment, the more flexibility you will have in the design and use of the room over time. It is much easier and less expensive to change wall coverings or furnishings than to install a new floor.

Good design is simple design—though simplicity is not always so easy to achieve. It requires a high degree of restraint, thoughtful planning, and careful execution. In some rooms, you may want a dramatic and exciting floor. If so, make it bold. Let it dominate; let it be the centerpiece for the rest of the room decor. More often, however, you will want the floor to play a subtle integrative role, pulling the other design elements together.

The most common types of floor covering are wood strip, wood block, resilient tile, resilient sheet, ceramic tile, and carpet. Each type is described fully elsewhere in the book.

Wood Strip and Wood Block: The traditional favorite, wood adds quality, permanence, and warmth to any room. The grain gives a floor texture. Wood-strip floors, especially wide planking, create a strong linear pattern. Wood-block and parquet floors create dynamic patterns.

Resilient Tile and Sheet Flooring: Very popular for kitchens, baths, and any other room where food and liquids are likely to be spilled, resilient flooring is durable, comfortable, and easy to maintain. Sheet materials come in room-size widths that create broad expanses of color and pattern.

Ceramic Tile: Tile and other masonry materials, such as brick and stone, are very hard on the feet, but create a feeling of permanence and substance. The effect can be either rustic or formal. Grout lines create a strong pattern. Choose a color and width for the grout lines to accentuate or subdue this pattern.

Carpet: Wall-to-wall carpeting and area rugs offer the advantages of softness, warmth, and comfort, and a wide choice of colors. Carpet is suitable for open expanses or intimate spaces and can be used in any room except the kitchen (manufacturer's claims notwithstanding). It does need to be vacuumed and shampooed on a regular basis, however, and is not as permanent as other floor materials.

FOOTINGS

A FIRM FOUNDATION FOR POSTS

Many auxiliary structures, such as decks and gazebos, require a foundation for each load-bearing post. These supports are usually called footings, although they are technically piers set on footings. To determine if your structure requires footings, refer to your local building codes.

Footing dimensions generally are a function of the height of the structure, the types of materials used, and soil bearing capacity. Because they support wood posts or beams which deteriorate with ground contact, piers typically extend above grade. They are usually cylinders or blocks, at least 8 inches across, with straight or beveled sides.

Footings are typically 18 inches square and at least 6 inches thick. They are buried at a depth prescribed by local building codes—anywhere from 12 inches to 6 feet or more, depending on the local depth of the frost and the stability of the soils in your particular area.

It is common practice to build a simple form for the pier and pour it along with the footing This unified concrete structure allows you to set metal anchors to connect the post to the pier. It also makes it easy to level the tops of piers at the same height.

For light, simple structures, you can eliminate the pier and set the post slightly above grade, provided the post lumber is pressure-treated. The use of an embedded post anchor or base is still a good idea.

SIMPLE FOOTINGS

Some projects, such as arbors, do not require footings capable of bearing large loads. They only need a firm aboveground support for posts. Posts set above ground will not be so vulnerable to decay, and they can easily be replaced or repaired. Always check local building codes to see if your structure requires footings that extend below frost level.

Make simple footings by excavating a hole in the ground and filling it with concrete. A simple footing does not necessarily need a pier to raise the post above grade if the post is pressure-treated lumber suitable for ground contact or a naturally durable species of lumber.

Excavating: Excavate holes at least 12 inches wide and 12 inches deep (or below the frost line).

Pouring Concrete: Fill the holes with concrete and fill each footing to the same level.

Positioning the Anchor: Tamp a galvanized post base or anchor into the fresh concrete when it has set enough to hold its shape but is still soft.

Leveling the Footings: Level each footing, sloping the fresh concrete away from the metal anchor so that water will drain away from the post.

Cylinder Piers: A deep footing hole will require pouring a tremendous amount of concrete. The most efficient way to deal with this problem is to pour pier and footing in one continuous unit, using a fiber forming tube. The round shape uses the least amount of concrete to attain the required cross-sectional dimension. Fiber tubes are available from concrete suppliers and lumberyards.

CODE REQUIREMENTS: FOOTINGS

Exterior walls must be supported on continuous solid masonry or concrete footings or other approved structural systems designed to safely support the building loads, considering the bearing capacity of the soil. Bedrock may act as the footing. All footings in areas subject to freezing must be below the maximum depth of frost.

A LASTING IMPRESSION

If you are building your own plywood pier forms, you can leave a lasting memory of yourself. Buy your initials in 4- or 6-inch-high wood letters at the hardware store. Coat them in oil and tack them to the inside of the form (in reverse, of course). When the form is stripped off, there you will be—forever!

If that's too pompous, then do the same thing with silhouettes of flowers, birds, cats, whatever. Have fun!

SITE-FORMED PIERS

1. Locating and Building Forms: Lay out the footings using string lines and batter boards. The lines should represent the outside edges of the posts—not the footings. Leave the lines in place—you'll need them when you place the metal post anchors.

To mark a footing location, drop a plumb bob from the intersection of two string lines. Mark the point with a nail—it represents the post corner. Hold a post in place and chalk its outline on the ground. Then chalk the outline of a footing around it.

2. Excavating Holes: Dig the footing holes carefully. A posthole digger will keep the sides vertical and prevent the hole from growing as you go deeper. Level the bottom of the hole and square the corners, using a square, rather than a pointed, shovel. Dig only to the required depth.

3. Building Pier Forms: If the footings are shallow and do not require a forming tube, build pier forms out of scrap lumber or plywood. Assemble them with ring-shank nails or wallboard screws and set them so that their top edges will be in the same plane.

To customize the piers with a graceful design, nail beveled strips of wood inside the four corners of the form, along the top edge, or both. The strips will leave beveled edges in the concrete when you remove the forms. If you don't want wood splinters in the cured concrete, paint the insides of the forms with vegetable oil to keep the concrete from adhering to the wood.

4. Mixing and Pouring the Concrete: Compute the total volume of your forms. If it is at least a cubic yard, have ready-mix concrete delivered. If not, mix your own, using the recipe: 1 part portland cement,

 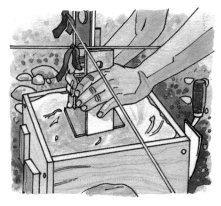

2 parts sand, and 3 parts gravel. Keep it stiff for maximum strength.

For tall piers, wire pieces of ½-inch reinforcing rod (rebar) into the forms so that they extend down into the footings. Fill the forms with concrete. Work a piece of rebar up and down in the concrete to consolidate it and remove air pockets. Also hammer the sides of the form several times on each face to release trapped air.

5. Setting the Anchors: Use a concrete trowel or a scrap of wood to smooth the concrete on the top of each form. Embed a post anchor in the wet concrete, aligning it with the string lines and using a level to make sure it is plumb.

6. Curing the Concrete: Leave the forms on the pier for at least three days. For the best cure, moisten the concrete two or three times a day, or cover it with plastic to retard evaporation.

Be careful when removing the forms to prevent chipping the edges.

SOIL BEARING CHARACTERISTICS

Type of Soil	Load Bearing, psf	Drainage	Frost Heaves
Bedrock	30,000	poor	low
Gravel and gravel-sand mixtures	8,000	good	low
Sands and gravelly sands	6,000	good	low
Silty sands, gravel, sand, silt mixtures	4,000	good	med
Clayey gravel, clayey sand	4,000	med	med
Inorganic silts and clays of low plasticity	2,000	med	high
Inorganic silts and clays of high plasticity	2,000	poor	med
Organic silts and organic silty clays	400	poor	med
Peats and other highly organic soils	0	unsat	med

LEVELING FORMS

There are several ways to level forms which are far apart. The first is to use a line level. This is a small cartridge-shaped device that hangs on a string and indicates how level the string is when it is pulled taut. It is quite accurate provided you pull the string very taut and place the line level dead center between the posts. You can

check the accuracy of a line level by turning it 180 degrees. If it doesn't indicate level both ways, the level needs adjusting.

The second method is using a water level. This is a long section of clear plastic tubing with colored water in it. When the two ends are held up, no matter how far apart they are, the

height of the water in one end will always be the same height as the water in the other end, as long as neither end is capped and the tubing is not partially in the shade and partly in direct sunlight (the part in the sun will receive more heat and expand more than the shaded end, giving a false reading).

FOUNDATIONS

HOW FOUNDATIONS WORK

ALSO SEE...
Concrete:
Pages 60–63
Drainage:
Pages 102–103
Footings:
Pages 142–143
**Gutters &
Downspouts:**
Pages 172–173
Insulation:
Pages 186–193

Laying or pouring a full house foundation is more work than you want to take on. Believe it! If you are skilled and determined, you might consider building the foundation for a small room addition. Even if you are not planning to lay a foundation, you should have a basic knowledge of what your foundation does and how to recognize serious problems.

It is important to keep the functions of a foundation in mind when inspecting it, analyzing problems, or planning extensive new work.

Understanding these functions will help you determine the design details and the materials you will need for any repairs.

The primary function of a foundation is to transfer and distribute the weight of the house to solid ground. Solid ground means undisturbed soil at least 12 inches below grade, and much deeper on steep grades or in soils subject to frost or expansion. Wide footings or deep piers carry the weight down to bedrock or more stable soil.

Second, the foundation holds the wood structure above the ground. Foundation materials, such as concrete, masonry, and pressure-treated lumber, must hold any other wood at least 8 inches above grade to prevent decay and insect damage.

A third function of the foundation is to compensate for an uneven site.

Fourth, the foundation anchors the house and protects it from wind and seismic damage. A house needs more than its own weight to hold it in place. The mass of the foundation and the fact that it is buried in the ground are what hold a house in place under stress—as long as the house is secured to the foundation and is tied together well.

Fifth, a foundation helps keep moisture out of the crawl space or basement. The foundation itself does not actually do this, but it provides a base for the application of waterproofing materials.

TYPES

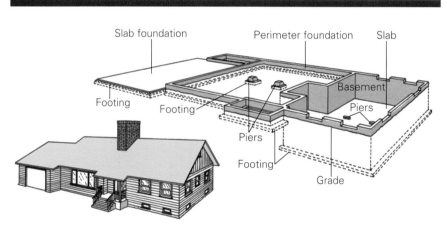

The house in the illustration rests on three types of foundation:

Perimeter: A perimeter foundation supports the exterior frame of the house and creates a crawl space under the house. Most perimeter foundations are made of poured concrete or concrete block, though it is not unusual to find brick foundations in older buildings. Piers, posts, or columns support girders and other concentrated loads within the perimeter.

Slab: A slab-on-grade (useful for garages and outbuildings) functions as both the foundation and the floor. It is economical but can only be used for "lightweight" structures or for homes in areas where soil conditions will permit

such construction. The slab must be thickened or have deep footings under its perimeter and bearing walls, and should keep the sill plate at least 8 inches above grade on the outside.

Basement: A basement foundation has walls high enough for habitable spaces. It is built on a footing and has separate footings for supporting columns. The basement floor slab is poured after the footings and basement walls are in place.

Pole: Not shown in the illustration, the pole foundation is appropriate for simple outbuildings and homes in rural areas. It relies on pressure-treated telephone poles, embedded to or below the frost depth, to both support a building and anchor it against uplift.

MINIMUM FOUNDATION DIMENSIONS

Critical	Stories		
Dimension	1	2	3
Depth	12"	18"	24"
Wall thickness	6"	8"	10"
Footing thickness	6"	7"	8"
Footing width	12"	15"	18"

LAYING OUT FOUNDATIONS

Foundation dimensions should be accurate to within ¼ inch, and the corners should be square. The layout technique described below uses batter boards at the four corners, with string lines representing the outside edges of the foundation. Once they are set properly, the lines can be taken down when in the way, but easily reestablished whenever needed.

Begin by establishing the corner where the ground is highest (point A) or at the edge of the house if you are laying out a room addition. Drive the batter boards 3 feet behind that point.

Then measure the approximate distance to point B and build another set of batter boards 3 feet behind it. Stretch a string line so it crosses over points A and B. Level the batter boards with a line level, transit, or hydrolevel (water hose with clear plastic tubes at the ends).

Build a third set of batter boards 3 feet behind the approximate position of point C, and stretch a string line back to the batter board behind point B. Use a 3-4-5 (or any multiple

thereof, such as 15-20-25) right triangle to square the two string lines.

Finally, build batter boards at point D and attach the last two string lines. All of the batter boards should be level with each other. The string lines will be used as a reference for leveling the forms later on. Adjust the string lines back and forth on the batter boards until the four intersections are exactly as far apart as the foundation dimensions. When the two diagonal measurements are equal, the corners are square.

Note: String lines should be made of nylon and not cotton

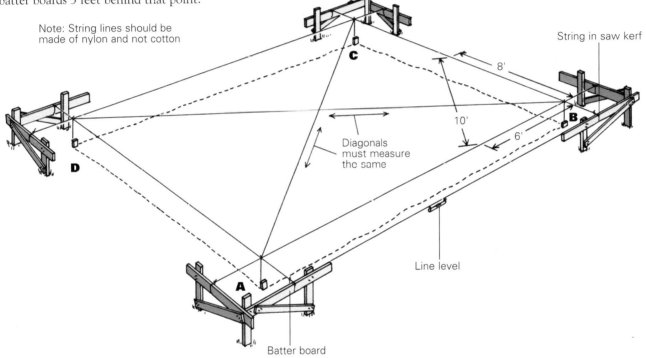

EXTENDING AN EXISTING FOUNDATION

An addition should have the same type of foundation as the rest of the house. Dig trenches for a perimeter foundation to the same depth as the house foundation footings. Drill ⅝-inch holes into the existing foundation, 7 inches deep, with a hammer drill (these can be rented). Cement anchor bolts or rebar into the holes with epoxy mortar. Build forms for the footing and wall to the height of the existing wall and place rebar. Clean the old wall with a pressure washer and a stiff brush. Thoroughly coat the old concrete with a latex-modified bonding agent before pouring the new concrete.

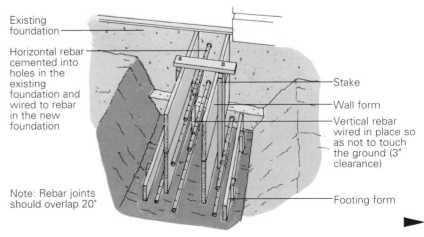

Note: Rebar joints should overlap 20"

POURED FOUNDATION

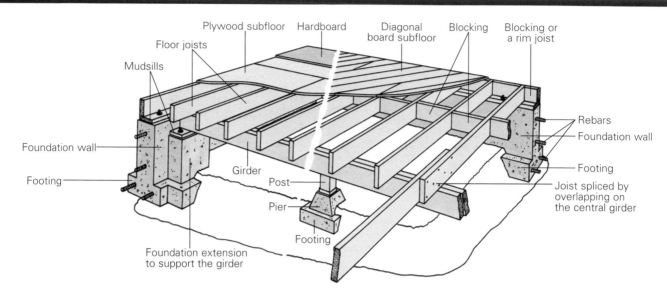

Plywood subfloor · Hardboard · Diagonal board subfloor · Blocking · Blocking or a rim joist

Floor joists

Mudsills

Foundation wall

Footing

Girder

Post

Pier

Footing

Foundation extension to support the girder

Rebars

Foundation wall

Footing

Joist spliced by overlapping on the central girder

When a continuous, poured concrete foundation rests on a continuous or stepped poured concrete footing, both wall and footing have to be reinforced with horizontal reinforcing rods (rebars). Both wall and footing may be poured at the same time, or the footing may be poured with a keyed slot that allows the wall to be poured later but locks the two together.

Footings must be at least 12 inches wide for one story and 15 inches for two, although 16 inches is the common practice. A footing must have at least the same thickness as the wall. The bottom of the footing must be below the maximum depth of frost or at least 12 inches below grade.

Most codes require that a foundation wall be at least 6 inches thick for a one-story house and 8 inches thick for two stories. Common practice is to not distinguish but to make any foundation wall 8 inches.

The wall must extend at least 8 inches above the final grade to afford the wood sill and sheathing protection from splash-back and vegetation.

Floor joists rest on the sill or a short cripple wall built on the sill. Clearance above the earth inside the foundation must be at least 12 inches beneath girders and 18 inches beneath joists.

Girder ends not resting on the sill or cripple wall usually rest in pockets formed into the foundation wall. The bottoms of any posts holding up the girder must be at least 8 inches above grade.

BUILDING A PERIMETER FOUNDATION

Most perimeter foundations are constructed from poured concrete, but foundations also can be built with concrete block laid on a poured concrete footing.

For a full-height poured wall, always hire a foundation contractor who has the forms and the know-how for the job. Build forms yourself for a short concrete foundation. First, lay out string lines to represent the outside edge of the wall (not the footing). Use orange spray paint to mark the outlines of the footing trenches for the excavator. Transfer the string line

positions to the ground with a plumb bob. Don't forget that the footing is wider than (generally twice as wide as) the wall.

Excavate to the code-required footing depth. If the soil is firm enough to maintain its shape when cut by a shovel, use it as a form. Level the bottom of the trench; make the sides straight, and the corners square.

Construct forms for the wall of ¾-inch plywood and 2×4 braces, or use 2-by lumber. (Make it the same size as the floor joists so you can use it later for that purpose.) Attach steel fence stakes driven into the bottom of the

INSPECTING AN EXISTING PERIMETER FOUNDATION

Before starting a major structural project in your home, make sure the perimeter foundation is in good shape. Inspect it for problems such as major cracks and bowing, and seek professional consultation if there seems to be a problem.

Older foundations may suffer from weak concrete caused by poor mixing or inferior materials. The rebars may even be exposed in some places. Brick or block foundations are also suspect. Look for crumbling mortar and evidence of excessive moisture.

Before separate, wide footings became the norm, most perimeter foundations were "battered" (or beveled) on the inside. Some had

no separate footings at all. These foundations tend to lean outward. This problem can be detected by stretching a string from corner to corner along the suspect walls.

Hairline cracks are natural and acceptable, but any crack wider than ¹⁄₁₆ inch is cause for further investigation. Make several continuous marks across the crack with a permanent magic marker and watch for movement through a full year. More movement indicates the absence of rebars and either settlement or upheaval of the soil beneath the footing. The problem is serious because it may continue to get worse with time. Consult a licensed building contractor.

trench, positioning them so the distance between the inside faces of the lumber will be 8 inches or the width required by your local code. Space the stakes every 3 or 4 feet.

To keep the concrete from spreading the form boards apart, insert metal form ties (available at masonry supply outlets) between them. These ties will become encased in the concrete, but you can free them from the concrete after it hardens. If your forms are plywood, paint the inside faces with oil to keep the concrete from sticking.

Set all the rebars in place before the pour and tie it securely with wire. Pour the concrete, insert anchor bolts for the sill, and let the concrete cure for at least 5 days before removing the forms.

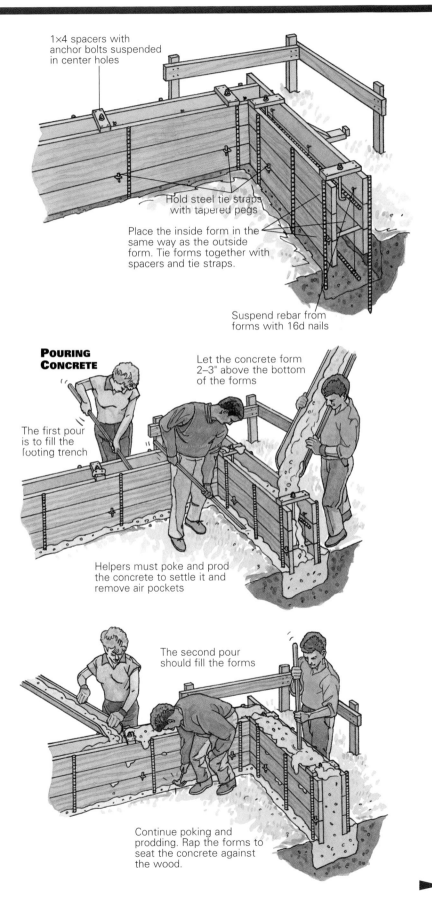

1×4 spacers with anchor bolts suspended in center holes

Hold steel tie straps with tapered pegs

Place the inside form in the same way as the outside form. Tie forms together with spacers and tie straps.

Suspend rebar from forms with 16d nails

POURING CONCRETE

Let the concrete form 2–3" above the bottom of the forms

The first pour is to fill the footing trench

Helpers must poke and prod the concrete to settle it and remove air pockets

The second pour should fill the forms

Continue poking and prodding. Rap the forms to seat the concrete against the wood.

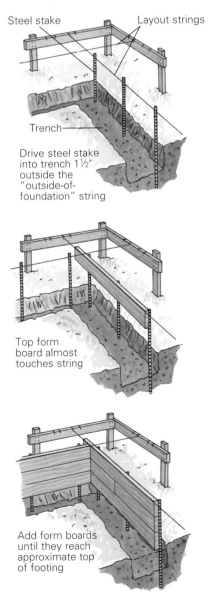

Steel stake   Layout strings

Trench

Drive steel stake into trench 1½" outside the "outside-of-foundation" string

Top form board almost touches string

Add form boards until they reach approximate top of footing

BLOCK FOUNDATION

In many areas of the country, foundation walls are built of concrete masonry units (concrete block) instead of poured concrete. The use of block eliminates the need for expensive forming.

THE BLOCK WALL

A block wall requires a continuous, reinforced concrete footing. Some building codes require that block walls be reinforced both vertically and horizontally with rebars, and that the block cores containing the rebars be filled with concrete. A course of blocks with horizontal rebars is called a bond beam; it uses blocks with holes at each end for the steel to pass through.

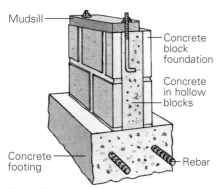

Note: Check local codes for footing depth

EXCAVATING FOR THE FOOTING

The simplest way to pour a footing is to excavate a trench to the required dimensions and fill it with concrete. This technique works where the soil is firm enough to maintain its shape when cut by a shovel. Otherwise, stake out 2-by lumber as forms.

A footing for concrete blocks must be perfectly level. To guide the

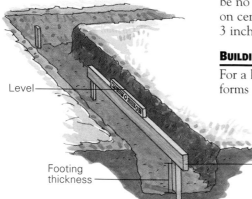

concrete finishing, make the tops of the forms level, or if using the soil as forms, set grade stakes inside the trench every 4 feet driven with their tops at the precise height of the footing.

The bottom of the trench should be roughly level as well. If the site is sloped, build the footing in steps. The height of each step must be exactly equal to the height of one or more blocks (including mortar joint), so that the courses will line up.

POURING THE CONCRETE

Place horizontal rebars in the trench. Wire them to dobies (small concrete blocks with wires attached) or rocks to hold them 3 inches above the ground and 3 inches in from the sides. Cut short sections of rebar for any vertical pieces. Bend the ends into an L shape and set them aside for inserting in the concrete later. Fill the trench with concrete, screeding it to the top of the forms or stakes.

Use a wood float to make the surface slightly rough. After the concrete has

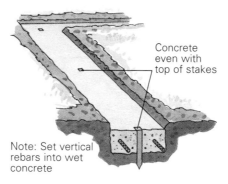

Note: Set vertical rebars into wet concrete

set a bit but is still soft, insert the bent vertical rebars in it. They should line up with the cells of the blocks and be no farther apart than 24 inches on center, and they should stick out 3 inches above the concrete.

BUILDING THE FOOTING FORMS

For a large job or unstable soils, build forms to reduce concrete waste and to

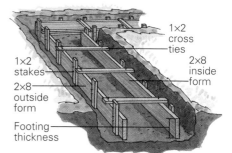

ensure a more accurate footing. Dig the trench at least 12 inches wider than the footing.

Once you've dug the trench, position the outside forms, staking them every 18 inches. Use 2×8 lumber for an 8-inch footing, keeping the lumber about ¾ inch off the ground because standard 2×8 lumber actually measures 1½×7¼ inches. Then build the inside forms, tying them to the outside forms with 1×2 strapping every 2 feet. Place horizontal rebars (supported by dobies) inside the forms and fill them with concrete, using the same method as for a trench. Screed the concrete flush with the top of the forms and place the vertical rebars. You can begin laying the concrete blocks the next day, but do not remove the forms for several more days.

When the footings are complete, begin laying the block. Concrete blocks are normally 8 inches wide, 8 inches high, and 16 inches long, although other sizes may be available. The sizes referred to are always nominal sizes. The blocks themselves actually measure ⅜ inch less to allow for a ⅜-inch mortar joint.

Half blocks, 8-inch cubes, are also common and are used to turn corners and to terminate walls at doorways or other openings.

LAYING OUT THE BLOCKS

The first step is to lay out a dry run, putting spacers between the blocks to make sure they fit. Then take the blocks off the footing and locate the two outside corners of the first course.

Mix your first batch of mortar. A good mix is 1 part masonry cement and 3 parts sand. Add water sparingly until you reach a good consistency (see Concrete, pages 60–63). Concrete

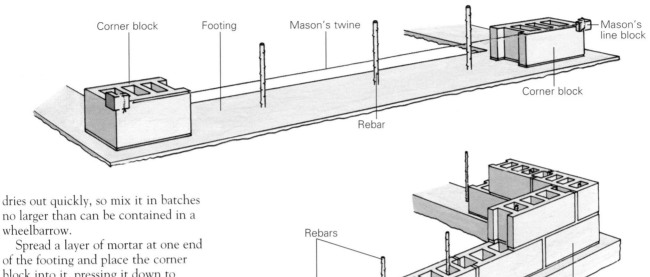

Corner block   Footing   Mason's twine   Mason's line block

Rebar

Corner block

Rebars

Block foundation wall

Footing

dries out quickly, so mix it in batches no larger than can be contained in a wheelbarrow.

Spread a layer of mortar at one end of the footing and place the corner block into it, pressing it down to within ³⁄₈ inch of the footing. Lay a block at the other corner, in the same way, and stretch mason's line between line blocks (available from masonry suppliers) as a guide while you complete the rest of the first row.

You can tell the top of a block because the web is wider than it is on the bottom of the block, providing a broader surface to lay mortar on for the next course.

SETTING THE BLOCKS

Spread mortar on the footing and butter one end of each block as you set it in place. Speed up the process by buttering several blocks at one time: Stand them on their ends near where you are working and spread mortar on all their ends at once.

As you lay each block, keep the buttered end raised slightly and then lower it snugly against the preceding block in one smooth motion (the mortar joint should be ³⁄₈ inch). Tap the block level, and scrape away excess mortar with the blade.

Constantly check your work to make sure each row is level, and hold the level vertically against the side of the wall as you build upward to be sure it is plumb. Build the four corners of the walls four courses high, then stretch mason's twine between line blocks as guides while you complete each course. After completing the four courses, build the corners again and repeat the process.

SETTING THE ANCHORS

Fill the cells with concrete after the finished wall has dried overnight. Even if the building code does not require concrete in every cell, you will need to fill them every 6 feet (4 feet in seismic areas) for setting sill-plate anchor bolts. The anchor bolts should be ½ by 10 or 12 inches. Embed the bolts 7 inches into the concrete while it is still fresh. Make sure there is an anchor bolt within 12 inches of the corners and at each end of the sill.

Wait at least 24 hours to install the pressure-treated sill over the anchor bolts. In some areas a metal termite shield must also be installed under the sill. If the wall encloses a basement or other heated space, place a thin layer of closed-cell foam "sill-sealer" between the concrete and the sill. In areas where codes do not require concrete within the wall, fill the blocks with insulating material, such as vermiculite, before the sill is installed.

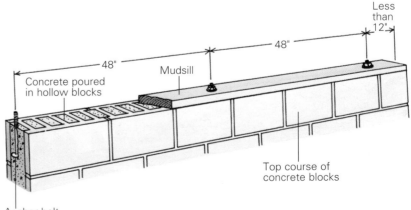

Less than 12"

48"

48"

Mudsill

Concrete poured in hollow blocks

Top course of concrete blocks

Anchor bolt

POLE FOUNDATION

While unacceptable to urban zoning and frowned upon by mortgage lenders in most cities, there is one superior type of foundation of which you should be aware. If you are building an outbuilding, a vacation home in the wilds, or a low-cost home for your family in a rural area, consider the pole foundation, developed by the U.S. Department of Agriculture as a low-cost rural option. It is easy to construct, inexpensive (no more than a few hundred dollars), as hurricaneproof and earthquakeproof as any, and long-lasting. Its single disadvantage is the lack of a freezeproof crawl space or basement space, making the protection of plumbing an exercise in ingenuity.

LAYING OUT THE FOUNDATION

Lay out the lines of a pole foundation using the procedure described on page 145. After you have established the outline of the building, it is a simple matter to establish parallel strings indicating the centerlines of the poles. Make the distance from the building edge to the centerline of the poles about 1 foot so the joists will overhang the sill beams by 6 to 8 inches. The overhang solves two problems. First, it accommodates variations in pole diameter. Second, it protects the wood poles from sunlight and rain, giving the poles an estimated lifetime of 100 years or more.

FOOTINGS

The spacing of the poles depends on the sizes of the beams that serve as the sills, and any local building codes. A 6- to 8-foot on-center spacing is usual. Once you have located the centers of the poles, mark them with a nail in the ground.

Excavate the holes for the footings to the frost depth, or to 2 feet, whichever is greater. For an 8-foot pole spacing, 20×20-inch or 24-inch-diameter footings are recommended.

Set the height of the pole at the highest location at 24 inches above grade to keep the bottoms of sill beams (which can be up to 12 inches deep) 12 inches off the ground. From that high point use a line level or a transit to determine the lengths of the rest of the poles.

SETTING THE POLES

Prepare the poles by driving several dozen 16d galvanized common nails around their fatter ends. Drop the poles into the footing holes, nailend down. Lay 2×4s along each side of the poles. Raise the poles a minimum of 8 inches (here is where several strong friends prove useful), and secure them plumb to the 2×4s with temporary 16d or 20d nails. When you are done, the poles should be suspended in air in their final positions.

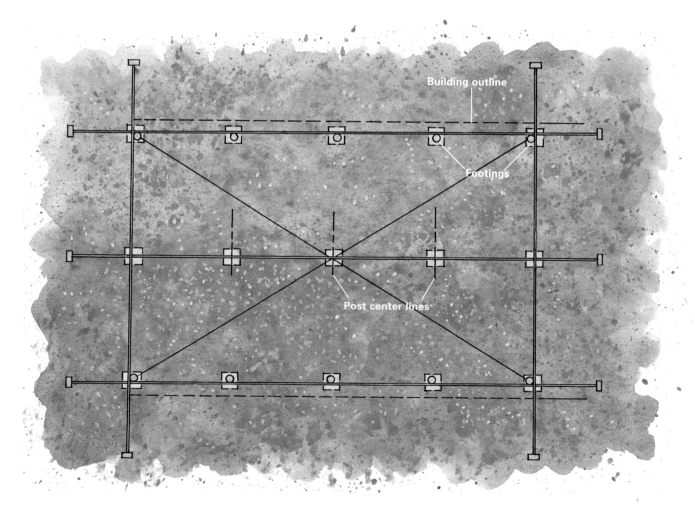

Pour ready-mix concrete under and around the poles until the nails are covered. Let the concrete cure for 24 hours, then backfill the holes. Be careful in backfilling not to disturb the poles until the floor system is in place.

ATTACHING THE SILLS

Using a line level or transit, mark the poles for the bottoms of the sill beams. Transfer these marks up the pole by about ½ inch less than the depth of the beams. Using a chainsaw, trim the poles to the higher marks. Then, using a circular saw or a handsaw, make a 1-inch-deep cut at the lower mark and chisel out a shoulder on which the beam will rest.

Rest the sill beam on the shoulder and fasten it to the pole with 20d spikes. After all sill beams have been nailed in place, drill ½-inch holes through the beams and poles at the midheight of the beams, and install ½×10 or 12-inch galvanized carriage bolts with the heads on the outside and washers and nuts on the inside.

ATTACHING THE FLOOR JOISTS

Assemble the floor joist and header system on top of the sill beams. Construct the entire system, but do not nail the joists to the beams. After the entire system is together, use a sledge to square it and straighten the headers. Once you are satisfied that the floor system is straight, level, and square, secure it to the sill beams by toenailing each joist/beam crossing.

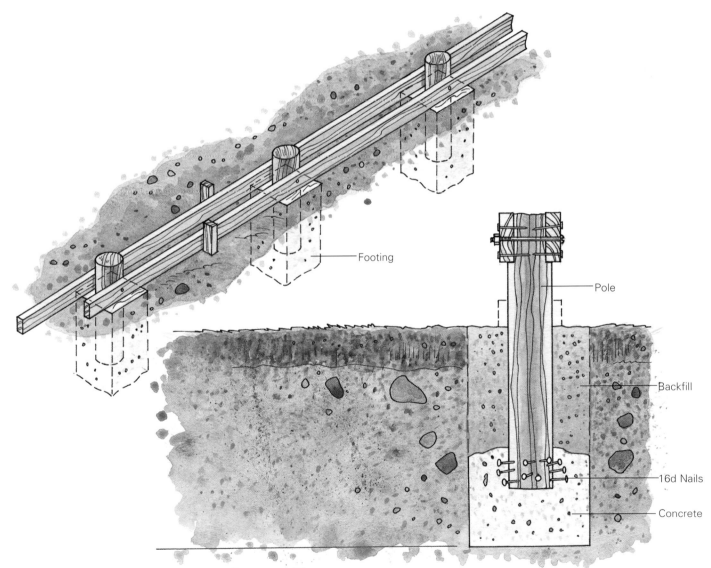

Footing

Pole

Backfill

16d Nails

Concrete

SECTIONAL VIEW

FRAMING

THE SKELETON OF ANY BUILDING

ALSO SEE...
Attics:
Pages 14–17
Bracing:
Pages 36–37
Fasteners:
Pages 122–125
Floors:
Pages 140–141
Roofs:
Pages 282–289
Span Tables:
Pages 326–331
Walls:
Pages 408–415
Wood:
Pages 446–453

Adding space, altering space, even cutting a hole in a floor, wall, or roof generally requires a knowledge of framing.

Never undertake a project involving framing until you understand the function of each framing member—and have taken out a permit. Your house should always be stronger when you finish than it was when you began. You may also need an inspection before covering up any of the new framing.

In new construction, such as a room addition, framing is a textbook operation. In remodeling an existing structure, however, you must be prepared to improvise and adjust to unique situations. You may find unorthodox framing conditions in a wall, under a floor, or in an attic, and you will have to either repair, replace, or work around them. Older homes, for example, may be constructed with lumber that is thicker and wider than lumber we use today but it will have the same nominal dimensions. To make sure surfaces and finishes match, you'll have to be aware of this potential problem and add shim stock.

The framing practices in this section reflect the requirements of most building codes and serve to illustrate the way framing works.

COMMON FRAMING SYSTEMS

Some homes are framed with heavy timbers, but most wood-frame houses use 2-by lumber. Older houses may be balloon-framed, a method in which long studs extend from the foundation to the roof, even in a tall house.

Today's standard is platform framing. The walls of each story are identical on identically framed floor platforms.

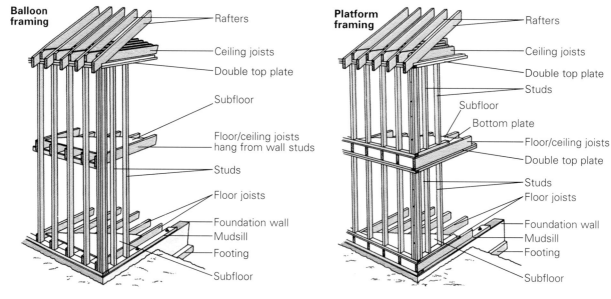

Balloon framing
- Rafters
- Ceiling joists
- Double top plate
- Subfloor
- Floor/ceiling joists hang from wall studs
- Studs
- Floor joists
- Foundation wall
- Mudsill
- Footing
- Subfloor

Platform framing
- Rafters
- Ceiling joists
- Double top plate
- Studs
- Subfloor
- Bottom plate
- Floor/ceiling joists
- Double top plate
- Studs
- Floor joists
- Foundation wall
- Mudsill
- Footing
- Subfloor

SILLS AND GIRDERS

Floor joists are supported at the building perimeter by mudsills, bolted flat to the perimeter foundation. In a pier or pole foundation, the sills must be beams or girders which can resist bending under load.

In the interior, girders provide intermediate support to the joists and load-bearing walls. These members must be sized for the loads they carry.

A girder can be solid lumber or several 2× boards nailed together—a built-up girder. Steel girders, such as I-beams, will span long distances. In all cases the posts are spaced according to the girder span, and they are always supported by footings.

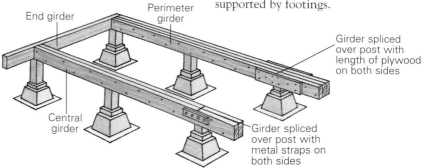

- End girder
- Perimeter girder
- Central girder
- Girder spliced over post with length of plywood on both sides
- Girder spliced over post with metal straps on both sides

FLOORS

Joists are the main framing members for floors. The ends of first-floor joists rest on either foundation mudsills or short-framed cripple walls, with large girders or beams supporting the joists at midpoint. Joists for upper floors rest on exterior and interior bearing walls. Joists are often doubled up where they carry a concentrated load, such as a bearing wall or bathtub.

Joists are always set on edge and fastened at their ends to rim or band joists to prevent them from rolling over. Deep joists (having depth-to-width ratios of 6 or more) are strengthened by blocking or cross-bridging over girders and every 10 feet along open spans.

INSTALLING JOISTS

Most codes specify allowable species, grades, sizes, and spacings of joists (see Span Tables on pages 326–331).

Always select the straightest lumber for the end and band joists. Assemble these perimeter joists, check them for square by measuring both diagonals, make any adjustments, then toenail the joists to the mudsill or cripple wall. Mark the locations of the interior joists on the rim joists and across the top of the girders, starting from the same end. End-nail each floor joist through the rim joist, then toenail the floor joists to the bearing surface. Floor joists must

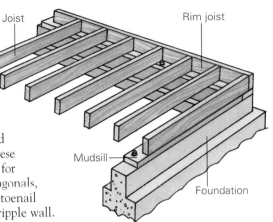

have at least 1½ inches of bearing surface over wood or steel, and 3 inches on concrete. Install joists with their crown, or curved edge, up.

SPLICING JOISTS

Floors often span lengths longer than joist stock and must be joined at a girder. Splice the joists with plywood or metal braces on each side, or lap them, extending each joist past the girder. Overlapped joists will not line up at the same points on both ends, which must be taken into account if you install a plywood subfloor. An alternative method is to attach the joists to the girders with joist hangers.

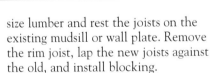

Joist spliced with plywood on both sides   Central girder

Central girder
Overlapped joists

EXTENDING AN EXISTING FLOOR

If you're building an addition whose floor will be at the same level as the existing floor and if you can install the new joists so that they run in the same direction as the old ones, use the same size lumber and rest the joists on the existing mudsill or wall plate. Remove the rim joist, lap the new joists against the old, and install blocking.

If the new subfloor or joists are a different dimension from the existing floor, install the new joists with joist hangers, taking the difference into account.

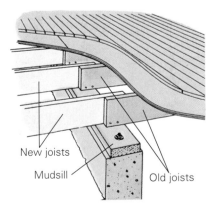

New joists
Mudsill   Old joists

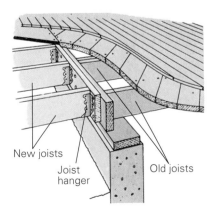

New joists
Joist hanger   Old joists

FLOORS *continued*

INSTALLING BLOCKING

Blocking helps keep joists from tipping and provides support for surfaces above. Cut blocking from joist material, measuring at the rim joists rather than where you will be installing it. Stagger the blocks so you can face-nail them at each end.

To use metal cross-bridging, attach the top, but wait until you set the subfloor before nailing the bottom of the cross-bridging.

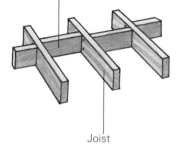

Staggered blocking with joist material

Joist

WALLS

Stud walls consist of a bottom plate nailed to the subfloor, vertical studs, and a double top plate, with extra studs and blocking added where walls intersect. Door and window openings are framed with headers and extra studs. Terminology may vary in different parts of the country, but the functions are the same.

Studs: Two-by-four studs usually are spaced every 16 inches on center; 2×6 studs 24 inches on center. If the wall is a bearing wall (supporting a wall above), the studs must be spaced no more than 16 inches on center. Studs are usually 2×4s, but must be 2×6 if the wall bears more than two floors. In cold climates, 2×6s are often used for exterior walls because they can hold more insulation.

The height of most ceilings is 8 feet, so studs are typically 92½ inches long to account for the added height

provided by the plates and ceiling material. Higher ceilings require longer studs. If you are ordering studs for a large project, figure one stud for every lineal foot of wall. The extras will get used up fast for blocking and cripple studs. Use standard framing lumber for most of the wall, but use kiln-dried studs to frame doors and windows to ensure that they will remain absolutely straight.

Plates: The bottom and top plates are the same size lumber as the studs. Use long lumber for plates, splicing lengths together for long walls. Although the bottom plate does not extend across doorways, if you are framing a wall on the floor and lifting it into position, it is easier to use a continuous bottom plate and then saw out the doorway section after the wall is in place. If you are building walls on a concrete slab, use pressure-treated

lumber for the bottom plates.

Bearing walls (all exterior walls except gable-end walls are bearing) require a double top plate, consisting of a top plate and a cap plate nailed to it. A single top plate is allowed on partition walls that are not load-bearing. When framing a wall, first attach only the top plate. Install the cap plates after all the walls are up, overlapping the top plate and cap plate at the corners, making a stronger connection. Center all top plate splices on a stud, and position splices in cap plates at least 4 feet from splices in top plates.

Openings: Frame openings with a header across the top. The header should be either solid 4× (nominal) lumber or two pieces of 2× (nominal) material sandwiched together with ½-inch plywood spacers between them. The vertical width of the header depends on its span. See Span Tables, pages 326–331, to select the size of headers.

Each end of a header rests on a shorter stud called a trimmer or jack stud, which must extend all the way to the bottom plate. Flank each trimmer stud with full-length studs, called king studs. Regardless of where an opening occurs, the 16-inch layout of joists continues from one end of the wall to the other. Cripple studs, used to fill in spaces above headers and below window sills, should follow the same on-center spacing to provide consistent lines for nailing sheathing and wallboard.

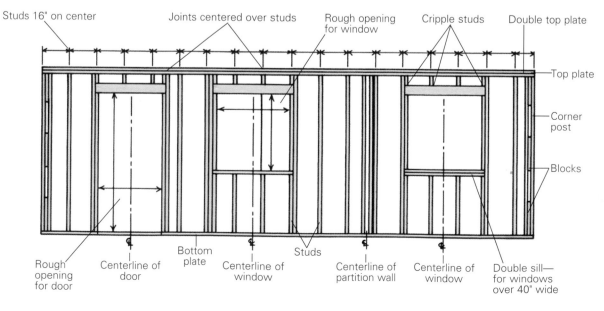

Studs 16" on center — Joints centered over studs — Rough opening for window — Cripple studs — Double top plate — Top plate — Corner post — Blocks

Rough opening for door — Centerline of door — Bottom plate — Centerline of window — Studs — Centerline of partition wall — Centerline of window — Double sill— for windows over 40" wide

LAYING OUT A WALL

Lay out the longest walls first. Begin by marking stud locations on the bottom and top plate. To ensure that the marks will line up when the plates are installed, clamp or hold the two plates together and mark them at the same time. If you're working in inches on center, begin at the end of the sole plate. If your marks represent the edge location for the studs, tack a scrap of ¾-inch wood on the end of the plates and hook the tape measure over it. This makes the first mark 15¼ inches from the end of the plates. Mark edge locations 16 inches thereafter.

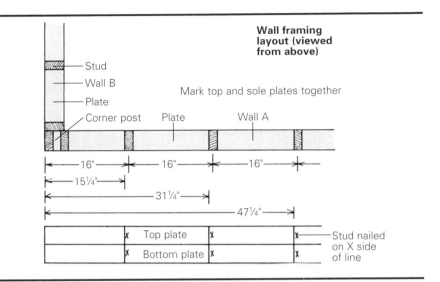

Wall framing layout (viewed from above)

Stud
Wall B
Plate
Corner post

Mark top and sole plates together

Plate · Wall A

16" · 16" · 16"

15¼"

31¼"

47¼"

	Top plate		
X		X	X
X	Bottom plate	X	X

Stud nailed on X side of line

BUILDING A WALL

Assemble walls on the subfloor before you raise them into place. Build the corner posts first, using two studs with short pieces of blocking in between. Frame door and window openings with a header, king studs, trimmer studs, and sill, if needed. Lay these assemblies in place, along with the rest of the joists, between the bottom plate and top plate, aligning them with the layout marks. Endnail each stud through the plates with two 16d common nails at each end. Install the cripple studs, toenailing each one into the header with four 8d nails.

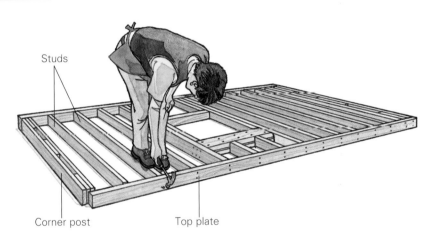

Studs

Corner post

Top plate

RAISING THE WALLS

Before lifting a wall, snap a chalk line onto the floor for aligning the interior edge of the bottom plate. Then lift the wall into place. Nail the bottom plate into the floor at every joist (every 16 inches). Using a plumb bob, plumb stick, or long level, align the wall so that it is plumb in both directions. Temporarily brace it to the deck with 2×4s (at right angles to the walls).

Leave the temporary bracing in place until you are ready to install permanent bracing and interior walls. Most codes allow three types of bracing: metal straps, 1× boards notched into the exterior face of the wall frame, and structural sheathing panels. Plywood sheathing is the strongest, but oriented strand board (OSB) is gaining in favor due to its lower cost.

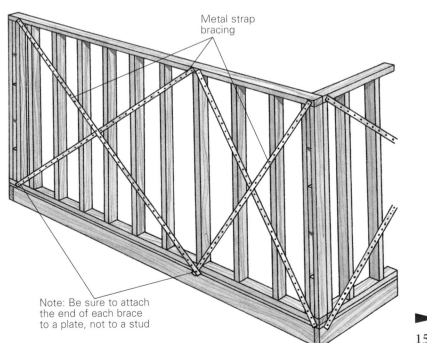

Metal strap bracing

Note: Be sure to attach the end of each brace to a plate, not to a stud

ROOFS

Most roofs are framed with ceiling joists, rafters, and a ridge board. When the rafters run parallel to the ceiling joists, the joists are nailed to the rafters to keep the weight of the roof from facing the walls outward. If the rafters are not parallel to the joists, rafter ties (also known as collar ties) connect the rafters to accomplish the same purpose. Never remove rafter ties without first providing an alternative solution. The ridge board stiffens the structure and provides a nailing surface for the rafters.

Roofs with cathedral ceilings require a different system. The rafters are supported on top by a ridge beam, at least 3 inches wide, supported at each end by a post or bearing wall.

The peaked gable wall at the end of a roof is framed like a standard stud wall, then short filler studs are cut to fit between the cap plates and the

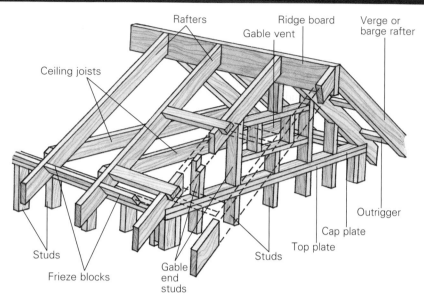

rafters. The eave that projects beyond the gable wall terminates in a pair of barge rafters, also called verge or rake rafters. They are held in place by

outriggers or lookouts, which are cantilevered 2×4s laid flat and placed into notches in the gable rafters.

LAYING OUT THE RAFTERS

To cut rafters you need to know the run and the slope. The run is half the width of the building. The slope is the number of inches of rise for every foot (12 inches) of run; it is expressed as "'x' in 12." For example, if a building is 24 feet wide (a 12-foot run) and the roof rises 6 feet in that 12-foot run, the slope of the rafters is expressed as 6/12, or at a 6 in 12 slope or pitch.

Mark the rafter plumb cut by setting a rafter square on one end of the board. As this is a 6 in 12 roof pitch, the tongue (the narrow part) intersects the edge of the board at the 6-inch mark and the blade (the wide part) at the 12-inch mark. Hold the square this way to make all the marks.

To determine the rafter length (from the peak to the bird's mouth), measure the rise and run, then use the formula $A^2 = B^2 + C^2$ (where B and C are the rise and run, both in feet).

Or, look at the tables stamped on the blade of the rafter square. The 13.42 under the 6-inch mark means that for every foot of run, you need 13.42 inches of length. On a 12-foot run, the rafter length for a 6 in 12 pitch is 12 times 13.42 = 161 inches, or 13 feet 5 inches.

Measure the rafter length from the plumb cut, and mark the top edge of the board. Set the 6 in 12 square against this mark and scribe a line.

Keeping the square in its 6 in

12 position, slide it back toward the original plumb cut line until it creates a line for the seat of the rafter exactly the width of the cap plate (3½ inches for a 2×4). Mark the position, then mark the tail cut by sliding the square beyond the bird's mouth the distance of the overhang.

Finally, move the original plumb line toward the bird's mouth by one half the thickness of the ridge board (⅜ inch for a ¾-inch-thick board). Then cut at your marked lines.

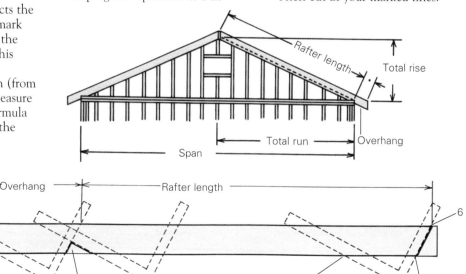

Mark the locations of the ceiling joists and rafters on the top plates. The first rafter will be flush with the outside of the gable wall. Inset the first ceiling joist by the width of a stud to leave room for the gable studs and to provide a nailer for the corner of the ceiling.

Size and cut the ceiling joists using the span tables on pages 326–331. Toenail them to the wall plates, giving you a platform to work on while you erect the rafters. In areas where wind or earthquakes are a hazard, you must use metal framing aids (see Framing Connectors, page 160–161) to connect the joists and rafters to the plates.

Lay out and cut the first pair of rafters. Hold the two rafters in place (with a scrap of ridge board) to see if the cuts fit snugly. Your ridge board should be one size deeper than your rafter stock (a 2×10 for 2×8 rafters, for

example). After making adjustments as needed, use these rafters as patterns for cutting the rest.

Lay out the rafter locations along both sides of the ridge board, allowing for the gable overhang.

Have at least two helpers when you install the rafters. Hold the first two rafters in place, with the ridgeboard sandwiched between, and nail each

end into the wall plate. Then nail the top ends into the ridge board, face-nailing one side and toenailing the other. Alternate this nailing sequence at the ridge as you work your way along the rafters.

Be sure the ridge board is level and centered over the house. If you have to splice it for a long roof, the splice must fall where a pair of rafters meet.

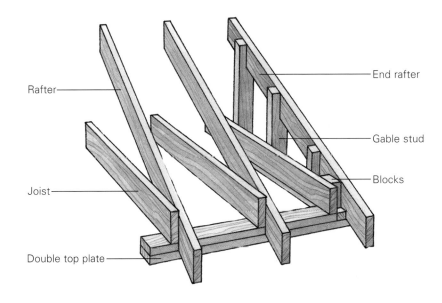

Rafter

End rafter

Gable stud

Joist

Blocks

Double top plate

TEMPLATE TEST

When cutting rafters, make a test pair first to check your calculations and layout. After you have put the pair up and verified their fit, take them down and use them as templates, rather than laying out the remaining rafters.

CODE REQUIREMENTS: FRAMING

Floors:

■ Joist, beam, and girder-end bearing must be at least 1½" on wood or metal and 3" on concrete.

■ Joist ends must be blocked, attached to a header/band joist, or nailed to an adjacent stud.

■ Joists with depth-to-width ratios of more than 6 must be blocked, bridged, or restrained at bottom at 10 feet on center.

■ Drilling and notching of joists must not exceed ⅙ of the depth at top or bottom, be in middle third of the span, or exceed ¼ depth at end ledger strip.

■ Holes in joists must not exceed ⅓ of depth or be within 2 inches of top or bottom.

Walls:

■ Top plates must be doubled, overlapped at corners and intersections, and overlapped at least 4 feet at joints.

■ Joists and rafters must fall within 5 inches of bearing studs if the joists or rafters are spaced more than 16 inches on center, and the studs are spaced 24 inches on center, unless the top plate is 2×6s, 3×4s, or is tripled.

■ Nonbearing partition wall studs may be 2×3s spaced 24 inches on-center or flat 2×4s spaced 16 inches on center, and may have a single top plate.

■ Studs may be notched 25 percent if bearing and 40 percent if nonbearing.

■ Studs may be drilled 40 percent of width if ⅝ inch or more from edge. Doubled studs may be drilled 60 percent of width.

■ Walls must be fire-stopped at top and bottom.

Roofs:

■ Rafter and ceiling joist end bearing must be at least 1½" on wood or metal and 3" on concrete.

■ Rafters and ceiling joists with depth-to-thickness ratio of more than 5 must have lateral support at points of bearing.

■ Rafters and ceiling joists with depth-to-width ratios of more than 6 must be blocked, bridged, or restrained at bottom at 10 feet on center.

■ Drilling and notching of joists must not exceed ⅙ depth at top or bottom, be in middle ⅓ of span, or exceed ¼ depth at end ledger strip.

■ Holes in joists must not exceed ⅓ of depth or be within 2 inches of top or bottom.

■ Openings in ceilings and roofs must be framed with headers.

■ Roofs subject to 20 psf or more of wind uplift must have trusses or rafters effectively connected to the foundation.

■ Rafters not parallel to ceiling joists must have rafter ties as close to plate as possible and spaced no more than 4 feet.

EXTENDING A ROOF

The techniques for tying new roof framing to the old vary with the design. If the addition continues at the gable end, frame the new rafters parallel to the old. Double the existing rake (end) rafter and use it to start the new rafter layout.

If the ridge of the new roof runs perpendicular to the ridge of the existing roof, you'll need to establish the location of the new ridge beam. First, strip away roofing material from the old roof, exposing the sheathing past the point of the new ridge. Then mark the sheathing at the point where the new ridge beam will intersect. Transfer the angle of the roof pitch to the new ridge beam, and cut it to fit. Nail that end in place and support the other end with temporary bracing. Install all full-length rafters between the new ridge and the top plates of the new addition wall.

When this portion of the framing is complete, add a pair of 2×4 plates laid flat against the old sheathing and cut to fit between the top of the new ridge and the new wall plates. Use a straightedge laid across the tops of the rafters to help align jack rafters between these 2×4 plates and the ridge. Finally, install the lookouts and barge rafters.

NAILING SCHEDULE FOR WOOD FRAMING

Item	Method	Number	Size	Type
Band joist to joist	End	3	16d	Common
Band joist to sill	Toe	16" OC	10d	Common
Joist to sill	Toe	2	10d	Common
Bridging to joist	Toe	2	8d	Common
Ledger to beam	Face	3/16" OC	16d	Common
Sole plate to stud	End	2	16d	Common
Top plate to stud	End	2	16d	Common
Stud to sole plate	Toe	4	8d	Common
Sole plate to joist	Face	16" OC	16d	Common
Doubled studs	Face	16" OC	10d	Common
Double top plate	Face	16" OC	10d	Common
Double header	Face	12" OC	12d	Common
Ceiling joist to top plate	Toe	3	8d	Common
Overlapping joists	Face	4	16d	Common
Rafter to top plate	Toe	2	8d	Common
Rafter to ceiling joist	Face	5	10d	Common
Rafter to hip rafter	Toe	3	10d	Common
Rafter to valley rafter	Toe	3	10d	Common
Ridge board to rafter	End	3	10d	Common
Rafter to rafter	Toe	4	8d	Common
Collar tie (2") to rafter	Face	2	12d	Common
Collar tie (1") to rafter	Face	3	8d	Common
Let-in brace to stud	Face	2 each	8d	Common
Corner stud to stud	Face	12" OC	16d	Common
Built-up beam (3 or 4)	Face	32" OC	20d	Common

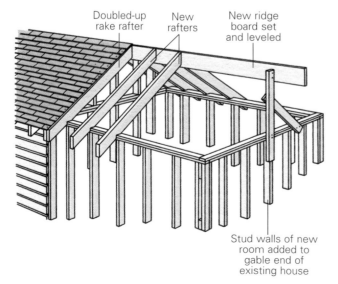

New roof ties to existing gable end

Doubled-up rake rafter

New rafters

New ridge board set and leveled

Stud walls of new room added to gable end of existing house

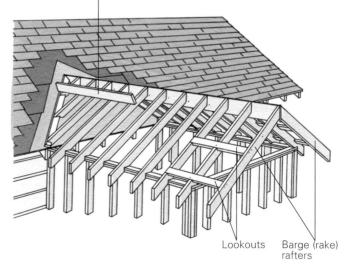

Line up and install jack rafters with a straightedge laid across other rafters

New roof runs perpendicular to existing roof

Lookouts

Barge (rake) rafters

As large-dimension framing lumber becomes increasingly expensive, roof trusses claim a greater share of the roof framing market. The illustrations at right compare the clear spans achieved with 2×6 rafters and ceiling joists with spans achieved using various truss designs.

Wood is much stronger in tension and compression than it is in bending. A roof triangle, formed by the two rafters and a ceiling joist, translates vertical roof loads into bending forces at right angles to the rafters and axial (tension and compression) forces in the rafters and joists.

The first illustration shows a simple roof triangle, consisting of rafters and a ceiling joist. Assuming roof loads of 10 psf dead (the roof itself) and 30 psf live, on-center spacing of 24 inches, and the use of No.2 Hem-fir lumber, the maximum span is 14'2".

The remaining illustrations depict trusses that break the rafter- and ceiling-joist span into smaller triangles. The tension and compression forces in the rafters (top chords of the truss) and the joists (truss bottom chord) remain the same, but the bending forces now act over smaller spans, so the total span (the sum of the smaller spans) increases dramatically. The modified queen post truss spans an amazing 42'3"! Up to a point, the larger the number of triangles, the larger the maximum span.

It's easy to understand why builders are turning to trusses. Economics 101: more span for the money.

Before you rush out and order trusses for your new addition, however, note that trusses pretty much eliminate the use of the attic as a useful space.

If you feel that trusses may solve a remodeling problem for you, talk to your local truss manufacturer. There are more than 400 manufacturers across the country, each offering free consultation services to help solve your problem.

WASTE NOT

Don't throw out crooked framing lumber until the job is done. You will be amazed at the number of short pieces the typical wall requires.

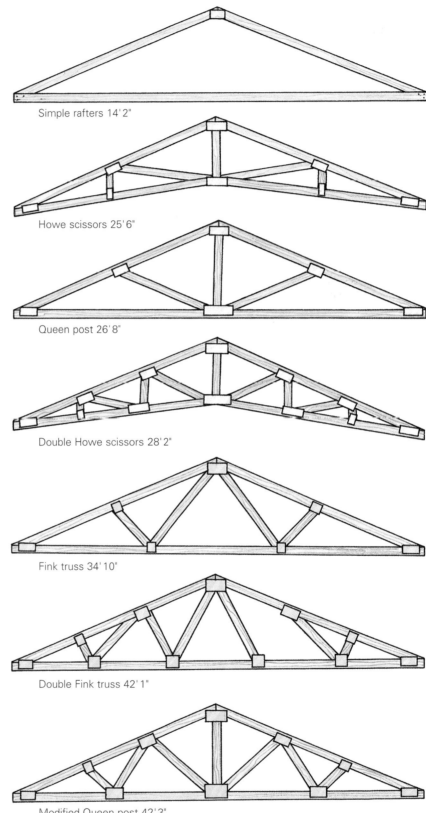

Simple rafters 14'2"

Howe scissors 25'6"

Queen post 26'8"

Double Howe scissors 28'2"

Fink truss 34'10"

Double Fink truss 42'1"

Modified Queen post 42'3"

FRAMING CONNECTORS

STRENGTHEN JOINTS QUICKLY AND EASILY

ALSO SEE...
Bracing:
Pages 36–37
Fasteners:
Pages 122–125
Floors:
Pages 140–141
Framing:
Pages 152–159
Roofs:
Pages 282–289
Walls:
Pages 406–413

Metal framing connectors were created as alternatives to traditional methods of toenailing, splicing, letting-in wood corner braces, and connecting large pieces of lumber. Used correctly, framing connectors make strong joints that withstand the exceptional amounts of stress that framing must endure. They are also valuable tools for creating buildings that must withstand extraordinary forces—exerted by hurricanes, tornadoes, earthquakes, and other localized phenomena.

Most framing connectors require specialized nails, sometimes called "teco" nails. These nails are designed to penetrate wood without splitting it, and they provide superior holding power. Use teco nails with the framing aids shown here to:

- Support joist and beam ends
- Brace walls against racking
- Strengthen splices and butt joints
- Provide earthquake and hurricane resistance
- Reinforce notches in joists and studs
- Keep wood from ground contact

DOS AND DON'TS

Metal joists hangers allow you to make strong joist connections—potentially. That potential won't be realized, however, unless they are installed to the manufacturer's specifications:

- Use the recommended number and size of fasteners.
- Make sure joists fit snugly between the hanger flanges to prevent rotation.
- The hanger must hang plumb so that the joist bottom bears evenly on the hanger.
- Allow no more than ⅛-inch gap at the joist end.
- With I-joists, make sure the joist top flange is restrained.

CODE REQUIREMENTS: CONNECTORS

There is little in the national building codes about the use of framing connectors. However, in areas of high wind (generally coastal and mountainous areas) and seismic regions, local codes generally require rafters to be tied all the way to the foundation through the use of a variety of metal framing aids.

If you are in such a region, make sure you understand the requirements and follow them.

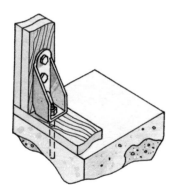

Anchor down

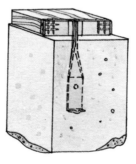

Foundation anchor

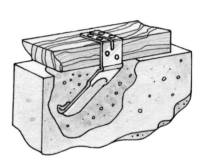

Foundation anchor

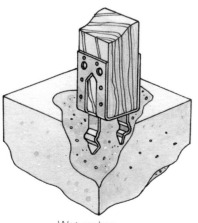

Wet anchor

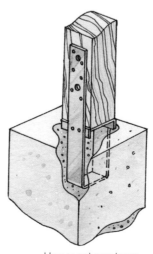

Heavy column base

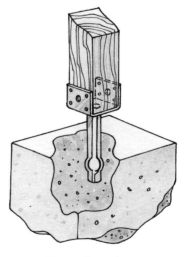

Elevated post base

Post beam cap

Post cap

Lally column cap

Multipurpose joist hanger

Joist hanger

Angle clip

Rafter / hurricane tie

Rafter / hurricane tie

Rafter / hurricane tie

Rolled strapping

Connector strap

Tension bridging

161

FURNACES

LOOK FOR EFFICIENCY AS WELL AS WARMTH

ALSO SEE...
Electrical Systems:
Pages 110–115
Energy:
Pages 116–117

Warm-air heating systems depend on a furnace to heat the air, using oil, gas, coal, wood, or electricity for fuel. Because of high heating costs and the relative inefficiency of older (10 years or more) furnaces, you should be interested in how you can increase the efficiency of your furnace and its distribution system.

Before turning your attention to the furnace itself, make sure the heating system is not wasting whatever heat the furnace produces. Insulate, caulk, and weather-strip your house. Be sure to insulate and seal leaks in all ducts that traverse unconditioned spaces. Balance the distribution of warm air throughout the house by adjusting the register dampers until each room is receiving just the amount of heat it needs. Finally, consider replacing an old thermostat with a new electronic model with setbacks.

By law, the efficiency of furnaces is rated by something called annual fuel utilization efficiency (AFUE)— the percentage of heat actually produced through the entire heating season compared with the heat potential in the fuel. The efficiency of most gas- and oil-fired furnaces installed twenty or so years ago is between 50 and 65 percent. Until a short time ago, new furnaces had ratings of 75 percent, but the current generation claims efficiency ratings of 90 percent or more. When it comes time to buy a new furnace, be a smart consumer. Read the section on Energy, page 116–117, and compare the long term savings of a more efficient furnace with the costs of the new equipment.

In the meantime, there are ways to improve the efficiency of an existing furnace without replacing it.

HOW FURNACES WORK

When your thermostat calls for heat, a heat source (gas burner, oil burner, electric coils, or heat pump) heats the heat exchanger. As soon as the heat exchanger reaches the appropriate temperature, the blower comes on, pulling cooled air through the return-air duct and furnace filter and pushing it through the heat exchanger. The warm air emerging from the heat exchanger enters the plenum where it is distributed to the individual ducts.

When the thermostat says, "enough," the burner turns off, but the blower continues sending air through the heat exchanger until its temperature falls.

If your house has central air-conditioning, its cooling coils will be located in the furnace plenum. By placing the coils inside the furnace, the air conditioner can share the blower and ducts with the furnace.

For the same reason, a central humidifier is often located in the plenum.

EFFICIENCY

You can install three devices that will have an impact on your fuel bills.

■ A flame-retention burner for oil furnaces operates at a higher rpm, burns more efficiently, and leaks less air up the chimney during off-times.

■ A gas conversion unit changes an oil-fired furnace to a gas-fired furnace, and will save money in areas where gas is cheaper per delivered Btu than oil.

■ An electronic spark igniter replaces the pilot light on a gas furnace, saving gas whenever the thermostat is not calling for heat (which is most of the time).

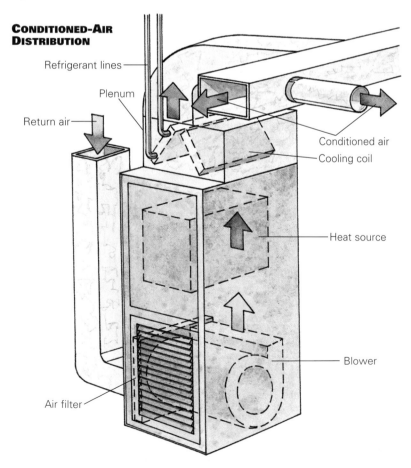

CONDITIONED-AIR DISTRIBUTION

Refrigerant lines

Plenum

Return air

Conditioned air

Cooling coil

Heat source

Blower

Air filter

HEAT DISTRIBUTION

A forced-air system blows heated air from the furnace to the living area through a system of ducts that end in room registers. The openings of these registers can usually be regulated by means of small levers that increase or decrease the amount of heat flowing into a room while the furnace is on. The air from the living space returns to the furnace through a separate set of ducts.

It is possible to divide the house into separate heating zones by installing thermostatically operated motorized dampers in the ducts.

EASY DOES IT

A dirty furnace filter makes your furnace work harder. Since the filter costs only a buck or two, you should change it every month during the heating season. To save trips to the home center, buy a case of filters at a discount.

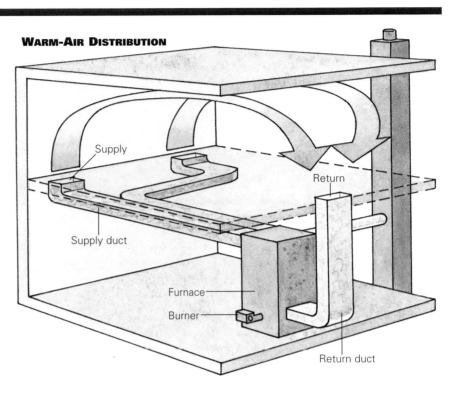

WARM-AIR DISTRIBUTION

Supply

Supply duct

Return

Furnace

Burner

Return duct

MAINTENANCE

No furnace will function efficiently for long if you don't maintain it. Ideally, you should have a furnace inspected and serviced annually by a qualified professional before the heating season begins. If you do your own maintenance, have it inspected professionally every three to five years.

The simplest maintenance chore is to clean or replace the furnace filter once a month. See the section below and the tip above about buying furnace filters.

Start every heating season with a thorough cleaning. Be sure the furnace is switched off (either the circuit breaker at the service panel or the red emergency switch near the furnace). Open the fan compartment and vacuum away all lint, dust, and debris. Then clean out the fire box or burner compartment. Use the vacuum brush attachment to remove soot and other debris from the walls of the chamber. Some walls are made of fragile fibrous materials, so vacuum carefully. If possible, remove the flue connection and vacuum it and the flue.

Next service the blower. Check the fan belt for tension; it should give about inch when you push down hard

with your finger. Adjust the belt tension by loosening the bolts and moving the motor mounting bracket.

You also can change the controls on the blower so it cycles the air at lower temperatures, allowing the blower to work even when the burner is not.

If the furnace is oil-fired, oil the bearings in the pump motor. Locate the fuel filter in the main oil line and change it once a year.

Every two to five years, the burners should be checked for proper adjustment, so the fuel and air mixture burns efficiently. This requires testing the flue gas for smoke. Black smudges around the inspection door to the burner compartment are a sign that an adjustment is needed. Even though gas burners can be adjusted by watching the flame, this should be done by a professional.

REPLACING FURNACE FILTERS

Changing a furnace air filter is a job that is easy and inexpensive. The filter keeps dust, soot, and other airborne grime out of the air that blows into your living area. Because air has more trouble passing through a dirty filter, your furnace has to work harder when

the filter gets dirty. Change the filter at least a couple of times during the primary heating season, and as often as every month if you live in a dusty area or if your furnace has to work long hours.

If you have central air-conditioning, you may have to replace the filter during the cooling season as well. The expense of a new filter—a dollar or two, depending on the size—will quickly be repaid by lower energy bills.

It isn't hard to change a furnace air filter. If, after reading the following instructions, you still have questions about how to do it, ask your furnace service person to demonstrate the process during the next routine visit, so you can do the task with confidence. First, turn off the thermostat. Then locate the metal panel near the blower that covers the filter. Remove the panel and slide the filter out. Slide the new filter in according to the air-flow arrows printed on it.

LOOKING FOR...
Garbage Disposers:
See **Sinks and Garbage Disposers,**
page 314

GLAZINGS

TYPES OF GLASS

ALSO SEE...
Cooling:
Pages 66–69
Greenhouses:
Pages 168–171
Insulation:
Pages 186–193
Solar Heating:
Pages 320–323
Windows:
Pages 432–441

Most of the windows in older homes contain sheet glass. It was manufactured in one of four thicknesses: single-strength ($\frac{3}{32}$ inch); double-strength ($\frac{1}{8}$ inch); and heavy ($\frac{3}{16}$ or $\frac{9}{32}$ inch). Plate glass, at least $\frac{1}{4}$ inch thick, was used for large windows, shelves, and tabletops. It was rolled into a flat plate while hot and plastic, then ground smooth and polished. Although plate glass is no longer manufactured by this method, the term is used generally to describe thick glass. Both sheet and plate glass have been replaced by float glass, made by pouring molten glass over a bed of molten metal. The glass floats on top of the metal and cools gradually. The resulting surfaces are smooth, parallel, and virtually free of distortion.

Safety Glass: Building codes require the use of specialty glass in "hazardous locations" such as doors and in windows within 18 inches of the floor (see Code Requirements, *below*). The code specifies the use of one of three types of specialty glass: tempered, laminated safety plate, or wire glass. Tempered glass is the most common. When it breaks, it disintegrates into small beads instead of large shards. Most manufacturers offer tempered glass as an option when you order prefabricated windows. The windows in a car are made of laminated safety glass. A thin adhesive film between two layers of glass keeps glass fragments from flying when the windows break. Wire glass is not often used in homes, but is an approved safety glass in many locations. It is a type of laminated glass with thin wire mesh between the layers.

Obscure Glass: Install obscure, or frosted, glass in bathrooms, entrance-hall windows, basement windows, and in any other setting where you desire privacy or diffused sunlight. Obscure glass is available in the same thicknesses as window glass.

Insulating Glass: Glass itself is a very poor insulator. The insulation provided by insulating glass is due almost entirely to an air space between two separate panes, not to an innate quality of the glass itself. The most effective insulating windows have the largest space between the glazings, up to $\frac{3}{4}$ inch. Units made of insulating glass are also called double-glazed or double-pane windows because each unit uses two sheets of glass. Triple-glazed windows are also available, but they have been largely replaced by double-glazed windows with low-E glass (see *below*). In the best windows, the manufacturer has also replaced all the air in the space with a gas which is a pool thermal conductor—usually argon. These units can provide up to 20 percent more insulation than units of regular insulating glass.

Windows with insulating glass are often expensive and difficult to replace when broken. It may be impossible to replace just the glass; instead, the entire sash (panes of glass and immediate frame) must be replaced.

Low-Emissivity Glass: Low-emissivity glass (or low-E glass, for short) has a clear, thin coating that admits most visible light but reflects on its interior surface some of the infrared (heat) energy that tries to escape. Low-E glass is particularly effective in double-glazed units where the coating is on the inside face of the exterior pane or is suspended on a thin plastic film between the panes. Most units carry insulating (R) values of 3 to 3.5, substantially more than double-glazed windows.

Reflective Glass: Reflective glass has a metallic coating that reflect half or more of direct sunlight. Reflective windows usually appear silver, bronze, or gray and are like one-way mirrors. Use reflective glass in rooms that are subject to overheating due to excess solar gain.

Tinted Glass: Tinted, or heat-absorbing glass, reduces sunlight and glare. The tinting material is not a coating but a metallic oxide that is mixed into the ingredients. Iron oxide produces a bluish green tint. Nickel oxide, cobalt oxide, and selenium produce a bronze or gray tint. The intensity of the color depends on the thickness of the glass. Tinted glass lets in more light than reflective glass, and its ability to reduce heat gain is therefore less.

Low-Iron Glass: Glass free of iron oxide admits a higher percentage of visible light than does ordinary window glass. The clarity of low-iron glass makes it a good choice for picture frames. Also use it where you desire solar heat gain, such as in windows that face south or in solar-collector panels. You can identify low-iron glass by its lack of the familiar greenish tint of ordinary glass.

CODE REQUIREMENTS: GLAZING

Glazing in hazardous areas must be of tempered or some other type of safety glass. Locations specified in the code:

■ Ingress and egress (entrance) doors, except jalousies
■ Patio doors
■ Swinging (revolving) doors
■ Storm doors
■ Unframed swinging doors
■ Doors and enclosures for tubs, showers, hot tubs, saunas, steam rooms, and whirlpools where the bottom of the glazing is less than 60 inches above the drain
■ Any area greater than 9 square feet with bottom edge less than 18 inches above the floor, top edge more than 36 inches above the floor, and within 36 inches horizontally of a walking surface
■ Walls and fences enclosing swimming pools where the bottom edge of pool side is less than 60 inches above and less than 36 inches horizontally from a walking surface
■ Any glazing in a railing

Exceptions:
■ Door openings less than 3 inches in diameter
■ Leaded-glass panels
■ Faceted and decorative glass
■ Mirrors mounted on flush or panel doors
■ Mirrors mounted or hung on walls
■ Louvered windows and jalousies at least $\frac{3}{16}$ inches thick and no more than 48 inches long with smooth edges

OTHER GLAZINGS

ACRYLIC (PLEXIGLAS®)

Acrylic is a lightweight plastic that actually passes more visible light than clear glass. Acrylic is easily scratched, however, and turns slightly yellow after a few years in direct sunlight. Acrylic also has a high thermal expansion coefficient, making large sheets difficult to seal against moisture. It insulates as well as or better than clear glass. Acrylic often is used in domed skylights and as a substitute for glass in certain situations, such as clear coverings for artwork in children's rooms, or as the clear panels for bookshelf doors or other pieces of furniture that may be subject to accidental knocks.

Acrylic sheets can be purchased at home-improvement centers. They come protected by a thin plastic film that helps prevent scratches during shipping. If you are cutting acrylic sheets, use a carbide-tipped power saw and leave the protective film in place until you have finished your cuts.

POLYCARBONATE (LEXAN®)

Polycarbonate plastic is much tougher than acrylic—so much so that it can be used as a substitute for tempered glass in code-defined "hazardous areas." Polycarbonate is also vulnerable to the ultraviolet rays in sunlight and is not quite as transparent as acrylic. Like acrylic, it expands and contracts with changes in temperature.

FIBERGLASS (FIBERGLAS®)

Polyester panels with fiberglass reinforcing fibers are available in flat or corrugated sheets. Easy to handle, easy to cut and drill, fairly stable in terms of thermal expansion, more transparent than glass to solar radiation, yet resistant to ultraviolet rays, fiberglass panels are excellent for greenhouse and solar-collector applications. They are not used for windows, however, because they are translucent rather than transparent.

FILMS

Films (thin sheets of plastic applied to glass surfaces) may improve the insulating, shading, or reflecting performance of your windows. Some films are clear and emulate low-E glass. Some are tinted bronze, gray, or gold. Other films are silver and reflective. Some films help glass retain interior heat while allowing maximum solar gain. Others block sunlight. Be selective in applying films. Each type serves a specific purpose—don't expect it to do more than one job.

Insulating films are most effective when applied on north-facing windows. If you wish to reduce heat gain, apply the appropriate film on windows facing east and west. Apply film to windows that face south only if heat gain is a problem all year. Follow the manufacturer's instructions carefully, especially if you apply the film to double-glazed windows.

LOW-COST SOLARIUM

Need a lot of high-R glass cheap, so you can construct a thermally efficient solarium for minimal cost? Try patio-door replacement units. These glazings are plentiful because they commonly are used by manufacturers to build patio doors. Because of the volume, they represent your best window deal. They come in three standard sizes: 28×76, 34×76, and 46×76. Call your local glass dealer for prices. You will be pleasantly astounded.

ENERGY RATINGS OF GLAZINGS

You can compare the energy performance of windows with these ratings, supplied by the manufacturers:

Unit "R": the average R-value of the entire unit.

Unit "U": the inverse of Unit "R."

Winter R-value: the R-value at the center of the glazing (ignoring the effects of the frame) with no sunlight and a glass temperature of 70°F.

Glass Shading Coefficient: the ratio of the total solar heat gain to the gain of a single ⅛-inch-thick clear glass.

Visible Light Transmission: the percentage of light in the visible spectrum that passes through the glazing.

Relative Heat Gain: the total heat gain, in Btu per hour, of 1 square foot of glazing when exposed to 200 Btu per square foot per hour of solar radiation and an outdoor temperature 14°F higher than inside.

HOW GLASS IS HELD IN SASHES

WOOD SASH

In a wood sash, the glass pane should be ⅛ inch smaller in both dimensions than the opening. The pane rests on a thin bed of glazing compound and is held in place by glazier's points. Glazing compound seals the glazing against rain.

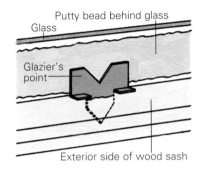

METAL SASH

In a metal sash the glazing is installed the same way as in a wood sash, except the glazier's points are replaced by metal spring clips.

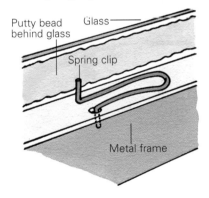

ALUMINUM STORM SASH

Aluminum storm sashes have extruded channels which slip over the glazing and a rubber or vinyl gasket. You have to take the frame apart to replace the glazing.

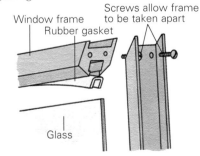

CUTTING GLAZINGS

PLASTICS

All plastics are so soft you can cut them with a saw. If they have protective paper or film attached, use it to mark the cut, and leave it on until you are finished cutting. Use a fine-toothed blade, or cut very slowly so that you don't fracture the plastic by taking too big a bite at once.

GLASS

If you need just a single piece, take your measurements to a glass shop or a good hardware store. Measure accurately because, once the glass has been cut, it is nearly impossible to trim it by anything less than a whole inch!

If you have a number of pieces to cut, however, it is worth learning to cut it yourself.

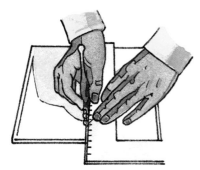

To cut glass, all you need is a steel framing square and a glass cutter. Practice the technique on a scrap

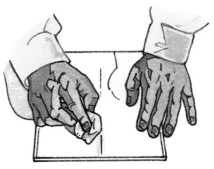

before cutting a large piece of glass. Mark the point where the cut begins by lightly nicking the glass with the cutter. Wipe the line to be cut with

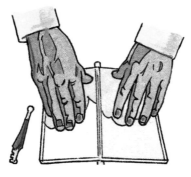

kerosene or turpentine, which helps reduce the chances of chipping the glass. Then hold a steel framing square along the line to guide your cutter. Make the cut in a firm, smooth, single pass. Just score the glass; pressing too hard will chip it. Don't ever go over the line a second time—you'll just get

a sloppy break. Instead, turn the glass over and score it on the other side.

Quickly, move the glass to the edge of the work table, or place a dowel under the score and bend it downward.

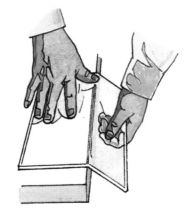

You must do this right away because—believe it or not—the glass will start to heal! If all goes well, the glass will snap cleanly along the scored line, and you will feel like a master glass cutter!

If the cut is less than perfect, however, nibble away little projections with the notches on the backside of the glass cutter.

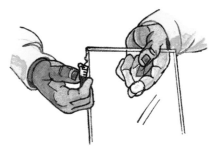

ENERGY CHARACTERISTICS OF GLAZINGS

Type of Glazing	Winter R-value	Shading Coefficient	Heat Gain Btu/Sq Ft-Hr	Light Transmission
SINGLE GLAZINGS				
Clear ⅛"	0.86	1.00	215	90%
Clear ¼"	0.88	0.95	204	88%
Heat-absorbing ¼"	0.88	0.69	154	41%
Heat-reflecting ¼"	0.88	0.71	157	52%
Acrylic (Plexiglas) ⅛"	0.94	1.02	—	92%
Acrylic (Plexiglas) ¼"	1.04	1.00	—	90%
DOUBLE GLAZINGS				
Clear ½" gap	2.00	0.82	172	80%
Heat-absorbing ½" gap	2.04	0.54	116	36%
Heat-reflecting ½" gap	2.04	0.56	119	46%
Low-E ½" gap	3.85	0.68	139	78%
Heat mirror HM88 ¼" gap	4.30	0.62	128	70%

WINDOWS WET?

Do you have a problem with moisture on your windows in winter? Here is a quick guide to the window R-value required to prevent condensation at different room relative humidities (RH):

RH	R-value 1	2	3	4
80%	60°F	49°F	38°F	30°F
70%	55°F	38°F	23°F	9°F
60%	49°F	27°F	6°F	-14°F
50%	42°F	13°F	-15°F	—
40%	34°F	-3°F	—	—
30%	24°F	-25°F	—	—

1 *Remove the shards of broken glass. If the window is merely cracked, apply masking tape in a big X, then break the glass further with a hammer.*

2 *Chip out old putty and points. If the putty is hard to remove, use a heat gun to soften it.*

3 *Coat bare wood with a primer recommended by the manufacturer of the glazing compound. This will help the compound to adhere.*

4 *Apply a thin cushion layer of glazing compound. The cushion also helps seal the glazing against moisture.*

5 *Press the glazing uniformly into the cushion layer, then fix in place with glazier's points.*

6 *Roll the glazing compound into a "snake" and press it into place. Don't worry about its appearance at this point.*

7 *Smooth with a firm, steady stroke of a putty knife. After the compound is dry to the touch, paint it, sealing it to the glass. Then scrape the excess off the glass with a single-edge razor blade.*

HELP FOR STICKY WINDOWS

Wood sash windows that don't operate smoothly probably are warped or have too much paint buildup. Strip sticky windows and repaint them. Check for warping with a straightedge. If the sash is warped, use a hand plane to remove the bow, then repaint the window. To help windows glide up and down, rub paraffin along the sash before reinstalling them.

GREENHOUSES

CREATE YOUR OWN GROWING ENVIRONMENT

A greenhouse, once a luxury within the budgets of only the wealthy, is today a structure almost anyone can build from scratch or from a kit. Different designs fit different spaces: a tiny backyard, rooftop, balcony, or even a window. The only thing that might stop you is lack of an unshaded southern exposure.

Though greenhouses have been traditionally found in the garden, you will enjoy yours more if it is attached to your home. With the right design and size, an attached greenhouse will expand the living space of the house and even help to heat it.

The benefits are evident whenever you set foot in a greenhouse; it is like entering another world—or at least another season. It may be snowing outside, but inside you work among exotic arrays of tropical flowers or enjoy a flourishing garden of ripening vegetables.

SITING REQUIREMENTS

Choose a site where the sun will not be blocked by houses, walls, or trees. Keep in mind that winter sun is lower in the sky than summer sun. The sun must shine directly on the greenhouse for at least four hours on December 21 if you plan to use it in winter.

In summer the hottest sun will come from directly overhead and slightly to the north of due west from 3 to 5 in the afternoon.

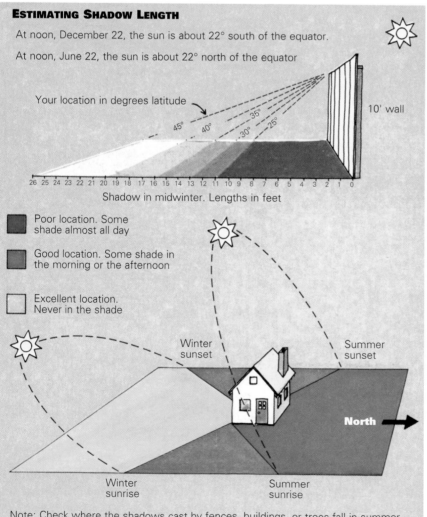

ESTIMATING SHADOW LENGTH

At noon, December 22, the sun is about 22° south of the equator.

At noon, June 22, the sun is about 22° north of the equator

Your location in degrees latitude

45° 40° 35° 30° 25°

10' wall

26 25 24 23 22 21 20 19 18 17 16 15 14 13 12 11 10 9 8 7 6 5 4 3 2 1 0

Shadow in midwinter. Lengths in feet

Poor location. Some shade almost all day

Good location. Some shade in the morning or the afternoon

Excellent location. Never in the shade

Winter sunset

Summer sunset

North

Winter sunrise

Summer sunrise

Note: Check where the shadows cast by fences, buildings, or trees fall in summer and winter. Locate a greenhouse where there is a minimum amount of shade.

IS A GREENHOUSE RIGHT FOR YOU?

PURPOSE

Start by identifying the primary purposes your greenhouse will serve. Do you want it to:

- Display plants
- Propagate and grow plants
- Extend the growing season for only one or two months
- Reduce your heating bill
- Provide a sunny living area

Some of these purposes are incompatible. Plants require a lot of moisture; houses can be damaged by too much moisture. If the greenhouse is primarily for growing plants, then it cannot provide much warm air to the house, nor will it be a very good living space. If warmth and a sunny space is what you want, go to Solar Heating, pages 320–323.

SIZE

A walk-in greenhouse should be at least 6 feet wide. The layout should allow you to walk through easily and provide room for benches on both sides.

STYLE

Greenhouses come in all shapes and styles. The type you choose depends on how permanent you want the structure to be, where you want to locate it, whether you live in a snowy climate, and the dictates of your taste and pocketbook.

The simplest greenhouse is an A-frame structure with two sloping sides joined at the top. An A-frame is relatively easy to construct and it sheds snow well, but provides limited room. The solution is bending the sides into an arch. Commercial greenhouse suppliers offer "Gothic-arch" tubular frames for this purpose.

ATTACHED OR FREESTANDING?

A greenhouse that attaches to a house wall is less expensive and easier to build than a detached greenhouse. There is one less wall to build, the house braces the flimsy greenhouse, utilities are nearby, and access is convenient. An attached greenhouse will help somewhat to heat the home, but you have to limit the infusion of moisture, and you must shut it off at night to prevent excessive heat loss.

KITS

Consider time, cost, and complexity of design in deciding how much of the work to do yourself. Kits for simple rectangular greenhouses can save time, particularly if you have limited carpentry skills. They can look like they've been installed by a professional, and manufacturers have worked out problems of decay resistance and ventilation. If you are knowledgeable about basic framing techniques, however, you can save more than half the cost of a kit by building from scratch.

ENERGY EFFICIENCY

Unless you plan to shut down the greenhouse in winter, it will need a secondary heat source, such as a gas or electric heater. Solar greenhouses include heat-absorbing materials, such as masonry or water barrels, a calculated ratio of glass area to potential heat gain, and window insulation that retains heat during cold periods. It is possible to include all of these features in your design.

CONTROLLING THE ENVIRONMENT

Greenhouse plants cannot survive long without care. Minister to your plants by maintaining, heating, cooling, and humidifying the greenhouse, as well as feeding, watering, and spraying the plants for insects. To minimize the time spent tending the greenhouse, automate as many of these systems as possible.

MAINTENANCE

Ensure that the greenhouse is as airtight as possible by weather-stripping the door and vents and sealing the joints between roof and walls with permanently flexible caulk. Check that all of the glazing is snug in its frame. In cold climates line the walls and roof with a layer of ultraviolet-resistant clear plastic sheeting (available through greenhouse supply companies) at least 4 mils thick. Staple it inside the glazing, leaving a 1 to 4 inch air space between.

HEATING

To determine the required heat output of your heating system, add up the total surface area (SA) in square feet of the ceiling and walls; do not include the floor. Next calculate the degree rise (DR)—the difference between the coldest outdoor temperature in the past several years and the minimum temperature you wish to maintain in the greenhouse. A typical minimum greenhouse temperature is 55° F. Now select the insulating factor (U). Assign a value of 1.0 to single glass and fiberglass glazings and 0.6 to a double layer of either. Multiply: SA × DR × U to yield the heat loss per hour in BTUs. The output of the heat supplied to the greenhouse must equal or exceed this heat loss.

Example: You are building a greenhouse which has 480 square feet of double-layered roof and walls. You want to maintain 55°F at the lowest expected outdoor temperature of -10°F. The output of the heater must be:

SA × DR × U =
480 × 65 × 0.6 =
18,720 BTU/hr.

To alert you when the fuel runs out or the heater quits for any other reason, install a battery-powered, temperature-sensitive alarm. If the greenhouse is attached to your home

and the heating system fails, you can at least prevent a freeze-up by blowing warm house air into the structure using a large box or window fan.

Reduce heating costs by installing thermal mass—any dense material that will absorb the direct rays of the sun, will prevent overheating during the day, and release the heat back to the structure at night. A concrete slab and stacked concrete blocks will store solar heat.

If a south wall greenhouse is freestanding instead of attached, construct a solid, rather than a glazed, north wall. Insulate it and incorporate thermal mass into it.

The air in a greenhouse should circulate for two reasons: (1) to allow the plants to breathe, by taking in carbon dioxide and giving off oxygen and water vapor and (2) to prevent hot air from collecting at the ceiling, while frigid air blankets the plants at floor level. A heater with a combination fan and thermostat is a favorite with greenhouse owners because it distributes warm air evenly throughout the structure. An inexpensive alternative is one or more ceiling fans.

COOLING

In most of the country, cooling the greenhouse in summer is a greater problem than heating it in winter. In a few areas, simple shades, fans, and an open roof vent are sufficient; where summer temperatures are constantly above 80 degrees, you need to install more elaborate cooling systems.

If you go with mechanical cooling, install an automatic system with thermostats. Buy a two-speed fan and use the lower speed during spring and fall. The thermostats should be designed for greenhouse use so humidity will not damage them. In addition, conditions may warrant thermal pistons that open and close vents, screens to block sunlight, and, in extremely hot regions, an evaporative cooler. As an alternative, move the plants outside and abandon the greenhouse for the summer.

▶

OUTFITTING THE GREENHOUSE

With the basic greenhouse structure and glazing in place, you are ready to install benches and other permanent structures. Place benches in long rows with an aisle down the center. Or place short benches at right angles to the center aisle. Since a greenhouse is primarily for growing plants, give up no more than one quarter of the floor area to aisles.

Benches can be attractive as well as functional. Build simple platforms by nailing ledges or backboards to the wall studs. At the ends build short box legs, then lay long planks over them. The benches should be easy to reach, no more than 36 inches deep. Place shelves above the benches on the back wall and below the benches on both sides according to your need for display and storage space.

Designate a shady area as a potting center. Build a rim around the bench to keep soil from spilling over. Other amenities include a sink, tool racks, shelves, and locked storage cabinets.

Your final chore before placing plants in the greenhouse is to sanitize it. You don't want to start right off with a plant disease or pest. The quickest and easiest way to sanitize is to wash everything down with a fresh solution of 1 part liquid household chlorine bleach to 10 parts water. Apply the solution with a sprayer. Scrub all surfaces, including crevices, crannies, benches, walls, and floors.

The greenhouse is now ready for plants, although you still need to fine-tune its environment.

A SIMPLE COLD FRAME

A greenhouse doesn't have to be a large walk-in structure. You can derive great pleasure from a mini version— a cold frame. The traditional cold frame has a clear top that is angled to directly face the low winter sun. It is often constructed with scrap lumber and discarded wood storm windows. If you don't have any old storms, you can buy them at a salvage yard for a couple of dollars apiece. Notch the horizontal mullions or dividers to allow standing water to escape.

White or silver paint on the inside helps reflect more light to the plants.

Don't, however, use aluminum foil because it can focus the sunlight and burn the plants.

Place a thermometer inside the frame and shield it from the direct rays of the sun. When the temperature is high, prop the top open to let the excess heat out. Close it again when the temperatures start to drop. This will conserve the radiation that has been absorbed by the soil.

In practice, cold frames are usually opened in the morning and then closed as soon as the direct rays of the sun have passed over.

THE WINDOW GREENHOUSE

Install a prefabricated greenhouse as a window in an existing or new opening. A window greenhouse provides an attractive addition that can be enjoyed by both the indoor grower and by people passing by.

The window greenhouse is a big step up from a windowsill garden. It is more than just a bay window with room for plants; it closes on the inside so the plants are in their own environment and not subject to the drying effects of the house. The small size of a window greenhouse can create a problem, however. As soon as sunlight hits the window, the greenhouse warms rapidly. At night, it cools quickly. Vents that connect to the outside and vents from the room enable you to keep the greenhouse environment stable.

The location of a window greenhouse depends on the effect you want to achieve and the plants you want to grow. To get maximum sunlight, especially during the winter months, choose a window that faces south. A window that faces east gets morning and midday sun. A western window gets midday and afternoon sun, and a northern window—forget the northern windows! If you put a unit where the plants you want to grow will not get enough sunlight, install fluorescent lighting to supplement natural light.

STEP-BY-STEP INSTALLATION

1. Measure the existing window and order a greenhouse at least 2 inches larger in width and height.

GREENHOUSE KITS

If you have a little extra money, but are short on time, patience, or basic carpentry skills, consider purchasing a greenhouse kit.

Kits range from models with simple tubing and polyethylene framing, all the way up to redwood and tempered-glass models. They frequently are advertised in gardening and home-improvement magazines, described as sunspaces, solar greenhouses, sun porches, or growing environments. Regardless of what they are called, all can be used as either living spaces or as greenhouses for plants.

A responsible kit manufacturer will make an effort to help you select an appropriate site. If the greenhouse is to be attached to your house, the manufacturer will advise you to select a kit that is compatible with your house and its exterior finish materials. Either a representative will visit your home or the manufacturer will send you forms and instructions that allow you to determine whether you have adequate direct sun and which size and model will fit your house.

The illustration *below* shows a typical add-on greenhouse. The panels

are modular, so that you can order a model 6, 9, 12, or 15 feet deep, with the length of your choice. The panels shown are designed to easily convert from double-glazed, insulating acrylic glazing for use during colder months, to screened panels for the summer. Many modular greenhouse kits have optional storage units for glazed panels or screens when they are not in use. Thus, the same structure can be a sunspace/greenhouse in winter and a screened-in porch in summer.

2. Remove the existing window sash by first removing one of the interior window stops.

3. If the greenhouse frame is larger than the exterior window trim, install a frame of 1×6 lumber. Slide Z-flashing under the siding and over the top of the frame.

4. Paint the frame to match the existing trim, and caulk it to the siding.

5. Weather-strip the frame where the greenhouse frame will be attached.

6. Lift the greenhouse into place and screw it firmly to the frame.

7. Install the interior shelves and the vents and shades that come with the greenhouse.

HUMIDITY CONTROL

Greenhouses—even small window units—are enclosed environments that trap humidity. While many varieties of plants enjoy moist, humid conditions, too much humidity can create conditions that encourage leaf mold and stem rot. Your greenhouse should include a ventilation system to promote healthy air circulation and prevent trapping excess humidity. Simple venting systems include a fresh-air intake located at the lower portion of a greenhouse wall, and an exit vent located near the uppermost portion. That way, natural warm-air convection currents will keep air circulating. Larger greenhouses may require power-assisted venting—fans—to help reduce excess heat.

GUTTERS AND DOWNSPOUTS

INTRODUCTION

ALSO SEE...
Drainage:
Pages 102–103
Roofs:
Pages 282–289

Gutters collect roof runoff and channel it into downspouts that direct water away from the house and foundation. Without gutters, water drips onto people's heads and the ground next to the foundation. The splash-back stains the siding and deposits dirt on the lowest courses. Worse, when the soil next to foundation walls becomes saturated with rainwater, moisture may seep into a crawl space or through basement walls.

COMPONENTS

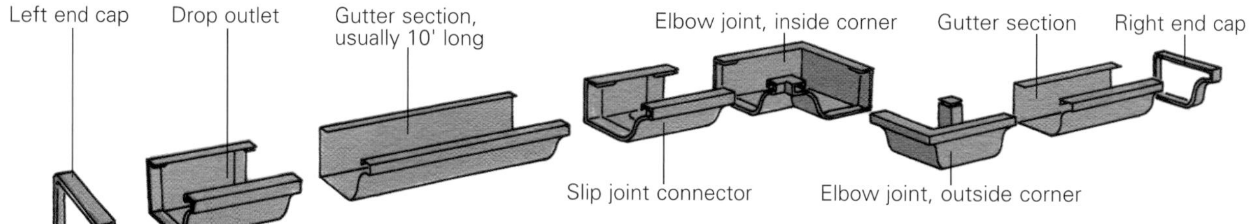

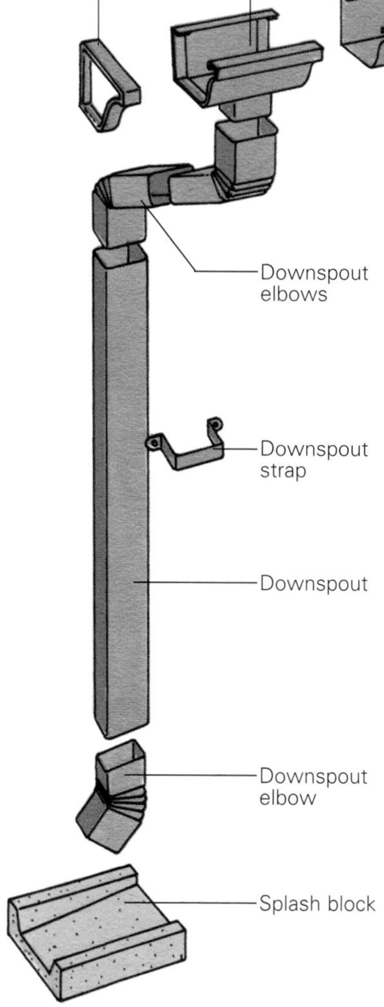

Left end cap · Drop outlet · Gutter section, usually 10' long · Elbow joint, inside corner · Gutter section · Right end cap · Slip joint connector · Elbow joint, outside corner · Downspout elbows · Downspout strap · Downspout · Downspout elbow · Splash block

Gutters and downspouts typically are sold in 10-foot lengths. Standard gutter widths are 4 inches, 5 inches, or 6 inches. As a general rule, a 4-inch gutter will handle the runoff from about 750 square feet of roof. You can double that to 1,500 square feet by sloping the gutter in opposite directions to two downspouts.

A 6-inch gutter will handle twice the load of a 4-inch gutter. However, all gutter components will have to match the 6-inch gutter.

The illustration shows all of the standard components required to install a complete gutter system. Note that in some systems, inside and outside corners are interchangeable, in others, they are not. If the downspout is square, a square elbow can be used to change direction to the right or left.

When buying parts for a complete installation, purchase more than you estimate you'll need and return any leftovers. It is easy to underestimate the number of hangers and connectors required.

HANGERS

If you live in a heavy-snow area, the weight of snow and ice your gutters will support at some times is considerable. To avoid droopy gutters install twice the number of gutter hangers recommended by the manufacturer.

AN EASY FIT

If you have difficulty getting vinyl gutter parts to mate, apply a little liquid detergent to the joint. The detergent acts as a lubricant, but will disappear in the first rainstorm (albeit in a cloud of bubbles!).

WHERE WILL THE WATER GO?

Before installing gutters, make sure you know where the downspouts will discharge. If it's directly into low spots next to the foundation, you might be better off with no gutters at all!

If the ground slopes toward the foundation, you can install leaders (sections of downspout) that lead the water far away from the house. A neat installation is to have the downspout discharge vertically into a 4-inch drainpipe which leads underground to a dry well, drainage ditch, or storm sewer.

SELECTING MATERIALS

Unless your home is historic or architecturally significant, use painted aluminum or vinyl gutters.

Home centers usually carry both types, including the dozens of fittings required for the average job.

Both aluminum and vinyl come in white and dark brown. Select the color that is most compatible with the color of your house. You can paint either, but by doing so you lose one of their greatest advantages—freedom from maintenance.

Your home center probably stocks only 10-foot lengths, 4-inch widths, and the colors white and brown. Greater lengths and widths and other colors may be available by special order, although at a significantly higher cost.

INSTALLATION

Measure the length of all eaves to calculate the number of 10-foot gutter sections. Plan to install one bracket every 3 to 4 feet (every 2 to 3 feet in snow country). Count the numbers of inside corners, outside corners, right end caps, and left end caps.

You will need a drop outlet for each length of gutter; place outlets no more than 40 feet apart. Each outlet will need three elbows and one or more lengths of downspout. Add a few extra lengths for elbows and bends. Don't forget the straps for the downspouts; plan to install a strap every 6 feet.

Now count how many slip connectors you need to join sections of gutter. You do not need connectors where gutter sections meet at corners or drop outlets. Finally, add up the number of splash blocks or leaders you will need under all the downspouts to divert water away from the house.

Installing the Gutters: Gutters should slope about 1 inch for every 20 feet. If you have a run of 40 feet or more, slope the gutters from the middle of the run and put a downspout at each end. To lay out the gutter slope, tack a nail to the fascia board at the high end of the slope. Measure the run, dropping 1 inch every 20 feet. Tack a nail at the final position and snap a chalk line between the two nails to use as a guide.

Lay out all the components on the ground. Measure the gutter runs and note the downspout locations. Cut the gutters accordingly, using a hacksaw. On painted gutters, use tin snips to minimize the shattering of enamel paint. To steady the gutters while sawing, slip a length of 2×4 in the gutter about one inch behind the cut. Then squeeze the gutter against the block. Use a file to remove burrs (ragged edges) from the cut edge.

If you do not have a helper, hang the far end of the gutter in a loop of string from a guide nail. When all of the pieces are secure, caulk each joint to prevent leaks.

Installing the Downspouts: Connect the downspout elbows to the drop outlet by drilling holes on opposite sides and inserting sheet-metal screws. Connect the elbows to the downspouts in the same manner. Bend the straps to fit the downspout, then screw them to the siding. Fit the elbow on the end of the downspout and place a splash block under it. If you wish to carry the water farther from the house, attach a length of downspout to the elbow.

REPAIRING GUTTER SUPPORTS

Most gutters droop and fail simply because the supports let go. The most common problem is the separation of the bracket from its supporting strap. There are three different methods of repair:

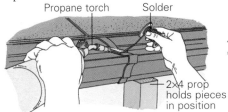

1 Soldering: This works only if the straps are galvanized steel or copper. Support the gutter temporarily in its desired position. Clean the bracket and strap with solvent so they are free of grease and dirt, then sand all of the oxidized surface off the metal. When the metal is bright, coat the two surfaces with flux, heat them with a torch, and touch the solder to the joint when it is hot enough to melt the solder.

2 Bolts: Drill a hole through both pieces and connect them with a galvanized stove bolt, washer, and nut.

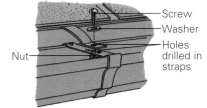

3 Sheet-Metal Screws: To attach a new aluminum strap, drill small pilot holes in the old bracket, and install the new strap with galvanized sheet-metal screws.

GUTTER GUARDS

DOWNSPOUT GUARDS

To prevent a downspout from filling with leaves and other debris, install a downspout guard. A downspout guard  is a perforated cover that you can insert in or over the drain hole. Or fashion your own from a piece of galvanized hardware cloth— a coarse screen. Clean guards out periodically to prevent the gutters from backfilling.

GUTTER COVERS

These are screens which keep leaves and other coarse debris out of the gutters so they won't accumulate, rot, and eventually dam the flow. Some gutter manufacturers offer matching gutter covers which slide into slots at the tops of the gutters. Otherwise, buy covers which slide under the first course of shingles and fit flush with the front of the gutter.

HANGERS

Gutters hang from eaves in a number of ways. You can use straps (these must be installed before the roofing is applied), brackets, or driven long spikes across the gutter through a spacer tube (ferrule).

Straps: Nail the strap to the roof beneath the first course of shingles. Insert the gutter from below and hook the hanger to itself under the gutter at the fascia.

Clips: Nail this hanger to the vertical fascia. Insert the gutter from above and snap the hanger clip across the top.

Spikes: Drive special gutter spikes through the gutter and spacer tubes, then into the fascia.

Spacer tube

NARROWING THE CHOICES

Hinges, pulls, catches, and knobs are basic hardware items that are chosen for their decorative value as much as for their practical function. The array of options is overwhelming, as you will see in visiting the cabinet hardware section of the nearest home center. The choices narrow considerably, however, when you consider the type of doors they will be used on and the overall design scheme.

Mounting hinges, pulls, catches, and knobs is usually about the last step in a kitchen- or bath-improvement project. Because these are the finishing touches, you might be encouraged to rush the installation. Don't. Haste leads to waste and to mistakes that will annoy you every day—when a door sticks, when pulls or knobs are not aligned, or when a door swings the wrong way. This is a job for thinkers and planners, as well as for those with a sense of design.

Most hardware requires only basic hand tools for installation, although a variable-speed drill with drill bits, plus a Phillips screwdriver will prove most useful of all. In addition, a router might be required to install certain recessed hinges.

A gimlet is a handy hand tool for starting screws; it resembles a screwdriver but has a conical threaded point at the end for making pilot holes without a drill. One size gimlet fits all screw sizes.

CABINET HINGES

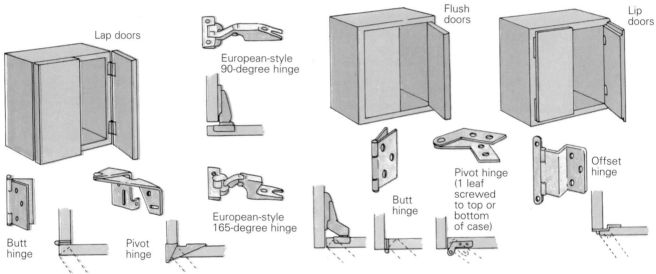

Lap Doors: Attach lap doors (square-edged doors which lap over the face of a cabinet) directly to the cabinet face with butt, pivot, or "European" hinges. Butt hinges can be seen from the side and require room beyond the edge of the cabinet for the doors to clear. Pivot hinges, screwed to the top and bottom edges of the door, don't require side clearance, but show their edges, top and bottom. The more expensive European-style hinges don't show at all. Instead, they are mounted entirely inside the cabinet body. Use European-style hinges with "frameless" cabinets for a sleek, contemporary look.

Flush Doors: Butt hinges for flush doors (doors whose faces are flush with the face of the cabinet) are mortised into the edges of the cabinet stiles and door to reduce the size of the gap. Pivot hinges are mortised into the top and bottom edges of each door. Decorative face hinges can be mounted to purposely show either one or both leaves. The Soss hinge, named for its inventor, is completely concealed.

Lip Doors: Lip doors (doors with rabbeted edges which partially overlap the cabinet face) use hinges that show one narrow leaf. They are not usually mortised into the doors or the cabinet frame. The popular bent-leaf, also called an offset hinge, comes in sizes to fit rabbets of different thicknesses, so be sure you have the right size. Like other types of hinges, one variation includes a spring for self-closing.

BUY IN BULK

If you are doing a whole kitchen, purchase knobs and hinges by the "contractor pack" at the home center. This generous supply will include enough hardware to complete a moderate-sized kitchen, and could save you about 50 percent!

START WITH THE DOORS

When installing cabinet doors, always mount the hinges on the doors first. You will find it nearly impossible to install a door on already-installed cabinet hinges without help.

PULLS

Be careful in selecting pulls. Nothing can date your cabinets more easily than out-of-style pulls. Because fads change, the safest designs to choose are simple or classical shapes. If a sleek and uncluttered look is desired, you can avoid pulls altogether, relying on finger grooves under the cabinet doors and drawers, and touch latches on full-sized doors. If the application is rustic or nautical, you can simply drill 1-inch finger holes through the door!

If you are changing the pulls or knobs on your cabinets, check to see whether the existing hardware is mounted with one or two screws. If two screws, make sure you measure the distance between the screws exactly. Unlike sink faucets, with cabinet pulls there are no standards for screw spacing. If you don't use the old holes you are likely to end up with at least one empty screw hole in the door or drawer.

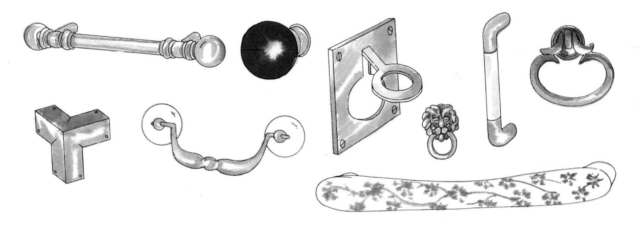

KNOBS

Some knobs have female threads to accept machine screws inserted from the backside of the door or drawer. Other knobs have clearance holes to accept either screws or machine bolts inserted through the knob into the door. Although less attractive (the head of the screw shows), the latter is the stronger because the screw can never break free of the knob internally. Also, the clearance hole makes it possible to use any type of screw or bolt that will fit through the hole, instead of having to match the thread.

CATCHES

There are three basic types of catches—the devices which keep a cabinet door closed.

■ Magnetic catches have a flat steel plate on the inside of the door and a loosely attached magnet inside the cabinet. Because the magnet "floats" within its case, this type of catch is very forgiving of misalignment and warping of the door.

■ Friction catches have a spring-steel tongue on the inside of the door and matching spring-steel jaws inside the cabinet. When the door is closed (it requires force), the tongue forces the jaws apart and is held there by friction. This type of latch is fussy, often requiring adjustment every year or so.

■ Roller catches are similar to friction catches with the spring-steel jaws being replaced by a pair of spring-loaded rollers. The catch is still fussy, but the rollers take less force to engage.

Magnetic catch

Friction catch

Roller catch

Hazardous Substances

COMMON HOUSEHOLD HAZARDS

ALSO SEE...
Paints & Stains:
Pages 232–241
Safety:
Pages 290–291
Ventilation:
Pages 386–387

Many homes contain carcinogenic chemicals and compounds that can seriously affect long-term health if not identified and handled or disposed of properly. The most common are paints with lead content, asbestos, naturally occurring radon gas, and various household chemicals.

Lead Paint: Most paints used to contain lead as a pigment. Since paint is rarely stripped from interior woodwork, most homes over 30 years old have one or more layers of lead-based paint on interior and exterior surfaces. Lead is also in the solder joints of older copper tubing.

Asbestos: Being noncombustible, asbestos was once used extensively as furnace, boiler, and steam-pipe insulation before its fibers were discovered to be carcinogenic. If you have heating pipes or ducts in the basement that are covered with thick, dense, cloth-covered white insulation, it may contain asbestos.

Radon: Radon is an odorless, tasteless, invisible gas which occurs naturally in many types of soil due to the radioactive decay of uranium in subterranean dirt and bedrock. The amount of radon present is usually negligible, but in some regions high concentrations of the gas may seep into basements during the winter.

Other Chemicals: Household cleaning fluids, paint strippers, and old batteries are just some of the dozens of chemicals most of us have in our homes. They obviously pose a risk to curious children, but, not so obviously, they also pose a risk to the environment unless disposed of properly.

LEAD PAINT

SOURCES

■ Painted wood surfaces, such as siding, moldings, baseboards, window and door casings

■ Drinking water, especially if your home has any lead pipes

■ Old painted toys and furniture

■ Hobbies such as refinishing furniture or making stained-glass objects

■ Food and liquids stored in lead crystal, lead-glazed pottery, or porcelain

DISPOSING OF OLD PAINT

The best way to dispose of old paint is to use it up. Use it to paint signs, dog houses, and birdhouses, or use it as a primer for a finish coat of another color.

If you can't use the paint, give it to someone or some group who can: neighbors, schools, theater groups, Habitat for Humanity.

If the paint has solidified completely inside the can, you can put it in the ordinary trash destined for a sanitary landfill. If it is not completely dry, however, leave the lid off until it dries, even if it takes months.

WHAT TO DO

Young children are considered to be at the greatest risk for lead poisoning because they often put things in their mouths out of curiosity. Paint chips and odd items coated with lead-containing paint dust usually are suspects. Young children exposed to renovation work on older homes are a high-risk group. Symptoms include headache, fatigue, and irritability. If you suspect lead poisoning, have your child tested. Lead poisoning can be reversed, but long-term exposure can lead to permanent brain damage.

Positive identification of lead in painted surfaces requires professional testing, typically at a cost of $200 to $400. Lead abatement for a whole house is a large, expensive process. Some surfaces can be effectively covered without disturbing lead-based paint underneath. Windows and doors should be replaced—opening and closing them causes friction that can release paint dust. Never use a belt sander, dry sandpaper, dry scraper, or propane torch on paint that might contain lead. Call 1-800-424-LEAD for advice on remodeling or renovating.

WHERE TO GET HELP

State	Telephone
Alabama	205-242-5661
Alaska	907-465-5152
Arizona	602-542-7307
Arkansas	501-661-2534
California	510-450-2424
Colorado	303-692-3012
Connecticut	203-566-5808
Delaware	302-739-4735
District of Columbia	202-727-9850
Florida	904-488-3385
Georgia	404-657-6514
Hawaii	808-832-5860
Idaho	208-332-5544
Illinois	800-545-2200
Indiana	317-382-6662
Iowa	800-972-2026
Kansas	913-296-0189
Kentucky	502-564-2154
Louisiana	504-765-0219
Maine	207-287-4311
Maryland	410-631-3859
Massachusetts	800-532-9571
Michigan	517-335-8885
Minnesota	612-627-5498
Mississippi	601-960-7463
Missouri	314-526-4911
Montana	406-444-3671
Nebraska	402-471-2451
Nevada	702-687-6615
New Hampshire	603-271-4507
New Jersey	609-633-2043
New Mexico	505-841-8024
New York	800-458-1158
North Carolina	919-715-3293
North Dakota	701-328-5188
Ohio	614-466-1450
Oklahoma	405-271-5220
Oregon	503-248-5240
Pennsylvania	717-782-2884
Rhode Island	401-277-3424
South Carolina	803-935-7945
South Dakota	605-773-3153
Tennessee	615-741-5683
Texas	512-834-6600
Utah	801-536-4000
Vermont	802-863-7231
Virginia	800-523-4019
Washington	206-753-2556
West Virginia	304-558-2981
Wisconsin	608-266-5885
Wyoming	307-777-7391

ASBESTOS

SOURCES (COMMON PRIOR TO 1970)

- Vinyl flooring
- Textured "popcorn" ceilings
- Cementitious sheets used to insulate walls from the heat of wood-burning stoves and furnaces
- Dry-mix furnace or boiler cement
- Gaskets for wood- and coal-burning stoves
- Stove mats and iron rests
- Duct connectors for central hot-air furnaces
- Laboratory gloves and pads
- Hot-water and steam-heat pipe insulation, usually 3- to 4-inch-wide "tape" wrapped around pipes
- Siding shingles characterized by wavy bottoms, usually 1 inch thick

WHAT TO DO

A qualified building inspector is trained to spot asbestos in its many forms, and can provide an inspection (that includes other aspects of your home) for $250 to $350. Confirmation of asbestos, however, may require testing that ranges from $200 to $500. Currently, there are no federal guidelines that mandate asbestos abatement within a home, even when you are selling your house. Your best defense is to contract a professional abatement contractor, or call 1-800-424-9065 and ask for your regional asbestos coordinator for information on removal, cleanup, and disposal.

RADON

SOURCES

- Underground rock formations which are rich in uranium. (The radon gas rises to the surface and infiltrates basements.)
- Water from underground wells. (The gas is released from the water when it is aerated, as in a shower.)
- Some older concrete block made from uranium mine tailings (very isolated source)

WHAT TO DO

Don't assume your test results will be the same as your neighbors; there are a lot of variables in addition to what lies under your home. For an initial test, purchase a charcoal-canister radon test kit from a home center or other retail outlet. Alternatively, hire a certified tester to conduct the test for you.

Place the test device in your basement during the winter when radon concentrations are the highest and air infiltration from the outside is usually at a minimum. If you don't have a basement (don't use a crawl space), conduct the test on the first floor. Keep all doors and windows on all levels of your home shut during the test, except for normal exit and entry. Do not operate ventilating fans or fireplaces during the test.

Run the test for a full 7 days. If the test result is less than 4 picoCuries per liter (4pCi/l), you have normal concentrations of radon that do not pose a health risk, and you won't have to do anything further.

However, if the result shows 4 to 8 pCi/l, have a professional radon tester conduct a more thorough test to confirm the problem. If the result is greater than 8 pCi/l, call in a certified radon-mitigation contractor to fix the problem. Call the number listed in the box on page 176 to get names and further advice. Or look in the Yellow Pages under Radon Mitigation.

DISPOSAL

Product	What to Do
Automotive batteries	Take to battery store, pay for disposal
Ammunition	Turn in to local police department
Artist and hobby paint	Save for special collection
Reusable house paints	Use up or give away
Unusable house paints	Let dry solid, then throw in trash
Alkaline batteries	Throw in trash
Nicad or button batteries	Save for special collection
Fabric dye	Save for special collection
Fireworks	Soak in water until saturated, then trash
Fluorescent bulbs and ballast	Save for special collection
Mothballs	Save for special collection
Photography chemicals	Contact your wastewater facility
Swimming pool chemicals	Save for special collection
Smoke detector (remove battery)	Throw in trash
Mercury thermometer	Save for special collection

FORMALDEHYDE ALERT

Formaldehyde is a superior bonding agent and a preservative that is used in the manufacture of many common building materials such as plywood, particleboard, and medium-density fiberboard. It is used for roof sheathing, cabinets, countertops, doors, and furniture. While not yet classified as carcinogenic, it is a type of chemical called a volatile organic compound, or VOC. A VOC readily vaporizes at normal temperatures and becomes a gas. These chemicals are responsible for a problem known as "outgassing"—the release of irritants into home interiors.

Lately, VOCs have come under close scrutiny by consumer safety groups as a possible cause of many kinds of ailments including nosebleeds, coughing, headaches, and skin rashes. If you suspect high levels of formaldehyde, consult a specialist by looking in the Yellow Pages under Environmental and Ecological Services.

Heat Leaks

HOW HOUSES LOSE HEAT

ALSO SEE...
Caulk:
Pages 50–51
Insulation:
Pages 186–193
Weather Stripping:
Pages 424–427

Want a shock? Stand in the middle of your home, imagine it to be a submarine under water, and look around for places you might expect water to pour in.

Under baseboards, around the window sashes, through the wall receptacles, around the door, down the chimney, though the dryer vent, the list goes on and on. But if water would come in, why not cold winter air?

It does! All of those places you identified—joints between building surfaces; movable cracks around doors and windows; floor, wall, and ceiling pipe and wire penetrations— are termed heat leaks by building scientists. Altogether, it has been estimated, the heat leaks in the average home add up to an astounding 2 square feet! The effect on your heating and air-conditioning bills is roughly equivalent to leaving a window sash up about a foot all year long.

The good news is that, once these leaks have been identified, they are easily and inexpensively sealed. All it takes is a roll of duct tape, a dozen $2 tubes of caulk, several hundred feet of inexpensive foam backer rod, and a weekend of your time.

FIELD GUIDE TO HEAT LEAKS

The illustration *at right* is a guide to where to look for heat leaks and their relative sizes.

The best way to confirm heat leaks (if you feel you need proof) is to wait until a very cold, windy day. Hold a lighted cigarette up to any suspect crack or hole. If it is a serious leak, the smoke will either be drawn into the crack or blown away from the crack. When you find an active leak, mark it with a piece of masking tape. Remove the tape only after you have sealed the leak.

JUST DUCKY

Which is it— "duck" or "duct" tape—that ubiquitous tape favored by backyard mechanics, sailors, and bank robbers everywhere?

No question about it. Although some enterprising company has undoubtedly named a product Duck Tape, duct tape originated as a tape for sealing the seams and joints in air-handling duct work.

FOAM FILLER BY THE FOOT

What if there were a product that looked like a foam rope, was very inexpensive, had infinite shelf life, left no messy residue, and could caulk any crack from ⅛ inch up to 1 inch?

Meet backer rod—flexible, compressible, extruded, closed-cell foam available in diameters from ⅛ inch to over 1 inch.

It's intended purpose is to fill large joints in masonry construction behind a surface application of caulk. Masonry supply companies sell it by the foot.

This, duct tape, and silicone caulk are all you need to seal 90 percent of all the heat leaks in your home.

A Field Guide to Heat Leaks in Buildings

Location/Number	Avg. Area, Sq. In.	Location/Number	Avg. Area, Sq. In.
Ceiling		21. Patio sliding door	16
1. General leakage per 100 sq. ft.	0.05	22. Entrance door, no weather stripping	8
2. Dropped ceiling, per 100 sq. ft.		Weather-stripped	6
With no continuous vapor barrier	78	With magnetic seal	4
With continuous vapor barrier	8	23. Attic access hatch, no weather stripping	6
3. Chimney/attic framing gap	12	Weather-stripped	3
Gap sealed	1	24. Air-lock entry (deduct)	-4
4. Whole-house fan with open louvers	8	25. Storm door (deduct)	-3
Covered with tight box	0.6	Windows (weather-stripped, each)	
5. Ceiling light fixtures (each)		26. Double-hung	0.8
Recessed in ceiling	4	27. Horizontal slider	0.6
Surface fixtures	0.3	28. Awning	0.2
6. Pipe or duct (each penetration)	1	29. Casement	0.2
Hole caulked	0.2	30. Fixed	0.2
Interior Walls		**Door and Window Frames (each)**	
7. Pocket door	5	31. In masonry wall, uncaulked	2
8. Pipe or duct inside wall (each)	2	Caulked	0.4
9. Recessed cabinet	0.8	32. In wood wall, uncaulked	0.6
10. Receptacle or switch, no gasket	0.2	Caulked	0.1
With cover gasket	0.03	**Vents and Chimneys**	
Exterior Walls		33. Kitchen range hood, damper open	9
11. General leakage per 100 sq. ft.	0.8	Damper closed	2
12. Wood sill on masonry foundation	65	34. Clothes dryer, damper open	4
Joint caulked	13	Damper closed	1
13. Box sill (Joist header on sill)	65	35. Bathroom vent, damper open	3
Joints caulked	13	Damper closed	1
14. Floor/wall joint	27	36. Fireplace, damper open	54
Baseboard caulked to floor	7	Average damper closed	9
15. Duct inside wall (each)	9	Tight damper closed	5
16. Pipe inside wall	2	With stove insert	2
17. Receptacle or switch, no gasket	0.2	**Heat and Hot Water**	
With cover gasket	0.05	37. Ducts in unheated space, untaped	56
18. Polyethylene vapor barrier (deduct)	-30	Ducts caulked and taped	28
19. Polystyrene sheathing (deduct)	-15	38. Furnace	
Doors		With retention head burner	12
20. Attic fold-down	17	With stack damper	12
Weather-stripped	8	With both of above	9
With insulated cover box	2	39. Gas or oil boiler or water heater	8

Heat Pumps

HOW A HEAT PUMP WORKS

If you understand how an air conditioner works, then you understand how a heat pump works: just reverse the valves and the functions of the indoor and outdoor coils, and you have it. The air conditioner moves heat from inside to outside; the heat pump moves heat from outside to inside. In fact, most heat pumps are reversible, providing heating in winter and air conditioning in summer.

If you don't understand air conditioners, then here is the longer explanation. First, know that a liquid will absorb large amounts of heat before expanding into a gas—a pot of water brought to a boil is an example. Conversely, a gas gives off a lot of heat when it is compressed into a liquid. Now all we need are a compressor, a refrigerant liquid that turns to gas at low (room) temperatures, an indoor coil, an outdoor coil, and various valves and controls.

In the heating mode, a fan blows air through the outdoor coil containing the refrigerant gas, which absorbs available heat from the air. The compressor then compresses the gas into a hot liquid and sends it to the indoor coil, where a second fan removes the heat. The cooled liquid now travels back to the outdoors where it expands into a gas again, absorbing heat. Even if the outdoor air is cooler than the indoor air, heat is removed from the outdoor air and released into the indoor air. Magic? No, it's good old thermodynamics.

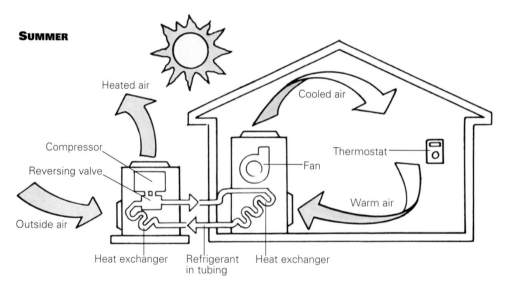

SUMMER

Heated air

Compressor

Reversing valve

Outside air

Heat exchanger

Refrigerant in tubing

Heat exchanger

Cooled air

Thermostat

Fan

Warm air

During warmer months the heat pump sends refrigerant liquid through the system where it gathers heat from inside the house in a heat exchanger and changes to a gas. In its gaseous state, the hot refrigerant loops to the outside where its heat is released with the help of a powerful fan. Once cooled, the refrigerant becomes a liquid again and is returned to the inside of the house to again gather heat in the heat exchanger.

During cooler weather the heat pump moves refrigerant liquid through a heat exchanger located outside the house. Even when it is cold outside, the refrigerant is able to absorb available heat and become a hot gas, aided by a compressor. Moving to the inside of the house, the hot refrigerant gives up its heat at the heat exchanger, aided by a fan. Cooled again to a liquid state, the refrigerant is cycled back outside to pick up more available heat.

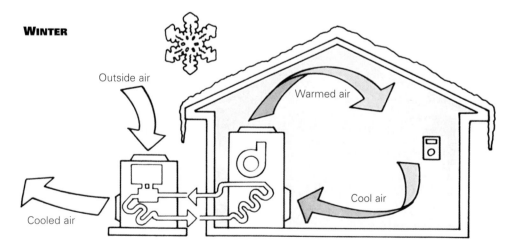

WINTER

Outside air

Warmed air

Cool air

Cooled air

The greater the temperature difference between inside and outside, the harder the compressor has to work to move the heat. At some lower outdoor temperature the efficiency of the heat pump falls below that of straight electric-resistance heating and is, therefore, uneconomical. For this reason, all residential heat pumps contain electric resistance coils, to which they automatically switch when the outdoor temperature falls to a predetermined point.

The resistance heater is needed also to take over while the heat pump is in its defrost mode. When the outdoor temperature falls to around freezing, the outdoor coil frosts up. To melt the frost the heat pump briefly and automatically switches to the air-conditioning mode, dumping heat into the outdoor coil.

If it's freezing outside and there is thick ice on the coil, the heat pump is not cycling. If instead, you never see frost, the unit is stuck in the defrost mode. Either condition may be caused by a stuck reversing switch. To unstick it try switching the house thermostat to "cool" for about 15 minutes and then back to "heat." If the heat pump doesn't resume normal operation, call for service.

If your electricity goes out for more than an hour during the heating season, don't restart the heat pump right away. The oil in the compressor may have thickened to the point where it would damage the valves when the compressor started up. Instead, turn the heat pump switch to "emergency heat" (electric-resistance heat) and leave it there for 6 hours while the compressor warms up.

TROUBLESHOOTING A HEAT PUMP

Problem	Possible Causes	What to Do
Pump doesn't run at all	Electricity off	Check circuit breakers or fuses.
		Check heat pump system disconnect switch.
	Thermostat not calling for heat	Check thermostat setting.
	Compressor overloaded	Press reset button in outdoor unit.
	Wiring loose	(If you feel qualified), check for loose or corroded wiring in control box.
Pump runs, but no heating or cooling	Dirty coils	Clean outdoor coils.
	Fan not running	Check fan; replace if burned out.
	Refrigerant leak	Call for service.
Pump heats but won't cool	Thermostat set to "heat"	Set thermostat to "cool."
	Reversing valve stuck	Set thermostat to "cool," wait 30 minutes, then reset to "heat." If still not cool, call for service.
	Refrigerant leak	Call for service.
Pump cools but won't heat	Thermostat set to "cool"	Set thermostat to "heat."
	Reversing valve stuck	Set thermostat to "cool," wait 30 minutes, then reset to "heat." If still not cool, call for service.
Heat feels uneven	Warm air from heat pump is cooler than from warm-air furnaces	Minimize temperature differences by balancing air flow in ducts to different areas. Also redirect air flow away from people.
Ice buildup on coils	Thermostat set to "heat"	Set thermostat to "automatic heat."
	Reversing valve stuck	Set thermostat to "cool," wait 30 minutes, then reset to "heat." If still not cool, call for service.
	Fins on outdoor coil flattened	Straighten fins.
"Emergency heat" light always on	Reversing valve stuck	Set thermostat to "cool," wait 30 minutes, then reset to "heat." If still not cool, call for service.
	Outdoor temperature sensor broken	Call for service.

HOODS AND VENTS

CLEARING THE AIR

ALSO SEE...
Kitchen Cabinets:
Pages 200–207
Ranges, Ovens, & Cooktops:
Pages 270–271
Ventilation:
Pages 386–387
Wire:
Pages 442–445

Ranges and cooktops require some means of removing smoke, grease, heat, and moisture from the kitchen. The most common is an overhead range hood, either hung beneath a cabinet or hung from the ceiling. Range hoods come in standard range widths and should be at least as wide as the range or cooktop. Down-draft venting, which is built into some models of cooktops and ranges, is the other type of venting device.

Most hoods and vents are ducted, venting all smoke, grease, heat, and moisture to the outdoors, through either the roof or the wall. Ductless hoods and vents filter out smoke and grease, but recirculate the heat and moisture through an activated-charcoal filter back into the kitchen.

The ducted vent does a much better job of removing smoke and moisture, but is sometimes difficult to install due to the location of the range. Whether you should install a ducted or a ductless vent depends on how much and what type of cooking you do.

Openings in vents are generally round and 4 inches in diameter, anticipating connection to standard 4-inch vent pipe. Some have more than one knockout to enable you to run the duct in horizontally or vertically.

Bathroom vents may also be vented through either a side wall or through the roof.

The Home Ventilating Institute (HVI) recommends bathroom ventilating fans be sized to 8 (as opposed to the Code's 5) air changes per hour. The HVI also recommends 15 ACH for kitchens.

RANGE VENT OPTIONS

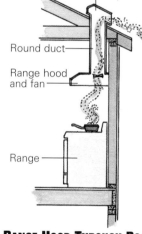
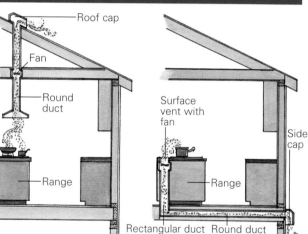

RANGE HOOD THROUGH WALL

If you are lucky enough to have an exterior wall right behind the range, installation couldn't be simpler. Use standard 4-inch aluminum vent pipe with a clothes-dryer hood or louvered vent on the wall.

RANGE HOOD THROUGH ROOF

Nearly as simple as venting back through the wall is venting straight up through an attic, crawl space, or closet to the roof. Vent fan manufacturers also sell roof vent kits.

ISLAND HOOD THROUGH ROOF

More expensive hoods are designed for center islands. They can be purchased directly from suppliers or custom-made by a sheet-metal shop and install an in-line booster fan in a piece of round duct.

ISLAND HOOD THROUGH ROOF

Some ranges feature down-draft venting. It takes a powerful fan to suck smoke and moisture downward. The ducts are large to handle the flow and often are routed between floor joists to an outside vent.

BATHROOM VENTS

Bathroom vents remove odors and excess moisture from the confines of bathrooms. Typically, they simply pull bathroom air up and vent it directly into the spaces between joists. Areas with heavy moisture, such as a steam sauna, should be vented directly to the outside.

WHAT IS A SONE?

The noise level of a fan is rated in sones. The average range hood over a stove rates 6 to 7 sones, and the vent fan in the restroom of the local gas station is probably between 4 and 5 sones. For a premium price you can find bathroom vent fans rated as low as 0.5 sones. That's less than a whisper.

GFCIs

Any electrical equipment installed over a tub or shower, including a bathroom ventilating fan—even though recessed into the wall, must be wired to a circuit that is protected by a ground fault circuit interrupter (GFCI) device. GFCI receptacles typically are required by codes in bathroom areas.

INSTALLING A RANGE HOOD

Range hoods are manufactured in a variety of styles and capacities. They typically are 18 to 24 inches deep, and their widths usually match standard range and cooktop widths of 30, 36, and 48 inches. Either they are made with decorative finishes, such as brushed stainless steel, and are designed to be a decorative part of the kitchen, or they are made to be installed inside an upper cabinet. For energy conservation, many include a spring-loaded damper that prevents room heat from escaping when the unit is off.

INSTALLING UNDER A CABINET

If you are mounting a ducted hood under a cabinet, cut holes in the cabinet for the hood outlet and duct before installing the cabinet. Mark holes for cutting by setting the cabinet upside down on the floor and laying the hood upside down on top of it. Trace the hood outlet onto the cabinet, cut it out with a saber saw, and cut another hole for the duct. If the cabinet is already hung, measure for the holes as carefully as you can before cutting them out.

WIRING

Run NM cable behind the wall and bring it out through a small hole in a place where the electrical junction box of the hood will cover it. The range hood motor is less than ½ horsepower, so the cable can come from any handy

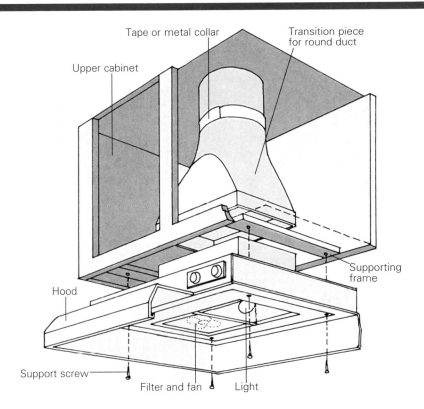

Tape or metal collar
Transition piece for round duct
Upper cabinet
Supporting frame
Hood
Support screw
Filter and fan
Light

nearby circuit. Strip away 6 to 8 inches of sheathing from the end of the cable and attach a cable clamp at that point, just outside the wall.

VENTING

Run a duct pipe into the cabinet from the attic or an exterior wall behind the cabinet. The pipe should vent all the way to the outside, terminating in a roof cap or wall cap. Secure each joint with sheet-metal screws and tape it with approved duct tape. Connect a transition fitting to the round duct for the rectangular opening in the hood, as well as any elbows needed for changing the direction of the duct in the cabinet. If an elbow won't fit, make a cardboard template showing cutouts and have a sheet-metal shop make up a metal box.

ATTACHING THE HOOD

Lift or prop the hood into place and mark where the screw holes line up against the bottom of the cabinet. Take the hood down and, on these marks, drill pilot holes for the screws. Lift the hood back up, feed the wires into the junction box, and screw it to the bottom of the cabinet.

Using wire nuts, connect the wires inside the junction box. Connect the ground wire to the grounding screw in the hood. Then connect the hood collar to the duct transition piece with sheet-metal screws and wrap the joint with duct tape.

AVOIDING GREASE FIRES

If you have a ductless range hood, remove the snap- or slide-out filter periodically and wash it with hot water and dishwashing detergent to remove built-up grease. Otherwise, if you have a fire in a frying pan, you may also have a fire in your range hood.

DOUBLE DUTY

Have you been holding off getting a microwave because you can't find a place to put it? Hold off no longer! Install a combination microwave/ductless range hood over your range. They cost little if any more than a countertop microwave and work just as well.

CODE REQUIREMENTS: BATHROOM VENTS

Bathrooms are required to have either an openable window or a mechanical ventilation system connected directly to the outside capable of providing 5 air changes per hour or a minimum of 50 cubic feet per minute (cfm). Bathrooms which contain only a water closet or lavatory or both may be ventilated with an approved mechanical recirculating fan or similar device designed to remove odors from the air.

Example: What is the minimum required cfm rating of a ventilating fan for a 8×10×8-foot bathroom?

Answer: Volume = 8×10×8
    = 640 cu ft
Required cfm = 640/5
    = 128 cfm

Hot Tubs, Spas, and Whirlpools

TAKING THE PLUNGE

ALSO SEE...
Bathrooms:
Pages 22–23
Decks:
Pages 74–81
Electrical Systems:
Pages 110–115
Plumbing:
Pages 256–263

Adding a hot tub or spa to your outdoor living area can afford much pleasure. A hot tub is less expensive than a swimming pool, uses less water, and is easier to install and maintain. Either is relaxing and conducive to socializing. A hot tub or spa fits into a small space, making it an ideal choice for an out-of-the-way corner. Many homeowners install their hot tubs or spas themselves.

Whether purchased as a self-contained unit or as separate components, the equipment includes a tub, pump, filter, heater, thermostat, piping, and insulated cover. Optional features include water jets and built-in lighting.

Even if you buy a complete unit, you will need to do more than just hook it up. A spa without a deck around it, steps leading up to it, and a privacy fence around it will look as ungainly as an unframed above-ground swimming pool. The whole point of having a spa is to be able to luxuriate in the soothing water. You will appreciate a spa more if you provide an appropriate setting.

If you don't have a good outdoor setting for a hot tub or spa, you can derive much of the same relaxation from a whirlpool bath. These closely resemble bathtubs, but have built-in water heaters to maintain the temperature and water jets to give your body a "hydro-massage." In addition to their lower costs, many whirlpools have the added advantage of being the same size as a standard tub (30 inches wide and 60 inches long), so they can directly replace an existing tub.

HOT TUB OR SPA?

Basically, hot tubs are wooden barrels and spas are shells manufactured of plastic materials. This distinction is complicated by the fact that some hot tubs have acrylic liners and some spas are freestanding units with wood skirting or are made from concrete. However, tubs and spas have other basic differences—in maintenance, durability, appearance, and operation—all of which are fundamental considerations.

Beveled wood staves held in place by tight hoops form the sides of a hot tub. A dado groove near the bottom of the staves holds the wood floor in place. Most tubs are made of redwood—usually vertical-grain, all-heart grades. Some are made from less expensive grades of species that include sapwood, cedar, and oak.

Depending on the species and grade of wood, a tub will last from 10 to 15 years. Make sure the wood is kiln dried so that it swells evenly when the tub is filled with water. The constant swelling of the staves renders the tub watertight.

A tub can be any size or shape, but round tubs 5 or 6 feet in diameter and 2½, 4, or 5 feet tall are most common. Some tubs are less than 4 feet in diameter and others are as wide as 12 feet. A standard 5×4-foot tub holds 500 gallons of water and weighs 5,000 pounds when full of water and bodies. This weight, spread evenly over the bottom of the tub, amounts to 250 pounds per square foot (psf). Compare that to the code-prescribed load on a wood deck of about 50 psf, and you can see why hot tubs require either a reinforced deck frame or a special foundation.

Tubs have a rustic and natural appearance; they blend well with decks, gardens, greenhouses, or patios. Hot tubs are harder to clean and maintain than spas because of the texture of the wood and the angles and corners inherent in their design. On the other hand, tubs are easier to relocate and generally cost less.

Early spas were made of fiberglass covered with gelcoat. Modern materials include formed acrylic reinforced with fiberglass and formed Centrex® thermoplastic, which needs no reinforcement. The outside of the spa varies. Some are designed to be installed in the ground or in a specially designed box that is filled with sand. Others are freestanding with wood skirting.

Colorful spas present more design options than hot tubs, ranging from straight-sided squares and octagons to circular, free-form shapes. Their sleek texture helps make them a distinctive element in any setting. Typical sizes are 5 to 6 feet across and 4 feet deep (spas are usually narrower across the bottom because of their seats).

Both hot tubs and spas are available as complete packages or as components that require assembly. The simplest installation is at grade level on an existing slab, and the most involved are in-ground spas or elevated hot tubs. Most building codes require a building permit for either installation.

CODE REQUIREMENTS

Barrier Requirements

Swimming pools (which includes hot tubs and spas under the Code) must be surrounded by a barrier where:

■ The top of the barrier is at least 48 inches above grade and the space between the bottom of the barrier and grade is less than 2 inches

■ The barrier may be either on the ground or mounted on top of the pool

■ If the barrier is on top of the pool, the space between the pool and the bottom of the barrier is less than 4 inches

■ Openings in the barrier will not pass a 4-inch ball

■ If the barrier has horizontal rails which are less than 45 inches apart, the spaces between the vertical members must be less than 1¾ inches

■ If the barrier has horizontal rails which are more than 45 inches apart, the spaces between the vertical members must be less than 4 inches.

■ Access gates must comply with the barrier requirements above, and be provided with a locking device.

LOCATION

There are many factors to consider when choosing a location for your tub or spa. The most important is privacy (unless you live in an isolated setting). Take advantage of plants, fences, walls, or existing screens, or build a fence or even an enclosed structure similar to a Japanese bathhouse.

Make sure the tub is close to a dressing area. The prospect of walking 100 feet from the house to the tub through winter air or a cold rain tends to dampen one's enthusiasm for a "taking a tub".

Take advantage of attractive vistas, and consider using the tub or spa as a focal point in a garden or patio. Install lighting in and around the tub so you can use it at night.

Climate is a major factor; consider sunlight, shade, wind, and snow. Generally, an outdoor spa should take advantage of late afternoon sunshine (unless you are in a hot climate) and be sheltered from prevailing breezes. In cold climates, the installation should have valves for draining the equipment and tub separately, so you can keep the equipment from freezing without having to drain the tub. Also avoid placing a tub or spa beneath eaves where snow will slide into it.

An indoor installation requires an adequate foundation for the tub and proper ventilation to reduce condensation. You will find that a 5×5 foot tub of steaming water can pump a lot of moisture into your home. At the very least, the tub must be covered when not in use.

INSTALLATION

Techniques for installing hot tubs and spas vary with manufacturer, but all share certain requirements. First, the tub or spa must be well supported. Tubs require a reinforced concrete slab, usually 6 inches thick, if installed on the ground. The slab needs to be only slightly larger than the tub. A freestanding spa should have the same type of slab, but if it is a sunken spa, excavate a hole, then backfill it with sand. If you install the tub or spa on a deck, double the joists under the unit and add at least four independent posts and footings to support them. The joists should be cross-braced or blocked, as well.

The tub or spa should also be convenient to plumbing. At the bottom is a drain that is the primary outlet for a pipe that goes to the pump. Most pumps are centrifugal, and must be large enough for the size of tub and number of jets (usually ¾ horsepower for one or two jets, 1 hp for three jets, 1½ hp for 4 jets, and 2 hp for six jets). The pipe is plastic, either PVC or CPVC, 1½ or 2 inches in diameter.

The pump moves the water through the pipe, which leads to the filter. Filters vary in their effectiveness. Cartridge filters have membranes of paper or fabric, are the least expensive, and require replacement about once per year. Sand filters work better, and the best filters of all use diatomaceous earth (DE).

The water must be heated as well as filtered. In some systems the heater is in the same circuit as the pump, usually between the filter and tub.

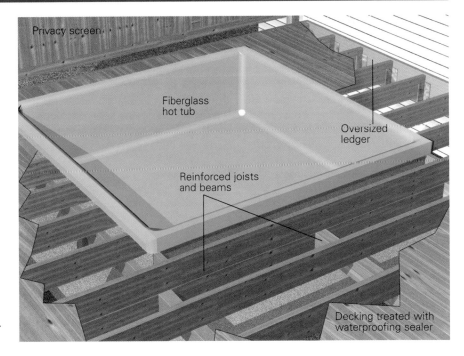

Privacy screen

Fiberglass hot tub

Oversized ledger

Reinforced joists and beams

Decking treated with waterproofing sealer

In other systems, water goes directly from the filter to the tub, and the heater is on a separate loop. Water circulates through the heater by convection, sometimes boosted by a small pump. With either system, the heater is powered by gas, or electricity. Models vary widely in their heat output and the speed with which they are able to warm up the tub.

The water jets are on a separate circulation system. The system includes a blower that introduces air into the pipes to create greater water pressure. The pipes that connect the various units have valves for draining or isolating different parts of the system as well as jets where the pipes connect to the tank. The system is usually closed; it is not included in the supply system of the house. In some cases, where the code allows, the filtering system may connect to house plumbing with a check valve that prevents backflow.

Wiring for a hot tub or spa must be in strict accordance with the National Electric Code. Electric heaters and most pumps are on their own circuits, usually 240-volt. Lights and auxiliary water-jet systems use 120 volts. GFCI (ground fault circuit interrupters) must protect all wiring, and switches must be outdoor types that are beyond the reach of anyone in the tub.

INSULATION

INCREASING COMFORT AND ECONOMY

Insulation slows down the transfer of heat. It helps make homes more comfortable and energy efficient. Although you may think of insulation as fluffy fiberglass blankets, the term also includes caulk, weather stripping, pipe wraps, and windows and doors.

New homes always include a good measure of insulation. In fact, state energy codes mandate it. But insulating an existing home is more complex. Don't start a complicated insulation project before installing less expensive or more effective materials.

A house can lose heat in the winter and gain heat in the summer in many ways. A single-glazed window, for instance, may allow as much as 10 times more heat to escape than the wall that surrounds it, even though the wall has more surface area than the window. One quarter of your entire fuel bill may depart through an uninsulated basement wall. Poorly sealed cracks around the foundation, sill, chimney, or siding can account for 10 percent of your heating losses, and a ¼-inch gap around a door is equivalent to a 2-inch-square hole in the wall. Many such cracks and gaps can add up to an opening the size of a window.

Start with projects offering the highest return on your investment. Use the list below. It ranks heat robbers from highest to lowest. By themselves, some materials, such as wall insulation, may be more effective than their position on the list indicates. But the cost of their installation lowers their position on the list.

- Heat leaks (see page 178)
- Caulk (see page 50)
- Weather stripping (see page 424)
- Insulating windows and doors
- Insulating attics
- Insulating floors or basement walls
- Insulating walls

THE THERMAL ENVELOPE

After plugging all your heat leaks, turn your attention to insulation. The basic principle of insulating a house is to surround the conditioned living space (occupied areas that are heated and/or air-conditioned) with insulating material.

The illustration *opposite* shows the surfaces you should insulate. Because heat rises, it is best to start at the top of the house and work down, but the type of construction may alter your priorities. For example, the perimeter of a concrete slab can lose tremendous amounts of heat in a single-story home.

Remember, you don't have to insulate everything at once. Do small amounts at a time and keep working away at the list until you have run out of insulation investments that pay high rates of return.

ATTIC AND ROOF

If the attic is not a living space, insulate the attic floor. This is a simple project that involves rolling out blanket insulation or having a contractor blow in loose fill.

If the attic is a living area, insulate the ceiling and walls, as well as the attic floor under the eaves. Some of these spaces are easily accessible; others may be covered with interior finish walls or ceiling material. If so, blow in loose-fill insulation from the outside or strip off the finish materials from the inside and install batt insulation.

Roofs are a primary source of heat loss. If roof rafters are covered with finish materials, blow in loose-fill insulation in the cavities. A more radical solution is to remove the roofing material, install rigid foam panels over the roof sheathing, nail ½-inch plywood over the insulation, and reroof.

CODE REQUIREMENTS: INSULATION

Flame-Spread and Smoke-Developed Ratings

All insulations are required to pass certain tests for flammability and amount of smoke generated during a fire. If the material is sold as insulation in a lumberyard or home center, you can be sure that it has passed these tests. Make sure you install it according to the manufacturer's instructions.

Foam Plastic Insulations

- Foam insulations must be separated from the building interior by a minimum of ½-inch wallboard.
- Wallboard covering foam insulation must

be installed with mechanical fasteners—not adhesives.

- A minimum of 1 inch of masonry or concrete can replace the required ½ inch of wallboard.
- When used in a roof, foam insulation may be protected by minimum ¹⁵⁄₃₂-inch tongue-and-groove plywood.
- In an attic with fixed-stairway access, foam must be covered by at least 1½ inches of mineral-fiber insulation, ¼-inch wood structural panels, ⅜-inch particle board or wallboard, or 0.016-inch corrosion-resistant steel.
- A ½-inch foam backer board may be used over existing siding, but if installed over sheathing, it must be separated from the interior

by at least 2 inches of mineral-fiber insulation or ½-inch wallboard.

Ventilation

- Attic and cathedral ceilings without vapor barriers must have ventilation openings equal to ¹⁄₁₅₀ of their areas.
- Attic and cathedral ceilings with vapor barriers must have ventilation openings equal to ¹⁄₃₀₀ of their areas.
- Ventilation area must be increased by 200 percent if the vents are covered with ¹⁄₁₆-inch screen; 225 percent if covered by louvers; 300 percent if covered by both.

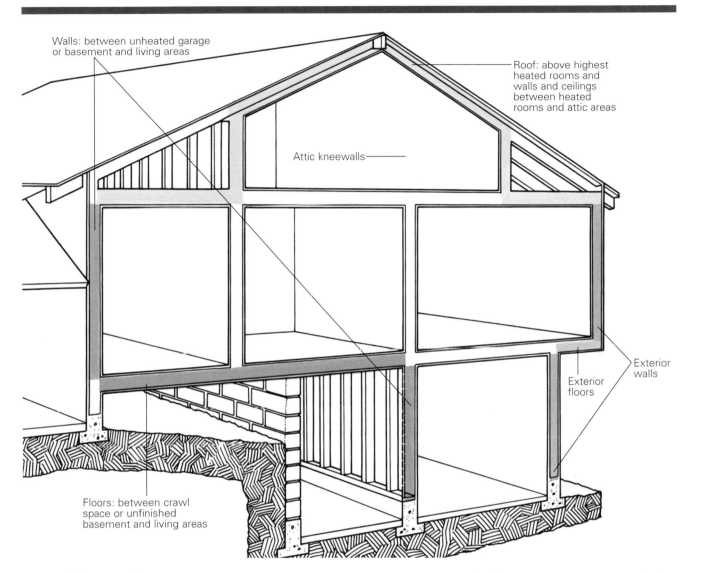

Walls: between unheated garage or basement and living areas

Roof: above highest heated rooms and walls and ceilings between heated rooms and attic areas

Attic kneewalls

Exterior walls

Exterior floors

Floors: between crawl space or unfinished basement and living areas

EXTERIOR WALLS AND WINDOWS

Insulating exterior walls is simple when the framing is exposed, but is a major project in an existing house. Most commonly, loose insulation is blown into the stud cavities through holes that are drilled in the exterior wall. Occasionally, rigid insulation is attached to exterior walls and new siding installed over it.

Windows can lose tremendous amounts of heat, even after they are caulked and weather stripped. Glass is a poor insulator—about R-1, compared with about R-4 for an uninsulated wall and R-11 to R-19 for an insulated wall. Increase the insulating capabilities of windows by adding another layer of glazing, installing storm windows, or by replacing the windows with double-

glazed units. Many window manufacturers make replacement units especially designed for retrofit situations.

EXTERIOR FLOORS

If a floor is cantilevered beyond a downstairs wall, blow in insulation from the wall side of each joist cavity. Or strip off the soffit boards, install blanket insulation between the joists, and replace the boards.

FLOORS OVER UNHEATED AREAS

Floors over unheated crawl spaces and basements are fairly easy to insulate, although the task is not very pleasant if the space is cramped. Install blanket insulation between the exposed joists, with the vapor barrier facing up. Hold the blankets up with vapor-permeable building wrap,

chicken wire, or netting improvised from fishing line or tie wire.

FOUNDATIONS AND BASEMENT WALLS

You can insulate basements and heated crawl spaces from the outside or from the inside. If the inside walls are already finished, and if excavating around the foundation won't be obstructed by plantings or trees, install rigid panels around the outside of the foundation. These panels also must cover the surface of the basement wall that extends above the ground. This is also the method that should be used for insulating around concrete slabs.

If the basement walls are unfinished, stud up wood-frame walls, insulate between the studs, and finish with ½-inch wallboard (see Basements, pages 18–21).

▶

INSULATION
continued

WHAT IS R?

All insulation products are required to have their R-value printed on them or on their packaging. So what is this R? It is a measure of the amount a given material restricts the transfer of heat.

You can calculate heat flow through a surface with the conduction equation

$$H = A \times (T_1 - T_2)/R$$

Where:
- H = British thermal units (BTU) per hour
- A = area of the surface in square feet
- T_1 = temperature on one side of the surface
- T_2 = temperature on the other side of the surface
- R = the R-value of the surface

Example: What is the heat loss through a 1,000 square foot attic roof insulated to R-20 when the inside temperature is 70°F and the outside temperature is 20°F?

Answer:
$$H = A \times (T_1 - T_2)/R$$
$$= 1,000 \times (70 - 20)/20$$
$$= 1,000 \times 50/20$$
$$= 2,500 \text{ BTU per hour}$$

T_1 (70°) T_2 (20°) H A 20' 50'

RECOMMENDED R-VALUES

The map *below* shows how much R-value the attic, floor, and wall insulation should have for homes in various regions of the country. The map is intended only to illustrate general differences among regions; it does not account for the significant variations that can occur within a region; nor does it account for cost differences between fuels. To find the recommended R-value for your area and fuel, consult with your local building department, utility, or state energy office.

Many states and counties have adopted rigorous energy standards for new construction and remodeling. Compliance with an energy code may be mandatory, so check your codes before you buy.

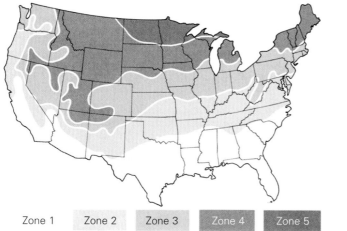

Zone 1 Zone 2 Zone 3 Zone 4 Zone 5

RECOMMENDED R-VALUES

Zone	Attic Floor	Floor Over Unheated Crawl Space or Basement	Exterior Wall
1	R-30	R-11	R-12
2	R-30	R-13	R-19
3	R-38	R-19	R-19
4	R-49	R-22	R-19
5	R-49	R-22	R-22

INSULATION CHARACTERISTICS

Which type of insulation is best for your project? Naturally, you want a high R-value. However, there are many other factors to consider:

Convenience: When doing the work yourself, choose the material that is easiest to install—usually fiberglass blankets or batts, since they are readily available and do not require specialized tools to install. Rock wool blankets have a slightly higher R-value, but are very difficult to find.

To install large amounts of loose-fill insulation, rent a blower. Call a few insulation contractors first before you do it yourself. You will probably find the cost of buying the material and renting the blower to be about the same as that of hiring a contractor.

Suitability: Consider the nature of the space to be insulated. If it has open framing spaced either 16- or 24-inches on-center, use blankets or batts. If the framing members are not spaced 16- or 24-inches on center, pour loose fill between them. If you're insulating a cavity enclosed by finished walls and ceilings, you will have to use blown fill. On the outside surface of a wall or roof, use rigid foam sheets.

Working Space: Rigid foam gives the most R-value per inch, making it ideal for tight spaces or where additional wall thickness must be kept to a minimum. If you have 2×4 stud walls and want to insulate to R-19, you may need to cover walls with rigid

INSULATION

Form	R/Inch	Materials	Uses	Method	Comments
Blankets and batts	3.2 3.7	Fiberglass Rock wool	Walls, floors, ceilings, attics, roofs	Fit between studs joists, and beams	Most common, by far. Fits 16- and 24-inch spacings
Loose or blown fill	2.2 2.4 2.7 2.9 3.3 4.0	Fiberglass Vermiculite Perlite Rock wool Cellulose Latex-bound Fiberglass	Floors, walls, hard-to-reach places, finished walls and ceilings	Poured or blown into place with specialized blowers	Best for irregular spaces; the only option for finished areas; should be installed by professional contractors
Rigid sheet	4.0 4.4 5.0 6.3 7.0	Molded polystyrene Fiberglass board Extruded polystyrene Urethane Polyisocyanurate	Unfinished walls, foundation walls, exterior walls under siding	Cut to fit and fastened in place; plastic foams must be covered with at least ½" wallboard	High R-value per inch; plastic foams are flammable

foam or fill the stud cavities with low-R material first and add thinner foam under the wallboard or siding.

Fire Protection: Plastic foams are flammable. When installing rigid panels between the exposed rafters of a sloped ceiling, cover the panels with wallboard or use fiberglass panels as a protection against fire (see Code Requirements, page 186).

Moisture Resistance: Some types of loose insulation, such as cellulose, compact and lose their R-value when wet. Compaction won't happen if the walls are properly sealed and protected with a vapor barrier, but may be a factor in humid regions or those subject to flooding. The most durable insulating material is polystyrene, which doesn't lose its insulating properties even if it's submerged.

ITCHLESS INSULATING

Does fiberglass insulation drive you wild? Then do as fiberglass workers in boatyards do—wear a Tyvek® painter's suit. These baggy, white coveralls cost less than $10 and filter out dust while passing perspiration. You can even get a matching hood to protect your head. Tape the wrists and ankles with masking tape and wear gloves. Use it for painting, too.

Better yet, buy the newest type of insulation—fiberglass batts wrapped in moisture-permeable polyolefin.

VAPOR BARRIERS

Buttoning up a house to resist infiltration and insulating it to trap warmth is so beneficial that it is hard to realize that it also causes a major problem in cold climates. It does a good job of keeping heat in, but unless your insulation is faced with a vapor barrier, moisture passes through it easily. Any water vapor passing through the insulation immediately condenses into liquid moisture when it

INSTALLING A VAPOR BARRIER

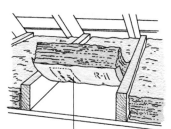

Vapor barrier toward living area

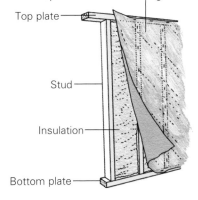

Top plate

Stud

Insulation

Bottom plate

hits cooler air, just like dew on grass on a cool night. The condensed moisture gets trapped and, provided it is still there when the temperature rises above 50°F, can cause wood decay and damage to foundations, roof, and walls.

One way to control this problem is to keep moisture from passing into the insulation by installing a vapor barrier between the insulation and the interior.

Many fiberglass insulations come with foil vapor barriers; closed-cell foam insulations are their own vapor barriers; and if the insulation doesn't have one, you can install polyethylene (poly) under the wallboard, or apply two coats of latex vapor-barrier primer paint to the wallboard. When installing poly sheeting, make sure that subsequent construction doesn't damage it or poke holes in it.

The other vapor control is to ventilate the spaces above attic and roof insulation so that the moisture can escape before causing damage.

The Uniform Building Code prohibits insulating attics and roofs unless they have 1 square foot of ventilation for every 150 square feet of ceiling area (1 per 300 if there is a vapor barrier). If you are insulating between the rafters with blankets or loose fill, maintain at least 1 inch of air space above the insulation and ventilate it at both soffit and ridge.

INSULATION

continued

INSULATING ATTICS

WITH LOOSE FILL

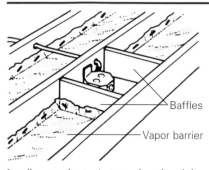

Install a vapor barrier (painting the ceilings below with vapor-barrier paint is the easiest and most effective) and install baffles to protect recessed light fixtures and soffit vents.

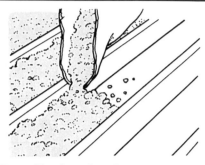

Pour or blow the insulation between the joists, making sure it gets into the corners and around bracings.

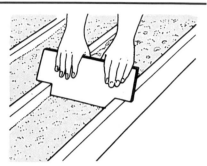

Spread and fluff the fill with a rake. Level it off with a board, notched at the corners to fit over the rafters.

WITH BATTS

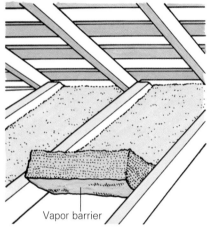

1 Beginning at one side of the attic, place the batts between the joists with the vapor barrier facing toward the living space you want to insulate. Take care not to cover any soffit vents.

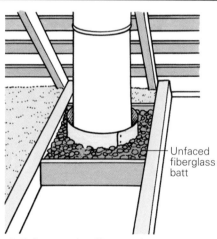

2 Only noncombustible materials can come within 2 inches of a chimney, so stuff the space between the framing and the chimney with unfaced fiberglass batt.

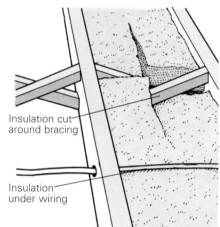

3 Place insulation under attic wiring. Separate the layers of insulation to surround cross-braces. A short, straight cut up the center of the batt allows you to tuck the insulation around the joist braces or pipes.

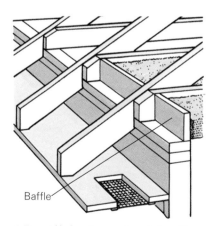

4 Do not block attic or roof ventilation. Place a baffle between the vent and the insulation and make sure both the baffle and the insulation don't touch the roof boards or block the air flow.

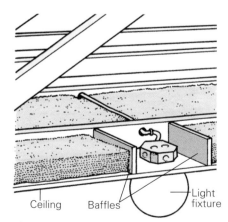

5 Keep insulation at least 3 inches away from recessed lighting fixtures unless the fixture is marked "I.C." (Insulated Ceiling). Otherwise, heat can build up to the point of starting a fire.

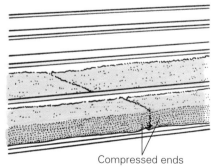

6 When you near the center of the attic, start over again from the eaves on the other side. Compress the ends together where they meet in the center of the attic.

INSULATING WALLS

Insulating studded walls is a relatively uncomplicated process. When adding fiberglass batts to a concrete or masonry wall, however, you may have to build a stud wall. If the insulation has no vapor barrier, cover the wall with 4-mil polyethylene sheeting, stapling the vapor barrier to the studs. Walls insulated with flammable insulation, such as polystyrene, should be finished with fire-retardant wallboard. See Basements, pages 18–21, for more on finishing basement walls.

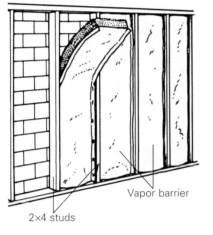

2×4 studs   Vapor barrier

CUTTING FIBERGLASS

If you have to cut a fiberglass batt or blanket, place it on a wide piece of plywood or other hard surface. Use a scrap board to compress the insulation at the cutting line and to act as a straightedge. Cut the insulation with a utility knife. If the utility knife is not long enough to cut through to the hard surface, any sharp, serrated kitchen knife will do.

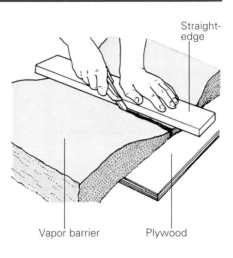

Straight-edge

Vapor barrier   Plywood

ADDING TO INSULATION

When adding to an existing layer of insulation, it is important to keep moisture from accumulating within and between the separate layers. If possible, add unfaced (without vapor barrier) blankets or batts. If the new insulation does have a vapor barrier, slash it. To block heat flow in any cracks, lay the new insulation perpendicular to the old insulation, with the slashed foil facing down.

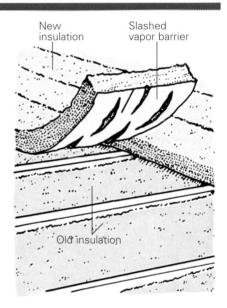

New insulation   Slashed vapor barrier

Old insulation

INSULATING FLOORS

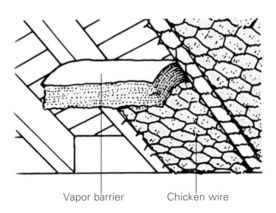

Vapor barrier   Chicken wire

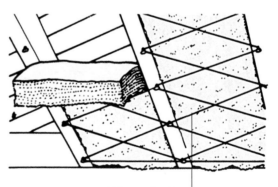

Wire netting hung on screws

To protect the living space above an insulated floor, make sure the vapor barrier faces up, toward the space you want to insulate. Hold the blankets up with vapor-permeable building wrap,

chicken wire, or netting improvised from fishing line or tie wire. If the underside of the floor is exposed to wind, protect the insulation with inexpensive paneling or plywood

sheathing. Perforate the sheathing with 1-inch-diameter ventilation holes spaced every 12 inches.

▶

INSULATING EXTERIOR FOUNDATION WALLS

A heated basement or crawl space should be insulated. So should the perimeter slab foundations. If the inside walls are finished and if there aren't obstacles around the foundation that prevent excavation, install extruded polystyrene foam panels on the outside of the foundation. This is a particularly good solution for moisture problems and allows you to install a drainage system or waterproof the outside of the walls.

Use foam at least 1 inch thick. Tongue-and-groove joints minimize heat leaks and make it easier to apply a protective surface. The above-ground portion of foundation is most important, because it loses the most heat. To prevent deterioration from sunlight, cover the exposed insulation.

How far to extend the insulation down the wall depends on your willingness to dig. Happily, you do not have to dig all the way to the footings to get good results; even 12 or 18 inches below grade helps. The most important area to cover is the foundation wall above grade.

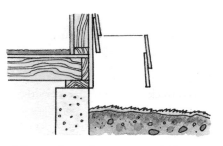

1 Remove the two bottom courses of siding. Vinyl and aluminum siding can be saved for reinstallation, but wood siding is difficult to remove without damaging it and probably will need to be replaced. Excavate at least 1 foot below grade.

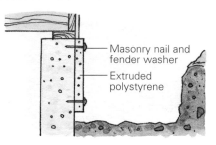

Masonry nail and fender washer
Extruded polystyrene

2 Fasten sheets of tongue-and-groove extruded polystyrene to the wall using special foam-compatible mastic or concrete nails and fender washers. Do not install the foam over tar-based foundation waterproofing, as the tar will dissolve the foam. Use special mastics, foundation waterproofing, and latex-modified exterior coatings available from masonry-supply outlets.

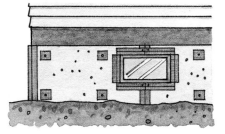

3 Sand the surface of the foam lightly to break through the tough skin and give the coating a "tooth" to adhere to. Apply self-adhesive fiberglass wallboard tape to all joints and corners.

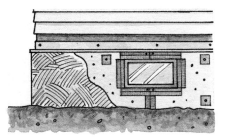

4 Install galvanized or aluminum Z-flashing against the sheathing and down over the top of the foam. Brush or trowel fiberglass-reinforced latex foundation coating onto the foam to several inches below grade. Replace the bottom courses of siding, and backfill the soil.

INSULATING WATER HEATERS

You can purchase insulating kits for water heaters at home centers, but better yet—make your own. All you need is duct tape and a roll of R-11 fiberglass. Cut three or four sections equal to the height of the heater and tape them together. Trim one edge so that the blanket fits snugly around the tank without the ends overlapping. Hold it in place, cut out openings for the controls and the drain faucet, and tape the ends.

You can cover the top of an electric heater, but don't cover the burner access at the bottom or the flue collar at the top of a gas heater.

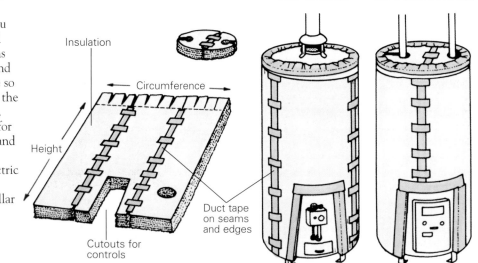

Insulation

Circumference

Height

GAS HEATER   ELECTRIC HEATER

Duct tape on seams and edges

Cutouts for controls

INSULATING DUCTS

1 Turn on the furnace or air conditioner to run air through the ducts. Check for leaks with your hand (wet it to make it more sensitive to moving air). Seal any leaks with duct tape.

2 Without crushing the insulation, wrap the blankets around the ducts with the vapor barrier on the outside.

3 Wherever the blankets meet, seal the seams with duct tape. Do not block any air intakes, and keep the tape and insulation out of contact with light fixtures, chimneys, and flue pipes.

4 At the ends of the duct, cut the insulation long enough so that it will fold across the front of the duct as shown. Cut the surplus from the top and bottom, fold the insulation over the end of the duct and tape it closed.

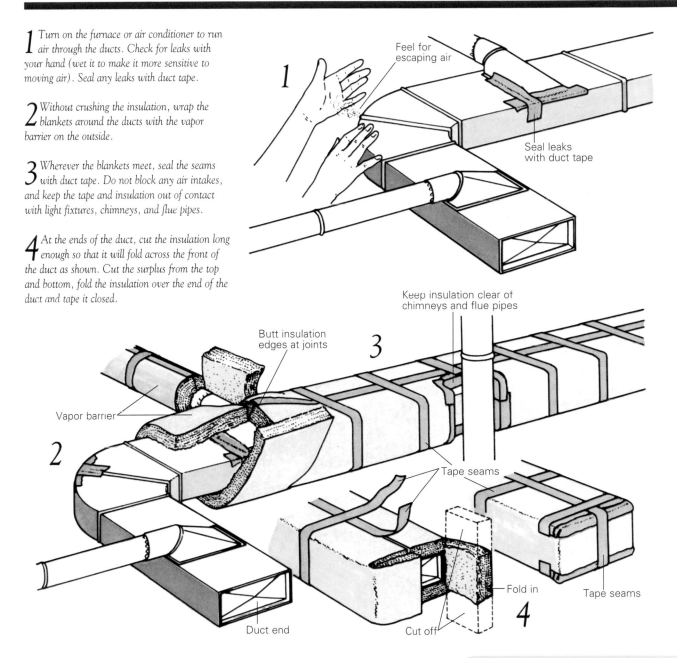

1

Feel for escaping air

Seal leaks with duct tape

Keep insulation clear of chimneys and flue pipes

Butt insulation edges at joints

3

Vapor barrier

2

Tape seams

Duct end

Cut off

Fold in

4

Tape seams

INSULATING PIPES

Metal pipes are good conductors and easily pass heat from hot water to the colder air. Insulate them so they won't lose heat to surrounding spaces.

Foam insulation for pipes comes in 6-foot lengths and sizes that fit all standard pipe diameters. The less expensive products are slit lengthwise, but you should tape all seams for the best efficiency. The more expensive products have adhesive in the slit so

you only have to press the seam together after slipping it over the pipe.

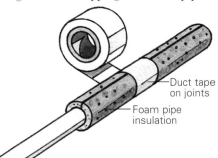

Duct tape on joints

Foam pipe insulation

LITTLE LEAKS, LOTS OF LOSS

When insulating, think of your house as a boat; the smallest leak can sink it. Just how bad is that 1-inch gap you left between the attic joists and the R-19 fiberglass batts you installed last fall? That gap is acting as a heat short circuit and has reduced your R-19 to an effective R-9!

It's not what kind or how much insulation you install that counts; it's the care with which you do it.

HOW JOINTS ARE MADE

Joinery is a task you may think you have little need for. But knowing how joints are made will add to your carpentry techniques and help you with tasks such as repairing cabinets and furniture, repairs that often involve failed joints. Making a fine wood joint requires care and patience, but the results are worth the effort.

You can make suitable joints with simple hand tools, such as a backsaw, sharp chisel, drill, and hammer, but power tools simplify and speed the process. You'll need three basic power tools to make most of the joints—a table saw, a router, and a power miter saw, sometimes called a "chop" saw. Serious woodworkers might consider buying specialized tools such as a

doweling jig, a dovetail template, and a biscuit joiner.

The keys to making a successful joint are precision cutting and secure fastening. Always use sharp tools and cut the pieces so that each joint closes tightly with gentle hand pressure. The snugger the fit, the stronger the joint will be.

For most joints, adhesives and screws or nails are sufficient fasteners. Woodworker's glue is adequate for most interior purposes, but for especially strong joints, use two-part epoxy. Clamp glued joints as soon as possible, and let them set overnight. Conceal nail heads by countersinking them, then fill holes with a stainable wood filler or putty that matches the color of the surrounding wood. Conceal screw heads by countersinking and plugging the holes with prefabricated plugs. You can also make your own by sawing dowels into short sections or by cutting plugs from scrap wood with a plug cutter.

DRAWBOLT JOINT

Drawbolt joints are very strong, easy to make, and are forgiving of minor imperfections. Pieces of wood joined with a drawbolt are easy to disassemble

and reassemble. They can be fashioned with a standard bolt, nut, and washers, or you can buy specialty parts for high-quality work.

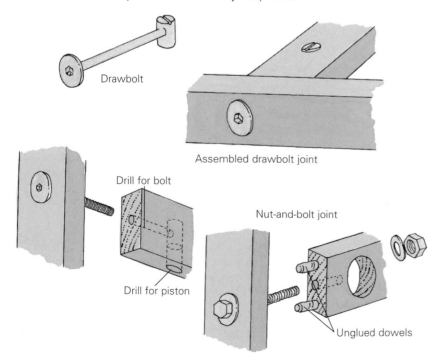

Drawbolt

Assembled drawbolt joint

Drill for bolt

Drill for piston

Nut-and-bolt joint

Unglued dowels

LAP JOINTS

FULL-LAP JOINT

This joint is excellent for fastening boards of different thicknesses at right angles. Mark the position of the thinner board on the sides and top of the cross-board. Cut the notch carefully with a sharp backsaw. Fit the lapping board in the notch and fasten with glue and screws or nails.

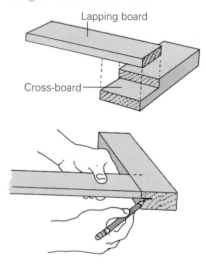

Lapping board

Cross-board

HALF-LAP JOINT

Use this joint to join boards of similar thickness. Lay the lapping board over the cross-board and mark the cross board. Turn the pieces over to mark the lapping board. Mark thicknesses on the sides of each piece. Check the marks for square with a try square. Cut out the notches using a sharp backsaw. If necessary, flatten the insides of the notches by shaving down any imperfections with a sharp chisel. Fasten the joint with glue and nails or screws.

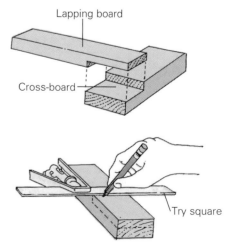

Lapping board

Cross-board

Try square

BLIND-DOWEL JOINT

Strengthen any joint with at least two dowels. To make a blind-dowel joint, clamp together the two pieces of wood to be joined with their faces parallel to each other. Check that all edges are flush, then mark both faces for the dowel locations. Unclamp the pieces and use a doweling jig to drill one of the pieces precisely. Drill the holes 1/16-inch deeper than the dowel length. Insert dowel centers in the holes, and tap the face of the other piece on them. Then drill the second piece at the marks left by the dowel centers.

Drive the dowels into one piece and tap the other piece onto them. If the joint fits square and snug, gently pry it apart and apply glue to the holes and mating surfaces—not the dowels—then clamp. If the dowels do not fit, fill the holes with new dowels, cut them flush, and start over again.

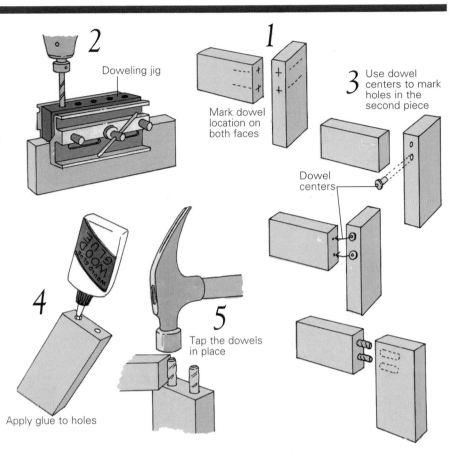

Doweling jig

Mark dowel location on both faces

Use dowel centers to mark holes in the second piece

Dowel centers

Apply glue to holes

Tap the dowels in place

MITER JOINT

This classic joint has dozens of applications around the house. It is used for picture frames, molding, shelf corners, handrails, and in any other project where you want to conceal the end grain of both boards.

The simplest and most accurate way to make the cut is with a power miter saw. Set the angle of the saw to 45 degrees for the first cut. Then rotate the saw to the 45-degree mark on the opposite side for cutting the second piece.

To cut freehand, work a 45-degree angle on the wood with a try square or combination square. Mark the board both across the face and down the side so that you can cut both dimensions accurately. Hold the blade of a backsaw square to the workpiece and cut one side, using a combination square as a guide. Then cut the other piece.

Mitered corners can be joined in several ways. The simplest— and weakest—is to glue both faces, pull them tightly together with a

picture-frame clamp, and drive two corrugated fasteners across the joint on each side. A method that is nearly as simple but makes the joint stronger is to glue the faces and then nail or screw them. The strongest method is to use dowels.

Cuts of 45 degrees make a right angle, but you can make any angle. Decide the assembled angle first. Then divide that angle in half for the cuts. Lay out and cut each board with the new angle, and then join them together with glue, nails, or dowels.

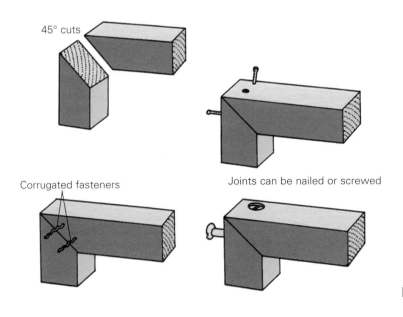

45° cuts

Corrugated fasteners

Joints can be nailed or screwed

DADO JOINT

PLAIN DADO

Dado joints are excellent for shelves, drawers, and similar cabinetwork where inside right-angle joints are required. Used on bookshelves, they stabilize the case and they make interesting edges when several joints show. Dadoes are best cut with a router or a power saw with dado blades. Make the depth of the cuts at least one-third but no more than half the thickness of the board.

RABBET JOINT

A rabbet joint is a dado cut at the end of the board. Rabbets are cut with the same techniques as a dado joint.

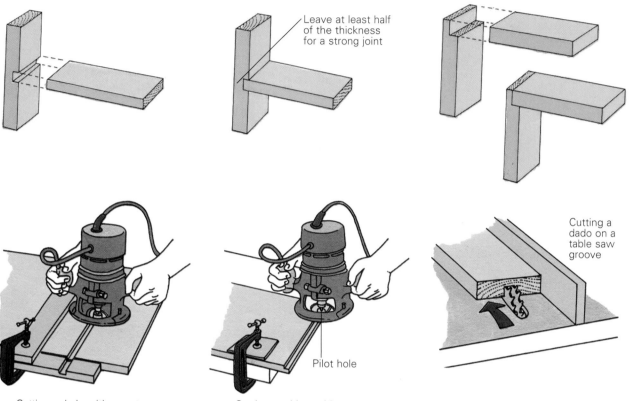

Leave at least half of the thickness for a strong joint

Pilot hole

Cutting a dado on a table saw groove

Cutting a dado with a router

Cutting a rabbet with a router

CUTTING A DADO BY HAND

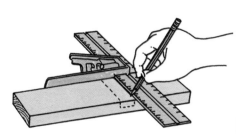

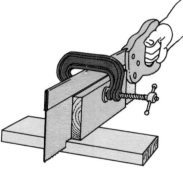

1. Mark and draw cut lines with a try square. Dado cuts usually are one-third to one-half the thickness of the board.
2. Clamp a guide board on a backsaw so that the amount of blade below the board equals the depth of the dado.

3. Cut the sides of the dado to the depth of the guide board.
4. Remove the waste with a chisel. Work from each side at an upward angle toward the center. Hold the chisel with the bevel side up.

5. Clean out remaining waste and smooth the bottom of the dado with the bevel side down.

BISCUIT JOINT

Biscuit joints are held together by thin elliptical wooden biscuits that fit in grooves in both pieces being joined.

Biscuits work well in three common joint applications:
■ Edge-to-edge, where adjacent panels are joined to make a larger flat surface, such as a table-top.
■ Mitered corners, such as in frames
■ Butt joints, where edge-and end-grained pieces come together, such as in cabinet-face frames.

A biscuit joiner has a small circular carbide blade with teeth whose thickness equals the thickness of pressed-wood biscuits.

The blade is plunged into the wood, making an elliptical slot. An identical slot is made in the second piece to be joined. When the two pieces are glued together with the elliptical biscuit in the slots, the joint is very strong.

Biscuits are made from dried compressed wood. When glue strikes the biscuit, it expands from its dry thickness of 0.148 to 0.164 inches. Since the slot is 0.156 inches thick,

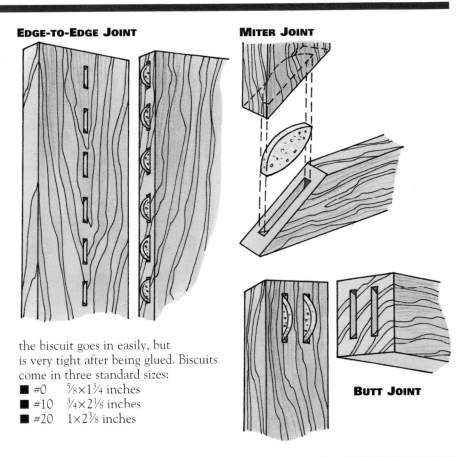

EDGE-TO-EDGE JOINT

MITER JOINT

BUTT JOINT

the biscuit goes in easily, but is very tight after being glued. Biscuits come in three standard sizes:
■ #0 $5/8 \times 1\frac{3}{4}$ inches
■ #10 $3/4 \times 2\frac{1}{8}$ inches
■ #20 $1 \times 2\frac{3}{8}$ inches

DOVETAIL JOINT

Best known for its application in cabinet drawers, the dovetail joint is very strong. You can make the cuts with a handsaw by laying them out with careful measurements on one piece, cutting them, and then tracing the "dovetails" onto the second piece.

It's easier, however, to use a router and dovetail template. The template holds the wood stock in either a horizontal or vertical position. Fit the router with a dovetail bit, which has

an inverted V shape. Clamp a piece of stock onto the template in the vertical position, butting the end up against the bottom of the fingered plate. Then run the router back and forth across the top of the stock, using the grooves as a guide. Make each cut by pushing the router toward the back and pulling it forward again; then move the router over to the next groove and repeat the process.

When the first piece of wood is

finished, clamp a second one into the jig in a horizontal position so that the end of it faces you and is flush with the front edge of the grooves. Rout it in the same matter as the first. Square off the inside of each cut with a saw and fit the two pieces together for a test. Mark the top and bottom for cutting so that the two pieces will be flush with each other at the joint. When you are satisfied with the fit, apply glue to all of the pieces and clamp them together.

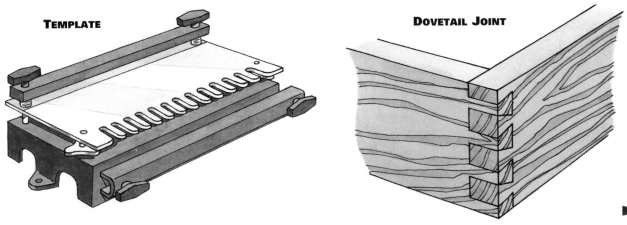

TEMPLATE

DOVETAIL JOINT

REPAIRS

CHAIR REPAIR

Repairing Stick Chairs: Even though a stick chair (or any chair, for that matter) may wobble in only one place, you may have to disassemble the entire chair in order to remove a single rung. The key to easy disassembly is to loosen the old glue. If your chair has been assembled with hide glue, you're in luck. Soften the glue with hot water or a hair dryer, then tap the parts with a rubber mallet to loosen them.

Remove all old glue from the dowels and sockets with a sharp knife, sandpaper, or a chisel. Be careful not to either reduce the size of the dowel or enlarge the dowel sockets.

Test-fit the joint before applying new hide glue or carpenter's glue. If it is slightly loose, coat the dowel with glue and wrap it tightly with a layer of thin cotton thread. Add more glue and insert the dowel into the socket.

If the joint is really loose, switch to a two-part epoxy, which can fill the void and still remain strong, or saw a kerf in the end of the dowel, partially insert a wedge of the same length as the depth of the kerf, coat the dowel with glue, and draw the joint together. The wedge will force the dowel apart, tightening the joint as it goes.

Clamp the joint with bar clamps or web clamps, or use bungee cords stretched as tightly as possible. Wipe off any excess glue with a damp rag; it will come off easily when wet, but you'll have to chip it off once it is dry.

1. Tap joints apart and twist out dowels

2. Remove old glue from dowels and sockets

3. Test-fit the dowels; if loose, wrap thread or shim with flat toothpicks

4. Glue and clamp the joints

CHAIR REPAIR

Repairing Frame Chairs:
The most common weakness in a frame chair is at the joint where the sides of the seat meet the legs and back. These joints are usually doweled. Gently spread the joint. If it is doweled, you will need to crack open the opposite joint and cut the dowels or drive off the other side rail with a padded mallet. Do not pound directly on the chair surface. Use wood blocks to protect it.

Once the joint has been disassembled, cut off the dowels flush with the surface.

Drill out the dowels on each side with a bit $\frac{1}{16}$ inch smaller than the dowel. Be careful not to drill too deep or enlarge the hole.

Clean out the dowel socket with a sharp chisel or screwdriver.

Test-fit the new dowels. If they don't line up perfectly, sand or drill the sockets slightly larger, then shim the dowel with flat toothpicks.

Glue and clamp the pieces, making sure that they are straight and correctly aligned.

Use a damp rag to wipe off any excess glue while it is still wet.

1. Pull joints apart; cut dowels flush and drill out

2. Clean out sockets

3. Test-fit new dowels; if loose, shim with flat toothpicks

4. Glue and clamp the joints

DRAWER REPAIR

Disassemble the loose joints, leaving the tight joints connected, if possible.

Clean off all old glue with a sharp chisel or knife, or sand it off (glue sticks very well to wood, but not very well to old glue). Take care to not remove any wood.

Apply carpenter's glue to the joint, following the manufacturer's instructions. Secure the glued joints with bar clamps, web clamps, or bungee cords wrapped tightly around the drawer.

While the glue is still wet, drill holes for small screws or nails through the joints. Install the screws or nails and countersink the heads just below the surface.

Reglue and clamp any loose corner blocks. If desired, you can install corner blocks in a drawer that doesn't already have them.

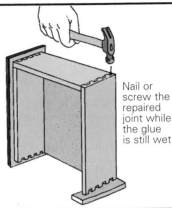

Nail or screw the repaired joint while the glue is still wet

TABLE LEG REPAIR

Table legs are usually attached with bolts or large screws and corner blocks. If the corner blocks are secure, you can fix loose legs by tightening the fasteners. If a corner block is loose, however, clean off the old glue and reglue it, using a screw or clamps to hold it in place while the glue dries.

If you use a screw, predrill the corner block with a hole slightly larger than the outer diameter of the screw threads so the screw will pull the block in tight. If the block is cracked, make a new one, using the old block as a template for cutting and drilling.

Table leg — Table leg — Corner block — Corner block — Lag screws

VENEER REPAIR

Furniture is often covered with veneer, a thin layer of decorative wood that over time may lift at the edges. Veneer that is lifting at the edges can be reattached. Veneer that is missing or damaged can be replaced or patched.

Repairing a Lifted Edge:

To reattach a lifting section, start by steaming the veneer by placing a barely damp towel over the loose section and heating it with an iron for 5 to 10 seconds. Repeat until the wood is pliable. Note that this may damage the finish, which will require subsequent repair; shellac is especially vulnerable to water.

Once the veneer is pliable, scrape out as much glue as possible and squeeze new glue into the crack. Hold the veneer down firmly and wipe up any excess glue. Cover the loose section with wax paper and a block of wood, then weight it down or clamp it until the glue dries.

Repairing a Blister: To repair a blister, carefully cut it open in the center—along the grain. Inject glue with a syringe (disposable plastic syringes are available at drugstores). Press the veneer flat, remove the excess glue, cover the blister with wax paper, and weight it down until the glue dries.

Replacing Veneer: Before attempting to replace veneer, use a scrap to practice matching the finish and grain of the surface. Stain the wood to match and with open-grained woods, such as mahogany, use a paste filler to smooth the surface.

Next, cut the patch. Trim it slightly larger than the damaged section. Align the grain of the patch with the surface. Use the patch as a template to mark the existing veneer, then cut out the outline of the patch. If the patch is thicker than the existing veneer, sand the back of the patch to thin it. Test-fit the patch and recut as required.

If necessary, stain the patch to match the existing color. Apply the same finish coat used on the original surface. Attach the patch with contact cement. If necessary, hide the seam with furniture putty that matches the veneer.

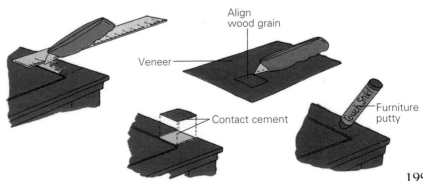

Align wood grain — Veneer — Contact cement — Furniture putty

199

KITCHEN CABINETS

KEY POINTS TO CONSIDER

Cabinets are a major design feature (and expense) in any kitchen remodeling project. Whether you are planning to build your own, buy and install ready-made units, or have the work done by professionals, there are many decisions you have to make before investing in cabinets.

Besides cost, the main factors to consider when planning and selecting cabinets are quality, appearance, efficiency, and capacity. When shopping for cabinets, research styles, models, and configurations. Visit home-improvement centers and kitchen-design showrooms to examine different cabinets and to understand how they are made. Make sure the brand you buy provides the features you want at a price you can afford. Look for guarantees that ensure your satisfaction for years to come.

PLANNING AND KITCHEN LAYOUT

The primary function of a cabinet is to provide storage. All cabinets perform this function, but some installations work better than others. Why? Because a well-designed arrangement of kitchen cabinets puts the storage where you need it, keeps stored items within reach, and creates an efficient work space with sensible traffic patterns. How do you plan the best layout for your kitchen conveniences? Here are some guidelines.

A good kitchen layout includes enough activity space, allows a smooth flow of traffic, organizes the work spaces into an efficient triangle, accommodates appliances well, stores food and cooking utensils exactly where they are needed, and provides adequate lighting. If the total space is not planned well, the cabinets will not work well either. The most beautiful cabinets cabinets in the world cannot overcome an inefficient kitchen.

The basis of kitchen design is the "work triangle," a set of imaginary lines that connect the three major appliances—sink, stove, and refrigerator. When configured properly, the traffic pattern between the sink, stove, and refrigerator should form a triangle that allows maximum efficiency of the space. Each leg should be from 4 to 7 feet long; the total length of all three legs should measure from 12 to 21 feet. The best arrangements attempt to place the sink at an equal distance from the other two appliances. Some kitchens, such as long, narrow galley kitchens in older homes, do not easily conform to work triangle ideals. If that's the case, use the work triangle as a helpful guideline.

Once you have laid out your work triangle, refine the size, placement and style of your cabinets with the following principles in mind:
■ Total frontage of base cabinets, not counting sink or corner cabinets, should be no less than 13 feet for small kitchens and 16 feet for medium and large kitchens.
■ Total frontage of wall cabinets should be at least 12 feet for small kitchens and 16 feet for medium and large kitchens.
■ Arrange cabinets so that every item is stored in the area where it is used. Put pots and pans near the oven and cooktop. Plates and glassware should be readily accessible to dining areas. Store dishtowels near the sink and dishwasher.
■ Base cabinets with large drawers and pull-out shelves are more efficient than fixed-shelf cabinets because you can reach their entire depth. Items are often "lost" at the back of fixed shelves.
■ Lazy-Susan cabinets are more efficient than fixed-shelf corner units. The type with doors attached to a revolving tray tend to pinch fingers. Diagonal or right-angle doors are safer.
■ Wall cabinets with adjustable shelves reduce wasted space. Put taller items at the bottom of the shelf unit; smaller, lighter items near the top.
■ Lower your reach—put the top shelf of a wall cabinet no higher than 6 feet.
■ Sink bases are available with a tilt-down front panel. The recess conceals a small tray for sponges and scrubbers.
■ Hang wall cabinets above a sink or stove no lower than 5 feet from the floor, including a range hood.
■ Make the cabinet over a refrigerator deep—24 inches instead of 12.

The increased depth provides storage space for large, seldom-used items.
■ If the minimum frontage for base and wall cabinets cannot be met, or if window space is of higher priority than wall cabinets, place a tall storage unit along a short wall. These units are 7 feet tall, 12 to 24 inches deep, and 18 to 36 inches wide. Some include small shelves in the doors or pull-out shelves and bins.
■ Although wall cabinets can be designed to extend to the ceiling, will you really use the upper shelves? An option is to use the tops of standard-height cabinets for displaying seldom-used items.

CONSIDER A PANTRY

Is there anything more frustrating than looking for that can of cashews you know is behind one of six cabinet doors? Or how about when you have guests, and they want to help out in the kitchen, but they can't because they can't find anything?

Enter the pantry—shelves and shelves with not a single cabinet door. If you don't mind having your kitchen look like a commercial kitchen, why spend thousands of dollars on fancy cabinets with doors?

USING USED CABINETS

We all know people with more money than sense—people who totally make over their kitchens once every ten years because they no longer look like the ones in the latest kitchen design publications.

Befriend people like this! Offer to dispose of their ten-year-old, $10,000 cabinets. If you are not fortunate enough to have friends like this, then look in your local buy/sell/swap publication. They are out there!

SIZES

Except for unique situations requiring a custom design, cabinet dimensions are standard throughout the industry. Base cabinets are always 24 inches deep (the countertop is usually 25½ inches), and 34½ inches high. When the 1½-inch countertop is added, it brings the total height to a comfortable 36 inches.

Wall cabinets are 12 inches deep and from 12 to 48 inches wide. Most are 30 inches high; when installed 18 inches above the countertop, the tops are 84 inches above the floor.

Wall cabinets also are available in 12-, 15-, 18-, and 24-inch heights for installations over sinks, ranges, refrigerators, and windows. Allow at least 30 inches of clearance above a cooktop, even when a range hood is under the cabinet. A bar counter is generally 42 inches high. Built-in desks or tables are usually 29 to 30 inches high—standard base cabinets won't work to support a built-in desk surface.

WALL CABINETS

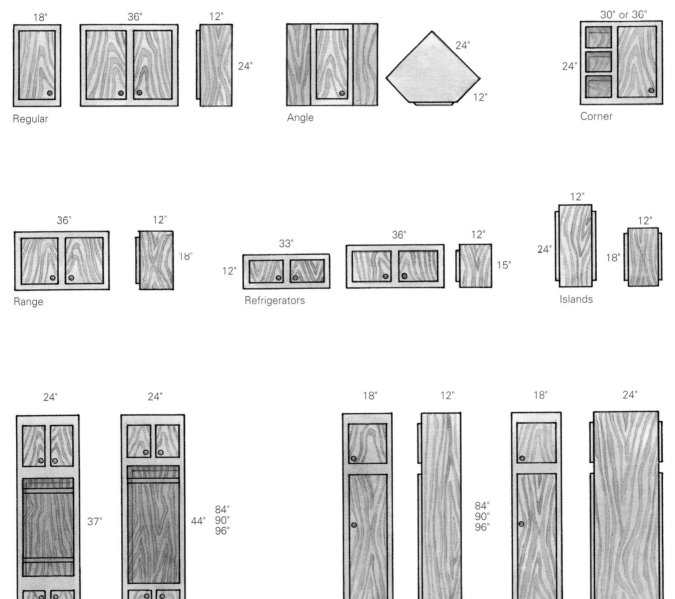

Regular

Angle

Corner

Range

Refrigerators

Islands

Wall ovens

Broom closets

SIZES *continued*

BASE CABINETS

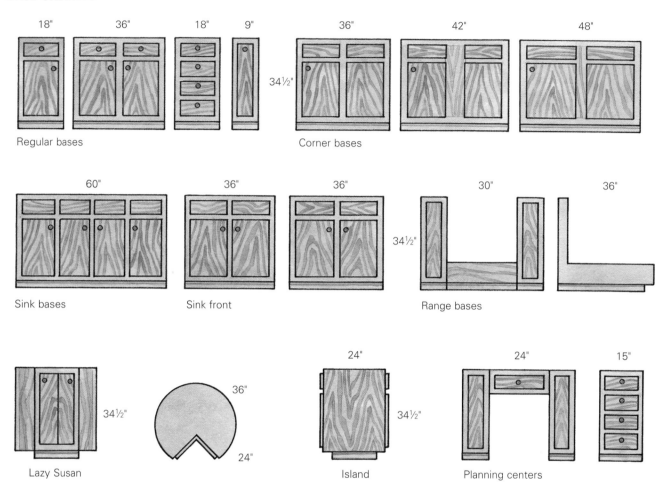

Regular bases

Corner bases

Sink bases

Sink front

Range bases

Lazy Susan

Island

Planning centers

EFFICIENCY AND CAPACITY

The primary function of a kitchen cabinet is to provide concealed storage and keep stored items free of dust. All cabinets perform this function, but some installations work better than others. Why? Because the storage is located where needed, and because it is easy to use.

The core of cabinet planning is a good kitchen layout—one that includes enough activity space, that allows a smooth flow of traffic, that organizes the work spaces into an efficient triangle, that accommodates appliances well, and that provides adequate lighting. If the total space is not planned well, the cabinets will not work well either. The most beautiful cabinets cabinets in the world can not

overcome an inefficient kitchen.

The size, placement, and style of the cabinets should be refined keeping all the following principles in mind:
■ Total frontage of base cabinets, not counting sink cabinets or corner spaces, should be no less than 13 feet for small kitchens and 16 feet for medium and large kitchens.
■ Total frontage of wall cabinets should be at least 12 feet for small kitchens and 16 feet for medium and large kitchens.
■ Cabinets should be arranged so that every item can be stored in the area where it is used.
■ Base cabinets with large drawers and pull-out shelves are more efficient than fixed-shelf cabinets.
■ Lazy-Susan corner cabinets are more

efficient than those with fixed shelves. The type with doors attached to a revolving tray tend to pinch fingers. It is better for corner cabinets to have diagonal doors or right-angle doors.
■ Wall cabinets with adjustable shelves reduce wasted space.
■ The top shelf inside a wall cabinet should be no higher than 6 feet for maximum accessibility.
■ Sink bases are available with a tilt-down front panel. The recess behind conceals a small tray for storing sponges and scrubbers.
■ Wall cabinets above a sink or stove should be no lower than 5 feet from the floor, including a range hood.
■ The cabinet over a refrigerator should be 24 inches instead of 12 inches deep, provided it is not

SOURCES

Cabinets are categorized as stock, modular, and custom.

Stock cabinets are mass-produced and commonly kept in stock by dealers. They are usually of low to medium quality.

Modular cabinets are displayed in kitchen showrooms. After you select and order the cabinets that fit your layout, they are assembled from modular components at a factory and shipped to you.

Custom cabinets are made to your specifications by cabinetmakers who build the units to fit your space and particular needs. Custom cabinets may be prove less expensive than buying from a kitchen showroom, even though the service and quality are comparable.

If you select custom cabinets, ask the cabinetmaker for references and apply the same standards of quality that you would to any expensive purchase.

TERMINOLOGY

There's more to cabinetry than "cabinets," and the terms applied to today's units can be confusing. Here's a set of definitions:

Appliance Garage: A small storage cabinet, typically installed directly on the countertop, it is used to hide small, frequently used appliances such as toasters or blenders. The tambour door of an appliance garage slides up much like a folding garage door.

Base or Base Frame: The pedestal on which the base cabinet rests—typically 4 to 4⅝ inches (higher for European cabinets).

Base Cabinet: A lower cabinet on which the countertop rests, typically 34½ inches tall and 24 inches deep.

Box: The main body of the cabinet, also referred to as a case or carcass. The box is made from plywood or particleboard, with a back for attaching to the wall and braces or "stretchers" across the top to which the countertop is attached.

Corner Cabinet: Either an upper or a base cabinet especially designed to form a 90-degree corner in a run of cabinets.

Deck: The permanent bottom shelf of a cabinet.

Double-sided Cabinet: An upper cabinet suspended over a peninsula and accessible from either side.

Face Frame: The front framework of a cabinet, consisting of horizontal rails and vertical stiles or mullions. It is usually made from the same material as the doors and drawer fronts. Not all cabinet styles have face frames.

End Panels: Decorative pieces of plywood or similar material that cover exposed cabinet sides.

Fillers: Narrow sections of face-frame material intended to fill the empty spaces when a row of cabinets does not quite fit wall to a wall. Fillers can be cut to the exact width of the space.

Island Cabinet: A freestanding base cabinet usually positioned in the center of a larger kitchen. For convenience, an island cabinet may have a second sink.

Lazy Susan: A turntable with rows of circular shelves—typically mounted inside a corner cabinet. A lazy susan rotates and provides access to stored items.

Peninsula Cabinet: Usually refers to a base cabinet that juts out into a kitchen space and is accessible from both sides. One end of a peninsula cabinet remains joined to the run of base cabinets.

Sink Front: A cabinet without a deck or a back to accommodate plumbing pipes and electrical hookups for appliances such as disposers.

Specialty Cabinets: These include corner cabinets (either "blind" or "lazy susan" units), island and peninsula cabinets, and built-in oven cabinets.

Toe Kick: A recessed space under base cabinets that allows you to stand close to the cabinet. It is usually 3 inches deep. It is automatically created when a base cabinet is positioned on a base frame of lesser depth.

Unfitted Cabinet: A freestanding cabinet made to look like a piece of furniture and designed to provide additional storage.

Utility Cabinet: A tall storage unit with shelves, or an open cabinet that functions as a broom closet.

Wall Cabinet: An upper, wall-hung cabinet, typically 30 inches tall and 12 inches deep.

connected to other 12-inch wall cabinets. The increased depth provides storage space for large items that are seldom used.

■ If the minimum frontage for base and wall cabinets cannot be met, or if window space is of higher priority than wall cabinets, place a tall storage unit along a short wall. These units are 7 feet tall, 12 to 24 inches deep, and 18 to 36 inches wide. Some include small shelves in the doors or pull-out shelves and bins.

■ While wall cabinets can be designed to extend to the ceiling, will you really use the upper shelves? An option is to use the tops of standard-height cabinets and display decorative items on the tops of the cabinets.

PAPER TIGER

Do you think the refrigerator is the biggest, ugliest thing in your kitchen, and that it dominates the space? And are you playful? If your answer is "yes" to both questions, then wallpaper the beast. That's right—wallpaper right over it. If it matches your kitchen wallpaper, you'll be surprised at how it seems to disappear.

And your friends won't think you are crazy; they'll be jealous.

KITCHEN CABINETS
continued

PREPARING FOR THE INSTALLATION

Whether you are constructing your own or purchasing ready-made kitchen cabinets, installing them is a meticulous and demanding task. All the units must be level, plumb, and square; all joints tight and flush; and all doors and drawers aligned. Before you begin, carefully study the following techniques and read the manufacturer's instructions. Note especially the differences between framed and frameless cabinets. There is no margin for error with frameless cabinets; if not perfectly square and straight, their doors and drawers will not open or close properly.

Make sure all the walls and ceilings are smooth, and finish the soffits. Install any rough wiring required for under-cabinet lighting. Complete the painting and hang the wallcovering. If the finished floor is down, protect it with plywood or cardboard while the cabinets are being installed.

When your cabinets arrive, inspect them for defects and measure them to verify they are the size you ordered. Make sure the doors fit, none of the boxes is warped, and all the drawers slide perfectly. Remove all doors, and mark on each the cabinet it belongs to.

LAYING OUT KITCHEN CABINETS

To start your cabinet layout, use a 4-foot level to locate the highest point of the floor the base cabinets will cover. If the highest point is not against the wall, use a level and a pencil to transfer the height of that point to the wall. Measure up 34½ inches from this mark and make a second mark indicating the top of a base cabinet. Allow for the thickness of the finished floor if it is not yet installed. Then mark the wall at 36 inches for the countertop.

Draw Lines. Using the straightedge and a level, draw lines on the wall to represent the tops of the base cabinets and countertop. The line will eventually be covered over by the counter or backsplash, so make it heavy enough that you can see it.

Draw another line at the level of the tops of the wall cabinets. Most wall cabinets start 18 inches above the countertop and are 30 inches tall. Therefore, for most installations, this line will be 84 inches above the highest point of the floor (36 + 18 + 30 = 84).

If the wall cabinets will extend to a soffit or the ceiling, you'll need to find the lowest point of the ceiling or soffit. Draw a level line on the wall at that height for the cabinet tops. You can now see how your wall unit will fit. You may have to trim its top (or base, depending on the manufacturer's recommendations) or cover a gap with molding once the cabinet is installed.

With the lines on the wall as a guide and using a level, mark the cabinet locations on the wall. Make sure they line up properly with each other and with windows, sinks, and appliances.

Mark Stud Locations. Next, find the studs—probe the wall with a nail until you locate both edges of the stud.

The wall below the line will be hidden by the cabinets, so don't worry about making nail holes. Mark the exact center of the stud on the wall. Using a level, draw a vertical line through this mark so you can see it above the top of the base cabinets. Most of the other studs should be either 16 or 24 inches on-center from the first stud. Mark the center of each stud behind the upper cabinets. If there is blocking between the studs, mark a horizontal line at the center of the blocking where the cabinets will be hung.

Typically, wall cabinets are installed before base cabinets. However, if you have a solid backsplash that will extend all the way up the wall to meet the wall cabinets, you'll need to install the base cabinets and the countertop first. It is also better to install the base cabinets first if there is a full-height cabinet in the middle of a run.

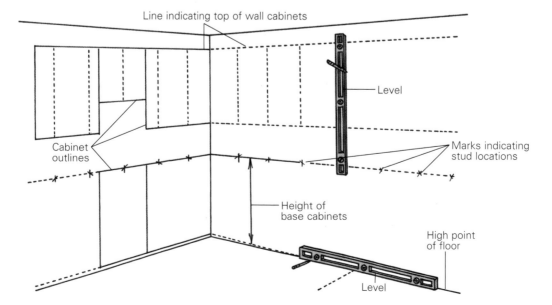

Line indicating top of wall cabinets

Level

Cabinet outlines

Marks indicating stud locations

Height of base cabinets

High point of floor

Level

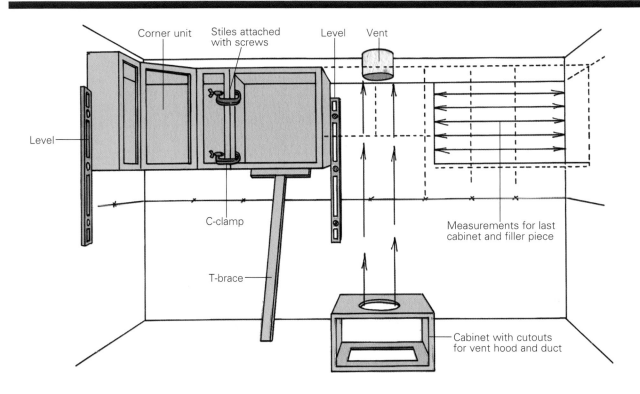

Corner unit — Stiles attached with screws — Level — Vent

Level

C-clamp

T-brace

Measurements for last cabinet and filler piece

Cabinet with cutouts for vent hood and duct

Start a run of wall cabinets with a full-height unit or a corner unit if you have one. Otherwise, start at whichever end will not require filler. The first cabinet must be perfectly level, plumb, and square or the entire run will be out of alignment.

Measure the stud placement behind the first cabinet and transfer these measurements to the inside of the cabinet at the top and bottom hanger rails (wood strips). At these marks, countersink and drill screw holes through the back of the cabinet.

If the cabinets are frameless, they may come with a metal support rail. Cut the rail to length and screw it securely to each stud at the height recommended by the manufacturer.

Hang the Cabinets: With a helper, lift the first cabinet into place and slide a prop under it. Attach the cabinet to the studs with 3-inch drywall screws, tightening only one of the top screws and leaving the others slightly loose. If the wall bows inward, shim the cabinet out next to a screw. Use a level to check that the cabinet is plumb in all directions and tighten the rest of the screws.

Now transfer the stud dimensions to the inside of the second cabinet and countersink and drill its screw holes. Drill two more holes through the stile on the side that will attach to the first cabinet. (Drill these holes where the door hinges will later cover the screw heads.)

Lift the second cabinet into place, support it, and clamp the two cabinets together so that the joint between them is tight and flush. (Use wood scraps to protect the cabinet finish from the clamps.)

Choose a drill bit slightly smaller than the shank of a 1½-inch drywall screw and center it in one of the holes you drilled in the stile. Drill two-thirds of the way into the adjoining stile of the first cabinet.

Do the same for the other hole and drive the screws firmly into the stile. If the cabinets are tall, or if the face frames do not align perfectly, drill more holes and add more screws. Then attach the cabinet to the back wall in the same way as you did the first cabinet.

Finishing Up: Repeat this process for the rest of the wall cabinets in the same run. If a vent hood will be mounted under a wall cabinet, cut holes in the cabinet for the exhaust duct before you install the cabinet.

In frameless cabinets, the stile holes are already partially drilled at the factory. All you have to do is complete the drilling. Special fasteners screw into each other through the holes, leaving a smooth head on each side that is covered with a plastic cap.

If the last cabinet ends at a sidewall, you may need to add a filler piece to close a gap. Fillers come in 3-inch and 6-inch widths and must be cut to fit snugly. Before you install the last cabinet, attach the filler to the stile as you would attach two cabinets together. Then take a series of measurements between the wall and the last cabinet installed. Transfer these measurements to the face of the final cabinet, marking them on the filler piece. Now connect the marks with a line. Cut along the line with a fine-toothed saber saw, angling the back of the cut toward the cabinet. The cut will follow any deviations in the wall so that the filler piece will fit perfectly. Filler pieces for corners need only be ripped to width, not scribed and cut.

▶

INSTALLING BASE UNITS

Both frame and frameless base units are installed the same as wall cabinets, but with the frameless cabinets there is no margin for error. Unless a cabinet in the middle of a run must be aligned with some other feature, such as a window, start with a corner unit.

Set the cabinet in place and shim the base until the top is even with the layout line. Countersink and drill through the top rail at each stud and attach the rail with 3-inch drywall screws. If the wall is not flat, place shims behind the cabinet, using a level to check the top, sides, and front. Hold the level against the frame, not against a door or drawer.

Set the second unit in place, shim it, and attach it to the first. Screw it to the back wall.

Complete the run of base cabinets, shimming each to bring its top to the horizontal line. On exposed cabinet ends, remember that gaps up to ½-inch wide between the cabinet and the wall surface will be hidden by trim (see Finishing Touches, *opposite*).

Some cabinets, such as lazy susan corner units and sink fronts, have no box to attach to the wall. They are held in place only at the face frames. (With frameless styles the sink fronts have sides that extend back just far enough to attach them to the adjacent cabinets.) Because these units have no backs, you will have to screw cleats of 1-by lumber to the wall just below the layout line to provide support for the back of the countertop.

If you want a deck under your sink, you will need to fabricate it. Cut it out of a piece of ½-inch to ¾-inch plywood and support it on cleats screwed to the wall and to the adjacent cabinets. Seal it or paint it before installing it.

If there is an appliance in the run, measure the actual appliance width before installing the cabinets (get dimensions from your supplier if the unit has not been delivered yet). Cabinets are mighty hard to move after they have been installed! To keep the cabinets on both sides of the appliance space aligned, bridge the gap with a long straightedge at the front and back. Finally, install fill pieces at the end of the run and at the corners, just as you did for the wall cabinets.

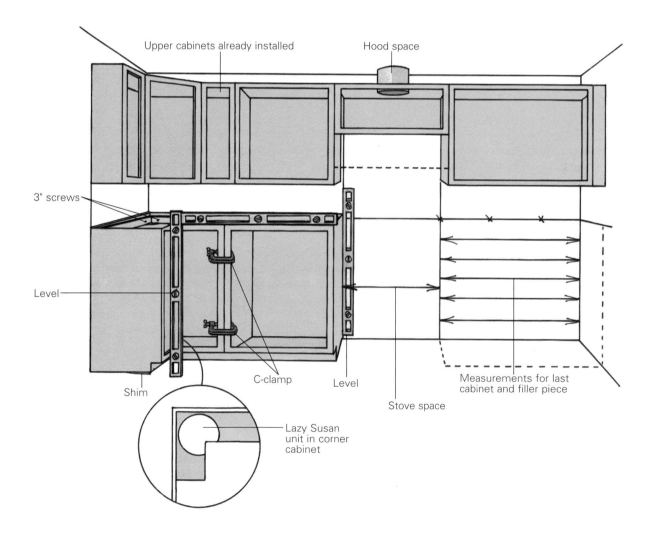

Upper cabinets already installed

Hood space

3" screws

Level

Shim

C-clamp

Level

Stove space

Measurements for last cabinet and filler piece

Lazy Susan unit in corner cabinet

FINISHING TOUCHES

Doors, trim, finish panels, and handles are all prominent features of kitchen cabinets. Attach them correctly the first time—it is very difficult to make adjustments later.

Finish Panels: Install finish panels on all exposed sides of the cabinets, except the face frame. The panels come either pre-cut or as a full sheet of plywood paneling from which you cut each piece. If the panels have grain patterns, match them carefully with the patterns on the adjacent cabinets.

Measure and cut each panel to size. Spread contact cement on the back of each panel and on the side of the cabinet. Let the glue on both surfaces set until dry to the touch. Press the panel in place, clamp it, and leave it overnight to dry.

Hinges: When you put the doors on the cabinets, some of them may not line up perfectly. Better-quality hinges include adjustment slots that allow you to loosen screws and move the hinges slightly without having to completely remount the hinges.

Trim: Before installing trim pieces, be sure that the cabinets are perfectly aligned and securely fastened. Cut the trim to length with a miter saw, and stain or paint the trim, including the cut ends, before attaching. Predrill and fasten the trim with 3d, 4d, or 6d finishing nails. Sink the heads with a nail set and fill the holes.

Attach frameless cabinet trim pieces from inside the cabinet, using screws. Predrill holes large enough to take the screws; use a smaller bit to drill pilot holes in the trim itself.

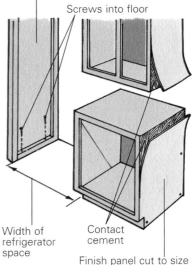

Back side of full-height refrigerator panel

Screws into floor

Width of refrigerator space

Contact cement

Finish panel cut to size

DOORS AND HINGES

FULL-OVERLAY DOORS

Attach overlay doors (square-edged doors which slightly lap the cabinet face) directly to the cabinet face with butt, pivot, or "European" hinges. The barrels of butt hinges can be seen from the side and are fastened just beyond the cabinet frame so the doors can clear. Pivot hinges, screwed to the top and bottom edges of the door, don't require side clearance, but show their edges. The more expensive European-style hinges don't show at all.

INSET DOORS

Butt hinges for inset doors (doors whose faces are flush with the cabinet face) are mortised into the edges of the cabinet stiles and door to reduce the size of the gap. Pivot hinges are mortised into the top and bottom edges of each door. Decorative face hinges can be mounted to purposely show either one or both leaves.

LIPPED DOORS

Lipped doors (doors with rabbeted edges which partially overlap the cabinet face) use hinges that show one narrow leaf. They are not usually mortised into the doors or the cabinet frame frame. The popular bent-leaf, also

called an offset hinge, comes in sizes to fit rabbets of different thicknesses, so be sure you have the right size. Like other

types of hinges, one style includes a spring for self-closing.

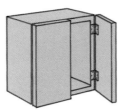

Full-overlay doors

Inset doors

Lipped doors

Butt hinge

Pivot hinge

European-style hinge

Butt hinge

Pivot hinge

European-style hinge

(1 leaf screwed to top or bottom of case)

Semiconcealed hinge

KITCHEN DESIGN

THE ESSENCE OF HOME

Hearth and home have always been synonymous. What was meant by hearth, however, was not the place Christmas stockings were hung, but the place where food was prepared. So "hearth" meant "kitchen."

The same is true today. The kitchen is the center of the home. Cooking, eating, and socializing happen there. Appliances, fixtures, work areas, storage spaces, and traffic corridors are all concentrated there. This focus of activity, combined with a bewildering choice of appliances and cabinetry, makes the kitchen the most complex room to plan.

Professional kitchen designers go through a series of steps in developing a plan: specification of the available space, an inventory of the occupants' habits and needs, the development of a floor plan, and finally, selection of the materials to achieve the desired look. This process entails many changes and refinements, and often much going back and forth between the planning steps. Some decisions involve functional considerations; others are concerned with taste and style; but the key to the entire process is the development of an efficient floor plan.

Start by drawing (on graph paper) an accurate floor plan. Then experiment with layouts until you find the most satisfying arrangement of appliances, furniture, and space. Trying dozens of layouts is more fun if you sketch them on tracing paper laid over the floor plan. Another time-saver is a kitchen design template, which contains scaled cutouts of cabinets and appliances that you can move around your floor plan like puzzle pieces. And don't overlook the computer. Many software manufacturers offer easy-to-use computer applications that help you plan creative kitchen layouts and configurations.

WHO USES THIS KITCHEN?

When architects design houses for clients, the first thing they do is determine the *program*—the list of everything the client desires in the design.

If you're going to be your own architect, your first task is to come up with your own program. Do you desire: a different stove, a different sink, more counter space, a nice window, more storage, better traffic patterns? Be as specific as possible about your needs. Some requirements jump to the front because you have lived too long without them. Some are ideas you have gotten from magazines or from friends' kitchens. Other needs may be less obvious because your present kitchen has them, but they are equally important, so don't forget to write them down. Try asking yourself:
■ How many cooks will work in this kitchen at the same time?
■ How tall are the cooks?
■ Do any of the cooks have particular physical needs?
■ Are the cooks right-handed or left-handed?
■ How often do you cook?
■ How often do you bake?
■ What kind of specialty cooking do you like to do?
■ How often do you entertain?
■ How many people do you typically invite when you entertain?

TAKE A TAPE

Would you buy a $10,000 suit or dress without knowing what size it was? Of course not! Then why would you do the same with a kitchen?

When you start getting serious about building or remodeling your kitchen, get in the habit of carrying a small tape measure and a sketch pad. When you see a kitchen you like, measure it and sketch it:
■ What are the dimensions of that island?
■ What are the lengths of the counters?
■ How wide are the passageways between counters?

Also, ask the owners what they like most and least about their kitchen. What would they do differently next time? Imagine their kitchen as your own. Then your design will incorporate all the experience of others who have done this before you.

■ Do you like to eat in the kitchen or in spaces nearby?
■ Do you like company in the kitchen or do you prefer to work alone?
■ Does your family congregate in the kitchen?
■ What other activities, such as homework, sewing, laundry, paying bills, and talking on the telephone, occur in your kitchen?
■ Do you want an office or a bill-paying station in the kitchen?
■ How often do you shop for groceries?
■ After shopping, where do you enter the kitchen with your groceries?
■ What kinds of items do you want to store?
■ What personal or decorative items do you want to display?
■ How often do you clean your kitchen?
■ What kind of emotional qualities do you assign your kitchen (tidy, busy, warm, sleek, etc.)?
■ What would you think of as your personal style—traditional, contemporary, country, or eclectic?
■ Is there access to the dining room and, if not, would you like there to be?
■ Do you have a deck where you like to entertain or eat with the family?
■ Do you need access to the garden or a place to dry herbs or flowers?
■ Do you want to look out to views?
■ Are neighbors or passersby close enough that privacy is an issue?
■ Do you want to open the windows?
■ Do you want sunshine in your kitchen?

Not all of these issues deal with strictly practical concerns. Some of the necessities of a kitchen have to do with your personal lifestyle and the needs of other members of your family. To keep all your ideas handy as you plan, start a scrapbook or file. Clip photographs from magazines that depict interesting ideas and store them in your file. When you shop, get product brochures and catalogs you can refer to for cabinets, appliances, and other kitchen items. Gather paint cards to help make color selections. If you are working with a design professional such as an architect or a certified kitchen designer, your file will help you communicate effectively.

If you are remodeling an existing kitchen, the location of existing pipes, wires, and ducts for the appliances may get in your way. Of course, given a large enough budget, you can change anything, but why spend a lot of extra money if you can work within the constraints? Move a sink a few inches without changing the rough plumbing by extending the supply tubing and drain arm. Move an existing gas stove or cooktop a few feet by lengthening the flexible supply pipe (but keep the shutoff valve accessible).

Range Hoods: If you cook light foods or cook very little, a ductless range hood will suffice. If you cook a lot with oil, however, you should have a range hood with at least 150 CFM capacity. Duct the hood to the outside through an exterior wall or through an attic directly overhead.

Electric Cooking: An electric range, oven, or cooktop must have its own 240-volt circuit; you cannot splice into an existing line. Run new wiring from the service panel or a new subpanel. Any fixed appliance, such as a dishwasher or trash compactor, also must have its own circuit.

Appliance Circuits: In addition to circuits for lighting, a kitchen must have at least two dedicated, 20-amp circuits for appliance receptacles. Lights can be on an existing general-purpose circuit. Other electrical needs include wiring for a smoke detector, telephone, intercom, and TV cable.

Ductwork: Since you may not be able to move existing heating and cooling ducts and registers, their locations should be a basic part of your kitchen plan. Floor registers can dump directly into the space beneath lower cabinets provided the front of the toe kick is partially removed to allow air flow. Cover any holes with register grills painted to match the kick.

COLOR CHOICES

Don't get caught in the color trap. You are going to have those appliances for 20 years. Remember how smart Avocado Green was back then?

There are only two colors that go with everything—black and white. In fact, black and white go pretty well together.

Single counter

Parallel counter

L-shaped

U-shaped

L-shaped with island

U-shaped with peninsula

There are six basic configurations for kitchen work areas:

1. The single-counter shape has work areas along one wall only. This configuration is often found in apartments and other small living areas.

2. A kitchen with two parallel counters is sometimes called a corridor kitchen. The work areas are confined along two facing walls and traffic passes through the middle. For this configuration to be effective, separate the lower cabinets by no more than 60 inches. That way, you'll have plenty of space for walking around open appliance doors. Make wider separations more convenient with a short peninsula counter.

3. L-shaped kitchens naturally direct traffic flows outside the work area. This basic and practical design keeps the work space within a conveniently confined area and makes for efficient use of space.

4. The U-shaped kitchen often is thought of as the ideal shape. All work surfaces are within handy reach, but interruptions for casual foot traffic are kept outside the work area.

5. An L-shaped kitchen with an island is actually a modified U that features an additional passageway for access to nearby areas.

6. A U-shape with a peninsula provides several work centers and is an ideal configuration for kitchens that regularly host two active cooks.

SALE AWAY

There are two reasons to purchase your appliances ahead of time: price and size.

Most appliance retailers have ongoing sales. Within a three- or four-month period, every appliance they carry will be marked down at least 20 percent. Most are so glad to get your check, they will gladly hold the appliances in their warehouse until you are ready to take delivery.

With advance purchases you know the exact size of your appliances. That way you won't be surprised by a 34-inch stove that turns out to be 34⅛ inches wide.

KITCHEN DESIGN
continued

STANDARD DIMENSIONS

Professional kitchen designers have developed time-tested standard dimensions and arrangements. Unless you have specific reasons not to, incorporate these standards in your floor plan.

WORK TRIANGLE

Position the three major appliances—sink, stove, and refrigerator—so that the traffic pattern between them forms a triangle. Each leg should be from 4 to 7 feet long; the total length of all three legs should measure 12 to 21 feet. The most efficient arrangement places the sink at an equal distance from the other two appliances. At the very least, place the sink and stove no more than three steps apart. In addition to the work triangle, think of each appliance as the center of its own work area, and try to provide at least 18 inches of adjacent counterspace on one side.

REFRIGERATOR

Allow a 33- to 36-inch space for the refrigerator, whether or not your present model is that wide. The door should swing so that you can reach into the refrigerator from the sink area (most refrigerators hinge on the right side, but some are interchangeable). Allow at least 18 inches of counter on the opening side, or no more than 48 inches across from the refrigerator if you prefer. Place the refrigerator at the end of a counter rather than where it would interrupt the flow of work from one side to the other. Make sure

that its door does not interfere with the doors of other appliances. Place other food storage cabinetry near the refrigerator.

RANGE

A range or cooktop should have at least 18 inches of heat-resistant countertop on one side. Heat-resistant materials include wood, tile, stone. Some solid surface materials are heat resistant, but may not withstand direct contact with a hot pot or pan. Refer to the manufacturer's recommendations. As an alternative, you can place a wood cutting board over a plastic countertop. The other side of the range worktop should have at least 12 inches of counter space to accommodate pot handles. If counters intersect near a range, allow at least 9 inches from the range to the corner. Store pots, pans, utensils, spices, and other seasonings in the vicinity of the range,

A microwave oven should have 15 inches of counter space nearby.

A built-in oven is not used nearly as often as a cooktop so feel free to place it outside the work triangle. The oven should have at least 18 inches of counter on one side, however. If possible, position it near a mixing center. Like the refrigerator, the oven is tall, so do not place it where it will interrupt the flow of work.

SINK

The sink is the most-often used utility and should, therefore, be accompanied

by the highest proportion of counter and storage space. Provide at least 24 inches of countertop on the side where you stack dishes (usually the left side) and another 24 inches where you drain them. A sink should be at least 12 inches from a corner (3 inches if there is 21 inches of counter around the corner). Average sink dimensions are 24 inches for a single bowl; 36 inches for a double sink. If you have a dishwasher, allow 18 to 24 inches of counter and 21 inches of standing space to either side.

MIXING AND FOOD PREPARATION

Allow each cook at least 36 inches of counter space for general food preparation. The mixing center may be a separate area or you may combine it with another work area. It should be near a sink. Other activity areas that may require at least 36 inches of counter space include an eating area and a desk work station.

PASSAGEWAYS

Where counters or appliances face each other, the space between them should be at least 42 inches; standard is 54 inches. To allow two people to work back-to-back comfortably, allow 60 inches. There should be at least 42 inches of clearance around all sides of an island counter. The space between a table and wall should be 26 to 36 inches; allow 30 to 44 inches if the space also serves as a passageway.

CABINETS

In selecting cabinets for your design, keep the following guidelines in mind:
■ Cabinets should be arranged so that every item can be stored in the area where it is used. Plan to store pots and pans near the stove or cooktop. Put dishes and glassware where they are readily accessible to dining areas.
■ Base cabinets with large drawers and pull-out shelves are more efficient than fixed-shelf cabinets because they make the space fully accessible.
■ Wall cabinets with adjustable

shelves are more efficient than those with fixed shelves. Place taller items on lower shelves; smaller, lighter items on higher shelves.
■ Lazy-susan corner cabinets generally are more efficient than those with fixed shelves.
■ The top shelf inside a wall cabinet should be no higher than 6 feet for maximum accessibility.
■ Wall cabinets above a sink or stove should be no lower than 5 feet from the floor, including a range hood.

If possible, plan this space without cabinets to prevent dirt and grease from building up on the underside of the cabinet.
■ The cabinet over a refrigerator should be 24 inches instead of 12 inches deep, provided it is not connected to other 12-inch wall cabinets.
■ If window space is of higher priority than wall cabinets, make up for the loss of storage with one or more tall storage units.

REMODELING IDEAS

L-SHAPE KITCHEN

The layout *below* illustrates a typical L-shape kitchen. It's a common layout, with predictable shortcomings. It would benefit from more storage and workspace. The lone window and central light fixture provide poor illumination. The columns at right show the potential for improving this space, first by making minimal structural changes, second by extensively altering the structure.

Few Structural Changes:
1. Add hood and roll-out shelves.
2. New upper and lower cabinets.
3. Side-by-side refrigerator/freezer.
4. Full height storage cabinet.
5. Open shelving.
6. Fold-up table encloses upper shelves.
7. Add track lighting.
8. Built-in bench with storage.
9. Doorway to dining room moved to allow counter.
10. Outside door replaced by desk and greenhouse window.
11. Glass-front wall cabinet.
12. Add a lazy Susan.

Extensive Alterations:
1. Cooktop moved for more workspace.
2. Closing hall allows for corner units.
3. Wall oven and microwave.
4. Side-by-side refrigerator/freezer with cabinet above.
5. Built-in bar and shelves.
6. Pocket door.
7. Pass-through to dining room with buffet counter.
8. French doors to patio.
9. Mobile chopping block with storage.
10. Open shelving over.
11. Extra-large sink.
12. New lighting panel.

EXISTING KITCHEN

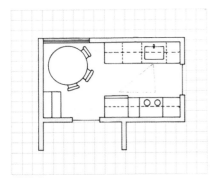

FEW STRUCTURAL CHANGES

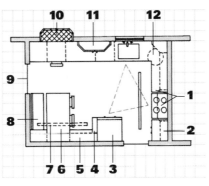

EXTENSIVE ALTERATION

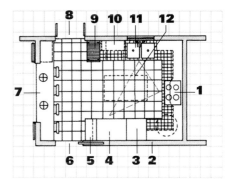

PARALLEL-COUNTER KITCHEN

The compact galley design *below* generally suffers from a lack of storage and countertop space. Cooks often find themselves working in their own shadows and bemoaning their solitude because there is room for only one person at a time. But look at the changes possible with minimal structural changes *below, center* and with major alterations, *below, right*.

Few Structural Changes:
1. Extend counter for wider sink.
2. Add track lighting.
3. Widen cooktop counter and tile for hot pots.
4. Move refrigerator to provide space for long baking center.
5. Remove hutch/change table.
6. Move refrigerator.
7. Add higher wall cabinets.

Extensive Alterations:
1. Replace dining-room half wall with full wall and add doors.
2. Increase counter depth.
3. Microwave over freestanding range.
4. Angle counter for access.
5. Recess refrigerator.
6. Build counter with track lighting.
7. Add lazy Susan.
8. Double sink.
9. Expand counter width.
10. Recessed spotlights.

EXISTING KITCHEN

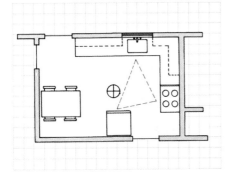

FEW STRUCTURAL CHANGES

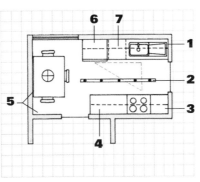

EXTENSIVE ALTERATION

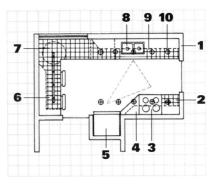

LIGHTING

BRILLIANT DESIGN

ALSO SEE...
Electrical Systems:
Pages 110–115
Switches:
Pages 352–355
Wire:
Pages 442–445

Lighting plays a key role in interior design. It affects not only the comfort and ambience of a room, but also your perception of every other design element. So don't take lighting lightly. Don't settle for just one ceiling fixture and some scattered table lamps.

Home lighting should be both varied and dramatic. Install lighting so the style, type, and intensity are appropriate to each activity area in the house (see Lighting Guidelines, pages 212–219). Connect incandescent fixtures to dimmer switches so that you can set the lighting to match your mood.

PRECAUTIONS

Besides the normal precautions you should take with all electrical wiring, there are some safety considerations unique to lighting.

Fire Hazards: Only 3 percent of the energy consumed by an incandescent lamp is given off as light; the remaining 97 percent turns into heat! If you think of light bulbs as little toaster elements, it won't be hard to keep fire danger in mind.

Do not cover recessed fixtures with insulation; allow at least 3 inches of clearance all around. Observe the limit the manufacturer places on the maximum wattage of a fixture.

Closet lights pose a fire hazard if clothing or other combustible material is too close. Lights should be installed on the ceiling or on the wall above the door. A surface-mounted fixture must be at least 18 inches from stored materials, and have unobstructed clearance between it and the floor. A recessed fixture must have a solid lens and be at least 6 inches away from stored material. A fluorescent fixture must have 6 inches of clearance.

Moisture: Lights in the bathroom should have moistureproof housings. Switches and hanging fixtures should not be near the tub or shower.

Height: The lights in children's bedrooms should be at a safe height so they will not be broken during normal play. Avoid lamps in the room of an infant or toddler.

Stairwells and Entrances: Illuminate stairwells and entrances well. Many low lights are better than one light, which may cast unsafe shadows.

FUNCTION TYPES OF LIGHTING

AMBIENT LIGHTING

Ambient lighting is the room's overall illumination, provided by windows and central ceiling fixtures, and reflected off the ceiling from soffit fixtures.

TASK LIGHTING

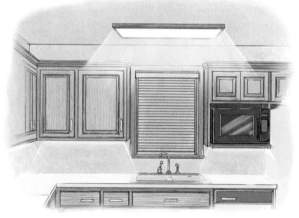

Task lighting focuses on a specific site—a desktop, sink, reading chair, or other spots where you need to see clearly for a specific task.

CODE REQUIREMENTS: LIGHTING

Fixtures in Clothes Closets: Surface-mounted incandescent fixtures may be installed on the wall above the door or the ceiling, with a minimum clearance to the storage space of 12 inches.

Surface-mounted fluorescents and recessed incandescents and fluorescents may be installed on the wall above the door or on the ceiling, with clearance to the storage space of at least 6 inches.

Fixtures in Wet Locations: Fixtures in wet or damp locations must be constructed so that water cannot enter or accumulate in wiring compartments or lampholders. They must be labeled "suitable for wet locations."

Hanging Fixtures and Tubs: Hanging fixtures and cord-connected fixtures must not be located within 3 horizontal feet and 8 vertical feet from the rim of a tub.

THE PRICE OF LIGHT

Do you have any idea how much it costs you to run a single 100-watt light bulb?

If you did, you would probably either turn the light off when you leave the room or install a compact fluorescent replacement bulb.

Let's do the calculation. Assume your per-kWh cost is 15 cents. Then:

Hour: $1 \times .1 \text{ kWh} \times \$.15 = \$.02$
Day (4 hours): $4 \times .1 \text{ kWh} \times \$.15 = \$.06$
Month: $30 \times 4 \times .1 \text{ kWh} \times \$.15 = \$1.80$
Year: $365 \times 4 \times .1 \text{ kWh} \times \$.15 = \$21.90$

LIGHT SOURCES

Consider the type of bulb when choosing fixtures.

INCANDESCENT

Incandescent bulbs produce a yellowish white light that flatters skin tones and highlights warm colors. The light is easy to direct. Incandescent bulbs cost more to operate and do not last as long as fluorescent tubes.

FLUORESCENT

Fluorescent tubes spread light, do not overheat, last a long time, and are about four times more economical to run than incandescent bulbs. They are available in many colors, from cool blues to full-spectrum white to warm tones. The initial cost of the fixtures is high, however.

QUARTZ HALOGEN

Quartz halogen bulbs produce a brilliant white light. One powerful bulb can illuminate an entire room, cast interesting shadows, and bathe a space in "sunshine." Because they put out so much heat, these bulbs must be used in special heat-resistant and thermally protected fixtures.

FIXTURE TYPES

Although there are many design variations of the fixtures shown, most fall into one of three categories:

Type of Lighting	Type of Fixture		Comments
Incandescent	Surface-mounted		Wall or ceiling; provide ambient or task lighting; attach each fixture to prewired electrical box
	Pendant		From chandelier to simple shade; offers flexibility in placing fixture
	Recessed		For downlighting, wall washing, or uplighting; canisters are usually installed before ceiling is finished, but retrofit units are available
	Track		Fixtures in a variety of shapes are snapped or clipped onto a track. Units can be positioned and directed individually
	Strip		Tiffany-type lights or incandescent tubes provide concealed lighting or dramatic accent lights
Fluorescent	Surface fixture		Primary lighting for bathroom or kitchen; tube or ring-shaped bulb
	Luminous ceiling		Light fixtures attached to ceiling and concealed by translucent panels held by grid suspended below lights
	Compact bulbs		Have screw-type bases for use in standard light fixtures in place of incandescent bulbs
Quartz halogen	Individual fixture		Uses halogen bulbs; requires transformer to step down house voltage

INSTALLING A CEILING FIXTURE

To install a ceiling light, first make sure the power to the fixture is off. Turn off the breaker or remove the fuse for the circuit. Then check the fixture with a simple circuit tester (available at any hardware store).

If you're installing a new fixture, disconnect the old one, then attach the mounting strap to the ceiling box in one of the two ways shown below. Either fasten the strap with the locknut on the threaded stud or screw the strap into the corner tabs of the box. If the box is plastic, ground the strap by connecting the bare wire to the green grounding screw.

Use wire nuts to connect the wires—black to black and white to white. If the fixture is metal, run a short pigtail from the grounding screw to the grounding wire.

Tuck the wires back into the box and screw the fixture base to the mounting bracket. Screw in the bulb and attach the globe.

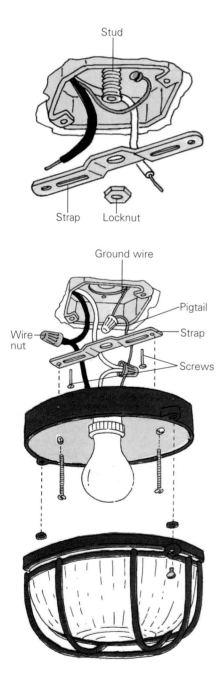

Stud

Strap   Locknut

Ground wire

Wire nut

Pigtail

Strap

Screws

RECOMMENDED LIGHTING LEVELS

Room	Application	Recommendation
Bath	General	100-watt incandescent or 40-watt fluorescent ceiling fixture
	Shower light	60-watt wet-location ceiling fixture
	Small vanity	60-watt incandescents or 20-watt fluorescents each side
	Large vanity	Three or four 60-watt incandescents in a 24-inch top fixture, or a 2- or 4-foot fluorescent instead
Bed	General	1 watt incandescent or .4 watt fluorescent ceiling fixture per square foot of bedroom floor space
	Bed reading	Individual 75- to 100-watt reading lamps with shade bottoms at eye level and 20 to 24 inches to side of book
Dining	Chandelier	200- to 300-watt incandescents 30 inches above table
	Buffet	25- to 60-watt shielded incandescents 60 inches above floor at either end
Entrance	Outside	25- to 60-watt incandescents 66 inches above porch floor at both sides, or a single lamp on the lock side
	Inside	For less than 75 square feet, 100 watts of incandescent; for larger area, 150 to 180 watts of incandescent
Hall		At least one ceiling or wall fixture every 10 feet
Kitchen	Ceiling	3-watt incandescent or 1-watt fluorescent per square foot
	Sink	Two 75-watt downlights spaced 18 inches apart
	Range	60-watt incandescent
	Cabinet	8 watts fluorescent per foot, installed at cabinet front
	Island	Two 75-watt downlights spaced 18 inches
	Dinette	100-watt hanging or track over table or counter
Living/ Family	General	1 watt incandescent per square foot in accent or wall-washing fixtures
	Reading	Individual 75- to 100-watt reading lamps with shade bottoms at eye level and 20 to 24 inches to side of book
	Television	Low level placed to avoid screen reflections
	Games	100-watt shaded incandescent hanging over table
Stairs		Ceiling or wall fixtures at each end on 3-way switches
Study	Desk	150-watt incandescent with shade bottom 15 inches above desk top, 12 inches from front edge
Workshop		Double 4-foot fluorescents 48 inches above workbench

TRACK LIGHTING

Track lighting adds both style and functionality to your lighting design. It puts light exactly where you want it. Track lighting consists of track, available in different lengths, and light units that snap or clip onto it. The track is connected to power at a junction box in the same way as a ceiling or wall fixture. You can purchase a kit consisting of one section of track plus three or four light units, or you can buy the track and light

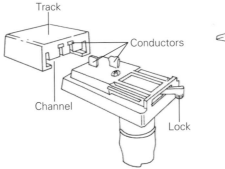

Track
Conductors
Channel
Lock

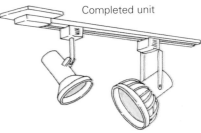

Completed unit

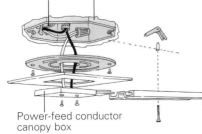

Ground wire   Ceiling box

Power-feed conductor canopy box

units separately. Sections of track can also be connected to make one long track.

INSTALLING TRACK LIGHTING

Turn off the power, test the circuit with a tester, and remove the old fixture from the ceiling box. Screw the track adapter plate to the corner tabs of the ceiling box.

Thread the wires from the canopy box through the adapter plate. Connect them to the wiring in the ceiling box with wire nuts. Tuck the wires in the box and screw the canopy box to the adapter plate.

Drill holes in a section of track for toggle bolts, slide the end into the canopy box, and screw the toggles into the ceiling.

Snap the light fixtures into the track wherever you want, and secure them in place. Some fixtures simply twist into place; others have locking levers, as shown. Turn on the lights and swivel and tilt them into position. If necessary, unlock the fixtures and slide them along the track until they are in perfect position. Relock the fixtures.

HANGING FIXTURES

Hanging fixtures such as pendant lamps and chandeliers can be difficult to install. It's not a complicated process, but tightening the mounting hardware with one hand while supporting the fixture with the other can be awkward. Some larger fixtures are heavy enough to require two people for installation—one to do the necessary tightening and the other just to hold the fixture as connections are made. Come prepared with a bit of patience.

Although there are many styles available, most hanging fixtures have similar parts: wire connections that are made in an electrical box inside the ceiling; a cover plate designed to hide the box and the hole in the ceiling; a chain, rod, or wire to support the weight of the fixture; and a threaded nipple that connects the support chain to the electrical box by means of a mounting strap. The electrical connections are simple and straightforward.

Hanging fixtures are mounted in much the same way as flush-mounted ceiling fixtures. First, turn off electrical power at the main service panel and test the circuit with a tester. Attach the mounting strap to the electrical box—the box should already be firmly fastened to a support arm or wood block installed between ceiling joists.

Once the mounting strap is in place, screw the nipple into the mounting strap. Secure the nipple with a retaining nut. Feed the fixture wires through the center of the nipple and connect them with wire nuts to the black, white, and bare circuit wires coming from the box. Carefully tuck all the wires into the electrical box.

While supporting the weight of the fixture, screw the fixture mounting bolt onto the threaded nipple. You may have to rotate the fixture as you do so. Then attach the cover plate. If the fixture hangs from a chain, thread the wire through the chain to make it less conspicuous.

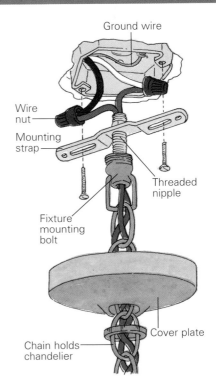

Ground wire

Wire nut

Mounting strap

Threaded nipple

Fixture mounting bolt

Cover plate

Chain holds chandelier

FLUORESCENT FIXTURES

Fluorescent lighting uses gas-filled bulbs that burn at relatively low temperatures and are more energy-efficient than incandescent light bulbs. For this reason they are popular for use in large buildings as a source of ambient or general lighting. The light from fluorescent bulbs is not as easily concentrated as incandescents and generally is not favored for task-lighting situations. You'll find three types of fluorescent lamps:

Preheat: In this oldest of the three types, the starter is separate from the ballast, and you can replace it without removing the ballast.

Rapid-start: This least-expensive type has the starter built into the ballast.

Instant-start: These fixtures have no starter at all. They are much less common than the other types and are distinguishable by the use of tubes with a single pin at each end.

Common repairs of fluorescent fixtures include replacing burned-out tubes, replacing the starter when the tubes flicker but never brighten, and replacing damaged or corroded sockets. Ballasts are rarely replaced because they cost as much as an entire new fixture. Just because a bulb goes out, don't assume it requires repair or replacement. More often than not, reseating the bulb in its sockets will bring it back to life.

TROUBLESHOOTING FLUORESCENT LIGHTS

Problem	Possible Causes/Symptoms	What to Do to Fix
No light at all	Switch off	Turn switch on
	Circuit breaker tripped	Turn circuit breaker on
	Bulb not seated	Remove bulb and reinstall
	Starter defective	Replace with new starter
	Tube defective	Replace tube
Partial light	Ends are blackened	Replace tube
	Ends light; center doesn't	Replace starter
	Uniformly dim	Replace tube
Light flickers	Temperature below 50° F	Wait until temp rises
	Lamp is failing	Replace tube
Fixture hums	Poor ballast connection	Tighten connections
	Ballast failing	Replace ballast or fixture

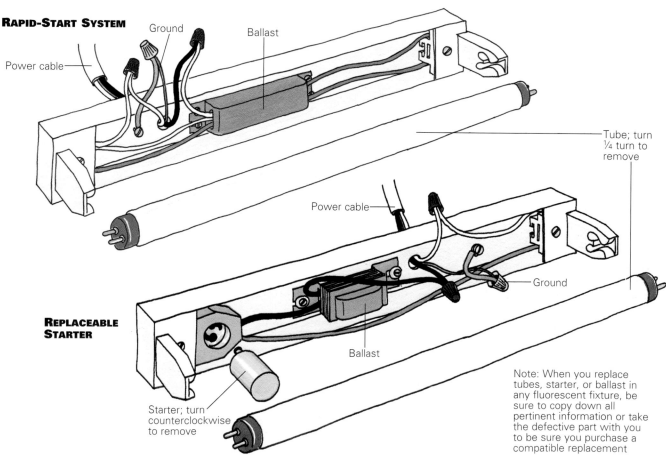

RAPID-START SYSTEM

Ground

Ballast

Power cable

Tube; turn ¼ turn to remove

Power cable

Ground

REPLACEABLE STARTER

Ballast

Starter; turn counterclockwise to remove

Note: When you replace tubes, starter, or ballast in any fluorescent fixture, be sure to copy down all pertinent information or take the defective part with you to be sure you purchase a compatible replacement

Installing outdoor lighting is much more than providing a fixture for the front porch and a security light over the garage door. A well-designed lighting system illuminates driveways, walkways, doors, stairs, and gates. It also provides security around the house by eliminating shadows where intruders could hide.

Lighting also enhances a garden after dark. It makes possible evening outdoor activities, such as entertaining. By lighting the landscape and allowing you to view it at night, it also brings the outside in, creating a graceful transition from indoor to outdoor space.

PLANNING A SYSTEM

When choosing outdoor lighting, you have two basic options: extending household circuits for 120-volt fixtures or installing low-voltage lighting. Low-voltage outdoor lighting is safe, inexpensive, and easy to install. Manufacturers generally include clear instructions with their systems. You will probably find planning the layout to be the most difficult part of the job.

Make sure the total wattage of the light fixtures doesn't exceed the capacity of the transformer. If it does, you will need to install one or more additional transformers.

The goals of a complete outdoor lighting system are to provide safe lighting for activities, to provide security, to illuminate plants, trees, pools, and other features, and to create moods and effects that enhance the character of the garden. You will find a great variety of outdoor fixtures at your local home center, but no matter what kind of system you install, always keep the following principles in mind:

Think Safety: Always install all wiring with proper permits and according to code. Outdoor electrical systems require special care, equipment, and materials.

Don't Overlight: A small amount of the right kind of lighting is much more effective than indiscriminate "ballpark" lighting.

Vary the Brightness: In some areas the lighting should be dim; in some, moderate; and in others, bright.

Define Space: Use light to define spaces and emphasize what's important. Bright lights that contrast with dimmer surrounding lights will point out pathways, steps, and activity areas for visitors, as well as illuminate interesting focal points.

Hide the Source: To avoid glare, place lights high above the ground, use fixtures with canopies close to the ground, shield fixtures behind plants or other features, reflect the light off light-colored walls, or use fixtures that have grills and baffles.

Keep the System Flexible: Use several circuits, each on its own switch, and use dimmer switches if possible.

Switches: Place switches at central indoor locations. If you want to be able to control the light at the point of use, install 3-way switches.

LIGHTING TECHNIQUES

You can alter three variables to achieve different lighting effects— location, direction, and intensity. The following techniques use these variables and should give you plenty of design tools:

Downlighting: Placing a light source high enough so it shines down on an object or a general area is most effective when the source is hidden. Use floodlights or filtered lights, depending on the mood desired, and locate them in trees or on high walls of the house. The effect is like moonlight filtering down through the trees.

Uplighting: Placing the source so that it aims light upward at an object produces an unnatural, startling effect which should be used with discretion. It is most effective for illuminating a special object or feature, or for lighting a tree so that it frames a particularly dramatic vista.

Safety Lighting: Light pathways, steps, and activity areas well enough for people to feel comfortable using them. Use downlighting or low path lights, depending on how large an area you want to illuminate. The light level should be bright enough to make hazards and heavily used areas stand out from their lighted surroundings.

Security Lighting: Lighting to discourage intruders does not have to be harsh and unpleasant. It should not cast shadows where an intruder could hide. Multiple sources work better than a single floodlight. Locate controls inside the house. Time clocks, photocells, and wireless controls all increase the system's effectiveness.

Area Lighting: Make sure activity areas, such as lawns, patios, and decks, have comfortable levels of illumination for entertaining, work, or play. Downlighting, either from floodlights or diffused low-voltage lamps, is efficient for lighting these large areas, but it should be combined with other techniques. Floodlights alone give a flat, dull look in which nothing is emphasized. In addition, if floodlights are too bright, they can cause irritating glare, overpower other lighting effects, and disturb the neighbors.

Diffused Lighting: If a light source is at eye level or in a direct line of vision, diffuse it to prevent harsh glare. Use frosted globes, plastic panels, or fabric or translucent shades around a fixture to soften the glare.

Emphasis: Emphasizing an object or surface can be achieved in several ways. If the object of your lighting has an attractive texture, such as brick, bark, or siding, direct a beam across the textured surface at an angle.

Highlight a specific plant or sculpture with a small spotlight. Direct the light onto a wall behind the object, creating a silhouette, or place the light so it casts a shadow of the object onto the wall behind it.

A long feature, such as a path or the edge of a pool, can be accented with a string of small lights following its contour.

Fill Lighting: Some areas of a garden may not need direct light, but should have low-level lighting to provide a background for the more interesting areas. If excess light from the main sources is not enough to light these areas, you can provide low-level lighting near the floor of the garden to fill in.

Lighting Water: Pools, fountains, and waterfalls are ideal candidates for lighting. Underwater lights create a diffused glow.

MATERIALS FOR OUTDOOR LIGHTING

BOXES AND CONDUIT

Outdoor electrical boxes are similar to their indoor cousins, except that they have solid walls and special gaskets and covers to make them weatherproof. Conduit, required for all aboveground outdoor wiring and some underground runs, must be joined with weathertight connectors.

LAMPS

Your main decision when choosing outdoor lighting fixtures will involve the type of lamp, or bulb, you plan to use. The choices are incandescent, quartz incandescent, and high-intensity discharge (HID).

Incandescent: Incandescent lamps include the "A" type bulb commonly used indoors and in various types of reflector lamps. The most common reflector lamp for outdoor spotlighting and floodlighting is the parabolic aluminized reflector (PAR) lamp.

Because of their wide availability, pleasing quality of light, and capacity for dimming, incandescent lamps are the most popular choice. Quartz incandescent lamps are a special type that give brighter light.

High-Intensity Discharge: HID lamps include mercury vapor, high-pressure sodium, and metal halide bulbs. They all give brilliant light and are energy efficient, but cannot be dimmed easily, and they vary in their color rendering. The high-pressure sodium lamp is not used widely for residential systems because of the orange hue that it casts. Metal halide lamps are very bright, with limited choice of intensities. The most versatile HID lamp for residential gardens is the mercury vapor, especially the clear, or "blue" type. If you use any of the HID lamps, you should supplement the lighting with incandescent lamps for greater warmth.

FIXTURES

Once you have chosen the lamps, choose fixtures that will accept the lamps and direct the light where you want it. Lamp types include simple sockets for floodlights, bullet lights that resemble canisters, well lights for partial burial in the ground, and decorative fixtures that are meant to be seen.

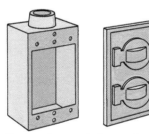

Outdoor receptacle box and cover

Outdoor
switch box

Extender
box

LV connector

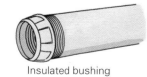

Insulated bushing

INSTALLING OUTDOOR LIGHTING

Before you string the wire, first plan the locations of all lights and receptacles. Consider safety and area lighting first, then accent and special-effects lighting.

Next, determine whether your system will provide enough lighting for security, and fill in areas where security lighting is deficient. Include the switch locations in your planning (security switches indoors), along with auxiliary outdoor switches in areas of high use.

Determine the number of circuits the lighting system will require. Outdoor receptacles should be on a separate 120-volt ground fault circuit interrupter (GFCI).

If the garden is small and there are only a few lights, you can probably extend existing 120-volt circuits. For a larger system, you will want a separate circuit for every 6 to 12 fixtures, depending on the total lamp wattage required for each circuit.

Plan circuits so you can group fixtures on the same switch, using dimmers for increased flexibility. You can also install motion detectors on security lighting circuits.

Once you have determined the location of all fixtures, switches, and receptacles, sketch a wiring plan—you'll need it to obtain the necessary permit. (Generally, codes allow low-voltage installation without a permit.) On the plan note all outlets, the size and type of wire, and the location of the main service panel. It is a good idea to have a professional electrician go over your plan first, even if you are doing the wiring yourself.

Bury 120-volt wiring runs or enclose them in conduit. Run low-voltage lines along the surface of the ground. You can bury underground feeder (UF) cable directly; nonmetallic-sheathed (NM) cable must be run through conduit. Your local codes may allow you a choice between rigid metal or PVC plastic conduit. Metal resists rodent damage and usually does not have to be buried as deeply as PVC, but it will also corrode in time. PVC is easier to work with, but must be buried at least 18 inches and is subject to chewing by rodents. For wiring aboveground, use metal conduit with weathertight connectors.

To run low-voltage wiring, just connect the transformer to a switch-controlled 120-volt outlet and then run low-voltage cable to the fixtures. Staple the line to trees, fences, or sheds. Lay it on the ground, or bury it.

INSTALLING OUTDOOR LIGHTING *continued*

TAPPING INTO EXISTING WIRING

For one or two outdoor lighting fixtures, you may be able to tap into an existing circuit at an inside outlet. If you're adding more than two fixtures, install a separate circuit. Outdoor receptacles must be on a dedicated GFCI circuit. In addition, it's a good idea to install GFCI receptacles at all outdoor locations.

If a fixture is already located on an exterior wall, you can extend the wiring to additional fixtures, but you'll need to open up the wall to do so. Any exposed wiring must be enclosed in conduit. The new fixtures will be controlled by the same switch as the original fixture.

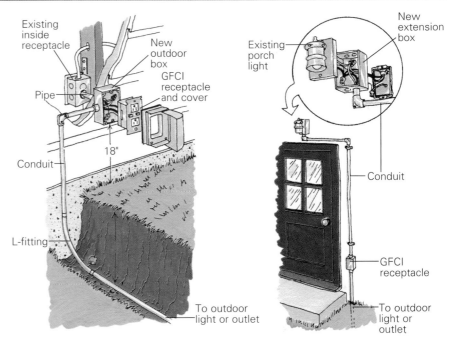

ANCHORING OUTDOOR FIXTURES

Freestanding outdoor fixtures and receptacles should be well anchored; use concrete or a concrete block. Make a 90-degree bend in the conduit at the point where your fixture will be and slide a block over it. The section of conduit aboveground, and which bends down through the block, should be metal. The buried portion may be either metal or PVC. After all of the conduit is in place, fill the cells of the block with concrete. Then attach the junction box, feed the cable or individual wires through the conduit, and install the light fixture or receptacle.

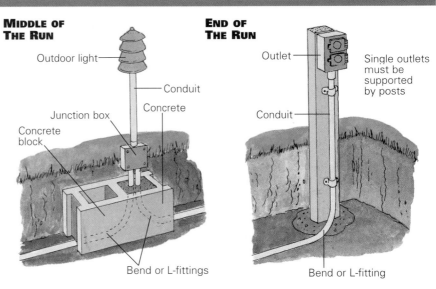

ATTACHING A FIXTURE TO A HOUSE

An outdoor fixture can be wired like an indoor light fixture, except that the fixture itself must be approved for outdoor use. Simply cut a hole in the wall, install an octagon box, run wiring through the attic to the nearest outlet or junction box, wire it to a switch, and attach the exterior fixture. Be sure to caulk any gaps between the electrical box and the siding.

219

KEYS TO HOUSEHOLD SECURITY

ALSO SEE...
Doors:
Pages 86–97
Security:
Pages 294–297

If you are concerned about security, first replace any glass-paned or hollow-core exterior door with a solid or steel-clad door. The jambs should be at least 1½ inches thick, with stops shaped as part of the jamb itself—not simply additional stock nailed on. If the stops are separate from the jambs, add extra nails or screws.

Next, turn your attention to locks. Door latches and dead bolts engage a strike plate that is set into the jamb. If the strike plate fails, the lock gives.

Most strike plates are made of a flimsy metal that is fastened to the jamb with ¾-inch screws. Buy large, heavy-duty reinforcement plates and extra-long screws that penetrate all the way through the jamb and into the studs of the door frame.

If a door swings outward (most don't), its hinge pins will be on the outside of the house. To prevent the pins from being pulled out by an intruder, open the door wide and drill through the knuckle and pin for a self-tapping screw. The screw will hold the pin in place and will be concealed when the door is shut. Do this for each hinge.

Burglars don't like to be seen by the neighbors, so give your back door more attention than your front door. Be sure it has a solid core, and reinforce the jambs, stops, strike plate, and hinges.

Avoid double-key locks, those which open from the inside only with a key. They make escape more difficult in emergencies, such as a fire. If you are considering a double-key lock because the door has glass panes, either replace the door or install polycarbonate plastic (Lexan®) in place of the glass. Polycarbonate is virtually smashproof, though its strength is no greater than the mullions that hold it in place.

LOCK TYPES

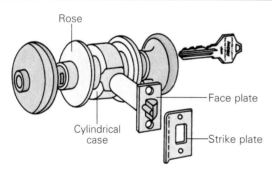

Rose

Face plate

Cylindrical case

Strike plate

CYLINDER LOCK

The cylinder lock, also known as the tubular or key-in-knob lock, has a wide barrel that extends through the door. The locking mechanism is in the knob. It is the most popular lock because it is easy to install

and quite inexpensive. It is also the easiest lock to force because of its rounded latch. If you have a damaged or malfunctioning cylinder lock, it is simpler to replace the entire unit than to repair it.

MORTISE LOCK

Having both a latch and a dead bolt, this unit offers greater security than the cylinder lock. But it is difficult to install, and the mortise that houses the mechanism weakens the door. Many older doors have this kind of lock. The most common problem is a broken spring, which can be replaced by removing and disassembling the entire lock. The mortise lock offers the additional advantage of having a replaceable key cylinder.

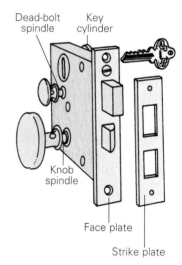

Dead-bolt spindle

Key cylinder

Knob spindle

Face plate

Strike plate

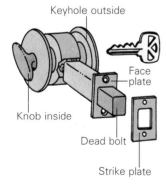

Keyhole outside

Face plate

Knob inside

Dead bolt

Strike plate

DEAD-BOLT LOCK

A dead bolt can be added to a door to increase security. The throw-bolt should extend at least 1 inch into the jamb, since prying open a door will usually force the lock no more than ½ inch. The lock exterior is difficult to jimmy because it is either flush with the door surface or protrudes as a tapered cylinder. Installation is the same as for a cylinder lock.

RIM LOCK

Like the dead bolt, this lock is installed in addition to the doorknob to augment security. It is mounted on the inside surface of the door, with the strike plate being secured to the casing as well as to the rim of the jamb. The assembly relies on gravity to hold the bolt in place.

Key cylinder

Lock case

Strike plate

INSTALLING A CYLINDER OR DEAD-BOLT LOCK

Doorknobs should be centered 36 inches above the finish floor. Dead bolts are usually installed 3 or 4 inches above the doorknob. When marking hole centers, measure from the side the door opens into (the edge away from the stop). If the door is already hinged, wedge shims under it to stop it from swinging. Install the lock or dead bolt first, then the strike plate.

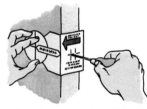

1 If the door has not been drilled, you will have to drill the holes for the locks yourself. Start by marking the edge of the door 36 inches from the finish floor. Extend the mark across the edge of the door on both

sides with a square. The holes will be centered on these lines.

The lock should come with a template. Hold the template against the edge of the door at the height of your marks to establish the exact centers of the holes. Drill the cylinder hole first, using a hole saw. To prevent splintering the face of the door, drill only half way through the door from one side and then complete the drilling from the other side.

Next, drill the hole for the latch or bolt. Use a spade bit, sized for the bolt, usually 1 inch. Make sure you hold the bit perpendicular to the edge of the door.

2 Insert the latch and trace its outline on the edge of the door.

3 Chisel out the mortise so that the latch face plate lies flush with the edge of the door.

4 Slip the latch or bolt mechanism into the bolt hole again and fit the face plate over it. Then insert the knob mechanism into the cylinder hole so that it engages the end of the latch. Push the other half of the knob mechanism into the other side of the door so that it lines up with the first half. Screw the two halves together, then screw the face plate to the door.

To install the strike plate, close the door and mark where the latch or dead bolt hits the doorjamb. Trace the strike plate onto the jamb so that its hole is centered where the bolt or latch is centered. Chisel out a mortise for the strike plate, drill a hole into the jamb (through it if the bolt is long), and fasten the strike plate with screws.

INSTALLING A MORTISE LOCK

1 Trace the outline of the lockset on the edge of the door.

2 Drill a series of holes to the depth of the lockset and ¹/₁₆ inch wider.

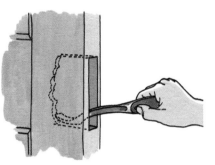

3 Chisel out the wood between the series of holes. If you have one, use a lock mortise chisel.

4 Insert the lock in the mortise and mark the outline of the lock's face plate. Chisel out the mortise for the face plate so that it fits flush with the edge of the door.

5 Using the template provided with the lock, mark and bore the holes for the cylinder and spindles. Note carefully which holes go all the way through the door and which don't.

6 Assemble the lockset in the door. Then mark, drill, and mortise for the strike plate on the jamb. Screw the strike plate into position.

Mantels

ARTISTIC ELEMENTS THAT SET THE TONE FOR ENTIRE ROOMS

ALSO SEE...
Fireplaces:
Pages 134–135
Moldings:
Pages 228–231

A mantel adds a touch of warmth to more than its fireplace; it often determines the style of the entire room. A massive hand-hewn timber laid across the top of a stone or hand-cut brick fireplace says *primitive*, *early-American*, or *country*, while an ornate frame trimmed at the brick fire box and smooth wall says *Victorian*.

There are many ways to add a mantel to your fireplace:

■ Install a used mantel; scout salvage yards and antique shops for a rescued treasure.
■ If you have the tools and skills, mill custom pieces and fabricate your own design.
■ Order a mantel kit from a building supplier that sells finish fixtures.
■ The easiest way of all is to make a mantel from stock pieces of molding.

Because the mantel is a focal point for the entire room, think of it as a piece of art. When making your own, make sure that every piece is smooth and fits well. The materials you choose depend on how you plan to finish it. If you want to paint it, make the mantel from pine. If you intend to leave the wood natural, use the same type of wood that is used throughout the room or add a different species for a visual accent. Oak, birch, walnut, and mahogany make handsome mantels. Consider mixing species or using stone. Tile makes an effective border, accent, or major finish covering for the mantel itself.

There are only a few distinctions in mantel design. The simplest mantel is a horizontal timber, usually 3 or 4 inches thick and 6 to 12 inches deep, that extends across the top of the fireplace. The timber may rest on top of a course of bricks, on two or three protruding bricks, or on brackets that attach to the wall.

The shelf of a more ornate mantel may rest at each end on vertical trim that either sits on edge or lies flat against the brick facing. Together with the shelf across the top, the side pieces frame the fireplace. Most mantels are variations of these simple designs, with extra molding added for decoration.

If you are not sure what kind of design to use, look through magazines and books to find one you like and have the skills to make. Just make sure it is in character with the rest of the room, whether ornate, austere, rustic, or tied to a particular architectural period.

Installation techniques vary with the design of the mantel, the dimensions of the fireplace, and the unique requirements of the room, but the steps shown here are typical.

CORBELED MANTEL SUPPORTS

If you are building a fireplace whose face will be surfaced in masonry veneer, decide how you will attach your new mantel. If the mantel is a single plank or a heavy timber, corbel the masonry for the supports. Corbeling means stepping in stages. For brick, use a two-step corbel. Project the first brick about 2 or 3 inches. The brick that rests on top of the first one projects outward an additional 2 to 3 inches. Provide enough supports to carry the weight of your mantel.

INSTALLING A MANTEL

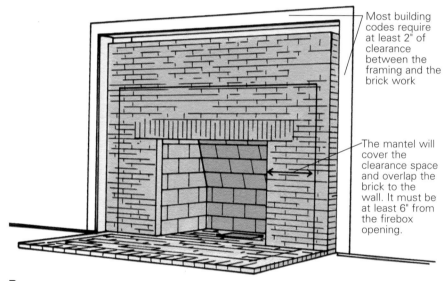

Most building codes require at least 2" of clearance between the framing and the brick work

The mantel will cover the clearance space and overlap the brick to the wall. It must be at least 6" from the firebox opening.

PREPARATION

Measure the fireplace opening and draw a plan to scale. Most mantels attach to a solid backer board that surrounds the firebox and covers the joint between the firebrick and wall. The backer board should be made of veneered plywood because a portion will remain in view. If you do not use a backer board, be sure there is wood to nail to behind the finished wall. You may have to strip away some of the wallcovering and install extra studs, plywood, or blocking between the existing studs.

INSTALLING THE SHELF

Choose a straight, knot-free board for the shelf and attach a piece of half-round molding or other trim to the front and side edges. Miter the trim at the corners. Or mill a decorative edge on the shelf with a router.

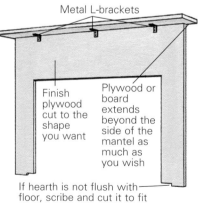

Metal L-brackets

Finish plywood cut to the shape you want

Plywood or board extends beyond the side of the mantel as much as you wish

If hearth is not flush with floor, scribe and cut it to fit

Fasten the shelf to the backer board with angle brackets or wood cleats spaced 24 or 32 inches on center. Attach the brackets or cleats to studs behind the wallcovering if you do not use a backer board. Cover the brackets or cleats with crown molding.

SHOPPING FOR USED MANTELS

Most major metropolitan areas have stores that buy and sell salvaged parts from beautiful old buildings. Any of these stores will have an ample supply of mantels in many styles that were saved from condemned homes and buildings. The great advantage of these parts is that they were typically built with style and care. Many of them feature hand-carved details and exquisite woods, and are completely intact. Best of all, they can be purchased for a fraction of what a newly made mantel of a similar style might cost.

To begin shopping, you'll need to know the size of your fireplace opening. Measure from top to bottom and from side to side. Carefully evaluate what style of mantel fits your house—even though it's beautiful, an ornate Victorian-style mantel would look out of place in a Colonial house.

If you buy an old mantel that still has its original paint, proceed with care. Don't sand the paint without taking precautions—old paint probably contains lead. If you like the patina of the old paint, seal it with two coats of clear polyurethane.

In most installations, the shelf should be approximately 16 inches above the firebox or about 5 feet above the floor. The length of the shelf will vary with the type of mantel and fireplace. The shelf should overhang the sides of the mantel assembly by 3 to 4 inches.

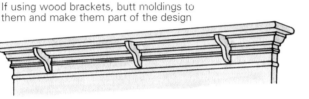

If using wood brackets, butt moldings to them and make them part of the design

WOOD BRACKETS

Instead of metal brackets, attach the shelf with wood brackets. You'll find stock items in many home centers or lumberyards; however, a jigsaw enables you to cut your own. Wood brackets do not have to be concealed by a crown molding. In fact, if you cut attractive-looking brackets, you will not want to cover them. Attach them to the wall by drilling pilot holes and screwing them into studs. Fill all holes with wood putty.

ADDING TRIM PIECES

If you use wood brackets, cut trim pieces to fit between them. Begin by installing the molding strips closest to the shelf and work down. Glue the moldings to the backer board with paneling adhesive and tack them in place with finishing nails. Miter any trim where it turns a corner, and be sure that the molding fits tightly before nailing it.

FINISHING THE MANTEL

Fill all the nail holes with wood putty. Then, unless the mantel is prefinished, sand the edges and apply stain and sealer that match the rest of the wood finish in the room. Use caulk or wallboard joint compound to fill gaps between the mantel and the wall or the brick facing.

CUSTOMIZING YOUR DESIGN

The range of custom mantel designs you can create with home-center stock is limited only by your imagination. Most suppliers stock dozens of standard moldings. You can butt simple pieces together to form more complicated designs.

If you use molding pieces made from different woods, stain the individual pieces so that they match or paint the entire mantel.

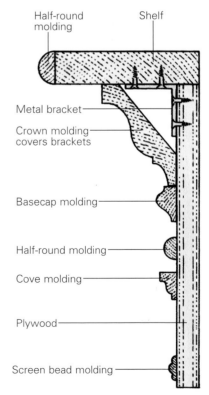

Half-round molding

Shelf

Metal bracket

Crown molding covers brackets

Basecap molding

Half-round molding

Cove molding

Plywood

Screen bead molding

Wood brackets

Miter moldings where they turn corners

223

METAL ROOFING

NEW MATERIALS AND METHODS

ALSO SEE...
Flashing:
Pages 136–139
Roofs:
Pages 282–289
Ventilation:
Pages 386–387

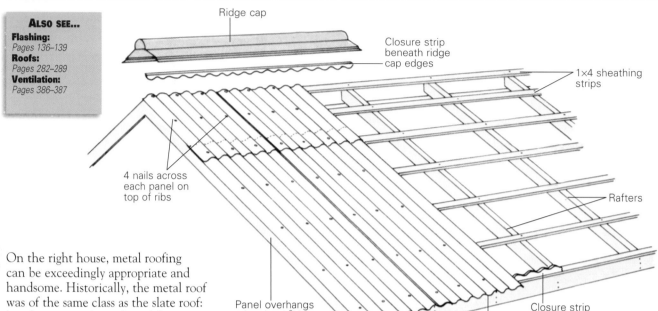

Ridge cap

Closure strip
beneath ridge
cap edges

1×4 sheathing
strips

4 nails across
each panel on
top of ribs

Rafters

Panel overhangs
rake about ⅜"

Closure strip

Panel overhangs eave by 2"

On the right house, metal roofing can be exceedingly appropriate and handsome. Historically, the metal roof was of the same class as the slate roof: handsome, stately, and good for a lifetime. Then corrugated metal panels became the roof of choice for new farm buildings. Since few people wanted their homes to look like budget-built barns, the metal roof fell out of favor.

But the metal roof is back—this time as an aluminum panel with a baked enamel finish, looking very much like the always-popular but expensive standing-seam roof.

The true standing-seam roof is superior, long-lasting, and expensive. Unfortunately, its installation requires the skills of a professional. The good news is that new aluminum look-alikes are inexpensive and no more difficult to install than asphalt shingles.

ROOFTOP BATTERY

Don't make a battery on your roof. Odd as that advice might sound, it makes sense.

Batteries are nothing more than dissimilar metals in a bath of conducting liquid. If your roof contains anything but a single type of metal, the electrochemically stronger metal will eat up the weaker one whenever it rains. A galvanized nail will eat a large hole through an aluminum panel in less than a year.

Make sure when buying your roofing that all of the fasteners and accessories are those recommended by the roofing manufacturer. Also, replace any existing roof flashings that aren't of the same metal.

INSTALLING A METAL ROOF

PREPARATION

Lightweight aluminum panels need support. For maximum strength and to dampen the sound of rain, install them over a solid deck of plywood or oriented strand board (OSB) sheathing, covered with 30-pound felt. Space the sheathing ⅛ inch at the joints to prevent buckling. For a shed or other unoccupied building, a lightweight roof can be supported by a grid of rafters and sheathing strips, as shown *above*.

APPLYING GABLE TRIM

Roofing manufacturers also supply trim for the gable edge and neoprene filler strips for the eaves. Start by applying gable trim to the edge of the roof which lies downwind of the prevailing storm winds in your area. Nail the trim every 12 inches, using the nails recommended by the manufacturer.

Next, apply a rubber closure strip to the bottom edge of the roof. Use only as many nails as you need to hold it loosely, as it will be nailed again when you install the roofing panels.

THE FIRST PANEL

Most aluminum roofing panels are available in lengths to 40 feet and are cut to the nearest inch when you place

your order. If they have not yet been cut, cut them to the length of the roof plus 2 inches. You can use circular saw with a metal-cutting blade or trim the panels with tin snips. (You will wish you had ordered them the exact size.)

Slide the panel edge all the way into the gable trim, and adjust the panel so that the bottom edge overhangs the eave by 2 inches. If the panel has an "anti-siphon" edge, make sure it is on the upwind side.

Fasten the panels with neoprene-washered nails or screws. Drive the fasteners through the panel ridges, not the valleys, and space them as recommended by the manufacturer.

Be careful not to overdrive the fasteners; compress the neoprene washer, but not the panel. Do not nail the last ridge or pair of ridges, as these will be nailed together with the overlapping edge of the next panel.

REMAINING PANELS

Lap the second panel over the first. Generally, the panels overlap by two ridges. You can tell what the manufacturer intended because the "gain" of each panel should be either 16, 24, or 32 inches. Again, use the special neoprene-washered fasteners

TWO STYLES OF CORRUGATED PANELS

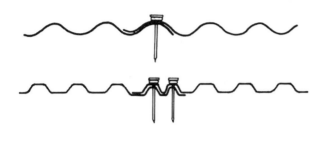

TWO KINDS OF RIDGE CAPS

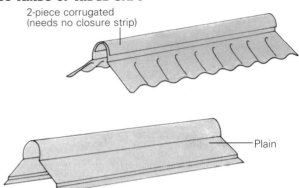

2-piece corrugated
(needs no closure strip)

Plain

and the spacing recommended by the manufacturer.

THE LAST PANEL

It is unlikely that the last panel will be exactly the right width to fit your roof. Lay it in place and mark where the edge of the roof falls. Take the panel down, lay it on a flat surface, and score it with a straight edge and a sharp utility knife. Bend the panel and it should break cleanly at the score.

Install the gable trim piece, then install the last roofing panel.

THE RIDGE

Ridge caps come in styles that match the pattern of the roofing panels.

Install the cap over the tops of the panels. Overlap sections of cap by at least 6 inches, and apply a bead of silicone caulk in the overlap.

Finally, plug the ends of the ridge cap with the flexible filler supplied by the manufacturer.

A METAL-ROOF MYSTERY: RAIN ON A CLEAR, COLD NIGHT

Metal roofing looks so impermeable and sheds rain so well that it is baffling when it seems to leak under a clear winter sky.

What is going on?

On a cold, clear night, metal surfaces radiate heat and become colder than the surrounding air. Moisture in the air condenses on these cold surfaces in the form of dew or frost. That's why you find so much frost in the morning on cars that have been parked outdoors overnight.

What is unique about metal roofing is that it has essentially zero R-value. Thus, the underside of the metal panels is just as cold as the top side, and condenses moisture, as well. When the sun comes out, this moisture drips down onto whatever is immediately below the roofing. If there is no waterproof layer to stop it, the roof may appear to be leaking.

The solution is a layer of 30-pound felt, overlapped like a second roof, to shed this "leakage."

ADDING AN AWNING

Need some low-cost shade over a patio or entry? Metal panels offer one solution. They are relatively inexpensive, and their light weight requires minimal framing lumber.

Support the frame at the house with a ledger, firmly attached to the studs, and on the other end with posts. Insert flashing under the house siding. Slide the awning's panels under the flashing and attach them to the frame.

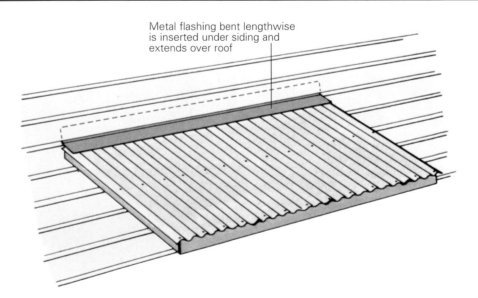

Metal flashing bent lengthwise is inserted under siding and extends over roof

Metal-Working Techniques

SHEETS, PLATES, AND BARS

ALSO SEE...
Tools:
Pages 374–383

Metal is used in many places around the house, such as flashing, metal door frames, and plumbing pipes. The common metals used in construction are steel, aluminum, copper, and brass.

Sheet metal is simply flat metal up to $3/16$ inch thick. Thicker flat metal is called plate. Bar metal may be round, T-shaped, L-shaped, flat, or other more unusual shapes, but anything called bar metal would be less than 12 inches wide if flattened out.

Basic metalworking skills are helpful for completing many ordinary home-improvement projects.

MEASURING AND MARKING

Create cardboard templates in the shape of the pieces you will need, or first cut the pieces oversized, then trim them to fit.

Sheet-metal thicknesses are often specified as gauge numbers, according to several standards (see Sheet Gauges, *below*). The only thing these standards have in common is that larger numbers indicate thinner metal. The inch equivalents shown are common, but not universal. Metal thicknesses can be given in inches or millimeters, too.

Metal can be marked with scribes, engraving tools, utility knives, center punches, or felt-tipped pens. Even a sharp nail will work in a pinch.

DRILLING

Mark the location of the hole with an X. Punch a small indentation at the center point with a center punch or an awl. If you don't, the drill will try to wander.

Clamp the piece firmly before drilling. Use a metal twist bit and apply a drop of oil to the indentation.

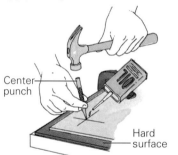

Center-punch

Hard surface

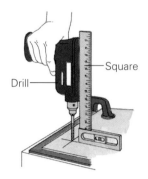

Square

Drill

Hold the drill perpendicular to the metal. If the bit slips off, stop drilling. Restrike the hole with the punch, or drill a pilot hole with a smaller bit.

As you drill, keep the hole lubricated with oil. Medium speeds work better than fast speeds when drilling through metal.

In thick sheet metal or metal plate, it is faster to drill a hole in stages. For example, to drill a $1/2$-inch-diameter hole in $3/8$-inch-thick steel, start with a $1/4$-inch bit, enlarge the hole with a $3/8$-inch bit, then finish with a $1/2$-inch bit. Cut holes larger than 1 inch with a hole saw.

SHEET GAUGES

Gauge	Uncoated steel	Stainless steel	Non-ferrous metals
1		.2813	.2893
2		.2656	.2576
3	.2391	.2500	.2294
4	.2242	.2344	.2043
5	.2092	.2188	.1819
6	.1943	.2031	.1620
7	.1793	.1875	.1443
8	.1644	.1719	.1285
10	.1345	.1406	.1019
12	.1046	.1094	.0808
14	.0747	.0781	.0641
16	.0598	.0625	.0508
18	.0478	.0500	.0403
20	.0359	.0375	.0320
22	.0299	.0313	.0253
24	.0239	.0250	.0201
26	.0179	.0188	.0159
28	.0149	.0156	.0126
30	.0120	.0125	.0100

WEIGHT OF SHEET METALS

Sheet Gauge	Pounds Per Sq. Ft.	
	Alum.	Steel
1	3.85	
2	3.43	
3	3.05	10
4	2.72	9.38
5	2.42	8.75
6	2.15	8.13
7	1.92	7.5
8	1.71	6.88
10	1.36	5.62
12	1.07	4.37
14	0.85	3.12
16	0.68	2.5
18	0.54	2
20	0.43	1.5
22	0.37	1.25
24	0.27	1
26	0.21	0.78
28	0.17	0.62
30	0.13	0.5

SAFETY TIPS

People who work metal with power tools and still have both eyes and all ten fingers observe the following rules:

■ Wear goggles or safety glasses when cutting, drilling, sawing, or soldering.

■ Clamp the piece being worked securely.

■ Wear leather gloves when cutting metal or installing metal with sharp edges.

■ File down burrs and sharp edges after cutting or drilling.

■ Use the safety features, such as shields, included with your tools.

■ Keep cutting tools sharp.

■ Don't force tools when cutting into metal.

CUTTING

The basic metal-cutting tools are the hacksaw and the tin snips, also known as aviation snips. Snips come in straight cut, right-hand cut, and left-hand cut models.

USING SNIPS

Wear leather gloves. Open the jaws fully, but never let them close completely because they will leave small bumps on the metal. Cut from the side, or select the tool that allows you to bend the work away from the cut, making room to operate the snips.

To make an inside cut, score the line, then drill a hole to start the cut.

SCORING

To cut thin sheet metal without snips, score it repeatedly with a utility knife and work it back and forth until it snaps. Wear gloves when bending.

USING A COLD CHISEL

You can use a sharp cold chisel to make rough cuts in fairly thick sheet metal. Score the cut line and clamp the piece to be cut over a wood or metal support. Hammer the chisel along the entire line. Repeat several times until the cut is done. File or grind the edges as needed.

BENDING SHEET METAL

You can bend sheet metal with homemade jigs or specialized tools.

SIMPLE STRAIGHT BEND

Clamp the metal between two pieces of wood so the edge of the wood is along the line of the bend. Use a third wood block and hammer the exposed edge over.

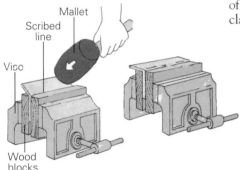

Mallet
Scribed line
Vise
Wood blocks

CURVED BEND

Using a band saw or jigsaw, cut a piece of wood to the desired curve, then clamp the metal between the two halves. Tap the metal over the wood to form the curve.

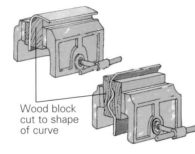

Wood block cut to shape of curve

ROUNDED EDGE

Make a 90-degree bend along the edge to be rounded, about ⅜ inch in from the edge. Clamp a piece of ⅛-inch hardboard against the bend, then bend the edge to 180 degrees. Remove the hardboard and continue bending the edge down to the surface.

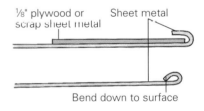

⅛" plywood or scrap sheet metal   Sheet metal

Bend down to surface

SOLDERING WITH AN IRON

Two soldering tools you'll find useful are the soldering iron (or gun) and the torch. Use a torch for large or heavy work, such as sweating joints in copper pipe; use an iron or gun for fine work.

TINNING THE TIP

It is not enough for the tip of an iron or gun just to get hot; it must be tinned and clean in order to conduct heat rapidly enough to do the work. If the tip is new or corroded, file it down to new metal.

Brush flux on the tip, clamp the soldering iron, and plug it in. Once the iron heats up, touch solder to the tip to coat it lightly.

SOLDERING

The pieces to be soldered also must be clean; use a file, sandpaper, or steel wool to make the joint shiny.

Test the pieces for fit, but don't touch the cleaned area with your fingers, or you will have to start over.

Coat the area to be soldered with flux. Clamp or position the pieces to be soldered. Hold the iron against the work (not to the solder). When the work is hot enough to melt solder, touch the solder to the joint. It should flow toward the heat.

Continue to move the iron along the edge of the work. When the entire edge is visibly soldered, let it cool, then wipe it clean with a wet sponge or rag. If staining is a concern, wipe off any last traces of flux.

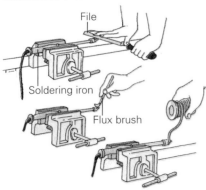

File
Soldering iron
Flux brush

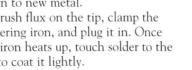

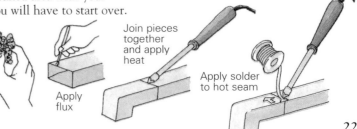

Clean and flux surfaces to be joined

Apply flux

Join pieces together and apply heat

Apply solder to hot seam

MOLDINGS

SHAPES OF AN ELEGANT AGE

Molding, also called trim, covers gaps and provides decorative relief for flat wall surfaces. Molding is used less in houses built today than in older homes, primarily because of its high cost. Molding in older homes is often elaborate. When remodeling, try to match the existing patterns.

Trim can be as simple as common boards, but most is milled to a decorative shape in a shaper, or molding machine. Most manufacturers use the standard profiles established in 1957 by either the Western Wood Products Association or the Millwork Producers. Ask your lumber supplier for a profile chart for the WP or WM series to see what is available. No lumberyard stocks all shapes, but your supplier can order most designs.

Moldings are typically milled of oak or pine, but some regional and local manufacturers use Douglas fir, larch, white fir, cedar, and hemlock.

Plastic moldings are also widely available. Vinyl moldings can be curved easily, but they cannot be stained and may not be paintable.

The best wood moldings are milled from a single piece. Choose one-piece molding if you plan to stain the trim. Consider less expensive finger-jointed molding if you plan to paint. The glue in the joints is not waterproof, so use finger-jointed moldings only indoors.

To remove old trim without damaging it, punch the finish nails through the molding with a nail set. If you must pry off the molding with the nails still in the wood, do not remove the nails by pounding them from the rear of the stock. Pull them through from the back with nippers to prevent damage to the face of the molding. Even if you don't plan to reuse the molding immediately, saving a few of the best long pieces for future use is advisable.

CHOOSING AND USING MOLDINGS

If you need to match a molding that is no longer available, try to make up the pattern with two or more pieces of stock molding from a lumberyard. If that won't do, see if a local millwork can mill the piece (they usually will if you are willing to pay the set-up cost). Or remove a replacement piece from an inconspicuous site in the house, and replace it with the closest match you can find.

In rare cases, you may have to restore plaster moldings. There are renovation suppliers and mail-order renovation houses that stock some of the old plaster patterns. As a last resort, create a new section of molding by making a template to match the old pattern and use that to mold a new one from plaster.

Moldings add character to a room, provided they are in keeping with the architectural style of the house. In a plain house, avoid ornate moldings, such as scallops or decorative friezes; likewise, don't use overly plain trim in a Victorian structure.

If you want to dress up door and window casings currently trimmed with boards (such as 1×4), add decorative molding across the tops of the casings. Then nail short pieces of the same molding at each end, and miter the corners.

Chair rail is another simple touch that dresses up a plain room. Install it 3 to 3½ feet above the floor or at the same height as the windowsills. Finish the wall below the rail with paneling or paint it a color different from the rest of the room.

Use moldings to break up large expanses of wall and add visual interest. They can make a room or hallway seem larger than it is. If you want the ceiling to appear higher, run horizontal molding near the ceiling at a height slightly lower than the tallest pieces of furniture. The horizontal line creates a feeling of space above the furniture. The deception works even better if you install molding around the top of the walls as well. To complete the artificial enlargement, add horizontal molding around the bottom of the wall, about 18 inches above the floor. At this height, the molding draws attention to the walls, and away from the furniture and windows.

In a small room with a vaulted ceiling, install molding at the same level as the tops of the doors and windows. The molding accentuates the beginning of the ceiling and, thus, emphasizes its height. Molding about 18 inches above the floor works with vaulted-ceiling rooms, too.

Architectural features such as fireplaces and alcoves can be framed in molding to add emphasis. Add molding to plain walls, too. Both techniques call attention to the room and can prevent furnishings or other features from overpowering the space. Use these tricks with caution, however. Molding alone will not solve fundamental design problems.

There are unconventional uses for molding, as well, such as trimming flush doors to make them resemble panel doors, or trimming posts and beams to make them appear carved. Don't be too clever, however. Molding is most effective when it enhances a home's existing architectural lines, not when it creates new shapes.

TO BE OR KNOT TO BE

Real wood moldings are extremely expensive because they are expected to be free of knots. But what if you don't care about knots? What if you plan to paint the trim or like a knotty-pine look?

If you are installing a lot of trim, as you would in building an addition, then order "run-of-the-mill" boards from a local mill. There will be unusable pieces, but the 90 percent that is usable will cost one-quarter as much as the fancy moldings in the home center.

TYPICAL MOLDINGS

The most common interior moldings are: *casing* around doors and windows; *baseboard* (mopboard) at the bottom of the wall; *crown molding* at the top of the wall; *picture molding*, usually about 1 foot below the top of the wall; and *chair rail*, covering the seam between wainscot paneling and the finished wall. Most home centers carry fairly simple, basic styles, but you can combine two or three different shapes to match the more ornate versions that are generally found in older homes.

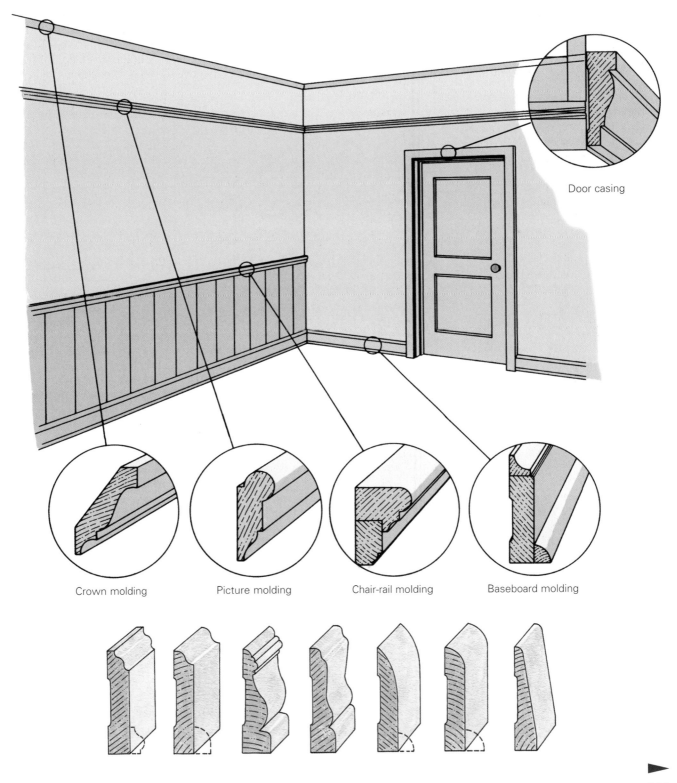

Door casing

Crown molding   Picture molding   Chair-rail molding   Baseboard molding

EXTERIOR MOLDINGS

Conformance with architectural design is even more important for exterior than for interior moldings. If you live in a historic district or historic house, you may have no choice but to follow historic guidelines. Even if you don't, however, seek advice from the local historic preservation group so your renovations will conform to the architectural character of your home.

Fashion the exterior trim for doors, windows, corners, and roof overhangs from standard boards. Make exterior moldings from redwood or other durable species. Fancier outdoor moldings include crowns and coves for joints under the eaves, brick mold for trimming doors and windows in brick or stucco walls, and one-piece corners.

Always prime the back of exterior trim. If you need to join two pieces end to end, miter them at 45 degrees. Miter vertical sections, too, and install the pieces so that moisture can drain away from the surface of the wall. Predrill the nail holes so that nailing does not split the trim. Apply a bead of caulk to the joint before nailing the molding, and set all nails below the surface.

Although the low price is seductive, never use finger-jointed moldings outdoors because the glue used in the joint is not always waterproof.

INSTALLATION TECHNIQUES

Before you install moldings, store them until their moisture content is equivalent to that of the house. Any subsequent shrinkage is sure to show. Prime the back of moldings before installation to minimize shrinkage. Save yourself time in the long run—prepaint or prestain all the pieces.

Use full lengths wherever trim will be prominent. If you have no choice but to join pieces end to end, miter both pieces at 45 degrees. Never use a butt joint.

Neat trim requires precision measuring and cutting. Make your marks with a knife blade or sharp scribe. Use the sharpest saw blade you can find. If you saw by hand, use a backsaw.

The most accurate power saw is the power miter saw. If you don't have one, beg, borrow, or rent one. Run the blade slowly through the wood for a smooth cut. An alternative tool is the miter trimmer, which slices instead of saws. You may be able to rent one from a picture-frame shop.

A finishing-nail gun will make installation easy. These air-powered nailers automatically sink the nail below the surface, eliminating any possibility of hammer dents. Regardless of the method you choose, nail moldings with 4d, 6d, or 8d finishing nails. Always countersink the nails and fill in the holes with wood putty or filler.

On irregular walls, use thin moldings or moldings with recessed backs so the trim will bend and hug the surface.

COPED JOINTS

In most situations where boards must be joined, the miter is the joint of preference. But miters do not work well in inside corners because the joint can open up and reveal an ugly gap. Butt joints work for square-edged moldings, but for moldings with a profile you need to use a modified butt joint known as a coped joint.

To make a coped joint, butt the first board into the corner. Using a piece of scrap, mark the contour of the molding on the back of the second board. Tape the front edge of the second piece to eliminate splintering and cut the profile with a coping saw. Fit the cut piece against the first and check the fit. Adjust the cut for a snug fit.

Continue around the room, alternating butts cuts and coped cuts until you are finished.

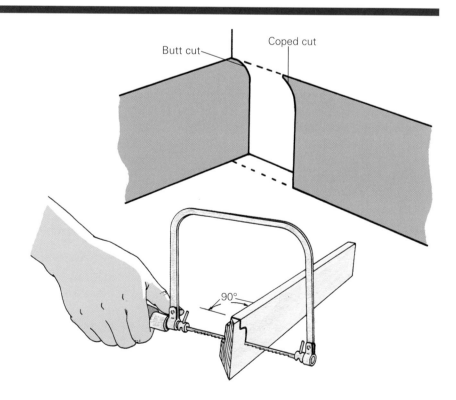

Butt cut

Coped cut

90°

BASEBOARDS

ONE-PIECE BASEBOARD

TWO-PIECE BASEBOARD

Baseboard

Base shoe

THREE-PIECE BASEBOARD

Base cap

Baseboard

Base shoe

Baseboards come in many configurations, from single pieces that are plain to multipieced moldings that create elaborate profiles. Ideally, base moldings should not be thicker than the door casing, so if you are installing a base shoe along the bottom edge, miter it to meet the door casing at its end.

Nail the baseboard to the wall about ¼ inch above the level of the finish floor—this ensures the nail will penetrate the bottom plate of the wall framing. Then position the base shoe against the baseboard, with a slight gap beneath it. Nail the shoe to the baseboard, not to the floor.

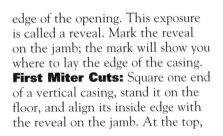

Bottom plate

DOOR AND WINDOW CASINGS

When installing square-edged lumber door casing, butt the vertical and horizontal pieces together. If the molding has a pattern, however, you must miter the casings.

Marking the Reveal: When installed, the casing should leave ¼ inch of jamb exposed around the edge of the opening. This exposure is called a reveal. Mark the reveal on the jamb; the mark will show you where to lay the edge of the casing.

First Miter Cuts: Square one end of a vertical casing, stand it on the floor, and align its inside edge with the reveal on the jamb. At the top, mark the casing where the vertical and horizontal reveals cross, and scribe a 45-degree line up from that mark. Make the cut with a miter saw, and nail the casing in place with 4d nails at the jamb edge and 6d or 8d nails on the outside edge.

Make a miter cut at one end of the head casing and hold it in position. At the other side, mark its bottom edge where the reveals intersect and scribe a 45-degree line up from that mark. Cut along the mark and tack the head casing in place. Don't nail it securely because you may have to remove the casing to adjust the cut.

Final Miter Cut: Square the end of the third piece and stand it in place. Mark both the inside and outside edges where they cross the head casing. Cut on the line—it should run at 45 degrees. If not, adjust the cut of the head casing so it matches the angle of the side casing. Remove the head casing, adjust the cut, and nail each piece securely.

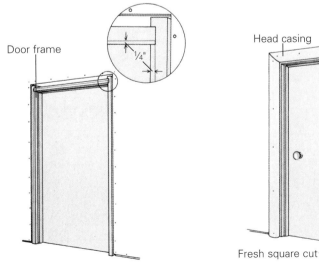

Door frame

¼"

Head casing

Miter cut

Fresh square cut

PAINTS AND STAINS

PROTECTION AND BEAUTY IN A CAN

ALSO SEE...
Caulk:
Pages 50–51
Hazardous Substances:
Pages 176–177
Shingle Siding:
Pages 308–309
Ventilation:
Pages 386–387
Wallboard:
Pages 394–399

Painting is inexpensive, quick, and offers you a dramatic way to improve your home, inside or out. With high-quality materials, the application process is as gratifying as the end result.

A good coat of paint will protect your home from weather and wear, but won't cure existing problems. Correct any moisture-damaged sections before you paint.

A well-chosen color has a positive, uplifting effect; a poor choice will haunt you until you paint it over. Select your color scheme carefully.

And don't scrimp on the other steps—preparing the surface, preparing the surface, and preparing the surface. The importance of the scraping, sanding, and washing cannot be overemphasized. They are vital steps that too many amateur painters skip.

TYPES OF PAINT AND STAIN

There are two basic types of paint: latex (water-based) and alkyd (solvent-based). Neither is best for all purposes. There are also primers and specialty paints to consider, as well as stains and sealers. But the first decision is usually whether to use latex or alkyd.

ALKYD PAINTS

On the positive side, alkyds:
■ penetrate wood and stick to smooth surfaces better
■ scrub better and last longer
On the negative side, alkyds:
■ fade quicker
■ don't adhere well to masonry or wallpaper
■ give off fumes
■ require paint thinner for cleanup
■ take from 8 to 12 hours to dry
■ should not be recoated in outdoor applications for 36 to 48 hours.

In general, use alkyds for interior woodwork, high-traffic areas, and areas subject to smoke and water staining.

LATEX PAINTS

On the positive side, latex paints:
■ are easy to use because water thins them and cleans them up
■ dry quickly and can be repainted within an hour or two
■ are particularly suitable as a covering for interior walls and ceilings where you want a flat finish
■ hold their color well
■ are semipermeable, allowing moisture to escape through the exterior wall coating
■ work well on masonry, such as stucco or concrete block
■ can be applied under damp conditions such as on a surface covered with morning dew.
On the negative side, latex paints:
■ don't wear as well, particularly under foot traffic
■ require surface preparation or a primer because latex adheres to the surface rather than penetrating it.

PRIMERS

Primers can have either oil or latex base. Choose the primer with the same base as the topcoat. Follow the manufacturer's recommendations; primers are formulated differently for different surfaces and topcoats. Some primers penetrate and change the composition of old paint to provide better "tooth." Others stick tenaciously to old paint. Painters usually use oil-based primers to repaint wood and save latex and acrylic primers for plaster and masonry.

SPECIALTY PAINTS

There are paints and primers made for hard-to-cover surfaces. If you are painting metal, concrete block, new masonry with a high alkali content, areas subject to mildew, nonporous surfaces (such as ceramic tile), or appliances subject to high temperatures (such as flue pipes or radiators), ask your paint dealer for recommendations.

PAINT TERMS

Acrylic: One of the synthetic resins used in some latex paints. Generally regarded as the best type of latex.
Natural Bristle Brush: A brush made from animal hair, usually hog hair. Natural bristle brushes are best for oil-based paints and stains.
Enamel: Any paint that forms an especially hard, smooth film. The term includes the full range of glosses in both alkyd and latex paints.
Epoxy Paint: Based on synthetic petroleum resins and cured by a catalyst. The most durable of paints.

Mineral Spirits: A petroleum-based solvent used to thin and clean up oil-based paints and other coatings.
Oil Paint: In these paints, oil is the basic ingredient. The term used to refer to paints with a linseed oil base, but now applies to alkyd paints as well.
Sealer: A base coat that prevents excessive absorption of later coats of paint of stain.
Solvent: The volatile portion of oil-based paints, it evaporates during drying. Water performs the same role in latex paints.

Stain: A finish formulated to color a surface without hiding it. Stains may be transparent, semi-transparent, or opaque, depending on the degree of hiding, and may be oil-based or acrylic.
Synthetic Brush: A brush whose bristles are plastic—usually polyester or nylon. Synthetic brushes are best used for latex paints, and deteriorate when used with oil-based paints.
Turpentine: A thinner derived from pine-tree resins. It has been mostly replaced by less expensive "mineral spirits," a petroleum-based thinner.

CHOOSING YOUR COLORS

Nothing affects the overall appearance of a home as much as its color.

EXTERIOR

Choose colors that harmonize with the character of your home and your neighborhood. To get ideas, tour the area and look through magazines and books. When you see a color scheme that works, don't be afraid to walk up to the door and ask the owner for the names of the paints. Remember the saying, "Imitation is the sincerest form of flattery?"

The design of a home often dictates how color can be used. If the architecture is strong, the walls plain, and your home far enough from the neighbors to not compete with their style, walls can become canvases for an imaginative, multi-color statement. For the majority of homes, however, two or three colors are usually sufficient.

Light colors won't get you in design trouble, but they tend to be dull and will look better with a contrasting trim color. If the foundation is distinct from the house, paint it a darker tone to give it stability and make it disappear.

Unless you want to make a bold statement, avoid bright, pure colors as well as combinations with equal intensities. Muted earth tones are very popular because they blend into the landscape. They also tend to last longer than pure hues.

INTERIOR

The color of a room affects its size, mood, and perceived temperature.

In general, light colors "enlarge" a room; dark colors "shrink" it. You can also enlarge a room by combining light and dark colors.

It is dangerous to use more than two colors, unless they are different intensities of the same hue. If one of the colors is off-white, choose a shade with a hint of color that matches the other colors in the room. And if two rooms are connected by a wide doorway, be sure to use compatible colors in both.

High-gloss paints are back in style and, due to their reflectivity, brighten a room. Experiment with them for up-to-the-minute fashion statements.

CHOOSING COLORS BY EXPOSURE

The amount of natural light in a room should affect your color choice. If a sunny room with windows facing west and southwest tends to feel hot and stuffy, use cool colors such as blue and gray. Rooms with windows facing north tend to be colder than other rooms and will benefit from warm colors such as red, orange, and browns. Rooms facing east can be painted in warm or cool colors depending on whether the morning sun needs a cheery boost or a cooling contrast.

Exposure is important, but it is not the only factor in choosing colors. The use of a room should also be considered—bright yellow may not be the best color for a living room, even if it faces north. Also remember that the wall colors must harmonize with the room's permanent features, such as a hardwood floor or large fireplace.

COLOR BY COMPUTER

Matching paint colors used to be a real art, gained only with years of experience. The computer has changed that. If you need to match new paint to an existing color, just take a flake or chip of the old paint to the store and a computer will analyze the color and print out a recipe for an exact match!

Of course the wise consumer will still buy and test a single quart or gallon before committing to the whole quantity.

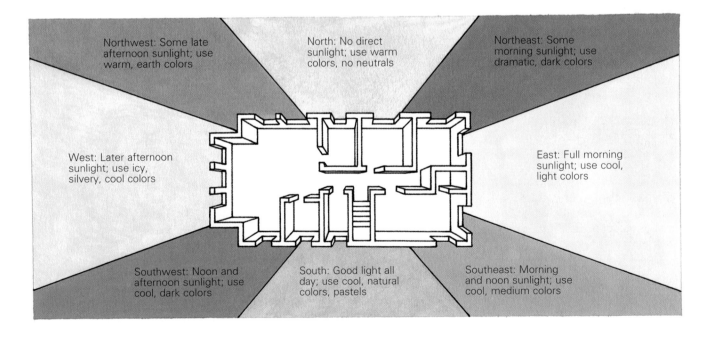

Northwest: Some late afternoon sunlight; use warm, earth colors

North: No direct sunlight; use warm colors, no neutrals

Northeast: Some morning sunlight; use dramatic, dark colors

West: Later afternoon sunlight; use icy, silvery, cool colors

East: Full morning sunlight; use cool, light colors

Southwest: Noon and afternoon sunlight; use cool, dark colors

South: Good light all day; use cool, natural colors, pastels

Southeast: Morning and noon sunlight; use cool, medium colors

APPLICATORS

The type of brush you use will depend on the kind of finish you're applying.

Use natural bristles with oil-based paints, varnishes, polyurethane finishes, and most chemical strippers. Use synthetic bristles for latex. A mix of 1½-inch, 3-inch, and 4-inch brushes will be all you need for most jobs. Brushes with flagged bristles (split ends) hold paint better and produce a smoother finish.

ROLLERS

Standard paint rollers are 9 inches wide. Choose a high-quality roller with nylon bearings, a threaded handle, and extension poles for reaching ceilings or other out-of-the-way areas.

Roller covers come in synthetic fibers, lamb's wool, and mohair. Synthetic covers work well with most paints, especially latex. Use lamb's wool covers with oil-based paints. Mohair produces the best results with high-gloss enamels and clear finishes.

Use a short-nap (¼-inch) cover for smooth surfaces, ½-inch nap for textured surfaces, and ¾-inch nap for very rough surfaces such as stucco or concrete block.

PAINT PADS

Spreader and trim pads apply paint slower than rollers, but faster than brushes, and they leave less texture than rollers. Their ease of handling, absence of spattering, and simple cleanup make them a joy to work with. Paint pads come in a variety of sizes.

THROWAWAY BRUSHES

You can buy ten of these cheap foam or bristle brushes for the price of one very good brush. Why would you use such cheap brushes? Because they work fine on most small jobs, and throwing them away is cheaper than buying the paint thinner to clean them. When painting takes five minutes and cleaning the brush takes ten, reach for a throwaway.

When using latex paints and stains, however, there's nothing to say you must throw away a throwaway brush. They clean up with soap and water. Keep a few of every size on hand.

BRUSH STYLES

4" wall   Sash   Sash/trim   Round   Foam   Foam

Birdcage frame

Trim roller

Roller cover

Extension handle

Pad painter

Paint tray

PAINT TRAYS

If you're painting with a roller or pad, you'll need a paint tray. Fill only the bottom portion of the tray with paint, leaving the upper, slanted portion for squeezing off excess and for spreading the paint evenly on your roller or pad.

Because paint in trays may sit out for extended periods of time, it often hardens along edges, making cleanup difficult. Make cleanup a snap with thin, plastic liners that fit the trays precisely. They cost only pennies each. When you're done painting, simply throw them away.

CAN CLEANUP

When it comes to paint projects, few things are as frustrating as cans of paint that slowly gunk up along the rim, prevent lids from being shut and, when opened, drop sticky bits of congealed paint back into the can. The culprit is the rim, which has an inverted groove. The groove works great to seal the can when it leaves the factory, but after it's opened, the same groove traps paint. To solve the problem, use a nail to punch three or four holes in the bottom of the groove. Excess paint will drain back into the can.

BUYING PAINT

Always buy high-quality paint. It will save you time (money in the long run) and frustration. Fortunately for the budget-minded, quality doesn't always mean high-priced.

To test paint quality, drop a stick into a well-stirred can of paint and lift it straight out. Ideally, ⅛ to ¼ inch of paint should cling to the stick, while the top surface runs off. If too much runs off too quickly, the paint will not cover; if the paint sticks without running off, it is too thick and you'll need more than necessary to do the job. Consumer's Union (CU) tests and reports on both interior and exterior paints on a regular schedule. Access their reports through subscription, your local library, their annual report (sold in bookstores), and their website.

Don't ever try to rely on your memory when it comes to colors. Bring old woodwork, swatches of fabric, magazine pictures, or wallpaper scraps with you to the paint store. Take home several color cards to see how they will look in the specific room. Use several cards showing identical colors and distribute the cards to different locations in the same room. Check to see how your color selection is affected by shadows and changing light patterns that occur throughout the day. Finally, buy small cans and paint test patches. Look at them for several days before making a final decision.

Calculate your needs by measuring the square footage to be covered. Have the dealer convert footage to gallons. Typical coverage is 300 square feet per gallon, but this varies according to the formulation. Buy a little more than you think you will need. In fact, if you select one of the standard pre-mixed colors, buy a lot more than you think you'll need, with the understanding that you can return unopened cans. Don't forget to save your receipt!

After you have picked your color, buy all of your paint at once. Batch-buying ensures a good color match from one can to another. Buying in 5-gallon buckets will also save money.

REMEMBERING COLORS

"What was the name of that color?" How many times have you heard yourself asking that question?

Take a tip from professional painters. Write the color name or formula on a gummed label and stick it inside the cover plate of the room's light switch.

Now... if you can just remember where you left that note!

MIXING PAINT

If your paint has just been tinted at the store, then you won't have to mix it much. Even if you're buying a stock color, have the store mix up the paint in their power shaking machine. If you bought the paint a month ago, the store will probably be glad to give it another shake if you bring it back.

If you have to mix the paint yourself, here's how.

Pour half the paint into an empty can. Stir the thick paint left in the can. While stirring, slowly pour the thin paint back. Then pour the mix back and forth between cans. If you have a variable-speed electric drill, purchase a paint paddle and mix at a slow speed. Power stirring is a lot easier on the wrists and arms!

To keep the groove around the top of the can from clogging with paint, pound a few nail holes in the bottom of the groove. Excess paint will drain through these holes.

Oil-based paints sometimes develop a thick skin on the surface. Don't try to stir or mix this skin into the paint. Instead, gently lift it off and pour the paint through a nylon stocking or cheesecloth strainer to get rid of any coagulated lumps.

Pour half the paint into an empty can

Stir the thick paint left on the bottom

Pour the paint in the second can back into the first.

235

PREPARING THE SURFACE

EXTERIOR SURFACES

A coat of paint generally lasts from four to seven years, depending on exposure (sunny exposures fade more quickly), color (darker colors fade faster), and surface preparation. Don't paint your house too often; the thicker the layers, the more likely they are to alligator and peel. Most exterior paint is formulated to wear away slowly, through a process called chalking. In many cases, removing the chalk by scrubbing or pressure-washing will renew a painted surface.

How do you tell when to repaint? When the existing paint has almost worn off, or is peeling, blistering, cracking, or alligatoring.

Preparing Wood Siding: Start by removing as much old paint as possible with a pressure washer. After the surface dries, remove any remaining stubborn spots with a paint scraper or power sander. Always wear a respirator and stand upwind because an older layer may contain lead.

If the original paint was peeling, eliminate the cause: moisture driven through the wall from inside the house. The solution: Install vents in the attic or ¾-inch vents near the top of the stud cavities. Also consider painting the interior surfaces of the problem walls with vapor barrier paint.

Set protruding nail heads and caulk cracks, seams, and joints. Sand high spots, and roughen shiny areas for better paint adhesion. You are now ready to apply the primer to bare spots.

Preparing Masonry Surfaces: To prepare masonry, pressure wash or scrub the walls with a wire brush and strong detergent. As moisture evaporates from masonry, it may leave salt deposits known as efflorescence. To remove these powdery salts, scrub the surface with a mixture of one part muriatic acid and three parts water. Wear gloves, safety glasses, and old clothing—the acid is caustic. (Note: never add water to acid; always pour the acid into water.) If the wall is too slick for paint to adhere to, scrub again with a stronger acid solution. If the wall is too porous, prime the surface first with a block filler.

> ### CUT OUT "CUTTING-IN"
>
> Nothing is more nerve-wracking than "cutting-in"—the process of applying paint to a joint without slopping it over onto the other finish. A lot of cutting-in can be eliminated if you exercise a little forethought and paint trim before you install it.

INTERIOR SURFACES

Prepare interior walls, ceilings, and woodwork by washing them with a solution of trisodium phosphate (TSP) and water. Let dry thoroughly, then patch any cracks or holes.

Don't paint wallpaper with alkyd paint unless you know you won't ever want to remove the paper. If the paper adheres well and is smooth, a latex primer and paint will probably cover it satisfactorily. If the wallpaper is damaged or doesn't adhere well, rent a steamer and scrape it off.

When repainting an enamel-paint or gloss surface, add some tooth for the new paint to grip. TSP may degloss the enamel sufficiently. Otherwise, roughen it by sanding with medium-grit paper and a pad sander. Use an oil-based primer, and then either an alkyd or latex finish coat.

If the details of your trim have flattened out under layers and layers of paint, you may want to strip it. Strip to bare wood if you want to restore the wood with a clear finish; partial stripping will be adequate if you are repainting.

If the trim is flat (and if you are lucky), you will be able to strip the wood with scrapers and a power sander. If not, you will have to use a chemical paint remover, following the instructions on the can. If you can find new molding with a pattern similar to the old molding, consider replacing the trim instead of stripping. Don't underestimate the labor and mess involved in stripping a heavy paint build-up.

WINDOWS

Scrape away loose paint with a putty knife or paint scraper. Remove loose putty around the glass, coat exposed wood with oil-based primer, and replace the old putty with new glazing compound (see Glazings, page 164).

If layers of old paint have frozen the sash to the window stops, cut through the paint with a utility knife so the window moves freely.

Look for damaged or rotten wood. If the damage is extensive, replace the sash. If the damaged area is small, chisel away the rotted wood and patch with epoxy filler. Spot-prime patches and bare wood.

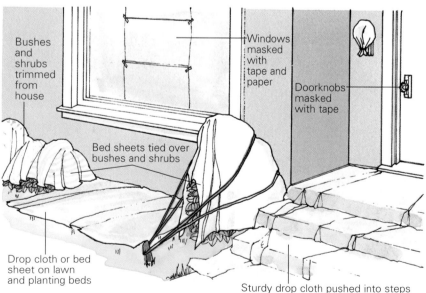

Bushes and shrubs trimmed from house

Windows masked with tape and paper

Doorknobs masked with tape

Bed sheets tied over bushes and shrubs

Drop cloth or bed sheet on lawn and planting beds

Sturdy drop cloth pushed into steps

The more you protect before you paint, the less you have to clean up afterward—and honestly, you know how messy your painting can be. Be smart about it this time.

PRESSURE WASHERS

A pressure washer is one of the best methods for removing dirt and peeling paint. It is also an effective way to remove dirt, grit, and chalky residue from old vinyl and aluminum sidings. But use it with care. A pressure washer is so powerful that it will erode soft wood in ridges, and will leave the surface rough and fuzzy.

You can wash an average-size house in half a day. Some scraping or sanding may still be needed, but washing provides a clean surface that paint will adhere to. You may not even need to repaint if the paint film is still intact; power washing not only removes residue. It can often rejuvenate the finish.

Power washers come with long wands for reaching high areas. Avoid using a ladder if you can—the force of the nozzle can knock you off balance. And stay at least 10 feet away from power lines. Prepare areas around power lines by hand, wearing rubber gloves and goggles, and use only wood or fiberglass ladders.

These tips will make power washing easier and safer:
■ Handle the power washer with caution. When you turn it on, the pressure will kick the wand back. Never point the washer at anyone or let children use it. The water pressure is hard enough to penetrate skin.

Rain gear Goggles Spray nozzle
Spray wand
Gloves
Water supply hose Gas-powered pressure washer

■ Keep the nozzle 12 inches from the surface and at a 45-degree angle. At this distance and angle, most peeling paint will come off without damaging the wood.
■ Cover fixtures and outlets in plastic.
■ Cover plants and tie them back from the wall.
■ Don't use the washer on windy days. The overspray will travel all over the neighborhood and leave deposits on automobiles.

■ Do not spray directly at windows from close range. The water pressure can even break glass!
■ Avoid spraying up under lap siding or into openings such as vents. If you do, you will have to wait a long time for the siding to dry enough to paint.
■ While you have the washer, clean patios, driveways, lawn furniture, and garbage cans. It does a fabulous job.

PAINTING TECHNIQUES

ROLLERS

Before you paint, wet the roller. Wetting primes it and helps to remove lint. Use water if you are using latex; use paint thinner with an alkyd. Then run the roller over a clean towel until it is dry to the touch. To load the cover with paint, roll it back and forth on a grid in a paint tray. The nap should be full but not dripping.

Paint ceilings first and walls from the top down, so spatters and drips will not mar already painted areas. First use a brush or paint pad to paint corners, and around trim, fixtures, and other obstacles. Then paint in the rest of the area with the roller. Use an extension pole to eliminate the need for a stepladder and keep spatter well away

from you. Wear a billed cap to protect your head and eyes.

To apply paint with a roller, spread the first few strokes in a W pattern. To reduce dripping, make the first stroke upward. Rolling slowly will cut down spattering. Increase pressure as you go to spread the paint evenly.

Then fill in the zigzag pattern. Use even, parallel strokes; take care not to roll too fast. As the zigzag disappears, feather the paint into adjacent areas, both painted and unpainted. Lift the roller at the end of each feather stroke.

BRUSHES

Dip the brush into the paint about half the length of the bristles. Lift the brush straight out of the paint and tap it

lightly against the inside edge of the rim. Resist the urge to draw the brush across the rim—that removes too much paint and clumps the bristles.

Hold the brush at a 45-degree angle. Deposit the paint with two or three strokes, then spread it evenly with long, light strokes. Use vertical strokes on walls; horizontal on lap siding. To produce a thin, feathered edge, lightly lift the brush as you finish each stroke.

Work in small sections—about 3 feet by 3 feet—and overlap previously painted sections slightly each time. Make sure the entire tip of the brush touches the surface. Always brush into the section most recently painted to avoid lap marks.

USING A PAINT SPRAYER

Paint sprayers can reduce your painting time drastically. They cover large areas quickly and apply paint smoothly—even to ornate or textured surfaces such as fences and carved woodwork. Spray painting, however, requires practice and your full attention. Sprayed paint can drift on a breeze, leaving a colorful trail.

High-volume sprayers utilize compressors that supply air under high pressure through hoses to a hand-held applicator. An airless sprayer has an electric pump in the hand-held unit.

Airless sprayers develop extremely high pressures—up to 3,000 pounds per square inch. If you accidentally pull the trigger while touching the tip of the nozzle, the sprayer may inject you with paint. Such an injury may not cause a loss of blood, but can result in severe tissue damage and blood poisoning. To prevent injuries, make sure the sprayer has a safety lock and guard, as well as a protective shield that keeps your fingers away from the tip. Never point the gun toward anyone, including yourself. Unplug

the sprayer before you try to unclog the tip, and store the sprayer in a locked cabinet when it is not in use.

Cover adjacent areas with drop cloths or masking paper; sprayers invariably produce overspray. To use a sprayer, first thin and strain the paint according to the manufacturer's specifications. Then test-spray a large piece of cardboard (save large shipping boxes in anticipation of spray painting) and adjust the spray so the paint covers evenly, without spattering.

To avoid lap marks, adjust the spray to an elliptical pattern—wide in the center and tapered at the ends. Hold the gun about 12 inches from the surface and move it back and forth horizontally, keeping the spray perpendicular to the surface. Don't spray one spot too long or the paint will become thick and sag. Several thin coats are better than one thick coat.

If a sprayer clogs, unplug the cord immediately. Follow the manufacturer's instructions to release the pressure and clean the tip. For final cleanup, use lacquer thinner instead of paint thinner because it is a stronger solvent.

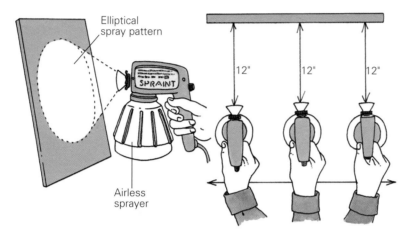

Elliptical spray pattern

SPRAINT

Airless sprayer

12" 12" 12"

PAINTING AND STAINING TRIM

When painting trim and woodwork, paint the horizontal surfaces before the vertical ones. Also, follow the "inside-out" rule—work from inner to outer sections. When using oil-based enamels, use a roller to save time, but finish missed spots with a brush while the paint is still wet. Always use a brush for applying latex enamel.

Since trim usually contrasts with the surrounding surfaces, paint a clean line between adjacent colors. As a general rule, paint trim before adjacent surfaces—cutting in a recessed flat surface is easier than cutting in a raised molding. Although you must paint the surrounding surfaces with care to avoid spatters, masking the trim or using paint shields is seldom necessary. Baseboards are an exception. Paint baseboards last and, if necessary, use a shield, such as a piece of stiff cardboard, to protect adjacent surfaces and leave a crisp edge. Change the

cardboard often to prevent smears.

To cut in trim or adjacent wall surfaces, hold the brush at an angle so all the bristles bend slightly (not too much) and make full contact. Then drag the brush slowly, twisting

it slightly so that the leading corner glides along the edge where the two colors meet. Once you've lined the edge, work away from it and brush on the remaining paint with long, even strokes.

PAINTING ORDER FOR OUTER SASH

1

Paint top half of lower window, then reverse windows and finish

2

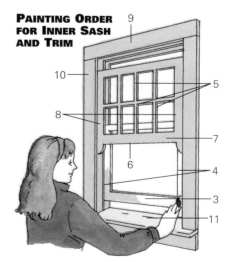

PAINTING ORDER FOR INNER SASH AND TRIM

9

10

5

8

7

6

4

3

11

It isn't always possible to paint all the exterior trim in one session. If you use scaffolds or a painter's fall, work from the top down, and complete an entire section before you move the equipment. Painting exterior trim and walls in one session may require cutting a new color into an existing edge when the first one is still tacky.

WINDOW TRIM

Mask each pane with common transparent tape, which works better than masking tape. Leave a 1/16-inch gap between the tape and the sash so the paint will seal against the glass. Work from the inside out, painting the muntins (dividers) and sash around the glass first. When painting double-hung windows, reverse the sash positions for easier access to each half.

PAINT EDGE FIRST

DOORS

Prime unpainted flush doors with a roller if you use oil-based paint; otherwise, brush on both the primer and topcoat. Spread the paint from the center to the outside edges, then immediately brush with long, vertical strokes. If the door is paneled, paint the panels first, then the trim.

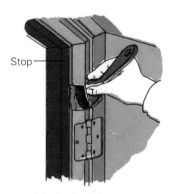

Paint horizontally, away from edge, then vertically

PAINTING ORDER FOR A PANELED DOOR

Make the patterned shadows cast by elaborate moldings much more dramatic by painting the door in a single, light color. Paint the latch edge of the door in the same color as the room into which it opens; the hinge edge should match whichever room it faces when the door is open. Paint the stop to match the surrounding frame.

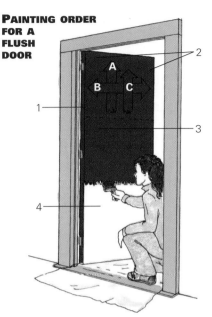

PAINTING ORDER FOR A FLUSH DOOR

BASEBOARDS

If the wall is papered, mask the edge with paper tape. Otherwise, use a paint shield as you work. Paint baseboards with an angled sash brush and start with the top edge. Next paint the bottom edge, protecting the floor with a shield or tape. Finally, paint the center portion with a larger brush, feathering the wet paint into the edges. Use long, horizontal strokes.

TROUBLESHOOTING EXTERIOR PAINT PROBLEMS

Problem	Likely Cause	What to Do
Alligatoring	Finish applied over wet primer	Sand or scrape to bare wood; repaint
Bleeding	Pitch coming out of knots in wood; usually found in siding	Apply white-shellac sealer over stains; repaint
Blistering	Finish applied over wet wall	Sand or scrape to bare wood; repaint with latex
Chalk	Paint designed to chalk	Pressure-wash before repainting
Checking	Excessive swelling and shrinking of siding	Sand or scrape to bare wood; repaint with latex
Mildew	Humidity, lack of direct sun	Scrub with 50/50 solution of house hold bleach; repaint with mildew-resistant paint
Peeling	Moisture source inside wall	Install inside vapor barrier (consider VB paint); install siding vents
	Paint applied when wall wet	Scrape and repaint
Rust stains	Non-rust-resistant nails	Apply white-shellac sealer over stains; repaint

Paints and Stains
continued

PAINTING A ROOM

Before you paint, remove everything from the room except items which are too large; move this big stuff to the center of the room and cover it with a tarp or plastic.

If the surfaces are greasy, wash them with trisodium phosphate (TSP) or detergent. TSP must be rinsed, but some detergents don't require rinsing.

Remove switch and receptacle cover plates, and mask the switches and receptacles with tape.

Patch cracks or holes with sandable spackling compound, except for small cracks that open seasonally. Paint these with an elastomeric primer. You can also use vinyl spackling compound, but smooth it with a damp sponge before it dries because it can't be sanded.

Caulk gaps between the trim pieces and the wall with paintable latex caulk.

Paint wood-frame windows, starting next to the glass and working outward. The paint should just touch the glass to seal the edge of the wood. Paint around the glass, then the rest of the sash, then the jambs, then the casing, and finally the sill and apron.

Next, paint trim with an angle brush. If you paint carefully, it won't be necessary to mask the walls.

Prime the patched areas and any new wall surfaces and let them dry. Use white-shellac primer/sealer on stains that won't wash out.

When the primer is dry and the trim painted, start the finish coat around the doors and windows and in the corners with a 2- to 3-inch strip. Fill in the remaining wall surface with a roller or large pad.

If you have panel doors, paint the panels first, then the trim. The door can be painted in place or taken down.

Remove the hardware and stuff the openings with paper towels.

COMMON MISTAKES

Where do amateurs go wrong? Creative folks can always find new ways, but these errors are the most typical:
- Not washing the surfaces before beginning to paint.
- Not using a primer where it's needed.
- Trying to economize by thinning and spreading the paint too far. Two thick coats will wear better than three thin ones.
- Ignoring the manufacturer's instructions
- Painting in the wrong sequence.
- Using the wrong type of brush for the paint base. Use natural-bristle brushes with oils and alkyds, and polyester or nylon for latex paint.

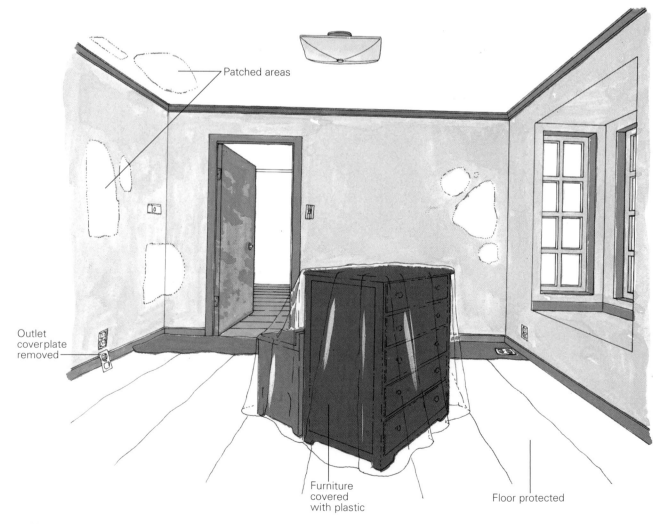

Patched areas

Outlet cover plate removed

Furniture covered with plastic

Floor protected

Seal cans which contain useful amounts of paint tightly and store them in a cool, dry cabinet out of the reach of children. Leave nearly-empty cans open in a dry, well-ventilated place, such as a garage, to let the remaining paint solidify. Do not dump thinners and solvents down the drain or sewer. Store thinners in a tightly sealed container. If you need to dispose of used solvents, ask your local waste management agency for disposal information (see "Hazardous Substances," pages 176–177). Do not dump them down the drain.

Don't rely on your memory to tell you what's hidden in the cans—label every can as to content. To clean rollers and paintbrushes used with oil-based paint, soak them in paint thinner for a few minutes, then flush them out by working the solvent into the bristles or nap and dipping them up and down in the solvent a few times. Repeat with fresh solvent until the solvent no longer runs with color.

SOAKING PAINTBRUSHES

You don't need to clean paintbrushes until you've finished painting. Store them temporarily in paint thinner when painting with alkyds; use water with latex paint. Suspend the brushes; don't stand them on the bristles.

Another short-term storage solution is to place the brushes in a plastic zipper bag and freeze them.

DRYING AND WRAPPING BRUSHES

To dry your brushes, spin them as shown below. Spinning inside a box or empty 5-gallon paint can will prevent spatter. Wipe the brushes with a clean rag and wrap them in plain butcher paper.

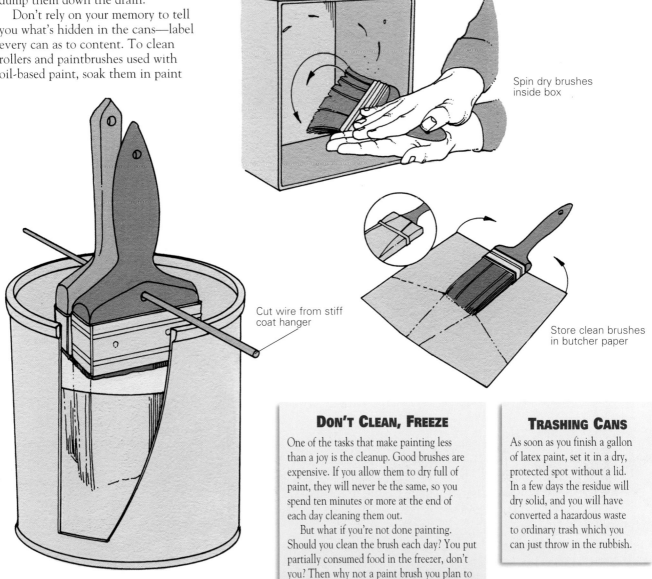

Cut wire from stiff coat hanger

Spin dry brushes inside box

Store clean brushes in butcher paper

DON'T CLEAN, FREEZE

One of the tasks that make painting less than a joy is the cleanup. Good brushes are expensive. If you allow them to dry full of paint, they will never be the same, so you spend ten minutes or more at the end of each day cleaning them out.

But what if you're not done painting. Should you clean the brush each day? You put partially consumed food in the freezer, don't you? Then why not a paint brush you plan to use the next day—especially if it's with the same paint? Wrap the brush in plastic wrap, or zip it up in a plastic storage bag, and throw it in the freezer. It will keep very well!

TRASHING CANS

As soon as you finish a gallon of latex paint, set it in a dry, protected spot without a lid. In a few days the residue will dry solid, and you will have converted a hazardous waste to ordinary trash which you can just throw in the rubbish.

PANELING

TRANSFORMING WHOLE WALLS

It is hard to generalize about paneling because it ranges from solid boards of the most expensive species down to fake "wood" paper-covered hardboard that fools no one.

Instead we'll leave the question of cost and taste up to you, the reader, and concentrate on techniques for its installation.

Installing paneling is a simple undertaking because the job requires few tools and fewer skills. The most difficult step would be the strapping and shimming of an irregular subsurface, were that required.

There are several advantages to using paneling rather than other finish wall materials. It is fairly durable—particularly solid boards—and nearly maintenance-free. Once installed, it needs little if any finishing.

The disadvantages are that, with the exception of minor scratches and blemishes, paneling is hard to repair, and a careless installation can result in shabby-looking seams and edges.

TYPES

BOARDS

Paneling used to consist of individual tongue-and-groove boards, but sheet panels made to resemble boards are more popular today.

TONGUE-AND-GROOVE

Tongue-and-groove paneling is usually made from softwood—pine, redwood, or cedar—but oak and mahogany are also available. Boards vary in thickness from ⅜ inch to 1¹⁄₁₆ inch and in width from 2 inches to 8 inches. Some are tongue-and-grooved on the ends as well. Often, single boards are made to look like two or three narrow boards by milling vertical grooves into the single board. Some types are rough-sawn on one side and planed ("dressed") on the other. Some boards can even be purchased prefinished.

SHEET PANELING

A great variety of paneling is available in sheets 4 feet wide by 8, 9, or 10 feet long. One type is basically plywood with one high-quality face veneer, and comes in thicknesses from ³⁄₁₆ inch to ⅝ inch. The other type is hardboard with a printed paper or plastic face and is ¼ inch thick. Some wood veneers are thick enough to have V-grooves.

EXTERIOR SIDING

Exterior sidings, including shingles, clapboards, and solid wood boards with shiplap and V-groove patterns, can also be used indoors. The boards can be installed vertically, horizontally, or diagonally, and can be painted, stained, or finished with a clear sealer.

TYPES OF PANELING

Type	Thickness	Cost	Description
Hardboard	⅛", ¼"	Low	Compressed and glued fibers, with a paper or plastic facing which is often printed to simulate real wood; fairly water-resistant; easy to install
Plywood	⅛", ⁵⁄₃₂", ³⁄₁₆"	Medium	Three wood plies; face veneer high quality soft- or hardwood; grooved to resemble boards; water-resistant; easy to install.
Boards	⅜", ¾"	High	Solid wood; edges may be plain, shiplapped, or tongue-and-groove; installation requires more time; very durable.

INEXPENSIVE 'BARN BOARD' PANELING

Do you like "barn-board" paneling? You can buy, for a lot of money, rough-sawn pine boards which have been bleached to resemble old barn boards. Or, you can bleach them yourself with a little help from the sun.

Purchase enough run-of-the-mill, 1×8, rough pine boards to cover your application. Have the mill shiplap the boards so that you won't be able to see through the cracks when they shrink. Also, specify the lengths (you can order any lengths from 8 feet to 16 feet, in

2-foot increments) to minimize the waste.

While you are at the mill, ask for an equal number of feet of sticking (the bark edgings). Lay out three rows of sticking and lay the boards on the sticks in direct sun. The boards will start nearly white. After a week they will be a pale yellow; two more weeks and they will be light tan, a month to fawn, and finally, after perhaps two or three months, a gray-tan. Spraying them with salt water will cut the bleaching time in half.

INSTALLING PANELS

To prepare a wall for paneling, locate all of the studs and mark their positions on the floor and ceiling. Then check for high and low spots with either a long straightedge or a taut string. If all areas are within about ¼ inch of a flat plane, apply the paneling directly to the wall.

If the wall is irregular, nail 1×2 furring strips 24 inches on-center and wherever panel seams will occur. If the framing is exposed, apply ½-inch wallboard before paneling. The wallboard will add weight to the wall and allow you to install the paneling with mastic instead of nails.

Take the paneling indoors several days before installation. It is susceptible to expansion and contraction and needs to acclimate to the home. Store it flat on the floor to avoid curvature, which will make it difficult to install.

Install full sheets wherever possible. Use filler pieces over doorways and windows. Place all edges over a stud or a furring strip. Install the first panel in the most visible corner. Use a 4-foot level to make sure the sides are plumb.

The easiest and best way to install paneling is with panel adhesive and a caulking gun. Apply a quick-drying adhesive immediately before each sheet goes up. Some adhesives require pushing the sheet against the adhesive, pulling it away to allow the glue to set, then pushing the panel into place. Even with adhesive, nail the panels along the top and bottom edges, which will be covered by trim.

Cut paneling with a handsaw, table saw, or circular saw. A handsaw should be a crosscut with at least 12 teeth per inch. When using a handsaw, table saw, or radial arm saw, cut paneling face-up. If using a circular saw, place the sheet face-down, and clamp a long straightedge to the panel for a guide.

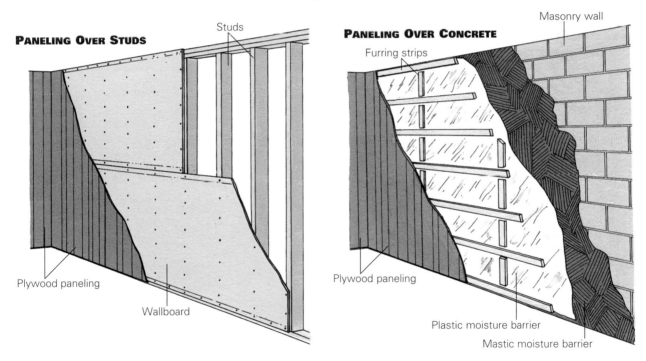

PANELING OVER STUDS

Studs

Plywood paneling

Wallboard

PANELING OVER CONCRETE

Masonry wall

Furring strips

Plywood paneling

Plastic moisture barrier

Mastic moisture barrier

FITTING AN IRREGULAR EDGE

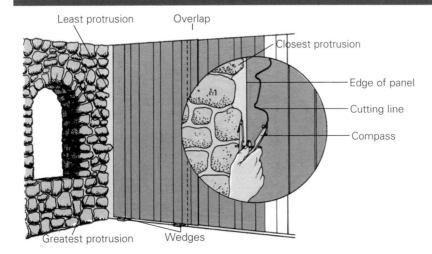

Least protrusion

Overlap

Closest protrusion

Edge of panel

Cutting line

Compass

Greatest protrusion

Wedges

Where paneling meets an irregular edge, such as a fireplace, cut it to fit. Wedge the panel so that its top jams against the ceiling, and its edge butts against the protrusion of the wall.

Use a compass and pencil to scribe a cutting line. Set the compass so that the legs bridge the widest gap between the panel and the irregular wall. Holding the compass rigidly in a horizontal position (don't let the legs swing), trace the contour of the wall onto the panel. Cut along the line with a saber saw.

PANEL SIDING

BEAUTY REALLY IS SKIN DEEP

ALSO SEE...
Fasteners:
Pages 122–125
Paints & Stains:
Pages 232–241
Shingle Siding:
Pages 308–309
Wood:
Pages 446–453

Panel siding is the easiest siding of all to install and, if it is structurally rated plywood, eliminates the need for sheathing. Apply it directly over the wall framing with galvanized nails.

In spite of a wide range of styles, the core of most panels is the same—either plywood or hardboard. Only the veneer—the thin top layer—distinguishes panel designs. More expensive panels have cedar, redwood, or Douglas fir veneers. Less expensive panels use lower grades of wood, resin-treated paper, or embossed hardboard. Because the veneer is so thin, paint or stain all panel siding for protection from the sun and rain.

TYPES AND SIZES

Plywood and hardboard panels are widely used because they are relatively low in price and can be installed very quickly. They come in a wide variety of patterns and designs, and some of the most popular are shown in the illustration (right).

Some designs include a rabbet along the edges and others are straight-edged. The kind of edge makes a difference in how the panels are installed.

Standard sizes are 4×8, 4×9, and 4×10. When estimating materials, remember that the bottom edge of the panel should overlap the foundation wall by at least 2 inches, but should not be any closer than 8 inches to the ground. For a house framed with standard 8-foot walls, you'll need 4×9 sheets.

Unfaced panel siding should be at least ⅜ inch thick; grooved material is heavier, ⅝ inch or thicker. When putting new siding over an irregular surface, such as shingles or horizontal siding, use the stiffer ½-inch or ⅝-inch panels. Use ⅜-inch panels over smooth surfaces, such as old panel siding or board siding with the battens (if any) removed.

ROUGH-SAWN AND BRUSHED

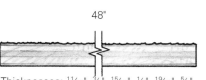

48"

Thicknesses: ¹¹⁄₃₂", ⅜", ¹⁵⁄₃₂", ½", ¹⁹⁄₃₂", ⅝"

KERFED ROUGH-SAWN

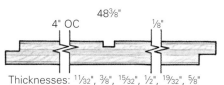

48⅜"
4" OC   ⅛"

Thicknesses: ¹¹⁄₃₂", ⅜", ¹⁵⁄₃₂", ½", ¹⁹⁄₃₂", ⅝"

TEXTURE 1-11 (T 1-11)

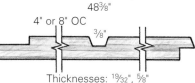

48⅜"
4" or 8" OC   ⅜"

Thicknesses: ¹⁹⁄₃₂", ⅝"

REVERSE BOARD AND BATTEN

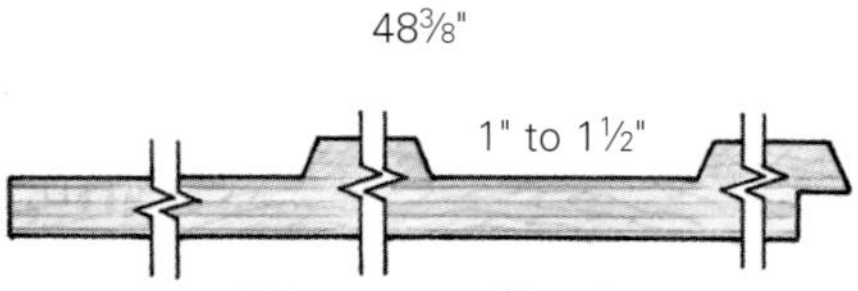

48⅜"
1" to 1½"

Thicknesses: ¹⁹⁄₃₂", ⅝"

CHANNEL GROOVE

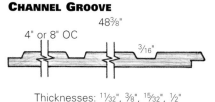

48⅜"
4" or 8" OC   ³⁄₁₆"

Thicknesses: ¹¹⁄₃₂", ⅜", ¹⁵⁄₃₂", ½"

FINISHING PANEL SIDING

Use any regular exterior-grade paint or stain for panel siding. If the panels have a rough-sawn surface, however, try stain. Stain penetrates the fibrous texture better than paint, and it won't flake or blister with age.

Because panel siding typically extends below the bottom plate and overlaps the foundation, coat the bottom 12 inches of each panel with a water sealer before painting or staining, making sure to soak all the edges.

INSTALLING PANELS

The primary problem with unfaced panel siding is what to do about the joints. If the panels have decorative grooves or rabbetted edges, only the end joints will show, but plain panels show all their joints

If you're installing the siding on a short wall, one long piece may do the trick—with only its end joints showing.

If that won't work, try to plan your installation so the joints are in an inconspicuous location, such as behind shrubbery, or a natural break, such as at the tops of the doors and windows. The best way to conceal joints, however, is to cover them with battens or trim.

Use either 6d stainless-siding or 6d hot-dipped galvanized (HDG) box nails for ⅜-inch panels. Use 8d or longer nails for thicknesses over ½ inch. Nail every 6 inches around the edges and 12 inches in the middle. Leave a ⅛-inch expansion gap between panels and a ¼-inch gap around windows and doors.

There is no need to add building paper between the studs and the siding in new construction, but 15-pound felt flashing should be applied around windows and doors. If you are covering existing siding, however, apply 15-pound felt first.

Panel siding is heavy and awkward to lift—don't try to hang it by yourself. Position each panel vertically—with joints over studs and blocking and a ⅛-inch gap along the edges. One person should hold the panel in place while the other person nails.

Align the first panel perfectly plumb. If you don't, all succeeding panels will be out of alignment.

If the panel won't square exactly with the structure, spread the corrections over several panels.

In new construction install the panel siding before the rafters. Make the panels flush with the top of the cap plate and notch the rafters to fit. The siding acts as structural reinforcement and braces the wall to take the weight of the rafters and roof.

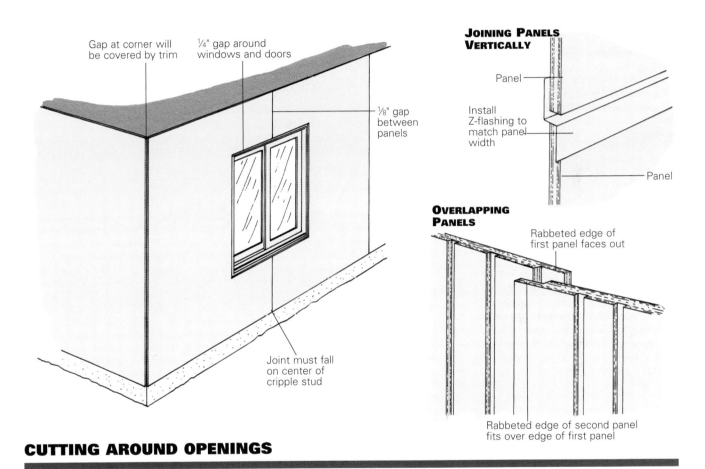

Gap at corner will be covered by trim

¼" gap around windows and doors

⅛" gap between panels

Joint must fall on center of cripple stud

JOINING PANELS VERTICALLY

Panel

Install Z-flashing to match panel width

Panel

OVERLAPPING PANELS

Rabbeted edge of first panel faces out

Rabbeted edge of second panel fits over edge of first panel

CUTTING AROUND OPENINGS

When working around openings, try to use full panels rather than cutting in a patchwork of smaller pieces. Remember to center the leading edge on a stud (including a cripple stud—the short stud above or below a window or door).

How you cut out the window or door opening depends on whether the window or door is already installed. If it isn't, nail a full panel in place directly over the opening. Then, with the framing of the opening as a guide, cut out the opening from the back, using a reciprocating or hand saw.

If the window or door is already installed, measure the opening on the panel before you hang it. Cut the opening ¼ inch larger all around to make fitting easier. To avoid splintering the front, cut from the back, making sure to reverse the measurements as you transfer them to the panel. Hold the panel up to the window or door before cutting just to make sure you have the proposed cutout in the right position.

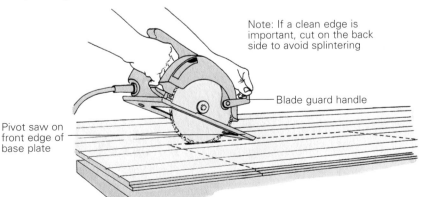

Note: If a clean edge is important, cut on the back side to avoid splintering

Blade guard handle

Pivot saw on front edge of base plate

PATIOS

DESIGN CONSIDERATIONS

ALSO SEE...
Bricks:
Pages 38–43
Concrete:
Pages 60–63
Drainage:
Pages 102–103
Tile:
Pages 360–367

A patio should be much more than a cold, hard square of concrete poured behind the back door. Like a deck, it should be an outdoor living space—a smooth transition that expands the activity area of a home and adds to the pleasures of outdoor living. It might be square, and it might be concrete, but it should be inviting.

The most obvious advantage of a patio is that there is no lawn to mow, no soil to till, and no mud to sink into. But remember that unrelieved pavement is awfully boring. Make it architecturally interesting by adding curves, angles, small planting areas, freestanding planters and garden furniture, as well as interesting paving texture and patterns.

Just as the transition from house to patio should be smooth, so should the transition from patio to the rest of the yard. Include in your plan steps and paths leading to the lawn or pool.

Whether you are building new or improving on the old, spend as much time planning as building so the space will suit your needs and your yard.

CONCRETE PATIO

LAYOUT

To prepare the patio site, lay out the perimeter with string lines, and drive grade stakes at 10-foot intervals. If the ground is rough, drive a stake every 5 feet. You will need these reference points to guide excavation and grading.

To establish pitch, stretch a line level from the house to the furthest stakes and mark level. From the level marks, drop marks on the furthest stakes 1 inch for every 10 feet. Now snap a chalk line along each row of stakes to establish the slope. Attach string to stakes at the level of the slope mark. Stretch strings across the patio area to form a grid that reflects the finished slope.

Determine the elevation of the patio. The lower edge should be slightly above the ground or flush with it, not below the ground. In southern areas plan the patio so that the edge closest to the house falls several inches below a doorway. In the snow belt, make the patio one or two steps below the door so that snow won't pile up and block the door. In either case, remember that the building code requires 8 inches of clearance between the finished patio and the bottom of the siding.

Determine how far below the strings the paving surface will lie. Add the thickness of the concrete and sub-base to this figure. The sum represents the distance from the string grid to the bottom of the excavation.

EXCAVATION

Remove all vegetation, debris, and loose soil down to the level you established. Be careful not to disturb the soil too much since the concrete slab must rest on compacted earth. Excavate deeper around the perimeter—a deeper footing will reinforce the outside edge of the patio. If the soil is subject to frost action, dig the footing to below the frost line and

CONCRETE PAVING FORMS

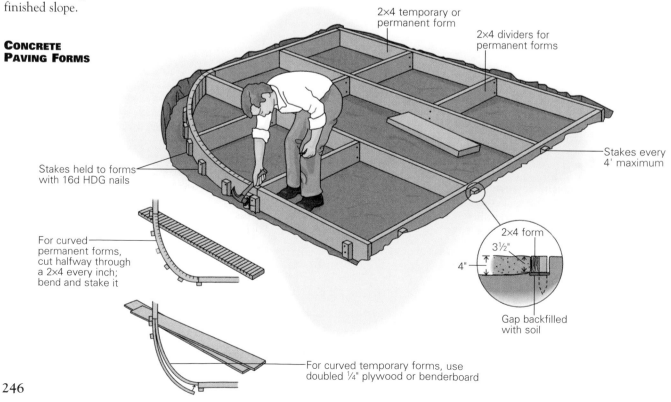

2×4 temporary or permanent form

2×4 dividers for permanent forms

Stakes every 4' maximum

Stakes held to forms with 16d HDG nails

For curved permanent forms, cut halfway through a 2×4 every inch; bend and stake it

2×4 form

3½"

4"

Gap backfilled with soil

For curved temporary forms, use doubled ¼" plywood or benderboard install perimeter drainage as if you were building a foundation.

If the patio will be above grade you need to fill rather than excavate. The best fill is a well-drained sand or gravel. You must always compact any fill that you add.

BASE

If the ground is particularly firm, you can pour concrete directly on it. Generally you need to put down and tamp a 2- to 4-inch deep sand bed. For problem areas—expansive soils or soils subject to freezing—put down 3 inches of pea gravel topped by 2 inches of sand.

FORMS

Forms can be simple 2×4s. If they are to remain in the concrete as decorative expansion strips, use pressure-treated lumber. Cover the top edges of the wood with masking tape to prevent concrete stains.

Drive a stake every 4 feet to hold the form. If you leave the forms in place, drive the stakes about 1 inch below the top edge of the forms. Use the string grid to set the top of the forms at the correct height.

To create sharp curves, cut saw kerfs halfway or more through one side of a 2×4 at intervals of 1 inch. For gentle curves bend 1×4s and stake them every 2 feet.

To control cracking, your patio should have expansion joints every 8 to 10 feet. Place either pressure-treated wood or vinyl expansion strips in the concrete when it is wet. Also, remember to install a strip of expansion material between the house and the patio.

Although patios generally do not require reinforcement, it provides extra insurance at small additional cost. Ask the ready-mix company to add fiber glass reinforcement to the concrete.

POURING AND FINISHING

To calculate the cubic yards of concrete you patio will require, see Concrete, pages 60–63.

Handle the concrete as little as possible. Have the ready-mix driver chute the concrete to where you need it, overfilling the forms slightly. Release trapped air by jamming a

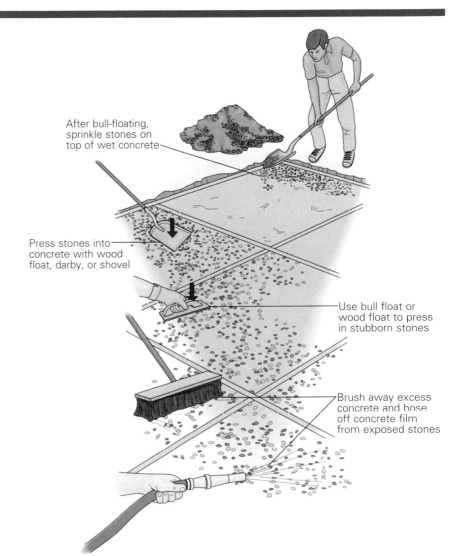

After bull-floating, sprinkle stones on top of wet concrete

Press stones into concrete with wood float, darby, or shovel

Use bull float or wood float to press in stubborn stones

Brush away excess concrete and hose off concrete film from exposed stones

shovel or stick up and down at various places, especially next to the form boards. Strike off the excess by dragging a long 2×4 across the tops of the forms with a sawing motion.

Immediately after strike-off, use a float to bring the surface to a preliminary smoothness. You may need a bull float with a long handle to reach the center of larger patios. Use a magnesium float for air-entrained concrete. Drag the float slowly across the surface, raising the leading edge slightly. Then run the tip of a trowel about an inch deep between the forms and concrete to clean the edge. Let the concrete set before finishing.

FINISHES

For a rough appearance and texture, the floated surface can be left as is. A broom surface, produced by dragging a damp pushbroom lightly across the floated surface, has very fine parallel lines and is skid-resistant. Edging with a special edging tool will add a finishing touch.

To add color, sprinkle on a dry-shake coloring agent after the excess water has evaporated from the slab. Add more color after each troweling. You may choose to paint or stain the patio after it cures.

You can also "seed" decorative stones into the surface after striking off the concrete. Wet the stones first, then spread them over the slab. Embed the stones in the surface with a float, level the surface, and wait for the concrete to set. Use a broom and fine spray from a hose to expose the tops of the seeded stones.

To cure the concrete, cover the slab with plastic sheeting. Leave the plastic on a full week. ▶

STONE PATIO

Flagstone and other natural stones make a great paving for large, rugged, earthy-looking patios. Compared to concrete the surface is very uneven, but the durability and natural look more than compensate.

Paving with flagstone is similar to paving with brick (see Bricks, pages 38–43), except that flagstones go down faster and must be installed with mortar or sod in the joints. Sand alone will not hold them because of the wide space between the stones. You may choose to lay the stones over a concrete and mortar base or a sand bed. Sand beds must be at least 2 inches thick to accommodate the irregular shape and thickness of the stones.

Permanent edging

Screeded sand (2")

Gravel base (4" to 8")

Groove scored with brickset or chisel

CUTTING FLAGSTONE

Flagstone is quite uniform in two dimensions and can be cut like brick. Use a broad chisel or a brickset and a hammer. Wear protective goggles because small chips of stone will certainly fly.

Mark the cut by scratching a line on the surface with the chisel, then score the line deeply. Repeat the process on the bottom.

Place the stone with the scored line just over the edge of a 2×4. Place the brickset on the line and give it a sharp rap. If the stone does not break, rap it in one or two more places along the line. Use the chisel to trim the cut.

If you prefer precise cuts, rent a wet-saw tile cutter from a tool-rental store or a store than sells quarry tile.

INSTALLING FLAGSTONE

Prepare the ground for flagstone as you would for a brick or concrete patio—mark the area with stakes and string, then level the site. Lay a 2-inch to 3-inch coarse sand bed; dampen and tamp it firm.

Build a border around the site. The border and the flagstones should lie flush with the ground.

After screeding the sand with a long, straight board, lay all the flagstones in their proposed positions to judge their final appearance. Space

the stones 1 to 3 inches apart if you will be infilling with mortar; space them farther apart if they will be separated by soil and grass.

A good dry-mortar mix for flagstone is 1 part portland cement and 3 parts sand. Mix the components with a mason's hoe (a hoe with several large holes in the blade) in a wheelbarrow until the mortar is a uniform color.

Spray the site with water so that the flagstones and the sand base are thoroughly wet. Let the stones dry, then spread the dry mix over the entire field of stone. Fill all the spaces completely. Sweep the mortar with a broom until it is smooth and level.

Set the hose nozzle to a fine spray and completely soak the joints. After 15 minutes, spray again to ensure that the water has penetrated all of the mortar. Top off settled areas with more dry mix and wet the newly added mortar.

After 24 hours, clean any mortar stains off the stones with a mixture of 1 part muriatic acid to 10 parts water. **Important:** Mix by adding the acid to the water; never add water to acid. Cover the patio with plastic sheeting for a week to let the mortar fully cure.

If you prefer grass between the stones, tamp the soil with the end of a 1×3; pack the soil tightly around the stones. Then lightly rake in grass seed

or encourage moss to grow between the stones.

You may also place flagstones directly in the ground without a sand base, except they will tend to sink into the ground and require periodic digging up and resetting. But if you do want to set them directly, lay the stones out in the pattern you desire. Then, one at a time, cut around their outlines with a trowel, remove the stone, and dig out the soil.

To create a more enduring installation, prepare a 3-inch concrete base. Lay out the stones on the base, then mix the mortar (1 part cement, 3 parts sand, plus water). Remove a few stones at a time, place the mortar, and replace the stones. Let the mortar set overnight; grout the joints the next day. Again, cover the entire patio area with plastic sheeting for a week to allow the mortar to fully cure.

Brick has long been a favorite paving material because it:
■ is is small and easy to handle
■ is modular in size, so can be set in a variety of patterns
■ is widely available
■ looks equally at home with casual or formal settings.

If laid in sand, the bricks should butt tightly. When set in concrete, the grout will become part of the pattern. (For a more detailed description of installation methods, refer to the Bricks, page 38–43.)

The marks of a professional installation are a level surface and precise alignment of the joints. This is not difficult for even an amateur to achieve—it will just take longer. Although large quantities of bricks are extremely heavy, an individual brick weighs only 5 pounds and is easy to handle. If you are laying your own brick patio, you can purchase and pick up small quantities and install a patio in stages, as your time and budget permit, or you can buy all of the bricks at once and have them delivered (see box, right).

Base: If you want your patio to remain level forever, you have no choice but to set the brick in mortar over a concrete base. A firmly packed sand bed yields a reasonable stable base, although you may have to relevel a few spots each year if the soil is of heavy clay or some other expansive material, or if the ground in your area freezes and thaws.

EDGING

Sand-base installations require a stable edge to hold the bricks. The best edging of all is a concrete or stone curb flush with the grade and tops of the bricks.

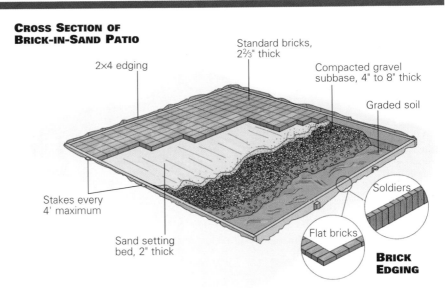

CROSS SECTION OF BRICK-IN-SAND PATIO

2×4 edging
Standard bricks, 2⅔" thick
Compacted gravel subbase, 4" to 8" thick
Graded soil
Stakes every 4' maximum
Sand setting bed, 2" thick
Soldiers
Flat bricks
BRICK EDGING

The next best edging is a concrete curb (below grade) topped with bricks. Set the bricks on the surface of the curb while the concrete is wet. Butt them together if the paving bricks butt. Otherwise, set curb bricks with the same spacing as paving bricks.

The third alternative is an edging of pressure-treated wood. Drive wood stakes around the perimeter of the patio at 2 feet on-center, then screw pressure-treated 2×4s to the stakes. Set the 2×4s flush with the tops of the bricks, and the stakes an inch lower so they won't be seen. Then spread the sand bed 2 inches below the level of the edging. Use a notched screed board to level the sand.

Whether you choose a concrete base or sand bed, prepare the grade and the bed as you would prepare for a concrete installation.

PATTERNS

The number of patterns you can lay is limited only by your imagination. Remember, however, that complex patterns may require more time, care, and material than simple, repeating patterns. Also, non-repeating and circular patterns are best laid in dry mortar due to the probability that you will be adjusting the pattern several times before you are ready to cast it in concrete.

WEIGHTY ISSUE

Before you drive the family car down to the home center to pick up bricks for your patio, calculate their weight.

A single 2×4×8-inch brick weighs approximately 5 pounds. Each brick, laid flat, covers 4×8 inches = 32 square inches, which is 0.22 square feet. There are, therefore, 4.5 bricks per square foot, or 450 bricks per 100 square feet.

At 5 pounds per brick, the weight of bricks is about 2,250 pounds per 100 square feet.

A lift of bricks (the quantity in which they are shipped) contains 500 bricks. If you order a lift direct from the brick distributor the shipping might be free. Call around and see.

CONCRETE

BOARD

BRICKS LAID FLAT

BASIC PRINCIPLES

The heart of a home plumbing system is pipe. Depending on the age of your home, you may find plastic, copper, or galvanized steel in the supply system, and plastic, copper, or cast-iron in the drain-waste-vent (DWV) system. Knowing how to measure and cut pipe is an important first step in mastering plumbing jobs.

Visit your local home center to find which pipe material your local code allows. Polyvinyl chlorine (PVC), polybutylene, and copper pipes are easy to handle. Threaded steel pipe is convenient if you can buy lengths that fit the installation exactly. No-hub cast-iron is also fairly easy to handle, but cutting it requires special equipment. Cast-iron pipe with leaded joints and gas piping are difficult to handle. If your project requires working with these materials, hire a pro.

A few simple fittings—couples, tees, and ells— allow you to make basic connections, but each shape has many variations for different applications. Some fittings are threaded, others have smooth hubs that slip over the ends of pipe, and others clamp to pipe.

Fittings for the supply system are different from those for the DWV system. Even if they are made of the same material and resemble each other, they are different. There are even fittings for joining pipes of different materials, such as plastic to cast iron or copper to steel.

CAST-IRON PIPE

Many DWV systems use cast-iron pipe for the main drain and stacks (although the smaller drain and vent pipes in a system will likely be galvanized steel or copper). Although most plumbing codes allow plastic DWV pipes, a few areas still require cast-iron, particularly if any plumbing will lie under a slab.

In older cast-iron systems, joints were sealed with molten lead. A more recent type of cast-iron pipe, called no-hub, joins with flexible fittings. Pipe, fittings, and bands are available in 1½-inch, 2-inch, 3-inch, and 4-inch sizes.

There are two methods for cutting cast-iron pipe. The first requires a soil pipe cutter (you can rent one) that has a chain that wraps around the pipe. By tightening a knob and rotating a handle, the chain snaps the pipe. The second method is to use a circular saw with a metal-cutting blade.

No-hub pipes join with a clamp that consists of a neoprene sleeve, a stainless steel shield, and two compression bands. Slip the band on both sides of a joint and use a plumber's torque wrench to tighten the nuts to 60 inch-pounds.

Making a molten lead joint for hubbed cast-iron is not for the inexperienced or the faint-of-heart. If you insist, however, rent a propane plumber's furnace and ladle. Clean both pipe ends thoroughly. Pack oakum into the hub, leaving 1 inch of space for the lead. If the pipes are horizontal, attach a joint runner against the hub to contain the lead. Melt the lead; if a scrap of newspaper dipped into the lead burns, the lead is too hot. Preheat the ladle before dipping it into the hot lead or the lead could explode. Ladle the lead into the joint. Be careful; lead spatters if it hits moisture on the pipe or ladle.

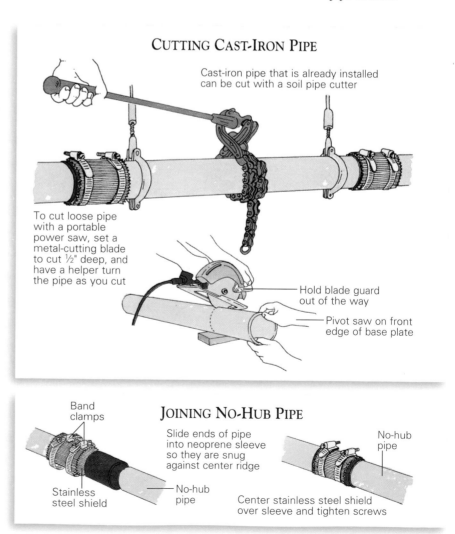

CUTTING CAST-IRON PIPE

Cast-iron pipe that is already installed can be cut with a soil pipe cutter

To cut loose pipe with a portable power saw, set a metal-cutting blade to cut ½" deep, and have a helper turn the pipe as you cut

Hold blade guard out of the way

Pivot saw on front edge of base plate

JOINING NO-HUB PIPE

Band clamps

Slide ends of pipe into neoprene sleeve so they are snug against center ridge

No-hub pipe

Stainless steel shield

No-hub pipe

Center stainless steel shield over sleeve and tighten screws

IRON PIPE AND FITTINGS

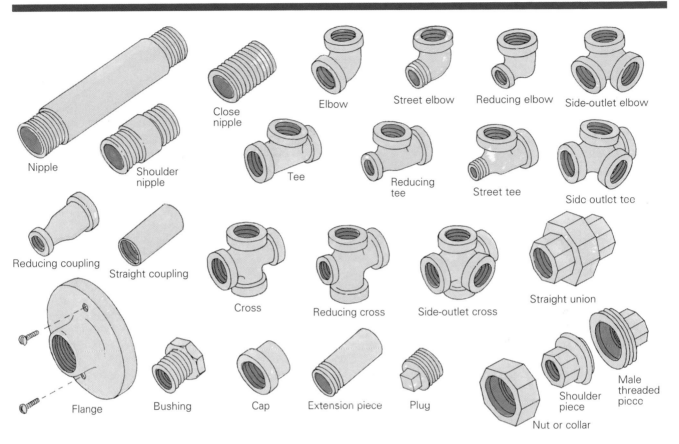

Nipple

Shoulder nipple

Close nipple

Elbow

Street elbow

Reducing elbow

Side-outlet elbow

Reducing coupling

Straight coupling

Tee

Reducing tee

Street tee

Side outlet tee

Flange

Bushing

Cross

Reducing cross

Side-outlet cross

Straight union

Cap

Extension piece

Plug

Shoulder piece

Male threaded piece

Nut or collar

Galvanized steel pipe, called "iron pipe," was used heavily for supply piping until about 40 years ago. Today, copper and plastic pipe are more common. Work with iron pipe only when repairing leaks or connecting an older system to new plumbing.

The fittings *above* are the most common for water supply piping. They all have iron-pipe (IP) threads. The most common sizes are ½-inch, ¾-inch, and 1-inch inside diameters.

Each length of iron pipe must be threaded at both ends. You must buy exact lengths of threaded pipe or rent threading equipment to cut, thread, and ream the pipe. Once you have the right lengths and fittings, iron pipe is easy to assemble. Coat the threads with pipe-joint compound or wrap them with Teflon tape and then screw them together. Use two pipe wrenches to tighten the joint. If you are running new pipe, work from the existing source toward the new fixtures. If you are putting new pipe into the middle of a run, you will need a union to make the last connection. (Note: unions are prohibited in gas lines.)

TEMPORARY PATCHES

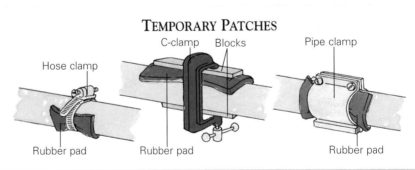

Hose clamp

Rubber pad

C-clamp

Blocks

Rubber pad

Pipe clamp

Rubber pad

REPAIRING LEAKS

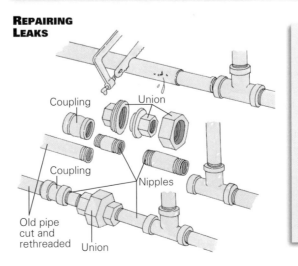

Coupling

Union

Coupling

Nipples

Old pipe cut and rethreaded

Union

CODE REQUIREMENTS

Pipes must be supported at intervals not to exceed:

Cast-iron	5'
Threaded steel	
<1"diameter	10'
≥1"diameter	12'
Copper	
<1-½"diameter	6'
≥1-½"diameter	10'
Plastic DWV	4'
Plastic rigid supply	3'
Plastic flexible supply	32"

▶

251

COPPER PIPE AND FITTINGS

Most water supply systems are made with copper pipe and fittings. Copper pipe is rigid, but you can purchase flexible copper tubing for use in slabs or in installations where pipes need to turn without fittings.

Copper pipe comes in the same nominal sizes as iron pipe—from ¼ to 2½ inch diameters. The outside diameter of the tubing is always larger than its nominal size, and the inside diameter varies with the thickness of the tube wall.

Supply tubing comes in three wall thicknesses, designated by the letters: "K" for the thickest wall, "L" for a medium wall, and "M" for the thinnest wall. Unless your local code prohibits its use, Type-M is adequate for home water supply systems. DWV pipe comes in larger sizes; it cannot be used as water supply piping.

WORKING WITH COPPER PIPE

When cutting pipe, measure the length between the faces of the fittings and add the depth of the fitting. Test flexible tubing for length before you cut—secure the starting end temporarily and run it exactly where you want it. Mark the cut, then allow a little bit of extra length before cutting. The extra length will allow you to make fine adjustments when you make the connection.

Cut copper pipe with a tubing cutter. This specialized tool is inexpensive, easy to use, cuts quickly, and leaves no outside burr. Its small

cutting wheel scores the pipe deeper and deeper as you tighten the handle while rotating the cutter around the pipe. Tighten the pressure slowly or you will distort the tubing and it won't fit the fitting. After you've cut the pipe, remove inside burrs with a reamer (they're built into most cutters) or a knife.

JOINING COPPER PIPE

Copper pipe is joined in two ways: with solder (in a process called "sweating"), or with compression fittings. To sweat a joint, first clean the pipe and fitting thoroughly with emery cloth or steel wool. Polish it

Clean the joint

until it is uniformly bright. Without touching the cleaned area with your fingers, apply a thin coat of flux to

Apply flux

inside and outside surfaces and slip the tubing into the fitting. Rotate the tubing and fitting to distribute the flux.

Set the assembled pipes in a stable position so the joint is accessible to

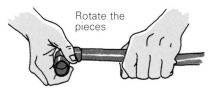

Rotate the pieces

Apply flame to fitting and pipe

the flame but away from combustible material. Use aluminum flashing as a heat shield between the joint and any nearby surfaces. Don't try to hold the pipes while you solder; they heat up very quickly. Heat the joint with a propane, MAPP gas, or acetylene torch. Heat both the pipe and the fitting until the flux begins to bubble. Then touch the end of the solder to the joint opposite the flame. When the solder melts, capillary action will

Flow in solder

draw it into the joint, even if the pipe is vertical.

When soldering existing pipes that have had water in them, be sure to drain the system thoroughly. Even a few drops of water in the pipe will cause steam that prevents the solder from taking. Leave a nearby faucet open so that steam can escape safely.

REPAIRING COPPER PIPE

To fix pinhole leaks, open a faucet or drain outlet to drain the pipe completely, clean the area, apply flux, and solder. For larger leaks, cut out the damaged section and sweat in a new pipe or install a compression coupling.

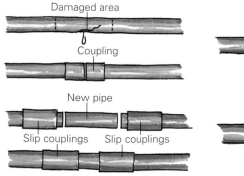

Damaged area

Coupling

New pipe

Slip couplings   Slip couplings

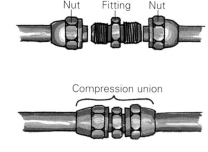

Nut   Fitting   Nut

Compression union

Plastic pipe is inexpensive, durable, and easy to work with. There are four types commonly used in plumbing systems: polyvinyl chloride (PVC), chlorinated polyvinyl chloride (CPVC), acrylonitrile-butadiene-styrene (ABS), and polybutylene (PB). Plastic has gained wide acceptance. Nearly all plumbing codes now allow it in Drain-waste-vent (DWV) systems. Some permit it for outdoor use only. Check your local codes first.

DWV System Pipes

DWV systems use either ABS or PVC piping, but not both. The two are incompatible and cannot be mixed. Diameters range from 1¼ inches to 4 inches and larger. DWV pipe is sized according to its inside diameter (i.d.). Plastic DWV pipes are fairly rigid, but fittings tolerate some misalignment.

ABS disintegrates from exposure to the sun's ultraviolet rays. Carbon black is added (accounting for its black color) to block UV. ABS commonly is used for vent pipes that penetrate the roof because it is less visible.

If horizontal runs of plastic DWV pipe are not well supported by plastic or wood straps (never use metal), they will sag. For 1½-inch pipe, position the straps or brackets no farther than 3 feet apart—4 feet apart with larger sizes. Install the supports loosely enough for the pipe to expand and contract freely.

Supply System Pipes

PVC and CPVC are both acceptable for cold-water pipes, but only CPVC can be used for hot. Flexible PB is acceptable for both, and installation is almost as easy as electrical cable; join it with compression fittings rather than solvents. Early PB proved susceptible to damage by chlorine and failed in many water systems. As a result, plumbers are wary of it. Unlike DWV pipe, the size of supply pipes refer to the outside diameter (o.d.).

Joining Plastic Pipe

When measuring plastic pipe for cutting, include the depth of the fitting sockets. With PVC and ABS this dimension is the size of the pipe. Mark the pipe and cut it with a hacksaw or

backsaw to ensure a square cut. Remove burrs by scraping with a utility knife, and clean all gloss and grease from the pipe with special plastic-pipe cleaner.

If you are assembling more than two pieces, dry-fit them in position before solvent welding and mark across the joint to indicate the final alignment

of pipes and fittings. This trick will prevent you from accidentally rotating them out of alignment when welding.

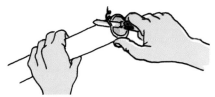

To weld a joint, use the brush supplied with the can to apply solvent cement to each surface—first inside the hub of the fitting, then to the end of the pipe. The solvent is not a glue; it actually dissolves the plastic so that both pieces fuse together. When both

pieces are coated, quickly join them and twist the pieces until your marks are aligned. You have only a few seconds to make adjustments before the joint is set. Hold the joint together for 15 seconds. Then wait two minutes before handling it again. Wait an hour or more before testing it with water.

The solvent in PVC and ABS cements contains combustible liquids and contaminants that can become airborne. Ventilate the space well while you are working.

Plastic also may be joined to copper, cast-iron, or iron pipe using adapters or no-hub clamps. Use Teflon tape on plastic screw fittings. Never use pipe dope on plastic pipe.

REPAIRING PLASTIC PIPE

To repair a pinhole or small leak, turn off the water, drain the pipe, and let it dry for a few hours. Force some plastic solvent cement into the hole and wrap the area tightly with electrical tape.

For larger holes or leaky joints, cut out the damaged section and install new pipe and fittings. There is usually enough play in plastic piping systems to allow insertion of the new fittings.

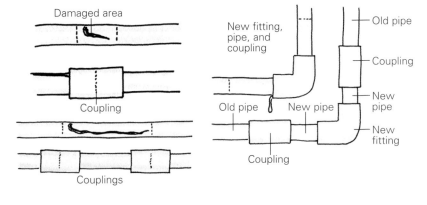

THE FUNCTIONS AND NAMES OF FITTINGS

Nothing is more confusing to first-time plumbers than the names of fittings.

Getting familiar with the various pipe fittings and their functions is an

important first step to completing home improvement plumbing projects.

SUPPLY FITTINGS

Couplings: Couplings join pipes in a straight line. Reducing couplings, also known as reducers, make the transition from one size pipe to another. Slip couplings can slide the length of the pipe and are ideal for repairing pin-hole leaks.

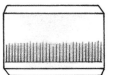

Coupling with stop Coupling without stop Reducing coupling

Elbows (Ells): Elbows change the direction of flow by either 22½, 45, or 90 degrees. You can change direction and pipe size at the same time with a reducing elbow. Street elbows have a female connection at one end and a male connection at the other end.

90° elbow 45° elbow 45° street elbow

90 elbow° street 90° reducing elbow

Tees: Tees allow you to tap into a straight run with a branch line. Reducing tees allow a simultaneous change of pipe size, while a street tee has a both male and female ends.

Straight tee Street tee Reducing tee

Caps and Plugs: Caps terminate a pipe. Plugs accomplish the same purpose, but insert into a fitting.

Cap Plug

Nipples: Nipples are lengths of pipe less than 12 inches long and threaded at both ends. The standard lengths run from 1 to 12 inches in 1-inch increments. The shortest available length of any pipe diameter, threaded at each end, is called a close nipple.

Close nipple Nipple

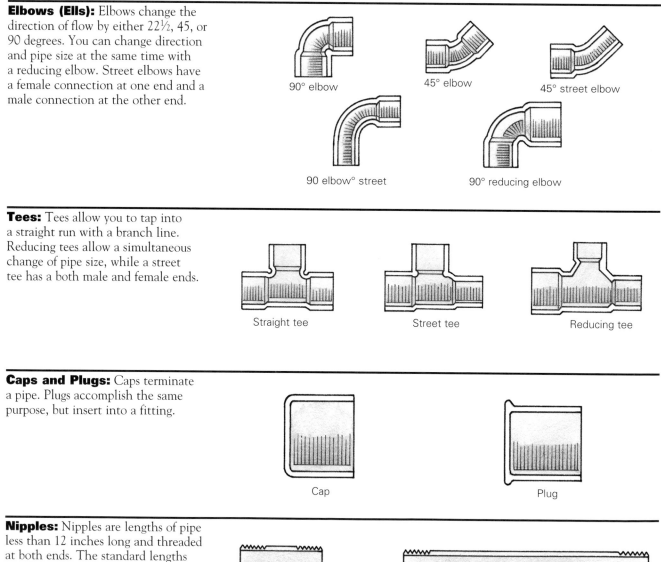

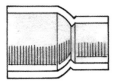

Unions: Unions allow you to disassemble threaded sections of pipe. They are used where repairs or replacement of an appliance, such as a water heater, is a possibility.

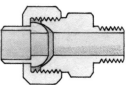

Copper to copper   Copper to pipe   Copper to pipe

DWV Fittings

Many drain-waste-vent fittings look entirely different from supply fittings because of the job they have to do. Drain water has no pressure behind it so the pipes must be designed to allow gravity to do its job. Thus, curves are gentle and always shoot the waste in the direction of the flow.

Couplings: Since they have no effect on flow, DWV couples are essentially the same as those for supply pipes.

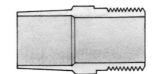
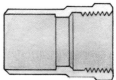

Male, copper to pipe   Female, copper to pipe

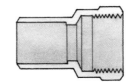
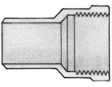

Reducing female, copper to pipe   Female street, fitting to pipe

Bends: Bends are the DWV equivalent of elbows. They change the direction of the flow—gently. The smallest direction change is 1/16 of 360 degrees, or 22½ degrees, accomplished with a 1/16 bend. Other bends (and their arcs) include:

- 1/8 bend (45 degrees).
- 1/6 bend (60 degrees).
- 1/5 bend (72 degrees).
- 1/4 bend (90 degrees).

As with most other fittings, the street version has both male and female ends. Long turns, or sweeps, allow water to run faster. Bends and DWV pipe are also useful for conduit.

1/8   1/8 street   1/4

1/4 street   1/4 long turn

Tees, Wyes, and Crosses:

The "sanitary" versions of these fittings are shaped for downward flow of waste. The "vent" versions simply intersect. You can use upside-down sanitary fittings as vent fittings, but not the other way around.

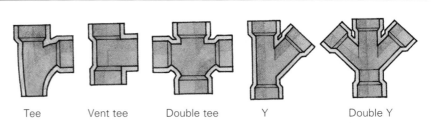

Tee   Vent tee   Double tee   Y   Double Y

PLUMBING

THREE ESSENTIALS: HOT, COLD, AND DOWNHILL

Plumbing is not really that complicated. As the old plumber's saying goes, "Hot on the left, cold on the right, and waste flows downhill."

A working knowledge of your home plumbing system makes plumbing projects proceed faster and more efficiently. But don't stop with a study of the house—basic knowledge of plumbing includes knowing relevant building codes as well.

A home plumbing system has three components. The water supply system brings water into your home and distributes it through pipes to various fixtures. Fixtures, such as faucets and spigots, regulate the flow of the water. The drain-waste-vent system collects and channels the waste water to a sewer or septic tank.

OVERVIEW OF THE THREE COMPONENTS

As shown below, in a public water supply cold water (blue) enters the house through a water meter which may be in the basement or outside the house. Private water supplies, such as a well, have no meter. Instead, cold water is pumped into a pressure tank.

Immediately after the meter there is a main shutoff valve. You should know its location in case you develop a leak or you want to drain the entire system when you leave home for a long while.

Trace the blue pipe in the illustration and you will see that it brings cold water to every fixture in the house, as well as to the water heater. A hot water pipe (red) runs from the water heater to every fixture that uses hot water.

FIXTURES

"Fixtures" is a term that covers all sinks, lavatories (bathroom sinks), water closets (toilets), bidets, showers, tubs, clothes washers, laundry tubs, and dishwashers. Outside spigots also are fixtures.

DRAIN-WASTE-VENT SYSTEM

Water which has been used in any way is known as "waste water" or simply "waste." With the aid of gravity alone, we must transport all of the waste water—including entrained solids—to the sewer or septic tank. Waste systems are complicated, involving traps to block sewer gas, pipe sizes and slopes, the angles at which pipes flow into each other, and the introduction of outside air to equalize air pressure. More than half of the Universal Plumbing Code (the national standard) is taken up by the rules for this rather tricky system.

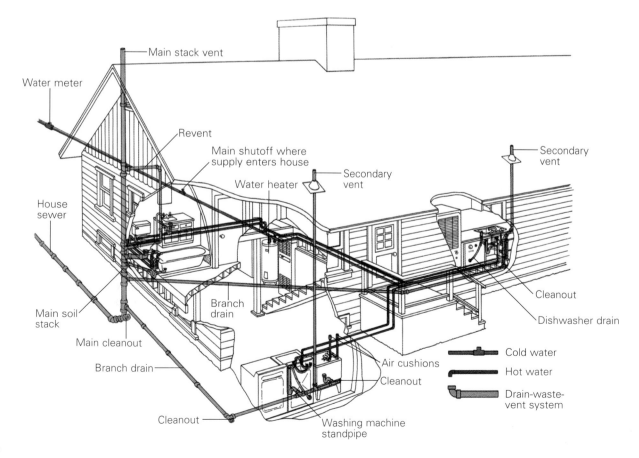

Main stack vent

Water meter

Revent

Main shutoff where supply enters house

Water heater

Secondary vent

Secondary vent

House sewer

Main soil stack

Main cleanout

Branch drain

Cleanout

Branch drain

Air cushions

Cleanout

Cleanout

Washing machine standpipe

Dishwasher drain

Cleanout

Cold water

Hot water

Drain-waste-vent system

SUPPLY SYSTEM

The supply system brings in cold water, heats some of it, and distributes both cold and hot water to fixtures. Since the supply system is pressurized, its pipes can run in any direction without regard to slope (although low points facilitate draining the system if necessary).

Normal "street pressure" is 40 to 55 psi (pounds per square inch), but may range as low as 30 psi or as high as 80 psi. If the street pressure is above 80 psi, the code requires a pressure reducing valve near the main shutoff. The main shutoff valve should be as close as possible to the supply line entry into the house.

Main supply lines are typically ¾ inch in diameter, larger if street pressure is lower than normal or if the house is taller than two stories. Use a ¾-inch line to feed the water heater and for all runs that feed more than one fixture. If a water softener is included in the system, the pipes serving it may be required to be one size larger than normal to make up for the drop in pressure it causes.

Fixtures usually are supplied with both hot and cold water. Dishwashers, however, are supplied only with hot water; toilets and hose bibbs are supplied only with cold. When both hot and cold water are supplied to a fixture, hot water is traditionally on

the left and cold on the right. To make repairs to fixtures easy, the supply pipes should stub out and terminate at valves, called shutoff valves, which are usually located under the fixture.

Sometimes pipes bang and chatter when you turn off a faucet quickly or when the clothes- or dishwasher draws water. This noise is called water hammer. To prevent it, your code may require shock-absorbing air chambers or their equivalent. Air chambers are

capped pipes extending perpendicular to and about 12 inches above the fixture supply stubs. The chambers trap air and cushion the shock of water hammer that occurs when valves are closed too quickly.

Dishwashers and washing machines need them because they use electric valves that snap shut. In addition, install air chambers for the kitchen sink and for the highest fixture in the bathroom.

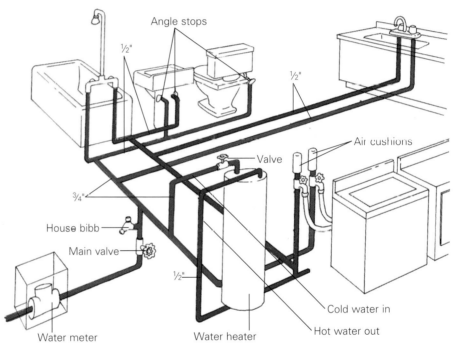

COMMON SUPPLY FITTINGS

1. Reducing tee, ¾×¾×½"
2. Reducing elbow, ¾×½"
3. 90° elbow, ½"
4. Valve body
5. Drop ell with threaded outlet
6. Shower arm
7. Threaded nipple, ½"
8. Shutoff valve
9. Supply tube, ⅜"
10. Type L pipe, ¾"
11. Type L pipe, ½"
12. Coupling, ¾"

See Pipe, page 254, for a description of the most common fittings used in copper supply-system piping. The illustration at left shows the use of these fittings in a typical bathroom.

If you enjoyed playing with tinker toys as a child, you will absolutely love plumbing your supply system!

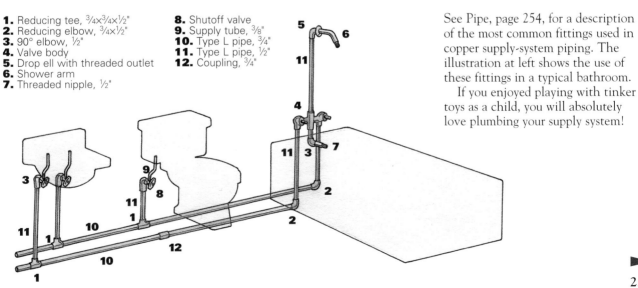

STANDARDS FOR FIXTURES

When remodeling, position new fixtures close to existing plumbing. Attach them to a wall that already contains plumbing or next to closets or utility chases that can hide new pipes. Run horizontal drainpipes between floor joists. If a drainpipe must run perpendicular to the joists, hang it below them rather than weakening the joists by notching. Conceal the pipes in a soffit.

A crawl space or unfinished basement allows you great flexibility in placing fixtures and running pipes. However, these spaces must be insulated or heated to prevent pipes from freezing. An upstairs floor, particularly one with few walls, will limit the design of the system.

Try to place bathroom fixtures so plumbing runs will be uncomplicated, but keep the layout efficient for your

family's use. Use plastic DWV pipes if your code allows them. Place the fixtures near the main stack, if possible. The toilet should be no more than 6 feet away unless it vents separately. If other fixtures drain into the same waste pipe as the toilet, the drain must connect upstream from the toilet or the toilet must vent before the connection.

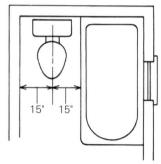

TOILET CLEARANCE

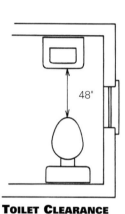

TOILET CLEARANCE

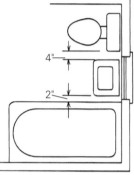

WASHBASIN CLEARANCE

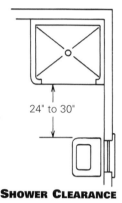

SHOWER CLEARANCE

CODE REQUIREMENTS: PLUMBING

Supply Piping:
■ A pressure-reducing valve is required when the incoming pressure is greater than 80 psi.
■ The service pipe must be ¾-inch minimum.

DWV Piping:
■ Horizontal drains must connect to vertical stacks through a wye, tee-wye, bend, sweep, or sanitary tee. Multiple fittings connecting two or more branches are allowed if the branches are the same size and are from similar fixture types or groups; exceptions are kitchen sinks and toilets.
■ Horizontal-drain connections to other horizontal drains must be made through a wye, tee-wye, bend, sweep, or equivalent long-pattern or combination fittings.
■ Vertical drains must connect to horizontal drains through a wye, tee-wye, bend, sweep, or other fittings of equivalent sweep.

Traps: Every fixture must have an individual trap except:
■ Fixtures with integral traps, such as toilets.
■ Multibowl sinks with outlets less than 30 inches apart.

Cleanouts:
■ Cleanouts are required at any change of direction greater than 45 degrees, but no more than one is required within 40 feet of run.
■ Cleanouts are required for cumulative horizontal runs of 75 feet.
■ Cleanouts must be accessible, with an 18-inch clearance for 3- and 4-inch cleanouts, and 12-inch clearance for smaller pipes.

Vent Termination:
■ Must not be located under a window or door, nor within 5 feet horizontally and 2 feet below a door or window.
■ Must extend at least 6 inches above the high side of the roof.
■ Must be at least 2 inches in diameter in areas where the winter design temperature is 0° F or less.

Water Closets (Toilets):
■ Must be water conserving (1.6 gallons/flush maximum).
■ Must have clearances of 15 inches from center to wall; 12 inches from center to tub; 21 inches minimum in front of the bowl.

Shower:
■ Floor must be at least 900 square inches and contain a circle with a diameter of at least 30 inches.
■ Flow must be limited to 2.5 gpm at a pressure of 80 psi.
■ Control valve must limit temperature to 120° F and be of the thermostatic or pressure balance type.

Water Heaters:
■ Must not be located in bedrooms, bathrooms, or closets, nor in spaces opening into bedrooms or bathrooms (exception: direct-vent heaters).
■ In a garage, must be protected from impact by automobiles, with switches and igniters at least 18 inches above the floor.

Gas Valves:
■ Appliance shutoff must be outside appliance, but in the same room within 6 feet of appliance.
■ Gas fireplace shutoff must be outside hearth, but in the same room within 4 feet of outlet.
■ Gas pipe penetrating a hearth or wall must be embedded 1½ inches in masonry or encased in a metal sleeve.

ROUGH-IN DIMENSIONS

Rough-in dimensions are the locations where supply and waste pipes come through the floor or wall. Sink supplies, for example, can come through either floor or wall as long as they're within the sink cabinet. Toilet, shower base, and tub rough-in dimensions depend on the size of the fixture. Be sure to check whether dimensions specified for the fixture are from the finish wall or from the face of the framing, or from subfloor or finish floor. Use the dimensions in the illustration below as preliminary guidelines—confirm with the manufacturer's information.

Toilet: The center of the flange for a standard toilet should be 12 inches

from the finished wall; elongated models require 14 inches. Always locate the shutoff valve on the left side, low enough to connect the supply tube to the tank. Wall entry for the supply line makes cleaning the floor easier than does floor entry.

Washbasin: Drain stubs usually are installed 15 to 17 inches above the floor. Supply stubs are usually slightly higher, but inside a vanity place the stubs lower so they are easier to reach.

Shower: The heights shown for the faucet and showerhead are standard, but feel free to adjust them to your personal preference.

Bathtub: Most drain locations are set 15 inches from the back wall and 8 to 10 inches from the end wall. You will need to cut a large hole in the floor to hook up the tub from below. If your tub will include a shower head that will be used frequently, you may want

to place the faucet control higher than normal for added convenience.

Kitchen Sink: Place the drain stub 15 inches above the floor and the supply stubs 19 inches above the floor (remember, however, that the supply also can rise through the floor). Installed stubs are usually 8 inches apart, unless the sink faucet is offset considerably or unless the hot-water stub must be close to a dishwasher.

Dishwasher: In most installations, the dishwasher waste drains into the garbage disposer under the kitchen sink drain. For dishwasher supply, rough in a hot-water stub through the floor under the dishwasher, either at the front or back, depending on the requirements of your model. If you have access through the floor, it is easier to locate the valve under the floor and run $\frac{3}{8}$-inch flexible tubing to the dishwasher inlet.

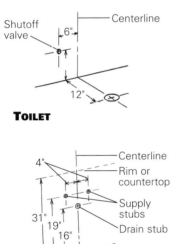

TOILET

WASHBASIN

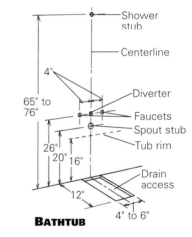

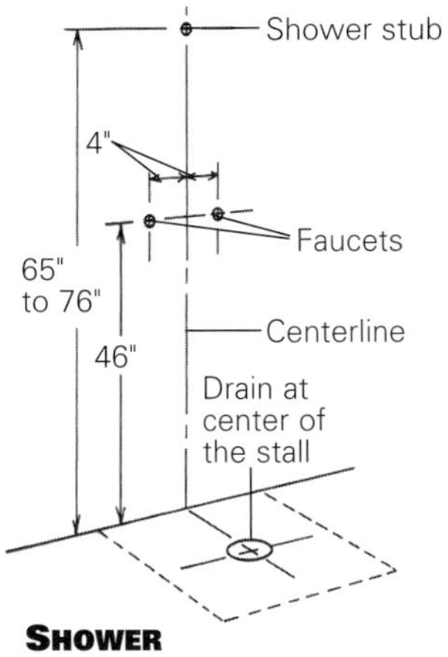

SHOWER

BATHTUB

FIXTURE UNITS, TRAPS, AND VENTS			
Fixture	**Fixture Units**	**Trap Size, Inches**	**Vent Size, Inches**
Water closet (toilet)	4	3	2
Bidet	2	1½	1¼
Bathtub	2	1½	1¼
Shower	2	2	1½
Washbasin	1	1¼	1¼
Washbasin pair	2	1½	1¼
Kitchen sink	2	1½	1¼
Kitchen sink and dishwasher	3	1½	1¼
Washing machine	2	2	1½

FIXTURE UNITS VS. PIPE SIZE

Building codes measure the flow of water through a fixture in fixture units. The chart summarizes typical code requirements for fixtures.

Pipe Size, Inches	Maximum Fixture Units	
	Horizontal Drain	**Vertical Vent**
1¼	1	1
1½	1	8
2	8	24
3	35	84
4	216	256

DRAIN, WASTE, AND VENT SYSTEM

The drain-waste-and-vent (DWV) system is completely independent of the supply system. Sometimes called the sanitary system, the DWV system includes all the drains and waste pipes in and under the house as well as the vents that extend through the roof.

Plumbing codes are very strict regarding the DWV system. All of the rules regarding pipe size, fitting orientation, trap location, slope, and fixture height are designed to keep contaminants—liquid, solid, or gas—out of the house.

If the installation of a DWV pipe and a supply pipe interfere with each other, the DWV has the "right of way" due to the stringent rules it must follow. For this reason, plumbers always install the DWV system before the supply pipes.

The DWV system is not pressurized; water and waste move because of gravity alone. For this reason the DWV system requires careful installation. "Upstream" and "downstream" are important directions; always keep your position in mind.

TRAPS

We are all familiar with traps because we have all, at one time or another, fished a contact lens or wedding ring out of one. But the real role of traps is not to collect precious objects. The real role is to function as a one-way waste valve with no moving parts. Water and waste flow through it easily, but gases from the sewer are blocked from entering the house because the water left behind after each use forms an airtight seal. If trap water were siphoned out, which can happen with an

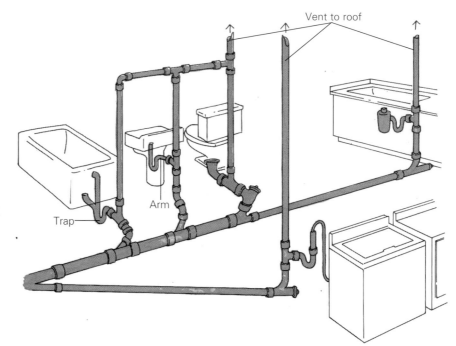

Vent to roof

Arm

Trap

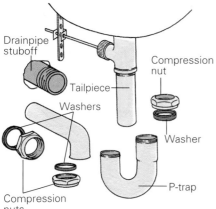

Drainpipe stuboff

Tailpiece

Washers

Compression nuts

Compression nut

Washer

P-trap

improper size or length of drainpipe, sewer gases could enter the house.

Each and every fixture must have a trap (although pairs of sinks and pairs of lavatories may share a trap). Some are visible (sink traps), while others are under the floor (bathtub and shower traps), in the wall (washing machine traps), or even inside the fixture itself (toilet traps).

Codes are specific about the maximum vertical distance between the fixture outlet and trap; the distance is usually 18 to 24 inches (toilets are an exception). The trap size should be the same as the fixture drain size. Codes also do not allow a fixture to have more than one trap.

P-traps, which have a short horizontal arm at the outlet, are the most common type. Codes no longer allow the S-trap and bell trap which were used in older construction. Traps concealed in a wall or under a floor cannot have cleanout plugs or slip joints.

CLEANOUTS

Cleanouts provide access to clogged pipes and should be provided at the upstream end of every horizontal run. Codes may contain more restrictive rules requiring a cleanout where the

house sewer connects to the public sewer, where the main drain joins the house sewer, and after every 75 feet of straight run.

In addition, most building codes mandate cleanouts immediately upstream of any single change of direction greater than 45 degrees and every cumulative change of direction in excess of 135 degrees. Fixtures and roof vents qualify as cleanouts.

All cleanouts must be accessible. Cleanouts that serve underground drains must extend to an accessible location. There must be at least 18 inches of space behind any cleanout on a 3- or 4-inch line; 12 inches on smaller pipe. If a cleanout is under the house or in an enclosed area, it must be within 15 feet of an access door.

ASK THE INSPECTOR

Are you afraid of the plumbing inspector? Don't be. His job is to keep you out of trouble.

Ask for his guidance. Tell him what you are trying to do, and he will probably show you how to to it "to code" and save you money at the same time!

Vents

The DWV system includes a number of pipes called vents that do not carry water. They have other functions—preventing vacuum siphoning of the traps, releasing sewer gases outdoors, and ensuring proper waste flow by equalizing air pressure in the system.

Each trap must be vented before the drain line reaches another fixture or a vertical drain. The distance allowed between trap and vent depends on the size of the drainpipe.

All vents terminate on the roof. A vent terminal must be at least 2 feet above and 5 feet horizontally from a window, door, or air intake.

In general, codes require that a vent pipe extending up from a trap arm cannot change to a horizontal direction within 6 inches of the flood rim of the fixture. Codes also specify vent distance for some fixtures—42 inches from the floor for sinks and washers, 24 inches for toilets and tubs.

A vent pipe that connects to a horizontal drain line from the side must connect above the center of the drain. A vent that serves a vertical drain must extend at a 45-degree angle, not straight up and down. Horizontal vent pipes should maintain the same slope as drainpipes ($\frac{1}{4}$ inch per foot) so that trapped moisture will drain away from the fixture.

Alternates for Toilet

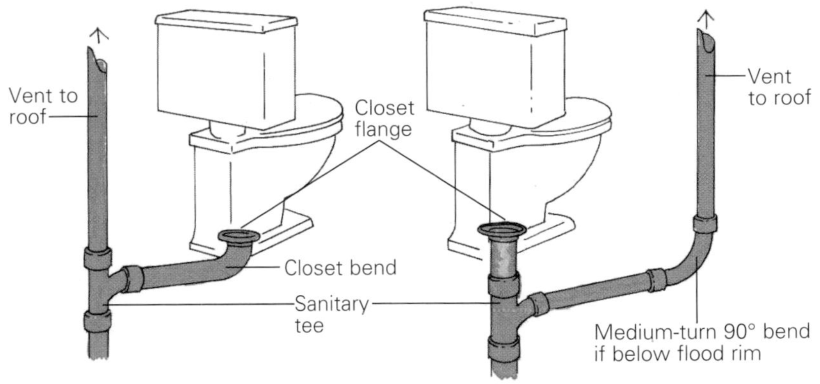

Vent to roof
Closet flange
Vent to roof
Closet bend
Sanitary tee
Medium-turn 90° bend if below flood rim

Fixture Venting

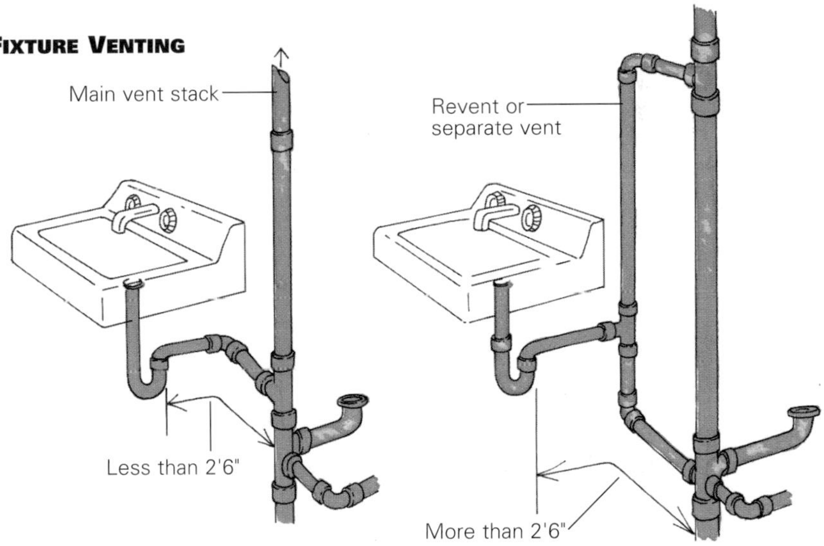

Main vent stack
Revent or separate vent
Less than 2'6"
More than 2'6"

Pipe Size

Most codes are very specific about the sizes of traps, drains, and vents, and the requirements depend on the amount of water flowing from the fixture. Codes measure flow in "fixture units", shown in the table on page 259. As the system picks up the waste of additional fixtures downstream, fixture units are cumulative, so the minimum pipe size increases accordingly.

DWV Fittings

DWV fittings have "direction" built into them; they can be installed only one way so that waste flows efficiently in the direction it's supposed to. In addition, the real angles of DWV fittings are not the same as the nominal angle of the bend. For instance, if you need a 90-degree change in direction, the fitting will actually be slightly more or less to account for the slope.

There are more than 100 DWV fittings, but you need to know only a handful. It is important to use the fitting that is made specifically for each connection, because only one will normally meet the code requirements for a specific installation. For example, a bend (also called a 90-degree bend) and sanitary tee are the only code-approved fittings for changing flow direction from horizontal to vertical.

Where the direction of flow changes from vertical to horizontal, the code allows a long sweep $\frac{1}{4}$ bend and the combination Y-branch. The closet bend for toilets is an exception. Because a closet bend must fit within the floor joists, codes do not require a sweep, or elongated, fitting.

Horizontal changes of direction use $\frac{1}{4}$ bends, $\frac{1}{5}$ bends, $\frac{1}{6}$ bends, $\frac{1}{8}$ bends, and $\frac{1}{16}$ bends, or the 45-degree Y. Always use the fitting with the most gradual bend when the pipe changes direction within its horizontal plane.

You can use reducers to change the size of an inlet to a smaller size, if necessary. Pipe size can never decrease downstream; it can only stay the same or increase.

PLUMBING
continued

PLANNING AN INSTALLATION

Before you install any pipes, plan the location of your fixtures carefully. Careful planning makes it easier to get a permit, ensures that you'll have all the required materials on hand before you start, and makes the job go faster. Don't hesitate to pay a plumber to help you plan the job, calculate runs, and create a materials list. Plumbers do this every day, and so can visualize the necessary components, as well as point out problems and suggest solutions.

Drain and Waste: You must maintain the required $\frac{1}{8}$- to $\frac{1}{4}$-inch-per-foot slope when putting in drain and waste pipes. And you must connect existing drains with proper fittings. Position cleanouts upstream of long (more than 75 feet) horizontal runs and make sure the cleanouts are accessible. (Remember that sinks, tubs, and toilets all qualify as cleanouts.) Start planning from the main drain and work upstream toward the fixtures.

Vents: Conceal vents in walls and ceilings. Here are some approved arrangements to make the job easier.

■ Adjacent fixtures can use the same vent if their traps are the same height.

■ A common vent consists of individual vents tied into one stack whose size is appropriate for the total fixture units.

■ A combination waste-and-vent stack is used if downstairs vents are revented into the stack above the highest fixture.

■ A wet vent is used (where codes permit) when one fixture with a low unit rating vents through the drainpipe of a vented fixture upstream.

Water Supply Line: Planning the water supply line is not as complicated as planning DWV lines. Supply lines follow the general path of the drain lines and easily run around obstacles. Keep the hot-water lines as short as possible—you will save energy and reduce the wait for hot water at the tap. Regardless of length, however, insulate hot-water lines—it always pays back in energy savings.

Back-to-Back: A new bathroom can back up to an existing bathroom and share the same stack.

Nearby Plumbing: A bathroom can share a toilet stack but requires a new vent for the tub and lavatory.

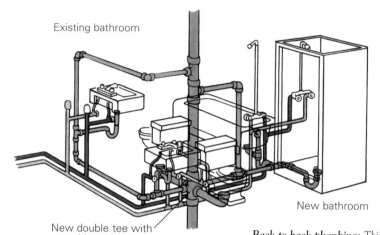

Back-to-back plumbing: This is an example of how a new bathroom can connect with an existing bathroom and use the same stack.

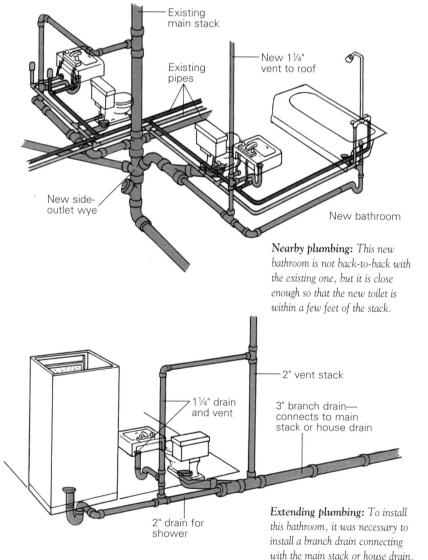

Nearby plumbing: This new bathroom is not back-to-back with the existing one, but it is close enough so that the new toilet is within a few feet of the stack.

Extending plumbing: To install this bathroom, it was necessary to install a branch drain connecting with the main stack or house drain.

INSTALLING ROUGH PLUMBING

You will need a plumbing permit to add a fixture or to extend a pipe. Don't regard this as an impediment; rather, use it as an opportunity to pick the plumbing inspector's brain!

After you have decided exactly the path of all the pipes, list the fittings and pipe lengths you will need. Make sure your supplier will accept the return of any unused materials, then buy extra fittings. (There is nothing more time-consuming than running out of materials.)

Install the DWV pipes first, then the supply pipes. Never cover any of the new pipes until they have been inspected and approved. Stub the pipes up through the floor and cap them off.

All horizontal DWV runs should slope between ⅛ inch and ¼ inch per foot. At shallower slopes, the flow is too sluggish to move solids; at steeper slopes the liquids will outrun the solids and cause them to accumulate.

Be careful to observe DWV fitting rules for changes of direction.

Hot- and cold-water pipes usually run parallel, 6 to 8 inches apart. Don't let them touch or the hot water will cool drastically. At places where they cross or make close contact, insulate the hot-water pipe or place a piece of rubber between them. Run the pipe perpendicular and parallel to framing members. Supply pipe is inexpensive, so there is little to be saved by running them diagonally.

TYING INTO A MAIN STACK

If you cannot tie into an existing drain or cleanout in the main stack, you will have to break into the stack. Before cutting the pipe, support it above and below the fitting with brackets fastened to the framing to hold it in place. Cut it and remove the unwanted section. If the pipe is cast iron, clamp a no-hub fitting in place. Similar fittings and bands are available for attaching plastic to cast iron or plastic to plastic.

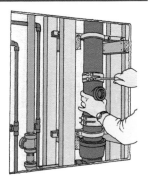

RUNNING PIPES THROUGH FRAMING

Don't notch or drill holes in framing indiscriminately. Observe the following guidelines to keep the structure strong.

JOISTS

■ Never notch or drill girders.
■ Never cut notches in the middle third of joists.
■ Limit notches in end ⅓ of joist to ⅙ of its depth.
■ Keep holes 2 inches from joist edges and limit to ⅓ of the depth.

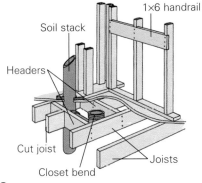

STUDS

■ Limit notches to 25 percent of width if bearing; 40 percent if non-bearing.
■ Limit holes to 40 percent of width and keep at least ⅝ inch from edges.
■ Limit holes in doubled studs to 60 percent of width and at least ⅝ inch from edges.

TOP PLATE

■ When drilling or notching more than 50 percent of its width, reinforce with 24-gauge steel angle.

Some pipes (the stack, for example) are too large to go through 2×4 plates. To widen a plumbing wall, use 2×6 studs or use 2×8 plates with a row of 2×4 studs turned sideways along each edge to accommodate the pipes.

PUMPS

HOUSEHOLD WORKHORSES

ALSO SEE...
Hot Tubs, Spas, and Whirlpools: *Pages 184–185*
Pipe: *Pages 250–255*
Plumbing: *Pages 256–263*

You probably have more pumps in your home than you think. Do you have a clothes washer? How about a dishwasher? What about an oil burner, forced hot water heat, a basement sump pump, or a private water supply? Each of them relies on a pump.

If you're installing a well pump, local codes may require that you hire a licensed professional to do the work, but you may be able to install, maintain, repair, or replace other pumps. Some pumps, such as those for sumps and decorative fountains and pools, simply plug into wall outlets.

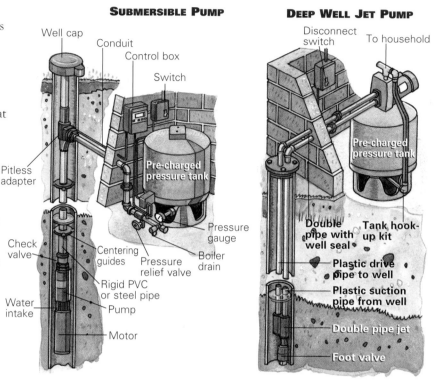

WELL PUMPS

Most wells use electric pumps to bring water to the surface and pressurize storage tanks. As the pump forces water into the tank, the water compresses the air in the tank. When you draw water, the compressed air forces the water into the supply pipe. When the pressure drops, the pump turns on again.

JET PUMP

The jet pump is located either in the house or at the well head. Shallow (less than 28 feet) versions need only a suction pipe. Deep (up to 100 feet) versions require two pipes: one brings water up under suction, and the other returns some of the water to a water jet at the intake to boost the flow.

SUBMERSIBLE PUMP

The submersible pump can be used in wells as deep as 500 feet. It requires at least a 4-inch well casing (most casings are 6-inch). At depths to 100 feet, you can pull the pump out by its flexible polyethylene pipe. Pumps deeper than 100 feet have a rope attached to enable you to pull the pump to the surface.

TROUBLESHOOTING PUMPS

Problem	Possible Causes	What to Do
Pump doesn't run at all	Electricity off	Check circuit breakers or fuses.
	Wiring loose or broken	If you feel qualified, check for loose, corroded, or broken wiring
	Float switch jammed	Clean debris from pit and float
Pump trips breaker	Short in wiring or pump	Call electrician
Pump runs too much	Plumbing leak	Check faucets, hoses, and toilets; check piping and pressure tank
	Pressure switch settings too close	Check that high and low settings are at least 20 psi apart
	Pressure tank waterlogged	Recharge the air in the tank
	Leaky check valve	Pressurize tank, shut off main shutoff, and watch gauge on tank; if pressure drops, replace the check valve between pump and tank
Pump won't quit	Pressure switch set too high	Adjust high-pressure cutoff
	Switch contacts stuck	Turn off fuse or breaker; take switch apart and check to see if contacts are stuck together

SUMP PUMPS

Sump pumps are designed to pump large volumes of water at low pressure from a sump pit. The water may be rainwater that has leaked into or under a basement, liquid effluent from a septic tank, or gray water—water from a washing machine, bathroom sink, shower, or bathtub.

The water runs into a concrete or plastic-lined sump pit. (Home centers sell both.) A float switch starts the pump automatically when water reaches a certain level in the pit. Some codes allow lines carrying uncontaminated underground seepage to terminate in a dry well or in a street gutter.

As a solution to flooded basements, sink the sump pit at the lowest point of the floor. For a sink or washer, put the pit at a location that is convenient for running the drainpipe. There are two kinds of sump pumps: the pedestal pump and the submersible pump.

PEDESTAL SUMP PUMP

The oldest, most common, and least expensive sump pump is an upright pump with an electric motor on top of a pedestal. The base of the pedestal contains the pump and discharge pipe and rests on the bottom of the pit. A float connects to the motor switch with a rod. When the water in the pit reaches a predetermined level, the float activates the switch. When the pump lowers the water level, the float turns off the switch, leaving about 6 inches of water so the pump won't be damaged by running dry.

SUBMERSIBLE SUMP PUMP

A submersible sump pump is more expensive but generally gives more reliable results than the upright pump. Flooding won't damage the submersible pump and it can run with a lower water level than an upright pump.

Submersible pumps are available with two types of switches. One is a float switch, activated when the rising water lifts a float. Because it has a moving part (the float), the float switch can be jammed by debris in the sump pit. A more desirable type of switch (and more expensive) is activated by water pressure alone.

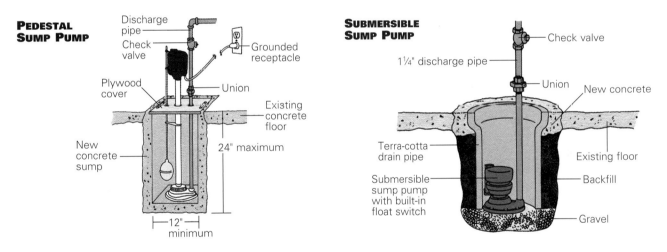

INSTALLING A SUMP PUMP

If you're not using a precast or plastic pit, you can side the pit with terra-cotta drain pipe (12 or more inches in diameter) or poured concrete.

In either case, break into the basement floor and dig a hole a little wider and 3 or 4 inches deeper than the pit will be. Add 3 or 4 inches of gravel and set a wooden form or a plastic pan into the hole. Pour concrete in the bottom of the hole and around the form.

Smooth and level the bottom, and smooth the concrete around the top so it is flush with the floor.

When the concrete has set, set in the plastic pipe or precast pit, and backfill. Then position the pump and make the necessary connections to the sewer or seepage pit. Install a check valve in the discharge line so water will not flow back toward the pump. Install a union below the valve so you can disconnect the pump easily. The pump should have its own grounded electrical outlet, with no other outlets or appliances on the same circuit.

Make a cover for the sump pit from ¾-inch exterior grade plywood. Drill three holes in the cover for a pedestal pump: one for the pedestal, one for the float rod, and one for the discharge pipe. Submersible-pump covers need only a hole for the discharge pipe. Saw the cover in half, cutting through the middle of the hole or holes. Fit the halves around the projecting pieces, and hold them together with straps of aluminum, galvanized steel, or wood held with screws.

BACKUP POWER

Many sump pump owners are distressed when, the first time they need it, the pump doesn't operate. If your basement floods in a hurricane or other major storm, chances are the electricity will be out as well. Back-up battery-operated power sources are available specifically tailored to sump pumps.

265

RADON

IT CAN CROP UP ANYWHERE, BUT YOU CAN CONTROL RADON

ALSO SEE...
Drainage
Pages 102–103
Energy
Pages 116–117
Fans
Pages 118–121
Foundations
Pages 144–151
Ventilation
Pages 386–387

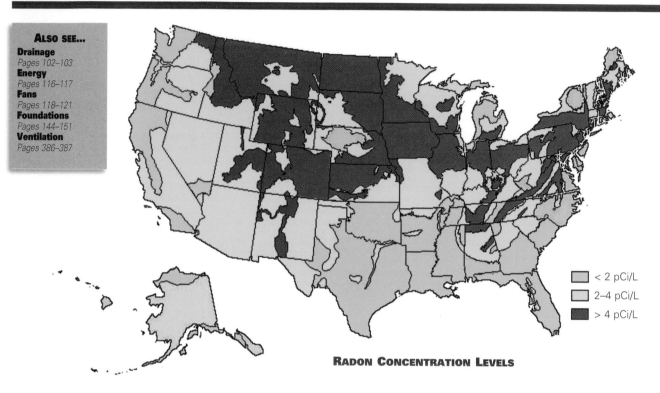

☐ < 2 pCi/L

☐ 2–4 pCi/L

■ > 4 pCi/L

RADON CONCENTRATION LEVELS

Radon is a colorless, odorless gas generated by the natural breakdown of uranium in soil and rock. It rises both as a gas and in groundwater. It enters homes through cracks and other holes in foundations and in water pumped from private wells.

WHAT'S THE FUSS ABOUT?

The two key problems are:

■ Radon tends to collect in homes.

■ Radon can cause lung cancer.

The U.S. Surgeon General has estimated that radon is the second leading cause of lung cancer, after smoking, resulting in 13,000 deaths per year. Your chances of getting lung cancer in a home having a high radon concentration are increased by spending more time in the home and greatly increased by smoking.

WHERE DOES RADON OCCUR?

Radon is in the air everywhere. The average concentration in the atmosphere is 0.4 picoCuries per Liter (0.4 pCi/L). Because homes trap and concentrate radon, its average indoor concentration is 1.3 pCi/L. It is recommended that radon mitigation (steps to reduce radon concentration) be performed on any home found to have a long-term average concentration in excess of 4.0 pCi/L.

The map above shows the potential indoor concentration of radon based on the types of subsurface rocks and soil, as well as predominant type of foundation. It must be stressed, however, that high levels of radon have been found in homes in every region. Thus the recommendation (and requirement at time of construction or sale in many states) that every home be tested.

If you are having a new home constructed, make sure the contractor anticipates a possible future need for mitigation and installs crushed stone under a basement slab and a vertical vent pipe from basement to roof.

If you plan to sell your home, check with your state's radon office well in advance for any test requirements and lists of certified testers and qualified mitigation contractors in your area.

TEST METHODS

The most meaningful test is one which measures the average concentration over the entire year. When selling a home, however, you generally don't have a year to wait. Tests are either long-term (over 90 days) or short-term (less than 90 days, but typically 48 hours to seven days).

The problem with short-term tests is their variability. Concentrations are generally much higher in winter when the house is buttoned up, and can be greatly reduced simply by operating a fireplace or by sleeping with bedroom windows open. Professional testers will insist that you follow a rigorous protocol during a short-term test so that the test results will be meaningful.

You can purchase a radon test kit at a hardware store, just as you can purchase a stethoscope at a drug store, but the value of the results in both cases depend upon the skill of the person performing the test. Most people would spend a lot of money to stop smoking in order to prevent lung cancer; why not spend a little more to find out whether you have a radon problem?

EPA TESTING CHECKLIST

Radon tests sanctioned by the federal Environmental Protection Agency must follow rigid, precise protocols. Among them:

BEFORE THE TEST:

Occupants of the structure must be notified of the test.

Testing devices must be EPA-listed.

Professionals assisting in the testing must be EPA-listed or state certified.

Implement methods to prevent or detect interference with the test conditions.

Any radon-reduction system in place must be operating 24 hours prior to the test.

Doors, windows and fireplace dampers must be kept closed, and fans that bring in outside air must not be run. Start the closed-house conditions at least 12 hours before the test.

DURING THE TEST:

■ Testing periods must last at least 48 hours.

Heating and cooling systems can operate normally; but for tests of less than a week, operate air conditioners on "recirculate."

Any radon-reduction system in place must operate throughout the test period.

Test devices must not be disturbed.

TAKE STEPS DURING CONSTRUCTION

Radon mitigation (reducing the amount of radon in your home's air) generally involves both cutting holes in your foundation floor or walls and running ventilation pipes up to the roof. Both can be done at minimal additional cost while a home is under construction, so do it then, even though you can't be certain you have a radon problem until the building is occupied.

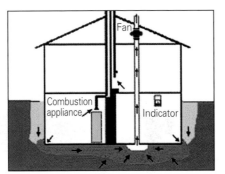

Active subslab suction draws radon gas from the soil before it can enter the house.

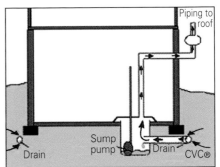

Sumphole and draintile suction take advantage of existing collection systems under the foundation.

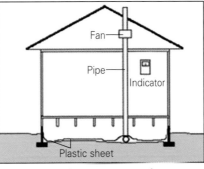

Submembrane depressurization substitutes a plastic membrane for a concrete slab over a dirt floor.

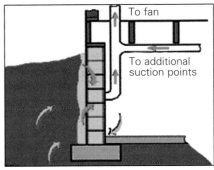

Blockwall suction collects radon from hollow concrete block walls before the gas enters the basement.

MITIGATION METHODS

The effectiveness of the various methods for reducing radon concentrations depends on the type of foundation, the condition of the foundation, and what is under the floor and around the foundation. The most common methods are shown above. Effectiveness and ranges of installation and annual operating costs are shown in the table below.

COMMON RADON MITIGATION METHODS

Method	Typical Reduction	Typical Cost of Contracted Installation	Annual Cost of Fan Electricity + Heat/Cool Loss
Active subslab suction	80–99%	$800–2,500	$75–175
Passive subslab suction (no fan)	30–70%	$550–2,250	Negligible
Sump hole suction	90–99%	$800–2,500	$100–225
Draintile suction	90–99%	$800–1,700	$75–175
Submembrane depressurization	80–99%	$1,000–2,500	$70–175
Blockwall suction	50–99%	$1,500–3,000	$150–300
Natural ventilation of crawl space	0–50%	$0–500	$0–150
Sealing of radon entry routes	0–50%	$100–2,000	Negligible

RAILINGS

DESIGN CRITERIA

ALSO SEE...
Decks:
Pages 74–81
Fasteners:
Pages 122–125
Stairs:
Pages 332–335
Steps:
Pages 336–337
Wood:
Pages 446–453

When designing railings, you must familiarize yourself with local building codes. Most codes, for example, specify a minimum height for the railing and a minimum allowable space between balusters. If you have questions, seek advice from your local building department or from a private building inspector familiar with local codes.

Next, consider the aesthetic character of your house and landscape. Is it formal? Does its design rely on straight lines or on flowing curves? Are angles prominent? Such questions will help you determine which railing designs fit better than others.

Don't build a railing without considering your lifestyle. Will you want to set food and drinks on it? Do you want privacy? Will flower pots or other small objects be placed next to the railing—objects that could slide under the bottom rail and fall?

By the time you have answered these questions, your railing may have designed itself, but you can get inspiration from magazine photographs or neighbors' designs. Your final task is to evaluate pictures and actual railings for ideas to satisfy your needs.

DECK RAILINGS

POSTS

If your deck posts extend above the decking, use them to support your railing. If you have to add posts, bolt 4×4s to the rim joists of the deck using two ⅜-inch carriage bolts per post. For a more finished appearance, notch the posts so they lap over the deck framing.

HANDRAIL (TOP RAIL)

Make handrails from 2×6s, using the longest lengths possible. Make sure that any joints in the handrail occur directly above posts. Cut joints at a 45-degree miter bevel so they overlap slightly, and the corners, too.

Rout a groove (⅜ inch deep and 1½ inches wide) on the underside of the handrail. Nail the rail to the top of the posts with 12d galvanized or stainless casing nails.

BOTTOM RAIL

Cut the bottom rails to fit between the posts, but do not attach them yet. Use a bevel gauge to mark the cutting angle if the rail is for a stairway.

ASSEMBLING

Assemble baluster sections by nailing 2×2 balusters to the bottom rail and to a length of ⅜-inch-thick lath to secure the tops. The lath will fit inside the groove you made in the handrail. Space the balusters as dictated by local code.

INSTALLING

Fit the lath of each baluster section up into the groove in the bottom of the handrail. Toenail the bottom rail to the posts.

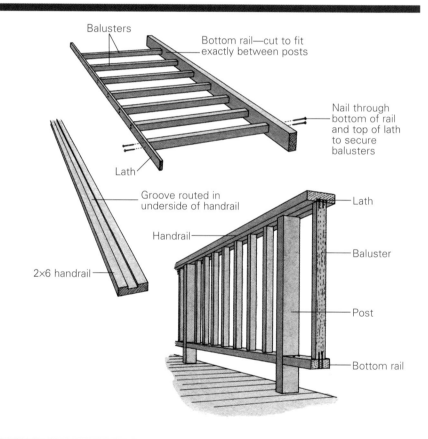

Balusters

Bottom rail—cut to fit exactly between posts

Nail through bottom of rail and top of lath to secure balusters

Lath

Groove routed in underside of handrail

2×6 handrail

Handrail

Lath

Baluster

Post

Bottom rail

CODE REQUIREMENTS: RAILINGS

Stair Handrails:
- The height must be between 30 and 38 inches, measured directly above the nosing of the tread.
- There must be a handrail available on at least one side of any stairway that has more than two risers.
- Stairways more than 44 inches wide require a middle rail in addition to the side rail(s).
- Handrails for spiral stairs must be fastened on the outside of the staircase.

- Handrails must be spaced out from the wall at least 1½ inches.

Guardrails:
- Any porch, balcony, or floor more than 30 inches above grade or another floor must have a guardrail.
- The minimum height of a guardrail is 36 inches.
- Guardrails must have intermediate closures (lattice or balusters) which will not pass a 4-inch sphere.

STAIR RAILINGS

When adding a stair railing to a deck, follow the design of the deck railing. Bolt the stair posts to the stringers with two ⅜-inch, galvanized carriage bolts.

To mark the angle that you need to cut on the posts and balusters, clamp a board across the sides of the posts and adjust its level until it is at a uniform, code-compliant distance above all tread nosings. Allow 1½ inches for the cap rail. Mark, then cut the posts. The handrail for the stairs must be easily gripped by hand, so make it from a 2×4. Toenail the handrail through each post with 12d hot-dipped galvanized casing nails.

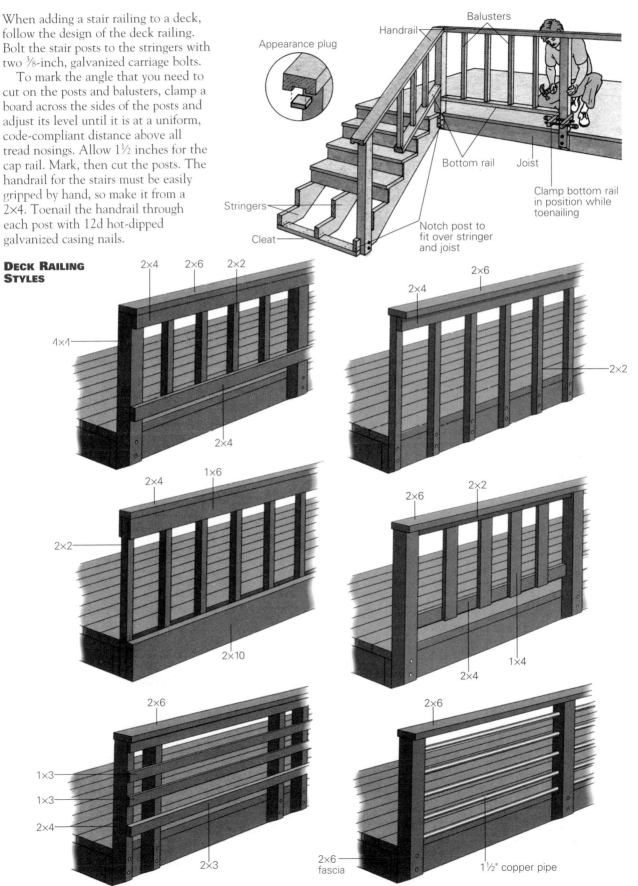

Appearance plug

Balusters

Handrail

Bottom rail   Joist

Clamp bottom rail in position while toenailing

Stringers

Cleat

Notch post to fit over stringer and joist

DECK RAILING STYLES

2×4   2×6   2×2

4×4

2×4

2×4   2×6

2×2

2×4   1×6

2×2

2×10

2×6   2×2

2×4

1×4

2×6

1×3

1×3

2×4

2×3

2×6

2×6 fascia   1½" copper pipe

RANGES, OVENS, AND COOKTOPS

CHOICES

From a cast-iron pot on the hearth to the latest microwave unit, the variety of cooking options seems endless, especially if you're trying to decide what to buy. It will help to begin with the basic question: gas or electric? Assuming both hookups are available, your choice comes down to a matter of preference.

Chefs generally prefer gas because it responds quickly, and the temperature is infinitely adjustable. Electric ranges and cooktops are getting faster, however, and you can set and reset a temperature by pushing a button.

Gas is cheaper, and offers an additional advantage—it stays on when the power goes out. Not only can you continue cooking, but—provided you have a battery-operated carbon monoxide monitor—you can keep your house from freezing by operating several cooktop burners. Gas units must have a venting arrangement—either a range hood or internal down-drafting unit.

The cost of gas and electric units is comparable. The final decision may boil down to choosing the type of hookup that is already in your kitchen.

RANGE OR SEPARATES?

Should you buy a range or individual cooktop and oven units? Here are a few things you should consider.

A separate oven and cooktop is more costly but more convenient. A built-in oven is at eye level. A separate cooktop offers convenient storage underneath, and lets you cook without having to stand in front of a hot oven.

If your work triangle is cramped, install a separate cooktop and move the oven somewhere else.

A slide-in range is prone to collect grease and debris in the crack between the counter and stovetop, but does have a distinct advantage: You can take it with you when you move.

WHICH TYPE OF COOKTOP?

Half of all kitchens in Europe now have smoothtop cooking surfaces, first introduced in the late '70s. Their great advantage is cleaning ease—they don't have drip pans which collect spills.

If you go with the smoothtop, you have a choice of three heating elements:

Radiant: The familiar resistance coil, but now flattened into a ribbon with greater surface area and faster response.

Halogen: An element that combines light energy with heat energy to provide more even heating with precise control.

Induction: Hidden coils that never get hot themselves (and thus cool instantly), but use electric fields to heat iron and steel pots indirectly.

INSTALLING AN ELECTRIC SLIDE-IN RANGE

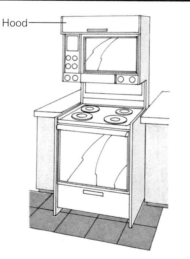

Hood

A slide-in electric range is easy to install. Strip off the packing carton, plug it into the special range receptacle, and slide it into place. To avoid scratching or tearing the floor, slide the unit on a piece of the cardboard carton.

A freestanding electric range comes equipped with its own cord for plugging into a dedicated 220-volt/ 50-amp circuit.

INSTALLING A GAS RANGE

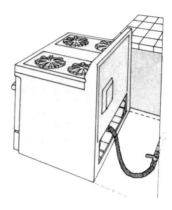

Before you install a gas range, get the installation specifications for the unit or, better yet, measure the floor model yourself, and make sure the gas cock in your gas line will fit in the recess in the back panel. The range can sit flush against the back wall only if the back panel and gas supply don't interfere.

To install the range, connect one end of a length of flexible gas tubing to the gas cock and the other end to the range stub. Slide the range into position. Most ranges also have a 120-volt electric cord for the clock, lights, and pilotless ignition, so be sure there is a regular 120-volt receptacle behind the range as well. Gas ranges do not require dedicated electric circuits.

ORDERING REPLACEMENT PARTS

Of course, given the model and serial number, you can always order replacement parts for your gas or electric range through the manufacturer. But anyone who has ever gone that route knows it to be a very trying and expensive process.

As with automotive parts, other manufacturers have stepped in to offer replacement parts. You can find the following parts for electric ranges at home centers and appliance repair centers:

■ Top burners
■ Trim rings for top burners
■ Drip pans for top burners
■ Generic knobs and switches
■ Bake (bottom) elements
■ Broil (top) elements

INSTALLING A DROP-IN RANGE

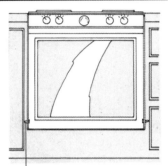

Screw into side cabinets

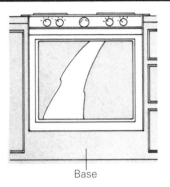

Base

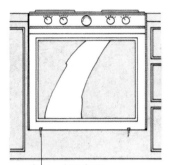

Screw into base

Drop-in ranges require a base cabinet with a front and counter cutout. The counter must have a matching cutout. On some units a flange around the cooking surface rests on the counter and supports the weight of the range. The edges of other models are flush at the top; screws hold them in place, either in the base or along the sides.

To install either type of drop-in range, connect the gas or electric supply first. (Use flexible tubing for gas.) Rest the range on the lip of the cabinet so you have room to reach behind and make the connections.

A gas range also needs a 120-volt receptacle for the lights, timer, and pilotless ignition.

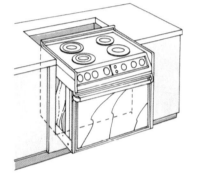

Most electric ranges have a heavy cord that fits into a 220-volt, 50-amp range receptacle. Some, however, have a flexible armored cable that wires into an electrical box behind the range.

INSTALLING A BUILT-IN OVEN

If you plan on a lot of baking, install a separate baking oven. You have the choice of conventional, convection, microwave, and combination convection/microwave.

A convection oven circulates oven air, and heats faster and more evenly. A microwave cuts cooking time by 75 percent, but fails to produce brown skins and crusts.

A combination unit has the advantages of both and cuts cooking time by 50 percent.

For a built-in, order cabinet units with cutouts and shelves of the right size. Most cabinet manufacturers offer standard units for the purpose. Oven models differ, so be sure that the specifications you have for roughing in gas and electric lines refer to the oven you plan to install. To install, slide the oven into the opening. Some ovens require screws to hold them in place. If there is a storage space below, you can connect the gas or electricity after the oven is in place.

INSTALLING A COOKTOP

Cooktops are either electric or gas and you can combine them. For example, you might install an electric oven and a gas cooktop.

Most residential cooktops drop into a cutout in the counter of a regular base cabinet. Commercial gas units—which professional cooks often use in their home—have a pedestal base and need to sit on a dropped section of counter so the cooking surface is flush.

Their installation requires custom cabinetry and a nonflammable surface material around the cooktop.

Commercial cooktops are available with two burners, four burners, and six burners. If your kitchen is regularly used by two cooks, consider installing a second cooktop set in an island away from the main cooking area.

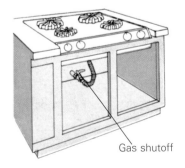

Gas shutoff

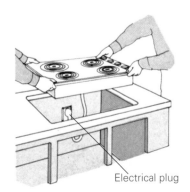

Electrical plug

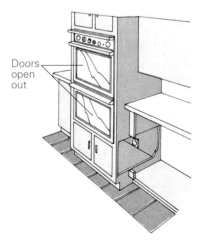

Doors open out

271

RECEPTACLES

READING A RECEPTACLE

ALSO SEE...
Electrical Boxes:
Pages 106–109
Electrical Systems:
Pages 110–115
Wire:
Pages 442–445

Receptacles have markings you should check before installing one. First, use only those with Underwriters' Laboratory (UL) approval. Then make sure that the amperage of the receptacle is compatible with its circuit (20-amp circuits can use receptacles rated at 15 or 20 amps, but 15-amp circuits can have only 15-amp receptacles). Finally, be sure your receptacle is compatible with the wire. Copper wire can be used with any receptacle. Copper-clad aluminum is compatible with those marked CU/AL. Use aluminum wire with receptacles marked CO/ALR.

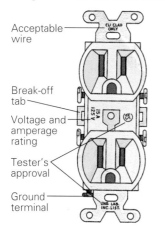

Acceptable wire

Break-off tab

Voltage and amperage rating

Tester's approval

Ground terminal

TYPES OF RECEPTACLES

Most of the circuits in a house are either 15-amp or 20-amp, 120-volt general-purpose circuits. These are wired with one hot wire (black), one neutral wire (white), and one bare ground wire. Install receptacles with the same rating as the circuit (check the breaker—it will tell you the circuit rating). The front of all receptacles has three slots to which the three wires are connected internally. The U-shaped hole is for the grounding prong, and the other slots differ in size. The short slot is hot and the long slot neutral. To remember this, associate the bigger slot with the safety function (neutral goes to ground and helps protect you from shocks). The distinction between hot and neutral is important because plugs for home electronic equipment are polarized, meaning that the neutral prong is wider, because the ground for the electronics and for the equipment case must be connected to the power-line ground.

Specific configurations in plugs for washing machines, clothes dryers, and electric ranges make it impossible to plug a 50-amp range into a receptacle intended for a 30-amp clothes dryer. There are more than 35 plug-and-receptacle configurations, ranging from the common 15-amp duplex receptacle to the four-prong 55-amp kitchen-range receptacle.

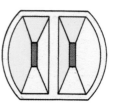

Ungrounded two-prong
(120 volts)

Grounded three-prong
(120 volts–15 amps)

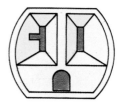

Grounded three-prong
(120 volts–20 amps)

Grounded three-prong
(120/240 volts–30 amps)

Grounded three-prong
(120/240 volts–50 amps)

Grounded three-prong
(240 volts–30 amps)

CODE REQUIREMENTS: RECEPTACLES

The code requires the following receptacles in new construction:

Convenience Outlets:
■ Are required in every habitable room
■ No point on a wall can be more than 6 feet from an outlet
■ "Wall" includes all walls wider than 2 feet as well as freestanding counters and dividers

Small-Appliance Outlets:
■ Two 20-amp circuits are required in kitchen, pantry, and dining room
■ Refrigerator and freezer included
■ Includes any 12-inch counter
■ No point on the counter can be more than 24 inches from an outlet
■ Face-up receptacles are forbidden

Specific Appliance Outlets:
■ Within 6 feet of appliance

■ Are required for washing machine and clothes dryer (electric dryer requires its own)

GFCIs (Required Locations):
■ Outdoors, at front and rear of house, if accessible from ground
■ Next to lavatory (one between two lavatories ok)
■ Within 6 feet of kitchen sink
■ In a garage
■ In an unfinished basement
■ Near a pool
■ Serving a whirlpool tub

Miscellaneous:
■ In basement, in addition to laundry
■ In attached garage
■ In hallways over 10 feet long
■ In attic or crawl space for servicing HVAC

WIRING 110-VOLT RECEPTACLES

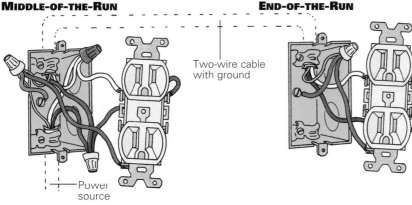

MIDDLE-OF-THE-RUN

END-OF-THE-RUN

Two-wire cable with ground

Power source

The illustration above shows wiring for middle-of-the-run and end-of-the-run receptacles. Notice the color of the screw terminals. Silver-colored screws take neutral (white) wires, brass-colored screws take hot (black) wires, and green screws take ground wires. If the colors are not obvious, remember that the longer slot is for the neutral connection.

To connect the wires, strip ½ to ⅝ inch of insulation from the ends. If the receptacle is a backwiring type, push the wires into the holes. If not, bend the ends of the wires clockwise around the screws and tighten the screws. Connect the bare ground wire to the green grounding screw.

When there is just one wire of any color in the box (the end-of-run), connect the wire directly to the correct terminal or receptacle. When there are two or more wires of each color, join them with a wire nut.

If a circuit has a single receptacle, the receptacle must have the same rating as the circuit. If the circuit has multiple receptacles, no receptacle rating can be higher than the circuit rating. The receptacles may have a lower rating, however. For example, on a 20-amp circuit, you may use a 15-amp receptacle. The National Electrical Code (NEC) doesn't restrict the number of receptacles on a circuit. Your local code may, however. As a

rule of thumb, it is common practice (and acceptable) to install up to 6 receptacles on small-appliance circuits and up to 10 outlets on general-purpose circuits. Strive to divide the receptacle load among as many circuits as possible.

WIRING 220-VOLT RECEPTACLES

The service panel contains two separate 110-volt hot sides which together supply 220 volts to large appliances.

A 220-volt circuit consists of two hot (black and black, or black and red) wires, plus a bare ground.

You will notice that both of the hot terminals on the 220-volt plug and receptacle have dark screws.

TESTER MAGIC

You don't have to be an electrician to use the little $5 plug-in tester sold at every hardware store. Three little colored lights immediately tell you whether:

■ There is power at all
■ There is a ground
■ The hot and neutral wires are reversed

SURFACE WIRING

If you need to add receptacles, but don't want to tear into the walls, raceways and plug-in strips are just the ticket.

Some metal raceways function as baseboards. To install them, remove the baseboard to a length equal to the raceway. Locate one end of the raceway directly under the existing receptacles which will serve as the power source.

Make sure the power is off, then open the outlet box and fish the raceway wires into it through a hole drilled at the base of the wall. Connect the wires, screw the raceway frame into the desired position, and snap on the cover plate.

If you use an extender or the box is surface-mounted, or if you use a plug-in raceway, you do not

have to drill through the wall. For an extender box installation, turn off the power, remove the wall plate and the receptacle, and attach an extender box to the existing one. Measure, cut, and

attach the raceway backing to the wall so that it joins the extender box. Connect the wiring to the existing receptacle, replace the receptacle, and attach the covers.

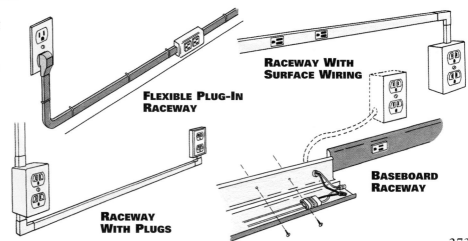

FLEXIBLE PLUG-IN RACEWAY

RACEWAY WITH SURFACE WIRING

RACEWAY WITH PLUGS

BASEBOARD RACEWAY

RESILIENT FLOORING

DESIGN CONSIDERATIONS

ALSO SEE...
Adhesives:
Pages 8–9
Floors:
Pages 140–141

Resilient flooring is practical and easy to install. Its patterns and textures range from glossy to matte, from lightly mottled to highly textured, from monochromatic to marbleized; and all are available in nearly any color. Few would want it as a living room or bedroom floor, but in the kitchen or bathroom—where spills are a common occurrence—the design flexibility and practicality are surpassed only by tile.

Most resilient flooring is made of vinyl or a vinyl composite, but rubber sheet and cork tile also qualify as resilient floorings. Solid vinyl and vinyl-covered cork are the most expensive and have the highest resiliency and sound-insulating qualities. Vinyl-composition flooring rates lower in these attributes and is less expensive.

These guidelines may be useful when selecting a pattern:

■ Don't use simulated natural patterns in places where the real material would never be used. For example, don't curve a Spanish floor-paver pattern up a wall.

■ Avoid patterns that overwhelm the space. The bigger and more elaborate the pattern, the larger the room must be. If you like an intricate pattern, but are concerned it may appear too busy in a large room, see if the same pattern is available in neutral, monochromatic tones.

■ If you need to seam sheet flooring in a prominent location, disguise the seam with a straight-line pattern, such as simulated tile with grouted joints.

Most resilient tiles measure 12 inches square and are sold by the piece. Resilient sheet is sold by the square yard and usually comes in 6- or 12-foot-wide rolls, although 9- and 15-foot widths may be available as a special order. Because seams are vulnerable to moisture penetration if not fused properly, sheet materials are preferred over tiles in these locations. Plan to install sheet flooring so that seams fall in the narrowest part of the room or away from highly visible, heavily trafficked areas.

When you measure the dimensions of a room to calculate square footage, include toe spaces under cabinets, spaces under movable appliances, any closets you want covered, and at least half the distance into every doorway. Add about 3 inches of extra length beyond the actual dimensions of a room for trimming and fitting. If you need to seam two or more pieces together, add a full overlap of one pattern for matching. Always bring a floor plan and accurate dimensions with you when you consult with your flooring dealer.

SAVE YOUR SCRAP

Typically, you'll have a substantial amount of scrap flooring left over when you are finished installing a resilient floor surface. Don't throw it away. If you can't find a place to store it, slip it under a rug where it will lie flat.

Why save it? Because there is a good chance that the bathroom or kitchen floor will suffer damage before it is worn out, and repairing small damaged areas is simple and far less costly than buying new flooring. And besides, you won't even remember the name of the pattern five years down the road; and if you do, there is no guarantee it will be still in production.

ADHESIVES

Which adhesive you use will depend both on the type of resilient flooring and the type of subfloor. Use only the formulation recommended by the manufacturer. The most common adhesive is a water-soluble paste, which can be used for wood floors or concrete floors above grade. Asphalt emulsion can be used below grade as well as above, but cannot be mixed with water. Other formulations include latex adhesive for moist situations; epoxy for places where extra strength and moisture resistance are needed; and adhesives for cove bases, rubber stair treads, and other specialty applications.

Always follow the manufacturer's instructions faithfully, and use caution with flammable adhesives. The room should be well ventilated and have no open flames such as pilot lights. Avoid using equipment that may cause sparks, such as electric motors, and do not smoke.

REMOVING OLD FLOORING

You can install vinyl flooring over almost any firm surface that is flat, level, and free of defects. Exceptions include ceramic tile and cushion-back or embossed vinyl. These floors must be removed or covered with plywood.

To remove ceramic tile, break it apart with a cold chisel and a hammer. If the tile is set in a mortar base, cut the flooring into sections using a circular saw equipped with a masonry blade. Pry up the sections with a pry bar and discard them or level the entire floor with a latex leveling compound.

To remove old embossed or cushion-backed vinyl, cut the material into strips with a utility knife. Pry up a corner with a pry bar and peel back each strip. Soften stubborn glue with a heat gun (not a torch) to help loosen it.

One trick is to cut the vinyl in 8-inch strips. Wind the strip onto a rolling pin and run the rolling pin the length of the floor, gathering up the vinyl as you go.

PREPARING THE FLOOR

Resilient flooring materials are thin—they reveal any dents, bumps, cracks, or depressions in the subsurface, including joints and recessed nail heads. Always make sure that the subfloor is smooth, level, and free of even minor imperfections.

Unlike floor coverings that are porous and allow small amounts of moisture to escape, a resilient floor traps it, deteriorating the adhesive bond and, eventually, the underlayment or subfloor. It must be installed over a surface that is free of moisture.

After making sure that the existing floor is sound and free of moisture problems, use the chart at right to prepare your floor. If the chart indicates that an existing floor covering must be removed, do so; then refer to the additional steps required to prepare the newly exposed subsurface.

If you're using sheet flooring, unroll it in the room for which it is intended, or in one heated to 70 degrees F, at least 24 hours before installation. When you are ready to install it, reroll it face side in. It tears easily, so roll carefully.

VINYL IN BATHROOMS

In bathrooms, always install resilient flooring before tubs, toilets, and showers are installed, and do not caulk around their bases. This accomplishes two purposes:
1. It eliminates the often-imperfect—and sometimes downright messy—caulk line.
2. It allows water from a leak under the fixture to escape onto the bathroom floor where it will alert you to the problem instead of silently rotting the floor away.

PREPARING FOR RESILIENT FLOORING

Caution: Old resilient tile may contain asbestos fibers, which are harmful if inhaled. Covering old tile with new flooring minimizes its potential hazard. If you must remove old tile, wear a respirator, minimize breakage, and do not sand.

Nature of Floor	Preparation
Exposed joists	**1.** Install ¾-inch T&G plywood or OSB subfloor.
	2. Install lauan plywood or ¼- to ½-inch rated underlayment.
	3. Fill all nail holes and joints and sand smooth.
Bare concrete	■ Level and smooth slab as necessary.
Wood floor/subfloor	**1.** Replace broken floor or subfloor boards.
over wood frame	**2.** Install lauan plywood or ¼- to ½-inch rated underlayment.
	3. Fill all nail holes and joints and sand smooth.
over concrete slab	**1.** Remove all wood materials.
	2. Level and smooth slab as necessary.
Resilient sheet/tile	■ If existing resilient is cushioned, remove and repair surface.
over wood frame	**1.** If existing resilient is loose, has wax or gloss surface, or is embossed, install lauan plywood or ¼- to ½-inch rated underlayment.
	2. Fill all nail holes and joints and sand smooth.
over concrete slab	■ If existing resilient is cushioned or loose, remove and level slab as necessary.
	■ If existing resilient is embossed, smooth the surface with a liquid leveler, otherwise, remove wax and sand smooth.
Ceramic tile	■ If possible, remove tile; or smooth with liquid leveler.
over wood frame	**1.** If removing tile, repair subfloor as necessary.
	2. Install lauan plywood or ¼- to ½-inch rated underlayment.
	3. Fill all nail holes and joints and sand smooth.
over concrete slab	**1.** If possible, remove tile; otherwise, smooth with liquid leveler.
	2. If removing tile, repair slab as necessary; if slab is uneven, smooth with liquid leveler.
Carpet	**1.** Remove carpet.
over wood frame	**2.** Repair subfloor as necessary.
	3. Install lauan plywood or ¼- to ½-inch rated underlayment.
	4. Fill all nail holes and joints and sand smooth.
over concrete slab	**1.** Remove carpet.
	2. After removing carpet, repair slab as necessary; if slab is uneven, smooth with liquid leveler.

INSTALLING TILE

Preparing for Installation:

After you have prepared the subfloor, remove the baseboards or shoes. If necessary, undercut the door casings so you can slide the sheet material under them—it's a lot easier than trying to cut the flooring to fit around such obstacles. Sweep and then vacuum the room carefully. The smallest particle of trapped debris will show up as a noticeable bump in the flooring.

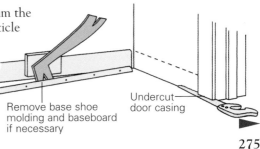

Remove base shoe molding and baseboard if necessary

Undercut door casing

RESILIENT FLOORING
continued

INSTALLING TILE *continued*

LAYING OUT

Use the quadrant method shown at right for laying out resilient tile, cork, wood block, and parquet tile

If the room has an irregular shape, alcoves, or protruding obstacles such as cabinets, start your layout in the largest clear rectangular portion of the room.

To begin, mark the midpoint of the two shortest opposing walls, and snap a chalk line between them. Mark the midpoint of the other two walls and use these marks to establish a midpoint on your chalked line. At this point, establish a perpendicular line, using the 3-4-5 method described in laying out foundations (see Foundations, pages 144-151). Snap a chalk line on the perpendicular.

A simpler and more accurate method is to use a 4×8 sheet of plywood as a large framing square. Thin plywood, such as ¼-inch lauan, is the lightest and easiest to maneuver.

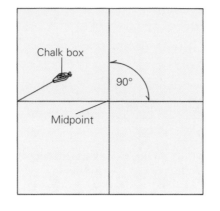

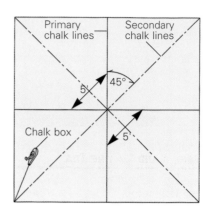

Place one corner of the sheet at the center mark and align one of the 4-foot edges with the chalk line. The 8-foot edge is now the perpendicular you are looking for. Mark it and extend it by snapping a second chalk line over it.

If you are laying the tile out in a diagonal pattern, first establish the guidelines just described. Then measure 5 feet out from the intersection along each axis and make marks. Find the midpoint between these marks, and snap chalk lines from the center of the quadrant through this midpoint (extended all the way to the walls). These lines will be 45 degrees to the original quadrant lines.

TRYING A TEST RUN

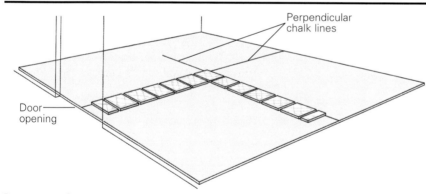

Lay dry tiles along both axes of one quadrant, starting at the center and working toward the walls. Adjust the guidelines until both borders have pieces at least half a tile wide (pieces less than half a tile wide are likely to loosen). If there is a doorway in the wall, adjust the guideline(s) so that the row meeting the high-traffic doorway consists of full tiles.

INSTALLING QUADRANTS

Vacuum all dirt from the floor. Apply the adhesive according to the manufacturer's directions. Remember the adhesive's open time—the period during which tiles can be laid before the adhesive becomes too dry. Some adhesives allow only enough time to set half a dozen tiles; with others, you will have enough time to set most of a quadrant in one application. Apply only the amount of adhesive for the tiles you can lay in the open time.

Start spreading adhesive in the center of the room. Avoid covering the chalk lines. The first tile locks you into the pattern, so position it so that it

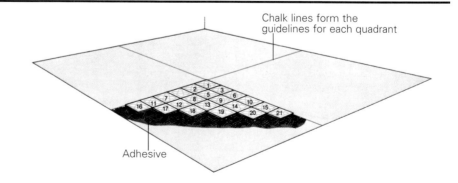

aligns perfectly with both chalk lines. Avoid sliding the tiles into position.

Cut the tiles to fit as you come to walls or obstacles. After laying the first quadrant, do the remaining quadrants.

As you proceed you will have to walk or kneel on newly laid tiles. Use a scrap of plywood to distribute your weight over them. Wipe up excess adhesive with a rag.

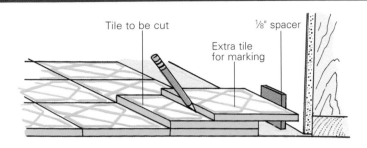

Tile to be cut | Extra tile for marking | ⅛" spacer

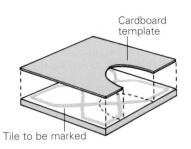

Cardboard template

Tile to be marked

MARKING AND CUTTING TILE

To cut a tile to fit against a wall, set it exactly on top of the last full tile. Place a second tile on top of it, butting it against the wall with a ⅛-inch expansion gap. Mark the cutting line on the first tile, then either cut it with

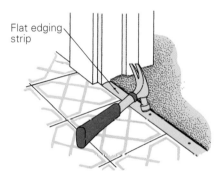

Flat edging strip

INSTALLING A METAL EDGING STRIP

Where resilient tile and other flooring materials meet, install a flat edging strip. Be careful not to dent the strip with your hammer.

a utility knife, or score and break it if it is too heavy to cut through.

Tiles are difficult to cut when cold and brittle. To make cutting easier, warm them briefly in an oven at the lowest temperature setting.

INSTALLING A WOOD BASEBOARD

After all of the tile is in place, nail baseboard or shoe molding around the edge to cover the ⅛-inch expansion gap. Keep the baseboard or shoe slightly above the flooring so that the resilient material can move freely.

INSTALLING A COVE BASE

If you're using vinyl cove base, cut sections to fit and glue them to the walls with the recommended adhesive. At inside corners, cut a V-notch in the flange and score the back of the strip.

MAKING A TEMPLATE

To fit tiles around an obstacle, such as a pipe, mark the tiles from a cardboard template. You may have to draw the template several times before you get it right, but it will be cardboard you are wasting—not tile.

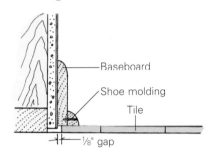

Baseboard

Shoe molding

Tile

⅛" gap

Wrap the base around an outside corner; the flange will stretch. Apply adhesive to the grooved back only; do not glue the flange to the flooring.

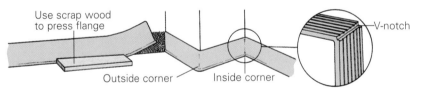

Use scrap wood to press flange

Outside corner | Inside corner | V-notch

INSTALLING SHEET VINYL

Sheet flooring is one of the simplest of all floors to install. Three methods for adhering resilient sheet are:
- gluing fully
- gluing just the perimeter
- laying loose with just a few edge staples.

Installations with seams must be glued at least around the perimeter and at the seam. The most difficult part of installing sheet vinyl is cutting it to fit around the edges. Baseboards are an absolute necessity for covering up imperfections and gaps at the edges.

CUTTING THE SHEET

To cut sheet vinyl to fit, make a paper pattern (butcher paper or kraft paper is

perfect for this) that exactly fits the room. Trim and tape strips together so that they form a continuous pattern around the edge of the room. Leave a ¼-inch gap at the walls. Then transfer the room outline to the flooring material. Some manufacturers supply a kit for this procedure.

Another method is to rough-cut the sheet 3 inches larger than room dimensions, then do the final trimming after putting the sheeting in place. This works if the material is quite flexible and easy to handle.

After cutting the sheet to its rough dimensions, roll it so that the face is inside, with the edge for the longest wall free. Position that edge so that

it curls up the wall slightly. Unroll the sheet, tugging and adjusting it so that it is centered and the pattern is square.

To make the sheet lie flat, make relief cuts at all the corners. Slit the curled margin with a knife, but just to the point where the floor intersects the corner. Do not cut beyond this point.

To fit the sheet around a pipe or post, cut a slit in from the edge of the flooring to make the sheet separate and close around the obstruction. Cut increasingly larger circles around the obstruction until the sheet lies flat on the floor and the two halves of the slit join back together again.

▶

INSTALLING SHEET VINYL *continued*

TRIMMING THE EDGES

Professionals sometimes can trim the flooring in one pass, but you will probably have to trim twice—first to remove most of the margin and then to perfect the fit. Heating the sheet with a hair dryer will make it more flexible and allow you to get closer to the edge of the floor. Make the cut freehand with a utility knife, but be conservative. You can always remove more on the second—or even third—cut, but you can never put back what

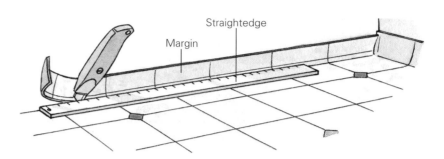

you have removed. Leave a ⅛-inch expansion gap at the edges. At

doorways without thresholds, trim the flooring at the centerline of the door.

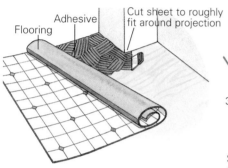

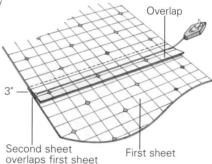

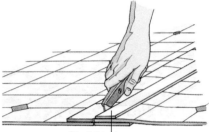

GLUING THE SHEET

To apply the adhesive, carefully lift the sheet along one edge and fold it loosely back on itself so that half of the floor is exposed. Apply adhesive to the floor with a toothed trowel, according to the manufacturer's directions. Work from the corners to the center of each wall if you are adhering only the edges. To glue the sheet fully, apply adhesive on the exposed floor up to the folded sheet. Then roll the sheet back into place; walk on it to press it into the adhesive. Repeat the process for the other half of the room. To ensure a tight bond with no air bubbles, roll the floor with a rented floor roller.

SEAMING TWO SHEETS

Trim and fit the first sheet in place, leaving 3 inches of extra material at the seam. Glue this sheet down, stopping 8 or 9 inches short of the seam location.

Next, trim and fit the second piece so that it overlaps the first by 3 to 6 inches. If the flooring has a pattern, be sure to position the second sheet so that it matches the pattern of the first sheet perfectly. Glue down the second sheet, applying the adhesive only to within 5 or 6 inches of the first sheet and letting the unglued edge of the second sheet overlap the first.

CUTTING THE SEAM

Use a straight line in the flooring pattern as a cutting guide, or snap a chalk line along the seam location after squaring it to the two side walls. Using a straightedge to guide the blade, cut along the line with a sharp utility knife.

Important: Don't cut twice: Press hard enough to cut through both layers of flooring on the first pass. Retracing the cut can cause slivers and unsightly gaps. Remove the scrap pieces and clean under the seam thoroughly, making sure there is no dust or debris on the floor.

ADHERING THE SEAM

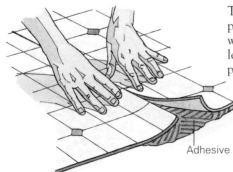

Test the seam by dry-fitting the two pieces together. They should abut without pushing the seam up or leaving a crack. Glue the seam by pulling back both edges of flooring

and spreading a band of adhesive along the floor. Then join the two edges together and press the seam into the adhesive. Immediately wipe off any adhesive that oozes up. Clean the seam with solvent recommended by the flooring manufacturer.

FUSING THE SEAM

After the adhesive has set, you can fuse the seam with a solvent that melts the

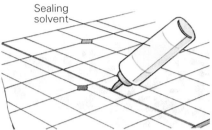

Sealing solvent

edges. The solvent comes in a bottle that includes a special applicator spout. Run the spout along the seam, according to directions, applying the sealer to the seam, not the flooring. A fused seam is completely waterproof.

INSTALLING BASEBOARDS

Install baseboards or base shoes around the room so that it covers the gap between the flooring and walls. Leave a slight space, about the thickness of a

matchbook cover, between the bottom of the baseboard and the surface of the floor to allow for movement.

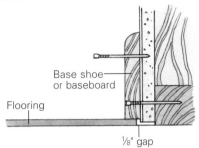

Base shoe or baseboard

Flooring

⅛" gap

REPAIRING DAMAGE

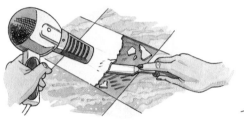

FIXING A BUBBLE

Every now and then you'll get a bubble in resilient flooring. Fixing it is easy.
■ Warm the bubbled area by placing a heating pad over it for half an hour.
■ Using a sharp utility knife, cut all the way across the bubble and all the way through the vinyl material.
■ Using a putty knife, lift one side of the bubble while you force vinyl tile adhesive into the pocket with a small brush. Repeat for the other side.
■ Slide the putty knife around inside the slits to spread the adhesive.
■ Wrap a rolling pin in plastic and roll the bubble from the edges toward the slit, forcing the excess adhesive out.
■ Clean up the excess adhesive with the solvent recommended by the manufacturer.
■ Weigh the area down for 24 hours; place waxed paper between the vinyl and the weight to prevent sticking.

REPLACING A TILE

This repair assumes you were smart enough to save a few of the original tiles or lucky enough to have found an exact replacement.
■ Warm the tile to be replaced with a hair dyer set to "high."
■ Chip the tile out using a sharp chisel. Be careful not to damage adjacent tiles, and rewarm as necessary to keep the tile soft.
■ Remove the old adhesive, using adhesive solvent if necessary.
■ Test fit the replacement tile. If it doesn't fit, sand its edges until it does.
■ Spread vinyl tile adhesive on the subfloor with a notched spreader. Press the tile into place and roll it with a plastic-wrapped rolling pin.
■ Clean up the excess adhesive with the solvent recommended by the manufacturer.
■ Weigh the area down for 24 hours; place waxed paper between the vinyl and the weight to prevent sticking.

PATCHING SHEET VINYL

Use a scrap of leftover flooring. If you don't have one, steal a scrap from under the refrigerator.
■ Slide the scrap around over the damaged area until the damage is covered and the patterns line up. Tape down the scrap with duct tape.
■ Taking care not to move your patch piece, use a very sharp utility knife and a straightedge, and cut through both layers of vinyl in a pattern that encompasses the damage.
■ Remove the tape and the top piece of vinyl.
■ Using a chisel, remove the damaged vinyl. Use adhesive thinner if necessary, and be careful not to damage the subfloor.
■ Apply vinyl adhesive to the back side of the patch and press it into place. Roll with a plastic-wrapped rolling pin.
■ Clean up the excess adhesive with the solvent recommended by the manufacturer.
■ Weigh the area down for 24 hours; place waxed paper between the vinyl and the weight to prevent sticking.

ROLL ROOFING

KNOW THE LIMITS

ALSO SEE...
Asphalt Shingle Roofing:
Pages 10–13
Flashing:
Pages 136–139
Roofs:
Pages 282–289

Single-coverage roll roofing is inexpensive and simple to apply, but it lasts only half as long as asphalt shingles. Double-coverage roll roofing, where each course overlaps the previous one by 19 inches, lasts about the same as asphalt shingles. Both typically have a Class C fire rating (A is the most fire resistant).

Roll roofing makes sense where cost is more important than appearance (as on farm buildings), or for low-slope roofing when contractor-installed built-up roofing is too expensive. It can be used for roof slopes down to 2 in 12 with the exposed-nail method, or to 1 in 12 with the concealed-nail method. Each method can be used with full-width mineral-surface (single-coverage) rolls or selvage-edge (double-coverage) rolls.

Roll roofing can crack in cold weather, so don't apply it when the temperature is less than 45 degrees F. If you have to do the job anyway, store the rolls in a warm place before you apply them, then unroll and cut them into strips no longer than 18 feet. Let them lie on the roof until they are flat.

Lay roll roofing over a plywood or orient strand board (OSB) deck, either perpendicular or parallel to the slope. Install plyclips (see Using Plyclips, page 281) on the sheathing edges. Let the roofing overhang the eaves by ½ inch.

An underlayment of felt roofing is optional. You will need 1 gallon of lap (not mastic) roofing cement for every roll, and 2 pounds of roofing nails for every square (one square equals 100 square feet). Use 1-inch nails for new roofing; use 1¼-inch nails for reroofing. Enlist the aid of one or two helpers to handle the long strips.

Valleys will be open, so flash them beforehand with two layers of roll roofing, the first an 18-inch-wide strip and the second 36 inches wide. Install the first strip upside down. Nail along one edge first, spacing nails ¾ inch in from the edge and 6 inches apart. Then nail the opposite edge. Overlap and cement end joints at least 6 inches.

CONCEALED-NAIL APPLICATION

The concealed-nail method is both more attractive and less likely to develop leaks than the exposed-nail method. The keys to achieving a tight, smooth-lying roof are applying the material when it is warm enough for full expansion and staggering the nails along the top edge of each course so that the 4-inch band that gets covered with lap cement is forced to lie perfectly flat.

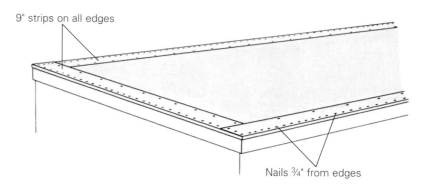

9" strips on all edges

Nails ¾" from edges

1 If necessary, install valley flashing consisting of an 18-inch strip followed by a 36-inch strip. If the sheathing is plywood, install 3-inch edge flashing to protect the edge plies. Cut 9-inch-wide strips and place them along the rakes, nailing ¾ inch from the edge every 4 inches.

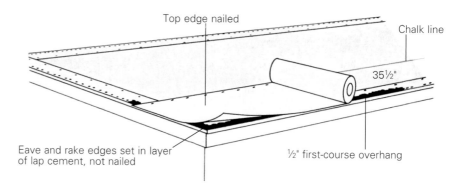

Top edge nailed

Chalk line

35½"

Eave and rake edges set in layer of lap cement, not nailed

½" first-course overhang

2 Snap a chalk line 35½ inches from the eave. Position the first sheet, and nail it across the top every 4 inches. To minimize gaps, stagger the nails along the top edge. Set the bottom and side edges with lap cement.

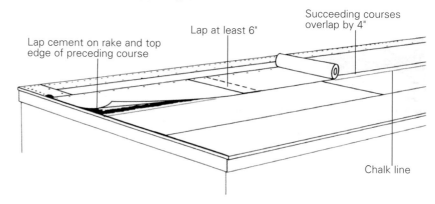

Lap cement on rake and top edge of preceding course

Lap at least 6"

Succeeding courses overlap by 4"

Chalk line

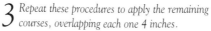

3 Repeat these procedures to apply the remaining courses, overlapping each one 4 inches.

EXPOSED-NAIL APPLICATION

Install preliminary valley flashings and edge flashings as required.

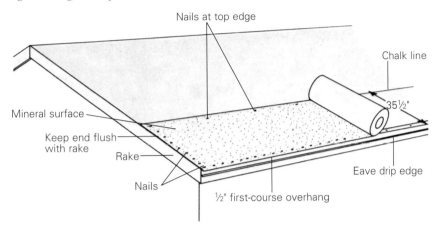

Nails at top edge

Chalk line

35½"

Mineral surface

Keep end flush with rake

Rake

Nails

½" first-course overhang

Eave drip edge

1 Snap a chalk line 35½ inches above the eave. Position the first sheet and tack the top edge every 2 feet. Nail the rake and eave edges every 3 inches, keeping the nails ¾ inch away from the edge.

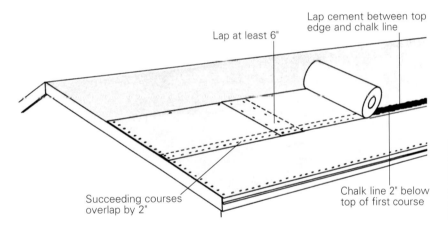

Lap cement between top edge and chalk line

Lap at least 6"

Succeeding courses overlap by 2"

Chalk line 2" below top of first course

2 Snap a chalk line 2 inches below the top of the first course. Tack the upper edge of the second strip. Then spread a 2-inch band of lap cement under the bottom edge. Nail the bottom edge every 2 or 3 inches.

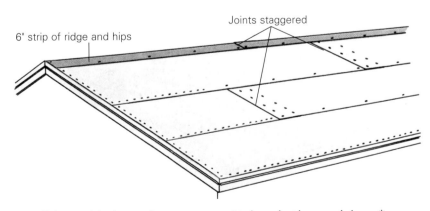

6" strip of ridge and hips

Joints staggered

3 Install the rest of the sheets in the same way, staggering end joints. Overlap end joints by 6 inches and apply cement before nailing every 4 inches in a double row. Add ridge and hip caps.

HIPS AND RIDGES

At hips and ridges, cut the roofing so that it meets but does not overlap at the joint. Snap chalk lines 5½ inches from the hip or ridge on both sides. For exposed-nail applications, spread a 2-inch-wide strip of lap cement from each line back toward the center. Cut a 12-inch strip of roofing the length of the hip or ridge. Bend it to fit the ridge, and nail it in place. For long hips that require more than one strip, work from the bottom up, lapping the top strip over the bottom strip by 6 inches. When using the concealed-nail method, apply lap cement to the entire area between the chalk lines; then embed the 12-inch strip in it. Only use nails in the top two corners.

VENT FLASHING

To flash roof vents, cut a hole in the roofing just large enough for the vent pipe and lay the strip in place. Then install metal vent flashing over the pipe, coating the roofing with mastic first so that the metal flange is embedded in it completely. Nail around the flange every 2 inches.

WORKING IN HOT WEATHER

Walking on roll roofing on a hot day with direct sun can seriously damage the roofing. Therefore, when working on a hot roof, lay down strips of plywood as walking surfaces. The plywood distributes your weight over a greater area, preventing damage even when the roof is hot.

USING PLYCLIPS

Roll roofing has little strength—particularly when it is hot—so it depends on a solid, uniform substrate for support. The most vulnerable spots are the joints between sheets of plywood sheathing. Stepping near the joint produces a shearing action: One edge deflects and the other doesn't.

To minimize this tearing, install plyclips. These little H-shaped extrusions clip onto the adjacent sheathing edges, forcing the two sheets to deflect together. Always install plyclips when you sheath a roof in either plywood or oriented strand board (OSB).

ROOFS

ROOFING WORK

Anyone who has ever been on a roof on a sunny summer day knows that the roof is an extremely hostile environment for building materials. It is a wonder that roofing lasts as long as it does.

The vast majority of residential roofs are covered with asphalt shingles, a material which represents a good balance of fairly low initial costs with moderate durability.

Those who are comfortable walking around on a modestly pitched roof can usually perform simple roof repairs.

However, if you are installing roofing on a new addition or replacing an entire roof, weigh several factors before deciding to do the work yourself. The first is labor costs versus time.

In most cases, the roof must go up quickly in case of rain. To estimate the installation time, allow two hours (if you're inexperienced) for the first square (100 square feet) of shingles, reduced to 1 hour after some experience. Total your time and figure that a professional will do the job in about half that time.

Also consider the type of roofing. Certain roofs, such as tar and gravel, slate, and metal with standing seams, should only be done by professionals. Roll roofing, composition shingles, tile, and wood shingles or shakes can be installed by a handy homeowner who has a little help handling the materials.

CODE REQUIREMENTS: ROOFS

Ventilation:
- Attic and cathedral ceilings without vapor barriers must have ventilation openings equal to $\frac{1}{150}$ of their areas.
- Attic and cathedral ceilings with vapor barriers must have ventilation openings equal to $\frac{1}{300}$ of their areas.
- Ventilation area must be increased by 200% if the vents are covered with $\frac{1}{16}$-inch screen; 225 percent if covered by louvers; 300 percent if covered by both.

Slope and Underlayment:
- Asphalt shingles with slope of at least $\frac{4}{12}$ must be applied over 15-pound felt. Shingles with slopes between $\frac{2}{12}$ and $\frac{4}{12}$ must be applied over two layers of 15-pound felt and be sealed.
- Wood shingles must be sloped greater than $\frac{3}{12}$. Shingles and wood shakes with slope less than $\frac{4}{12}$ must be applied over 15-pound felt or have reduced exposure.

PARTS OF THE ROOF

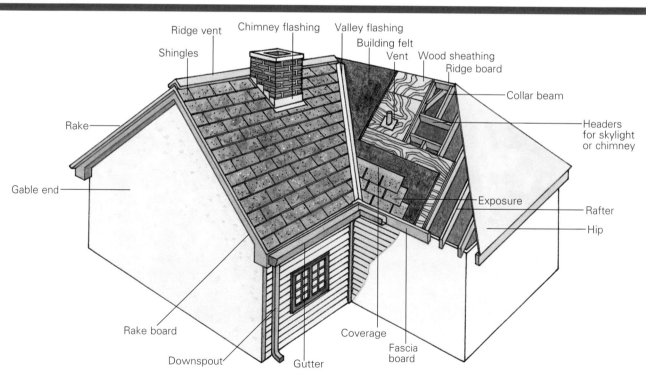

The roof is the first line of defense against rain and other forms of precipitation. Architects refer to the roof as a building's umbrella, but "duck's feathers" is a better term. Unlike an umbrella, a roof is made from hundreds of pieces, all lapped like duck's feathers to shed water.

At the top is the ridge, followed by shingles or sheets of impervious material, overlapped so that any water that falls on the surface flows over each course in turn, until it finally falls off the roof to the ground or into a gutter. Anything that penetrates the roof, such as a vent or chimney, is flashed—sometimes quite ingeniously—to keep the water on the surface of the roof.

The illustration above shows the terms you need to know to discuss roofing materials and construction.

SLOPE

Before you install new materials you need to know the slope of your roof. Slope, sometimes mistakenly called pitch, is the number of inches the roof rises for every 12 inches of horizontal distance. Slope is expressed as "× in 12." The simplest way to measure slope is to place the edge of a board against the roof, level the board with a level, and measure down to the roof from a point on the level exactly 1 foot from its end.

The reason you need to know the roof slope is that roofing materials vary widely in their ability to keep water out at low slopes. For this reason, the Universal Building Code specifies the minimum slope for each:

- Built-up roofing (BUR) 0/12
- Double-coverage 2/12
- Roll roofing 2/12
- Metal panels 2/12
- Asphalt shingles
  double underlayment 2/12
  single underlayment 4/12
- Tile 3/12
- Wood shingles 4/12
- Wood shakes 4/12

With a good pair of rubber-soled athletic shoes, you can generally walk around on a roof pitched up to 6 in 12, although tools start to slide off at around 4 in 12. However, keep safety first. No repair is worth a fall. Use a safety line that runs over the ridge and is firmly anchored on the other side. As you work, have a helper adjust any slack in the line, retrieve necessary tools, and pass materials up so you can keep movements to a minimum.

At slopes steeper than 6 in 12, roofing installation is difficult—especially if there are a number of dormers, hips, and valleys. Either hire professionals for such a roof or plan on a long and tedious job.

WHAT'S THE PITCH?

The slope of a roof is the total rise divided by the run of the rafters. The pitch of a roof is the total rise divided by the total span of the roof. So, for the ordinary gable roof, pitch is half of slope.

PREPARATION

First you'll need to know how much roofing to order. The most accurate way to estimate the area of your roof is to take measurements on the roof itself, then calculate the total square footage. If the roof is steep or complex, however, you can get a good estimate from the ground. Measure the ground-floor area of the house and add the area of eaves and overhangs. To account for the slope, multiply the total by the appropriate coverage factor from the table, right.

You will need at least one sturdy ladder and roof jacks if the slope is steeper than 6 in 12. Prepare for rain with plastic tarps or a roll or two of plastic sheeting. Wear soft-soled shoes, such as sneakers, rather than shoes with hard rubber soles that might damage the roofing. Most roofing can be laid with a hammer, tape measure, chalk line, utility knife, and flat bar. Buy a roofer's hatchet if you are installing wood shingles or shakes.

If you plan to install your own roofing, have the materials delivered to the roof. A 2,000-square-foot roof will require over 4,000 pounds of shingles—more than sixty 70-pound packages. Having them delivered to

AREA MULTIPLIERS FOR SLOPED ROOFS

Slope (in 12)	Multiplier
1	1.01
2	1.02
3	1.04
4	1.06
5	1.09
6	1.12
7	1.16
8	1.21
9	1.25
10	1.31
11	1.36
12	1.42

the ridge saves your back and 60 risky trips up a ladder. Even better—there is usually no charge for the delivery! Shop around until you find a supplier who has the equipment. Make sure, however, that you have removed the old shingles and properly prepared the roof before the delivery!

REMOVING OLD ROOFING

If you are roofing over existing shingles, check to see how many applications are already installed. Most building codes allow a total of two existing roof thicknesses, plus one new. To determine how many your roof has, inspect the edge at the gable end. Each application consists of two-plus layers. If there is only one application and it is not made of shakes, you can reroof over it.

If the new application will put your roof over the "layer limit," or if you're installing a heavy material such as tile, tear off all of the old roofing before installing the new.

To remove old asphalt shingles, first rent a debris box and specify delivery under the center of one eave to minimize the distance you have to carry the old shingles.

Starting at the ridge and working your way down, scrape off all the roofing, including underlayment, with flat, serrated roofing shovels. Pitch the debris into the debris box. This is a perfect job for enthusiastic helpers with very strong backs and no fear of heights.

Line the ground around the base of the house with tarps or drop cloths to catch scraps, nails, and other debris that misses the box. After the job is complete, fold up the cloths and shake them off in the debris box.

▶

ROOFING MATERIALS

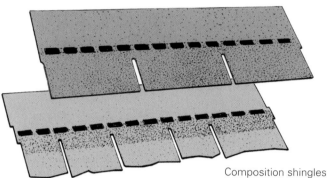

Composition shingles

COMPOSITION SHINGLES

Composition shingles, also called asphalt shingles, come in a wide array of colors, weights, tab sizes, textures, and edge configurations. The most common are three-tab shingles, which are 12 inches wide and 36 inches long. Shingle weight and the fabric used for the central core determine durability. Shingles weigh from 215 to 300 pounds per square (100 square feet installed) and last from 15 to 30 years. The most durable have a fiberglass—rather than felt—core. Fiberglass core shingles also have a Class A fire rating (felt shingles are Class C), and are required by some local building codes.

Laminated fiberglass/asphalt shingles (also known as dimensional, heavyweight, or architectural shingles) are gaining popularity. The exposed lower half of each shingle is double thickness, designed to create shadow lines or to imitate random wood shingles. Because of their double thickness, they last up to 40 years and are, naturally, more expensive than standard shingles.

Most shingles have strips of roofing cement to seal the tabs of the course applied above them. After the shingle is installed, the heat of the sun melts the cement and bonds the shingles.

ROLL ROOFING

Roll roofing is essentially the same material as composition (asphalt) shingles but comes in installed 36-foot rolls. It doesn't last as long as composition roofing because it is installed in only one layer, compared to the three layers created by overlapping shingles.

There are two basic types of roll roofing: full-width mineral-surface, and selvage. Ninety-pound mineral-surface roll roofing is 3 feet wide and is installed with a 2-inch overlap so it covers one square. It also can be used as flashing and is commonly put in valleys under metal flashing.

Selvage rolls are also 3 feet wide, but are installed with a 19-inch overlap, so it takes two rolls to cover a square.

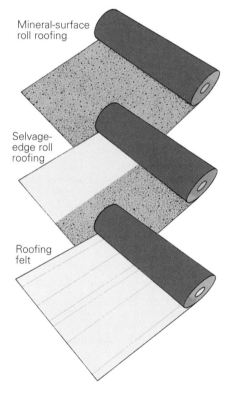

Mineral-surface roll roofing

Selvage-edge roll roofing

Roofing felt

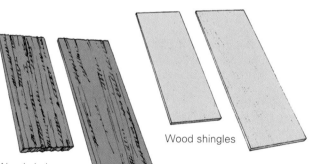

Wood shingles

Wood shakes

WOOD SHINGLES AND SHAKES

Natural wood shingles, applied correctly, can last 40 years or more—longer than the best asphalt shingles. They are also expensive. Shingles are smaller, thinner, and lighter than shakes, and are sawn on both sides. Shakes are split by hand; some are resawn or flat on one side only.

Shingles and shakes are graded by number: 1 (the best), 2, and 3. Use only number 1 shingles on roofs, because they are decay-resistant heartwood and free of knots.

Your local fire code may require fire-retardant treated shingles.

WOOD-FIBER SHINGLES

Resembling wood shingles, wood-fiber shingles are made of compressed and glued hardboard and come in 4-foot panels. They are much less expensive than wood shingles and shakes, but are typically guaranteed for 25 years. The panels install quickly because they cover a large area at once, and they have alignment marks that make it unnecessary to measure each course.

ROOFING FELT

This tar-impregnated paper, also known as tar paper, is used for underlayment with such materials as composition shingles, shakes, and tile. The 36-inch wide rolls are classified by weight per square, usually 15 pound or 30 pound. One roll covers either two or four squares, depending on the weight.

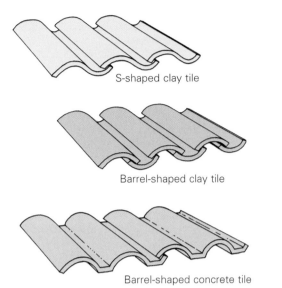
S-shaped clay tile

Barrel-shaped clay tile

Barrel-shaped concrete tile

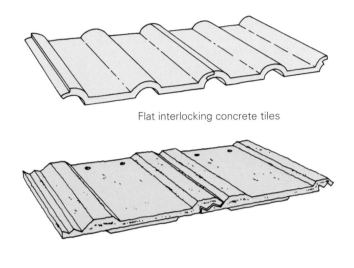
Flat interlocking concrete tiles

CLAY AND CONCRETE TILES

Traditional clay-tile roofs have long been the standard of a durable, attractive—and heavy—roof, outlasting many of the houses on which they were installed. But clay tiles are now being challenged by concrete tiles. Concrete tiles are lighter (750 to 900 pounds per square, compared with over 1,000 pounds), cost less, and are easier to install than clay because each one is molded with a ridge on the back that simply hooks over spaced sheathing.

Concrete tiles come in many shapes: flat, barrel shaped, or in forms resembling wood shakes. They also come in a wide range of colors, from traditional reds and browns to glazed surfaces of bright blue, red, or green.

If you are installing clay tile on a roof that previously had a lightweight covering, you may need to reinforce the roof with additional framing, purlins or doubled rafters to take the extra weight. Some tile distributors will send out a sales consultant to evaluate the roof for suitability. Virtually any new roof built to today's code, however, can easily handle the weight of concrete tile.

METAL ROOFS

Metal roofs are experiencing a revival. Unlike the shiny or tarred, corrugated barn roofs of the past, the new metal roofs are attractive, durable, and practical for many homes. The most durable roofs are flat sheets joined by a standing seam and should be installed by professionals, but there are standing-seam look-alikes that are easily installed by the competent homeowner. Other aluminum or steel materials resemble shingles and shakes; they should also be installed by professionals. One particular metal roof made in Sweden is strong enough to span between rafters without wood sheathing. This saves one complete step in building a new roof.

BUILT-UP ROOF (BUR)

Used primarily on flat—or nearly-flat—roofs, this kind of roof is made of alternating layers or roofing felt and hot tar. The top layer of tar is covered with a layer of light-colored gravel to prevent direct sunlight from evaporating the solvents in the tar. When a built-up roof begins to leak, usually in 15 to 20 years, another one can be put directly over it, to a maximum of three roofs.

COLD-MOP ROOFING

Cold-mop roofing is an inexpensive version of built-up roof, but it is less effective than hot tar. The material is

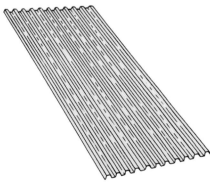
Corrugated steel panel

a liquid with an asphalt base. It does not have to be heated because it lacks the clays and other hardening agents that are part of a hot-tar roof. This type of roofing is little used today except for repair work; standard roofing materials such as composition shingles, shakes, and tile are better choices.

ELASTOMERIC ROOFING MEMBRANES

Many roofing systems have been developed for commercial and industrial use that can solve thorny residential applications, such as a flat roof over a deck. Most are tough membranes that are applied in liquid form or as solid sheets. They are usually applied in stages—a primer coat plus two or three follow-up coats. These proprietary systems are typically installed only by licensed roofing contractors. Consult the Yellow Pages for the names of companies in your area.

▶

SHEATHING

SPACED SHEATHING

Spaced sheathing is used under wood shakes and shingles because it allows the surface material to breath and dry out. If you're laying shingles or shakes, nail 1×4s directly to the rafters with an on-center spacing equal to the surface exposure. For example, wood shingles with a 5-inch exposure (the part of the shingle exposed to the weather), requires sheathing spaced exactly 5 inches on-center to catch the roofing nails.

Where appearance is important, use attractive starter boards, such as V-rustic, for the eaves and rakes, or install a soffit underneath. On shingle and shake roofs, cover the 18 inches just below the ridge with solid boards to provide an adequate nailing surface.

PLYWOOD SHEATHING

Plywood sheathing provides a smooth base for composition shingles and roll roofing. It is also used with spaced sheathing on roofs that require diagonal strength or under tile to provide a solid wind barrier.

Use ½-inch plywood sheathing for rafter spacings of 16 and 24 inches. Install the panels perpendicular to the rafters and leave ⅛-inch gaps at all edges to allow for expansion. Stagger the end joints by 4 feet.

Special "plyclips" are available to lock the panel edges together between rafters. Nail plywood with 8d nails spaced every 6 inches along the edges and 12 inches in the center.

TONGUE-AND-GROOVE SHEATHING

If the sheathing will be visible from inside the house, as it is in cathedral ceilings, use tongue-and-groove roof decking—1×6s or 1×8s for 16- and 24-inch rafter spacings and 2×6s for spacings of 32 and 48 inches.

Install the first board along the eaves with the tongue edge facing toward the ridge. Use a 2-foot scrap piece of tongue-and-groove as a hammering block to knock boards into place. Stagger butt joints so that they do not line up over the same rafter, and leave ¹⁄₁₆ inch at each joint for expansion. Some decking is made with tongue-and-groove ends as well, so you can place butt joints anywhere.

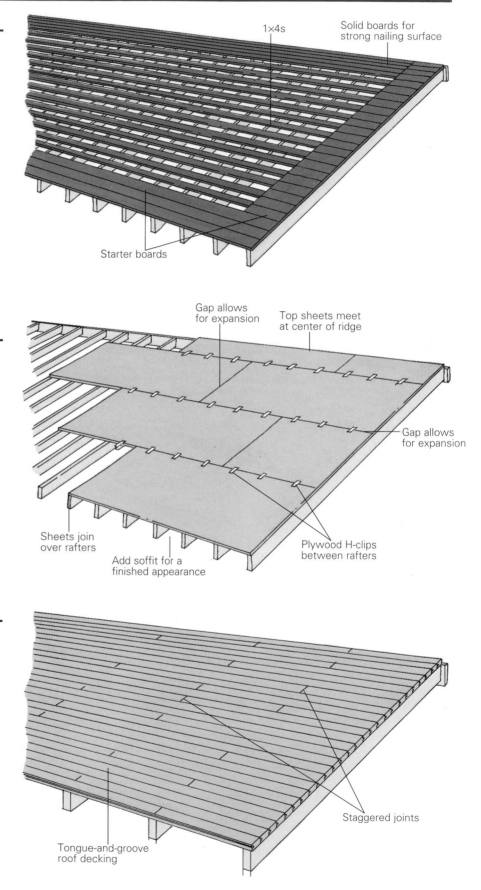

1×4s

Solid boards for strong nailing surface

Starter boards

Gap allows for expansion

Top sheets meet at center of ridge

Gap allows for expansion

Sheets join over rafters

Add soffit for a finished appearance

Plywood H-clips between rafters

Staggered joints

Tongue-and-groove roof decking

VENTILATION AND ICE DAMS

THE PROBLEM

When a house suffers from ice dams, most homeowners regard them as inevitable. They tack up heating cables to melt the ice or climb ladders to hack at the buildup with hatchets. If ice dams are inevitable, why do some roofs not have them? The whole secret is in ventilation.

Study the illustration (right) showing how the ice dam forms, blow by blow.

First it snows. Snow is, surprisingly, a very good insulator. Assuming it's as good an insulator as the attic insulation, it helps keep the temperature halfway between the outside temperature of 0 degrees F and the inside 70 degrees F, or 35 degrees F. That's warm enough to begin melting snow on the roof. Meltwater flows down the roof toward the eave, but when it reaches the uninsulated eave it encounters roof that is more like 0 degrees F, where it freezes. As this process continues the ice at the eave continually builds up, eventually forming a dam.

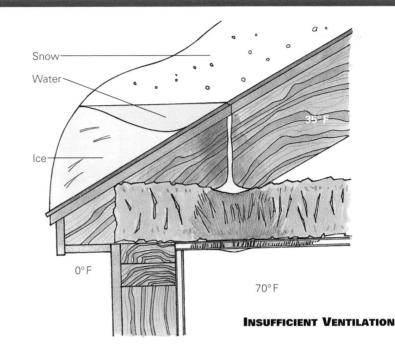

Snow

Water

Ice

35°F

0°F

70°F

INSUFFICIENT VENTILATION

So far no harm has been done and the homeowner is probably unaware of the events unfolding. As soon as the meltwater backs up beyond the top of the first row of shingles, however, leaks can occur. The water flows down through the roof sheathing and the attic insulation, soaking the plaster or wall board of the ceiling. Suddenly, water is dripping from the ceiling; water is running down the walls; the wallpaper and paint are both peeling.

THE CURE

Of course a homeowner can shovel the snow off the roof, install heating cables at the eave to melt the ice dam, or go up a ladder with a hatchet and chop the ice off. But why not fix the problem once and for all? What is needed is roof ventilation.

By installing screened soffit vents at the bottom, ridge or gable vents at the top, and baffles to prevent the insulation at the eave from blocking the natural air flow, we can force the temperature of the roof sheathing to be the same as the outdoor air everywhere. As a result, the snow will no longer melt or, if it does, will not freeze when it reaches the eave. Voila! No more ice dams!

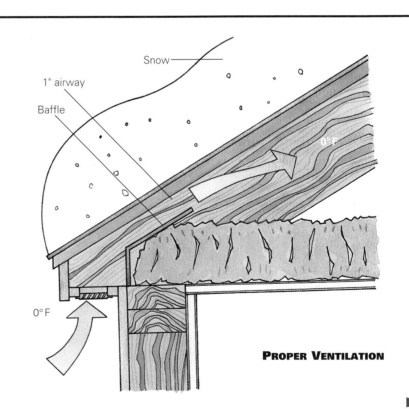

Snow

1" airway

Baffle

0°F

0°F

PROPER VENTILATION

ROOF REPAIRS

INSPECTING THE ROOF

Inspect your roof once a year, looking for cracked shingles, rusted flashing, open joints, or brittle mastic. The prime problem areas are valleys and chimneys. Other likely places to find defects are ridges, hips, vent flashing, and other flashings.

Naturally, if your roof is very high or very steep, you may be reluctant to conduct an on-site inspection. Fortunately, you can conduct just as effective an inspection from inside the attic—particularly on a rainy day. Any serious leaks will be seen coming through the roof sheathing overhead.

SPOTTING A LEAK

Rarely does a leak in the ceiling come from a spot directly above it. With access to the attic, you can trace the leak. Mark the rafter with bright chalk where the water is coming through the roof, so that you can go back during better weather and poke a long nail or straightened coat hanger up through the sheathing. If you cannot search for the leak during a storm, have someone spray the roof with a hose while you look for the leak.

SEALING VALLEYS

Valleys require special attention because so much water rushes into them during any rainfall. There are two types: Closed valleys conceal the underlying metal flashing with shingles. Open valleys leave the flashing exposed.

Closed Valleys: In some valleys the shingles butt together to conceal the metal flashing. This method is not as effective as a full-lace valley because water can rush down one side of the roof fast enough to overshoot the valley and seep under the shingles on the opposite side.

To repair leaks, slip diamond-shaped pieces of flashing under each course of shingles, starting at the bottom. Cut the few nails you run into with a hacksaw blade. Nail each shingle and seal the nailheads with mastic.

Open Valleys: First, clean all debris from the valley. Then make sure the existing roofing material is cut in a smooth, straight line on each side and that the distance between the shingles widens from ridge to eave at a rate of ⅛ inch per foot of valley on each side. Trim the shingles straight and to the required separation, if necessary. Then lift the shingles, one by one, and coat the area where they lie on the valley with roofing cement. Next, use a cartridge gun to run a bead of roofing cement down the valley next to the shingles. If the shingles are made of wood or other inflexible material, run a bead of roofing cement down the edges.

Shingles butted

Slide diamond-shaped pieces of aluminum under shingles. Overlap at least 2"

Bead of roofing cement   Roofing cement

COMPOSITION SHINGLES

Pick a warm day to repair composition shingles so they will lift and bend easily. If you must do the repair on a cold day, warm the shingles with a heat gun so they won't crack.

Broken Shingles:
1. Pry out nails.

3. Cut notches in the new shingle to match any nail tears in the old one.

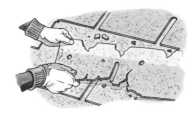

2. Pull out the damaged shingle.

4. Slide the new shingle into place and nail it.

Cracks: Fill cracks with roofing cement.

Curled edges: Put roofing cement under curled edges.

BUILT-UP ROOFING

BUR roofs can develop air blisters that eventually leak. Repair them by slitting the blisters down the middle, inserting roofing cement, and patching.

HOLES

1. Clean off gravel. Remove the damaged portion, and fill with roofing cement.

2. Cut one patch to fit the hole and one 6 inches larger all around.

3. Nail smaller patch, cover it with cement, and nail larger patch on top.

4. Cover larger patch with roofing cement and replace the gravel.

VENT FLASHING REPLACEMENT

1. Remove old flashing and one or two shingles above the vent. Slide new flashing underneath.

2. Nail flashing in place. Place nails where they will be covered by shingles.

3. Replace shingles. Seal joint between flashing and vent with roofing cement or caulking.

WOOD SHINGLES OR SHAKES

Repair a bowed shingle by carefully splitting a thin strip out of the middle with a sharp utility knife. Make sure the new split is not directly over a joint in the underlying course.

When replacing several rows of shingles, remove the top course first and work down. Install the

replacement shingles from the bottom up. If necessary, cut nails with a hacksaw.
1. Pull out damaged shingle, and saw off nails with a hacksaw blade.
2. Slide in a new shingle and nail it. Cover nails with roofing cement.

SAFETY

PRIORITY NUMBER ONE

Even if you're not considering a home renovation for stylistic reasons, you should take a safety inventory and make improvements to keep your house safe. Some hazards, such as fire, electrical shock, or falls are obvious and can be identified with a quick home inspection. Locating and removing others, such as asbestos, radon, and lead paint, are not so obvious (see Hazardous Substances, page 176) and may require the assistance of professionals.

Use the checklist below to perform your own inspection. Include all family members in your tour. Keep in mind that the most common home accident is a fall and that two thirds of all home fires start in the kitchen. Many problems can be rectified immediately. Others, such as installing lights, should move to the top of your to-do list.

HOME SAFETY CHECK LIST

To evaluate your family's overall safety at home, review specific areas individually. Each room has a distinctive list of safety considerations.

ENTRANCE

■ Is the floor slippery?
■ Are rugs secure or do they have non-skid backings?
■ Is the lighting adequate?

STAIRS

■ Is there light over the stairs, with switches top and bottom?
■ Are railings secure and installed no higher than 32 inches above the risers?
■ Is there a second, low rail for children?
■ Are balusters spaced 4 inches maximum?
■ Are the stairs free of clutter?
■ Is there a smoke detector at the top? Are risers no more than 7½ inches high? Are treads at least 9 inches deep?
■ Does a door open over the stairway? If so, the door should be 3 feet from the top stair or reversed to swing away from the stairwell.

LIVING/FAMILY ROOM AND DEN

■ Are there any one-step changes in floor level? If so, are they marked prominently with a change of flooring material or with accent lighting?
■ Do all windows within 18 inches of the floor have tempered or safety glass?
■ On stairs, is there a second, lower handrail for the children?
■ Does the fireplace have a fire screen or glass doors?
■ Are all guns unloaded and stored in a locked cabinet?

CODE REQUIREMENTS

Smoke Detectors:
■ Smoke detectors must be installed in every sleeping room and outside sleeping rooms in the vicinity of the sleeping areas.
■ There must be a smoke detector on every floor of a building, including the basement, but not an uninhabitable attic.
■ In new construction, smoke detectors must be line-powered with a battery backup; in old construction, battery power is acceptable.
■ In new construction, all smoke detectors must be interconnected.
■ Whenever work on a building requires a permit, smoke detectors must be installed throughout the building, although they are not required to be interconnected, nor line-powered.

Bedroom Egress:
■ Every sleeping room must have at least one openable window or exterior door approved for escape, openable without a key or special tool.
■ Egress windows must have a minimum net clear opening of 5.7 square feet (5.0 for grade-level windows), minimum net clear width of 20 inches, minimum net clear height of 22 inches, and maximum sill height above floor of 44 inches.

■ Is there an accessible fire extinguisher near the fireplace?
■ Does the fireplace hearth extend at least 20 inches into the room and 12 inches to the sides? (Fireplaces of less than 6 square feet opening must extend 16 inches in and 8 inches to sides.)
■ Has the chimney been cleaned within the past year?
■ If there is a wood-burning stove, has it been inspected?
■ Are there enough electrical outlets?
■ Do extension cords avoid runs under carpet or across doorways?
■ Are all valuables stored in a fireproof safe?
■ Are ashtrays convenient?
■ Are light bulbs the correct wattage for each fixture? Use 60-watt bulbs if you're not sure.
■ Are dangling electrical cords tied up beyond a child's reach?
■ Are tippy lamps and furniture secure?
■ Do electrical receptacles have childproof sockets?

■ Are any houseplants poisonous?
■ Are choking hazards—things small enough for a child's throat—removed?

HALLWAYS

■ Is there adequate lighting, with switches at both ends of the hall?
■ Is the hallway free of clutter?
■ Are rugs secure or made with non-skid backings?

KITCHEN

■ Are key telephone numbers (emergency, family doctor, poison control center) posted by the phone?
■ Is a Class B:C fire extinguisher handy, visible, and up to pressure? (It should not be next to the cooktop.)
■ Have curtains above or behind the cooktop been removed?
■ Can you grab utensils easily without reaching over the cooktop?
■ Are large lids available close to the cooktop for smothering a grease fire?
■ Are the cooktop controls childproof?

■ Is the cooktop away from doors that swing inward and windows that open over it?

■ Is a smoke detector positioned between the kitchen and living areas?

■ Are main traffic paths out of the way from the main work area?

■ Are floors and work surfaces well lighted?

■ Do you have a first-aid kit?

■ Are tablecloths that toddlers might pull removed from tables?

■ Are cleaning supplies and other dangerous materials kept in locked storage cabinets?

■ Do cabinet doors and drawers have childproof latches?

■ Are electrical outlets next to the sink GFCI-protected?

■ Are sharp tools (knives, scissors) stored out of reach?

■ Are matches and other lighters stored out of reach?

■ Is there a play space for toddlers close to the kitchen, but not in the main work area?

BATHROOMS

■ Does the bathtub have a nonskid bottom?

■ Do electrical outlets have GFCIs?

■ Are light and fan switches beyond reach from the tub or shower?

■ Do rugs have nonskid backing?

■ If there is a portable heater, is it approved for "wet" locations?

■ Does the shower door have safety glazing (tempered, laminated, or hard plastic)?

■ Are the towel racks securely mounted?

■ Does the tub or shower have an anti-scald faucet?

■ Does the shower have a grab bar?

■ Can the door be unlocked from the outside with a nail or common object?

■ Does the medicine cabinet have a locked section?

■ Does each toilet lid have a latch?

BEDROOMS

■ Does each bedroom have safe egress—an openable window with a clear opening at least 20 inches wide and 22 inches high and a sill within 44 inches of the floor?

■ Does each second-story bedroom have a second escape?

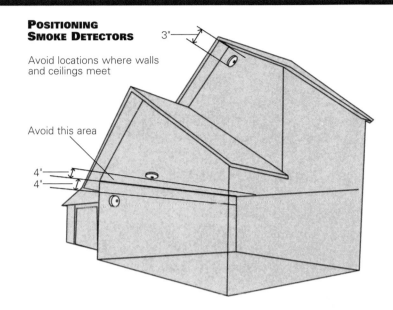

POSITIONING SMOKE DETECTORS

Avoid locations where walls and ceilings meet

Avoid this area

3"

4"
4"

■ Is the path to safety clear of clutter, for quick exit in the dark?

■ Is a lamp or wall switch within reach of each bed?

■ Are flashlights within reach of beds?

■ Is smoking in bed prohibited?

■ Does the phone have emergency numbers displayed or stored?

■ Are the smoke detectors working? (Have at least one per floor, outside sleeping areas; test monthly with smoke and replace batteries yearly.)

■ Is the crib safe (no "doodads" on top of corners; slats no more than 2⅜ inches apart; lead-free paint; mattress fits snugly against sides; bumper pads around the inside of the crib, attached by snaps)?

■ Are windows childproof (cannot be opened more than 5 inches and no climbable furniture nearby)?

■ Are bath and bedroom light switches low enough for a child to reach?

GARAGE/BASEMENT

■ Does the automatic garage door have a safety reverse?

■ Is the floor dry? Free of debris?

■ Are gasoline and flammables stored in approved containers?

■ Are they stored away from appliances with pilot lights?

■ Is a fire extinguisher handy?

■ Are ladders safe and solid?

■ Are appliance pilot lights at least 18 inches above the floor?

■ Is the area around furnace free of combustible material?

■ Does the furnace have adequate air intake and flue?

■ Is the dryer vent clean?

■ Is the area behind the dryer free of lint and rubbish?

■ Is the water heater temperature no higher than 120 degrees if children or older persons live in the home?

■ Does everyone know how to shut off gas and electricity to the house?

■ Are outlets in the unfinished basement GFCI-protected?

■ Is a smoke detector installed in the basement?

■ If the electrical service involves a fuse box, are any fuses the wrong size, and are extra fuses of the right amperage handy?

■ Are workshop areas well lit?

■ Do workshop areas have enough receptacles? GFCI protection?

■ Are power tools locked up?

■ Are hazardous materials locked up?

OUTSIDE

■ Do all electrical receptacles have GFCI protection?

■ Are walkways, entrances, and steps well lighted?

■ Do decks and stairs higher than 30 inches have railings?

■ Are spaces between deck-railing members no wider than 4 inches?

■ Is the swimming pool or spa fenced, with a door alarm on patio doors?

■ Are any of the plants poisonous to eat?

SCREENS

FIRST IMPRESSIONS

ALSO SEE...
Doors:
Pages 86–97
Windows:
Pages 432–441

A screen door in need of repair makes your home look frayed around the edges. And a ripped screen door is nearly as bad as no door at all for keeping bugs at bay.

Screen doors are fragile compared with solid-core or sliding glass doors and—with everyday use—screening will tear, break, sag, or simply come out. But repair is easy. The only skill required to replace screen material is knowing how to get the new screening smooth and taut.

SCREEN MATERIALS AND SIZES

Screen for windows and doors is manufactured from many different materials: fiberglass, nylon, polyethylene, galvanized steel, stainless steel, aluminum, and bronze. Most of the products sold by home centers, however, are fiberglass or aluminum.

If you are concerned about quality and longevity, special order bronze screen (you may have to order a full 100-foot roll) from your local lumberyard or hardware store.

Hardware stores and home centers sell screen by the square foot, usually from rolls that are 24, 30, 36, 42, 48, 60, and 72 inches wide. Standard mesh sizes are 16×16, 18×14, and 18×16 wires per inch, but a retailer is likely to stock just one size. The higher the number of wires per inch, the tighter the screen. All mesh sizes keep most insects out, but if your area is home to pesky, nearly invisible black flies, make sure you buy 18×16 or 18×14 material.

When you replace a screen, be certain that you are not combining metals that are incompatible. Dissimilar metals will corrode quickly.

Use either fiberglass or aluminum screen with aluminum doors, not bronze or galvanized steel. If you attach screen to a wood door frame, use copper nails for bronze screen, aluminum nails for aluminum screen, and galvanized nails for galvanized screen. Use staples on fiberglass or galvanized screen only if they are corrosion resistant or protected from direct exposure to the weather.

FIBERGLASS SCREEN

Fiberglass screen (in gray or black) is the most flexible and the easiest screen to work with. It is not as durable as metal screen, but is the least

expensive. Most homeowners prefer black because it is nearly invisible in place and is the easiest to see through.

GALVANIZED SCREEN

Galvanized screen is the least expensive metal screen and the least resistant to corrosion. When new, it is very strong, but the zinc coating wears off fairly quickly, allowing the steel to rust and cause stains.

ALUMINUM SCREEN

Slightly more expensive than fiberglass, aluminum screen is stronger and almost as resistant to corrosion. The wire consists of a high-strength, alloy core coated with a more corrosion-resistant aluminum.

Aluminum will corrode near salt water and tends to turn a dark color in smoggy areas. In most cases, soapy water cleans it effectively.

BRONZE SCREEN

Bronze screen is the most expensive and the most durable. It is available with one of two finishes: bright or antique (dark brown). A coat of varnish covers the finish and prevents staining, but it wears off in a few years. At that point, the screen may stain the floor or nearby surface. A new coat of varnish or lacquer will renew the screens. If you coat bronze screens, thin the coating so it will not clog the spaces.

REPAIRING TEARS

SMALL TEARS

For tears less than an inch long in any type of screening:
■ Restore the strands or wires to their untorn positions.
■ Smear model airplane cement over the torn area.
■ Quickly poke holes through the cement film to clear the holes. (Have a box of toothpicks on hand.)

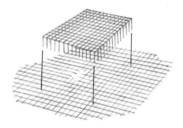

LARGE TEARS IN METAL

■ Cut a patch of the same type of screening large enough to cover the tear.
■ Placing the patch over a sharp, square edge, bend the wire ends of the patch down at a right angle.
■ Carefully position the patch so that the wire ends line up with holes in the screen, and push down.
■ Bend the patch wires over to secure the patch.

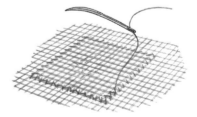

LARGE TEARS IN FIBERGLASS

■ Cut a patch of the same type of screening large enough to cover the tear.
■ Position the patch over the tear.
■ Use a tapestry sewing needle and thin nylon fishing line to lace the patch to the screen.

REPLACING STAPLED SCREENING

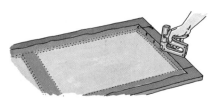

1. Start by removing the door. Lay planks over a pair of sawhorses and lay the door on the planks.

Pry up the molding around the screen, being careful not to break it. (It's not costly to replace, just aggravating. If you break it, purchase screen bead or quarter-round—whichever matches the type on your door.)

2. Use a small screwdriver or the corner of a putty knife to remove the staples holding the old screen.

3. Cut a new piece of screen so it overlaps the opening by at least 1 inch all around. Attach the screen across the bottom edge of the door, using a staple gun. Be sure the screen is straight and the staples are snug.

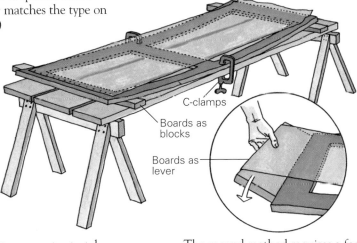

C-clamps
Boards as blocks
Boards as lever

4. Staple the sides, then the other end of the screen.

There are two ways to stretch screening. The easiest is to bow the door by placing sticks under each end of the door and clamping the middle down to the planks. Staple the top of the screen in place, release the tension slowly, then staple both sides. Do not staple the center rail until last. Trim the excess screen with a sharp utility knife and replace the molding.

The second method requires a foot of extra screen at the top. With the door flat, butt a 1×6 or 2×6 against the top of the door frame, tilt the board up at about 30 degrees, pull the screening over the raised edge of the board, and staple the screening to it. Push the board flat to stretch the screen tight, and staple the screen to the top of the door frame.

5. Replace the molding over the edge of the screen, covering the staples.

REPLACING TUBULAR-SPLINED SCREENING

Screening on an aluminum screen door or window is held in place by flexible rubber or vinyl splines that fit into channels.

To remove the old screen, use a screwdriver to pry a corner of the spline from its channel. Pull the spline straight up and out. Be careful so you can reuse the spline material. Cut replacement screening 1 inch larger all around than the opening in the frame.

Using the convex wheel of a spline roller, press the screening loosely into

the channel. Press one end of the spline into the corner, then, with the spline roller's concave wheel, roll the remaining spine, pressing the screening tightly into the channel. Keeping the door square, work your way up one side with the spline and all the way around the door. The combination of pressure from the tool and the spline compressing into the channel will stretch the screen taut. Trim off the excess screen with a utility knife.

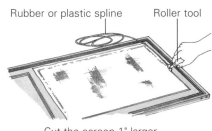

Rubber or plastic spline   Roller tool

Cut the screen 1" larger than the opening

293

Security

CAUTION: BURGLARS AT WORK

ALSO SEE...

Doors:
Pages 86–97
Glazings:
Pages 164–167
Lighting:
Pages 212–219
Locks:
Pages 220–221
Windows:
Pages 432–441
Wire:
Pages 442–445

Most of our impressions of burglars are images formed largely by movies and television. After all, how many of us have actually met a burglar, much less seen one at work? Contrary to what we see on the screen, most burglars don't operate exclusively at night and they don't use high-tech equipment to drill through safes.

What they rely on is their understanding of human nature—that most of us are creatures of habit, following the same routine day after day; that we don't think it strange to see a person dressed as a repairman walking in broad daylight around a neighbor's house; that most of us forget to lock a window or two and even, occasionally, the back door; and that most of us keep jewelry in the bedroom, rather than a safe.

About half of all burglaries occur in broad daylight between 8 a.m. and 5 p.m. Why shouldn't they? That's when a house is most likely to be empty.

Front doors are not attacked if there is any other option, because front doors are usually visible from the street.

In more than 40 percent of burglaries, there is no forced entry. When forced entry does occur, it is usually accomplished by kicking in a door or destroying a lock cylinder with a pry bar or large wrench. Once inside, burglars head straight for the master bedroom, because this is where they expect to find valuables such as jewelry and cash.

Your best defense is plain common sense. Knowing that burglars are logical will help you defend your castle, utilizing the tricks—and some of the equipment—described here.

HOME SECURITY CHECKLIST

■ Are there any areas of deep shadow next to your house?
■ Do shrubs offer thieves a hiding place next to a window or door?
■ Do tree limbs offer thieves access to second-story windows?
■ If you have just moved, have you changed the locks?
■ Does your answering machine indicate when you will be home and away?
■ Have you hidden any keys under the doormat or under a flower pot?
■ Are all of your windows locked securely?

■ Do you have exterior lights that are activated by infrared or motion sensors?
■ Does everyone in your home know what to do in case of a break-in?
■ Does your community have a Neighborhood Watch program?
■ Have you engraved IDs on your valuables?
■ Are your ladders locked away so a thief can't use them?
■ Do you have automatic timers on some inside lights when you go away?
■ When you go away, do you have mail and newspaper deliveries stopped?

LANDSCAPING

To gain entry into your home, a thief has to go through a door or window. If the door or window is locked, he will have to do something which will invite the neighbors' attention, such as force the door with a crowbar, break a window, or put a ladder up to a second-story window.

If you provide cover for him at the window or door, such as high bushes, or an almost totally dark side of the house, he will thank you and take advantage of your hospitality.

To make sure you haven't inadvertently aided a thief:
■ Trim all high bushes anywhere near the house.
■ Install flood lights activated by motion detectors on dark sides of the house, and make sure bushes don't block the light.
■ Cut down tree limbs that are heavy enough to support a thief and close enough to allow access to a second-story window.

LIGHTING

In spite of the fact that most burglaries are committed during the day, outdoor lighting is still a worthwhile deterrent. Many daytime burglaries occur only after the burglar discovered the location of an unlocked door or window on a previous night. Security lighting prevents such prowling.

You don't need bright searchlights to deter a burglar. Pick a lighting system suitable for all of your outdoor needs: a variety of intensities coming from a variety of sources. The key is to eliminate areas of deep shadow near the house.

There also is no need for your yard to resemble a mall parking lot all night. Inexpensive floodlights activated by motion—and very slight motion at that—are available at home centers. After a short duration, usually between two and 10 minutes, they shut off automatically.

Such lights are also a convenience. They automatically light the path from the street to your door, or from your car to your back door. Install several of these double-bulb floodlights at the peak of the house, at the peak of the garage, even on a big tree in the yard. And wire them to switches in the house so you can turn them on and off manually.

RECORDED INVITATIONS

Never leave a recorded phone message stating that you are away on vacation. Instead say, "We're not able to come to the phone right now, but ..."

NOT CLEVER ENOUGH

No matter how clever you think you are, never leave a hidden key outside your home. Thieves have seen it all—after all, it's their business.

DOOR LOCKS

CYLINDER LOCK

Also known as the key-in-knob lock, a cylinder lock is the least expensive and, therefore, most common lock of all. Unfortunately, it is also the easiest to jimmy. The latch is beveled so that it will automatically retract when the door closes. The only tool a thief needs is something stiff and thin enough to slip between the door and the casing—in other words, a credit card.

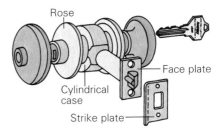

Rose
Face plate
Cylindrical case
Strike plate

PROTECT YOUR VALUABLES

Provide extra protection for valuables such as jewelry, keys, art objects, and silverware. Buy a good fireproof home vault that is too heavy for a thief to carry away. Engrave your ID on all electronic equipment, power tools, and other valuables. Your police department can loan you an engraving tool, or you may be able to buy one cooperatively with your Neighborhood Watch group.

CREATIVE ILLUSIONS

Make it look like someone is at home when you go away:
- Leave a car in the driveway.
- Have a neighbor empty your mailbox. and pick up your newspaper every day.
- Leave a radio playing loudly.
- Set timer switches to turn on several lights and a television at night.

NEIGHBORHOOD WATCH

Neighborhood Watch is a national volunteer organization that has proven to be extremely effective. Thieves are not as likely to hit a neighborhood where the residents have been trained to identify and report suspicious behavior. Contact your local police department for information about starting a program in your area.

What about a dog to keep burglars away? Experts agree that they help to deter intruders, but unless they are trained, they generally make poor security guards. Thieves who know how to handle dogs can generally "disarm" the ordinary household pet.

You can easily disassemble a cylinder lock and replace it with a similar model. However, the sizes and spacings of the required holes in a door vary between manufacturers. If you are thinking of changing locks, take the old lock and a drawing of the hole pattern with you when you buy the replacement.

DEAD-BOLT LOCK

Unlike a cylinder lock, a dead-bolt is square and typically extends an inch into the jamb, making it nearly impossible to jimmy. When shopping for dead bolts, get the one with the longest bolt throw. If you are installing a new door, purchase a matched cylinder/dead-bolt pair so you need only one key.

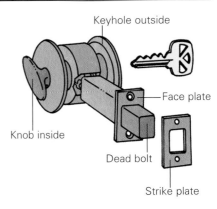

Keyhole outside
Face plate
Knob inside
Dead bolt
Strike plate

MORTISE LOCK

The mortise lock combines a spring latch (so the door will automatically latch when closed) with a dead-bolt, all in the same unit. Mortised locks are often found on doors in older homes. It has fallen out of favor, except for restoration work, however, because their housing requires a huge mortise that weakens the structural integrity of the door.

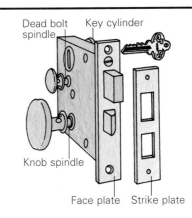

Dead bolt spindle
Key cylinder
Knob spindle
Face plate
Strike plate

RIM LOCK

After the credit card/cylinder lock trick, the burglar's next favorite trick is forcing the door and casing apart with a crowbar far enough to disengage the latch. The vertical bolt of a rim lock engages a strike plate which is screwed to both jamb and casing, making it impossible to wedge the door and jamb apart. In addition, the vertical bolt uses gravity to resist thieves' attempts to slide it open.

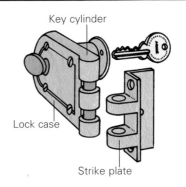

Key cylinder
Lock case
Strike plate

WINDOW LOCKS

Since you don't ordinarily enter your home through a window, you don't need the convenience—and the complexity—of a key and a latch. The most difficult aspect is simply remembering to latch them again after use.

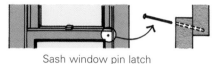

Sash window pin latch

Sliding window pin latch with key

SASH LOCK

The common sash lock, found universally on older double-hung windows, does a good job of pulling the window closed for a tight seal, but the older models are easily jimmied by inserting a thin blade (like a putty knife) between the sashes and pushing sideways. Modern versions of the sash lock, installed on all new prehung windows, cannot be opened this way.

SASH WINDOW PIN LATCH

Nothing could be simpler to install than a pin latch. Close the sashes tightly (with the sash lock) and drill nearly through the meeting sashes at a slight downward angle (so the pin won't fall out). Insert the pin and a thief can't open it without breaking the sash.

KEYED PIN LATCH

If you want to prevent unauthorized opening of a window from inside (such as an upper-story window in a child's room), install this pin latch—it requires a key to operate.

SLIDING GLASS DOOR LOCKS

Although technically a door, the slider, or patio door, operates more like a window than a door. Both of the window pin latches described for double-hung windows work equally well on the sliding glass door.

A simple and strong lock for a patio door is a wood broom handle, cut to fit in the tracks adjacent to the door, or laid in the track at the bottom.

Unfortunately, while the broom handle prevents opening a sliding door sideways, it does nothing to stop its removal by wedging it up into the overhead track and swinging the bottom free of its tracks. To prevent lifting of the door, screw several large sheet-metal screws into the overhead track and adjust them to just allow the door to slide freely back and forth.

Patio doors are good locations for exterior motion-detector security floodlights. This type of light includes a sensor that switches on the lights when movement is detected.

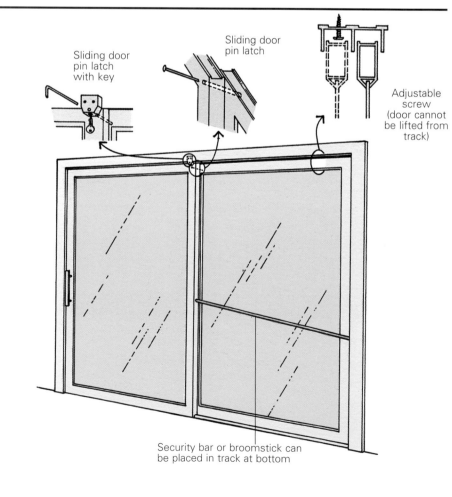

Sliding door pin latch with key

Sliding door pin latch

Adjustable screw (door cannot be lifted from track)

Security bar or broomstick can be placed in track at bottom

ALARM SYSTEMS

No home can ever be made completely burglarproof, but you can go a long way toward securing your home from intruders by investing in a home-security device. But remember—home security is more than something you buy at a store and install. The best security system is not much good unless you have installed effective door and window locks, eliminated deep shadows around your home, and adopted common-sense personal security habits.

Alarm systems vary widely in sophistication and price, but there are just two basic types:
■ Perimeter protection, which trips an alarm whenever an outside door or window opening is compromised
■ Space protection, which trips an alarm whenever motion is detected inside the house.

Both systems consist of sensors, a central control panel, and the alarm itself. In lower-cost systems the sensors are connected to the control panel with wires, which must be concealed and protected against cutting but

which are otherwise reliable. In more expensive systems the sensors transmit radio signals to the control panel. This system is quite sophisticated, and should be installed by a professional.

Perimeter-defense sensors should be installed at every exterior door and every ground-level or over-porch window. Space-protection sensors should be located where a thief would be sure to go—the stairway to the master bedroom, for example.

Both systems connect the central panel to one or both of two types of alarm:
■ An audible alarm, which is intended to scare the intruder away before anything can be removed.
■ A security alarm, which silently dials either a security service or the local police and delivers a recorded message.

Home security systems are available through home centers and consumer electronics stores, as well as through security companies which will tailor and install a system specifically for your needs.

You can install most alarm systems yourself if you have basic wiring skills, but get professional advice from several sources before you buy and install the system. Many insurance companies reduce their premiums with the installation of a security alarm.

Small, individual infrared sensors and motion detectors are also available. These devices are battery operated and cost about $10 each. To operate them, flip the switch to "On" and place the device near a typical entry point, such as a patio door or a lower-level window. If the device senses movement, it gives out a piercing alarm—loud enough to wake you from a deep sleep and loud enough to scare off intruders.

Because these devices are battery operated, you might want to reserve their use for specific situations, such as when a spouse is traveling out of town and you're alone in the house.

As with any motion-detector, make sure that pets won't wander into the field of detection in the middle of the night. You might be rudely awakened!

SUPPLEMENTAL SECURITY

In addition to the primary security measures described on these pages, here are a few additional measures that will help make your home safe and secure.
■ Replace entry door sidelight glass panes with shatterproof acrylic. For insulated panes, try removing the stops from the inside of the glazing unit and covering the inside of the glass with a

sheet of clear acrylic. Replace the stops—you may have to shave them down to accommodate the new thickness.
■ If you don't have an easy way to view visitors at your front door, make one by installing a wide-angle peephole viewer—the kind often found in motel-room doors. Peephole viewers are easy to install. You'll only need to drill one hole. The inside and the outside pieces of the viewer screw together.
■ Any door is vulnerable to forced entry. Make forcing more difficult with bar or barrel bolts at the tops and bottoms of the doors.
■ A door with exterior hinge pins can be taken apart from the outside. Keep hinges intact by removing one set of opposing screws. In one screw hole, drive a double-headed (duplex) nail. The nail head will protrude. Drill a hole in the opposite screw location so that the nail head will slip into it

when the door is shut. The nail head will act as a pin, preventing the hinge from being taken apart.

Basement windows are another choice point of entry for intruders. Secure any basement windows with one of the following methods:
■ Install hasps on the window and secure them with padlocks or combination locks. If you use a keyed lock, make sure the key is nearby and in plain sight in the unlikely event you'll need to make an emergency escape. However, don't keep the key where an intruder might see it.
■ For in-swinging louver windows, screw a wooden stop inside the window frame so the window can't be opened more than a few inches.
■ In areas of high crime, consider having custom-made iron grills professionally installed over the outside of your basement windows. Grills can be made so you don't lose aesthetically while you gain peace of mind.

PHOTO EVIDENCE SHOWS YOUR LOSS

It's not enough just to carry insurance for your valuables. The insurance company may be reluctant to cover losses unless you can document your ownership of the items. One way to document items is to lay them out on the floor and photograph them. Or walk around the house, describing items as you videotape. Keep the photographs or the video in a safe deposit box, or have a neighbor hold them for you, because they will document your loss in case of fire, as well as theft.

SHAKE ROOFING

A TRADITIONAL FAVORITE

ALSO SEE...
Flashing:
Pages 136–139
Roofs:
Pages 282–289

The rustic charm of a shake roof makes it a favorite material for both casual cottages and more formal homes. Cedar shakes are made from all-heart, western red cedar— a remarkable natural roofing material that resists decay much longer than other woods. In fact, shake roofs have been known to last over 100 years.

Aside from high initial cost, its single drawback is that it burns readily. Many codes do not allow shakes in wooded areas or on homes with a fireplace. Shakes that have been treated for fire resistance, however, may satisfy your local code. Check with your building codes official.

Shake Grade	Length (")	Butt Thickness	Maximum Exposure	Nails for New Roof	Nails for Reroof
No. 1	18	½–¾	7½	6d	7d
hand split	18	¾–1¼	7½	7d	8d
and resawn	24	⅜	10	6d	7d
	24	½–¾	10	6d	7d
	24	¾–1¼	10	7d	8d
No. 1 taper split	24	½–⅝	10	6d	7d
No. 1	18	⅜	7½	6d	7d
straight split	24	⅜	10	6d	7d

CEDAR SHAKE GRADES

EXPOSURE

Shakes can be applied at slopes down to 3-in-12. At slopes between 3-in-12 and 5-in-12, they must be applied over 15-pound felt or have reduced exposure. They function best, however, on roofs with at least a 6-in-12 slope.

Shakes measuring 18 inches long are overlapped 10½ inches, leaving an exposure of 7½ inches; 24-inch-long shakes are overlapped 14 inches, exposed 10 inches. This amount of overlapping provides standard two-ply coverage. You will have a markedly better roof with three-ply coverage, however, which means a 12½-inch and 16½-inch overlap, respectively.

Allow a ½-inch gap between shakes for expansion during the rainy season.

PREPARING THE ROOF

Shakes are normally laid over 1×4s or 1×6s battens to create gaps below them for air circulation. Because shakes are irregularly shaped, however, drying air readily circulates beneath them when they are installed over solid sheathing or an existing composition roof.

Solid sheathing, such as plywood, should be used in areas which get wind-driven snow or in earthquake areas where racking resistance is needed in the roof structure.

To cover an existing roof, cut back all roofing at the eaves and rake edges to make room for 1×6 trim boards. The trim boards provide solid edges for the shakes to rest on and conceal the unsightly edges of the existing roof.

Flash all valleys with 18-gauge galvanized steel flashing with a center crimp and ½-inch edge returns before applying roofing felt.

Unlike regular wood shingles, 18-inch-wide shakes require 30-pound roofing felt to be interleaved between the courses of shakes. This method of using felt assures that any water that penetrates under the shakes will quickly be carried out to the roof surface. If you can't find rolls of 18-inch-wide felt in your area, cut a full 36-inch-wide roll in half with a circular saw. Clean the tar off the blade with gasoline.

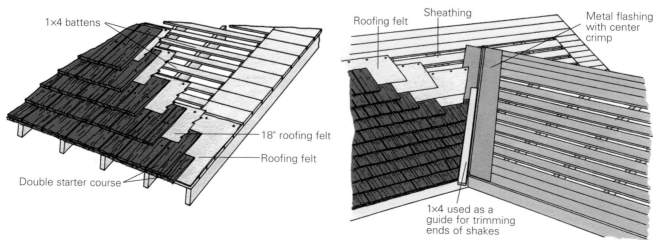

1×4 battens

18" roofing felt

Roofing felt

Double starter course

Roofing felt

Sheathing

Metal flashing with center crimp

1×4 used as a guide for trimming ends of shakes

ROOFING AROUND VENTS

To apply shakes around a roof vent, carry the course up to the vent pipe. With a saber saw, notch shakes to fit on each side of the pipe so that the standard gap of ½ inch between their edges is maintained. Slip the flashing over the pipe, and lap the next course of shakes over the top edge of the flashing, again notching the shakes with a saber saw to fit around, but not touch, the pipe collar.

If you don't wish the metal of the vent flashing to show between the shakes, paint the metal before applying it so it blends with the roof. If you try to conceal the flashing by covering with shakes on the bottom, they will dam the water and cause problems.

If the vent interferes with the bottom edges of the next course of shakes, notch them also. If there is too much of a gap between the bottom of the shakes and the pipe, slide one or more shakes down to cover the gap.

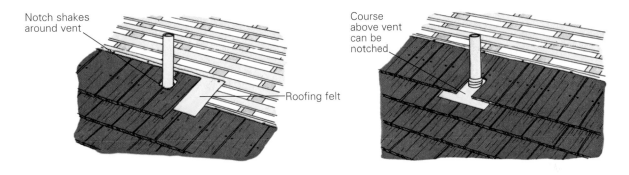

Notch shakes around vent

Roofing felt

Course above vent can be notched

APPLYING HIP SHAKES

Alternating overlaps

As each course of shakes meets a hip, cut them with a saber saw so that they meet at the centerline of the hip.

You can buy shakes for covering hips and ridges that are factory assembled and made to match a variety of roof pitches. They require 8d nails or longer. Place one hip shake at the bottom of the hip and one at the top, and snap a chalk line between their centers as a guide for placing the rest of the hip shakes.

Apply two hip shakes at the eave. Cut the bottom shake of the pair so that its top edge butts against the next course of shakes. Proceed up the hip, alternating the overlaps of the mitered corners. Lap the roofing felt over the hip, trimming it before applying the next course of shakes.

APPLYING RIDGE SHAKES

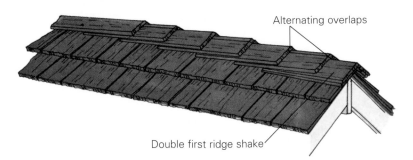

Alternating overlaps

Double first ridge shake

Apply ridge shakes in the same way as hip shakes. Fasten a ridge shake at each end of the roof and snap a chalk line between them to guide alignment of the remaining ridge shakes. Work toward the end of the ridge that receives the worst storms, or, for a symmetrical design, work from both ends toward the middle.

SHEDS

THE RIGHT SHED FOR YOU

ALSO SEE...
Concrete:
Pages 60–63
Doors:
Pages 86–97
Foundations:
Pages 144–151
Framing:
Pages 152–159
Roofs:
Pages 282–289
Shingle Siding:
Pages 308–309
Windows:
Pages 432–441

If you're planning to build a shed, make sure it meets the following criteria:
■ It should fit in with your overall storage plan, especially your needs for outdoor equipment and tools for your lawn and garden.
■ Its size and design should be in keeping with the amount of time, effort, and money you are willing to invest.
■ Its style should be appropriate to your site and, if possible, suited to the architectural style of your house.

Whether designing a custom shed or buying a prefabricated shed kit, consider how it will look—its floor area, its height, and its location on your property. Contemplate the best positions for doors, windows, and utility hookups. And think about the multiple purposes your shed may serve—a springtime planting prep area and winter workshop, for example.

When it comes to construction, your options include:
■ building your own structure
■ assembling a kit
■ buying a finished shed
If your time and skills are limited, buy as complete a kit as possible. If you want a custom size or shape and you enjoy a challenging outdoor project, design and build it from scratch.

Be sure to locate the shed where the access is convenient and where there is good drainage. You should also check with local building codes before starting any construction.

BASIC WOOD-FRAME SHED

This is the perfect shed for sharpening your construction skills in anticipation of building an addition. It is a simple but versatile freestanding structure that can be used solely for storage or for storage combined with a workshop, a garden center, or a child's playhouse.

An experienced builder with one helper could put the shed up in less than two days. A novice without help should plan on at least six days or three weekends to allow time for head-scratching.

Builders always try to simplify construction and eliminate waste by designing around the standard sizes of building materials. The dimensions of the shed shown are 12 feet by 8 feet. If you wish to alter the size, make all changes in 4-foot increments.

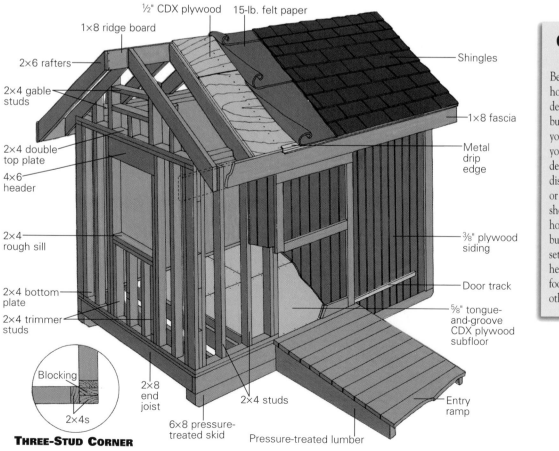

½" CDX plywood — 15-lb. felt paper
1×8 ridge board
2×6 rafters
2×4 gable studs
2×4 double top plate
4×6 header
2×4 rough sill
2×4 bottom plate
2×4 trimmer studs
Blocking
2×4s
THREE-STUD CORNER
2×8 end joist
6×8 pressure-treated skid
2×4 studs
Pressure-treated lumber
Shingles
1×8 fascia
Metal drip edge
⅜" plywood siding
Door track
⅝" tongue-and-groove CDX plywood subfloor
Entry ramp

CHECK LOCAL CODES

Before you just haul home, or have delivered, or start to build a little shed in your yard, consult with your building code department. You may discover that your city or town considers sheds to be real, honest-to-goodness buildings, subject to setback requirements, height restrictions, and footprint limits, among other things.

DESIGN CONSIDERATIONS

DOOR AND WINDOW PLACEMENT

The placement of doors and windows nearly always requires an architectural compromise. From the exterior, a pleasing appearance demands symmetry. On the inside, however, storage capacity and access to stored items is most important.

Having them in the right place is important because they will affect the way you enter, move around in, and use the shed. Experiment with sketches to see if a proposed arrangement is the best use of space.

From a structural standpoint, doors and windows can go anywhere, as long as you frame them properly—with headers, side jambs, and sills. Modifying a plan to add a window or shift a door isn't difficult.

INTERIOR PARTITION WALLS

If your shed will serve more than one purpose, interior partition walls may help define spaces clearly and separate activity areas. For example, a solid wall across the midpoint of the shed allows you to incorporate a child's playhouse on one side while keeping the kids safely away from the tools and chemicals stored on the other side.

You can erect interior walls anywhere in the shed. They act as simple barriers rather than load-bearing walls, so frame them the same as exterior walls, nailing them to the floor and the wall framing at each end.

BUILT-INS

Built-in storage cabinets and shelves increase storage significantly. They are a simple, inexpensive way to keep things neat.

■ Plan storage cabinets to house supplies. Use locking cabinets to safeguard pesticides or other potentially hazardous substances.
■ Add wall racks for tools, fishing rods, and garden hose.
■ Install hooks in the rafters for ladders and bicycles.
■ Give each of the children a bin for their toys.

In other words, customize the interior of your shed so that the whole family gets maximum use from the storage space.

METAL SHED

Metal sheds have the advantages of being inexpensive and easy to erect. They're usually not very pretty, however. They stand out simply because painted steel isn't common to residential construction. By taking great care to integrate yours into its surroundings with a new coat of paint, pathways, plantings, and other landscape elements, you can have a metal shed that shares your outdoor living spaces discreetly and serves your storage needs well.

They come in a variety of sizes, but you can't modify the design the way you can with wood. If you live in an area where strong winds or heavy snowfall is frequent, you must also realize that metal sheds can blow over unless tied down, dent under high roof loads, and rust.

You will have to provide the floor for the shed—either a concrete slab, a temporary wood floor, or a permanent wood floor on its own foundation.

Peak cap
Ridge cap
Peak cap
Roof panels
Roof panels
Roof beams
Wall angle assembly
Side roof trim
Side roof trim
Front panels
Gable assembly
Front frame assembly
Door track
Side panels

BUILDING EXPERIENCE

If you have no building experience, yet dream of creating an addition to your home, what better way to gain experience than to assemble a shed?

Sheds are just little buildings and, as such, contain most of the elements of bigger buildings: footings, floor joists, studs, rafters, sheathing, siding, roofing, flashing, window(s), door(s), and perhaps even a light or two.

Even if it's from a kit, building a shed will build your skills and tell you whether you will enjoy the process of planning and constructing a building.

▶

FOUNDATIONS

Whether you buy a preassembled shed or build one from scratch, you will have to prepare the site and provide some sort of foundation.

The site should be level, firm, and well drained so the shed will sit squarely, settle evenly, and be protected from dampness. If the site is not level, you can compensate by constructing a stable, level foundation.

Depending on the requirements of your local building codes, you may have several choices for foundation materials (see Footings on page 142, and Foundations, page 144): pressure-treated wood such as railroad ties, a layer of patio blocks, a bed of gravel, a concrete slab, or piers. Anchor the shed firmly to its foundation. If the foundation is not sunk into the ground, you may have to provide tie-downs.

Some prefabricated sheds come with flooring, but most do not. Therefore, your floor will be either a slab foundation, gravel, or a finish floor installed over joists.

RUBBISH BOX

These rubbish barrels are neatly stored in a low shed that is backed up to—and painted the same color as—the nearby fence. The raised concrete slab makes it easy to occasionally hose down spills. Tight-fitting doors with latches keep varmints out.

The box may be constructed of boards or of ⅝-inch tongue-and-groove Texture 1-11 (T1-11) exterior-grade plywood.

LEAN-TO

This small lean-to shed clings to the back of a house. It is convenient to the back door, and its location is ideal for storing patio furniture, cushions, the barbecue, and other summer furnishings that require winter shelter.

You can easily modify the length, depth, or height to fit your storage needs. However, make sure you choose proportions that harmonize with the overall architecture of your house, as well as the particular wall on which it is placed. Finish it with materials that complement those used on the house.

POOLSIDE CABANA

This poolside cabana is walled through the middle to create two separate spaces. The front half of both sides has dressing rooms with benches for changing. The high windows provide light yet ensure privacy. Between the dressing rooms, there is a cabinet for towels and pool toys.

The back space has its own entrance. In one half, the mechanical equipment for the pool hums away out of sight; the other half houses general household or garden storage. There's also room for pool chemicals, long-handled pool skimmers, and vacuums.

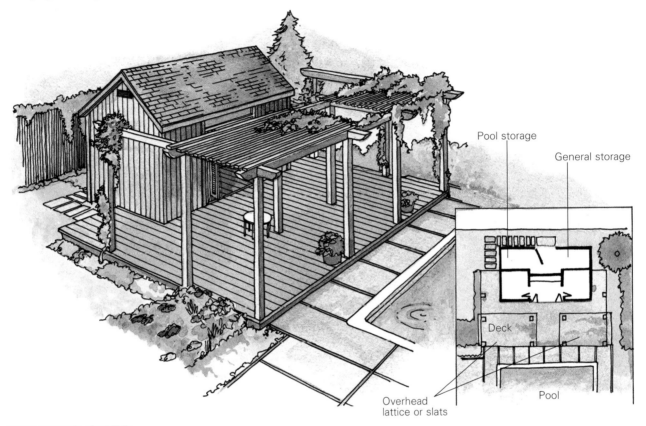

Pool storage

General storage

Deck

Overhead lattice or slats

Pool

POTTING SHED

The long bench next to the south-facing windows in this simple garden workshop offers ample space for potting tools and the activity of potting plants. When not being used as a garden prep center, the bench provides space for seedling trays.

Potting soil can be stored in a large bin or barrel in a corner, and a drain in the concrete floor makes it easy to water new plants and to hose away the dirt.

Lawn

Potting bench

General storage

Patio pavers

Vegetable garden

303

SHELVING

AN EVER-EXPANDING NEED

Most of us are like pack rats: We never want to throw anything away. When we run out of room for additional junk, we hold a yard sale, to which others run to make our stuff their stuff. And, aside from a section of kitchen counter and the table where you eat, when was the last time you saw a clear horizontal surface in your home? We seem to have infinite need for surfaces on which to drop or display things: the mail, our keys, books and magazines, houseplants, collections.

You can always use additional shelves, both for storing items that don't need to be seen and for showcasing collections of things that you do want seen. You need shelves in cabinets, shelves in storage areas, shelves in closets, shelves for books, shelves for records and tapes, shelves in the kitchen and the bathroom—the list is endless.

Building your own shelves is a simple and immensely gratifying way to hone your carpentry skills and create something useful at the same time. To make your efforts worthwhile, use high quality materials. It is surprising how simple it is to build complicated-looking shelves, and how good the shelves look when they are built with quality materials.

BASIC BOOKCASE

The shelves in this freestanding bookcase fit into dadoes cut in the uprights. Properly made, a dado joint provides stability and an interesting edge detail. For increased stability, enclose the back in lauan plywood or tempered hardboard. Notice the toe space beneath the bottom shelf; toe space is usually 3 inches high. The top shelf is rabbeted into the sides. Glue reinforces all joints.

An alternative to rabbeted joints and dadoes is butt joints, but the load that a butt-jointed shelf can support is severely limited. Secure any joint with glue and screws for maximum strength.

MATERIALS

You can build your shelves from dimension lumber, plywood, or some type of fiberboard. Dimension lumber is a solid and attractive choice, but the grades required for any but the crudest cellar shelves are quite expensive.

Plywood costs from a quarter to about half as much as good dimension lumber, depending on whether you intend to paint a construction grade or show off the hardwood veneer of a cabinetry grade. However, plywood edges need to be concealed.

The fiberboards, all relatively inexpensive, have limited use because they tend to sag and don't hold screws or nails well. Prefinished shelving of medium density fiberboard (MDF) is relatively attractive and inexpensive, however, and can be used for short spans or light loads.

Hardboard—a thin, strong fiberboard—works well as a backer board to close bookcases and keep them square.

PLYWOOD SHELVES

If you decide to use plywood for shelving, make it ¾ inch thick. That way you can rip ¼-inch strips of 1× dimension lumber (which is also ¾ inch thick) to hide the ugly plywood edges.

Another option is edging the plywood with hardwood veneer tape, an inexpensive way to get the look of solid hardwood shelving.

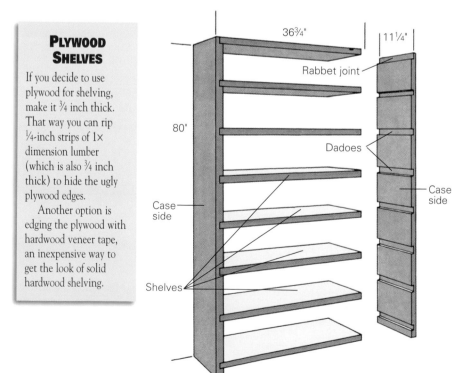

36¾"   11¼"

Rabbet joint

80"

Dadoes

Case side

Case side

Shelves

SHELF SPACING	
Stored Object	**Typical Height**
Hardback book	11"
Paperback book	8"
Oversize hardbacks	15"
Oversize paperbacks	16"
Audiocassettes	5"
Compact disks	5"
Videotapes	8"
Slide carousels	10"

SHELF SPANS	
Shelf Material	**Maximum Span**
⅜" glass	18"
½" acrylic (plexiglas)	22"
¾" particleboard	28"
¾" plywood	36"
1×12 lumber	24"
2×10 lumber	48"
2×12 lumber	56"

FRAMED BOOKCASE

This handsome bookcase features face frames on both front and back so it can serve as a room divider, accessible from either side. Face frames also hide the edges of the case, making it possible to use plywood with hardwood face veneers such as cherry, oak, mahogany, or birch. You can install fixed or adjustable shelves, and hide their exposed edges with ¼×¾-inch hardwood strips of the same species.

The dimensions given here are for a unit made to sit on a 30-inch (table-height) or 36-inch (counter-height) cabinet. Adjust the dimensions to suit your purpose. The ¾-inch plywood shelves should be no longer than 40 inches for light loads, 36 inches for average books, and 32 inches for heavy books. To alter this design so the case will stand on the floor, construct a pedestal of 1×3s and attach it to the bottom.

To build the unit, precut all the pieces. Drill evenly spaced holes in the sides if you're planning adjustable shelves. Assemble the top and bottom shelves with butt joints, using carpenter's glue and finish nails. Assemble the face frames with doweled joints and glue them to the case, using clamps or nails. The outside edges of the frames should be flush with the outside edges of the case. Sand all edges smooth. Fasten the edge strips to the front and rear edges of the shelves using glue and brads. After the glue sets, sand and finish all components and install the shelves.

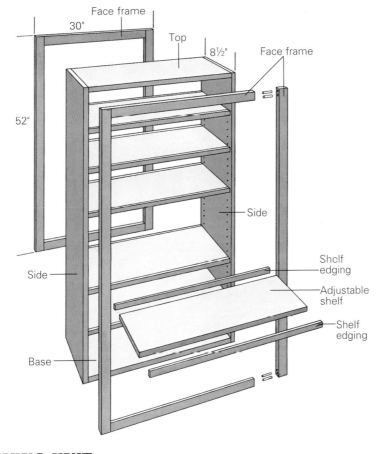

SHELVING UNIT

This unit, suitable for bedroom storage, consists of two freestanding cases with additional shelves hung between. Shelf tracks and clips allow shelf-height adjustment. Some track is made to install one way only (the top has a screw hole closer to the end). Line up all of the tracks so you don't install one or more upside down.

Use a combination square to align marks for the first top screw holes. After all of the tracks are hung from their top screws, use a level to plumb the tracks before applying the remaining screws.

Stabilize the end sections by installing 1×4 cleats across the back edge of the top and bottom shelves and screwing them to the wall or by gluing and nailing lauan plywood to their backs.

To obscure the contents without the trouble or expense of hanging cabinet doors, attach either roll-up blinds or simple cloth curtains to the tops of the cases.

CUBBYHOLE SHELVES

This cubbyhole case made to be suspended over a desk (by about a foot) requires a lot of patience and very accurate measurements. Assembling it, however, is easy.

The unit is 10 inches deep and is made of ¾-inch plywood featuring a hardwood veneer.

Cut the parts using a table saw, a power miter saw, or a radial arm saw with a high-quality blade. Equipped with a dado blade, these saws will cut accurate dado grooves.

Identical ¼-inch-deep dadoes on opposite sides of the same vertical partition will make the partition fragile until assembly, so handle the partitions carefully during construction. A lauan plywood backing makes the case stronger and easier to hang.

To hang the unit, install a 1×2 cleat on the wall, fastening it directly to the wall studs. Place the case on the cleat, secure it with a screw driven through the backing at one end. Then level the unit, drive a screw at the other end and every 6 inches in between.

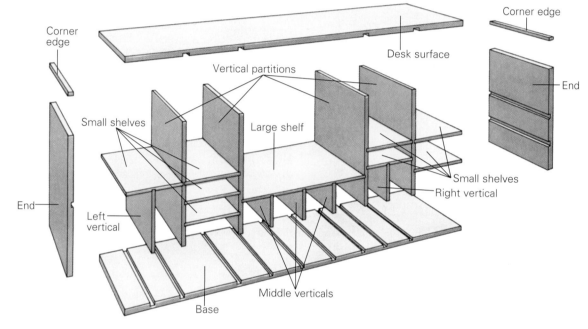

SPORTS CLOSET

Closets with a single hanging pole waste a lot of space unless you find a use for the roughly 3-foot empty area beneath the clothes. These lockerlike modules make use of that wasted area by adding shelves. They are simple to make and will house a variety of sports equipment as well as clothes. Separate the individual units with horizontal blocking, and use the narrow spaces behind the blocking for storing items like hockey sticks, lacrosse sticks, baseball bats, and tennis rackets.

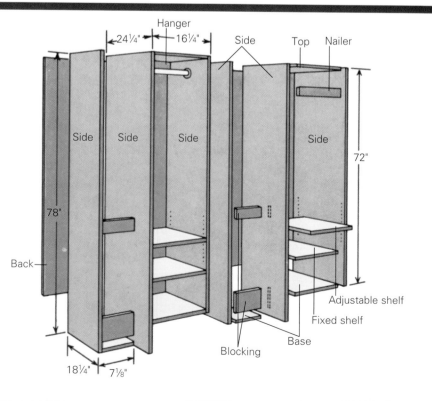

METHODS FOR SUPPORTING SHELVES

Arguably, the most elegant storage is also the simplest—horizontal shelves fitted to dadoed vertical standards. But simplest doesn't equate to easiest; just ask any cabinetmaker who makes Shaker furniture replicas. Cutting the dadoes to fit the shelves exactly requires precision tools and experience. Fortunately, there are a number of other shelf supports that are reasonably attractive, yet easy to install:

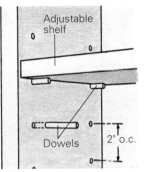

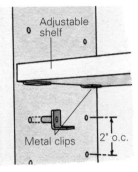

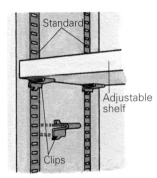

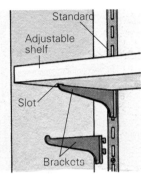

Wood Dowels: The simplest of all is hardwood dowels fitted into holes of the same diameter. The weight of the shelf keeps the dowels from falling out; no fasteners are needed. By drilling pairs of holes at intervals (say 2 inches on center), the shelves are adjustable as well.

Metal or Plastic Dowel Clips: Similar to wood dowels, these clips require holes drilled to the diameter of the clip post. The shelves need to be about ¼ inch shorter than the span to accommodate the clips.

Adjustable End Standards: Rather than drilling a series of evenly spaced holes (a difficult trick to do accurately), install a pair of slotted standards that accommodate metal clips. Screw the metal standards to the surface of the wood, or recess them in dadoes for a more attractive look.

Adjustable Shelf Brackets: These metal standards may be screwed directly to a wall. The shelf ends may cantilever over the brackets, achieving greater spans and a lightweight look.

This system of brackets and standards can support surprisingly large loads.

LIPPED SHELVES

Shelf tracks and bracket arms can provide flexible and strong open shelving. For heavy storage, such as a plant-potting area, make sure to use enough brackets and enough screws in the tracks to support the weight of pots filled with earth.

Glue and screw a lip to each shelf to make sure that the heavy, stored items don't slip off. The lips can be made of ¾-inch lumber, plywood, or particle board and should be securely glued and screwed to the shelves.

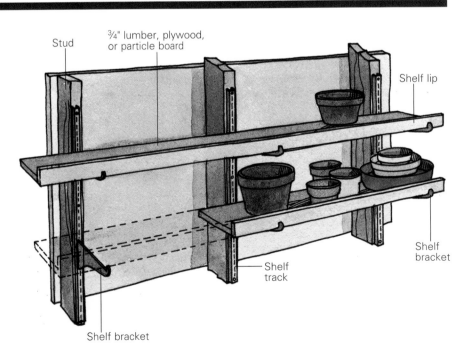

SHINGLE SIDING

SLOW TO INSTALL AND SLOW TO WEAR OUT

ALSO SEE...
Fasteners:
Pages 122–125
Paints & Stains:
Pages 232–241
Wood:
Pages 446–453

Wood shingles have been a popular siding material for centuries. They are extremely attractive and long lasting, and lend themselves to both traditional and contemporary styles. They are more expensive than most other sidings, but require virtually no maintenance for up to 50 years.

Installation of shingle siding is simple but time-consuming. Professional installation adds to the overall expense, but professionals use time-saving equipment such as fast-firing staple guns and scaffolding. So if you are considering installing wood shingles, it's worth it to ask a few contractors to submit bids for the entire job.

Don't paint wood shingles. The paint will trap moisture inside, causing decay. You also will have to repaint them—just like any other painted siding—about every four years. If you need color, choose a light-bodied, oil-based stain; consult with your local dealer for other recommendations. Otherwise, let shingles weather to their natural color—a deep, silvery gray.

CODE REQUIREMENTS

Application:

■ Shingles must be applied to wood or plywood sheathing that is at least ½ inch thick, or to 1×3 or 1×4 wood furring strips over ½-inch nonwood sheathing.

■ Wood or plywood sheathing must be covered with a weather-resistant, permeable membrane, such as building wrap.

■ The spacing between shingles must not exceed ¼ inch, and the offset between joints must be at least 1½ inches.

■ Each shingle must be fastened with two hot-dipped, zinc-coated aluminum or stainless steel nails or staples.

■ Fasteners must penetrate the sheathing or furring strips by at least ½ inch.

MAXIMUM EXPOSURE

Length	Single Course	Double Course
# 1 GRADE		
16"	7½"	12"
18"	8½"	14"
24"	11½"	16"
# 2 GRADE		
16"	7½"	10"
18"	8½"	11"

THE PRICE OF BEAUTY

How many $5,000 shingling jobs have you seen ruined by little black streaks running down silver-gray shingles? Would you be willing to spend an extra $50 to $100 to avoid those streaks? If the answer is "yes," buy stainless steel siding nails.

CEDAR SHINGLE SPECIFICATIONS

Shingle Grade	Butt Thickness, Inches	Length, Inches	Bundles per Square
RED CEDAR			
No. 1, blue label	0.40	16	4
Premium grade, 100% heartwood	0.45	18	4
100% clear, 100% edge grain	0.50	24	4
No. 2, red label	0.40	16	4
Good grade, 10" clear on 16" shingle	0.45	18	4
16" clear on 24" shingle	0.50	24	4
No. 3, black label	0.40	16	4
Utility grade, 6" clear on 16" shingle	0.45	18	4
10" clear on 24" shingle	0.50	24	4
No. 4, undercoursing (for bottom	0.40	16	2 or 4
course in double-coursed walls)	0.45	18	2 or 4
No. 1 or 2 rebutted-rejoined (machine-	0.40	16	1
trimmed, square-edged, top grade)	0.45	18	1
WHITE CEDAR			
Extra (perfectly clear)	0.40	16	4
1st clear (7" clear, no sapwood)	0.40	16	4
2nd clear (sound knots, no sapwood)	0.40	16	4
Clear wall (sapwood, curls)	0.40	16	4
Utility (undercoursing only)	0.40	16	4

TYPES, GRADES, AND SIZES

Two types of cedar shingles are most commonly used:
■ White cedar usually weathers to silvery gray.
■ Red cedar weathers to silvery gray, medium brown, or dark brown, depending on climatic conditions.

Each type comes in three grades:
■ No. 1, premium shingles, is usually used exclusively for rooftop surfaces.
■ No. 2, with some sapwood, is used for most sidewall shingling.
■ No. 3, with sapwood and knots, is mostly used for utility buildings or interior walls.

The chart, *above*, further explains the specifications of the different shingle grades.

PREPARING THE WALL

For new construction, install ½-inch plywood sheathing to the wall framing. Install the doors and windows, along with 15-pound felt flashing and any casings. Cut and fit metal Z-flashing over the door and window casings.

As you shingle, install building paper on each wall, wrapping it around the corners. Paint corner, door, and window trim before shingling so that you don't have to cut the paint in.

Prepare existing walls that are flat and sound in the same manner as plywood sheathing. For rough walls, such as stucco or existing shingles, nail 1×3 horizontal furring strips to the wall and nail jamb extenders to the windows. Space the strips at the same interval as the shingle exposure. Except for stucco, it is generally better to remove the old siding.

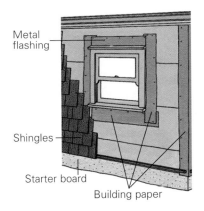

Metal flashing

Shingles

Starter board

Building paper

APPLYING THE SHINGLES

If possible, plan the shingle coursing so that the shingle butts will align with the tops and bottoms of window and door frames. This not only looks neater, but minimizes the number of shingles you have to cut.

The first course across the bottom should be doubled and should have a water table board or a starter board behind it. To keep this course level, nail a shingle at each corner of the building with the butt an inch below the starter board. Tack a small nail to the bottom of each shingle and stretch a string line to align the starter course.

If you are shingling an old house that is not level, the first course should follow the slant of the house rather than be level; otherwise it will emphasize the irregularity. Adjust each successive course by ⅛ inch until the courses become level. The slight change will never be detected.

NAILING

Use 3d (5d for double courses) stainless siding nails, two per shingle. Nail them approximately ¾ inch from each edge. Space shingles to allow for expansion. Normal spacing is ⅛ inch. Vertical gaps should be offset by at least 1½ inches between courses, and no two gaps should line up with less than three courses between them. Do not let a shingle gap line up with the edges of any windows or doors.

CORNERS

The fastest way to shingle corners also gives the most effective weather protection: Use trim boards for both the inside and outside corners—2×2s

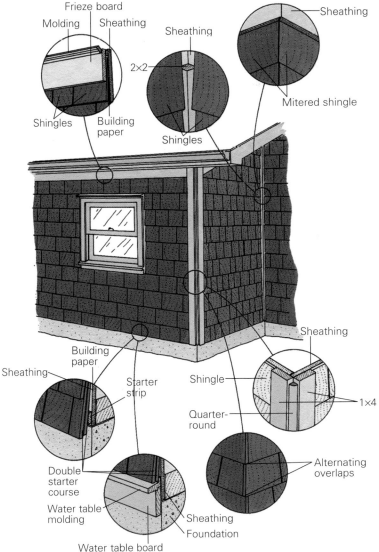

Frieze board
Molding
Sheathing
Shingles
Building paper

Sheathing
2×2
Shingles

Sheathing
Mitered shingle

Building paper
Sheathing
Starter strip

Double starter course
Water table molding
Water table board

Shingle
Quarter-round
Sheathing
Foundation

Sheathing
1×4
Alternating overlaps

for the inside and at least 1×4s for the outside. Pick redwood or cedar if you want the boards to weather with the shingles; use pine if you paint the trim.

If you shingle to the corners, the easier method is to "weave" the corner so that each course of shingles alternates in overlapping the edge.

SHOWERS

STYLE AND LIGHT—YOU HAVE CHOICES

ALSO SEE...
Bathroom Design:
Pages 22–23
Bathtubs:
Pages 24–27
Faucets & Valves:
Pages 126–129
Framing:
Pages 152–159
Plumbing:
Pages 256–263
Tile:
Pages 360–367
Wallboard:
Pages 394–399

You have four choices when installing a new shower:

■ Single-piece prefabricated fiber glass shower stall.

■ Shower base plus a set of panels you install for an enclosure.

■ Shower base, around which you build and tile an enclosure.

■ Building everything from scratch, including a tiled floor.

There is no reason why a shower should be dark and cavelike, unless you choose to have it so. Even if you have limited space, you can transform a simple shower stall into a luxurious spa by adding a skylight, lowering the partition walls so they do not reach the ceiling, installing a fan and light unit overhead, or installing a small window near the top of the stall.

If you have enough space, you can add a second shower head to create a shower room for two people. Installation techniques will vary with your choice, but the basic plumbing is all the same.

FREESTANDING UNITS

A freestanding shower can be placed anywhere: in a corner, along a wall, even in a large closet. That is an advantage, but most are probably flimsier than you would like. They are typically made from enameled steel, which is noisy and prone to rusting and chipping. Others are made from plastics, such as polypropylene or ABS, or from fiberglass with an aluminum frame. The drain pan is usually of a heavier material that resembles marble.

Freestanding units come in a variety of sizes and shapes, including 32- and 36-inch squares, corner units with a rounded or angled front, and circular units for installation away from walls. Most come in sections (fixtures not included) and need to be assembled.

SECTIONAL UNITS

These come with a door and either three or four wall panels. Most include a matching four- or five-sided drain pan, but you can also order the wall panels without drain pan.

Unassembled, the sections can be carried through any doorway. Some panels are even designed so that the size of the assembled unit can be adjusted to fit a range of opening sizes.

'THIS END UP'

Some models of shower/tub controls are easy to install upside down. If you do so, you will find the tub filling rather slowly! So check.

ONE-PIECE STALLS

These shower stalls are molded from fiberglass or acrylic and must be installed in framed openings. They may be 32-, 36-, or 40-inch squares, 32×48-inch rectangles, or five-sided corner units, either 36 or 40 inches on the long sides.

Before you buy one, make sure you can get it through the doors to your bathroom!

Also, there are two reasons why you should not frame the opening completely before setting the unit in place:

1. Their sizes sometimes vary quite a bit from the nominal (a "36×36" stall might measure 35¾×36½).

2. The valve stems of the shower control stick into the shower space, so if all three walls and the control valve are pre-installed, it may be impossible to slide the enclosure into place.

INSTALLATION

After building a frame and roughing-in the plumbing, installing a prefab shower goes fairly quickly.

■ Lift the shower unit into place, centering the drain fitting over the roughed-in 2-inch drainpipe. Some manufacturers recommend setting the unit on a ½-inch bed of mortar or quick-setting plaster compound for maximum support.

■ Nail the top and side flanges to the studs with galvanized roofing nails.

■ Secure the drain fitting by slipping the gasket down around the drainpipe

and tightening the retaining ring.

■ Finish plumbing the faucet and showerhead. Apply caulk around cutouts; then attach the fittings and escutcheons to the rough plumbing.

CODE REQUIREMENTS

For showers:

■ The floor area must be at least 900 square inches and contain a circle of diameter at least 30 inches.

■ The flow rate is limited to 2.5 gpm at a pressure of 80 psi.

■ The control valve must limit temperature to 120°F and be of the thermostatic and/or pressure balance type.

INSTALLING A CUSTOM-BUILT SHOWER

A custom shower built from scratch offers unlimited choice of size, shape, color, and materials, but it also requires a lot of time and effort. It can be as small as 32 inches square, or it can resemble the shower room at a "Y" with several shower heads and tile on the ceiling as well as the floor and walls.

The really critical part of any shower installation is the shower pan. Although it is possible to make the floor any size or shape imaginable and then cover it with tile, this process requires that an elaborate custom-

fabricated waterproof pan be under the tile. A far easier route is to use a molded plastic, fiberglass, or terrazzo shower pan for the floor. The size and shape of the stall will then be dictated by the size and shape of the pan.

Most custom-built shower stalls are tile, because tile is readily available in many attractive designs, is easy to clean and maintain, and can be installed over awkward shapes. The only drawback is that the grout lines are not totally waterproof, but this is not a problem, provided the backing is sound.

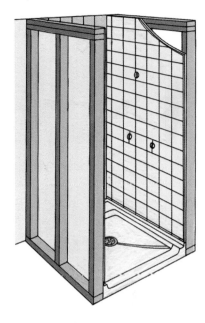

SHOWER PAN AND PLUMBING

Shower bases, or pans, usually come in 32-, 36-, and 40-inch squares, 32×48-inch rectangles, and five-sided corner showers. Many other sizes and shapes are available as special orders, however. All are molded to slope toward a drain hole that receives a standard shower drain. If a drain fitting is not included with the pan, get the kind with an internal compression sleeve for connecting to the rough plumbing stub. Before installing rough plumbing, frame the back wall and faucet wall.

Use 2-inch PVC or ABS pipe and fittings for the rough plumbing. The trap should be below the floor, with the trap inlet positioned directly in line with the shower pan drain hole. Do not go by the specification sheet for the drain pan; carefully measure the location of the drain hole on the actual unit, because a difference as

small as ¼-inch may make the hookup difficult.

If you have not done so already, cut a hole in the floor for the shower drain to fit through, then connect a short stub to the trap just long enough to slip the drain fitting over. Next, install the drain fitting in the base. Put a ring of plumber's putty around the hole first, insert the fitting into the hole, and screw the tightening ring very snugly against the bottom of the base. Then set the base in position so that the drain fitting slips down over the stub-out. Tighten the neoprene compression sleeve by turning the tightening ring with a screwdriver and the special tool that comes with the drain assembly.

The supply pipes are usually ½-inch copper or CPVC. Install the shower control valve at a comfortable height 42–48 inches above the pan. Your local code may require shutoff valves for the hot and cold supply lines, either in the basement, or from an access panel behind the wall. As with a tub, an access panel behind the control valve is essential.

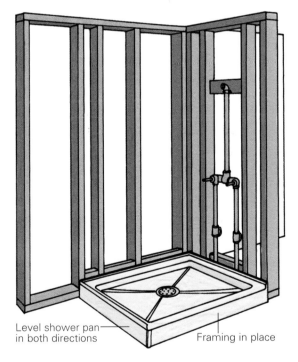

Level shower pan in both directions — Framing in place

CLEANING IRON STAINS

Iron in your water produces rust stains in your sinks, toilets, and shower. Since they are porcelain, the sinks and toilet can take scrubbing without scratching. Most showers stalls however, are gel-coated fiber glass, a material easily scratched by abrasive cleaners.

So what will remove the stain? Acid! Relax, that doesn't have to mean dangerous, caustic chemicals. Cola is acidic. So are lemonade, orange juice, and vinegar. The cheapest solution will be a citric-acid cleaning solution found in the household cleaner section of your super market.

The riser pipe to the drop-ell fitting for the showerhead should be 54–78 inches above the floor, depending on your preference. If you later find that the shower arm is too low, you can replace it with a "shower-up" extension that raises the shower head approximately 12 inches. This would be a good point at which to test for leaks, since corrections later will prove much more difficult.

▶

311

INSTALLING A CUSTOM-BUILT SHOWER *continued*

FRAMING THE STALL

Use 2×4s to frame in the rest of the shower. Studs should be a minimum of 16 inches on center, and the walls should have a soleplate and top plate.

If you want a low ceiling in the shower, nail 2×4 cleats to the walls at the level of the new ceiling and put short 2×4 joists between them. If you want the top of the stall to be open, build the partition wall so that it does not go all the way to the ceiling. However, you will have to brace it somehow. One way is to add a header across the top of the door opening, which can either be exposed or covered with finish material. Another bracing technique is to back up a counter or linen-storage closet or shelving to the unattached wall.

All of the corners need some sort of backing for the edges of the wallboard. In addition, install blocking to back up toilet paper holders, towel racks, grab bars, or door enclosures. Finally, nail 2×4 blocking between the studs at the

top of the shower stall. Secure the top by nailing or screwing its flange to the studs.

Be sure the shower stall has proper clearances. There should be at least 18 inches (preferably 24) between a stall with a shower curtain and any plumbing fixture on the opposite wall. If the stall will have a door, there must be at least 28 inches of clearance for the door to swing open. The minimum floor area of a shower is 30 inches square.

Custom Bases: When installing a custom tile floor rather than a prefabricated base, build a curb across the doorway of 2×4s. Nail ½-inch plywood to the inside of the curb and all around the bottoms of the walls. Have a shower pan fabricated from a code-approved material: copper sheet with soldered seams (from a sheet-metal shop), or a continuous rubberized membrane (from a roofing company that specializes in EPDM

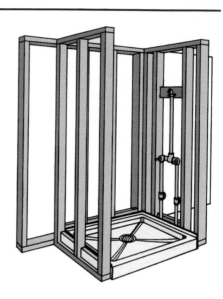

roofing). The shower pan should lap over the curb and up the walls at least 3½ inches higher than the curb. It should also slope toward the drain.

TILE BACKER BOARD

Although moisture-resistant wallboard (greenboard) has been widely used as a backing for tiled showers, it will not hold up indefinitely if water seeps into it through cracks, grout joints, or any other path. A more durable type of panel is a sandwich panel with a lightweight concrete material on the inside and mesh reinforcing cloth on each face. You cut and nail it like wallboard, attach it with roofing nails, and tape the joints with fiberglass mesh tape.

Don't rest the backer-board panels on the lip of the base. Leave about a ¼-inch gap above the base so that any water that might seep behind the tile will not wick up into the backer board. This space will be covered with tile and sealed with caulking or grout.

Before you install the panels, seal all cut edges with a special sealer or the joint compound specified for moisture-proof wallboard. Cut holes for the faucet stems and shower arm so there is approximately ¼-inch clearance. Do not put a vapor barrier behind the backer board. Nail the panels directly to the studs with coated wallboard nails, 8 inches on center. Then tape

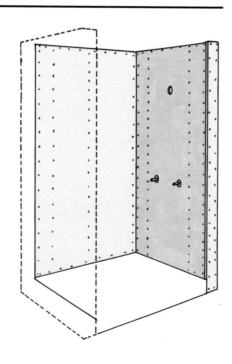

and fill the joints and cover all the nail heads. Use the joint compound specified by the backer board manufacturer.

FINISHING

Tile is the material of choice for custom-built showers. Start the tile layout at the bottom. Lap the first course of tiles over the shower pan, but leave an ⅛-inch gap above the floor for sealing with caulking. The tile should extend at least 6 feet above the floor. If it terminates before the ceiling, use bull-nosed tiles or radius trim pieces for the top row.

Cut the tile holes for the faucet stems and shower arm with nippers or a wet saw. Then grout the joints. To ensure proper curing, cover the grouted tile tightly with plastic sheeting for a few days. When completely cured and dry (approximately two weeks) apply a clear grout sealer, available where you buy your tile.

If you want to trade elegance for labor savings, you can finish shower walls with plastic panels. Kits are available for standard-sized showers and tubs, although you may need to cut the panels to size. Use adhesives to glue the panels to the wallboard. Seal the joints with caulking.

If you're into rustic (as, for example, a log cabin) it is also possible to finish shower walls with wood siding, but this requires sealing the backing and using naturally durable woods such as redwood or cypress. Several coats of penetrating sealer must be applied to the wood surface, and it must be maintained diligently.

The final step is to install faucet handles and a showerhead. Fill the gaps around the faucet stems with caulk, slip the escutcheons (cover rings) over them, and attach the handles. If the shower valve has a single-handle, remove the temporary plastic tile spacer from the valve, apply a bead of caulking around the back of the cover plate, and screw the plate into the valve. Then attach the handle. For the showerhead, screw the arm into the drop-ell (elbow with ears) behind the wall. Use a rag to prevent pliers from scratching the finish. Then screw the showerhead to the arm.

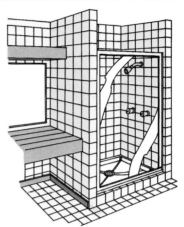

SUPPLY PLUMBING

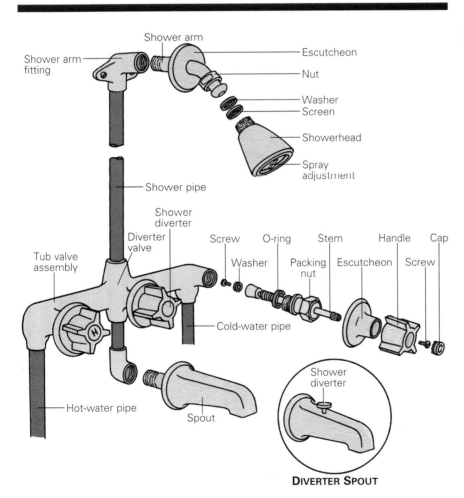

DIVERTER SPOUT

The exploded view, *above*, shows a tub/shower control for a combination bathtub/shower installation. Water can be diverted from the spout to the showerhead either with a third handle on the valve or a pull-up diverter on the spout.

The same unit can be used just for a shower or just for a tub simply by plugging the unused outlet.

The other type of tub/shower control is the single-handle, which works just like a single-handle faucet for a sink. It, too, can be used just for a shower, just for a tub, or for both.

INSTALLING A DOOR OR ENCLOSURE

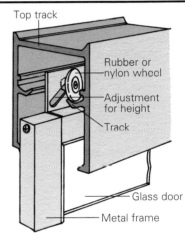

The simplest and least expensive way to close off a shower is with a shower curtain. However, these last only a few years and tend to mildew. Many styles of shower door and tub enclosure are also available. All have aluminum frames, although the color of the metal may be gold, bronze, or silver. Glass shower doors must be tempered, and may be either clear or opaque.

Installation depends on whether the door rolls on a track or swings on a hinge, but several techniques are the same for both. First, be sure to install blocking behind the rail locations when you frame the walls (use expansion bolts when installing doors for an existing shower).

Most installations also require drilling through tile so that the side rails can be screwed into the walls. If possible, locate the screw holes in the joints because grout is much easier to drill. In any case, use a masonry bit with a carbide tip, and be prepared to drill for a long time!

313

SINKS AND GARBAGE DISPOSERS

CHOOSING A SINK

ALSO SEE...
Countertops:
Pages 70–73
Dishwashers:
Pages 82–83
Faucets & Valves:
Pages 126–129
Kitchen Design:
Pages 208–211
Plumbing:
Pages 256–263

Sinks present a broad range of choices. Besides material and size, you need to select the number and sizes of bowls, the color, the mounting detail, and the number of holes for the faucet and accessories.

A single-bowl sink is suitable for any installation that requires a sink less than 28 inches long. Double-bowl sinks offer more flexibility. The bowls in some double sinks are the same size, while others have unequal bowls. Three-bowl sinks are also available.

To select a size that will fit your needs, consider how often you fill large pots, whether you like to keep one bowl free, and how often other members of the household interrupt the cook to use the sink.

In addition to stainless steel, kitchen sinks come in enameled cast iron, synthetic marble, porcelain-coated steel, and slate. Because stainless steel is durable, inexpensive, and easy to clean, it is used universally in restaurants and institutional kitchens. Stainless sinks come in 18-, 20-, and 22-gauge. The lower the gauge, the thicker the metal. Choose 18- or 20-gauge to minimize vibration from the disposer. It comes in three finishes: polished, matte, and brushed. Matte and brushed are easier to maintain.

Enameled cast iron is durable, heavy, and expensive. A rainbow of colors is available, but remember that you may want to replace your expensive sink if you decide later to change your kitchen's color scheme.

Sinks come with three, four, or five holes on the back rim for mounting faucets, spray hoses, and soap dispensers. Matching plugs cover holes that you choose not to use.

Drain holes are identical on all modern sinks and accommodate standard strainer drains and all garbage disposers.

Disposers require a dedicated 110-volt circuit, operable from a switch near the sink. Your local code may specify the location of this switch.

INSTALLING A SINK

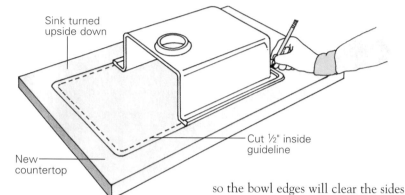

Sink turned upside down

New countertop

Cut ½" inside guideline

MARKING FOR THE CUTOUT

Kitchen sinks are designed to be installed in countertops.

Place the sink upside down on the countertop and set it in position. Be sure to center it over the sink cabinet so the bowl edges will clear the sides of the cabinet. For a standard 25-inch countertop, leave 1½–2 inches at the front edge. For a wider counter (an island or peninsula, for example), leave 3–4 inches. Pencil a line around the edge of the sink and lift it off. Then draw a second line ½ inch inside the first outline.

TYPES OF SINK RIMS

SELF-RIMMING

Most sinks are of this style because they are so easy to install. Simply lay a bead of tub-and-sink caulk around the opening. Set the sink into the opening so the rim rests in the caulk. From underneath, install the clamps provided by the sink manufacturer. Space the clamps about 4 inches apart. After the caulk has set, score around the edge of the sink with a knife and remove any caulk that oozed out.

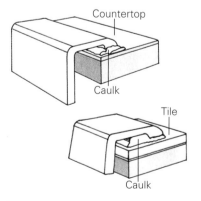

Countertop

Caulk

Tile

Caulk

SURFACE MOUNTED

A surface-mounted sink comes with a separate stainless mounting rim. Lay a bead of tub-and-sink caulk around the cutout. Set the sink into the opening, support it temporarily, and insert the

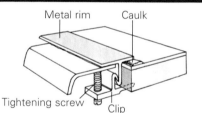

Metal rim   Caulk

Tightening screw   Clip

rim around it. Working from underneath the sink, install clips every 4–6 inches around the edge.

RECESSED

A recessed installation is similar to the installation of a self-rimming sink without the clips. The tile will hold the recessed sink. Sometimes a bullnose edging surrounds the sink. Other sinks have a rim that allows the installation of full tiles with tops flush with the top of the sink.

Single-wall stainless steel sinks expand and contract more than tile. As a result, a good seal on a tile counter is difficult. Single-wall stainless sinks are, therefore, not recommended for recessed installation.

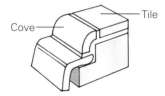

Tile

Cove

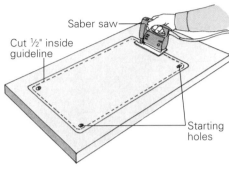

Cut ½" inside guideline — Saber saw — Starting holes

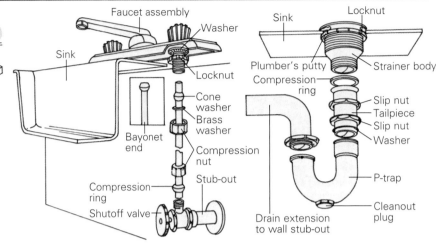

Faucet assembly — Washer — Sink — Locknut — Sink — Cone washer — Brass washer — Bayonet end — Compression nut — Compression ring — Shutoff valve — Stub-out

Sink — Locknut — Plumber's putty — Strainer body — Compression ring — Slip nut — Tailpiece — Slip nut — Washer — P-trap — Drain extension to wall stub-out — Cleanout plug

CUTTING THE OPENING

Drill a ½-inch hole at each corner of the inside line. Using a saber saw, cut between the holes along the inner line, supporting the cutout toward the end of the cut so the weight does not crack the countertop. If you don't have a saber saw, use a handsaw for the straight runs and a keyhole saw for the curves. The edges do not have to be perfectly straight nor smooth—the rim of the sink will cover them.

Before installing the sink, attach the strainer assembly, the faucet, and all accessories.

HOOKING UP THE FAUCET

Before hooking up the sink faucets to the hot and cold stops, note whether you will also be installing a dishwasher or icemaker. If a dishwasher will get its hot water from the same supply pipe, install a tee fitting, then two stops— one for the hot faucet and one for the dishwasher. Use the same method on the cold-water side to split the supply between the faucet and an icemaker.

HOOKING UP THE DRAIN

Apply plumber's putty around the sink's drain opening, insert the strainer bowl, and tighten the locknut. Hook up the P-trap assembly, connecting it to the drain stub-out with a slip nut and to the strainer tailpiece with another slip nut. Tighten the nuts by hand. A garbage disposer installs in same way (see below).

INSTALLING A DISPOSER

Before you install the disposer, record the model and serial number from its nameplate, which may be inaccessible after mounting it under the sink. Also, if you plan to drain a dishwasher through the disposer, remove the knockout from the dishwasher drainhose connector.

A garbage disposer includes a mounting bracket that conveniently detaches from the unit. Apply plumber's putty around the sink drain. Install the bracket in the drain hole before installing the sink.

After installing the sink, attach the disposer to the mounting bracket with its discharge elbow lined up in the direction of the drain stub in the wall. Most units are held by mounting screws. Some have a quick-mount feature; merely twist the lock ring.

Now attach a 1½-inch trap adapter to the disposer's discharge elbow and hook up the P-trap the same way that you would hook up a regular drain.

Finally, connect the hose from the dishwasher.

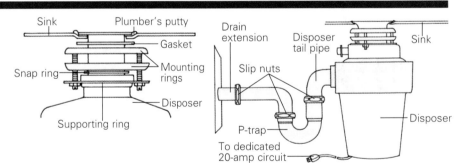

Sink — Plumber's putty — Gasket — Mounting rings — Disposer — Snap ring — Supporting ring

Drain extension — Disposer tail pipe — Sink — Slip nuts — P-trap — Disposer — To dedicated 20-amp circuit

TROUBLESHOOTING GARBAGE DISPOSERS

Problem	What to Do
Makes an odd sound	Turn the unit off and remove the object making the noise.
No sound—not even a hum	Press the reset button on the disposer.
	Check the circuit breaker at the panel
Hums but doesn't turn	Try turning flywheel from the bottom with the special tool that came with the disposer.
	Lost the tool? Use an Allen wrench.
	Try turning the flywheel from the top with a broom handle.
	Call for service or replace the unit.

SKYLIGHTS AND ROOF WINDOWS

REACH FOR THE SUN

ALSO SEE...
Flashing:
Pages 136–139
Framing:
Pages 152–159
Glazings:
Pages 164–167
Roofs:
Pages 282–289

Nothing alters the character of an interior space more dramatically than a skylight. It brightens any space in your home, especially areas that are naturally dark, such as hallways, interior bathrooms, stairwells, back bedrooms, and even closets. Because it faces upward, a skylight will admit four times as much light as a wall window of the same size. Therefore, it does not have to be especially large to make a difference.

CODE REQUIREMENTS

Definition: A skylight is any transparent or translucent glazing installed at a slope of at least 15 degrees from vertical.

Permitted Glazings:
■ Laminated glass
■ Tempered glass
■ Heat-strengthened glass
■ Wired glass
■ Rigid plastic

Screens: Tempered or heat-strengthened glass requires a screen beneath the glass, except when:

■ The area of glass is 16 square feet maximum and its highest point is no more than 12 feet above an accessible area.

■ The area of glass is more than 16 square feet, the slope is no more than 30 degrees from vertical, and its highest point is no more than 10 feet above an accessible area.

Curbs: Any skylight installed in a roof with a slope of less than 3/12 must be mounted on a curb extending at least 4 inches above the roof.

HEAT GAIN AND LOSS

Direct sunlight through a skylight is intense and can pose a problem, particularly in summer when the sun is high in the sky. Fabrics fade, the room heats up, and the strong light creates an uncomfortable glare. Here are a few solutions:

■ Install a unit with a low shading coefficient (SC): the ratio of the total solar heat gain to that of single 1/8-inch clear glass. Clear double-glazed glass has an SC of 0.82; heat-absorbing glass an SC of 0.54. Be aware, however, that reducing heat gain also decreases light and is somewhat self-defeating.

■ Install a retractable shade screen. Many manufacturers offer this option, and homemade variations are possible.

DUCKING DRIPS

Regardless of how much you spend for a skylight, if you live in the cold north country you will, from time to time, have condensation on the inside of the glazing. This is why you won't want to install the skylight directly over your sleeping pillow or over the tub.

■ Use deciduous foliage. Plant a fast-growing tree or take advantage of a tree that already shades part of the roof during the hotter months.

■ Locate skylights on the north side of the roof. This will cut out most of the glare, except during June and July.

■ Accept the light, but vent the heat. If direct sunlight is your goal, make the most of it, but make sure the skylight opens to exhaust excess heat.

In northern areas, heat loss is more serious than heat gain. Skylights can lose enormous amounts of heat to the cold night sky. To minimize heat loss:

■ Install a skylight with low-E or Heat-Mirror glazing (see Glazings, pages 164–167). With winter R-values of R-3.8 and 4.3, these glazings lose only 23 and 21 percent as much winter heat as a single-glazed piece of glass.

■ If you can't—or don't want to—buy low-E or Heat Mirror units, install movable insulation that you can put up each night. Buy quilted shades or make shutters out of rigid insulation.

LIGHT SHAFT VARIATIONS

You do not need to build a shaft in a room with a cathedral ceiling; but in a room with a dropped ceiling, you will need the shaft to funnel the light down to the room. The shape of the shaft is a matter of aesthetics and the degree to which you want to maximize the light. Generally, the smaller the skylight, the more you should flare the shaft.

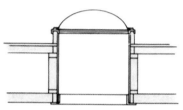

STRAIGHT SHAFT/FLAT ROOF

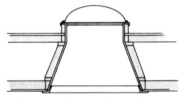

FLARED SHAFT/FLAT ROOF

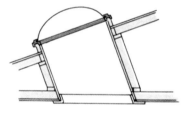

ANGLED SHAFT/PITCHED ROOF

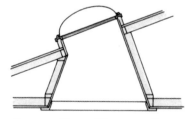

FLARED SHAFT/PITCHED ROOF

COMBINATION SHAFT/PITCHED ROOF

SKYLIGHT FRAMING PATTERNS

The illustrations, *below*, show three ways of framing a roof opening for a skylight. If possible, plan to use existing rafters rather than jack rafters to frame sides. If you add jack rafters, secure them with joist hangers.

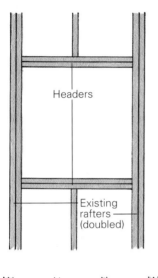

Headers

Existing rafters (doubled)

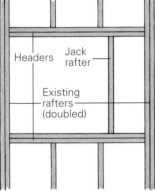

Headers   Jack rafter

Existing rafters (doubled)

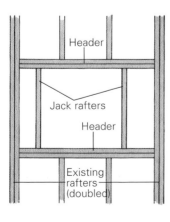

Header

Jack rafters

Header

Existing rafters (doubled)

PREPARATION

Most skylights are designed for easy installation. On roofs with a slope of 3-in-12 or less, your building codes may require that the skylight be installed on a 4-inch-high curb. If you install a curb yourself, it's a good idea to hire a professional roofing contractor to seal around the curb with hot mop roofing. The best installers add a waterproof membrane at the corners.

Installation should take from half a day to three days, depending on how many interior alterations are involved and the type of roofing material. If the room has a cathedral ceiling—with the interior finish attached directly to the undersides of the roof rafters—the installation should go quickly. If not, you will need to build a light shaft between the rafters and the ceiling joists. If the skylight spans more than two rafter bays, you will need to strengthen the rafters before installing the headers. If the roof is framed with trusses, consult a professional building contractor before cutting any framing members.

The key to an easy installation is preparation. Have all materials on hand and the preparatory framing completed before cutting a hole in the roof. You can break through the ceiling and install the framing for the light shaft and the skylight before cutting the hole. The actual cutting of the roof hole and installation of the curb and skylight should not take more than a few hours.

LAYING OUT THE OPENING

After determining where you want the skylight, drive a nail through the ceiling at the center of where the light shaft will be. In the attic, drop a plumb bob from the underside of the roof deck to the nail in the ceiling to find the center of the roof opening. Mark that point, then lay out the dimensions of the roof opening on the underside of the roof, taking care to account for any additional framing, such as a curb, that will be necessary. Refer to the manufacturer's directions for creating an opening of precisely the right width and length.

Nail marks center of ceiling opening

FRAMING THE OPENING

After laying out the opening, include 3 inches for the double headers at the top and bottom of the layout, and mark the rafters for cutting. If you are cutting more than one rafter, support the roof by nailing 2×4s across the rafters above and below the location of the opening. These temporary supports should span at least two rafters to either side of the opening. Use duplex nails. Cut the rafters with a handsaw or reciprocating saw and nail the jack rafters and headers in place, as shown.

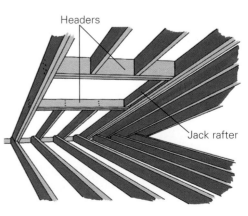

Headers

Jack rafter

▶

INSTALLING A SKYLIGHT *continued*

Cut shingles 2" out
from curb outline

Inside edge of curb

Flange

Roofing
cement

Toenail curb
into place

Caulk

CUTTING THE OPENING

Make sure no attic wiring or obstructions on the roof are in the way of the cutting. If the roof is steeper than 6-in-12, see if you can cut the opening from the attic side with a reciprocating saw, using the headers and rafters as a guide. Otherwise, make the cut from the roof side. Lay out the cut by drilling holes or driving nails up from the attic at the four corners of the opening. On the roof, snap chalk lines between the holes. Use a reciprocating saw to cut through the roofing and the sheathing. If you use a circular saw, equip it with a nail-cutting blade.

INSTALLING A SELF-FLASHING SKYLIGHT

Remove the shingles around the sides and top of the opening so that the flange lies flat on the roof sheathing. Coat the edges of the opening with roofing cement and lay the skylight in place, lapping the bottom flange over the shingles along the bottom edge of the opening. Make any adjustments in alignment and nail the top and sides of the flange with galvanized roofing nails spaced every 6 inches. Coat the top of the flange with roofing cement and replace the shingles around the skylight.

INSTALLING A CURB

Most skylights are mounted on a curb. Build a frame of 2×4s, with outside dimensions equal to the inside dimensions of the skylight, less ⅜ inch in each direction for clearance. Remove enough shingles around the roof opening for the curb to sit directly on the sheathing. Using 8d nails, toenail the curb down through the sheathing into the headers and rafters. Make sure that the curb is absolutely square, using a framing square if the skylight is small, equal diagonals if large. Also, make certain that the top of the curb is on a flat plane. Correct any sagging corners with shims.

INSTALLING THE SKYLIGHT

Flash the curb with step flashing on the sides and with collars at the top and bottom. Have the top and bottom collars fabricated by a sheet-metal shop if they don't come with the skylight. Install the bottom collar first, then the step flashing, followed by the top collar. Then put a bead of caulk or closed-cell foam weather stripping on the top edge of the curb and set the skylight on it. Drive nails through the sides of the skylight into the curb, using special aluminum nails with neoprene gaskets. Most skylights have holes drilled in the sides for this purpose.

CUTTING THE CEILING JOISTS

Drop a plumb bob from each corner of the framed roof opening to the ceiling and mark. These locations define the inside edges of the opening in the ceiling. Note: Use these points to establish the size of a flared opening (see Light Shaft Variations, page 316).

Provide temporary bracing for the ceiling joists by fastening 2×4s that span at least two joists in each direction. If possible, fasten these temporary supports with drive screws—hammering may loosen or crack the ceiling finish below.

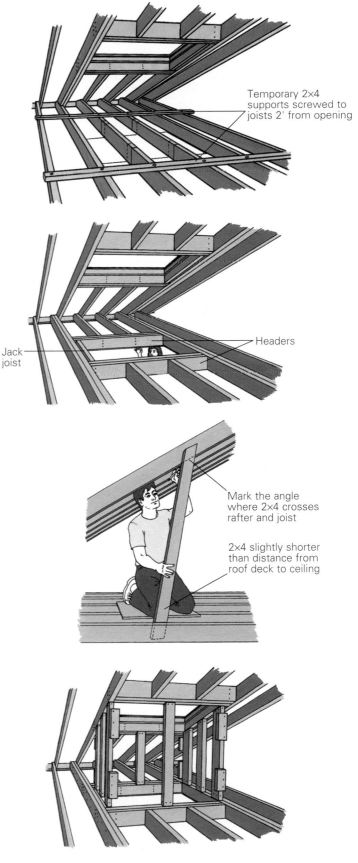

Temporary 2×4 supports screwed to joists 2' from opening

FRAMING THE CEILING OPENING

Cut through the joists. Be careful if you use a power saw because the blade may bind as the joist sags. Avoid this problem by using a reciprocating saw with a long blade, beginning the cut under the joist and cutting upward. Take care to protect the room below from damage caused by falling debris. After cutting, install headers and double up the side rafters, as shown. If you are cutting through only one joist, single headers will suffice. Double up the side joists when they are longer than 8 feet or if you are cutting through two or more joists.

Jack joist

Headers

FRAMING THE LIGHT WELL

Use 2×4s, spaced no more than 24 inches apart, to frame the walls of the light shaft. To mark them for cutting, hold them in place against the rafter and joists at whatever angle you want the light well to be. You may have to cut them to approximate length first for them to fit for marking. Mark each stud separately. Toenail the tops of the 2×4 studs to the rafters and the bottoms to the joists.

Mark the angle where 2×4 crosses rafter and joist

2×4 slightly shorter than distance from roof deck to ceiling

FINISHING THE LIGHT WELL

Because rafters and ceiling joists do not always align, proceed with care. You may have to consider each stud as an individual project of measuring, cutting, and nailing. When the framing for the shaft is complete, install faced blanket insulation between the studs, with the face toward the shaft. Then staple a plastic vapor barrier to the inside of the framing, install wallboard, and finish the shaft with paint and trim.

319

SOLAR HEATING

A BRIGHT IDEA WHOSE TIME HAS COME—AGAIN

Sunlight is a benign, abundant, and free source of energy. Solar energy is not a new technology, but an ancient idea that has been revived. During the last century we have relied, directly or indirectly, on fossil fuel for our heating, cooling, and lighting needs. The volatility of cost and finite amount of these sources prompted the search for alternatives. Initial experiments with solar energy produced many residential applications, from off-the-shelf hardware to homes designed completely around the idea of solar heating. Some resembled space-age fantasies, but most attempted to integrate solar features into traditional home design.

In the minds of some, solar energy requires high-tech hardware and futuristic house design. While research projects may involve these elements, great improvements can be made to the residential use of solar energy without gadgets or unsightly hardware.

Solar energy is not new to any of us—we experience it when our car warms up in a sunny parking lot, when we gravitate toward sunny rooms in the winter, or when our west-facing dining room is too uncomfortable for dinner during the summer. We can consciously design our homes to make use of the sun throughout the day and through the four seasons. A solar home is one that works in harmony with the sun, whether we want sunshine to heat and cool or simply to enjoy.

SOLAR WEATHER

The map *below* shows the pattern of solar-energy potential to lower heating bills across the continental United States. The zones reflect the amount of sunshine and the severity of the cold.

The area designated "Zone 1" shows the greatest potential for savings, "Zone 6" the least. For actual savings potentials, read further.

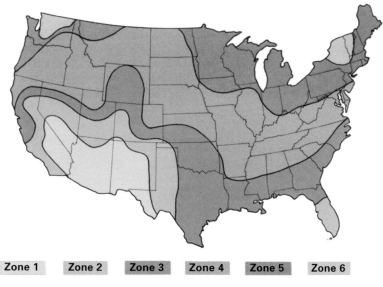

Zone 1   Zone 2   Zone 3   Zone 4   Zone 5   Zone 6

FIRST THINGS FIRST

Don't even think about solar design until you have incorporated the following energy-conservation steps into your house:

- Insulate floors, walls, and roofs to your state's energy code standards (see Insulation, page 186).
- Reduce air infiltration with continuous air/vapor barriers, careful caulking, and thorough weather stripping.
- Install insulated exterior doors.
- Install triple-glazed, Low-E, or Heat Mirror windows, or add moveable window insulation to double-glazed windows.
- Reduce the number and areas of windows on the north side of the house
- Use deciduous trees or overhangs to admit winter sun, but block most of the summer sun.

STORING SOLAR HEAT

Once the rays of the sun reach the inside of your house, you want them absorbed by massive objects. They store heat and release it after the sun goes down. Heat from the sun is reflected by thin objects, which warms the air around them immediately. Therefore, heavy objects should have high absorptance; lightweight objects low absorptance. For your guidance:

Material	Absorptance, %
Flat black paint	95
Dark gray slate	89
Dark brown paint	88
Dark blue paint	88
Brown concrete	85
Medium brown paint	84
Light gray paint	75
Red paint	74
Plain concrete	65
Medium yellow paint	57
Medium blue paint	51
Light green paint	47
White semigloss paint	30
White gloss paint	25

GET TO KNOW TRUE SOUTH

To maximize solar heat, face the wall with the most windows directly south—the direction of the sun at solar noon (midway between sunrise and sunset). Here's how to find "due" south:

- From the newspaper or TV weather, write down the time of sunrise and the time of sunset.

- Add the two, for example 6:20 a.m. plus 6:10 p.m. equals 12:30. Then add 12 hours to your total: 24:30.
- Divide the total in half and you have the time when the sun lies due south (in the example, 24:30/2=12:15.

PASSIVE SOLAR HEATING

In simple terms, "passive solar" design involves creating or changing interior space to maximize its potential as a solar collector. A passive design uses:
■ South-facing windows to capture the greatest warmth of sunlight.
■ The building's mass to store the captured solar energy.
■ Insulation and air-tightening to minimize the loss of heat.

Discounting extreme designs, which most would find unappealing, there are three basic passive solar building types: direct gain, isolated sun space, and integrated sun space.

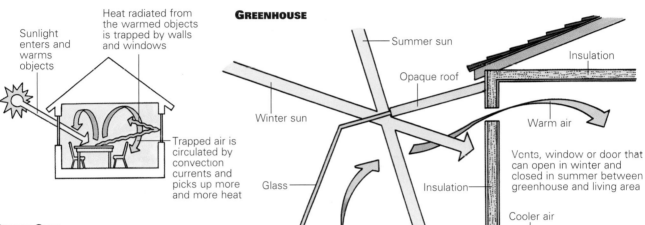

Sunlight enters and warms objects

Heat radiated from the warmed objects is trapped by walls and windows

Trapped air is circulated by convection currents and picks up more and more heat

GREENHOUSE

Summer sun

Opaque roof

Winter sun

Insulation

Warm air

Vents, window or door that can open in winter and closed in summer between greenhouse and living area

Glass

Insulation

Cooler air

Insulation

DIRECT GAIN

If you have ever lived in a house that has one especially sunny room, you have already experienced direct-gain solar heating. On a sunny winter day, the sun streams through the windows, heating the first surface it strikes, which, in turn, heats the air in the room. In other words, direct-gain design incorporates materials that utilize direct exposure to sunlight.

In direct-gain design, south-facing glass, thermal mass (ability to absorb heat with small rise in temperature), absorptivity of surfaces, and heat loss of the building are optimally balanced to reduce the heating bill without overheating the spaces.

The more extreme designs utilize maximum glass, absorptions, and mass to capture several day's worth of heat during an eight-hour period.

The two most common heat-storage masses are:
Masonry: concrete, tile, slate, and brick—typically used in floors and structural walls.
Gypsum wallboard: often applied as a double layer in walls and ceilings.

Most direct-gain designs feature open plans so that all of the floors, walls, and ceiling of the house participate in heat storage.

ISOLATED SUN SPACE

People love sunny spaces during the winter. Add-on sunrooms and solar greenhouses are two popular structures that can bring the comforts of sunlight into an existing home.

When a sun space is designed into a home from the beginning, there are two ways to maximize its benefit. In the first, the sun space is isolated from the main living area by a wall and glass doors. The temperature in the sun space is allowed to swing higher during the day and lower during the night, than in the rest of the house.

During the day, while the sun space is warmer than the house, heat can either be stored in a masonry separating wall, or blown directly into the living space with fans. At night the process reverses, with heat flowing back into the cool sun space from the wall, and—optionally—blown in from the heated living space. The isolated sun space can also be used as a solar greenhouse, since the humidity required by the plants can be kept out of the house where it would cause mildew.

INTEGRATED SUN SPACE

The second design integrates the sun space into living areas. With no wall between the sun space and the rest of the house, it is similar to the direct-gain design, except that tilted windows reach out and grab maximum sun. The integrated design is appropriate when the sun space is intended primarily as a living space.

With its tilted windows, integrated sun spaces are subject to overheating during the summer when the sun is high overhead. The best remedy for overheating is large deciduous trees. Their leaves block the sun in the summer; in the winter, their bare branches let the sunlight in.

SOLAR WATER HEATING

EVER THINK YOU'D CONTEMPLATE HOME THERMOSIPHONS?

Americans are relatively new to the solar energy game; in fact, most of us don't even know how the game is played. However, solar energy has been used to heat water for domestic use in many parts of the world for half a century.

Unless you live in a hot, sunny climate, meeting all of your hot water needs with solar energy is impractical. It makes a lot of sense, however, to produce the first and easiest 40–80 percent with solar collectors. The payback period for a solar hot water system is very short compared to elaborate space heating systems.

In most systems the solar collector only preheats the water before it enters a conventional heater. In others the solar-heated water is hot enough—anywhere from 120° to 160° F—to be used directly.

The three basic systems for heating water are flat-plate collectors, batch heaters, and thermosiphons.

CODE REQUIREMENTS

Pressure and Temperature Relief: All system components containing fluids must be protected with pressure- and temperature-relief valves. The system must be plumbed such that no section can be isolated from a relief valve.

Vacuum Relief: All system components subjected to pressure drops below atmospheric pressure (a vacuum) must be protected by a vacuum-relief valve.

Protection from Freezing: All system components must be protected from damage from freezing of heat-transfer fluids at the lowest ambient (surrounding the equipment) temperatures that occur during operation.

BATCH HEATER

The batch collector actually contains the storage tank—usually a black tank enclosed in a box with glazing. The nonglazed interior surfaces of the box have a shiny surface to reflect solar energy onto the tank from as many sides as possible. The large size of the tank and dual glazing generally prevent the water from freezing overnight.

BATCH HEATER SYSTEM

Because the batch collector holds water all the time, it is not suitable for northern climates subject to extreme cold unless it is used only seasonally.

A batch heating system does not heat water as quickly as a flat-plate system, but it does heat the water all at once. It relies on intermittent rather than continuous use.

Water, under pressure from the domestic water system, circulates through the batch collector and into a conventional water heater. That's it.

The appearance of batch systems has been a major drawback, but units are now available that fit into the roof structure and resemble a skylight. Others can be enclosed within interior spaces so they are less obtrusive and are protected from freezing.

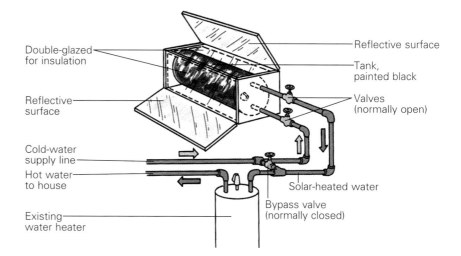

Double-glazed for insulation · Reflective surface · Cold-water supply line · Hot water to house · Existing water heater · Reflective surface · Tank, painted black · Valves (normally open) · Solar-heated water · Bypass valve (normally closed)

THERMOSIPHON COLLECTOR

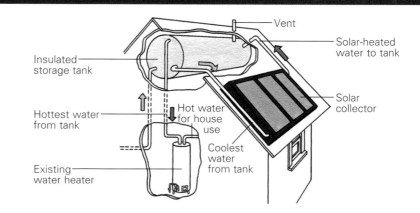

Insulated storage tank · Hottest water from tank · Existing water heater · Vent · Solar-heated water to tank · Solar collector · Coolest water from tank · Hot water for house use

From the street, a thermosiphon system looks the same as a flat-plate collector system. That is because they both use collectors on the roof. The thermosiphon collector must be mounted below the tank, however, so the heated, less-dense water will rise naturally to the storage tank without the assistance of a pump.

If your home's framing is not rugged enough to support the weight of the storage tank, you can locate the

FLAT-PLATE COLLECTOR

A typical flat-plate collector panel is an enclosed metal box with clear glazing on top and a black absorber plate inside with attached tubes. The tubes are spaced for the most efficient collection of heat from the flat plate. The heat-transfer fluid enters a single pipe (bottom manifold) at the bottom of the collector, spreads out into the smaller tubes where it is quickly heated by the absorber, and rejoins in a top manifold through which it leaves the collector. Circulating fluid can reach 120–160 degrees F. Water that stagnates inside the collector can reach temperatures as high as 400 degrees F.

Most collectors heat about a gallon of water per day per square foot of glazing on a clear day. If one person uses 10–20 gallons per day—a typical amount in a home with a clothes washer and dishwasher—then a typical household of four people requires two 4×10 foot panels to satisfy up to 80 percent of their hot water needs.

Although it is possible to make your own collectors, considering the stresses they must endure in the hostile rooftop environment, it is better to buy them from an established manufacturer. Besides freezing and boiling, they must resist corrosion from the mating of dissimilar metals, endure snow and wind loads, and resist leaks.

Collectors are usually mounted high on roofs in order to be out of the way

FLAT-PLATE COLLECTOR SYSTEM

A small circulator pump pushes heat-transfer fluid up into the collectors where it is heated by absorber plates. The heated fluid flows down through a heat exchanger inside a storage tank, then back to the pump.

Sensors are located at the collector outlet and the pump inlet. When the system control senses that the temperature in the collector is higher than the outlet of the heat exchanger, it turns on the pump.

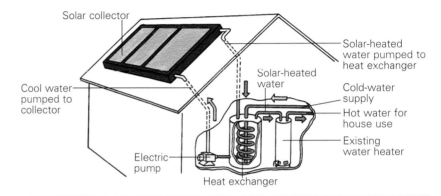

Solar collector

Cool water pumped to collector

Solar-heated water pumped to heat exchanger

Solar-heated water

Cold-water supply

Hot water for house use

Existing water heater

Electric pump

Heat exchanger

and to avoid being shaded. They should face within 30 degrees of true south. The altitude (angle of tilt above the horizon) should be the same as your latitude, which ranges from roughly 25 degrees near the southern border of the continental United States to approximately 50 degrees at the northern border. In determining the tilt of your collector, remember to include the slope of your roof. A slope of 12/12 equals 45 degrees.

The greatest danger to a collector is freezing. A solar collector, designed to absorb solar energy during the day, will just as efficiently radiate energy back to the cold night. So even when the air temperature at night is well above 32 degrees F, collectors can freeze. You can prevent this by using antifreeze instead of water as the heat transfer fluid. Use non-toxic propylene glycol ("RV antifreeze") rather than ethylene glycol, and test it every two years.

A second way to prevent freezing is to design the collector to drain back into a holding tank whenever the circulating pump is off. In milder climates you can use a simpler system that drains the water on command from a temperature-controlled valve. In very mild climates you may prevent freezing simply by allowing the water to continue circulating through the collector on cold nights. The water loses heat, but the alternative—a freeze—could ruin the system. The last two methods are vulnerable to power failure, so you must have a warning system with manual backup valves.

Flat-plate collector systems always include a storage tank. The typical solar water tank has a 120 gallon capacity and a heat exchanger coil. The tank is filled from the home water supply. Hot fluid from the collector flows through the heat exchanger, which transfers the heat to the water in the tank, and then back to the collector. Water in the storage tank is thus preheated to some degree for the regular water heater down the line.

collectors on or near the ground with the storage tank on a nearby stand.

THERMOSIPHON COLLECTOR SYSTEM

Like the other solar water heaters, a thermosiphon system works best when you schedule use of hot water around periods of greatest availability—late afternoon and early evening.

This system combines the efficiency of flat-plate collectors with the simplicity of a batch system. However, it only works if the tank is several feet above the top of the collectors in order to generate sufficient flow. Considering that the typical 120 gallon tank weighs nearly 1,400 pounds full of water, this can pose a structural problem.

The advantage of this system over a batch heater is that water can be

recirculated constantly through the collectors, raising the temperature in the storage tank until it is needed. Water is tapped from the top of the tank, where it is warmest.

DOUBLE-DUTY SYSTEM

You will collect a lot more heat if you consider your solar water heater as a pre-heater, instead of the whole water heater. There are lots of times (just after sunrise, before sunset, and on cloudy days) when the sun's rays are not strong enough to heat water to 120°F, but can preheat your cold incoming water to 80°F. So don't shut it off on cloudy days; just top off the heat with a regular water heater.

SOUND CONTROL

HOW SOUND TRAVELS

ALSO SEE...
Caulk:
Pages 50–51
Framing:
Pages 152–159
Insulation:
Pages 186–193
Wallboard:
Pages 394–399

There are three ways to reduce unwanted sound:
■ generate less
■ absorb more
■ transmit less.
Sound travels as waves, just like the ripples from a pebble tossed into a pond. When sound waves (vibrations) spread through the air and strike a door or wall, they cause it to vibrate as well. If the object is rigid, and if there is enough sound energy, the far side vibrates and passes the energy on to the air of the next room.

REDUCING SOUND GENERATION

Water pipes, appliances, duct work, furnaces, heating pipes, and other sources produce sound that can be reduced.

■ Hammering water pipes can be quieted with arresters, which act like shock absorbers. They are generally installed at the appliances causing the problem by too quickly closing their supply valves.

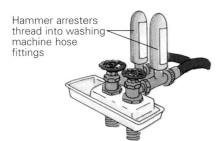

Hammer arresters thread into washing machine hose fittings

■ Rattling water pipes can be supported with hangers.

Pipe hangers isolated with felt weather stripping

■ Plastic pipes that squeak when they rub against framing can be silenced by stuffing fiberglass insulation between the pipe and the framing.

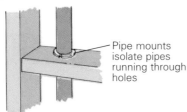

Pipe mounts isolate pipes running through holes

■ Low-noise toilets are quieter than standard ones, but more expensive. If the local building code requires ultra-low-flow toilets, test one before you buy. Some are very noisy.
■ Appliances can be supported on rubber vibration pads. You can also use sheets of foam or fiberglass sound deadener to reduce some of the higher-frequency noise.
■ Air-conditioning will let you close the windows when it is noisy outside. Whole-house units are quieter than room units.
■ Heating and cooling ducts can act as sound tunnels, transmitting blower-fan and room-to-room noise. They may also creak and pop. Oil the furnace pulleys and replace filters and fan belts to help quiet the furnace. Reroute straight ducts so they have bends and install a flexible rubber boot at the furnace output and cold-air return plenums. Readjust sections of duct work that pop. If that doesn't work, lightly score the surface of the duct in an X pattern. This allows the metal to flex without popping.

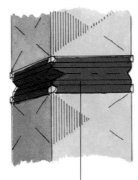

Rubber boot between sections of forced-air duct

ABSORBING SOUND

You can reduce the sound energy in a room by absorbing it instead of letting it bounce from wall to wall.

The absorption coefficient of a surface is the fraction of sound energy it absorbs. Since this figure varies with the frequency of the sound, engineers use a single figure, called the Noise Reduction Coefficient (NRC), the average of the absorption coefficients at 250, 500, 1,000, and 2,000 Hz.

The table, below, lists the NRCs of common home materials.

NRCs OF SURFACES

Material		NRC
Brick	Bare	0.04
	Painted	0.02
Carpet	On slab	0.29
	On foam pad	0.55
Concrete	Bare	0.36
	Painted	0.07
Fabric	10 oz velour straight	0.14
	14 oz velour pleated	0.56
Floor	Bare concrete	0.02
	Resilient on concrete	0.03
	Bare wood	0.09
	Parquet on concrete	0.06
Furniture	Bare wood or metal	0.06
	Plastic upholstered	0.50
	Fabric upholstered	0.55
Glass	Plate	0.04
	Double strength	0.16
Wall	½" gypsum drywall	0.07
	Marble or glazed tile	0.01
	Plywood paneling	0.15
Plaster	Smooth	0.03
	Rough	0.04

STC AND SPEECH PRIVACY

STC	Effect on Hearing
25	Normal speech heard clearly
30	Loud speech heard well
35	Loud speech audible but not understood
40	Loud speech heard as murmur
45	Loud speech barely heard
50	Loud speech not heard at all

QUIET WALLS

A wall 6 inches thick and filled with sand would give an STC rating of about 60. Referring to the table STC and Speech Privacy, however, shows that an STC of 45–50 is quite acceptable for the home. An STC of 45 can be achieved by covering a standard stud wall with ½-inch sound-deadening board on both sides, then finishing with ⅝-inch wallboard.

Another method is to use resilient channel on the studs and cover the wall with ½-inch wallboard. This will give an STC of approximately 50.

A third method is to build a double-row stud wall. Stagger the studs, weave fiberglass insulation between them, and cover with ½-inch wallboard. This will also give an STC rating of about 50.

In all walls, keep the number of receptacles and registers to a minimum.

Storm windows will dramatically block street noise.

INSULATED DOUBLE-ROW STUD WALL

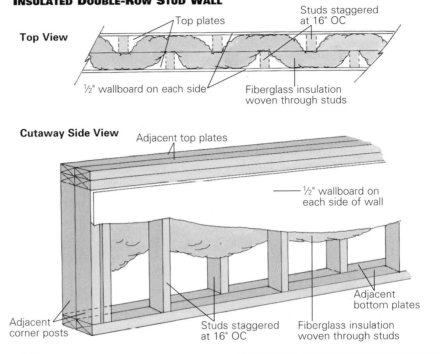

Top View — Top plates — Studs staggered at 16" OC — ½" wallboard on each side — Fiberglass insulation woven through studs

Cutaway Side View — Adjacent top plates — ½" wallboard on each side of wall — Adjacent corner posts — Studs staggered at 16" OC — Fiberglass insulation woven through studs — Adjacent bottom plates

QUIET FLOORS AND CEILINGS

SUSPENDED CEILING

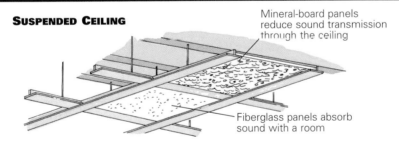

Mineral-board panels reduce sound transmission through the ceiling

Fiberglass panels absorb sound with a room

The easiest way to quiet a floor is to install a thick pad and carpet. A more expensive method, if the structure can support the weight, is to build the floor up with wallboard or a layer of sand.

A suspended ceiling of fiberglass panels or mineral-fiber tiles, will reduce sound transmission.

A better ceiling method is to use resilient channel on the joists. All existing material must be removed from the ceiling so the channel can be attached directly to the joists. If you can't attach the channel to the joists, add layers of wallboard to the ceiling (provided the structure can support the added weight). Resilient channel requires at least 3½ inches of air space above it to be effective. The greater the air space, the better it performs.

When attaching wallboard to resilient channel, be careful not to use screws long enough to reach and penetrate the ceiling joists, which cuts the effectiveness of the channel.

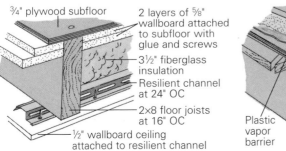

¾" plywood subfloor — 2 layers of ⅝" wallboard attached to subfloor with glue and screws — 3½" fiberglass insulation — Resilient channel at 24" OC — 2×8 floor joists at 16" OC — ½" wallboard ceiling attached to resilient channel

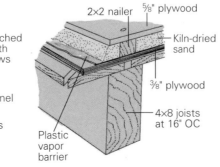

2×2 nailer — ⅝" plywood — Kiln-dried sand — ⅜" plywood — 4×8 joists at 16" OC — Plastic vapor barrier

SOUND TRANSMISSION

The transmission of speech through walls is rated by Sound Transmission Class, STC (*see box*). Transmission through ceilings and floors is rated by both STC and Impact Insulation Class, IIC. For either measurement, the higher the number, the less sound transmitted. A rating of 45–50 is reasonable; at this level, loud speech is barely heard as a murmur.

Materials for reducing sound transmission should be either heavy or nonrigid or both. Sand is a material having both properties. Its heaviness prevents the sound waves from vibrating the material; the non-rigidity absorbs and dissipates the sound.

The lower the pitch, the more difficult it is to block a sound. If high-pitched sounds are transmitting from room to room, there are probably air gaps letting the sound waves through. A one-inch gap in a wall can reduce the STC rating from 50 to 30.

The walls and ceilings of wood-frame buildings are light and rigid and, thus, need interrupted assemblies to block sound. This is easy with walls, since double-row stud walls are effective in preventing sound transmission. It is harder with ceilings.

325

Span Tables

SELECTING LUMBER TO FIT THE JOB

Building codes include span tables, which define what sizes of what species and grade of lumber will support loads of various weights. Each table is specific to a situation. The table on page 330, for example, is for roof rafters carrying light roofing (shingles or metal panels), but no finished ceiling, in areas of design snow loads of 20, 30, and 40 pounds per square foot (psf). Check you local building department for the requirements in your area.

To understand the table headings on the next five pages, you'll need to be familiar with these terms:

Maximum Allowable Span: The maximum allowable distance, in feet and inches, between supports for a joist or rafter.

O.C. Spacing: The distance between framing members, measured from the center of one to the center of the next, called "on center."

Species Group: The group of species the lumber falls within, as specified in its grade stamp.

Sel. Str., No. 1, No. 2, No. 3: An abbreviation for "select standard," followed by the grade of the lumber, ranked by quality.

Example: You are building an addition, and wish to purchase the lumber for your first-floor family-room floor joists. The joists will be spaced 16 inches on center, and they will span a distance of 11' 8". Your local lumberyard carries mostly Hem-Fir No.2 framing lumber. What size (cross-section) must the joists be?

Answer:

1. Find the appropriate span table for floor joists (see pages 328–329).

2. Find the row for Hem-Fir, 16" o.c.

3. Scan across to find the maximum allowable spans for all four of the No. 2 grade sizes:

2 × 6	9' 1"
2 × 8	12' 0"
2 × 10	15' 2"
2 × 12	17' 7"

The smallest size that will span 11' 8" safely is a 2×8.

THE STRENGTHS OF WOOD

Structural engineers use six measures of a timber's strength when calculating its ability to carry a "live load" (people, furniture, wind, snow) or a "dead load" (static building materials such as the exterior walls, siding, roofing, and windows). The six factors are:

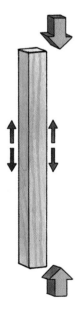

Tension Parallel to Grain (Ft): Occasionally, such as in roof trusses, a member is in tension: a force that tries to pull things apart.

Compression Parallel to Grain (Fc): The cross section of a post carries all of the weight on the post. If Fc is too small, the fibers will separate and the post will collapse.

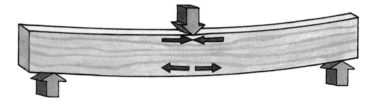

Fiber Stress in Bending (Fb): A load on a beam makes it bend, resulting in compression in the upper fibers and tension in the lower fibers. Fb is the design maximum tension allowed in the lowest fibers, in pounds per square inch (psi).

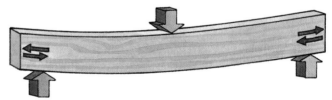

Horizontal Shear (Fv): When a beam bends downward, its upper fibers compress while its lower fibers elongate. Thus, its middle fibers are subject to a sliding or shearing action. If Fv is too small, the beam will split into two pieces along the zone of maximum shear.

Compression Perpendicular to Grain (Fc⊥): The last few inches of a joist bear half of the total weight carried by the joist. If the joist's compressive strength (Fc⊥) is too small, the bearing surface of the joist will crush.

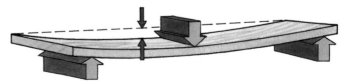

Modulus of Elasticity (E): E is a measure of the timber's stiffness, i.e. how far it will deflect as weight is applied. Floor joists with too low an E will be "bouncy."

BASE DESIGN VALUES FOR U.S. DIMENSION LUMBER, PSI (2–4" THICK × 2" AND WIDER)

Species Group	Grade	Extreme Fiber Stress in Bending Fb	Tension Parallel to Grain Ft	Horizontal Shear Fv	Compression Perpendicular to Grain Fc⊥	Compression Parallel to Grain Fc	Modulus of Elasticity (million psi) E
Douglas Fir-Larch	Sel. Str.	1,450	1,000	95	625	1,700	1.9
	No.1	1,000	675	95	625	1,450	1.7
	No. 2	875	575	95	625	1,300	1.6
	No. 3	500	325	95	625	750	1.4
	Construction	1,000	650	95	625	1,600	1.5
	Standard	550	375	95	625	1,350	1.4
	Utility	275	175	95	625	875	1.3
	Stud	675	450	95	625	825	1.4
Hem-Fir	Sel. Str.	1,400	900	75	405	1,500	1.6
	No. 1	950	600	75	405	1,300	1.5
	No. 2	850	500	75	405	1,250	1.3
	No. 3	500	300	75	405	725	1.2
	Construction	975	575	75	405	1,500	1.3
	Standard	550	325	75	405	1,300	1.2
	Utility	250	150	75	405	850	1.1
	Stud	675	400	75	405	800	1.2

ALLOWABLE DESIGN VALUES FOR SOUTHERN PINE, PSI

Lumber Dimension	Grade	Extreme Fiber Stress in Bending Fb	Tension Parallel to Grain Ft	Horizontal Shear Fv	Compression Perpendicular to Grain Fc⊥	Compression Parallel to Grain Fc	Modulus of Elasticity (million psi) E
2–4" thick, 2–4" wide	Sel. Str.	2,850	1,600	100	565	2,100	1.8
	No.1	1,850	1,050	100	565	1,850	1.7
	No. 2	1,500	825	90	565	1,650	1.6
	No. 3	850	475	90	565	975	1.4
	Stud	875	500	90	565	975	1.4
2–4" thick, 4" wide	Construction	1,100	625	100	565	1,800	1.5
	Standard	625	350	90	565	1,500	1.3
	Utility	300	175	90	565	975	1.3
2–4" thick, 5–6" wide	Sel. Str.	2,550	1,400	90	565	2,000	1.8
	No.1	1,650	900	90	565	1,750	1.7
	No. 2	1,250	725	90	565	1,600	1.6
	No. 3	750	425	90	565	925	1.4
	Stud	775	425	90	565	925	1.4
2–4" thick, 8" wide	Sel. Str.	2,300	1,300	90	565	1,900	1.8
	No.1	1,500	825	90	565	1,650	1.7
	No. 2	1,200	650	90	565	1,550	1.6
	No. 3	700	400	90	565	875	1.4

FLOOR JOISTS IN SLEEPING ROOMS AND ATTICS: 30 PSF LIVE, 10 PSF DEAD

Species Group	Spacing in. o.c.	2 × 4				2 × 6				2 × 8				2 × 10			
		Sel. Str.	No.1	No.2	No.3	Sel. Str.	No.1	No.2	No.3	Sel. Str.	No.1	No.2	No.3	Sel. Str.	No.1	No.2	No.3
Douglas Fir-Larch	12	12-6	12-0	11-10	9-8	16-6	15-10	15-7	12-4	21-0	20-3	19-10	15-0	25-7	24-8	23-0	17-5
	16	11-4	10-11	10-9	8-5	15-0	14-5	14-1	10-8	19-1	18-5	17-2	13-0	23-3	21-4	19-11	15-1
	19.2	10-8	10-4	10-1	7-8	14-1	13-7	12-10	9-9	18-0	16-9	15-8	11-10	21-10	19-6	18-3	13-9
	24	9-11	9-7	9-1	6-10	13-1	12-4	11-6	8-8	16-8	15-0	14-1	10-7	20-3	17-5	16-3	12-4
Hem-Fir	12	11-10	11-7	11-0	9-8	15-7	15-3	14-6	12-4	19-10	19-5	18-6	15-0	24-2	23-7	22-6	17-5
	16	10-9	10-6	10-0	8-5	14-2	13-10	13-2	10-8	18-0	17-8	16-10	13-0	21-11	20-9	19-8	15-1
	19.2	10-1	9-10	9-5	7-8	13-4	13-0	12-5	9-9	17-0	16-4	15-6	11-10	20-8	19-0	17-11	13-9
	24	9-4	9-2	8-9	6-10	12-4	12-0	11-4	8-8	15-9	14-8	13-10	10-7	19-2	17-0	16-1	12-4
Southern Pine	12	12-3	12-0	11-10	10-5	16-2	15-10	15-7	13-3	20-8	20-3	19-10	15-8	25-1	24-8	24-2	18-8
	16	11-2	10-11	10-9	9-0	14-8	14-5	14-2	11-6	18-9	18-5	18-0	13-7	22-10	22-5	21-1	16-2
	19.2	10-6	10-4	10-1	8-3	13-10	13-7	13-4	10-6	17-8	17-4	16-5	12-5	21-6	21-1	19-3	14-9
	24	9-9	9-7	9-4	7-4	12-10	12-7	12-4	9-5	16-5	16-1	14-8	11-1	19-11	19-6	17-2	13-2

Maximum Allowable Span, ft.–in.

FLOOR JOISTS IN ALL ROOMS BUT SLEEPING ROOMS AND ATTICS: 40 PSF LIVE, 10 PSF DEAD

Species Group	Spacing in. o.c.	2 × 4				2 × 6				2 × 8				2 × 10			
		Sel. Str.	No.1	No.2	No.3	Sel. Str.	No.1	No.2	No.3	Sel. Str.	No.1	No.2	No.3	Sel. Str.	No.1	No.2	No.3
Douglas Fir-Larch	12	11-4	10-11	10-9	8-8	15-0	14-5	14-2	11-0	19-1	18-5	17-9	13-5	23-3	22-0	20-7	15-7
	16	10-4	9-11	9-9	7-6	13-7	13-1	12-7	9-6	17-4	16-5	15-5	11-8	21-1	19-1	17-10	13-6
	19.2	9-8	9-4	9-1	6-10	12-10	12-4	11-6	8-8	16-4	15-0	14-1	10-7	19-10	17-5	16-3	12-4
	24	9-0	8-8	8-1	6-2	11-11	11-0	10-3	7-9	15-2	13-5	12-7	9-6	18-5	15-7	14-7	11-0
Hem-Fir	12	10-9	10-6	10-0	8-8	14-2	13-10	13-2	11-0	18-0	17-8	16-10	13-5	21-11	21-6	20-4	15-7
	16	9-9	9-6	9-1	7-6	12-10	12-7	12-0	9-6	16-5	16-0	15-2	11-8	19-11	18-7	17-7	13-6
	19.2	9-2	9-0	8-7	6-10	12-1	11-10	11-3	8-8	15-5	14-8	13-10	10-7	18-9	17-0	16-1	12-4
	24	8-6	8-4	7-11	6-2	11-3	10-9	10-2	7-9	14-4	13-1	12-5	9-6	17-5	15-2	14-4	11-0
Southern Pine	12	11-2	10-11	10-9	9-4	14-8	14-5	14-2	11-11	18-9	18-5	18-0	14-0	22-10	22-5	21-9	16-8
	16	10-2	9-11	9-9	8-1	13-4	13-1	12-10	10-3	17-0	16-9	16-1	12-2	20-9	20-4	18-10	14-6
	19.2	9-6	9-4	9-2	7-4	12-7	12-4	12-1	9-5	16-0	15-9	14-8	11-1	19-6	19-2	17-2	13-2
	24	8-10	8-8	8-6	6-7	11-8	11-5	11-0	8-5	14-11	14-7	13-1	9-11	18-1	17-5	15-5	11-10

Maximum Allowable Span, ft.–in.

CEILING JOISTS, DRYWALL, NO FUTURE ROOMS AND NO ATTIC STORAGE: 10 PSF LIVE, 5 PSF DEAD

Species Group	Spacing in. o.c.	2 × 4				2 × 6				2 × 8				2 × 10			
		Sel. Str.	No.1	No.2	No.3	Sel. Str.	No.1	No.2	No.3	Sel. Str.	No.1	No.2	No.3	Sel. Str.	No.1	No.2	No.3
Douglas Fir- Larch	12	13-2	12-8	12-5	10-10	20-8	19-11	19-6	15-10	27-2	26-2	25-8	20-1	34-8	33-5	32-5	24-6
	16	11-11	11-6	11-3	9-5	18-9	18-1	17-8	13-9	24-8	23-10	23-0	17-5	31-6	30-0	28-1	21-3
	19.2	11-3	10-10	10-7	8-7	17-8	17-0	16-7	12-6	23-3	22-5	21-0	15-10	29-8	27-5	25-8	19-5
	24	10-5	10-0	9-10	7-8	16-4	15-9	14-10	11-2	21-7	20-1	18-9	14-2	27-6	24-6	22-11	17-4
Hem-Fir	12	12-5	12-2	11-7	10-10	19-6	19-1	18-2	15-10	25-8	25-2	24-0	20-1	32-9	32-1	30-7	24-6
	16	11-3	11-0	10-6	9-5	17-8	17-4	16-6	13-9	23-4	22-10	21-9	17-5	29-9	29-2	27-8	21-3
	19.2	10-7	10-4	9-11	8-7	16-8	16-4	15-7	12-6	21-11	21-6	20-6	15-10	28-0	26-9	25-3	19-5
	24	9-10	9-8	9-2	7-8	15-6	15-2	14-5	11-2	20-5	19-7	18-6	14-2	26-0	23-11	22-7	17-4
Southern Pine	12	12-11	12-8	12-5	11-6	20-3	19-11	19-6	17-0	26-9	26-2	25-8	21-8	34-1	33-5	32-9	25-7
	16	11-9	11-6	11-3	10-0	18-5	18-1	17-8	14-9	24-3	23-10	23-4	18-9	31-0	30-5	29-4	22-2
	19.2	11-10	10-10	10-7	9-1	17-4	17-0	16-8	13-6	22-10	22-5	21-11	17-2	29-2	28-7	26-9	20-3
	24	10-3	10-0	9-10	8-2	16-1	15-9	15-6	12-0	21-2	20-10	20-1	15-4	27-1	26-6	23-11	18-1

CEILING JOISTS, DRYWALL, NO FUTURE ROOMS AND LIMITED ATTIC STORAGE: 20 PSF LIVE, 10 PSF DEAD

Species Group	Spacing in. o.c.	2 × 4				2 × 6				2 × 8				2 × 10			
		Sel. Str.	No.1	No.2	No.3	Sel. Str.	No.1	No.2	No.3	Sel. Str.	No.1	No.2	No.3	Sel. Str.	No.1	No.2	No.3
Douglas Fir- Larch	12	10-5	10-0	9-10	7-8	16-4	15-9	14-10	11-2	21-7	20-1	18-9	14-2	27-6	24-6	22-11	17-4
	16	9-6	9-1	8-9	6-8	14-11	13-9	12-10	9-8	19-7	17-5	16-3	12-4	25-0	21-3	19-10	15-0
	19.2	8-11	8-7	8-0	6-1	14-0	12-6	11-9	8-10	18-5	15-10	14-10	11-3	23-4	19-5	18-2	13-8
	24	8-3	7-8	7-2	5-5	13-0	11-2	10-6	7-11	17-1	14-2	13-3	10-0	20-11	17-4	16-3	12-3
Hem-Fir	12	9-10	9-8	9-2	7-8	15-6	15-2	14-5	11-2	20-5	19-7	18-6	14-2	26-0	23-11	22-7	17-4
	16	8-11	8-9	8-4	6-8	14-1	13-5	12-8	9-8	18-6	16-11	16-0	12-4	23-8	20-8	19-7	15-0
	19.2	8-5	8-3	7-10	6-1	13-3	12-3	11-7	8-10	17-5	15-6	14-8	11-3	22-3	18-11	17-10	13-8
	24	7-10	7-6	7-1	5-5	12-3	10-11	10-4	7-11	16-2	13-10	13-1	10-0	20-6	16-11	16-0	12-3
Southern Pine	12	10-3	10-0	9-10	8-2	16-1	15-9	15-6	12-0	21-2	20-10	20-1	15-4	27-1	26-6	23-11	18-1
	16	9-4	9-1	8-11	7-1	14-7	14-4	13-6	10-5	19-3	18-11	17-5	13-3	24-7	23-1	20-9	15-8
	19.2	8-9	8-7	8-5	6-5	13-9	13-6	12-3	9-6	18-2	17-9	15-10	12-1	23-2	21-1	18-11	14-4
	24	8-1	8-0	7-8	5-9	12-9	12-6	11-0	8-6	16-10	15-10	14-2	10-10	21-6	18-10	16-11	12-10

RAFTERS: MEDIUM ROOF COVERING, NO CEILING

Species Group	Spacing in. o.c.	2 × 4 Sel. Str.	No.1	No.2	No.3	2 × 6 Sel. Str.	No.1	No.2	No.3	2 × 8 Sel. Str.	No.1	No.2	No.3	2 × 10 Sel. Str.	No.1	No.2	No.3
20 PSF LIVE, 15 PSF DEAD																	
Douglas Fir-Larch	12	11-6	10-9	10-1	7-7	18-0	15-9	14-9	11-2	23-9	19-11	18-8	14-1	29-4	24-4	22-9	17-3
	16	10-5	9-4	8-9	6-7	16-4	13-8	12-9	9-8	20-9	17-3	16-2	12-2	25-5	21-1	19-9	14-11
	19.2	9-10	8-6	7-11	6-0	15-0	12-5	11-8	8-10	19-0	15-9	14-9	11-2	23-2	19-3	18-0	13-7
	24	9-1	7-7	7-1	5-5	13-5	11-2	10-5	7-10	17-0	14-1	13-2	10-0	20-9	17-3	16-1	12-2
Hem-Fir	12	10-10	10-6	9-11	7-7	17-0	15-4	14-6	11-2	22-5	19-5	18-4	14-1	28-7	23-9	22-5	17-3
	16	9-10	9-1	8-7	6-7	15-6	13-3	12-7	9-8	20-5	16-10	15-11	12-2	24-11	20-7	19-5	14-11
	19.2	9-3	8-3	7-10	6-0	14-7	12-2	11-6	8-10	18-8	15-4	14-6	11-2	22-9	18-9	17-9	13-7
	24	8-7	7-5	7-0	5-5	13-2	10-10	10-3	7-10	16-8	13-9	13-0	10-0	20-4	16-9	15-10	12-2
Southern Pine	12	11-3	11-1	10-9	8-1	17-8	17-4	15-5	11-11	23-4	22-3	19-11	15-3	29-9	26-6	23-9	18-0
	16	10-3	10-0	9-4	7-0	16-1	15-4	13-4	10-4	21-2	19-4	17-3	13-2	27-1	22-11	20-7	15-7
	19.2	9-8	9-5	8-6	6-5	15-2	14-0	12-2	9-5	19-11	17-7	15-9	12-0	25-5	20-11	18-10	14-3
	24	8-11	8-5	7-7	5-9	14-1	12-6	10-11	8-5	18-6	15-9	14-1	10-9	23-6	18-9	16-10	12-9
30 PSF LIVE, 15 PSF DEAD																	
Douglas Fir-Larch	12	10-0	9-6	8-10	6-8	15-9	13-11	13-0	9-10	20-9	17-7	16-5	12-5	25-10	21-6	20-1	15-2
	16	9-1	8-3	7-8	5-10	14-4	12-0	11-3	8-6	18-4	15-3	14-3	10-9	22-5	18-7	17-5	13-2
	19.2	8-7	7-6	7-0	5-4	13-3	11-0	10-3	7-9	16-9	13-11	13-0	9-10	20-5	17-0	15-11	12-0
	24	7-11	6-8	6-3	4-9	11-10	9-10	9-2	6-11	15-0	12-5	11-8	8-9	18-3	15-2	14-2	10-9
Hem-Fir	12	9-6	9-3	8-9	6-8	14-10	13-6	12-10	9-10	19-7	17-2	16-2	12-5	25-0	20-11	19-10	15-2
	16	8-7	8-0	7-7	5-10	13-6	11-9	11-1	8-6	17-10	14-10	14-0	10-9	22-0	18-1	17-2	13-2
	19.2	8-1	7-4	6-11	5-4	12-9	10-8	10-1	7-9	16-5	13-7	12-10	9-10	20-1	16-7	15-8	12-0
	24	7-6	6-6	6-2	4-9	11-7	9-7	9-1	6-11	14-8	12-1	11-6	8-9	18-0	14-10	14-0	10-9
Southern Pine	12	9-10	9-8	9-6	7-2	15-6	15-2	13-7	10-6	20-5	19-8	17-7	13-5	26-0	23-4	21-0	15-10
	16	8-11	8-9	8-3	6-2	14-1	13-6	11-9	9-2	18-6	17-0	15-3	11-8	23-8	20-3	18-2	13-9
	19.2	8-5	8-3	7-6	5-8	13-3	12-4	10-9	8-4	17-5	15-6	13-11	10-7	22-3	18-5	16-7	12-6
	24	7-10	7-5	6-8	5-1	12-3	11-1	9-7	7-5	16-2	13-11	12-5	9-6	20-8	16-6	14-10	11-3
40 PSF LIVE, 15 PSF DEAD																	
Douglas Fir-Larch	12	9-1	8-7	8-0	6-1	14-4	12-7	11-9	8-11	18-10	15-11	14-10	11-3	23-5	19-5	18-2	13-9
	16	8-3	7-5	6-11	5-3	13-0	10-10	10-2	7-8	16-7	13-9	12-11	9-9	20-3	16-10	15-9	11-11
	19.2	7-9	6-9	6-4	4-10	11-11	9-11	9-3	7-0	15-2	12-7	11-9	8-11	18-6	15-4	14-4	10-10
	24	7-3	6-1	5-8	4-3	10-8	8-11	8-4	6-3	13-6	11-3	10-6	7-11	16-6	13-9	12-10	9-9
Hem-Fir	12	8-7	8-4	7-11	6-1	13-6	12-3	11-7	8-11	17-10	15-6	14-8	11-3	22-9	18-11	17-11	13-9
	16	7-10	7-3	6-10	5-3	12-3	10-7	10-0	7-8	16-2	13-5	12-8	9-9	19-11	16-5	15-6	11-11
	19.2	7-4	6-7	6-3	4-10	11-7	9-8	9-2	7-0	14-10	12-3	11-7	8-11	18-2	15-0	14-2	10-10
	24	6-10	5-11	5-7	4-3	10-6	8-8	8-2	6-3	13-4	10-11	10-4	7-11	16-3	13-5	12-8	9-9
Southern Pine	12	8-11	8-9	8-7	6-6	14-1	13-9	12-4	9-6	18-6	17-9	15-11	12-2	23-8	21-1	19-0	14-4
	16	8-1	8-0	7-5	5-7	12-9	12-3	10-8	8-3	16-10	15-5	13-9	10-6	21-6	18-3	16-5	12-5
	19.2	7-8	7-6	6-9	5-1	12-0	11-2	9-9	7-6	15-10	14-1	12-7	9-7	20-2	16-8	15-0	11-4
	24	7-1	6-9	6-1	4-7	11-2	10-0	8-8	6-9	14-8	12-7	11-3	8-7	18-9	14-11	13-5	10-2

Maximum Allowable Span, ft.–in.

HEADER SPANS, EXTERIOR WALLS, FOR DOUGLAS FIR-LARCH, HEM-FIR, AND SOUTHERN PINE

Roof Live Load (psf)	Size	20 Building Width, ft.			30 Building Width, ft.			40 Building Width, ft.			50 Building Width, ft.		
		20	28	36	20	28	36	20	28	36	20	28	36
Headers Supporting Roof & Ceiling	2-2×4	3-6	3-2	2-10	3-3	2-10	2-7	3-0	2-7	2-4	2-10	2-5	2-2
	2-2×6	5-5	4-8	4-2	4-10	4-2	3-9	4-5	3-10	3-5	4-1	3-7	3-2
	2-2×8	6-10	5-11	5-4	6-2	5-4	4-9	5-7	4-10	4-4	5-2	4-6	4-0
	2-2×10	8-5	7-3	6-6	7-6	6-6	5-10	6-10	5-11	5-4	6-4	5-6	4-11
	2-2×12	9-9	8-5	7-6	8-8	7-6	6-9	7-11	6-10	6-2	7-4	6-4	5-8
	3-2×8	8-4	7-5	6-8	7-8	6-8	5-11	7-0	6-1	5-5	6-6	5-8	5-0
	3-2×10	10-6	9-1	8-2	9-5	8-2	7-3	8-7	7-5	6-8	7-11	6-10	6-2
	3-2×12	12-2	10-7	9-5	10-11	9-5	8-5	9-11	8-7	7-8	9-2	8-0	7-2
Headers Supporting Roof, Ceiling, & One Floor (with Center Bearing Wall)	2-2×4	3-1	2-9	2-5	2-10	2-6	2-3	2-8	2-4	2-1	2-6	2-2	2-0
	2-2×6	4-6	4-0	3-7	4-2	3-8	3-3	3-11	3-5	3-1	3-8	3-2	2-11
	2-2×8	5-9	5-0	4-6	5-3	4-8	4-2	4-11	4-4	3-11	4-8	4-1	3-8
	2-2×10	7-0	6-2	5-6	6-5	5-8	5-1	6-0	5-3	4-9	5-8	4-11	4-5
	2-2×12	8-1	7-1	6-5	7-6	6-7	5-11	7-0	6-1	5-6	6-7	5-9	5-2
	3-2×8	7-2	6-3	5-8	6-7	5-10	5-3	6-2	5-5	4-10	5-10	5-1	4-7
	3-2×10	8-9	7-8	6-11	8-1	7-1	6-5	7-6	6-7	5-11	7-1	6-2	5-7
	3-2×12	10-2	8-11	8-0	9-4	8-2	7-5	8-9	7-8	6-11	8-3	7-2	6-6
Headers Supporting Roof, Ceiling, & One Floor	2-2×4	2-8	2-4	2-1	2-8	2-3	2-0	2-6	2-2	2-0	2-5	2-1	1-10
	2-2×6	3-11	3-5	3-0	3-10	3-4	3-0	3-8	3-2	2-11	3-6	3-0	2-9
	2-2×8	5-0	4-4	3-10	4-10	4-3	3-9	4-8	4-1	3-8	4-5	3-10	3-5
	2-2×10	6-1	5-3	4-8	5-11	5-2	4-7	5-8	4-11	4-5	5-5	4-8	4-3
	2-2×12	7-1	6-1	5-5	6-11	6-0	5-4	6-7	5-9	5-2	6-3	5-5	4-11
	3-2×8	6-3	5-5	4-10	6-1	5-3	4-9	5-10	5-1	4-7	5-6	4-10	4-4
	3-2×10	7-7	6-7	5-11	7-5	6-5	5-9	7-1	6-2	5-7	6-9	5-10	5-3
	3-2×12	8-10	7-8	6-10	8-8	7-6	6-8	8-3	7-2	6-6	7-10	6-10	6-1
Headers Supporting Roof, Ceiling, & Two Floors (with Center Bearing Wall)	2-2×4	2-7	2-3	2-0	2-6	2-2	2-0	2-5	2-1	1-11	2-3	2-0	1-10
	2-2×6	3-9	3-3	2-11	3-8	3-3	2-11	3-6	3-1	2-10	3-4	2-11	2-8
	2-2×8	4-9	4-2	3-9	4-8	4-1	3-8	4-5	3-11	3-6	4-3	3-9	3-4
	2-2×10	5-9	5-1	4-7	5-8	5-0	4-6	5-5	4-9	4-4	5-2	4-7	4-1
	2-2×12	6-8	5-10	5-3	6-7	5-9	5-2	6-4	5-7	5-0	6-0	5-3	4-9
	3-2×8	5-11	5-2	4-8	5-10	5-1	4-7	5-7	4-11	4-5	5-4	4-8	4-2
	3-2×10	7-3	6-4	5-9	7-1	6-3	5-7	6-10	6-0	5-5	6-6	5-8	5-2
	3-2×12	8-5	7-4	6-7	8-3	7-3	6-6	7-11	6-11	6-3	7-6	6-7	6-0
Headers Supporting Roof, Ceiling & Two Floors	2-2×4	2-1	1-10	1-7	2-1	1-9	1-7	2-0	1-9	1-7	2-0	1-9	1-7
	2-2×6	3-1	2-8	2-4	3-0	2-7	2-4	3-0	2-7	2-4	2-11	2-7	2-3
	2-2×8	3-10	3-4	3-0	3-10	3-4	2-11	3-9	3-3	2-11	3-9	3-3	2-11
	2-2×10	4-9	4-1	3-8	4-8	4-0	3-7	4-7	4-0	3-7	4-7	3-11	3-6
	2-2×12	5-6	4-9	4-3	5-5	4-8	4-2	5-4	4-8	4-2	5-3	4-7	4-1
	3-2×8	4-10	4-2	3-9	4-9	4-2	3-8	4-9	4-1	3-8	4-8	4-1	3-7
	3-2×10	5-11	5-1	4-7	5-10	5-1	4-6	5-9	5-0	4-6	5-8	4-11	4-5
	3-2×12	6-10	5-11	5-4	6-9	5-10	5-3	6-8	5-10	5-2	6-7	5-9	5-1

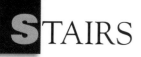

STAIRS

YOUR FIRST STEP

ALSO SEE...
Framing: *Pages 152–159*
Joinery: *Pages 194–199*
Railings: *Pages 268–269*
Steps: *Pages 336–337*

Installing a formal hardwood stairway is no weekend project. The job requires meticulous planning, mathematical calculations, and finish carpentry skills. But anyone with at least some carpentry experience can build a simple, straight stairway for the attic or basement.

If you're in doubt about your skills or don't have the time, consider these options:

■ Get a local manufacturer to prefabricate and deliver the stairway as a unit.
■ Hire a contractor to install prebuilt stairs or to custom build them on site.
■ Take your stair dimensions to a building supplier or a stair specialty company and order precut parts.

DESIGN CONSIDERATIONS

WHERE TO LOCATE A STAIRWAY

A stairway is a funnel for transporting people from one group of living spaces to another on a different level. When planning a new stairway, make sure its location is close to the center of traffic patterns in each area.

Also consider the structural modifications you'll need to make to accommodate a new stairway.

On levels with sloping ceilings, be sure to leave enough headroom at the top of the stairs and three feet beyond the top stair.

Finally, except for basement and attic access stairs, always treat stairs as a major design element rather than a utilitarian afterthought. Going up and down stairs is a dramatic transition. Plan an appealing view at the top—a window or attractive alcove rather than a stark hall or blank wall. Also consider the view as you descend. Likewise, place a window or an inviting space where the steps lead.

The least disruptive place to locate a new stairway is directly above an existing stairway. Place a new set of attic stairs above the main stairs or basement stairs, for example. If this isn't practical and you are forced into cutting a hole in the floor or ceiling, try at least to run the flight parallel to the joists. If the stairway must run perpendicular to the joists, position it along a bearing wall or add a new wall or posts to support the trimmer joists.

CONFIGURATION OPTIONS

Stairways take up a lot of space! A typical straight-run stairway from one floor to the next requires about 40 square feet of floor space (3 feet wide, 12 to 13 feet long), not to mention an additional 9 square feet of floor space for a landing at the bottom. The well opening eliminates another

CALCULATING DIMENSIONS

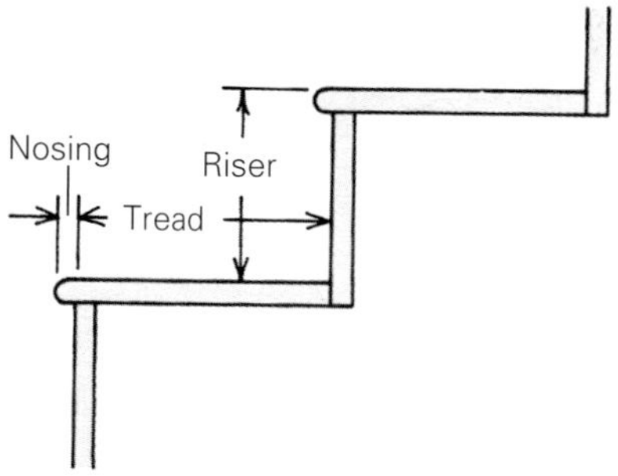

RISER HEIGHT AND TREAD WIDTH

Here's how to calculate risers and treads:

1. Measure the distance from floor to floor (total rise), allowing for the depth of finish flooring.

2. Divide the total rise by 7½ (an appropriate riser height) to get the approximate number of steps. Round up the answer to the nearest whole number.

3. Divide the rounded number back into the total rise. The answer should be 7 and a fraction—that's the actual height each riser must be.

4. To find the tread width, subtract the riser dimension from 17½ inches.

Example:

A total rise of 98" divided by 7½ equals 13.067. Rounding up gives approximately 14 steps. Dividing the total rise again, this time by 14, yields a riser height of exactly 7 inches. Subtracting the riser height from 17½ gives a tread depth of 10½ inches.

STAIR DIMENSIONS

Total Rise, feet/inches	Number of Steps	Riser inches	Tread inches	Total Run, feet/inches
7' 6"	12	7½"	10"	9' 2"
7' 7"	13	7"	10½"	10' 6"
7' 7½"	12	7⅝"	9⅞"	9' ⅝"
7' 9"	12	7¾"	9¾"	8' 11¼"
7' 10¼"	13	7¼"	10¼"	10' 3"
7' 10½"	12	7⅞"	9⅝"	8' 9⅞"
8' 0"	12	8"	9½"	8' 8½"
8' 1½"	13	7½"	10"	10' 0"
8' 2"	14	7"	10½"	11' 4½"
8' 3¾"	14	7⅛"	10⅜"	11' 2⅞"
8' 4¾"	13	7¾"	9¾"	9' 9"
8' 5½"	14	7¼"	10¼"	11' 1¼"
8' 7¼"	14	7⅜"	10⅛"	10' 11⅝"
8' 8"	13	8"	9½"	9' 6"
8' 9"	14	7½"	10"	10' 10"

36 feet of floor space upstairs. Such a stairway occupies 84 square feet. At $75 per square foot (a national average cost for renovations) the stairway will cost $6,300, not a sum to be taken lightly.

Steeper stairs, spiral stairs (you can buy prefab units), and winders will save space, but making stairs steeper to save room is safe only to a point. Keep the angle of ascent to the preferred angle—from 30 to 35 degrees. A 9-foot stairway within that range requires a run of 13 feet, 5 inches. A steeper stairway angled at 38 degrees would require only 10 feet, 7 inches.

Prefabricated spiral stairs come with diameters ranging from 4½ feet to 6 feet. Some codes restrict spiral stairways to serve only as a secondary flight if the upper story contains more than 400 square feet. Consider whether your spiral stairway will prevent you from moving beds or other essential large items between floors.

Winders save space by eliminating the 3×3-foot platform where the stairs turn 90 degrees. Codes have strict requirements regulating the size of winders, however (see Code Requirements, below).

CODE REQUIREMENTS: STAIRS

Width: The minimum widths of stairways are:
- 36" between walls
- 32" between a single handrail and opposite wall
- 28" between handrails on opposite walls

Headroom: The minimum headroom above any portion of a stairway is 6' 8", measured above the tread nosings

Treads and Risers:
- Minimum tread, nose to nose, is 10"

- Maximum tread variation is ⅜"
- Maximum slope of tread is 2%
- Maximum riser height is 7¾"
- Maximum variation of risers is ⅜"

Tread and Riser Profile:
- Nosing must be ¾" to 1¼"
- No nosing is required if the tread is over 11"
- Risers can be zero to 30 degrees from vertical

Winder Stairs:
- Tread must be at least 10" at point measured

12" from the narrow side
- The tread must be at least 6" deep
- A handrail is required on narrow side

Spiral Stairs:
- The minimum width for any stair is 26"
- Treads must be at least 7½" at point measured 12" from the narrow side
- Maximum riser height is 7¾"
- The minimum headroom above any portion of the stairway is 6' 6"

STAIRWAY OPENING

Determine the total length of the stairway (the total run) by multiplying the tread depth times the number of treads minus one. To find the length of the stairwell opening, subtract the headroom from the ceiling height and determine how many risers and treads will fit. Then subtract the combined width of those treads from the total length of the stairway.

If there is not enough room for the opening or for the total length of the stairs, try another design that uses higher risers and narrower treads.

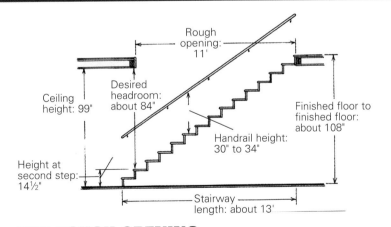

THE ROUGH OPENING

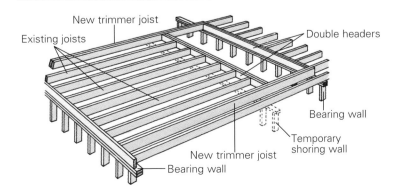

If the opening runs parallel to the joists, you need to cut through only one or two joists. If the opening is perpendicular, support the joists temporarily with shoring, then install trimmers and a new bearing wall or double headers.

To frame the opening, nail trimmer joists to the end joists with 16d nails 12 inches on center. Make sure the joists are supported at both ends. Mark the cut for the opening. Allow enough room for the framing, finish materials, and handrails.

▶

STAIRWAY INSTALLATION

Use only straight, clear, high quality 2×12s for stringers. To mark the first stringer, set the tongue (the short leg) of a framing square at the riser dimension, and the blade (the long leg) at the tread dimension. Scribe the outline of the square on the wood. Continue this process until you have marked all risers and treads. Mark carefully; the height of each finished riser must measure within 3/16 inch of every other riser to conform to code.

To make the bottom step the same height as the others, trim the bottom of the stringer by the thickness of one tread, and cut a notch for a 2×4 cleat.

Place the stringer in the rough opening to see if it fits properly. Adjust it if necessary. Then use it as a pattern to cut a second stringer. If the stairway is wider than 32 inches, you need to cut a third stringer.

Install the stringers, using a ledger or joist hangers at the top. If you nail one of the stringers to wall framing, add a

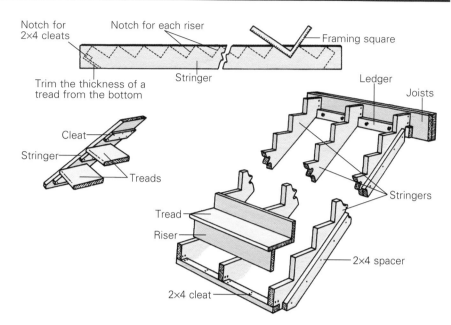

2×4 spacer for wallboard and finish trim. Install two or three risers at a time. Then, starting from the bottom, attach the treads. Fasten them to the

stringer with construction adhesive and 8d nails. In addition to face-nailing, drive nails from the back of the risers into the treads.

BALUSTERS

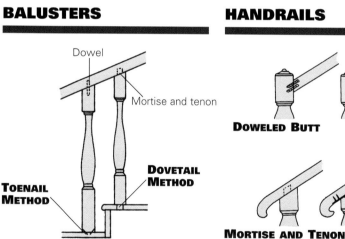

ATTACHING BALUSTERS

Traditional carpenters dovetail balusters into treads and cover the joint with molding. It's easier, however, and within the capabilities of most do-it-yourselfers, to drill pilot holes at an angle into the baluster, and toenail through the holes into the tread. There should be two balusters per tread, because codes specify a maximum opening between balusters of 4 inches. Position and fasten the handrail to the posts and balusters with dowels or mortise-and-tenon joints.

HANDRAILS

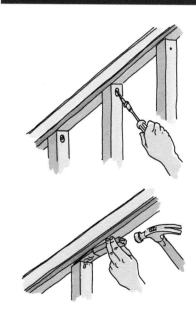

ATTACHING A HANDRAIL

You can attach the handrail in several different ways: with doweled butt joints, mortise-and-tenon joints, countersunk and plugged screws or bolts, or metal straps.

With the handrail clamped securely in position, mark the location of each baluster by dropping a plumb bob to baluster marks on the treads. Also mark the correct angle to guide you when drilling dowel holes or cutting mortises. Drill the holes and install the new handrail.

TIGHTENING HANDRAILS

To tighten a loose handrail, squeeze glue into the gap and predrill the baluster for countersunk drywall screws. Tightening the screws also will provide pressure for the glue.

If the gap is too large, drive a glue-coated wedge between the rail and the baluster and then fasten with screws.

REPAIRING LOOSE OR SQUEAKY STAIRS

Japanese emperors used to surround their sleeping quarters with specially designed porches and stairs that creaked loudly if anyone set foot on them. So you have a choice: You can fancy yourself a Japanese emperor or you can fix your squeaky stairs.

Stairs squeak when two pieces of wood rub together or wood rubs against a nail. Locate the problem area and lubricate it with graphite powder (lock lubricant). Repeat the application until the squeak stops.

Loose stairs require a little more work. Because of warps or settling, the edge of the tread sometimes separates slightly from the riser. You can live with squeaks, but a loose step is potentially hazardous and you should fix it immediately.

Whenever possible, repair a staircase from its underside. Because the repairs will not be seen, you can use heavy wood pieces and metal framing aids. Install metal brackets or glue-coated blocks tightly against the tread and screwed to the riser. Have a helper stand on the tread to press the tread and the riser firmly together—then glue and screw the joint.

If you must make repairs from above, predrill nail and screw holes to avoid splitting the wood.

With Nails: Angle each pair of nails in opposite directions. Recess the heads with a nail set and fill the holes with putty.

With Screws: Drill pilot holes and countersink them. Tighten the screws and fill the holes with putty before repainting.

With Wedges: Remove any molding and drive small, glue-coated wedges between the tread and the riser as shown. Note that the direction you drive the wedge depends on the type of construction.

After the glue dries, cut the wedges flush with the surface using a utility knife. Cover the gaps with decorative molding.

Trim molding

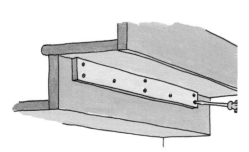

With Cleats: Have a helper stand on the loose step while you are working. From the underside, position an adhesive-coated cleat against the tread, then screw it into the riser. Be careful that the screws don't poke through the front face of the riser.

STEPS

DESIGN CONSIDERATIONS

If your lot slopes at all, you can use a few steps. First, they make walking on slippery ground safer. Second, they add an interesting design element to your landscaping.

Your major consideration, however, should be safety:

■ Use nonskid paving materials.
■ Never install a single step, because it is too easy to miss and trip over.
■ Make risers at least 4 inches high.
■ Risers and treads in the same flight should match within ⅜ inch, just as with interior stairs
■ provide a handrail if there are more than four steps in a flight and install lighting nearby.

Width should relate to the scale of the total area. As with interior stairs, 3 feet is the minimum, while 8 feet—the length of railroad ties—is a suitable maximum. Also, consider how to treat the edges of the steps. Will they remain bare or will you line them with planters or other barriers?

RISER-TREAD DESIGN

Interior stairs have to fit a floor-to-floor total rise; exterior steps have, instead, to match the slope of the ground. To determine the best riser-tread relationship, you first need to find the total vertical rise and total horizontal run. Use a long board or a line level to find these dimensions. If the distance is too great for a single measurement, take a series of measurements between intermediate points along the slope. Draw these measurements carefully on graph paper to give you a cross section of the slope to scale. If the slope changes over the total run, consider building the steps in several runs of differing slope.

After you have plotted the total rise and run of a set of stairs on graph paper, you can use a simple formula to find a ratio that conforms to the slope without being too steep or too flat. The formula: $2 \times \text{Riser} + \text{Tread} = 27$. For example,

$$\begin{aligned}
\text{Riser} &= 4 \text{ inches} \\
\text{Tread} &= 27 \text{ inches} - (2 \times \text{Riser}) \\
&= 27 \text{ inches} - 8 \text{ inches} \\
&= 19 \text{ inches}
\end{aligned}$$

$$\begin{aligned}
\text{or Riser} &= 8 \text{ inches} \\
\text{Tread} &= 27 \text{ inches} - (2 \times \text{Riser}) \\
&= 27 \text{ inches} - 16 \text{ inches} \\
&= 11 \text{ inches}
\end{aligned}$$

Arriving at a standard is a little easier with outdoor steps than with indoor stairways because you can adjust the grade level a few inches at the top or bottom of the slope to create a full step if necessary.

In some cases an outdoor flight presents at least one fixed point, such as an existing path, sidewalk, deck, patio, or driveway. In that case, start or end your steps at that level, just as you would with an interior stairway.

WOOD STEPS

NOTCHED STRINGERS

First, don't even think about constructing exterior stairs of anything but pressure-treated lumber unless, of course, you want to go through the whole exercise again in about ten years.

If the stairway has more than two treads, construct it with stringers. Most stringers are made from 2×12s. Leave the riser spaces open to provide better drainage and air circulation, or close them to conceal an undesirable view.

The tops of the stringers attach to a house wall, deck joist, or small platform. The base should rest on either a concrete pad or a partially-buried railroad tie.

To build stringers, calculate the riser dimension that will produce a whole number of steps. Determine the best tread width to go with the riser size using the formula given earlier:

$2 \times \text{Riser} + \text{Tread} = 27 \text{ inches}$

Use a framing square to lay out each step on the 2×12. Position the square so that the mark showing riser height

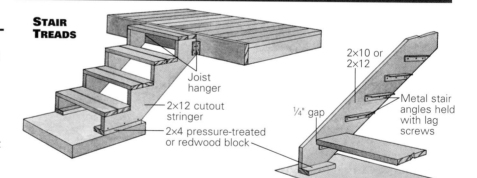

STAIR TREADS

Joist hanger

2×12 cutout stringer

2×4 pressure-treated or redwood block

2×10 or 2×12

¼" gap

Metal stair angles held with lag screws

and tread width end at the edge of the stringer. Cut out the stringer. Check that it fits; when it does, use it as a pattern for the other stringers.

Install all the stringers and make sure they are level. For further protection against decay and splitting, coat all the stringer edges with sealer or primer. Then attach the treads with 3-inch galvanized decking screws or 16d galvanized box nails. If you use risers, the tread nosings should overhang them by 1½ inches.

SOLID STRINGERS

The treads, which should not be wider than 3 feet, are suspended between two stringers by cleats. Stringers can be 2×8s, but should be at least 2×10s for spans longer than 10 feet.

Mark risers and treads on the stringers as if you were going to cut them. Use the marks for the tread bottoms as guides for the tops of the cleats. Fasten the cleats with 2-inch galvanized decking screws. Each tread should overhang the one below it by 1½ inches.

Many materials work well as steps, including brick, stone, concrete block, poured concrete, railroad ties, and lumber.

Brick Steps: Excavate to accommodate a concrete footing, or build the new steps over an existing concrete stairway. If you pour a new base, make sure that the brick layout fits the chosen riser height or you will have to cut the bricks. Start laying the bricks at the bottom and work up. Set

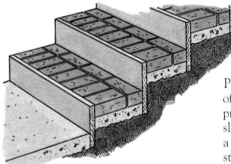

the board risers in place, lay down a thick mortar bed, then lay the tread bricks on the mortar. Grout all the joint spaces after you are finished.

Loose Fill: Use pressure-treated 2× lumber, timbers, or concrete pavers on edge as risers and then backfill with a contrasting material for an interesting effect. The riser should be wide if the backfill is a soft paving material that easily gives way. The tread area should be well drained, preferably with a gravel base. Predrill the riser timbers and drive rebar pins at least a foot into the ground to hold the riser boards in place.

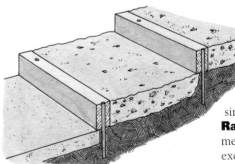

Stepping-Stones: Where conditions permit, set concrete blocks, heavy log rounds, thick flagstones, or similar materials directly in the soil. The slope must be gentle and the soil stable. Pour a concrete landing at the bottom of the steps to anchor them and prevent the entire stairway from slipping. Excavate to accommodate a gravel or sand sub-base that will stabilize each paving unit.

Platforms: If you need only a few steps, the simplest way to build them is to construct small platforms using 2×6s or 2×8s as joists. A 2×6 is 5½ inches

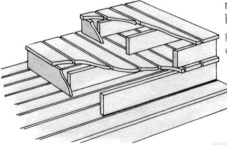

high; a 2×8 is 7½ inches high. Both heights are common for risers. If you use one step to separate two deck platforms, run the decking boards perpendicular to each other. Define the edge of the platform with a fascia board to make the step easy to see. Note: your local building code may not permit a single step on a deck.

Railroad Ties: Most railroad ties measure 7×9 inches, 8 feet long. To excavate a bench for each step, stretch a level string line above the stairway. Deter-mine the point at which each nosing will lie, and measure down the distance to the step plus the thickness of the tie. Dig a level bench from this point back into the hill. Start at the bottom of the stairway and work up, one tie at a time. Take measurements from the string line, then double-check by measuring from one tie to the next.

Drill a ¾-inch hole at both ends of each tie with a ½-inch electric drill bit or a brace and bit. Pound a 30-inch length of pipe or rebar into each hole to secure the step.

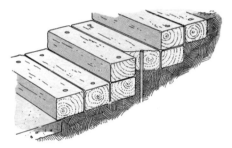

Make treads by laying several ties together, or use ties for the risers and backfill with brick, gravel, or a ground cover such as grass or dichondra. Some plants will not grow well because of the creosote in the ties. Check with your local nursery.

THE SECRET OF LONG LIFE

Why is it that wood shingles, only about ½-inch thick, can last 50 years, but much thicker wood exterior steps often rot in a decade? The key is standing water. Shingles, whether on a roof or a wall, shed their water and dry immediately, while a horizontal stair tread will absorb water standing on its surface and then rot.

There are three things you can do to make steps last longer:
■ Slope them ¼ inch per foot.
■ Fasten them heart-side up.
■ Use pressure-treated lumber.

SPACE— THE NEXT FRONTIER

Have you ever met anyone who thought they had enough storage? What seemed enough when you moved in quickly becomes woefully deficient. It just doesn't take long for space to fill up.

Storage space is a major concern when potential buyers shop for a new home. Most buyers look carefully for adequate closets and shelves for clothes, linens, seasonal items, toys, tools, garden implements, building materials, and exercise and other sporting equipment.

If you're remodeling, it's time for a different look at storage space. You will be surprised at how much usable space is still available in existing nooks, insets, gaps, and crannies. Once you have an idea how to look for possible storage space, you'll be able to see the potential in your own home.

SHOES UNDERFOOT?

Shoes—so many shoes! How do we keep them from being underfoot?

Have you ever tried plastic milk crates? These handy, lightweight, and durable containers are used by distributors of dairy products to ship cartons of milk to store locations. Once used, they are often discarded, although their popularity is making them more valuable to dairies and their distributors alike.

Fortunately, you can buy inexpensive copies in a variety of colors in merchandise outlets. They provide a good solution to many storage problems, since they are:
- modular and stackable
- color-coded
- well-ventilated
- "cool," even by kid standards
- able to hold loose items easily

WHERE TO FIND MORE SPACE

If you're looking for more space, there usually is an unused corner you can convert into extra storage.

If your imagination is coming up short, attend a boat show. Get into a 30-foot sailboat and look at all of the clever storage compartments. People live in these things—full time.

Next look at the illustration, *right*. Compared to a 30-foot boat, your home is a veritable warehouse of potential storage space.

Dormers: Place a storage bench or chest under the window. Make it tall, so the cat can sit in the window and look out.

Eaves: Unless there is already built-in kneewall storage, install cupboards along a wall where insufficient headroom won't allow use of the floor space.

Fireplaces: The fireplace is a focal point. Frame it even more dramatically with built-in bookshelves.

Unfinished Basement and Garage Ceilings: Sling a hammock to store yard equipment. In the summer, move it outside, along with its contents.

Garage Space: A garage is the ideal spot for a workshop. With its concrete floor, it doesn't matter if you make a mess.

Beds: What could you do with an additional 30 square feet of storage space? That is what you have under every double bed in your house. Put this to use by placing a mattress on top of drawer units. Hide-a-bed kits are available in many designs. They're perfect for guest bedrooms or under the bed of a son or daughter who has gone to college but still comes back often.

Bathroom Cabinets: Add roll-out shelves under sinks. They do not have to be full depth if the plumbing gets in the way.

Kitchen Cabinets: Make use of the space between the wall cabinets and the base cabinets with narrow shelves or bins.

Countertops: Hide the clutter and trailing cords in an appliance garage.

Under Counters: Many appliances now come in undercounter versions. A roll-around cabinet provides extra counter space when pulled out, can be moved to where it's needed, and tucks neatly away when it is not in use.

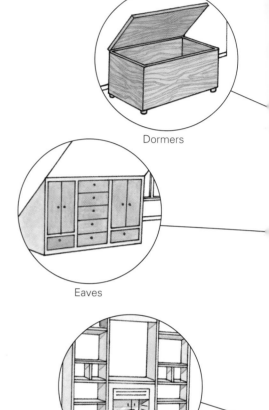

Dormers

Eaves

Fireplaces

Stairways

Unfinished ceilings

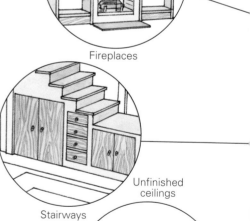

Under Sinks: If it stands on a pull-out shelf, the garbage can be close at hand and out of sight beneath the kitchen sink.

Utility Room: Mount deep shelves or cupboards above the washer and dryer. These can house supplies, such as bleach bottles and detergent, and are convenient for storing linens.

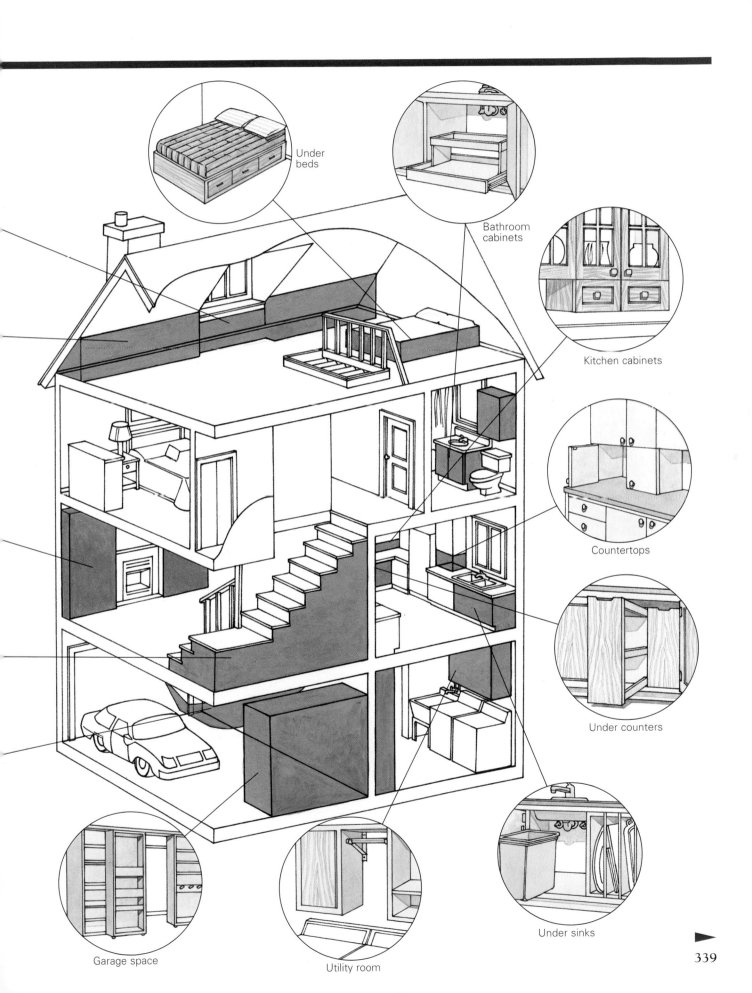

Under
beds

Bathroom
cabinets

Kitchen cabinets

Countertops

Under counters

Under sinks

Garage space

Utility room

CLOTHES DIMENSIONS

Item	Length from Pole, inches
MEN'S CLOTHING	
Coverall	66
Pants, folded	32
Pants, unfolded	48
Shirt	38
Ski jacket	40
Ski pants (bib style)	66
Suit	40
Ties, folded	32
Topcoat	56
Travel suit bag	60
Winter coat	55
WOMEN'S CLOTHING	
Bathrobe	52
Blouse	36
Dress, everyday	58
Dress, formal	69
Skirt	35
Suit	37
Ski jacket	40
Ski pants (bib style)	66
Winter coat	52
ACCESSORIES	
Cane	36
Garment bag, folded	48
Garment bag, unfolded	60
Shoe bag	36
Umbrella	36

LINEN DIMENSIONS

Item	Maximum Size, inches
Bath mats	9×10
Bath towels	13×14
Beach towels	18×20
Blankets	22×27
Dish towels	10×16
Fitted sheets	11×18
Flat sheets	14×15
Hand towels	6×10
Pillowcases	7×15
Washcloths	7×7

A BUILT-IN DESK

Many older homes have alcoves intended for china cabinets or seating nooks. This built-in desk and storage unit puts alcove space to good use—from floor to ceiling. Doors and drawer fronts close to form a sleek facade.

Use a finish-grade plywood or laminate the drawer faces and doors. If you want a little more color, paper the upper doors and the bottom of the desk with a mural, so it looks like a picture when closed up.

If the alcove once contained a solid-core door, make the drop-down desk from a door section. Build the overhead shelves and doors as a separate unit, and trim the outside of the unit with molding that harmonizes with the rest of the room.

AN UNDERSINK ROLLOUT

Are you wasting the undersink in your bathroom and kitchen? If you design a storage drawer around the plumbing, you can have nearly as much space as in other base cabinets. Build a lipped roll-out platform and top it with a shelf just low enough to clear the plumbing. Screw the shelf to the platform. Mount the platform on a partial-extension slide; it will stop the platform with about 4 inches inside the cabinet.

And the next time you install plumbing, keep the pipes high to give you more room.

A SEWING CLOSET

The seamstress in the family will love this closet. Open it and you'll find a whole sewing room. The closet door has been removed to accommodate a cabinet that rolls in and out on casters. A hinged panel attached to the cabinet unfolds as a work surface. Another cabinet on casters supports the work surface at midspan.

The tabletop is ¾-inch plywood topped with plastic laminate. Piano hinges extend the full width.

Construct the rolling cabinets from ¾-inch paint-grade plywood with ½-inch plywood inserts and sides. Make the rollout bin for storing fabric from three pieces of ¾-inch plywood mounted on full-extension drawer rollers. Pieces of fabric hang on ⅝-inch dowels.

The upper part of the doorway consists of swing-out shelving. The sides and dividers are ½-inch plywood; the back is ¾-inch plywood. A piano hinge allows the upper section to close until the back is flush with the opening. The upright on the latch edge angles inward so that the unit clears the door frame.

Shelves on the inside of the closet complete the work space. Shelf track enables you to adjust the heights. One shelf should be at the same height as the tabletop—30 to 36 inches high.

Before renovation

HANGING IN A HAMMOCK

Increase your garage storage by suspending a net or hammock over the hood of your car. Store bulky, soft things that would not mar the car if they fell. Camping supplies such as sleeping bags and pads, baseball gloves, and beach toys are good examples.

If the garage walls are too far apart to serve as attachment points, attach pulleys overhead and tie the hammock to pulley ropes. Raise and lower the hammock to any height you wish.

HIDING UNDER THE BED

Most people slide a few boxes and loose items under a bed, but built-in, roll-out storage is far more efficient because you can see and access the items more easily. Multiple units and levels are better than a single unit. Enclosed storage also keeps those infamous "dust bunnies" from accumulating under the bed.

Create the storage platform by building or buying several small units of the same height and clustering them together. Small units are easier to transport than one bed-sized unit. The drawers do not need to be as deep as the entire width of a large bed.

Support the mattress with one or more sheets of plywood screwed down to the tops of the storage chests. Flush drawers create a clean profile.

It also is a good idea to include a toe kick to allow you to get closer to the bed when changing the linens.

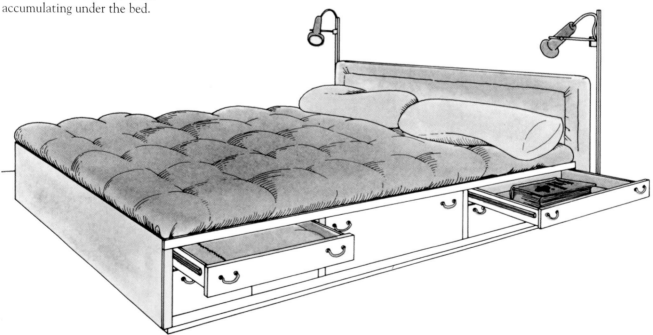

KITCHEN STORAGE OPTIONS

Storage systems should be practical, but they should also be in keeping with the style of the room. This is no less true in the kitchen than in other rooms.

Kitchen storage is generally:
■ open shelves that display whatever is placed on them, or
■ traditional cabinetry that not only defines the kitchen design but also provides a wealth of concealed storage.

The style shown at right is a mix of "high-tech" open, stainless steel shelving and sleek contemporary cabinets. The scheme is supplemented with open racks and steel grills for hanging kitchen utensils and cooking equipment. In addition, a movable, centrally located work table features a stainless steel frame topped by a butcher-block surface. All the storage components utilize grids, modules, or repetitive elements to suggest organization and order.

Vinyl coated steel grids have become very popular and are available

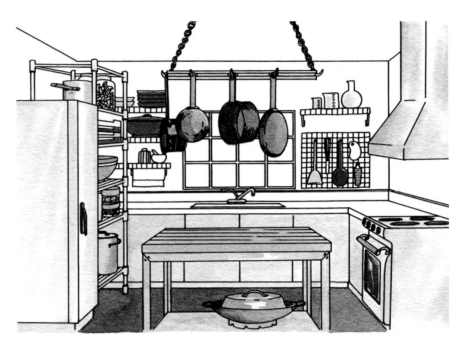

in all home centers. These grids provide flexible storage possibilities. Add S-hooks and hang kitchen utensils on them, or add baskets and fill them with spice jars, coffee mugs, or items you want near at hand.

A KITCHEN CABINET

Kitchen base cabinets with fixed shelves are inefficient because the back of each shelf is inaccessible and there is usually wasted space above the stored items. The illustration, *right*, shows how you can transform such a space waster into a more useful storage unit. The cabinet—once a two-shelf unit—now contains four shelves and a work surface.

Face a slab of butcher block with a drawer front and attach rollers to make a sliding cutting board that frees counter space. Vertical dividers (lauan plywood routed into mortises at the top and bottom) enable you to store cookie sheets, large lids, and other flat items on end.

A bank of roll-out trays increases storage space and makes every item easy to find. Lips keep items from sliding off the front. Divide the trays for even more organization for utensils and other small items.

343

AN APPLIANCE GARAGE

You don't always have to create additional space to improve storage; concealing items can create the illusion of more space. An "appliance garage" keeps a countertop from appearing cluttered.

Most kitchens have a herd of appliances that need corralling: coffee maker, blender, can opener, toaster. Line them up to see how much space each one needs and decide which ones you use the most.

Install your appliance garage in front of an electrical receptacle so appliance cords will also be hidden.

The "garage doors" and pulls should match the style of the rest of the cabinets. Order door replacements for your cabinets and cut them to size or use plywood and face or finish it to match. Use piano hinges at the edges and magnetic catches on the doors.

LINEN STORAGE

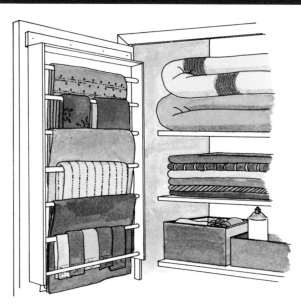

Linens stay fresh and uncreased when you hang them on a lift-up door-back frame. The rack also makes it possible to spot linens easily, rather than rifling through a stack on a shelf.

Make the frame of 1×3 clear lumber, 6 inches narrower than the door. Bore ½-inch holes on 4-inch centers in—not through—the sides. Glue ½-inch dowels into the holes before attaching

the top of the rack. Mount the rack at a convenient height with a piano hinge fastened to a 1×3 cleat on the back of the door.

Swing the rack up and the space between the towels will increase, allowing you easily to add or remove a towel. When the door is closed, the rack lies flat against the door surface.

DOOR POCKETS

The backsides of closet and cabinet doors offer a lot of convenient storage space. Before you construct the shelves, however, make sure you know how deep they can be without interfering with the existing shelves. Soup cans are slim; several rows of lipped shelves for these will store and display all the soup you will consume in a month.

If the door has a hollow core, first attach ½-inch plywood to beef it up; canned and bottled goods weigh a lot.

Older homes sometimes have high ceilings and large entrance halls. Of course, if your entry is already very handsome and ornate, you won't want to alter it. But if it is rather mundane, consider using a portion of its wasted volume for storage.

In the illustration below, what was once a plain wall with a door in the center has become a hall closet for coats and boots, a mail center, and a set of cubbyholes overhead for rarely used bulky items such as suitcases and sleeping bags.

The construction consists of three plywood cabinets that enclose the door. On one side is a hanging closet with shelves above. On the other side are two large cabinets with adjustable shelves. The upper cabinet door is covered by a mirror so you can check your hair before flying out of the house. The upper and lower units are separated by a drop-down shelf— an ideal place for letters, stamps, envelopes, keys, and all those other little things you need just as you go out the door.

The vertical cabinets consist of four sides of ¾-inch plywood, two backs of ¼-inch plywood, and bases and tops of ¾-inch plywood. Build each unit on a pedestal of 2×4s laid flat.

Install shelves, dividers, and closet poles as needed. Cut 1×2 or 1×4 lumber in half to form door frames. Within the frames, use hollow-core flush doors or make your own doors of ¾-inch plywood of lumber-core construction. Hang them on 2-inch butt hinges.

The upper cabinet is framed with ¾-inch plywood on all sides, including the back. Make sure the sides line up with the sides of the lower cabinets, and install molding around the edge of the frames.

GARAGE WORKSHOP

Your workshop wall is an ideal spot for adding storage and workspace. Here's a unit that combines both features in one installation. Two cabinets with a flush work surface between them create a practical workbench.

If you plan to do serious work on this bench, fasten a second layer of ¾-inch underlayment-grade plywood to the first with plenty of construction adhesive and 1¼-inch drywall screws applied from beneath. Don't let the tips of the screws penetrate the upper layer of plywood.

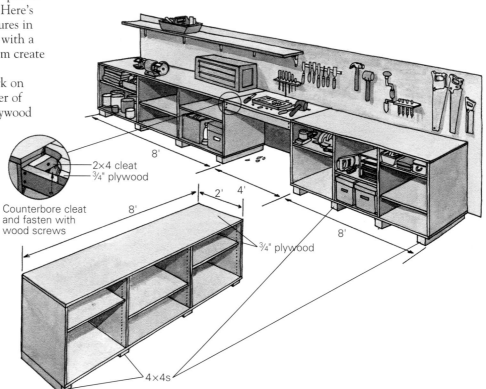

2×4 cleat
¾" plywood

Counterbore cleat and fasten with wood screws

8'

2'   4'

8'

8'

¾" plywood

4×4s

GARAGE WALLS AND CEILING

Do you have a two-car garage, but one or both cars are parked outside because there is no room for them inside? Open your garage door and look at the floor. It's probably covered with "stored" items. Of course, you can't bring all those big and messy items into the house, but you can't use the floor for both storage and cars, either.

The walls and the ceiling are your way out. Install racks, hooks, and shelves to prevent sports equipment from getting damaged, hoses from getting tangled, and bikes from falling over. Suspend large items, such as canoes, on a hook and pulley system.

SUSPENDED PLATFORMS

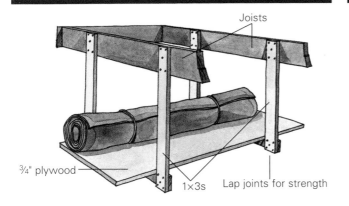

Joists

¾" plywood

1×3s

Lap joints for strength

A suspended platform transforms overhead space into storage for light loads. It's ideal for garages, basements, attics, and crawlspaces.

To make the platform, make up two U-shape slings (three-sided frames) out of 1×3s. Tack one of the uprights to a joist with a single nail. Hold a level on the crosspiece to determine the correct position for the second upright and tack it in place. For permanent fastenings, use drywall screws. Hang the second sling in the same way using a level to make sure the crosspieces are on the same plane. Slide a piece of plywood between the two slings and tack it loosely in place.

HANGING TOOL RACKS

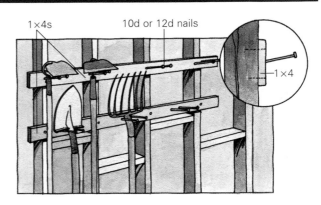

1×4s

10d or 12d nails

1×4

To store long-handled garden tools, hang them. Nothing fancy is needed, so forget those expensive designer tool racks you may see in the mail-order catalogs. Instead, build simple racks from 1×4s nailed or screwed across the studs. For hangers, try pairs of 12d nails driven at a slight upward slant.

If you prefer the look of wooden dowels, get four-foot lengths of hardwood dowel at your hardware store or home center. Cut them into appropriate lengths. As with the nails, the dowels should have a slight upward slant. To make sure that the angle is always the same, make a drilling template out of a block of wood. Drill all of the holes using the template as a guide.

UNDER AN ENCLOSED DECK

A second-story deck on plain posts can look ungainly and will likely benefit from some form of enclosure. Latticework (in 4×8-foot panels) affords an inexpensive solution. But for secure and weatherproof under-the-

deck storage you need to frame the space and sheath it, as shown below.

Waterproof it in one of two ways:
■ Build a sloping roof with double-coverage roll roofing, and then frame the deck above it.

■ Build a flat, sheathed roof, have it professionally covered with a rubber membrane roofing, and then lay the deck on sleepers over the roofing.

STUCCO

MATERIALS FOR A STUCCO WALL

ALSO SEE...
Framing:
Pages 152–159
Paints & Stains:
Pages 232–241
Shingle Siding:
Pages 308–309

Stucco is a surface mixed from portland cement, sand, lime (to keep the mixture pliable), and water. For small jobs, buy premixed sacks at a home improvement center, or mix your own bulk ingredients (see box, opposite page) for a large job.

A stuccoed wall consists of three separate coats applied over metal lath:
■ The first—or scratch—coat (so named because scratches etched in its surface provide support for the next coat) is about ¼ inch thick and is supported by the lath.

■ A brown coat (it used to contain sand), is ⅜ to ½ inch thick.
■ The finish coat is about ¼ inch thick.
The lath is either an extruded screen or a wire similar to chicken wire. Furring nails with fiber washers hold the lath away from the sheathing. Self-furring lath doesn't require washers and attaches with roofing nails.

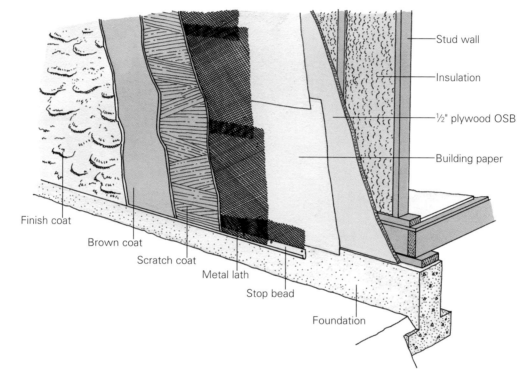

Finish coat
Brown coat
Scratch coat
Metal lath
Stop bead
Foundation

Stud wall
Insulation
½" plywood OSB
Building paper

WHEN TO APPLY

Weather conditions affect stucco—choose your workday with these factors in mind. If hot sun bakes the wall, the stucco will dry too rapidly and shrink, causing cracks. Apply stucco only when there is little direct sun, or hang shade cloths from the eaves. The best temperature range is 50–80 degrees F. Never apply stucco at less than 40 degrees F; the mixture will be too stiff and difficult to work with. If it freezes, it will be wasted.

Don't apply stucco until after the interior wallboard is nailed into position because the hammering could jar the stucco material loose. If you don't have a choice, apply the wallboard with screws.

MIXING AND APPLYING

To mix stucco easily, buy premixed ingredients and rent a mixer. What you pay in rent you save in time.

If you buy and combine bulk ingredients, use the recipe on the next page. Add the water slowly because the amount you will use will vary with the initial moisture content of the sand.

MIXING

Pour the dry ingredients into the mixer and turn until the stucco is an even color. Slowly add water until you think you have almost enough, then mix some more. The goal is a soft, pliable consistency that you can squeeze and hold in your hand without dripping.

Employ at least one helper and carry the mix to the work site in a wheelbarrow. If you work slowly, cover the wheelbarrow with plastic so the stucco won't dry before you get to it.

LOADING THE TROWEL

Chop the stucco with the edge of the trowel, lift a trowel-full, and spread it evenly around the center of the hand-held carrier, known as a hawk. Tilt the hawk down while you scoop the slice of mortar onto the trowel.

APPLYING STUCCO

As with painting, start at the top of the wall. Press each trowel of mortar into the lath with an upward motion, tilting the top edge of the trowel back slightly. Blend adjacent areas with smooth horizontal strokes.

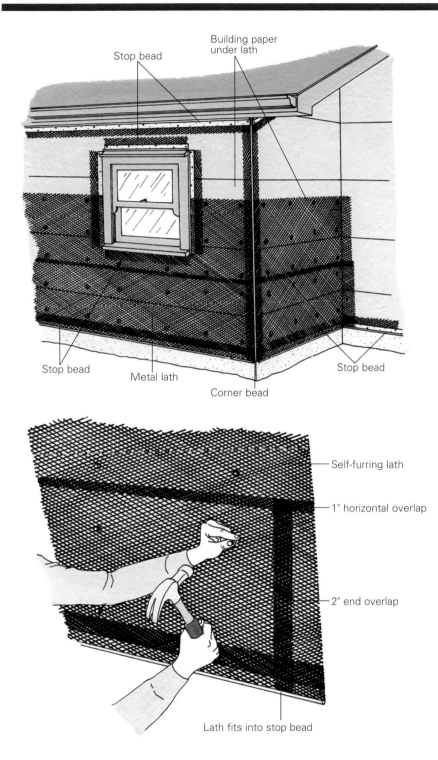

Building paper under lath

Stop bead

Stop bead

Stop bead

Metal lath

Corner bead

Stop bead

Self-furring lath

1" horizontal overlap

2" end overlap

Lath fits into stop bead

SHEATHING

The best base for stucco is ½-inch exterior-grade plywood or OSB sheathing. Apply 15-pound felt or kraft paper over the sheathing. Trim windows and doors with stucco mold, which has a groove for locking the stucco into place.

STOP BEAD

Stucco should not extend to the ground. A stop bead, also called a weep screed, supports the stucco and allows moisture to escape. Stop bead comes in 10-foot lengths, and different products are made for fastening to concrete or to wood. Beading made for sheathing applications has a flange that is covered by your building paper. Install the bead before the lath.

INSTALLING LATH

Start from the bottom at one corner and work up. The first course of lath rests in the stop bead. Working from the center of a section of lath, hook a nail in the wire, and drive the nail. Stretch the mesh each time you hook a nail. At the corners, nail a corner bead. The metal strip should protrude from the edge by ¾ inch. Use a level to plumb the bead, and if you use more than one length, align the ends carefully because the beads serve as guides when you apply stucco.

Self-furring lath saves time. It comes in rolls that include the building paper and attaches with roofing nails. Horizontal wires on the back enable you to install it directly over studs. The extra paper along one edge laps over the previous course.

Overlap lath courses by 1 inch horizontally and by 2 inches at the ends. Place furring nails (they have washers close to the nail head) every 6 inches on the lath. Hook the wire between the nail head and washers, and drive the nail home.

The job goes a lot faster with a helper to pull on the lath as you nail.

Apply masking tape to door and window casings to protect them as you apply stucco.

STUCCO MIX

Component	Lb.	Cu.Ft.	Gal.
Sharp sand	200	2	15
Ptld. cement	47	½	3¾
Lime	12	⅓	2½
Clean water	48	¾	6

STUCCO CURING TIMES

Coat	Keep Moist	Total Set
Scratch	12 hours	2 days
Brown	12 hours	7 days
Finish	12 hours	2 days

APPLYING THE SCRATCH COAT

Apply the scratch coat by sweeping the stucco into the lath with a trowel. Check for uniform thickness and correct bulges and pockets.

Before the stucco dries, rake it horizontally with a scarifying tool to provide texture and help the next coat adhere. The tines should bite deep enough to nearly touch the lath, but not expose it. Keep this coat moist for 12 hours before proceeding.

APPLYING THE BROWN COAT

PREPARATION

Ensure the brown coat is even by taking two preparatory steps: First, stretch strings tightly across the wall between nails driven into the corners. The strings will be held out ⅜ to ½ inch from the scratch coat by the protruding corner bead. One string should be near the top of the wall, one near the bottom, and one near the center. Then, drive roofing nails flush with the inside of the string every 5 feet. The nail heads will give you reference marks for a level coat of stucco. After the nails are in, remove the strings.

APPLYING SCREEDS

Trowel on narrow vertical strips of stucco (screeds) spaced every 5 feet. The screeds should just cover the nail heads. After applying each strip, run a straight board over it to eliminate any high or low spots.

APPLYING THE BROWN COAT

After 24 hours (keep the screeds damp during this time), spray the wall lightly with a mist, dampening only as much of the surface as you can coat in an hour. Apply the brown coat from top to bottom. Feather the stucco into the screeds with smooth, even strokes so no joint is visible. Smooth the mortar over the corner beads and stop beads.

Allow each section between screeds to dry for about an hour; then go over it in circular motions with a wood float. Rub lightly until you feel the sand at the surface.

Allow to dry for at least 24 hours, misting with water every four hours.

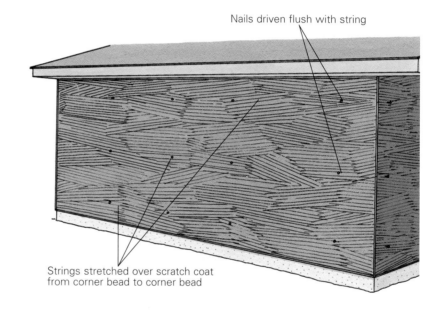

Nails driven flush with string

Strings stretched over scratch coat from corner bead to corner bead

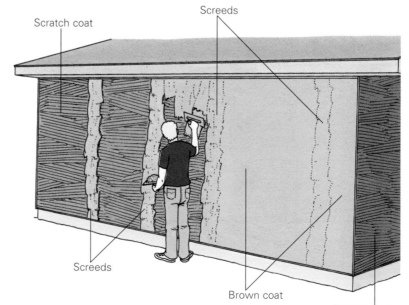

Scratch coat

Screeds

Screeds

Brown coat

Scratch coat

APPLYING THE FINISH COAT

Color and texture the finish coat to your taste. To achieve a pure white finish, use white cement and white sand. For shades of brown, tan, or off-white, mix a dye available from a stucco or masonry supplier with the final coat. If you paint the stucco, coat the cured finish with a stucco primer, and use a compatible latex paint.

Here is how to achieve a variety of finish textures:

Travertine Finish: First, float the finish coat. Then jab the bristles of a whisk broom into the finish while it is still damp (keep the bristles horizontal). After the stucco sets up slightly, go back over the surface with a steel trowel. Smooth it with long, horizontal strokes so that the top of the rough ridges flatten but the valleys and craters remain.

Wood float

Standard Smooth Finish: *While the stucco is still wet, smooth the surface with a wood float. Repeat the process while the stucco is still damp, working the float in a circular motion without leaving a pattern.*

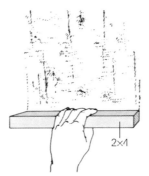

2×4

Modern American Finish: *Apply a float finish to the wet stucco, and let it set just slightly. After the surface moisture disappears, scrape the finish coat in vertical strokes with a foot-long 2×4. Press firmly to roughen the stucco without tearing it.*

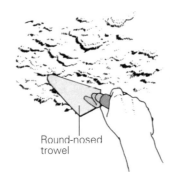

Round-nosed trowel

Old English Finish: *This style requires a thin finish coat. After the finish has dried for about an hour, use a round-nosed trowel to apply irregular gobs of mortar. Work quickly for a spontaneous, rugged look.*

Snap brush against stick

Spatter Finish *(also called a dash finish): Mix a small batch of wet stucco, dip a large, stiff brush in the mixture, and snap it against a stick to spatter stucco onto the wall. Wear gloves, old clothes, and safety glasses; the stucco will splatter on you, too. Let the first application dry one hour, then repeat the process.*

REPAIRING A CRACK

Clean out the crack with a wire brush.

Undercut the crack in an inverted V and dampen the area.

Apply a mortar patch of one part cement to three parts fine sand. Keep the patch damp for two days.

REPAIRING A HOLE

Cut out the hole and weave in a patch of new wire lath. Wet the area, then apply the scratch coat. When it begins to set, score with a scarifier. Keep the patch damp for 48 hours.

Apply the brown coat layer to within ⅛ inch of the surface. Keep the patch damp for two days, then cure for five more days.

Dampen the wall before applying the finish coat complete with colored pigment. Keep the patch damp for another two days.

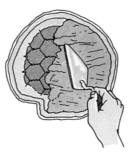

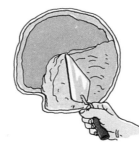

SWITCHES

SWITCH BASICS

ALSO SEE...
Electrical Boxes:
Pages 106–109
Electrical Systems:
Pages 110–115
Lighting:
Pages 212–219
Wire:
Pages 442–445

Switches connect and disconnect electrical loads from current in the ungrounded (hot) conductor. Most switches may look similar, but there are significant distinctions. Furthermore, identical switches can be wired differently in different situations.

The most useful things to know is how many switches control a particular fixture and whether the hot wire from the service panel goes first to the switch or to the fixture.

Although switches vary in style and some have features specific to their use, there are really only four basic types (see The Four Basic Switches, below). And of those, only two—the single-pole and the three-way—are generally used in residential wiring.

SPECIALTY SWITCHES

Dimmer: Dimmers vary the intensity of light by regulating the amount of voltage the fixture receives. They should not be used in undersized or overcrowded boxes. Dimmers extend lamp life significantly. In addition to standard single-pole incandescent light dimmers, there are special three-way dimmers and other dimmers for fluorescent fixtures.

Time Delay: Once switched on, this switch automatically turns off a light fixture after a pre-set amount of time, usually between 45 seconds and five minutes. It is useful in a garage or laundry where you often have your hands full.

Time Clock: A switch with a time clock can be set to go on and off at any time, making it appear that the home is occupied. Wire time clock switches directly into an existing circuit or use the type that plug into wall receptacles. These time-clock devices act as receptacles for lamp plugs.

Key Operated: This switch prevents unauthorized use of power tools or other appliances, and is recommended if you have young children. The key fits into a slot and moves the switch toggle up and down.

Pilot Light: The light in this switch shows when a light or other electrical equipment in a remote location—such as the basement—is on.

Remote Control: This low-voltage switch operates by infrared or by electronic pulse to turn on and off a full-current switch elsewhere in the home. Wiring for a remote-control switch is 16- or 18-gauge. Hand-held models are battery-operated.

CODE REQUIREMENTS: SWITCHES

Lights and Resistive Loads: Loads on switches must not exceed their rating.
Motors: Switches must not control motor loads of more than 80 percent of their rating.
Aluminum Wire: Switches directly connected to aluminum wire must be labeled CO/ALR.
Grounded Conductors: Switches must never interrupt the grounded (white) conductor. If a white wire is used as an ungrounded conductor, its end must be painted or taped black to indicate its use.
Access: The center of a switch toggle must not be more than 6½ feet above the floor.

Door-Operated: Opening a door activates this push-button switch. You often see them in cars and refrigerators. They are also handy for closets and storage areas.

COLOR CODE FOR SWITCH TERMINALS

Single-Pole Switches:
■ Brass (2)—black wires
■ Green (1)—bare ground wire
Three-Way Switches:
■ Brass (2)—travelers
■ Dark (1)—common
■ Green (1)—bare ground wire

THE FOUR BASIC SWITCHES

Single-Pole: Use a two-way, or single-pole, switch when only one switch operates a fixture. A single-pole switch has on-off markings on the toggle and two terminals (besides ground).

Double-Pole: Used for 240-volt equipment or to operate two circuits at the same time. Has on-off markings and four terminals.

Three-Way: Used in pairs, to control a fixture from two separate locations. The toggle can be on or off in either position, so it is not labeled. Has three terminals.

Four-Way: Used between a pair of three-way switches to control a fixture from three separate locations. Toggle is on or off in either position, so is not labeled. Has four terminals.

PRINCIPLES

There are so many configurations for two-way, three-way, and four-way switches, you would never be able to memorize what wires go where. To simplify things, we show eight different configurations, one of which should cover any situation in your home. Just find the diagram that matches the switch-fixture arrangement you want to install (or repair) and connect the colored wires exactly as shown.

There is, however, one principle common to all switch configurations—the neutral wire must never be switched. If you are wiring with cable, there are times when you may need to use the white wire as a hot conductor (the switch loop shown below is an example). In such cases, you must blacken both ends of the white wire to indicate that it is being used as a hot wire. Use either electrical tape or paint.

The switch-fixture connections are sometimes only part of larger circuits; some installations require switches in the middle of a circuit that extends elsewhere in the house.

Also, be aware that there may be wires in a box that are entirely independent of the circuit you are working on. Make sure you know where all the wires go before you disconnect any of them.

SWITCH CIRCUITS

TWO-WAY SWITCH: SOURCE THROUGH SWITCH

The cable from the source has a black (hot) conductor, a white (neutral) conductor, and a bare ground wire. The black wire is connected to the switch (the switch makes and breaks the current in the hot wire), but the white wire continues—through a wire nut connection—uninterrupted through the box. The green ground wire is pigtailed to the bare wires and lead to the box (if it is metal) and to the green screw of the switch. This switch can control additional lights if the wires continue to them from the fixture shown.

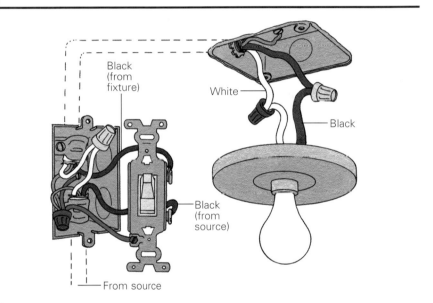

Black (from fixture)

White

Black

Black (from source)

From source

TWO-WAY SWITCH: SOURCE THROUGH FIXTURE

In this installation, the black (hot) wire from the source goes through the fixture first. It must be sent down or "looped" though the switch in order for the switch to interrupt it. Notice that the wire leaving the switch to feed the fixture is a white wire functioning as a hot wire and must be painted black.

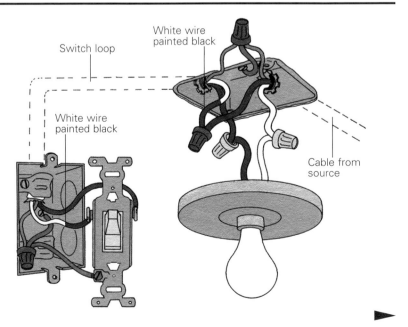

Switch loop

White wire painted black

White wire painted black

Cable from source

SWITCH CIRCUITS *continued*

THREE-WAY SWITCH: SOURCE THROUGH ONE SWITCH

Here, three-way switches have three terminals: a dark terminal called the "common" and a pair of brass-colored terminals called "travelers." The common terminal is color-coded dark because it is always connected to the black wire. The travelers of the first switch are always connected directly to the travelers of the second switch. One of the traveler wires is red; the other traveler wire may be either white or black, depending on the configuration. As always, the bare ground wire is pigtailed to green ground wires to the switch and to metal boxes.

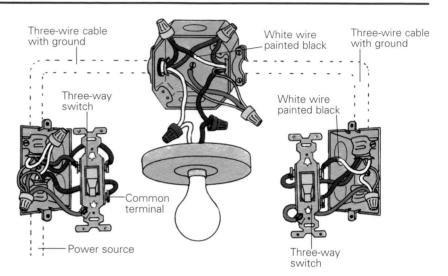

Three-wire cable with ground

White wire painted black

Three-wire cable with ground

Three-way switch

White wire painted black

Common terminal

Power source

Three-way switch

THREE-WAY SWITCH: SOURCE THROUGH CENTRAL FIXTURE

In this configuration, the hot wire from the source is not wired directly to the fixture. It is wired through the fixture box and is connected to the common terminal of one switch. The two wires leaving this switch—called traveler wires—are wired through the fixture box all the way to the second switch. The common terminal of the second switch is wired to the hot side of the fixture. Both switch circuits are switch loops and have no neutral wires.

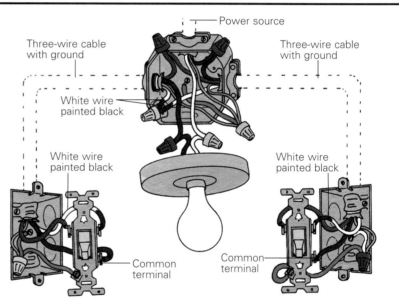

Power source

Three-wire cable with ground

Three-wire cable with ground

White wire painted black

White wire painted black

White wire painted black

Common terminal

Common terminal

THREE-WAY SWITCH: SOURCE THROUGH FIXTURE

Again, the hot wire from the source cable is wired through the fixture box to the switches. Both switches are part of a single switch loop, with no neutral wires in their boxes.

Notice that a two-wire cable (with ground) is sufficient for the leg between the light and nearest switch, but the leg between the switches requires three-wire cable.

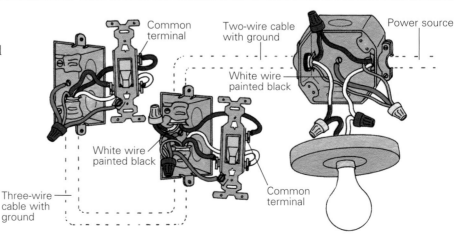

Common terminal

Two-wire cable with ground

Power source

White wire painted black

White wire painted black

Three-wire cable with ground

Common terminal

THREE-WAY SWITCH: SOURCE THROUGH SWITCHES AND LIGHT TO RECEPTACLE BEYOND

This circuit shows how switch and fixture boxes can serve as junction boxes for circuit wiring that extends to other points. Current from the hot wire of the source must serve both the switch and the light system, but also travel through to the receptacle without being switched.

To wire this type of switch, use a four-wire leg (plus ground) between the two switches. If you use conduit, pull white, black, red, and blue wires and use the blue conductor as a continuous feed for the receptacle. With cable, use two two-wire cables (plus ground).

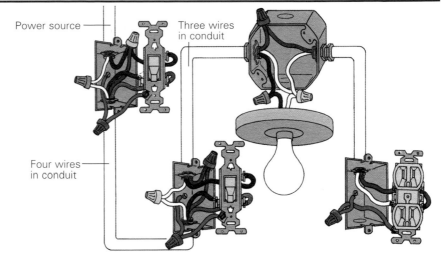

Power source — Three wires in conduit

Four wires in conduit

FOUR-WAY SWITCH: SOURCE THROUGH FIXTURE

To control a light from three points, use a four-way switch and a pair of three-way switches. The four-way switch, with four terminals, is always in the middle. The hot source conductor connects to the common (dark) terminal of the first three-way switch, which then sends two travelers to the four-way switch. The travelers connect to the top two terminals. Travelers of the same colors connect to the bottom two terminals of the four-way switch and proceed to the second three-way switch. The four-way switch simply redirects current between travelers.

In the diagram, all the wiring is in conduit, which provides a continuous ground. If you wire with cable, use three-wire cable, with bare ground, and substitute its white wire (painted black at its ends) for the blue wire.

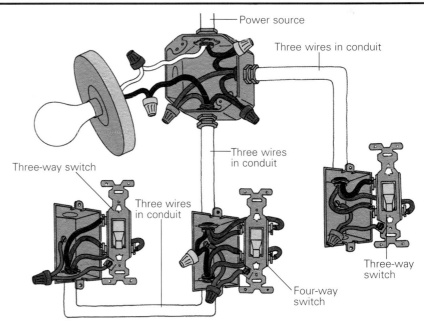

Power source

Three wires in conduit

Three wires in conduit

Three-way switch

Three wires in conduit

Three-way switch

Four-way switch

SPLIT-CIRCUIT RECEPTACLE

In some rooms, the switch controls a receptacle (into which you plug a light) instead of a permanent light fixture. This diagram shows how to wire the receptacle so only half of it is controlled by the switch and the other half is always hot.

Duplex receptacles have a breakable fin on the hot side for split-circuit wiring. If there is one on the neutral side as well, do not break it or there may be no return path for the electricity and a serious ground fault could occur.

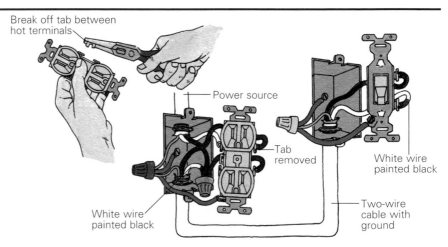

Break off tab between hot terminals

Power source

Tab removed

White wire painted black

White wire painted black

Two-wire cable with ground

355

TELEPHONES

INSTALLING A NEW PHONE

ALSO SEE...
Security:
Pages 294–297
Wire:
Pages 442–445

Buying and installing telephones is easier and less expensive than ever. Hardware stores, home centers, and even drug stores sell phones, wires, jacks, and other hookup supplies. Some inexpensive phones cost as little as $10, making them virtually disposable when something fails.

Installing an additional telephone jack is a home improvement task that you can complete in as little as an hour. Installing a jack is easy even if your home improvement skills are modest. Best of all, you'll save money.

Planning a telephone installation is simple because phones and their connectors are modular. Standard jacks allow you to move a telephone from one room to the next simply by unplugging from one jack and plugging into another.

Flat line cord is used only to plug a phone or a computer modem into a telephone jack. It is made in many lengths for different-size rooms and situations. Telephone cable is round and runs from a wire junction to the telephone jacks. It usually has four color-coded wires (see chart, opposite).

Make sure all of your equipment and wiring works properly before you extend wiring. Otherwise, you will not be able to determine if new problems result from faulty connections or malfunctioning equipment.

Although there should be no danger of shock, phone companies recommend a few precautions:
■ Don't work on phone lines during thunderstorms.
■ Avoid touching bare wires or terminals.
■ Use tools with insulated handles.
■ Disconnect the house system from the phone company's network before you patch into an existing outlet.
■ Don't work on telephone wiring if you wear a pacemaker.

REPLACING A MODULAR CORD

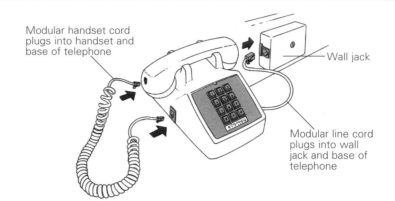

Modular handset cord plugs into handset and base of telephone

Wall jack

Modular line cord plugs into wall jack and base of telephone

Twenty years ago, telephones were hard-wired, with wires wrapped around terminal screws in the telephone and the wall jack. Newer telephone equipment is modular, with four-wire cords, plugs, and sockets. If a cord goes bad, simply buy a replacement cord. Coiled handset cords are available in many colors. Line cord is available in lengths from 6 feet to 25 feet.

CONVERTING A JACK TO MODULAR

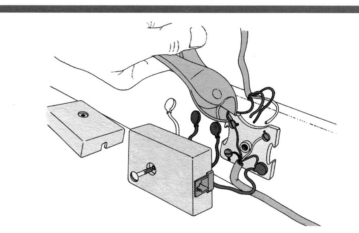

Phone sets that are not modular are hardwired—you can't unplug them. If you have a new telephone with a modular plug, all you need is a new modular cover; you do not have to replace the base.

Remove the old cover. Identify the incoming wires so you don't disconnect them, then snip the wires that connect the telephone. If the wires of the new cover have snap fittings, simply push the color-coded caps onto the screw terminals of the matching colors.

If the cover wires are terminated in spade lugs (U-shaped lugs), loosen the terminal screws in the base, insert the lugs under the screw heads (matching the wire colors), and retighten the screws.

When you are finished, screw the cover to the base and plug in a phone.

FOUR-PRONG ADAPTERS

A precursor to the modular plug is the four-prong plug and jack. Converting these to modular is a simple matter of plugging in a four-prong-to-modular adapter, available wherever telephone supplies are sold.

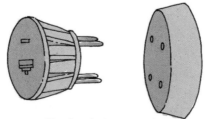

Plug-in adapter converts 4-prong jack to modular

There are two ways to install a modular jack in a new location: breaking into an existing cord you find running along a baseboard, and running a new cord from an existing jack or junction box.

A third possibility is that the new jack will be so close to the old that all you need is a T-adapter that plugs into an existing modular jack.

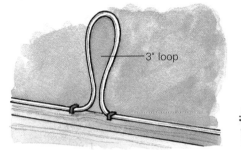

3" loop

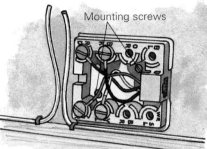

Mounting screws

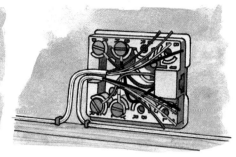

BREAKING INTO A LINE

Find a cord running along a baseboard near where you want the new jack. Next, trace the cord to see where it comes from. See if there is a shorter way to run the cord, such as taking a diagonal route instead of running along a beam and joist at right angles. If so, loosen the staples to that point and pull the excess cord into a 3-inch loop. Cut the loop at its top. Mount the base of the new modular jack next to the cut loop, remove a knockout, strip the cord sheathing, and feed the two sets of wires through the knockout. Strip the wire ends and insert the pairs of color-coded wires under the matching color-coded terminals. Tighten all connections.

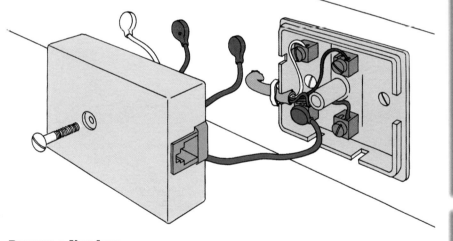

RUNNING A NEW LINE

Begin by making sure that neither wires nor plumbing lie behind the wall or baseboard where you will install the new jack. Then drill pilot holes where the jack will fasten. Screw the base to the wall or baseboard. Strip 3 inches of sheathing from the length of wire and 1 inch of insulation from each conductor.

Attach the appropriate conductors to the color-coded screws.

Run the wire along the top of the baseboards, behind them, or under the house to the nearest modular jack. Secure the wire with rounded staples every 8 to 12 inches; do not let the staples penetrate the wire.

To attach the new wire to an existing modular jack, first remove the cover from the existing jack. Strip 3 inches of sheathing from the new wire, then strip 1 inch of insulation from each conductor. Attach the conductors to the color-coded screws in the same manner as the existing wire connects. If the jack is not modular, now is a good time to convert it.

PLANNING FUTURE USE

If you are adding on, don't forget to wire for phones and TV. Just place a regular plastic receptacle box anywhere you think you might want a phone or TV hookup in the future, and run telephone and video cable to each box from a central location in the basement. You don't have to hook them up until you need them. Just attach blank cover plates to those you are not using. When you wish to activate an outlet, purchase the appropriate cover plate (with phone, TV, or phone plus TV jacks), and make the connection.

Try not to run the cable close to your electrical cable, however, to avoid powerline interference.

TELEPHONE WIRE COLOR CODES

Illustrations on these pages show the most common color codes for four-wire telephone wire: red, green, yellow, and black. You may encounter other codes. The table below shows how to match up the other colored wires.

Most Common	Variation 1	Variation 2
Red	Blue	Blue/White
Green	White/Blue	White/Blue
Yellow	Orange	Orange/White
Black	White/Orange	White/Orange

RUNNING TELEPHONE CABLE

TYPES OF CABLE

There are three main types of telephone cables or cord. Standard cable is the general-purpose cable used to wire houses. It runs inside walls and through framing members, and connects the centrally located telephone junction to individual telephone jacks. It includes four wires: red, green, yellow, and black. Normally, only the red and green wires are used, with the yellow and black reserved for a second phone line.

Modular cable, also called flat line cord, is the flat cable used to connect phones to jacks.

Multiwire cable consists of more than four wires arranged in pairs and twisted together.

CONCEALING CABLE

Besides the ways one would run concealed electrical cable (under the floor, through walls, or through the attic), additional methods are possible for telephone cable because it carries such a low voltage:
■ Under the edge of wall-to-wall carpeting, between the tack strip and the wall.
■ Under the bottoms of cabinets, through the cabinets at the back, or under the toe kick.

■ Through the backs of closets.
■ Through a cold-air return duct or alongside pipes in plumbing chases.
Remember—these are only for telephone cable, not electrical!

PRACTICES TO AVOID

Do not:
■ Run telephone cable in electrical conduit or in a junction box with electrical wiring because it will pick up 60 MHz hum
■ Run phone lines in wet locations.
■ Run phone lines where they will contact hot pipes.
■ Splice telephone cable; it causes noise on the line.

FISHING CABLE

When running telephone cable through walls, choose interior partition walls if possible. They are not insulated and usually don't contain fire blocks or bracing.

Drill a 1/16-inch pilot hole into either the basement or attic next to the wall where the new jack will go. Try to center the location between two studs. Push a clothes hanger or a long piece of wire through the hole so it will be easy to find. Locate the hole under the floor or in the attic and measure over to where the center of the wall should be. Drill a hole at least 3/8 inch in diameter through the top or bottom plate into the stud bay.

Cut the hole for the phone jack to fit an electrical remodeling box.

If you are running the cable from the attic, hang a weighted string down past the box opening and hook it with a bent clothes hanger.

If you are running the cable from beneath the floor, a fish tape is useful because it is stiff enough to reach up into the wall. If you don't have a fish tape, suspend a weight on a string from the box opening and hook the string from below.

Once the string is hooked, pull it through the jack opening. Securely tape the phone cable to the string and pull the cable through.

Install the electrical box. Strip the cable back 3 inches, connect the wires to the color-coded terminals of the

modular jack (mounted on a cover plate), and install the cover plate.

Connect the other end of the wire

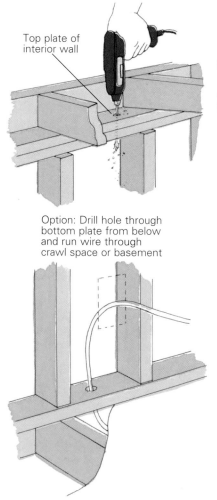

Top plate of interior wall

Option: Drill hole through bottom plate from below and run wire through crawl space or basement

to the phone block or another jack. When all connections are complete, hook up a phone and test the line.

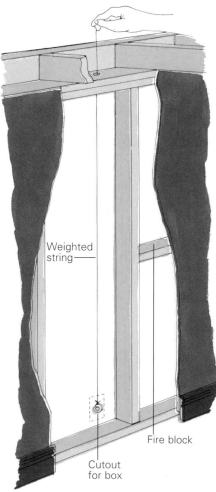

Weighted string

Fire block

Cutout for box

TROUBLESHOOTING YOUR CONNECTIONS

TESTING

If you suspect a problem, begin by testing the line with a phone that you know is in good working order. Plug the phone into the jack. If there is a dial tone, try to call a number. If the dial tone won't stop, the red and green wires are reversed. If there is no dial tone, follow the wire run and look for a short circuit. Short circuits occur when bare wires touch each other, or a staple or other type of metal fastener has penetrated the telephone cable at some point. Open connections occur when a wire is not secured to a terminal or a wire has broken during the installation.

In the rare instance that the red or green wire is broken, substitute the yellow and black wires for the red and green, or replace the cable completely.

WHO'S RESPONSIBLE FOR REPAIRS?

Homeowners are responsible for telephone repairs from the main wiring block into the house. Fortunately, many common problems are easy to diagnose and fix.

When a problem occurs, first determine whether it is inside or outside the house (if it is outside, the telephone company will repair it).

TROUBLESHOOTING TELEPHONES

Problem	Possible Causes	What to Do
No dial tone at all	Telephone broken	Plug a different phone into the jack. If you now get a dial tone, the first phone is broken. Throw it away.
	Phone company problem	Plug a phone directly into the network interface module (the first box the phone line enters as it comes into your home). If there is no dial tone, the problem is in the phone company's wiring. Call the company.
	Loose or broken wire	If there is a dial tone at the network interface, the problem is a loose or broken wire between the interface and the jack. Remove the covers from both the interface and the jack, then replace the red and green wires with the yellow and black wires at both ends: yellow for red, and black for green.
Continuous dial tone on just one phone	Red and green wires reversed at the jack	Remove the cover from the jack and reverse the red and green wires.
Continuous dial tone on all phones	Red and green wires reversed at the network interface	Remove the cover from the network interface and reverse the red and green wires.
Noise or interference	Loose splice	Look for splices in the phone wire between the network interface and the troublesome jack. Resplice the wires.
	Wet connections	Find a wet connection and dry with a hair dryer. Remove or divert the source of moisture.
	Electrical interference	Look for places where the phone cable touches a water pipe or conduit, or runs next to an electrical cable. Move the phone cable. If you still have noise, call the phone company.

CORDLESS COMFORTS

Portable phones (not to be confused with cellular phones) are simply wonderful. If you are working in a room or in the yard where there is no phone, just take the portable with you. No more running to reach the phone before the caller hangs up or the answering machine picks up. Since they are battery-operated, you can even use them in the tub. The two types are:

■ 43 to 49 MHz; the original type, suitable for around the home with a range of 100 to 150 feet.
■ 902 to 928 MHz (nominally 900 MHz); a newer, more expensive type, for ranging up to 1,000 feet or more.

Wiring an existing home for phones in every room is a difficult project involving fishing wires through walls. Consider the option of one or more cordless phones. It may, in fact, be cheaper than a hard-wired phone in every room.

A REEL SOLUTION

Although cordless phones are all the rage, phones with cords are still the most popular type of phone. There's no doubt, however, that those spring-coiled cords can still be a nuisance. A better solution is to install a spring-loaded cord-coiler. Lightweight and compact, a cord coiler replaces your old cord. It reels out up to 15 feet of line, and when you replace the receiver it automatically reels the line back in.

TILE

INSTALLATION BASICS

ALSO SEE...
Access:
Pages 4–7
Adhesives:
Pages 8–9
Bathtubs:
Pages 24–27
Countertops:
Pages 70–73
Floors:
Pages 140–141
Showers:
Pages 310–313
Wallboard:
Pages 392–397

Tile is a classic, beautiful, and sturdy material for finishing walls, floors, countertops, tub backs, showers, and hearths. The wide range of its colors, textures, sizes, and shapes makes it suitable for installations that vary from simple and angular to warm and textural. You can use tile as the main feature of a large area or they can be used in small accent panels with other materials.

Whether its installation is easy or difficult will depend mostly on the shape of the surface to be covered and the type of backing required. Most homeowners can do their own worry-free installations using thin-set techniques, although the areas around showers, tubs, and sinks require careful attention.

No tile installation is automatically waterproof. Tiles themselves vary in their absorption characteristics, from nonvitreous (highly absorbent), to semivitreous, to vitreous (low absorption), to impervious (won't even absorb dye). The grout can be even more vulnerable to water absorption. Most portland cement grouts include waterproofing additives, but you should still seal these grouts in wet areas after they have cured.

Grouts made from silicone or polyurethane are extremely waterproof. Manufacturers grout sheets of tile with it, and you can purchase it in tubes for application with a caulking gun. Waterproof grouts with resin or epoxy bases, used for industrial installations, are rarely used in home applications.

TYPES OF TILE

There are several ways to classify ceramic tile. Examples include glazed wall tile, mosaic tile, quarry tile, pavers, and marble and granite tiles.

Glazed Wall Tile: Standard glazed wall tiles are waterproof, making them excellent for walls, tubs, showers, vanities, and kitchen countertops. Watch out for handmade tiles, however; some have soft glazing, which is not suitable for tubs, showers, or counters. Sizes of imported tile vary, but domestic sizes are 4¼ inches and 6 inches square.

Mosaic Tile: Mosaic tiles are small—usually 1 or 2 inches across—although some are as small as ⅜ inch square. Because they come in one-foot squares with a mesh backing, their installation is no more time consuming than solid, one-foot square tiles. Mosaics come glazed or unglazed, and usually are made by the dust-press method—a process that forms tiles by compressing clay dust under extreme pressure.

Quarry Tile: Quarry tile is for floors and hearths. It generally is unglazed and vitreous to semivitreous. Most quarry tiles are manufactured by an extrusion process that is not as meticulous as the dust-press method.

Pavers: Pavers are quarry tiles made by the dust-press method. They can be glazed or unglazed, and are intended for patios and floors. Those made in the United States are generally 12 inches square and about ¾ inch thick. The European equivalents are about 13¼ inches square. If used indoors, they should be sealed to prevent staining. Beware of using them outside in areas with severe winters; expansion and contraction due to freezing and thawing is likely to crack them.

Marble and Granite: These are popular floor and accent tiles. In addition to natural stone, there are composites made of marble or granite chips mixed with epoxy resin. You'll need a water saw to cut them—rent one from a rental center or tile outlet.

CHANGING FLOOR LEVELS

If you are replacing a sheet-vinyl floor with tile, floor levels may need some modification to meet the requirements of the Americans with Disabilities Act. According to the act:
■ Abrupt changes in floor level must be less than ¼ inch.
■ Beveled changes in floor level of less than ½ inch must have a slope of less than ½.

Remember that quarry tile is about ½ inch thick. If you lay additional plywood or cement backer board to stiffen the floor for the tile, you are adding at least another ½ inch. You'll need to take this new height into account where new tile floors meet older surfaces. A beveled strip of neutral material, such as painted or natural wood, will bridge the gap.

MARKING TILE FOR CUTTING

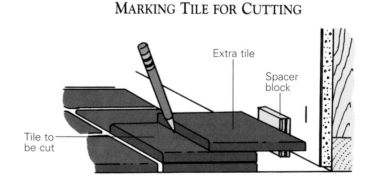

Extra tile

Spacer block

Tile to be cut

Thin strips of tile are weaker than full tiles, so try not to end up with pieces that are less than half a tile. This is especially important in high-traffic areas, such as in front of doors. Also, short rows look better when they are equal on both sides of the centerline. The best-looking tile layouts result from careful planning.

When a row must end with a cut tile, use the method shown, *above*, to mark the tile accurately. Mark each tile as you go in case there are variations in the wall. The spacer must be as thick as the grout on both sides of the cut tile.

Tile requires a firm, inflexible base. For that reason, tile in wet areas needs a backing that will not deteriorate if moisture seeps through the tile or grout. Common backing materials are concrete, a bed of mortar, wallboard, plywood, and glass-mesh backerboard (panels of cement material sandwiched between two layers of fiberglass mesh).

WALLS

In dry areas you can install tile over any smooth wall surface using thin-set organic adhesives. Install a new backing material—such as wallboard—over walls with cracks or irregularities. Some surfaces—such as new wallboard—should first be sealed with a primer that is compatible with the adhesive. Existing wall surfaces must be free of dirt, wax, grease, efflorescence, or other residues, and should be lightly sanded if they are glossy or painted.

Wet locations, such as tub and shower enclosures, require a waterproof backing such as glass-mesh backerboard. Tape the backerboard joints with self-adhesive fiberglass-mesh tape, fill them with an appropriate compound, and use dry-set or latex/portland cement mortar to lay the tiles.

You can install tiles over concrete or wood floors, but the surfaces must be prepared properly. For new construction, space joists at 12 inches on-center rather than the normal 16 inches. Install a subfloor of ⅝-inch tongue-and-groove plywood covered with an underlayment of ⅜-inch plywood (⅝ inch for epoxy adhesives).

You can set tile directly over noncushioned vinyl that is over plywood, provided you remove all wax and sand the surface lightly so that the adhesive will bond.

On old tile set on solid floors, roughen the surface to ensure tight bonding. Then apply a liquid underlayment (if you are using mastics) or epoxy mortar to level any irregularities.

Concrete floors make excellent bases as long as they are dry, smooth, level, and well cured. You will also need to remove wax, oil, and any curing compounds. Remove any old floor materials first and roughen the surface to ensure adhesion. If the floor is cracked or damaged, repair the damaged section and fill the void with latex leveling compound. Let the compound dry, then sand it smooth.

Tile will adhere directly to smoothly finished slabs with the use of organic adhesives or dry-set mortar. Epoxy or portland cement mortar is a better substrate for rougher surfaces.

COUNTERTOPS

For thin-set organic and epoxy adhesives, use ¾-inch plywood. However, plywood may deteriorate in wet locations if the tile is not well sealed. A better solution is to use either dry-set or latex/portland cement mortar over glass-mesh backerboard over exterior-grade plywood. The best installation of all, however, is a reinforced mortar bed floated over ¾-inch exterior-grade plywood.

TILE ADHESIVES AND MORTARS

Type	Composition	Conditions for Use	Comments
ADHESIVES			
Type I Mastic	Solvent based	Damp areas	Thin-set; ready to use, flammable, may irritate skin and lungs
Type II Mastic	Latex based	Dry areas only	Easy to clean up, nonflammable vapors
Epoxy Adhesive	Two-part epoxy	Good adhesive for wet areas. Use over plywood or existing resilient floor coverings	Expensive, toxic to skin, works best between 70 and 85 degrees F
MORTARS			
Portland Cement Mortar	Traditional mortar bed—portland cement mixed with sand and water	Good adhesive for wet areas or where subfloor is uneven	Thick (¾" to 1¼") bed, reinforced with wire mesh, long lasting, waterproof, good structural strength, requires careful installation
Dry-Set Mortar	Portland cement mixed with sand, additives, and water	For concrete or glass-mesh backerboard; not for over wood or resilient floors	Not water-resistant, nonflammable, easy to clean up, rigid, impact-resistant
Latex-Portland Cement Mortar	Portland cement mixed with sand and liquid latex, sometimes diluted with water	For concrete or glass-mesh backerboard; not for over wood or resilient floors	More water-resistant than dry-set mortar, easier to work with, less rigid, tends to move more
Epoxy Mortar	Epoxy resin mixed with hardener, sand, and portland cement	Good adhesive for wet areas. Use over concrete or existing ceramic tile	More body and chemical resistance than adhesive; levels uneven subsurfaces

CUTTING TILE

If you have just one or two cuts, it is easiest to pay your tile supplier to make perfectly smooth cuts with a water-cooled saw. If you have many cuts to make, rent the water saw and make them yourself. For amounts in between, cut them by hand or use a snap cutter (which you also can rent—cheaper than a water-cooled saw).

To cut tile manually, score the tile using a tile-scoring tool. Place the score mark over a pencil or dowel and snap the tile with quick, forceful pressure on both sides.

A snap cutter makes straight cuts quickly and accurately. The handle has a small cutting wheel which scores the tile as you pull the handle across it. An extension arm on the handle then forces the sides of the tile down to snap it. Large models are effective for cutting tiles up to 12 inches square.

ROUND CUTS

1. To make round cuts by hand, mark the diameter of the circle, then score and cut the tile along this line.
2. On each half tile, score around the half circle. Also make crosshatch scores all over the area to be cut away.
3. Using pliers or nippers, break out waste in small chips. Be sure to wear safety glasses.

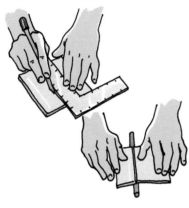
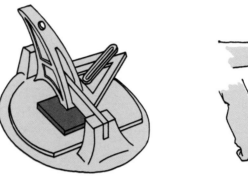

SETTING THE TILE

Spread adhesive over an area approximately 3 feet by 3 feet, using the appropriate notched trowel (see the table at right). For floors that tend to be damp, apply a first coat of adhesive over the entire surface with a smooth trowel, let it dry, then apply a second coat with the notched trowel. Set the tiles into the wet adhesive with a firm, twisting motion. If adhesive fills the joint to the top of the tile, you're using too much. Insert spacers between the tiles and wipe off any excess adhesive immediately.

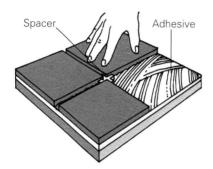

Spacer   Adhesive

NOTCHED TROWEL SIZE GUIDE

Type of Tile	Trowel Size and Type
Mosaics and smaller tiles	3/16"×5/32" V-notched, 1/4"×3/16" V-notched
Wall tiles	1/4"×1/4" Square-notched
Flat-backed floor tiles	1/4"×1/4" Square-notched
Irregular or lug-backed tiles	1/4"×3/8" Square-notched, 1/2"×1/2" Square-notched
Marble and granite	1/4"×1/4" Square-notched, 1/4"×3/8" Square-notched

ESTIMATING GROUT—SQUARE FEET PER POUND

Tile Size	Joint Width, inches 1/16	1/8	1/4	3/8	1/2	3/4
1"×1"×1/4"	5.0	2.5	1.0	–	–	–
2"×2"×1/4"	10.0	5.0	2.0	–	–	–
4¼"×4¼"×5/16"	14.5	7.0	3.0	–	–	–
6"×6"×1/4"	25.0	12.0	5.0	3.5	2.4	–
6"×6"×1/2"	12.5	6.0	2.5	1.7	1.2	–
4"×8"×1/2"	11.0	5.5	2.2	1.5	1.0	–
8"×8"×1/4"	33.0	17.0	6.6	4.5	3.0	2.4
8"×8"×3/8"	22.5	11.5	4.5	3.0	2.0	1.6
8"×8"×3/4"	11.0	5.5	2.2	1.5	1.0	0.8
12"×12"×3/8"	28.0	14.0	7.0	4.5	–	2.0
12"×12"×3/4"	14.0	17.0	7.0	–	–	1.0
16"×16"×3/8"	45.0	22.5	9.0	5.7	3.7	3.0
24"×24"×3/8"	65.0	32.5	13.0	9.0	6.0	4.8

APPLYING GROUT

After the adhesive has dried, remove the spacers. Mix cement-based grout according to the type of tile: stiff for mosaic tile, loose for most white-bodied tiles, and runny for red-bodied tiles. Force grout into the cracks by spreading it diagonally across the tiles with a rubber float or squeegee. Work it into joints using the rounded end of a toothbrush handle.

Remove as much excess as possible, and wipe off the remainder with a wet sponge. Wait 30 minutes, let a haze form, and polish the surface with a soft

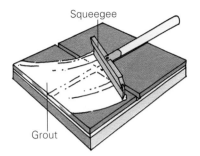

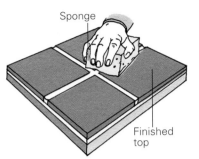

cloth. To cure, keep the grout moist by covering the tiled area with plastic sheeting or spraying it at regular intervals for two or three days. Do not

apply pressure or walk on the tiles during this time. Seal after two weeks.

INSTALLING A TILE FLOOR

STARTING THE LAYOUT

Find the midpoint of two opposite walls, and snap a chalk line down the center of the room. Snap another chalk line, perpendicular to the first, at the centerline of the other two walls.

Starting with a full tile at the doorway, lay a dry run of tiles along the first line. Use spacers between every tile for uniform joints. If you do not have enough room for a full tile at the end, adjust the row of tiles so that you have equal cut tiles at both ends or widen the grout spaces. Repeat the process along the second chalk line, readjusting both lines so that they intersect at a tile corner.

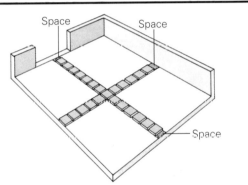

INSTALLING TEMPORARY STRAIGHTEDGES

After you have established the tile pattern, draw a line on the floor to mark the outside edge of the last full tile at the doorway. This line must be perpendicular to the first chalk line and perfectly straight, even if the wall is not. Use a full sheet of plywood as a giant framing square to make sure the lines are perpendicular.

Extend the line along the length of the wall. Repeat this process for the other walls. Set long 1×2s or 1×3s (these will be your outside edge guides) on the outside of each line and nail or screw them to the floor.

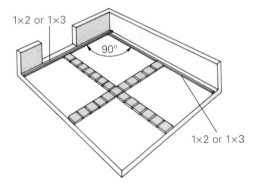

SETTING THE TILES

Starting in the corner where the boards intersect, spread a 3×3-foot adhesive area with a notched trowel, then press the corner tile into place with a slight twisting motion. Continue setting tiles in the numeric order shown, inserting spacers between them to keep the alignment straight. Molded plastic tees (you can buy them from your tile supplier) are best because they set the space in both directions and won't stick to the adhesive.

Tamp down any uneven tiles with a rubber mallet or beat on a 2×4 wrapped in a towel with a hammer. Wipe any excess adhesive off of the tile surface immediately because it will be difficult to remove later. Allow the adhesive to set, remove the straightedges, and install cut tiles along the edges, leaving a ⅛-inch gap along the wall.

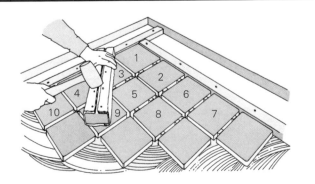

INSTALLING A TILE WALL

LAYING OUT WALLS

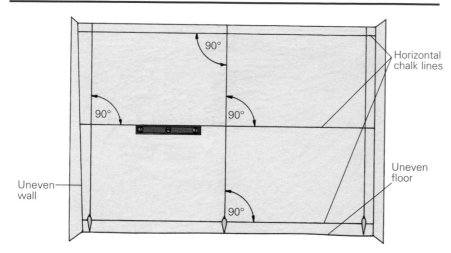

USING LAYOUT RODS

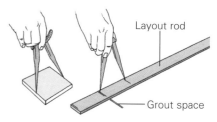

Cut two straight 1×2s—one for the height and one for the width of the wall. Put a tile, a spacer, and a second tile together on the floor. Using a compass, measure the gain—the total length of one tile and one spacer—as exactly as you can. Then mark both layout rods at this increment. If you don't end up with even tiles (or at least a half tile) at both ends, adjust the grout spacing until you are satisfied with the layout.

Wall layouts require the same centering and dry run techniques that a floor installation does, but wall layouts are made easy with a layout rod. First, find the center of the wall by centering perpendicular lines on the midpoints of the height and width. Snap a plumb line (using a plumb bob to make sure) from the ceiling to the floor through this midpoint, and two more plumb lines close to the edges of the wall.

Snap a chalk line through the center point of the wall perpendicular to the first line. Check the angles between the horizontal line and the three vertical lines to be sure they are all square. Then snap two more horizontal lines as close to the floor and ceiling as possible. Check the angles again. This grid will show you where you need tapered tiles to conform to uneven walls. The grid also gives you the centerlines for starting the installation.

If you are using special tiles or trim pieces as a border, be sure they are included at the proper ends of the rods.

Transfer the marks from each layout rod to the wall by holding the rod against the parallel lines you've drawn at the edges of the wall. These marks will guide the installation.

SETTING WALL TILES

Begin the installation on the bottom row, starting at the centerline. Apply enough adhesive for the first few tiles, but leave the baseline and centerline visible for accurate alignment. Set the first tiles in place and insert spacers between them. For a thinner grout line than the one allowed by a spacer, use plywood, coins, or any other uniformly thin material.

After the tiles have set, let the adhesive dry for a full day before grouting the joints. For wide joints, use cement-based grout with sand added for bulk. Grout narrow joints with cement, epoxy, or elastomeric grouts. Use the rounded end of a toothbrush handle to pack it in tightly.

When grouting a bathtub or shower, plug the drain with a rag to keep grout out of the plumbing, and use a drop cloth to keep the grout off the tub. To cure the grout, keep it damp for at least 72 hours by covering it with plastic sheeting and misting it twice a day with water from a spray bottle.

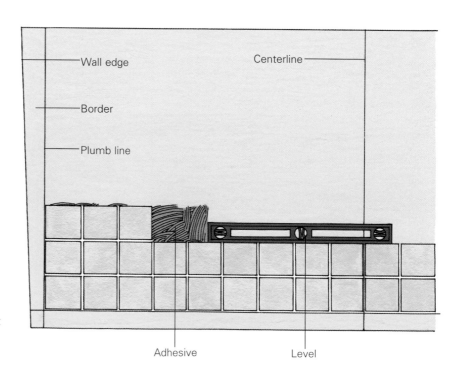

INSTALLING MOSAIC TILE

Most mosaic tile comes in sheets (usually 1-foot square), held together with paper on the face or mesh on the back. Some are bonded together with a rubberlike grout. Prebonded tile is excellent for tub and shower enclosures, but should not be used for food-preparation surfaces.

Mosaic tiles require less cutting because the units are typically only an inch square and, thus, lend themselves more easily to tight fits. Use the same surface preparation and layout guidelines as described for floor and wall tile.

LAYOUT

Plan your layout by setting full sheets in place. Avoid tugging on corners and distorting the spacing. Instead, set one edge of the sheet down and unroll the rest. Remember to keep the space between sheets the same as the space between tiles.

The paper face makes marking cuts simple; just sketch the cut lines on the paper surface.

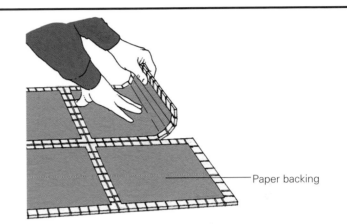

Paper backing

OBSTRUCTIONS

To fit a sheet of mosaic tile around an obstruction, use a utility knife to cut the paper or mesh and remove whole tiles. Any remaining gaps can be filled later with individual cut tiles.

Utility knife

BORDERS

To fill border spaces, slide a sheet over the space, and mark it, allowing for a ⅛-inch expansion gap. Cut along the line with a water saw, or cut single tiles with nippers or a hand cutter.

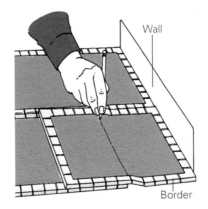

Wall

Border

SETTING THE TILE

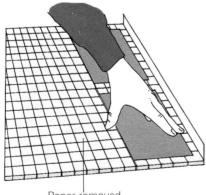

Paper removed

Spread adhesive with a ³⁄₁₆×⁵⁄₃₂-inch or ¼×³⁄₁₆-inch V-notched trowel, carefully embedding the sheets of tile in it. Unroll the sheets to prevent sliding them around in the adhesive. Press them into place.

Grout mosaic tile the same way you would other kinds of tile. Force the grout into the cracks with a rubber float or squeegee, working across the tiles diagonally to prevent the squeegee blade from dipping into the tile joints. You will need a lot more grout to fill the joints around mosaic tile than you would for an equivalent area covered with larger tiles.

If the tiles are attached with paper glued to the top surface, soak the paper with warm water and gently peel it off after the adhesive dries.

INSTALLING A TILE COUNTERTOP

Tile is a popular finish for bathroom and kitchen countertops. Its clean, durable surface has a special, textural beauty. Best of all, it is not difficult for the average do-it-yourself homeowner to install.

Tile on countertops has two inherent drawbacks, however:
■ Glass and other fragile objects can break if dropped on the tile surface.

■ Grout joints tend to collect dirt and stains, although less so if the grout is colored and well sealed.

Make sure you select the highest-quality tiles your budget will allow, and install them securely on a moisture-proof surface that has been carefully prepared.

Install glazed or semivitreous tile around sinks, food preparation areas, and where water splashes because unglazed tile readily stains.

When the surface is properly prepared, tile can be installed over many different materials. If you are installing it over ¾-inch plywood, make sure the tile and grout are waterproofed. Mounting glass-mesh backerboard over the plywood is one of the best methods.

TRIM

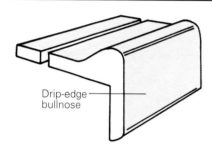
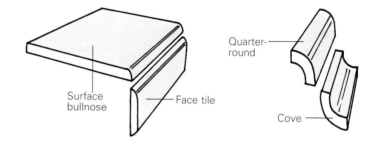

Drip-edge bullnose · Surface bullnose · Face tile · Quarter-round · Cove

There are many kinds of trim pieces tailored for countertop edges, corners, backsplashes, and sink openings. When you select your tile, make sure that the trim you need is available in the same pattern and color, or comes in a complementary color. Buy extra pieces

so you have replacements if a tile breaks or chips in the future.

Try to use only whole tiles on your countertop. If this proves impossible, install a self-rimming sink so the rim will cover the cut edges.

A second option is to trim the edge of the counter with a hardwood stained

and finished to blend with the tile. Adjust the width of the trim and the widths of the grout joints so that whole tiles butt against the trim.

The backsplash can be one tile high, extend farther up the wall, or you can fashion it from wood instead of tile.

LAYOUT

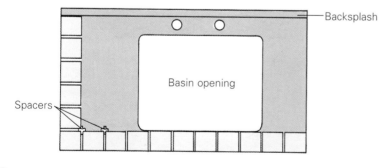

Backsplash · Basin opening · Spacers

Lay out the tile pattern and test it with a dry run. Start with trim pieces or bullnose tiles first. If the counter is L-shape, start the layout with a full tile at the inside corner and work outward in both directions. All trim pieces should be laid out so the grout lines follow the grout lines of the rest of the tiles.

CUTOUTS

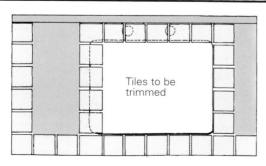

Tiles to be trimmed

When you are satisfied with the layout for the front and back edges, lay out the tiles around the sink. If the sink is self-rimming or has a metal rim, mark the tiles for the sink cutout by laying them in their proper place and marking the cut lines from beneath the counter.

If you have a recessed—instead of self-rimming—basin, set it in place and cut tiles and trim pieces to fit around it. Try to buy a sink that contains faucet holes, so you won't have to fit tile around the faucets.

SETTING THE TILE

When you know where all of the tiles will go and have marked them for cutting, make all the cuts before starting installation. Apply adhesive over a small area with the proper notched trowel (see Notched Trowel Size Guide, page 362).

Adhesives take different amounts of time to dry, so check the product directions. Don't spread adhesive over an area larger than you can cover in the adhesive's working time. Be mindful of safety precautions regarding ventilation and open flames.

On straight counters, start the installation with bullnose tiles or trim pieces at a corner, using spacers between the tiles. If it is an L-shape countertop, start at the inside corner.

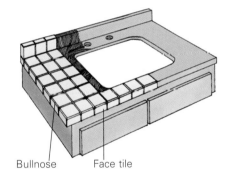

Backsplash

FINISHING THE APPLICATION

Use nippers to cut tiles so they will fit around obstructions. As you finish each row of tiles on the horizontal surface, work your way up the backsplash or wall. End with a row of bullnose tiles or full tiles edged with moldings. As you finish setting groups of tiles, remove any excess adhesive as quickly as possible. Let the adhesive dry for at least one full day.

Bullnose   Face tile

GROUTING JOINTS

Press grout into the grout joints using a rubber squeegee. Run the applicator diagonally across the tiles so the joint is filled flush with the tile. Force the grout firmly into the joints, using a small tool such as a toothbrush handle.

Remove the excess grout with a damp sponge, rinsing the sponge frequently. After rinsing the entire surface at least twice, let the surface residue dry to a haze, then polish the tile with a soft cloth.

Cover the countertop with polyethylene sheeting for two or three days to let the grout cure properly. After two weeks, apply a grout sealer with mildew protection.

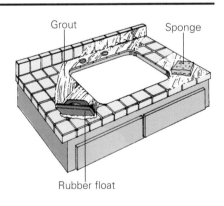

Grout   Sponge

Rubber float

REPLACING GROUT

Dig out the old grout with any sharp tool (an old-fashioned beer-can opener works well) or rent a grout saw.

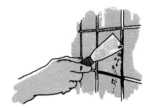

Apply new grout with your finger. Smooth and wipe off the excess.

REPLACING A TILE

Wear eye protection. Break the tile with a hammer. Don't hit hard enough to damage the underlying wallboard.

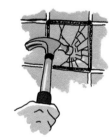

After removing the chips, scrape off the old adhesive. If it's hard, warm it with a heat gun.

Apply adhesive and set the new tile. Wedge it in place with toothpicks. After a day remove the toothpicks, mist joints with water, and apply grout.

TILE ROOFING

A CLASSIC GETS EASIER

ALSO SEE...
Flashing:
Pages 136–139
Roofs:
Pages 282–289

Tile roofs are fireproof, beautiful, and long lasting—and many new styles are surprisingly easy to install. Their heritage makes them prevalent in the South and West, but tile roofs are suitable in any climate.

Installation varies with the type of tile and the manufacturer. Some clay tiles must be installed over a "hot mop" tar roof; others can be laid over sheathing. The easiest type to install is interlocking flat tile, shown here.

PREPARING THE ROOF

Traditional glazed tile can weigh 10 pounds per square foot. The newer concrete types weigh half as much. For glazed tile, sheath the roof with ⅝-inch tongue-and-groove plywood; for concrete tiles, ½-inch plywood is sufficient. Whether to install 30-pound felt underlayment depends on slope. The minimum recommended slope for tile is 3/12. Consult the manufacturer's directions.

Some tiles are made to nail directly to the sheathing; others have lugs that hook over 1×2 battens. For the battens, use redwood or pressure-treated southern yellow pine, spaced at the required exposure—usually 14 inches.

Regardless of the type, install metal drip flashing under the felt along the eaves and over the felt along the rake edges. Flash valleys with copper W-flashing at least 25 inches wide laid over 90-pound mineral surface roofing. Make sure your nails are copper as well. Cover hips and ridges with a double layer of felt that overlaps at least 6 inches on both sides.

Nail a 2×2 to the framing along the center of every hip and ridge to support the cap tiles. Also nail a 1×2 along the outside edges of the rake rafters to hold the rake tiles away from the rafters. Finally, nail a 1×2 along the edge of the eaves. If the tiles are not flat, this starter strip can become a dam for water blown under curved tiles, so cut drainage notches.

INSTALLING THE TILES

The First Course: Snap a chalk line to align the top edge of the tiles. Beginning at the right-hand rake edge, install the first course with the tiles overhanging the starter strip, Nail the tiles with copper nails long enough to penetrate the roof sheathing fully.

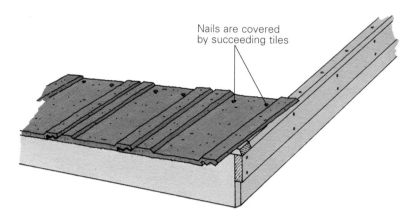

Nails are covered by succeeding tiles

Clips: Use metal clips on every fourth row for roofs steeper than 6/12; use clips on every row for roofs steeper than 10/12. The clips are provided by the manufacturer to fit the type of tile and are nailed directly to the sheathing. Clips are also available for high-wind areas to hold down the side of each tile.

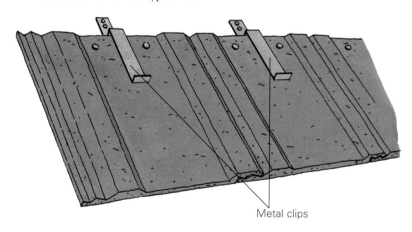

Metal clips

Trim Tiles: Cover the rake edges with the special end tiles or metal trim provided by the manufacturer. The metal trim may be designed to be concealed by a fascia board.

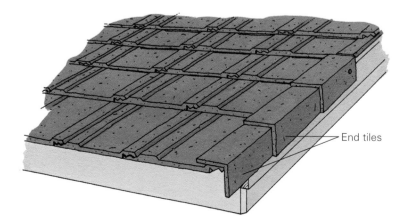

End tiles

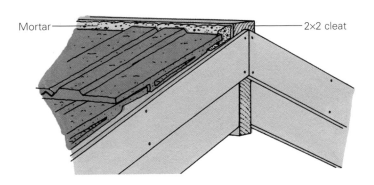

Mortar

2×2 cleat

The Final Course: Trim the final course of tiles at ridges and hips 1½ inches short of the 2×2. Cut the tile using a circular saw with a masonry blade. Lay a bed of mortar against the 2×2 and embed the top of the tile in it as you nail it in place. Cover the nail heads with mastic. Some manufacturers recommend a ½-inch gap between the 2×2 and the tile, and some specify mastic instead of mortar.

Cap Tiles: Starting at the bottom of a hip (or at the end of the ridge facing prevailing storms), cover hips and ridges with special cap tiles. They come in various shapes, but should cover at least the top 3 inches of each side. Nail the cap tiles into the hip or ridge 2×2, and apply mastic over the nail head and end of tile that will be covered by the next cap tile.

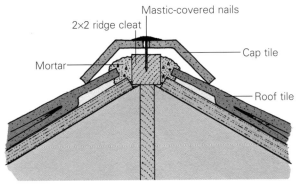

Mastic-covered nails

2×2 ridge cleat

Mortar

Cap tile

Roof tile

Blade guard handle

Masonry blade

Tile

Cutting Around Vents: Cut the tiles to fit snugly around the vent pipe, using plunge cuts with a circular saw. Hold the blade guard out of the way and, keeping the front edge of the shoe steady against the tile, lower the blade slowly into each tile. The saw blade will not cut cleanly to the corners, so just tap out the remainder with a hammer.

Vent Flashing: Vent flashings for tile roofs should be made of lead at a sheet-metal shop. After placing a cut-out tile over the vent pipe, apply mastic to the tile. Then drop the flashing down over the pipe onto the mastic, and press the lead flange to conform to the profile of the tile pattern. The course of tiles above should lap over the top edge of the flashing, just like vent flashing for shingles and shakes. Finally, seal the top of the flashing to the pipe with silicone or other non-hardening sealant.

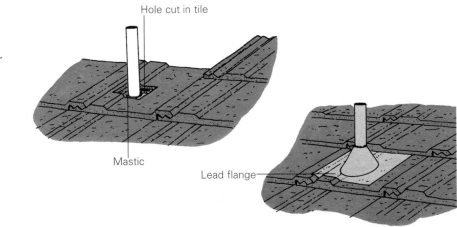

Hole cut in tile

Mastic

Lead flange

NEW MODELS OF EFFICIENCY

ALSO SEE...
Bathroom Design:
Pages 22–23
Faucets & Valves:
Pages 126–129
Plumbing:
Pages 256–263

Few things in your home are simpler to repair or replace than a toilet. You probably already have the few tools required, and the nearest home center or hardware store has all of the replacement parts.

If you're replacing your toilet entirely, you will find that new toilets are required to be water-saving models. Building codes now require that toilets use no more than 1.6 gallons per flush.

If you have heard that these toilets won't flush, don't believe it. In fact, due to some advanced hydraulics engineering being applied to the problem, you will probably find that a new toilet will flush better than your old 5- to 8-gallon guzzler.

HOW TOILETS WORK

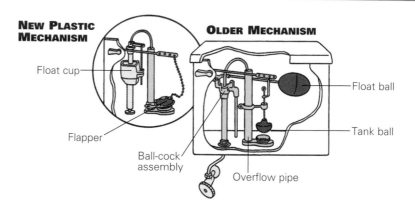

Pushing the handle down raises the flushing lever. The lever lifts the tank ball or flapper, which lets the water in the tank rush into the bowl. When the loop behind the bowl fills with water, a siphon is established, which then empties the bowl.

Meanwhile, as water in the tank empties, it lowers the float ball (or float cup). The ball is attached to an arm which opens the intake valve in the ball-cock assembly. When the tank ball or flapper descends far enough, it closes the tank outlet and water fills the tank. The float rises with the water level and closes the intake valve when the water reaches the right level. While the tank is refilling, water is also squirting through a tube clipped into the overflow pipe. This water flows down the pipe into the bowl, refilling it after the initial flushing.

All toilets are variations on one of the following types:

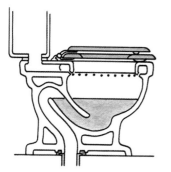

Reverse-trap toilets have deep traps and flushing holes only around the inside of their rims.

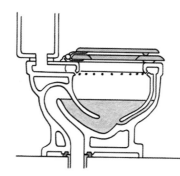

Siphon-jet toilets have a small hole below the waterline which directs a jet of water into the trap to start the siphon quickly. These are quieter and use less water than reverse traps.

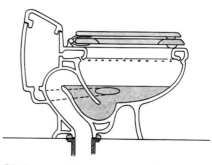

Siphon-action or one-piece toilets are the quietest, most efficient, and most expensive toilets. Instead of a small hole and a jet of water, they have an elongated hole on one side of the bowl. Water swirls powerfully to rinse the bowl and to create a siphon.

Low-flow toilets, required for all new installations or replacements, use 1.6 gallons of water per flush (GPF) compared with 3.5 to 8 GPF for older toilets. New toilets look pretty much like the old ones; the better flushing action is due to steeper bowl sides, a smaller amount of water in the bowl, and generally better hydraulic design.

TACTIC TO SNAG RIGID OBSTRUCTIONS

If your toilet backs up but still drains slowly, chances are someone has flushed a rigid object, such as a comb, down the bowl and the object is hung up in the trap.

First try plunging the bowl with a downward pressure. If that fails to dislodge the stoppage, flush the toilet and, as the water slowly exits the bowl, allow the end of a hand towel to follow the flow into the trap. When the towel has gone as far as it will, quickly pull the towel out. If you are lucky, the end of the towel will snag the object.

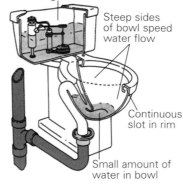

TROUBLESHOOTING TOILETS

Problem	Possible Causes	What to Do
Tank won't fill	Tank ball or flapper not falling	Check the entire linkage from the flush handle to the flush bowl or flapper to make sure nothing is hanging up. You may need to tighten the handle, adjust a length of chain, or shift the linkage-rod guide arm.
Water runs constantly after the tank is full	Float ball set too high or waterlogged	Flush the toilet and pull the float ball up hard. If the water shuts off, the float ball is set too high or is waterlogged. For the former, bend the ball arm down; for the latter, replace the ball or replace the whole ball-cock assembly with a plastic float cup.
Water runs awhile after the tank is full	Flush ball or flapper fouled or worn	Clean the flush ball or flapper and the ball seat; if ball or flapper is worn, replace; if the seat is corroded, replace the whole ball-cock assembly with a plastic float cup.
Water on the floor	Tank filling too high	Flush the toilet and observe the tank as it fills. The water should shut off when it rises to ¾ inch below the top of the overflow tube. If it rises to the top of the tube, bend the float-ball arm down until it fills properly.
	Condensation on tank around the toilet	Flush the toilet and feel the sides of the tank after 10 minutes. If they are wet, you have condensation due to the cold water in the tank. The solution is to install a foam insulation kit or to replace the tank with an insulated model.
	Tank is leaking	Let the tank warm to room temperature to eliminate the possibility that condensation is the cause. Wipe the bottom of the tank dry with paper towels. Check again after 10 minutes. If the bottom is wet again, the tank is leaking. Empty the tank and remove it; take the old gaskets to the hardware store and get replacements; install replacements, reinstall tank, and test.
	Wax gasket is leaking	Dry the floor around the toilet, the tank, the supply tube, and the supply fittings thoroughly with paper towels. After an hour, check all for water. If there is no water, the problem can only be the wax gasket. Replace the gasket (described under Installing a New Toilet, page 373).

REPLACING A VALVE ASSEMBLY

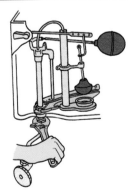
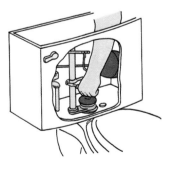

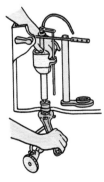

1 Close the shutoff valve. Flush to empty the tank and sponge out any remaining water. Loosen the nut beneath the tank that connects the supply tube to the ball cock assembly and pull the supply tube out of the way.

2 Unclip the refill tube from the overflow pipe and remove the ball-cock assembly and the old rubber washers.

3 Install the new valve according to the manufacturer's directions, making sure the new rubber washers are seated tightly. Clip the end of the refill tube inside the overflow pipe.

4 Reconnect the supply tube and turn the water back on. Check for leaks at the bottom of the tank. Adjust the float level with the spring clip.

REMOVING AN OLD TOILET

WALL-MOUNTED TOILET

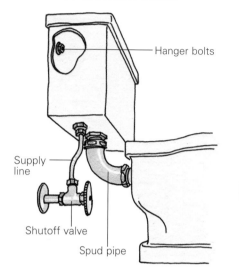

Hanger bolts

Supply line

Shutoff valve

Spud pipe

BOWL-MOUNTED TOILET

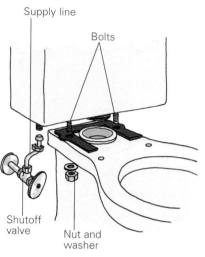

Supply line

Bolts

Shutoff valve

Nut and washer

Rough-in distance from bolt to wall

Bolt cap

Washer

Bolt

Nut

1 Turn off the water at the shutoff valve under the tank and then flush the toilet. Use a sponge and a bucket to remove the remaining water from both tank and bowl.

2 Disconnect the supply line from the fitting at the bottom of the tank.

  If the tank is mounted on the bowl, remove the two connecting bolts and lift the tank off the bowl. (If the tank is wall-mounted, remove the spud pipe or elbow connecting it to the bowl. Then, unscrew the nuts inside the tank and lift it off the wall.)

3 The bowl is connected to the closet flange (under the bowl) with two bolts. Unscrew the connecting nuts (they may be concealed by decorative bolt caps which you can pry off).

  Before you remove the bowl, measure the rough-in dimension as shown; on most toilets it is 12 inches, but it may be as much as 14 inches for an elongated or wall-hung toilet. Be sure that the new toilet has the same dimension.

CONDENSATION CULPRIT

If you find water around the base of your toilet in summer—particularly toward the rear—don't assume that the tank is leaking. The tank is more likely condensing moisture out of the warm, humid summer air every time it refills with cold water.

  To test, wipe the tank dry with a paper towel, then flush the toilet. Come back in 10 minutes and run your hand over the lower side of the tank. If it comes up wet, you have found the culprit.

  What to do? First, don't let anyone talk you into running hot water to the tank. That trick will work, but it will also cost you at least $100 per year in hot water bills. Instead, install a foam tank liner kit, or replace the tank entirely with a factory-insulated model.

Rock bowl to break seal with floor

4 After removing the nuts from the closet flange bolts, you are ready to remove the bowl. Straddle it and rock it from side to side. This will loosen the wax seal.

Twist from side to side, then lift straight up

Stuff soil pipe with rags to contain sewer gas

5 Once the bowl is free, lift it straight up so water doesn't spill from the trap. Scrape all wax and debris from the closet flange with a putty knife. Before installing a new wax ring or toilet, check the condition of the flange bolts. If they are questionable, buy brass replacement bolts.

INSTALLING A NEW TOILET

First, make sure the rough-in dimension for the flange (distance from center of flange to wall) is correct for your new toilet. Also make sure that the flange is screwed securely to the subfloor and that the subfloor is sound and in good condition.

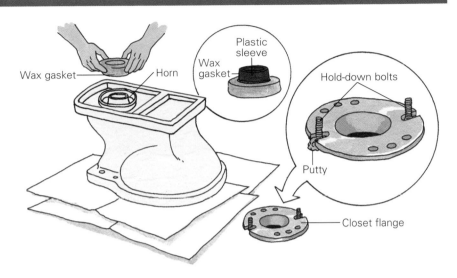

Wax gasket — Horn

Plastic sleeve

Wax gasket

Hold-down bolts

Putty

Closet flange

1 *Place a new wax gasket (available at the hardware store) around the horn of the outlet opening, pressing it firmly into place. If the closet flange is recessed, use a wax gasket with a plastic extension that reaches down into the pipe.*

Slip brass bolts into the slots on the floor closet. If necessary, press plumber's putty around the heads of the bolts to hold them in place.

Untightened nuts

Shims

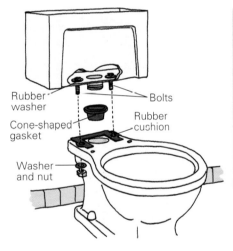

Rubber washer — Bolts

Cone-shaped gasket

Rubber cushion

Washer and nut

2 *Straddling the flange and sighting the closet bolts through the holes in the toilet base, carefully set the toilet straight down over the flange. Do not sit on the toilet at this point because you may overcompress the wax ring. Instead, tighten the closet bolts alternately until the toilet is flat on the floor. If the floor is not flat, slip thin shims under the base to give the toilet more support against rocking. When tightening the nuts on the flange bolts, be careful. You want the nuts to be tight, but not too tight or you will crack the bowl.*

3 *Place the rubber cushion on the bowl so that it lines up with the bolt holes. Push the cone-shaped rubber gasket over the flush outlet with the narrow end down. Set the tank in place on the bowl. Put the rubber washers on the ends of the bolts and screw on the nuts. Tighten the bolts but not tight enough to crack the bowl.*

If the old supply tube no longer fits, take it to the hardware store and purchase a flexible, braided, stainless-steel supply tube of slightly greater length and with the same size end fittings. Hook up the supply tube between the shutoff valve and the tank. Turn on the supply and look for leaks.

WHEN INSTALLING NEW FLOORS

If your remodeling plans call for a new floor in your bathroom, you'll want to remove your toilet so the new flooring material can be installed underneath it. If your new flooring material is fairly thick, such as ceramic tile or wood, you'll be raising your toilet off the flange. To compensate, buy a new wax ring that is extra-thick. Extra-thick wax rings are made specifically for retrofits.

DON'T CAULK JOINT

Some experts will advise you to caulk the joint between the toilet and the floor. But what are you keeping in or out? If the toilet leaks at the wax gasket, the caulk will keep the water trapped under the toilet so you will never see it. Soon, you will be making structural repairs to a rotted floor in addition to replacing the toilet gasket. It's better to see the leak as soon as it happens, so don't caulk.

TIPS FOR TOOL BUYING, RENTING, AND CARRYING

> **ALSO SEE...**
> *Most entries provide information on the appropriate tools*

There is no sense owning expensive specialty tools, such as a pneumatic flooring nailer, that you will use rarely. These kinds of tools can be rented.

You should, however, equip yourself with basic carpentry tools. These tools are essential for completing the many tasks and projects that face homeowners on a regular basis.

Always purchase the best tools your budget allows. Poor-quality tools end up costing you more in both frustration and replacement costs.

In addition to the basic tools shown here, you may occasionally need inexpensive specialty tools when you work with plumbing, electrical, wallboard, tile, and masonry materials. As you build a collection of tools, provide safe and well-organized storage for them.

Don't purchase a single, very large tool box to hold all of your tools. You won't be able to carry it! A better idea is to have small tool boxes, or buckets with canvas pockets—one for each group of tools.

CARPENTRY TOOLS

HAMMERS

Hammers come in many weights. For household home improvement tasks, you should have at least three: 13-, 16- and 20-ounce hammers. The 13-ounce is good for light carpentry and easy jobs such as hanging a framed picture. The 16-ounce is an all-around utility hammer. The 20-ounce is for pounding big 12d and 16d nails for framing jobs.

You also have a choice of the type of claw: curved or straight. The curved claw gives you more leverage when pulling nails and is good for amateurs. Professional carpenters prefer the straight claw, however.

Handle choices include wood, fiberglass, tubular steel with a rubber grip, and solid steel with leather grip. The differences affect strength, comfort, and durability; your choice is a matter of personal preference, although the only hammer you are not likely to break in a year of full-time use is the solid steel with leather handle.

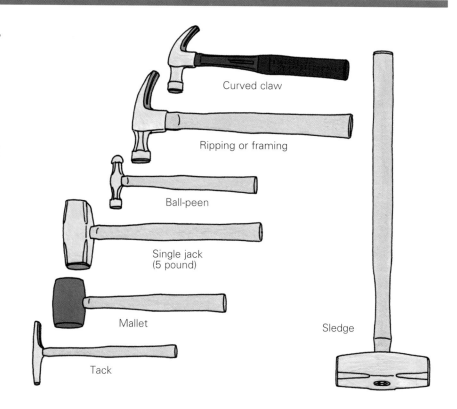

Curved claw

Ripping or framing

Ball-peen

Single jack (5 pound)

Mallet

Tack

Sledge

NAIL PULLERS

A cat's paw is essential for removing nails already driven completely into the wood. The wrecking bar pulls nails easily once the heads are clear of the surface. Wrecking bars are also used for prying apart adjacent building materials, such as two studs that have been nailed together, or for removing old flooring and wall coverings.

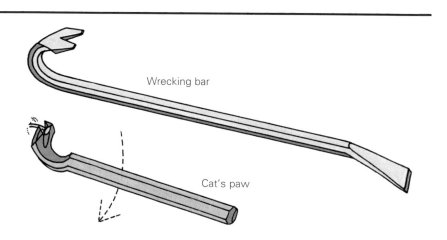

Wrecking bar

Cat's paw

SQUARES

A carpenter's square helps you check right angles. It is also used for laying out stair stringers, calculating rafter lengths, and evaluating edges for straightness. Usually, one leg is 24 inches, the other 16 inches long.

A combination square is small enough to sling from your tool belt and enables you to mark materials for cutting at 90 degrees and 45 degrees. The bevel gauge makes it possible to duplicate any angle and transfer it to materials for cutting.

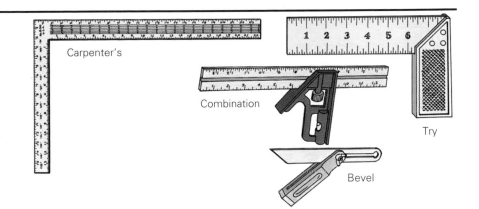

Carpenter's

Combination

Try

Bevel

SCREWDRIVERS

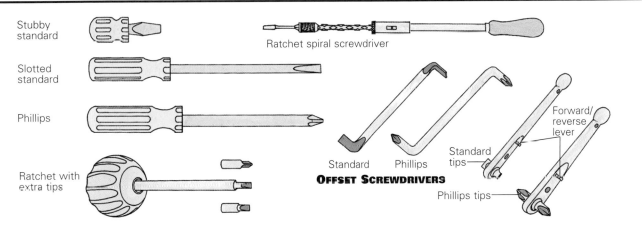

Stubby standard

Slotted standard

Phillips

Ratchet with extra tips

Ratchet spiral screwdriver

OFFSET SCREWDRIVERS

Standard

Phillips

Standard tips

Phillips tips

Forward/reverse lever

There are two general types of screwdriver tips—slotted and Phillips. In order to do basic work you will need a medium-size slotted and a No. 2 Phillips. Eventually you will want at least three sizes of each, as well as handles and shanks of various lengths, which could mean a large collection. Even good screwdrivers are inexpensive when bought in sets, however, so bite the bullet here and go for a complete set.

Specialty screwdrivers with interchangeable tips eliminate the need to carry a large collection of screwdrivers in your tool pouch. If your work involves a lot of screws of different types and sizes, buy a very good ratcheting screwdriver with an assortment of tips.

MARKERS

A plumb bob is a heavy brass weight which hangs from a length of string and indicates true vertical, or plumb. Use a plumb bob to locate the corners of a foundation and determine a starting line for hanging wallcovering.

A chalk reel consists of about 50 feet of cotton string wound inside a container of powdered, colored chalk. When the chalk-coated string is stretched taut between two points and snapped briskly, it makes a long, straight line. Chalk reels can be used as crude plumb bobs if the wind isn't blowing too hard.

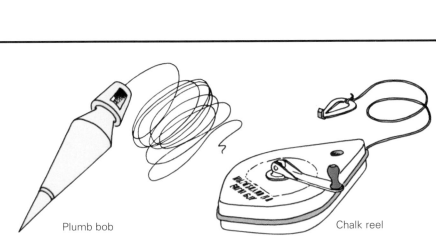

Plumb bob

Chalk reel

CARPENTRY TOOLS *continued*

TAPES AND RULERS

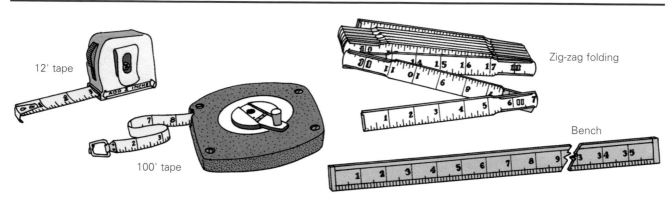

12' tape

100' tape

Zig-zag folding

Bench

A 12-foot steel tape measure with a ¾-inch-wide blade is adequate for general household use, but choose a 25- or 30-foot tape measure with a 1-inch-wide blade for building projects. You may also need a 100-foot tape measure for laying out a room addition or landscaping project. Rulers are seldom used except for fine carpentry.

LEVELS

A 2-foot carpenter's level will handle most jobs around the house, but if you are doing extensive framing or working with brick or concrete block you also should have a 4-foot level with a tough aluminum housing. A heavy wood mason's level costs more, but survives drops better. The very best levels are wood with steel or brass edges and adjustable level bubbles.

A small torpedo level is handy for your tool apron, especially for plumbing. Use a line level or a water level for layout, fences, and footings where a transit is not available.

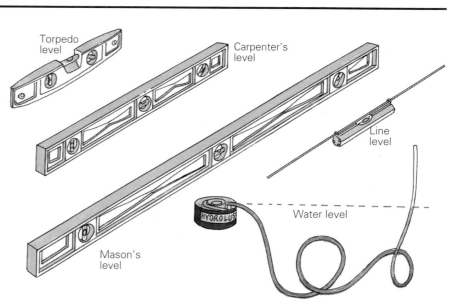

Torpedo level

Carpenter's level

Line level

Mason's level

Water level

CHISELS

Keep chisels sharp and use them only for their intended purpose—cutting and shaping wood (or soft plastics).

To start your chisel collection, buy a medium-priced framing chisel, either 1 inch or 1½ inches wide. Use it for cutting off protruding dowels, shaving sticky doors, and cutting mortises for locks and strike plates.

Only framing chisels are built to withstand the strike of a hammer. The steel of the blade turns into a stout rod that runs through the handle and will withstand hammer blows. Use a wooden or rubber mallet to strike any other type of chisel.

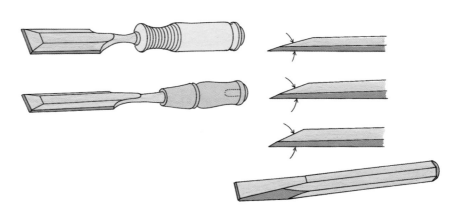

CLAMPS

Most homeowners start off with an assortment of useful and inexpensive C-clamps. Other types of clamps are particularly handy for specialty jobs. Pipe or bar clamps have large capacities and are especially useful when gluing wide, flat pieces of wood. Hand screws have wooden jaws that won't mar fine woodwork. Web clamps hold odd-shaped objects for gluing. Spring clamps have powerful jaws and can be operated with one hand. Use a miter clamp for 45-degree angles.

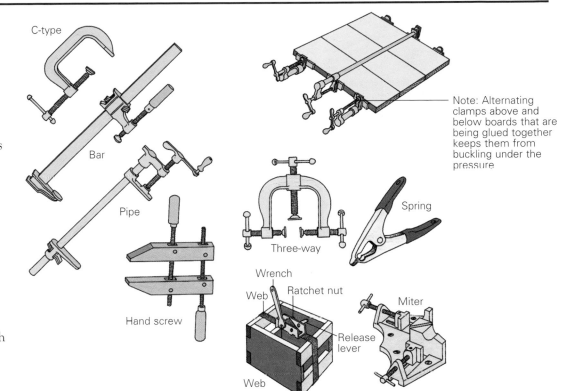

C-type

Bar

Pipe

Hand screw

Note: Alternating clamps above and below boards that are being glued together keeps them from buckling under the pressure

Three-way

Spring

Wrench

Web

Ratchet nut

Release lever

Web

Miter

FILES AND RASPS

Files smooth metal; rasps smooth wood. Use them to give professional-looking results to your projects. The four-in-hand rasp is easily carried in your tool belt and has a variety of textures for smoothing wood. The Surform has replaceable flat or rounded blades in two degrees of coarseness.

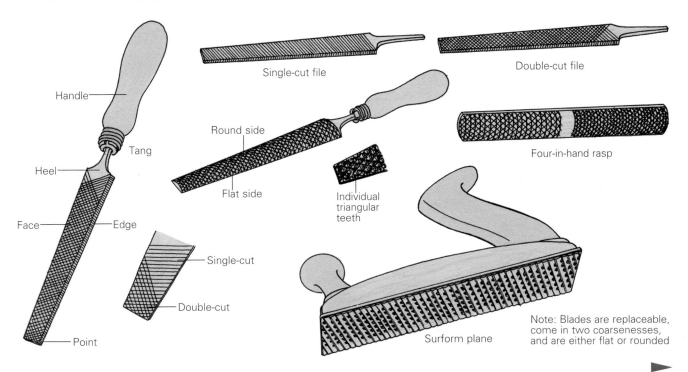

Handle

Tang

Heel

Face

Edge

Point

Single-cut file

Round side

Flat side

Single-cut

Double-cut

Individual triangular teeth

Double-cut file

Four-in-hand rasp

Surform plane

Note: Blades are replaceable, come in two coarsenesses, and are either flat or rounded

CARPENTRY TOOLS *continued*

PLANES

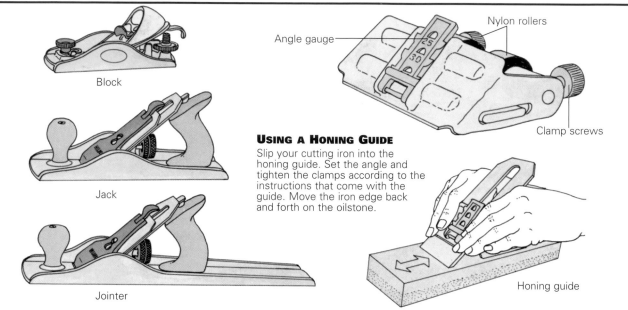

Block

Jack

Jointer

USING A HONING GUIDE
Slip your cutting iron into the honing guide. Set the angle and tighten the clamps according to the instructions that come with the guide. Move the iron edge back and forth on the oilstone.

Angle gauge

Nylon rollers

Clamp screws

Honing guide

For the most part, hand planes have been replaced by accurate table saws, jointers, and belt sanders. A medium-sized jack plane or a block plane will be sufficient for most projects.

Like a chisel, the plane requires a very sharp blade for good results. In addition, the double plane iron (the beveled cutting piece), the level cap, the depth-adjustment screw, and the lateral-adjustment lever must all be carefully set by hand for the plane to function properly. Choose a plane with high-quality steel and buy a stone for honing it periodically.

HANDSAWS

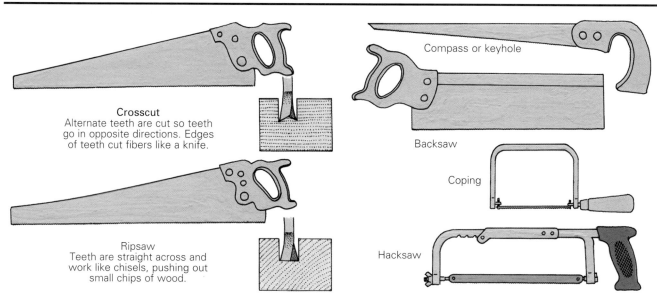

Crosscut
Alternate teeth are cut so teeth go in opposite directions. Edges of teeth cut fibers like a knife.

Ripsaw
Teeth are straight across and work like chisels, pushing out small chips of wood.

Compass or keyhole

Backsaw

Coping

Hacksaw

Handsaws are good for making quick, accurate cuts in wood. An eight-point crosscut saw has eight teeth per inch and is a good all-around saw for cutting boards across the grain.

You are not likely to need a ripsaw if you own a power circular saw.

A compass or keyhole saw comes in handy for many remodeling tasks—rough-toothed versions are used for cutting holes in wallboard. A 12-point backsaw is essential for making very fine, smooth cuts across the grain. Use a bow-backed coping saw for cutting delicate curves in wood.

A hacksaw with interchangeable metal-cutting blades is indispensible for plumbing projects, cutting the heads off stubborn bolts, and for most metal-cutting tasks. You can use the same blades for cutting small pieces of wood, such as moldings, as well as plastics.

PLUMBING TOOLS

PLIERS

Basic and indispensible, a pair of slip-joint pliers might be the most-used tool in a homeowner's toolbox. Use groove-joint pliers for really big nuts, such as on slip-joint fittings and shower drains. Locking pliers have a special ratcheting mechanism that allows the jaws to hold extremely tightly. An adjustment nut permits fine-tuning the jaws.

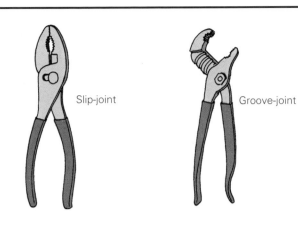

Slip-joint

Groove-joint

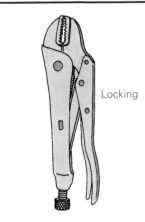

Locking

WRENCHES

Wrenches tighten and loosen nuts of all sizes and types. A 10-inch adjustable wrench fits most nuts and bolt heads around the house. Pipe wrenches have loose lower jaws that grab tightly to round plumbing pipes. Open-end and box wrenches are sized to fit corresponding nuts precisely. Ratcheting wrenches have interchangable sockets of various sizes. Use a basin wrench for reaching under sinks to tighten faucet-supply nuts.

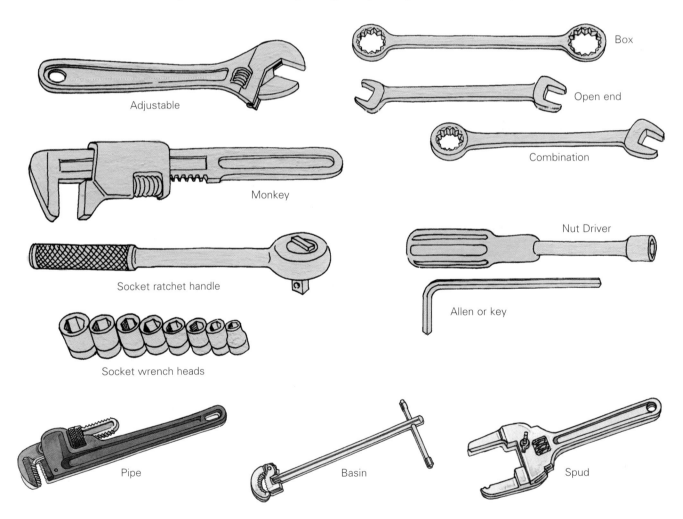

Adjustable

Box

Open end

Monkey

Combination

Nut Driver

Socket ratchet handle

Allen or key

Socket wrench heads

Pipe

Basin

Spud

TOOLS
continued

WIRING TOOLS

For basic electrical jobs you'll need diagonal-cutting or machinist's pliers and long-nose pliers for cutting and bending wire. An electrician's pliers performs these tasks and also has special holes for stripping the insulation from the ends of wires.

To test wiring, a neon circuit tester quickly determines if a circuit is live, a receptacle tester tells if a receptacle is wired correctly, and a multitester accurately measures volts, amps, and ohms.

Machinist's pliers

Needle-nose pliers

Electrician's pliers

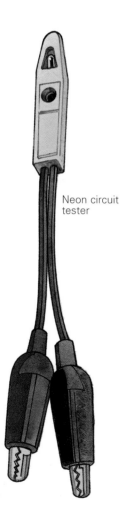

Neon circuit tester

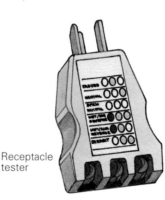

Receptacle tester

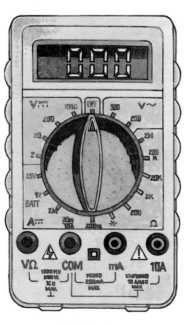

Multitester

POWER TOOLS

ROUTER

A router has a motor that turns a shaping bit at high speed, enabling you to make decorative edges, cut dovetails, and trim laminate. There are hundreds of different bits you can buy. The best, longest-lasting bits have carbide cutting edges. They cost three or four times as much as identical bits with steel edges, but they last much longer and never need sharpening

Router with bits

WELL-OILED MACHINERY

You will lose your tools to rust before you wear them out. Unless you keep them oiled, that is.

Keep an oily rag in your toolbox and periodically wipe your tools down. Use an oil that won't evaporate too quickly. Automatic Transmission Fluid (ATF) is perfect.

DON'T LET TOOLS WALK

"Tools have legs" is a favorite saying among carpenters and machinists. The problem is not thievery; rather, it is because so many workmen have identical tools.

The solution is to paint a spot of "your color" on every tool you own. Painted tools don't walk.

CIRCULAR SAW

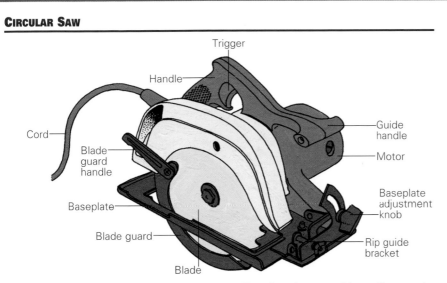

A circular saw is a carpenter's workhorse, so buy the best quality you can afford. A heavy-duty model is less likely to buck or kick back, and is safer to use, but choose one that feels most comfortable to you.

Your best buy—and best all-around saw—is one with a 7¼-inch carbide-tipped blade. Unless you are building a whole house, and if you avoid sawing dirt and hit only a few nails, the original blade should last a lifetime.

RECIPROCATING SAW

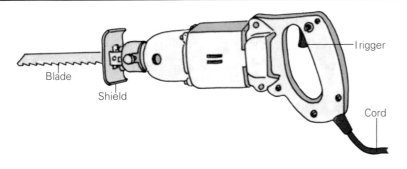

This saw is essential for demolition and extensive remodeling. It works like a saber saw, but is much faster, more powerful, and makes cuts that are less refined. Blades are available for cutting wood, metal, plastics, and a variety of specialty materials. Extra-long blades reach into tight spaces.

ELECTRIC DRILLS

A ⅜-inch variable speed drill is as essential as a circular saw. It will bore holes through wood or metal, drive screws, and mix paint. You can even buy a stand, as shown, to turn it into a bench-model drill press.

Drill bits are as important as the drill. Don't waste your money on low-cost twist bits. Buy a complete set of high-speed bits, ranging from 1/16 to ⅜ inch, in increments of 1/32 inch. If you plan on drilling steel, consider upping your investment to cobalt-steel

bits, which last 10 times longer. For larger diameter holes in wood, get a set of inexpensive spade bits, ranging from ⅜ inch to 1½ inches.

A battery-operated, variable-speed, reversible drill is handy when driving drywall screws, hanging pictures, and doing work outside. Select a model that is rated at 12 or 14.4 volts, and purchase a battery charger and a spare battery. That way, you'll always have a fresh battery when one runs low.

SABER SAW

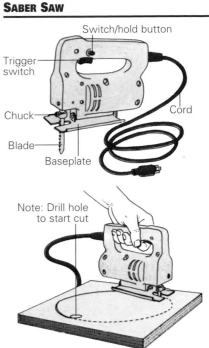

Note: Drill hole to start cut

The small blade of the saber saw is ideal for cutting out circles or making curved cuts. Different kinds of blades are available for cutting wood, plywood, plastic, and metal.

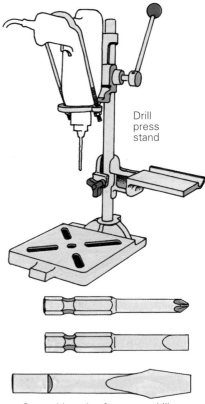

Drill press stand

Screwdriver tips for power drills

POWER TOOLS *continued*

SANDERS

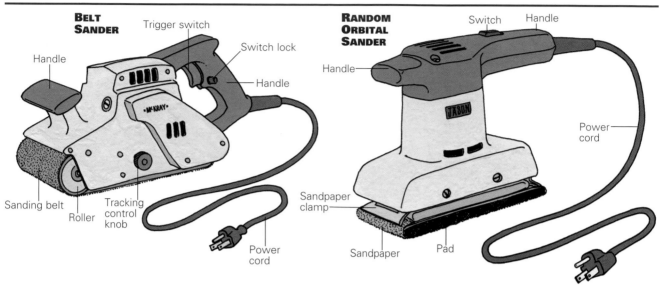

BELT SANDER

Handle

Trigger switch

Switch lock

Handle

Sanding belt

Roller

Tracking control knob

Power cord

RANDOM ORBITAL SANDER

Switch

Handle

Handle

Power cord

Sandpaper clamp

Sandpaper

Pad

Use belt sanders to smooth large areas fast. They work especially well on flat surfaces, such as plywood sheets or flush doors. A model that uses a 3×21-inch belt is good for general use.

Sanding belts come in many grits for different degrees of finished smoothness. A coarse 50-grit belt will move lots of wood in a hurry but leave

a rough texture. A finer, 120-grit belt produces a finish surface that is smooth to the touch and ready for paint or stain. Be careful using a belt sander on surfaces smaller than the width of the belt. It is difficult to hold a belt sander at precisely 90 degrees.

Random-orbital sanders—sometimes called finish or palm sanders—vibrate

very fast and typically are used to put a finishing touch on wood surfaces. They can be used for heavier sanding work but are much slower than belt sanders. They use precut sandpaper disks and pads that are easy to change. Some models use hook-and-loop-backed sandpaper that sticks instantly and simply peels off when worn.

TABLE SAW

Particularly effective at cutting plywood or paneling and for ripping long boards to length, the table saw requires a lot of space. If you are ripping 8-foot lumber, for example, the operation requires more than 16 feet in total length.

Blade sizes range from 6½ inches to 12 inches in diameter, but the two most popular sizes are 8 inches and 10 inches. The 8-inch table saw, with a very sharp blade, is sufficient for most carpentry work. At half the weight and cost of the 10-inch version, many contractors actually prefer the more portable 8-inch version.

The blade can be moved up and down to control the depth of cut, and set to any angle up to 45 degrees. A sliding miter guide allows you to make angled cross-cuts. The ripping fence acts as the primary guide, allowing you to repeat long, accurate cuts.

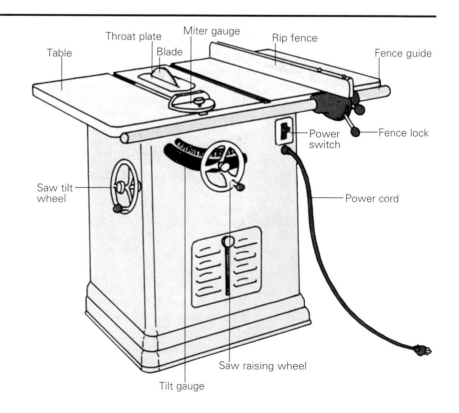

Throat plate

Miter gauge

Rip fence

Table

Blade

Fence guide

Power switch

Fence lock

Saw tilt wheel

Power cord

Saw raising wheel

Tilt gauge

POWER MITER SAW

Sometimes called a "chop saw," this versatile tool makes fast, accurate cuts in moldings and lumber. As its name implies, it is ideal for cutting angles. A compound miter saw is a more expensive version that makes complex miter cuts, while the sliding compound miter saw is a miniature version of the radial saw, allowing much wider cuts.

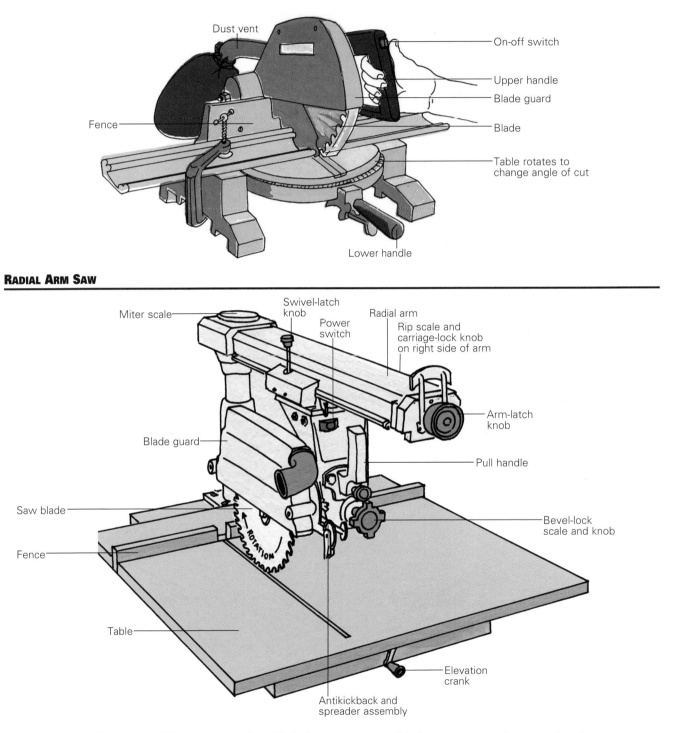

Dust vent

On-off switch

Upper handle

Blade guard

Fence

Blade

Table rotates to change angle of cut

Lower handle

RADIAL ARM SAW

Miter scale

Swivel-latch knob

Power switch

Radial arm

Rip scale and carriage-lock knob on right side of arm

Arm-latch knob

Blade guard

Pull handle

Saw blade

ROTATION

Fence

Bevel-lock scale and knob

Table

Elevation crank

Antikickback and spreader assembly

A radial arm saw has a powerful motor, a 12- or 14-inch circular blade, and a large cutting capacity that makes it ideal for working on large pieces of lumber. With the proper type of blade, a radial arm saw will also cut dadoes and rabbets. Once a basic tool for woodworkers and carpenters, the radial arm saw often is replaced by a variety of smaller, more portable tools that include a table saw and miter saw.

Vanities

STORAGE AND STYLE IN ONE BOX

ALSO SEE...
Bathroom Design:
Page 22
Kitchen Cabinets:
Pages 200–207
Countertops:
Pages 70–73
Faucets & Valves:
Pages 126–129
WashBasins:
Pages 416–417

A bathroom vanity provides the washbasin (lavatory) with an attractive base and creates useful storage space. Many sizes and styles are available, and their installation is a relatively easy project. Most cabinets are open in the back, fitting around the usual supply and drain piping.

Most of the major manufacturers of kitchen cabinets offer vanity cabinets, as well. Since they are bulky, pre-assembled units are expensive to ship. If you are on a strict budget, consider the easily-assembled vanity packages that cost roughly half as much. Home centers offer a variety of these units in sizes to 36 inches wide.

Combine two or more cabinets to create a wider vanity than is available as a standard unit. The standard height, including countertop, is 30 inches.

MATERIALS

Although you can build your own cabinet from plywood and finish it with paint or a stain and sealer, it is much easier and no more expensive to buy a prefinished cabinet and attach the countertop of your choice.

The most popular one-piece countertop materials are plastic laminate, synthetic marble, real marble or granite, and tile. Most synthetic marble countertops have washbasins molded into them and are solid-colored so that surface scratches can be sanded.

Tile is also an excellent countertop material and is easy to install yourself (see Tile, pages 360–367). The trickiest part is making clean and accurate cuts. Rent a water-saw to make these cuts. Many tile suppliers rent water saws to their customers for less than tool-rental companies.

STANDARD SIZES

Standard height for a vanity without top is 29 inches; the standard depth is 21 inches, although smaller units are sometimes 18 inches deep.

Single vanities are available in widths to 36 inches. A double vanity should be 48 inches wide.

Standard dimensions are well suited to vanities in guest suites or powder rooms, where they'll be used by people of all sizes. But a private vanity, such as one located in a master suite, can be tailored to your individual stature. Cut down or build up your vanity's base to add a new dimension of comfort, but remember that you may need to adjust the length of plumbing lines as well.

ACCESSIBLE COUNTERTOPS

Access guidelines for kitchen countertops call for a maximum counter height of 34 inches and a minimum knee clearance of 27 inches. With a height of 36 inches (including countertop), standard manufactured kitchen cabinets won't work. But standard bathroom vanities will; they're just 30 inches tall. For clearance underneath, simply install a countertop across two narrow cabinets, giving 29 inches of knee room.

INSTALLING VANITY CABINETS

If you are installing more than one cabinet, you first need to establish a level line. To do so, use a long level or a level on a long board, to find the highest point of the floor. From this point, measure up 29 inches and mark the wall to indicate the top of a vanity base. Add an allowance for the thickness of the finished floor if it is not yet installed.

Using a straightedge and a level, draw a line on the wall along the location of the top of the cabinet. The line will be hidden by the vanity top or backsplash.

Next, below the line, probe with a hammer and nail until you locate both edges of a stud. The wall below the line will be hidden by the cabinets, so don't worry about making test holes. Mark the exact center of this stud on the wall above the line. Using a level, draw a line through this mark and down to the floor. Find and mark the rest of the studs by measuring 16 or 24 inches on-center from the first one.

Set the cabinet in place and shim under its base until the top is even with the layout line. Drill through the top rail at each stud and attach the rail to the stud with 2-inch drywall screws. If the wall is not straight, place shims

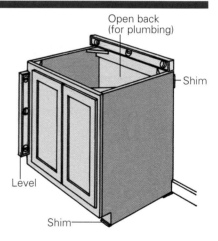

To elevate a vanity, turn it over and screw wood cleats to the bottom.

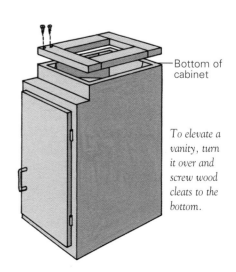

Open back (for plumbing)

Shim

Level

Shim

Bottom of cabinet

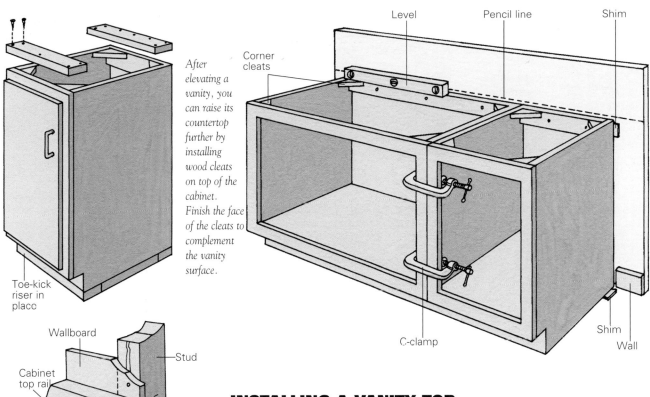

After elevating a vanity, you can raise its countertop further by installing wood cleats on top of the cabinet. Finish the face of the cleats to complement the vanity surface.

Level — Pencil line — Shim

Corner cleats

Toe-kick riser in placc

Wallboard

Cabinet top rail

Stud

Wood screw

C-clamp

Shim

Wall

behind the cabinet. Use a level to check the top, sides, and front. Hold the level directly against the frame, not against a door or drawer.

Set the second cabinet unit in place, shim it, and screw it to the first. Then screw it to the back wall just as you did the first.

INSTALLING A VANITY TOP

The simplest vanity top to install is a one-piece synthetic marble with a molded washbasin. Run a bead of silicone caulk around the top edge of the cabinet and set the top onto it. For other vanity tops, such as plastic laminate or tile over plywood, cut a hole for the washbasin and attach a backsplash. Then mount the top to the cabinet. Synthetic marble does have one disadvantage, however—you can't change the location of the washbasin.

VANITY TOPS WITH CUTOUTS

To cut the hole for a washbasin, trace an outline of the basin on the countertop. Next draw a line ½ inch inside the outline (so the basin will have support). Drill a starting hole inside the cutout and use a saber saw to make the cut.

Drill pilot holes and attach plywood backsplash and sidesplash pieces to the countertop with silicone sealant and screws. Set the completed countertop in place and drive screws into the underside through the corner cleats of the cabinet.

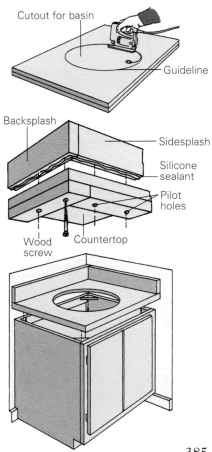

Cutout for basin

Guideline

Backsplash — Sidesplash

Silicone sealant

Pilot holes

Wood screw — Countertop

MULTIPLE VANITIES

Standard vanity cabinets are available in widths to 60 inches. While this sounds wide, it is marginal when you install side-by-side lavatories. The usual solution is to combine two identical "his and her" cabinets, but beware of the drawer arrangements: If you select identical vanities having doors on one side and drawers on the other, you will find it impossible to install the lavatories symmetrically because the drains can not run through the drawers. The solution is to pick vanities that are mirror images of each other or to use three or four smaller vanities.

VENTILATION

WHAT VENTILATION DOES FOR YOUR HOME

ROOFS AND ATTICS

In hot weather, roof and attic ventilation reduces the heat buildup in the attic and subsequent flow of heat from attic to living space. The same ventilation in winter helps prevent moisture from condensing in the insulation, structural members, shingles, or on the roof (see Ice Dams, right).

Codes and standard practices vary, but a rule of thumb is to figure on 1 square foot of free vent area for every 150 square feet of attic. Ventilation area must be doubled if the vents are covered with $\frac{1}{16}$-inch screen; increased by a factor of $2\frac{1}{4}$ if covered by louvers; and tripled if covered by both.

You can reduce the required vent area by half if half of the vents are soffit vents in the eaves and the other half are located at least 3 feet from the attic floor.

Roof and gable vents are easy to install. You need only measure and cut out a piece of the roof or wall and then insert the vent into the hole. You should frame any hole cut into the roof or wall with a system of 2×4s, and use caulk or flashing to seal the hole around the vent after it's installed.

If the rafters are insulated, as in an occupied attic or a vaulted ceiling, the rafter space must be ventilated at the eave and ridge. There must be at least a 1-inch air gap between the top of the insulation and the bottom of the roof sheathing. A continuous ridge vent is best here.

CRAWL SPACES

Locate foundation vents for the crawl space on every wall, within 3 feet of each corner. The net free vent area should be at least 1 square foot for every 150 square feet of floor area. Placing an effective vapor barrier over the ground helps reduce the ratio to 1 square foot of ventilation for every 1,500 square feet of floor area. Heated crawl spaces and basements are exempt from these requirements.

CODE REQUIREMENTS: VENTILATION

Roofs and Attics:
■ Attic and cathedral ceilings without vapor barriers must have ventilation openings equal to $\frac{1}{150}$ of their areas.
■ Attic and cathedral ceilings with vapor barriers must have ventilation openings equal to $\frac{1}{300}$ of their areas.
■ Ventilation area must be increased by 200 percent if the vents are covered with $\frac{1}{16}$-inch screen; 225 percent if covered by louvers; 300 percent if covered by both.
Crawl Spaces: The space between the earth and the bottom of the floor joists, except in a basement, must be ventilated:

■ The minimum net free ventilation opening must be $\frac{1}{150}$ of the area of the floor.
■ When the ground is covered with a vapor barrier, the minimum net free ventilation area is $\frac{1}{1,500}$ of the floor area.
■ There must be a ventilation opening within 3 feet of at least three corners of the foundation.
Living Spaces: Habitable rooms, including bathrooms, require either an open-window area of at least 5 percent of the floor area, or mechanical ventilation equivalent to 0.35 room air exchanges per hour.

ICE DAMS

THE PROBLEM

To prevent ice dams, you first have to understand how they occur:
1. Suppose the temperature inside the house is 70 degrees F, while the temperature outdoors is a little below freezing. Since snow is as good an insulator as the insulation on the attic floor, the temperature of the roof boards and roofing is a little above freezing.
2. The snow next to the roof slowly melts, and the meltwater flows down the roof toward the eave.
3. When the water reaches the eave, it encounters uninsulated roof at the same temperature as the outdoor air, so it freezes.
4. The ice at the eave builds up continually, eventually forming a dam.

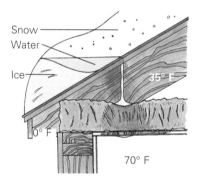

5. The meltwater backs up behind the dam to beyond the top of the first row of shingles, allowing the water to flow down through the roof sheathing and the attic insulation, soaking the wallboard of the ceiling.

THE CURE

Shoveling the snow off the roof, installing heating cables at the eave to melt the ice dam, and going up a ladder to chop the ice off are not cures but temporary holding actions. The permanent solution is proper ridge-and-vent ventilation.

Screened soffit vents at the bottom and ridge or gable vents at the top allow outside air into the attic and force the temperature of the roof sheathing to be the same as the outdoor air. As a result, the snow will no longer melt and refreeze when it reaches the eave.

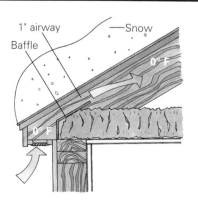

TYPES OF VENTS

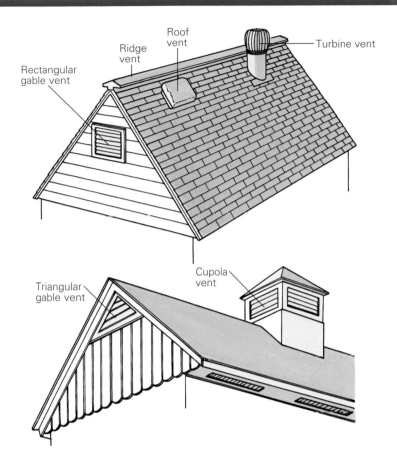

Rectangular gable vent · Ridge vent · Roof vent · Turbine vent

Triangular gable vent · Cupola vent

Vents work best when they work together—one letting the air in, the other letting it out. The illustrations *below* show the different types of vents and the effectiveness of various pairs in moving air through an attic.

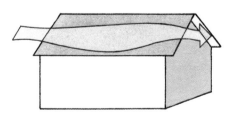

GABLE END VENTS ONLY

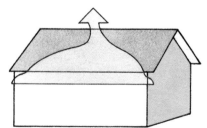

SOFFIT AND TURBINE VENTS

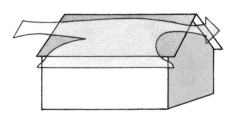

GABLE END AND SOFFIT VENTS

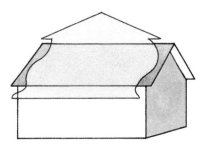

SOFFIT AND RIDGE VENTS

INSTALLING GABLE VENTS

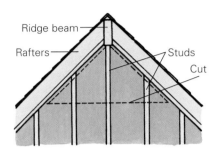

Ridge beam · Rafters · Studs · Cut

1 Using a reciprocating saw, cut a hole to the size indicated by the manufacturer.

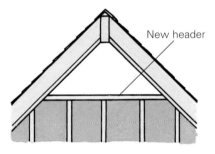

New header

2 Nail in the 2×4 or 2×6 header.

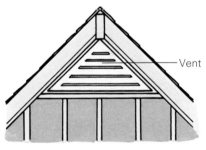

Vent

3 Install the vent according to the instruction sheet provided by the manufacturer. Caulk all the outside edges.

STOPPING AIR MOVEMENT

Ventilation and insulation can work at cross purposes. On the one hand, roofs and attics are required by code to have ventilation (see Code Requirements, opposite). On the other hand, fiberglass insulation depends on still air for its insulating value.

A little ventilation doesn't hurt, but if you are in a windy location and you can actually feel the air moving in your attic, lay down vapor-permeable building wrap over the exposed fiberglass blanket, batt, or loose fill to keep the air currents from stealing your heat.

387

VINYL SIDING

ADVANTAGES OF VINYL SIDING

ALSO SEE...
Caulk:
Pages 50–51
Shingle Siding:
Pages 308–309

Whether you are doing new construction or planning a major facelift for your home, you should choose siding with the same care you give to the interior of your home. Factors to consider are your taste, the style of your house, the prevailing styles of homes in the neighborhood, durability, cost, and ease of installation.

Vinyl siding has been popular from its introduction because it is less expensive than good quality wood siding, and it eliminates the need to paint.

The earliest types of vinyl were easy to identify: They were usually white, somewhat shiny, and too perfect. Siding manufacturers have been busy, however. It is now possible to buy vinyl sidings which closely resemble natural wood. Some mimic stained or bleached cedar clapboards.

Here are the major advantages and disadvantages of vinyl siding.

Advantages:
■ Low cost
■ Simple, fast installation
■ Elimination of painting

Disadvantages:
■ May sag when very hot
■ Is brittle and in some cases may break when cold
■ Shows unevenness in walls

INSTALLATION

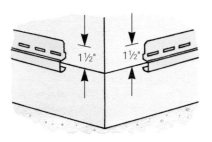

STARTER STRIP

Using a line level, find the lowest corner of the old siding or sheathing. Drive a nail part way in, 1½ inches above this lowest point. Using the line level again, partially drive nails at each corner of the house at this same level. Snap chalk lines from nail to nail, all the way around the house.

Measure the widths of inside and outside corner posts.

Position a starter strip with its top edge along the chalk line, and its end the width of a corner post plus ¼ inch from a corner. Nail the strip in place with the nails midway in the nailing slots and with ¹⁄₁₆ inch of play between the nail head and the vinyl. As you add starter-strip sections, leave ¼ inch between the ends to allow for thermal expansion.

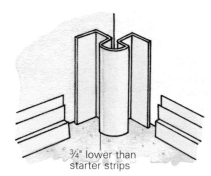

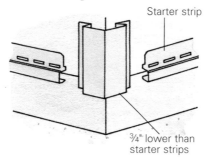

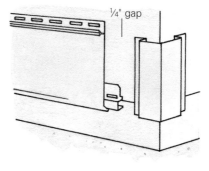

INSIDE CORNERS

Install inside corner posts from ¼ inch below the starter strip to ¼ inch below the soffit. Begin nailing at the top, allowing the corner post to hang from the top set of nails. Locate the remaining nails in the centers of nailing slots spaced every 8 to 16 inches. If more than one section of corner post is required, allow a ¼-inch space between ends for thermal expansion.

OUTSIDE CORNERS

Install outside corner posts from ¼ inch below the starter strip to ¼ inch below the soffit or eave. Begin nailing at the top, allowing the corner post to hang loosely from the top set of nails. Do not drive the nails so tight that the post cannot move. Loosely drive the remaining nails in the centers of nailing slots spaced every 8 to 16 inches. If more than one section of corner post is required, allow a ¼-inch space between ends for thermal expansion.

FIRST SIDING PANEL

Starting at the bottom, snap the bottom of the first panel into the starter strip, then nail the centers of the nailing slots at the top. As usual, leave ¹⁄₁₆ inch between the nail head and the vinyl so that the panel can slide when it expands.

At every corner post, leave a ¼-inch gap so that the panel can expand into the post without buckling.

To overlap panels, cut back one of the top nailing flanges 1¼ inches, and overlap the panel faces by 1 inch, leaving ¼-inch gap between the ends of the nailing flanges.

REMAINING PANELS

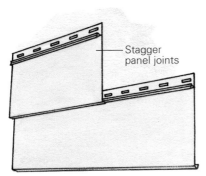

Stagger panel joints

After completing the entire first row of panels, begin working your way up, snapping each course into the preceding course and nailing the top flanges. Cut some of the whole panels into halves and some into thirds so that successive overlaps are staggered by at least 2 feet. Lap the panels away from the street and from major entrances so that the joints will be less visible.

J-CHANNELS

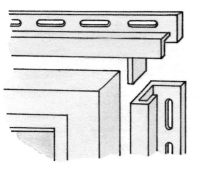

J-channel goes entirely around windows and doors to catch the cut ends of the panels. The illustration shows how to make a square corner at a door or window top so that the channel acts as a flashing. J-channel is nailed loosely in the same way as the corner posts.

REPAIRING VINYL SIDING

Of all the siding materials, vinyl is one of the most difficult to repair. Remember that particular shapes and colors of vinyl siding quickly go out of style, so the home improvement center or store where you originally purchased your siding may not have replacement materials. As with other important building materials that you install in your home, keep leftover pieces of vinyl siding to use for repair jobs.

The key to repairing damaged vinyl siding is the zip tool, an inexpensive hand tool made specifically to unlock the horizontal edges of vinyl runs. Insert the zip tool at an end joint of the damaged piece and pull the tool along the horizontal seam to release the locking joint. Do the same to the joint over the damaged area. Wedge wooden spacers between the panels to keep them apart, then use a flat pry bar to remove the siding nails. Use tin snips to cut out the damaged piece. Slide in a replacement piece that is 2 inches longer than the damaged piece. Overlap the ends and renail—it's easiest if you can drive the original fasteners back in their original holes. Use the zip tool to relock the horizontal edges of the siding.

FITTING PANELS AROUND DOORS AND WINDOWS

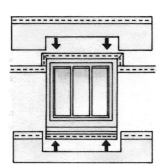

When you reach a window, you will probably have to cut a notch out of the panel. Make sure the panel extends beyond the window on both sides. Hold the panel under the window and mark the vertical cuts, allowing a ¼-inch gap on each side. Next, snap a scrap piece onto the panel below the window and slide it over to the window. Mark the depth of the cut on the scrap and use the scrap as a guide when making the long horizontal cut.

As you proceed up the sides of the windows and doors, just remember to leave a ¼-inch gap for thermal expansion of the panels.

When you reach the top of the door or window, cut the notch in the top panel exactly the same way as you did the bottom panel.

TOP COURSE

At the top of the wall, install lengths of undersill trim. To measure the amount to cut from the top siding panel, measure the distance between the inside top of the undersill trim and the bottom of the lock strip of the panel below. After cutting the panel to this width, it will no longer have a nailing flange.

Insert the cut panel into the undersill trim and draw a pencil line where they meet. Remove the panel and, using a snap-punch tool, punch the panel every 6 inches just above the pencil line so that the raised dimples are on the outside face.

Lock the bottom of the top panel into the panel below with its top in the undersill trim. Push up until the dimples snap into place, holding the panel up.

389

BACK FROM THE PAST

Wainscoting is panels of wood typically installed over the lower portion of a wall. When you think of wainscoting, you might have visions of elegant home libraries and black-tie dining rooms. Until recently, that would not be far from the truth. Wainscoting made of solid hardwood is expensive, and the cost of a well-trained finish carpenter needed to install it properly is considerable.

Not any more! Most home improvement centers carry inexpensive wainscoting homeowners can install:
■ Back from the past—beaded pine paneling which adorned Victorian bathrooms and porch ceilings.
■ Kits, including raised panels, rails, and stiles made of medium density fiberboard, finished with select hardwood veneers.

These types of materials are available as boards or plywood panels. Whether you are building new or just redecorating a room, you can now have a home like the rich and famous—give or take a few servants.

BEADED PINE BOARDS

Beaded pine boards are available in 3-foot lengths for wainscoting and 8-foot lengths for paneling an entire wall or ceiling. Its 5/16-inch thickness makes it easy to install:

1. Dado enough baseboard stock to finish the entire wall you are going to wainscot. Make the dado 3/8×3/8 inches. Install the baseboard with the dado at the top, facing in.

2. Dado enough top rail to match the length of the baseboard.

3. Determine the finished height of your wainscoting, including cap rail, if any.

4. Subtract the height of the undadoed baseboard, top rail, and cap rail from the finished height. The result is the length to cut the strips of beaded pine. Cut enough strips to cover the wall.

5. Insert the first strip into the dado of the baseboard with its grooved edge in the corner. Using a level, plumb the strip and tack it lightly at the very top.

6. Continue installing the remaining strips with the tongues snug in the grooves. Tack the tops as necessary to hold the strips in place. Check vertical periodically, and adjust as necessary.

7. When all the strips are in place, place the top rail with its dado over the tops of the strips, and nail to the studs using 6d finish nails.

8. Attach the cap rail (if any) with 6d finish nails down into the top rail.

9. Finish all parts with paint or stain. If painting, prime any knots first with two coats of white shellac primer/sealer.

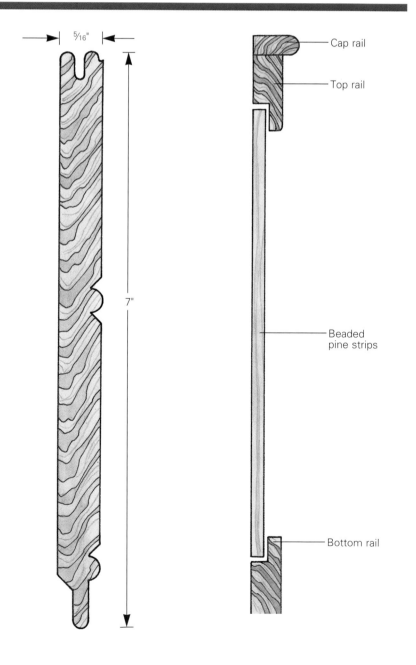

5/16"

7"

Cap rail

Top rail

Beaded pine strips

Bottom rail

RAISED-PANEL WAINSCOTING KITS

An accent wall of raised-panel wainscoting is a striking, yet inexpensive, addition to a dining room, living room, or study. Kits containing everything you need—raised panels, top and bottom rails, stiles, cap rails, and shoes—are available at most home improvement centers. The kits are affordable because the panel material is made of medium density fiberboard overlaid with hardwood veneer.

INSTALLING AN ACCENT WALL

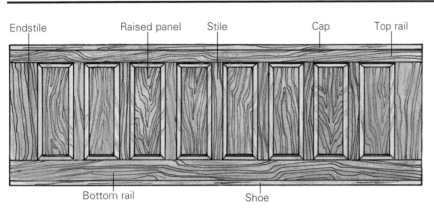

Endstile   Raised panel   Stile   Cap   Top rail

Bottom rail   Shoe

1 Find and mark the locations of wall studs with a pencil (any trial holes will be covered by panels). Mark at both the floor and the wall above.

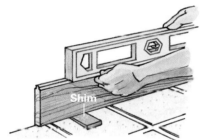

Shim

2 Cut the bottom rail to length, place it on the floor, and shim it until level (the shoe will cover up to a ½-inch gap at the floor). Predrill and nail the shoe with 8d finish nails.

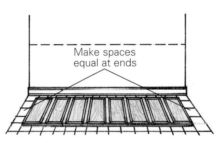

Make spaces equal at ends

3 Lay out alternating panels and stiles. Adjust until you have equal gaps of up to 10 inches at the ends. If electric outlets fall outside flat panel areas, shift the layout a few inches or move the boxes.

Rabbet behind baseboard

4 Apply a small amount of construction adhesive to the back of a center panel, insert its tongue into the base rail, and press into place. Adhere the remaining panels and stiles.

5 At an outlet, slide the panel upward to mark the horizontal location and sideways to mark the vertical location. Drill holes at the box corners and cut with a saber saw. See Tip Box, right.

6 Measure the gap at each end, adding ¼ inch for the panel tongue, and trim a 10-inch stile to the total width. Install the end stile and repeat at the other end of the wall.

Nailing grooves

7 After all of the panels and stiles are in place, cut the top rail to length and slide it over the tongues. Predrill the rail at stud locations and fasten it with 8d finish nails.

8 Cut the cap rail to length and install it over the top rail with adhesive. Predrill the cap and fasten it to the top rail with 4d finish nails.

9 Cut the base shoe to length and predrill it at stud locations along the floor. Fasten the shoe with 8d finish nails, pressing down so that it follows the contour of the floor.

EXTENSIONS FOR RECEPTACLE BOXES

Adding wainscoting means making a portion of your walls thicker. At receptacles, you'll need to unscrew the outlet fixture and reattach it flush with the surrounding surfaces. For safety, add a box extension. As the name implies, a box extension is made for just this sort of job. It has four sides and slips into the old box to make a deeper, code-compliant box.

Walks and Paths

GETTING THERE IS HALF THE FUN

ALSO SEE...
Bricks:
Pages 38–43
Concrete:
Pages 60–63
Decks:
Pages 74–81
Lighting:
Pages 212–219
Steps:
Pages 336–337

Paths bring to mind leisurely strolls across flower-filled meadows, warm welcomes, and mysterious walks through shadowy forests. The word "path" is often a metaphor for life. No wonder professional gardeners and landscape designers use paths to direct eyes and feet toward focal points, and as overall design elements.

Walks and paths do not have to be complicated or difficult to construct. The simplest paths are just stepping-stones or mulches such as gravel and bark. Pavings, such as stone, brick, and concrete, are also fairly easy to install. The design of a path may be more of a challenge than its construction.

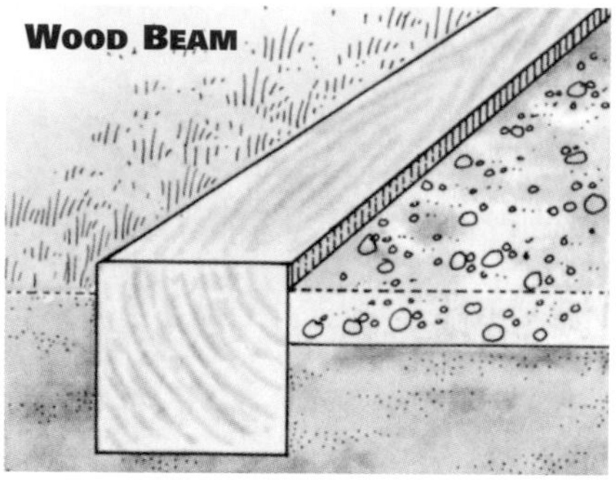

WOOD BEAM

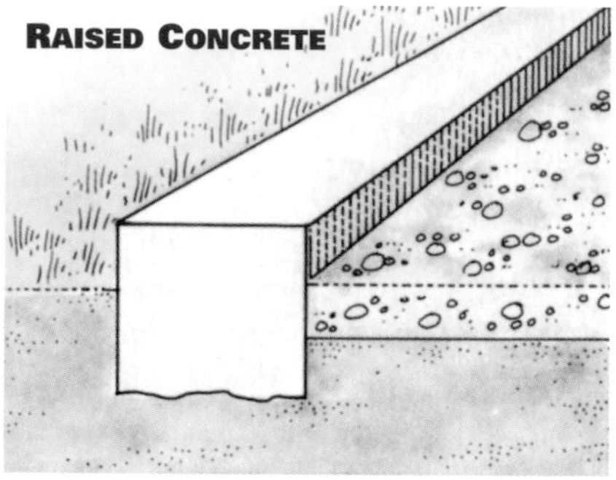

RAISED CONCRETE

FLUSH CONCRETE

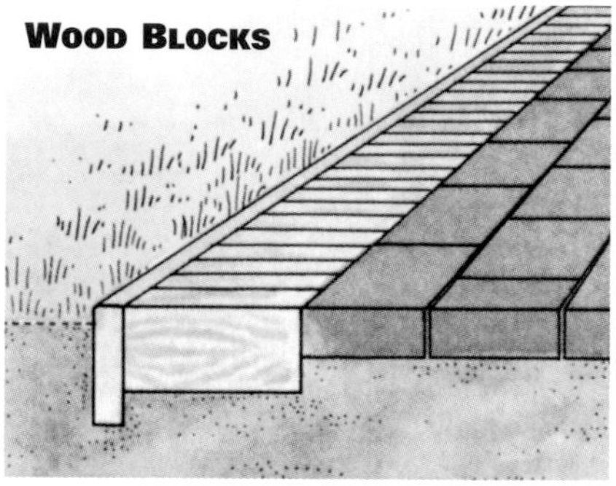

WOOD BLOCKS

MATERIALS

Paths may be categorized as soft or hard according to the materials with which they are surfaced. The table below lists the characteristics of common surface materials.
Soft Paths: A soft path is one finished with loose materials such as wood chips or gravel, or covered with natural grass or moss. Such a path is inexpensive and easy to construct. The drawback is maintenance: Moss is fragile; grass requires clipping; wood chips and gravel settle and scatter.
Hard Paths: A hard path is one finished with masonry: brick, stone, or concrete. These paths require significant investment of both material and time. On the other hand, the path will probably last into future generations and become an integral part of the property's architecture.

SURFACE MATERIALS FOR WALKS AND PATHS

Material	Cost	Labor	Maintenance	Life	Other
SOFT PATHS					
Wood bark	Low	Low	Medium	5 yr	Very rustic
Wood chips	Low	Low	Medium	5 yr	Very rustic
Grass	Low	Low	High	—	Needs moisture, cutting
Moss	Low	Low	Low	—	Fragile, requires shade
Crushed rock	Low	Low	Medium	10 yr	Hard on bare feet
Marble chips	Medium	Low	Medium	10 yr	Scatters, bright white
Shells	Medium	Low	Medium	10 yr	Scatters, can cut feet
HARD PATHS					
Brick	High	High	Low	50 yr	Use only modular pavers
Flagstone	High	High	Low	25 yr	Square or uncut random
Cobblestone	High	High	Low	50 yr	Very uneven surface
Concrete pavers	Medium	High	Low	25 yr	Look unnatural
Poured concrete	Medium	High	Low	25 yr	Commercial look

EDGINGS

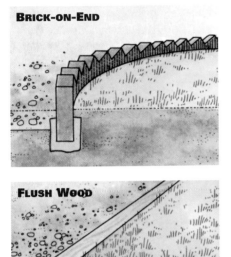

BRICK-ON-END

FLUSH WOOD

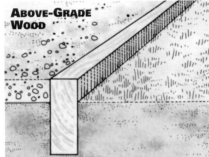

ABOVE-GRADE WOOD

Edgings are often used to:
- contain loose surface material
- prevent the spread of grass
- provide a visual border.

They can be constructed of a variety of materials, from brick to wood to concrete. They can be set flush with the soil surface, inset below grade, or installed above ground.

If it is a lawn that needs an edge, consider installing convenient plastic-strip edging below grade to all but eliminate the need for hand edging and trimming.

Railroad ties, 2×4 redwood or pressure-treated lumber, and doubled layers of bender board are also popular.

More permanent edges may be constructed of brick or concrete. A concrete edge can be installed as many inches above grade as you wish.

The illustration (at right) shows a wide variety of possible edgings.

SPACING STEPS

In placing stepping stones, first rake the area, then walk across it at a casual pace. Center one stone over each footstep and you will find your stepping-stone path very easy to traverse.

LET THE PURPOSE DEFINE THE PATH

The nature of a path should be determined by its purpose:

Entrance: The path to the door you wish strangers to use should be straight, wide, welcoming, and obvious.

Utility: Walks leading to the garage, clothes line, and trash storage should be straight and free of obstacles you could run into or trip over in the dark or while loaded with packages.

Outline: Paths through and round your property outline its major areas and functions. Plan the uses and sizes of each lawn or garden area before laying down any paths.

Stroll: A path for strolling should encourage you to slow down and enjoy the surroundings. It should meander, ideally with a destination that is not obvious as the start. And it should be flanked with interesting plants and other diversions.

Shortcut: Unless you want ugly paths worn into your lawn, place stepping stones —or barriers— wherever you discover people are consistently taking shortcuts.

DESIGN PRINCIPLES

Besides the choice of surface material and pattern, a few simple design principles are essential to the success of any walk or path:

Proper Width: Wider paths are naturally more costly and time-consuming to construct. For this reason the majority of residential paths are too narrow. Make side-by-side paths and walks at least four feet wide, and set bordering plants back so they won't encroach on the path.

Slopes and Steps: Slopes greater than 1 inch per foot are slippery when wet and should have steps. Avoid single steps because they are easy to overlook and trip over. Instead, on gentle slopes, alternate level stretches with sets of two or three steps. Also, within any set of steps, make the rise (height) of each step the same.

Straight or Curved? Straight paths should lead to something—a door, a gate, a sculpture, or a view, for example. Curved paths, on the other hand, work best when their destination is not obvious. In fact, they may lead back to their origin and still have performed their function of making the stroller slow down and enjoy the view.

Space Definition: Because you can see to the end of straight paths, they define the limits of a property. Curved paths have the opposite effect; because you can't see where they end, they make a property seem limitless–or at least larger. The curved-path effect is magnified by high shrubbery which totally eliminates any sense of distance.

PREORDAINED PATHS

Install walks where people want to walk. This may seem obvious, but how many times have you seen paths worn bare through people's lawns? If there is any question where these natural paths should be, scratch the bare soil around your house and wait for the footprints to appear!

WALLBOARD

USING WALLBOARD

Wallboard—also called drywall, gypsum board, gypboard, and Sheetrock (a brand name)—is a versatile and inexpensive building material. Since nearly all walls and ceilings today are finished with wallboard, it is used in a wide variety of home improvement projects.

Wallboard has many characteristics that make it a primary choice as a finish material for home interiors.

Advantages:
- Inexpensive
- Fireproof
- Dimensionally stable
- Cuts with a knife
- Easy to install
- Provides thermal mass
- Increases sound insulation
- Easy to repair
- A perfect surface for painting and wallpapering

Disadvantages:
- Requires skill to finish well
- Heavy, difficult-to-handle panels
- Monotonous, unless decorated

WALLBOARD FASTENERS

The "drywall screw" (Type W screw) has proven so technically superior in nearly every carpentry situation that we often ignore the existence of other wallboard fasteners:

Fastener	Application
Ring-shank nail	Single layer of wallboard to wood framing
Cup-head nail	Single layer of wallboard to wood framing
Type S screw	Wallboard to sheet metal studs or furring
Type G screw	Wallboard to wallboard or wood framing

ESTIMATING WALLBOARD SUPPLIES

Wallboard sheets	Nails, pounds 1¼"	1⅝"	Screws, pounds 1¼"	1⅝"	Compound, gallons	Tape, feet
8	1.0	1.4	0.8	1.0	2	95
10	1.3	1.7	1.0	1.3	2	118
12	1.5	2.0	1.2	1.6	3	142
14	1.8	2.4	1.4	1.8	3	166
16	2.0	2.7	1.6	2.1	4	190
18	2.3	3.1	1.8	2.4	4	213
20	2.6	3.4	2.0	2.6	4	237
22	2.8	3.7	2.3	2.9	5	260
24	3.1	4.1	2.5	3.1	5	285

PLANNING A JOB

Installing wallboard is a fairly simple process. However, taping and finishing joints requires skill and patience. If possible, learn by finishing an out-of-the-way location, such as a closet or a laundry room wall, before attempting a highly visible living or dining area. Professionals do the job in a quarter of the time it would take a novice, with far superior results, and at a very reasonable cost.

The first planning step is to calculate the placement of panels so that you can order the sizes you need. For a large project, calculate the total square footage, allow a small percentage for waste, and order an equivalent square footage in the largest size panels you will be using. For a small project, draw a layout diagram and figure the exact number of panels of each size. It is a good idea to order a few extra sheets, since wallboard is a relatively inexpensive material.

Having the right tools will make the job proceed more efficiently. A variable-speed, reversible drill with a ⅜-inch-capacity chuck is invaluable for installing wallboard. A battery-operated model keeps cords from getting underfoot. Buy several #2 Phillips bits so you can use the drill as a wallboard screwdriver.

You will also need extra blades for your utility knife, a wallboard saw, a metal straightedge or wallboard T-square, and a foot lever to snug the heavy panels up against the ceiling.

PREPARATION

You do not want to have to move wallboard panels after they have been delivered. To protect the finish faces, the panels come taped together, finish-face to finish-face. A pair of common 4×8 sheets weighs 80 pounds! Therefore, be prepared to instruct the delivery crew where you want how many of each type of wallboard. The contractor usually leaves a large window opening on the second story of a new house project so a crane can place the sheets directly upstairs.

Before you begin installing panels, make sure the walls and (or) ceilings are ready. Examine the framing. Make sure it is on 4-foot centers so that each joint will have a stud or joist for backing. Remove all nails.

Check for crooked studs. Sister them with straight studs or, if they contain wiring or plumbing, straighten them by sawing halfway through and then nailing short pieces of lumber or plywood on each side. Check room corners carefully to make sure they have backing to nail both intersecting panels into; alternatively, use wallboard clips.

Check the alignment of ceiling joists to be sure they form a smooth, flat plane. If not, and you have access from above, install a "strongback"—a 2×8 laid on edge across the tops of the joists, with all the joists screwed (with long wallboard screws) up into it. Push the low joists up against the strongback before fastening the two pieces with

TYPES OF WALLBOARD

Type	Thickness, inches	Lengths, feet	Typical application
Regular	¼	6 to 12	Walls and ceilings in dry locations.
	⅜	6 to 16	Not for fire-rated applications.
	½	6 to 16	
	⅝	6 to 16	
Fire-rated	½	6 to 16	Walls and ceilings where fire-rating
(Type-X)	⅝	6 to 16	is required by code.
Water-resistant	½	8, 11, 12	Moist areas such as bathrooms and
(Type-W)	⅝	8, 11, 12	showers, as a base for ceramic tile.
Foil-backed	⅜	6 to 16	Walls and ceilings in dry locations.
	½	6 to 16	Foil qualifies as a vapor barrier.
	⅝	6 to 16	

TYPES OF WALLBOARD

Wallboard is made of gypsum sandwiched between two layers of heavy paper. One side is smoother than the other, and the two shorter edges are beveled slightly to create a recessed cavity when two panels butt together. This cavity makes it possible to cover the joint with a special tape and layers of taping compound. Done properly, the result is a smooth wall with no visible joints.

The four types of gypsum wallboard are: regular, fire rated (Type-X), moisture resistant (Type-W), and foil-backed. Building codes specify where fire-rated and moisture-resistant panels must go. Typically, fire-resistant panels must be used in residences for common walls and ceilings between garages and living spaces, for closets under stairs, and in closets with gas water heaters. Moisture-resistant panels must be used behind bathtubs, sinks, and other high-moisture areas. They are an acceptable backing for tile, although glass-mesh backerboard is recommended by most tile manufacturers. Moisture-resistant panels require a special joint compound and a sealant for coating all cut edges.

Most walls and ceilings are covered with ½-inch-thick panels. Use ¼-inch or ⅜-inch-thick panels to cover plaster walls or for special applications such as round corners. For better fire resistance and sound insulation, use ⅝-inch-thick panels to span stud spacings greater than 16 inches.

CUTTING

Wallboard does not have to be cut for a perfect fit because the joints are covered with tape. In fact, it is better to cut the wallboard with a gap of about ⅛ inch at the joints.

Cuts can be made using either a knife or a saw. Use a utility knife and straightedge for long, straight cuts (professionals are experienced enough to use only a chalkline), and have plenty of extra blades on hand for big jobs. Saw the first leg of L-shaped cuts and holes. The best kind of saw is a wallboard saw (a keyhole saw with coarse teeth). The sharp tip makes it possible to start a cut in the middle of a panel by punching the blade through the board without having to drill a starter hole.

Cutting wallboard is simple. Most mistakes are due to errors in measuring, not cutting. To minimize such errors, draw a simple mini-sketch of the shape you need to cut right on the panel. Then write in all the dimensions, measuring twice for each one. Be especially careful with ceiling pieces, because it is easy to reverse the dimensions when measuring something over your head.

Straight Cuts:

1 Score the panel on one side with a single, straight, firm cut using a sharp utility knife.

2 Turn the panel over and break it along the score. Then slit the paper to complete the cut.

---

screws. A bar or pipe clamp will draw the joist to the strongback easily. Correct twisted joists with blocking nailed between joists at several points. Finally, make sure there are nailers at the tops of walls that run parallel to the joists.

Plan the panel layout carefully. End joints lack tapered edges, so your aim is to minimize the number and lengths of these joints. Professionals use the longest possible lengths in horizontal runs so that rooms up to 16 feet wide have end joints only in the corners.

If you are installing wallboard over existing plaster walls, rather than removing casings, moldings, and baseboards, consider leaving them in place and closely fitting ¼- or ⅜-inch

wallboard to the trim. On exterior walls, create a vapor barrier by sandwiching a sheet of poly between the plaster and the wallboard.

To prepare old plaster walls, first remove any bulges by carefully chipping away excess plaster with the claw end of a framing hammer. You won't have to worry about small holes. Simply cover holes up to 12 inches in diameter with new wallboard. Larger holes that expose joists or studs may require a solid backing.

Next, turn off the electrical power. Remove the cover plates from all outlets and switches, unscrew each device from its box, and pull it out enough so that it can be fed through the hole you will cut in the wallboard.

CUTTING *continued*

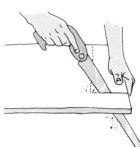

L-Shaped Cuts:

1 *Cut through the shorter leg using a saw. Cut the longer leg with a utility knife, just as you would a straight cut.*

Cutting Holes with a Saw:

1 *Measure and mark the hole carefully with a pencil and either a square or an electrical box as a template.*

2 *Push the point of the saw through the wallboard at a corner and saw around the line.*

Cutting Holes with a Utility Knife:

1 *Draw the outline of the hole, then carefully score the wallboard along the line and draw an "X" between the corners.*

2 *Holding the wallboard up, sharply rap the center of the "X" with a hammer to break the core.*

3 *Turn the wallboard over and slit the paper to remove the pieces.*

Scribing an Irregular Cut:

Occasionally, you must butt a piece of wallboard against an irregular surface, such as a wall that is not plumb. To make the wallboard fit precisely, you must scribe it for cutting. Set the end of the panel in place. Adjust a compass so the pencil and point are 2 inches apart. Holding the point against the irregular surface, pull the compass so that the pencil reproduces the irregular shape on the panel. Cut the line with a wallboard saw.

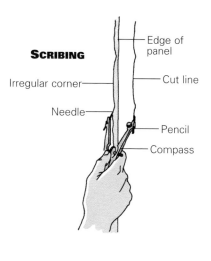

SCRIBING

- Edge of panel
- Irregular corner
- Needle
- Cut line
- Pencil
- Compass

NAILS, SCREWS, AND ADHESIVES

Nails are the less expensive fastener but are subject to aggravating "nail pops." Nail pops occur when wallboard is not tightly fastened to the stud underneath. If the wallboard is free to flex, the nail heads push outward, causing unsightly bumps. Screws are stronger, go in as quickly as nails, and hold wallboard tightly to studs.

Ring shank (annular ring) nail

Cement-coated, cup-head nail

NAILS

Wallboard nails are either ring shank or cup-head. Both are designed to hold drywall well. Nails must penetrate the framing or furring at least $\frac{3}{4}$ inch, so the most common length is $1\frac{1}{4}$ inches. If the framing is not dry, you must install 1×3 furring, spaced 16 or 24 inches on center. If you nail directly to wet framing, the nail heads will later pop out, requiring tedious resetting and spackling.

Nails should be placed 7 inches apart for ceiling panels and 8 inches apart for walls.

SCREWS

Space $1\frac{1}{4}$-inch type W screws 12 inches apart on ceiling panels and up to 16 inches apart on wall panels.

Type W wallboard screw

INSTALLING PANELS

CEILINGS

If you are installing more than a half dozen ceiling panels, consider renting a wallboard jack. This device raises or lowers a full sheet of wallboard with a simple crank. It has wheels to position the wallboard easily. With a jack, one person can install ceiling panels.

Ceiling panels are installed first so that the wall panels support the ceiling panel edges. Install them parallel to the joists. If possible, use panels long enough to span wall to wall.

Before installation, mark the location of ceiling joists on the top plates of the walls so you'll know where they are when they are covered up.

Lift the first panel into place and attach it to the joists with $1\frac{1}{4}$-inch type W screws (or $1\frac{1}{4}$-inch ring-shank nails). Begin in the center of the panel and work outward. Stagger any unavoidable end joints at least 16 inches. If you cut any panels full length, place the cut edge against the wall and leave a slight gap.

POSITIONING FASTENERS

Both nails and screws must be no closer than ⅜ inch to panel edges. If the head of a nail or screw breaks through the paper, place another nail or screw next to it. Embed all nail and screw heads far enough into the paper for compound to cover them.

If there are no nailers behind a corner, use drywall backup clips. Contractors use the clips because they replace extra studs and blocking.

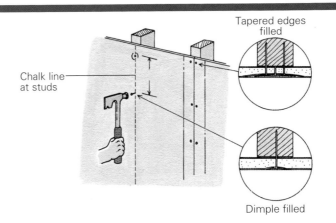

Chalk line at studs

Tapered edges filled

Dimple filled

ADHESIVES

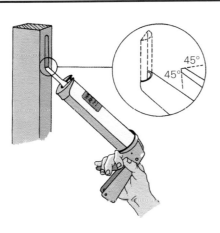

45°

45°

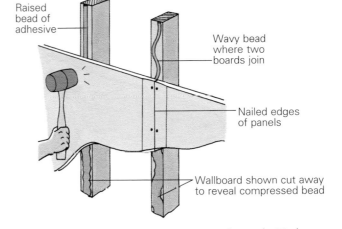

Raised bead of adhesive

Wavy bead where two boards join

Nailed edges of panels

Wallboard shown cut away to reveal compressed bead

Used together with nails or screws, adhesive improves a wallboard installation. It eliminates most of the nail holes that have to be covered with joint compound, keeping nail pops to a minimum. It also reduces vibration

and makes a wall more soundproof.

Cut the nozzle of an adhesive cartridge with two 45-degree cuts. Apply a bead of adhesive along each stud, one panel at a time. Then position the panel and press it firmly

against the studs. Nail or screw the outer edges only. To ensure contact and to spread the adhesive, hold a 2×4 over each glue line and strike it with a hammer.

WALLS

Wherever wiring or plumbing pass through studs, make sure they are protected by at least 1¼ inch of stud or a metal protector plate. Mark stud locations on the floor and ceiling.

If you are installing panels horizontally, place the top panel first so that it is snug against the ceiling. Then install the bottom panel so that it touches the top panel. Fill any space below the bottom panel (up to 2 inches) with strips of wallboard.

If the filler space is more than 2 inches, it is better to install panels vertically. Snug them up against the ceiling with a foot lever.

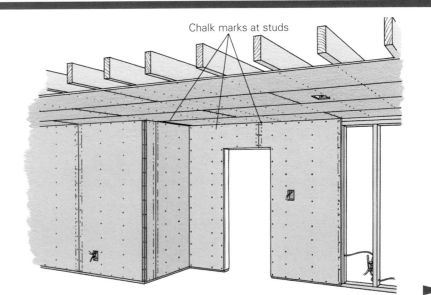

Chalk marks at studs

WALLBOARD
continued

FINISHING JOINTS

Once the wallboard is installed, all nail holes are filled and sanded, and the seams between the sheets are covered with wallboard tape and joint compound. Using the proper techniques will leave a smooth, uniform surface that completely disguises all seams and nail holes.

To tape and fill joints, use a series of putty knives, usually 3- or 4-inch, 6-inch, and 12-inch; a right-angled corner knife; a tray for holding compound, a sanding block, sandpaper, wallboard tape, and joint compound.

All-purpose premixed compound is adequate for most home improvement projects. The compound, also called mud, comes in 1-, 2-, and 5-gallon containers. To use the compound, scoop a small amount into a wallboard tray and work from the tray, rather than directly from the bucket. Keep the remainder of the compound covered. Clean your tray often; and don't return unused compound to the container. Otherwise lumps of dried-out compound will plague you by making drag marks when you try to get a smooth surface.

OUTSIDE CORNERS

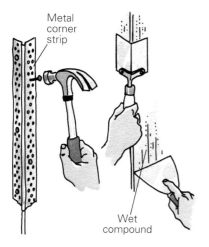

Metal corner strip

Wet compound

1 Nail on a metal corner strip (corner bead). Make sure it fits the corner tightly without any raised edges, or "fishmouths."

2 Apply compound with a putty knife or a corner trowel.

3 Finish as for a taped joint.

TAPING A STRAIGHT JOINT

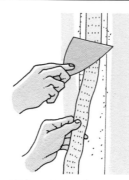

1 Spread a 3-inch strip of compound along the entire length of a joint.

2 Lay tape into the wet compound and smooth it with a 3- or 4-inch putty knife. Wet the tape to reduce binding.

3 With a 4-inch knife, apply a thin layer of compound over the bedded tape. Feather the edges carefully.

4 Fill and smooth all dimples with a layer of compound. Let the compound dry completely, then sand it smooth.

5 Apply a second coat of compound. Smooth and feather it with a 6-inch knife. Sand smooth when dry.

6 Apply a third coat with a 12-inch wallboard knife. When the compound is dry, sand it lightly. (Two coats are sufficient under wallcoverings.)

INSIDE CORNERS

Fold the paper joint tape in half lengthwise and press it into the wet compound, using a corner knife. Apply one or more coats of compound. Let each coat dry and sand it lightly before applying the next coat.

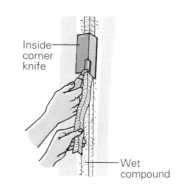

Inside corner knife

Wet compound

TEXTURING

Texturing is done after the joints are taped, the dimples are filled, and all compound is dry and sanded smooth.

First, mix the compound to a consistency that will give the roughness or smoothness of texture desired. Experiment on large leftover scraps of wallboard before tackling the whole wall or ceiling. Apply it randomly to the wallboard surface, using a sponge, roller, or trowel to get the right effect. If you want a rough, bumpy finish, leave it alone at this point or swirl patterns into it with a sponge. If you want a "knock-down" finish, drag a wide trowel over the wet compound to flatten the high spots and produce a uniform texture.

REPAIRING HOLES

SMALL HOLES

Holes that are more than just dents—but no more than an inch across—can be patched with wallboard tape and compound.

1 Cut strips of paper or self-adhesive fiberglass mesh tape to cover the hole and extend several inches beyond its edges.

2 Spread joint compound around the hole and press the tape into it, covering the hole. Smooth more compound over the tape, letting it ooze into the hole as much as possible.

3 Feather the edges with a 6-inch knife, let it dry and sand it smooth. If drying causes cracks or shrinkage, smooth another layer of compound over the patch with a 12-inch knife, let it dry, and sand it smooth.

MEDIUM HOLES

Holes 1 to 4 inches across are best "plugged" with another piece of wallboard.

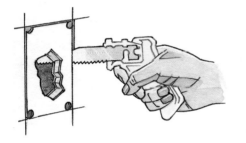 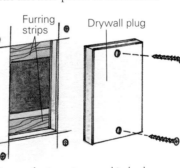 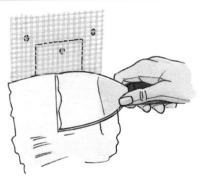

Furring strips   Drywall plug

1 Draw a rectangle around the damaged spot, drill ½-inch holes in the four corners with a spade bit, and cut the rectangle out with a keyhole saw.

2 Cut two furring strips several inches longer than the cutout's width. Insert the strips through the hole and draw them up tight with wallboard screws. Using the cutout section as a template, make a plug of wallboard to fill the hole.

3 Tape and finish the patch as you would a normal wallboard joint.

LARGE HOLES

Holes that span most of a stud cavity are best patched by removing a rectangle back to the centers of the studs.

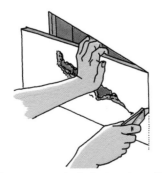  

1 Use a saw to make the horizontal cuts (be careful in case there is wiring behind the wall) and a knife to cut the sides. If the hole is near the floor, cut the rectangle all the way to the floor to give the patch more support.

2 Measure the hole and cut a new piece of wallboard to fit. Hammer it to the studs.

3 Tape and fill the joints. When dry, sand, texture (if needed), and paint the patch so that it matches the surrounding wall.

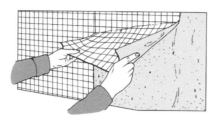

WALLCOVERINGS

CHOOSING WALLCOVERINGS

ALSO SEE...
Paints & Stains:
Pages 232–241
Paneling:
Pages 242–243
Wallboard:
Pages 392–397
Walls:
Pages 406–413

Wallcoverings are the basis for interior design schemes. They provide the color, texture, and background for the other elements of the room. Although the process of applying wallcoverings is somewhat complicated, the more difficult task is choosing from the thousands of styles and patterns.

First consider the character of the room. Is it traditional, contemporary, country, or eclectic? What style are the furnishings? Wallcoverings should harmonize with other elements of a room: furniture, rugs, and artwork.

Are you stuck with floorcoverings or other permanent features which you can't change? If so, choose a wall covering which includes some of the same colors as well as another color which will provide a complementary tie to the new elements.

Also consider the condition of the room. Are the walls bumpy? Are the corners or ceiling lines irregular? If so, stay away from stripes, straight-line patterns, and shiny materials such as foil wallcoverings. These materials will make irregularities in the wall all the more visible.

ESTIMATING COVERAGE OF SINGLE STANDARD ROLLS

Peri-meter, feet	Rolls for walls		Rolls for ceilings
	8 feet high	10 feet high	
36	9	11	3
40	10	13	4
44	11	14	4
48	12	15	5
52	13	16	6
56	14	17	6
60	15	19	7
64	16	20	8
68	17	21	9
72	18	22	10

REMOVING OLD WALLCOVERINGS

STRIPPABLE PAPER

Some wallcoverings are strippable—they are made for easy removal.

To strip the "strippables," lift a bottom corner with a scraper, then pull up and away from the wall steadily and slowly.

Remove all the covering, wash the walls with warm water, and scrape off remaining glue with a broad knife. Rinse the walls with clear water and allow them to dry thoroughly.

TYPES OF WALL COVERING

Commonly available wallcoverings are machine-printed in widths ranging from 18 to 27 inches. The length of a single roll times the width (the area) always equals 36 square feet. Most are pretrimmed and many are prepasted.

Paper wall coverings (wallpaper) are the least expensive. As a general rule, the more colors in the material, the higher the price, since the paper has to be run through the printer once for each color.

Vinyl wallcoverings are more durable than wallpapers. They are resistant to stains and dirt and can be washed if necessary. Some are tough enough for scrubbing. The best vinyl coverings are entirely vinyl instead of vinyl-coated paper. Both types tend to stretch when stressed but resist tearing.

Wallcoverings are also made with foil or cloth; cork veneers are also available. They can be flocked, embossed, or multistrip murals. Consult with your dealer about any special installation techniques or adhesives that are required for the covering you choose.

CHEMICAL REMOVERS

Chemical removers, available from wallcovering dealers, soak the paper off the wall by dissolving the underlying paste. Removers may be sold as a ready-mixed solution or liquid and powders requiring the addition of water. Be sure to follow the manufacturer's instructions about gloves, safety glasses, or other protective measures.

First pierce the wall covering with a perforating tool (a small wheel with sharp teeth) to allow the remover or steam to get behind the covering. After soaking the wallcovering, use a broad knife to lift it away from the wall. Flush the walls with a trisodium phosphate (TSP) solution, rinse with fresh water, and allow to dry before continuing.

STEAMERS

Rent a steamer from your dealer if you do not have a chemical remover or if you need to remove several layers of wallcovering. Lift the covering away as you steam, working a small section at a time. If the wallcovering is vinyl, it will lift more easily if you pierce it thoroughly with the perforating tool.

PREPARING WALLS

If you're considering applying a new covering over the old, consider the risks. First, any seam which is obvious in the old covering will show right through. Second, if the first covering is loose, the second might pull it away farther. Listen while you run the tips of your fingers over the surface. If you hear a crackling noise, the covering is too loose and should be removed. Another test is to flick the edges of a strip with a broad-bladed putty knife. If huge areas peel off easily, remove all the old paper.

Preparing a wall or ceiling for wallcovering involves filling holes and cracks the same as you would prepare for painting. There are, however, two considerations unique to wallcovering.

First, the wall should be as smooth as possible; the degree to which any roughness will show through will depend on the thickness and texture of the new covering. To smooth the wall, you may have to remove existing paper or attach a special underlayment.

Secondly, you must seal or size the wall so it neither draws too much moisture from the paste nor permits alkalis or corrosive elements to leach to the surface and discolor the wallcovering. Premixed primer-sealers accomplish both tasks.

Paint the trim and ceiling before starting, overlapping the area that will be covered by about ¼ inch.

Remove wax or grease stains from an existing wall covering with trisodium phosphate (TSP) or other strong cleanser, and finish the entire wall with an oil-based enamel undercoat before you apply the new covering.

THE TEST OF TIME

When you think you have found your wall covering, take the time for one final test. See if the store will give you a large sample—say 2 feet by 2 feet. If not, then ask if you can remove the sample page from the book.

Tape the large sample to the wall for at least 24 hours. Observe it under natural light throughout the day; then observe it under the room lights at night. After 24 hours, do you still like your choice?

PICKING THE STARTING POINT

There is little chance that the area you want to cover is evenly divisible by the width of your wallcovering. If you plan to cover all four walls, you eventually will end up with a mismatched pattern. Plan your hanging pattern so that the mismatch falls in an inconspicuous location.

If you think it is worth it, you can carefully measure around the room and mark where each seam will fall. However, if you have to lap a seam in order to stay plumb, this will throw off your layout. It's best to choose starting and ending points where the mismatch will not be obvious.

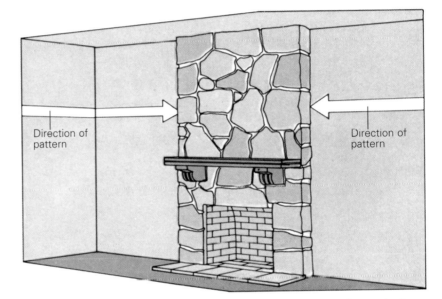

The best place to plan for pattern mismatch is where a wall is interrupted. If a bookcase or fireplace extends from floor to ceiling, it provides an ideal ending point so patterns won't have to meet.

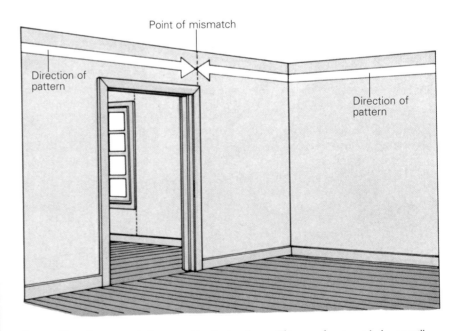

The second best place to start is down one side of a door frame. This way, the mismatched seam will occur above the door where it will be a foot long at most.

MARKING PLUMB LINES

Wallcovering should be hung plumb. Even if the pattern is forgiving, crooked seams are always obvious. Correct alignment is especially important for the starter strip because this will control the alignment of all subsequent strips.

To get the first strip plumb, snap a chalk line or use a straightedge, a level, and a pencil. (You can improvise a chalk line by rubbing colored chalk along a length of string, tying a weight to its end, and hanging it from a pushpin or nail near the ceiling.) Snap the chalk line about ¼ inch away from the edge of the first strip so you can see it while you hang the strip.

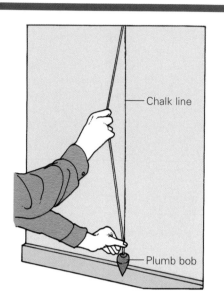

Chalk line

Plumb bob

APPLYING PASTE

Set up a work surface that is about 6 feet long (a 30-inch by 80-inch hollow-core door is perfect), prepare the paste, and let it sit according to the directions on the package.

Cut a length of wallcovering equivalent to the length to be covered plus several inches. Lay the strip pattern-down on your work surface and clamp the top. Using a paste brush or thick-nap roller, apply paste to the strip. Spread it evenly, holding the covering down with your free hand. Work the paste out toward the edges. Use a damp sponge to wipe excess paste off the work surface.

When you've finished the top half, unclamp it and fold the pasted end

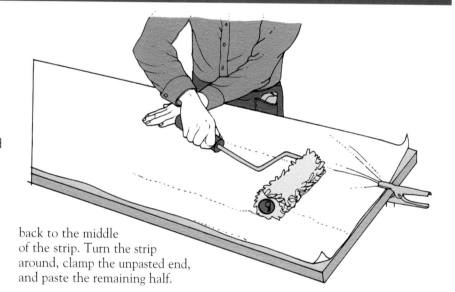

back to the middle of the strip. Turn the strip around, clamp the unpasted end, and paste the remaining half.

BOOKING AND CURING

When you have applied paste to the entire strip, unclamp and lightly fold the second half so the ends meet— but do not overlap—near the middle. Align the edges, but do not crease the folds. This folding process, called "booking," reduces water evaporation while the paper cures. Curing takes about 10 minutes and allows the paper to soften and expand. In the unlikely case the covering has strips of unprinted area along the edges (selvage), trim them off with a straightedge and a utility or razor knife

while the paper is booked. Use a fresh blade every time and cut carefully, because your cut will become the seam.

PREPASTED COVERINGS

Prepasted wallcoverings require wetting, typically in a plastic or metal trough. Fill the trough halfway with lukewarm water, then place it on the floor at the base of the area to be covered. When you measure a strip from the roll, add 2 inches at the top and 2 inches at the bottom. Cut the strip and reroll it, from bottom to top. Immerse it in the trough, soaking according to the manufacturer's directions (usually about one minute), and pull it out from the top.

Book the wetted, prepasted wallcovering just as you would unpasted material. Let it cure for 10 minutes before applying the wallcovering to the wall.

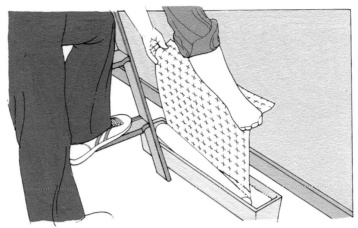

Some professionals apply paste to prepasted coverings to guarantee long-term adhesion. If you want to do this, mix 2 parts premixed vinyl adhesive with 1 part water and apply as if the paper was unpasted.

HANGING THE FIRST STRIP

1. Standing on a stable surface, unfold the top section of your booked covering and gently hold it up to the top of the wall, overlapping the ceiling by about 2 inches. Gently tack the section in place by wiping it lightly with a damp sponge or brush; do not smooth it flat. (If the paper is flocked or embossed, pat it lightly with a folded cloth.) Adjust the edge of the strip so it aligns with the plumb line.

2. Stroke the aligned top section flat against the top of the wall with your smoothing brush. Then smooth the covering with downward strokes, working from the center outward in both directions. Smooth out all wrinkles.

When you reach the center of the strip, release the fold and slide the bottom half of the strip into position.

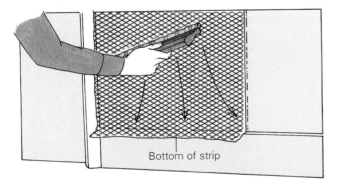

3. Recheck the alignment and make any necessary adjustments. Smooth the remainder of the strip with your brush, working down and out from the center.

4. After you have brushed the strip smooth, go over it with a damp sponge to remove excess paste and force out air bubbles. Work from the center toward the edges.

TRIMMING EDGES

Using a 6- or 10-inch broad knife as a guide, trim the edges with a razor knife. Hold the razor knife in one hand, and the broad knife in the other hand. Press the broad knife flat against the wall and into the corner, and pull the razor along the edge of the broad knife. Then, without lifting the razor knife from its cut, "leapfrog" the broad knife to the next position. Continue leapfrogging until you complete the cut. Change blades after every long cut. Expect to use 30 or 40 blades in a room. That's cheaper and less frustrating than tearing wallcovering.

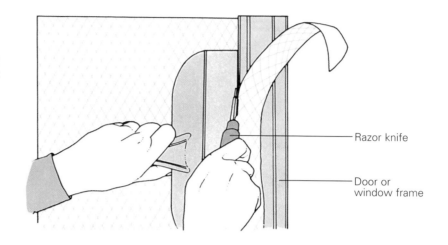

Razor knife

Door or window frame

SEAMING

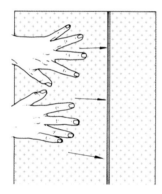

BUTTING THE STRIPS

Strips of wallcovering are usually joined with butt seams. Slide the new strip tightly against the first until the edges form a tight ridge (you can feel the ridge with your finger) but do not overlap the edges. Make sure the pattern matches, and don't stretch the paper as you adhere it to the wall.

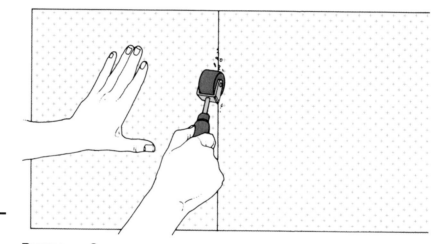

ROLLING THE SEAM

Flatten the seam with a seam roller. Use a cloth or sponge on flocked or raised coverings to prevent crushing the raised pattern. Sponge away excess paste and air bubbles.

Trim the top and bottom edges with the broad knife and razor knife either before or after rolling the seam. Be sure to continue the trim cut from one strip to the next without interruption.

ALTERNATIVE SEAMS

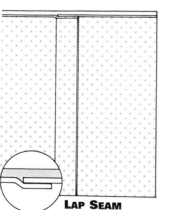

LAP SEAM

Straightedge

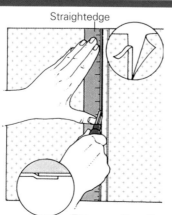

DOUBLE-CUT SEAM

The butt seam doesn't work well at corners or on all-vinyl wallcoverings. In these instances, use a lap seam or a double-cut seam.

Use the lap seam at inside and outside corners. It produces a slight pattern mismatch, but guarantees there will be no gap between the strips.

Use the double-cut seam for vinyl unless you use special vinyl-to-vinyl adhesive. To make the seam, hang the second strip over the first with a ½-inch overlap. Then use a straightedge and a razor knife to cut cleanly through both layers of the overlap. Remove the narrow cutout from both layers, then flatten the seam with a seam roller.

TURNING AN INSIDE CORNER

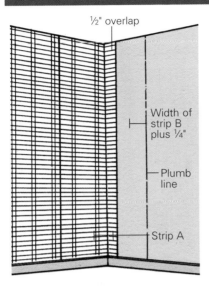

½" overlap

Width of strip B plus ¼"

Plumb line

Strip A

Tempting as it may be, don't try to wrap a full width of wallcovering around an inside corner; you're likely to end up with wrinkled paper and a severely out-of-plumb edge. Instead, cut a piece of wallcovering lengthwise into two strips and hang them separately. The steps below will help you avoid problems.

1. Measure the distance between the last strip hung and the corner at both top and bottom.

2. Add ½ inch to the wider dimension. Cut a strip of covering—strip "A"—to this dimension.

3. If the remaining strip is wider than 6 inches, use it on the other side of the corner. If it is narrower, throw it away and use a new strip for the other side of the corner.

4. Apply paste and press strip "A" into the corner so it aligns with the previous strip. Smooth the ½-inch excess around the corner onto the next wall.

5. Before you cut and hang the second strip, measure the width of strip "B" and add ¼ inch. At this measurement from the corner, snap a vertical chalk line.

6. Align strip "B" between the corner and the new plumb line, producing an overlapping seam. If the covering is all-vinyl, make a double-cut seam instead because vinyl doesn't stick to itself.

TURNING AN OUTSIDE CORNER

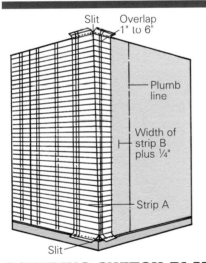

Slit

Overlap 1" to 6"

Plumb line

Width of strip B plus ¼"

Strip A

Slit

1. Measure the distance from the last strip to the corner at both top and bottom. Add 1 inch to that measurement (add 6 inches if the covering is particularly stiff, as are some vinyls and foils).

2. Cut a strip of covering to that width, using a new razor blade and a straightedge.

3. Paste and hang strip "A," smoothing it into place on the first wall. Use your razor knife to slit the excess at the top and bottom of the strip so you can bend it around the corner.

4. After you fold the covering around the corner, smooth it and trim the excess from both top and bottom.

5. Measure strip B and add ¼ inch. If it is narrower than 6 inches, use a full width strip. From the corner, measure this distance and snap a new plumb line at that point.

6. Hang strip "B" so the edge lies ¼ inch in from the plumb line. Double-cut the seam if the covering is all-vinyl.

COVERING SWITCH PLATES

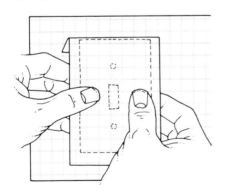

If you want switch plates to disappear, it is a simple job to cover them.

1. Remove the plate before covering the wall, covering right over the switch or outlet box.

2. Cut an X across the box, stopping about ¼ inch from the corners. Cut off the flaps to make a hole slightly smaller than the opening.

3. Choose a scrap of wallcovering large enough to cover the switch plate and matching the pattern on the surrounding wall.

4. Cut the scrap ½ inch larger than the plate all around, fold it lightly over the top of the plate and match the top edge to the covering on the surrounding wall.

5. Slide the plate down ⅛ inch and fold the wallcovering cover around the bottom. (This ⅛ inch distributes the mismatch caused by the curve of the plate.)

6. Repeat the procedure to make side folds.

7. Place the covering face down and paste it. Center the cover plate inside the folded lines, cut away the corners, and wrap the plate, pressing firmly.

8. When the plate is dry, cut an "X" for each toggle, pasting the untrimmed flaps onto the back of the plate. Use a pin to find the holes for the plate's mounting screws.

▶

TRIMMING AROUND OBSTACLES

WINDOWS AND DOORS

Fitting a wallcovering around any obstacle—a door, a cabinet, a built-in bookcase, or a window—is easiest when you trim the covering after it's up.

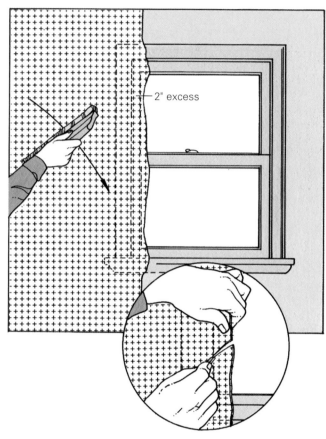

2" excess

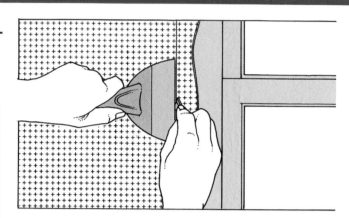

2. Press the covering against the edge of the molding with the smoothing brush. Use a broad knife and a razor knife to trim away the excess, as close as possible to the molding. On older, uneven molding, it is better to follow the irregular contours by hand.

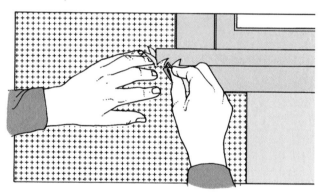

1. Hang a full prepared strip, letting it overlap the window frame. Butt the seam against the previous strip and smooth the strip so it adheres loosely on all wall areas. Cut away all but a few inches of any overlap that covers the window. Then, slice diagonal slits at the molding corners to release the covering and allow it to lie flat against the wall.

3. Trim around the rounded edge of the window sill by making a series of small incisions in the covering and pressing it tightly against the wall with your fingers. Trim flush to the molding.

4. Finally, apply wallcovering to the areas above and below the window, making sure the pattern matches.

BEAMS

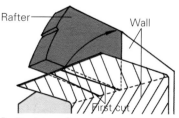

Rafter — Wall — First cut

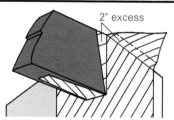

2" excess

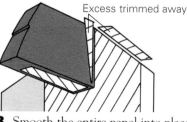

Excess trimmed away

1. Position the wallcovering at the ceiling with the normal 2-inch excess and smooth it against the bottom of the beam or rafter. Slit the covering, from the point it meets the bottom of the beam back to the wall at a slight angle.

2. Smooth the covering into place against the wall. Slit the covering at the other side of the beam (a mirror image of the previous cut).

3. Smooth the entire panel into place, then trim off excess wallcovering around the beam.

ARCHES

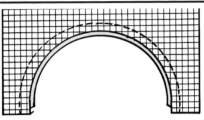

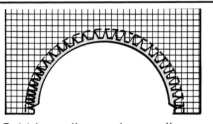

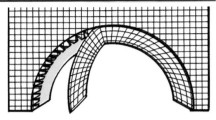

1. Cover the area above and around the arch as you would any wall, allowing the wallcovering to hang into the archway opening. When you have covered the full width of the arch, trim the excess to within 2 inches of the archway edge.

2. Make small triangular cuts all around the arch, spacing the cuts more closely where the curve is sharpest. Turn the edges under, smoothing the "tongues" firmly against the inside of the arch. Using a new razor blade, trim them off to a length of ½ inch.

3. Cut a strip of wallcovering just slightly narrower than the thickness of the arch (to avoid an edge that might lift and peel). Paste it into place, covering all of the tongues.

RECESSED WINDOWS

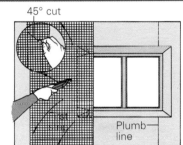

Triangular pieces pasted into corners

First strip Plumb lines

45° cut

Wallcovering

2" excess

Window

Plumb line

1. If possible, plan your layout so that the first panel overlaps the window edge by the depth of the recess plus a couple of inches. Cut triangles from scrap wallcovering, fold them in half, fit them into the corners of the recess from front to back, and paste them in position.

2. Smooth the first strip on the wall right over the window opening. Using your fingers, feel through the paper and locate the upper corner of the window opening. With a fresh razor blade or shears, cut a 45-degree slit from the corner to the edge of the covering. Do the same at the bottom corner of the window opening. Tuck and smooth the wallcovering into the top, side, and bottom of the recess, pressing it firmly against the casing.

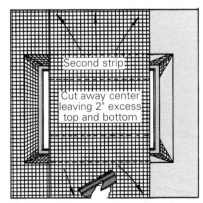

Second strip

Cut away center leaving 2" excess top and bottom

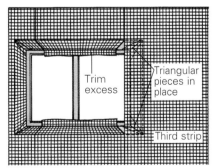

Trim excess

Triangular pieces in place

Third strip

3. Hang the second panel as if you were covering a solid wall. Cut away the center portion, leaving enough to fold back into the recess, plus about 2 inches.

4. Smooth the strip into the recess and against the casing. (Hang as many strips as needed to reach the far side of the recess.)
5. Repeat steps 1 and 2 at the other side of the window.

CEILINGS

Covering a ceiling is as simple as covering a wall and is done in the same way. Follow the same steps for preparation, plumb lines, cutting, pasting, smoothing, and trimming.

Two additional considerations apply to ceilings, however. The first is physical difficulty—you will be fighting gravity. Not only is this tiring, but it is hard to keep a tacked-down strip in place while you check the pattern match. Don't do this alone; enlist the aid of a helper. One person can hold the booked end of the panel against the ceiling with a T-brace or broomstick while the other matches the pattern and positions it.

The second consideration is the direction in which you should run the strips. How is the pattern on the ceiling going to relate to the walls? In a small-scale installation and with an all-over pattern, the direction of the strips may not matter, but if the pattern is striped one way will definitely look better than the other. Generally it is best to cover a ceiling with the fewest seams. If the pattern looks good and the strips don't get so long that they are unmanageable, apply them with the seams running parallel to the longer walls.

407

Walls define spaces. If you want to alter the spaces in your home, you will have to alter walls, and that means opening them up, removing them, or building new ones.

You probably think of walls as permanent structures so you may be apprehensive about changing them. But working on walls requires more common sense than technical skill, more finesse than brute strength, and more general construction knowledge than specific answers for every situation.

But before you get out the tools, ask yourself how changing the wall will affect the structure of the house? What is inside the wall?

Before opening up a wall or removing it, do some detective work. Although it is impossible to predict every detail, you should be able to get the general picture.

Cutting an opening for a medicine cabinet will have no effect on structure as long as you don't cut any studs.

Cutting a large opening in a wall—for a window or door, for example—or completely removing a wall can have a major impact on the structure, however. First determine whether the wall is bearing or nonbearing. You also need to know if diagonal bracing or structural sheathing provides the wall with its shear strength. If you interrupt the bracing, you will have to replace it with the same bracing.

Walls always have studs. To locate the studs, use an electronic stud finder or drive pilot nails near the baseboard until you hit a stud. Find the center of the stud by finding its edges. Find the center of other studs by measuring 16 inches on-center from the first stud. Check your measurements with the stud finder or nails, since older homes don't always have regular stud spacings.

Look for electrical outlets, switches, and fixtures. Even if the wall has no visible outlets or switches on either side, look in the attic or basement for wires that go into the wall.

Also look for plumbing pipes and heating ducts. Even if the wall has no plumbing fixtures on it or next to it, check in the attic and basement to see if any lines enter into the wall.

Electrical lines are easy to reroute; pipes and ducts are considerably more difficult. You may, in fact, decide to change your plans rather than move the plumbing.

LIFTING WALLS

When raising walls, it may be tempting to emulate those pictures you see of Amish barn raisings—hordes of family and friends pushing up huge walls in celebration of their growing community.

The spirit is right, but walls are heavy, and an accident could spell disaster. Have an experienced contractor on hand to supervise the raising, or raise the wall in sections no longer than 16 feet and spike them together after they are up and braced.

CODE REQUIREMENTS: WALLS

Energy: Energy conservation standards are set by each state. The standards specify separate minimum R-values required for floors, walls, roofs, and windows, or specify an overall performance of the building, considering R-values, infiltration, and solar gain. For specifics, contact either your building code official or your state energy office.

Bracing: All bearing walls must be braced against shear (racking) caused by both wind and seismic forces. See the table (below) for the code-specified minimum bracing requirements for exterior residential walls.

Framing:

■ Top plates must be doubled, overlapped at corners and intersections, and overlapped at least 4 feet at joints.

■ Joists and rafters must fall within 5 inches of bearing studs if the joists or rafters are spaced more than 16 inches on-center and the studs are spaced 24 inches on center, unless the top plate is 2×6s, 3×4s, or is tripled.

■ Nonbearing partition wall studs may be 2×3s spaced 24 inches on-center or flat 2×4s spaced 16 inches on-center, and may have a single top plate.

■ Studs may be notched 25 percent of width if bearing and 40 percent if nonbearing.

■ Studs may be drilled 40 percent of width if ⅝ inch or more from edge. Doubled studs may be drilled 60 percent of width.

■ Walls must be firestopped at top and bottom.

EXTERIOR WALL BRACING REQUIREMENTS

Seismic Risk Areas	Type of wall	Type of brace	Where
Most of the continent uses these.	Top story 1st of 2-story 2nd of 3-story	1×4 let-in brace or structural sheathing	Each corner and at least every 25 feet
Check your local codes	1st of 3-story	Structural sheathing	4-foot-wide panels at each corner and every 25 feet
Western regions	Top story	1×4 let-in brace or structural sheathing	Each corner and at least every 25 feet
more prone to quakes	1st of 2-story 2nd of 3-story	Structural sheathing	25 percent of wall length
use these	1st of 3-story	Structural sheathing	40 percent of wall length

RECOGNIZING A BEARING WALL

Bearing walls hold up floors, roofs, and other walls; nonbearing walls merely divide interior spaces. All exterior walls are bearing walls.

GENERAL RULE

To determine if an interior wall is a bearing wall, look in the attic or basement. If the ceiling joists run perpendicular to the wall, it is a bearing wall. If you can't inspect the wall from above, look under the floor. Walls located directly over girders and doubled joists are usually bearing walls. Posts and footings within the perimeter of the foundation usually support bearing walls as well.

EXCEPTIONS TO THE RULE

Short walls, such as those enclosing a closet, may be perpendicular to the joists, but are not necessarily bearing walls. When a central hallway runs the length of a house, only one wall will be a bearing wall. Look in the attic to see which wall the ceiling joists overlap.

Also look in the attic for strongbacks: beams or 2× lumber set on edge to hold up joists. The ends of strongbacks bear on walls that run parallel to the joists.

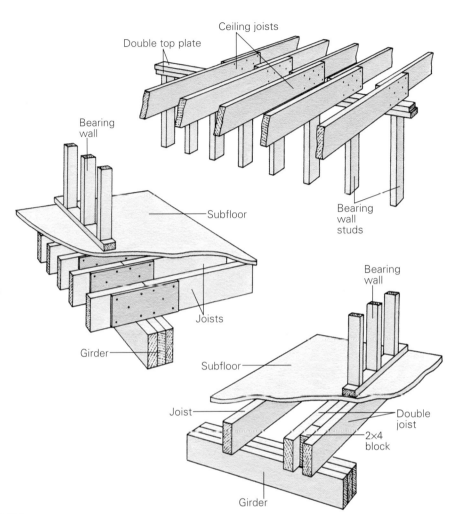

CUTTING INTO WALLBOARD

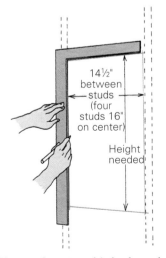

1 Using an electronic stud finder, locate the studs and mark the outline for the cutout between them.

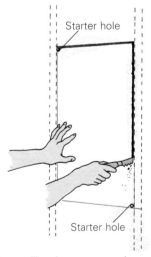

2 Use a wallboard saw to cut out the opening. Start it by drilling pilot holes or by plunging the point of the saw through the wallboard.

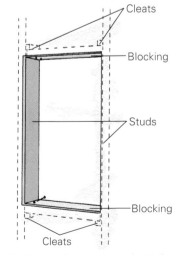

3 Cut blocking to fit between the studs. Nail cleats or drive 8d nails into the studs to brace the blocking, then toenail each block into place.

REROUTING UTILITIES

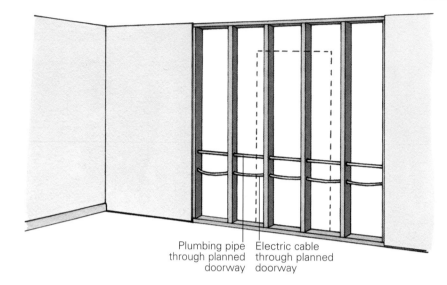

Plumbing pipe through planned doorway

Electric cable through planned doorway

WIRING

Before cutting into a wall, make sure the power to that area is shut off. To identify the right circuit, plug a radio into an outlet on the wall. As you flip the circuit breakers in the basement or garage, you will hear the radio go off when you hit the right breaker.

If you are framing a fairly high window, the wiring may be at receptacle level where you will not be removing any studs. If you are framing a door or low window, you will have to reroute the wires over the header.

Code forbids splicing wires inside walls or even in junction boxes that have cover plates not accessible to the outside. The easiest way to splice cable

CUTTING INTO LATH AND PLASTER

If you're remodeling an older home, your walls are likely to be lath and plaster. Composed of layers—wooden lath nailed to the studs, and a heavy coat of plaster over the lath—a lath-and-plaster wall is like a continuous membrane. Rough handling of one lath in one section can create cracks nearby. Make each cut carefully and deliberately.

To cut an opening in lath and plaster, follow these steps:

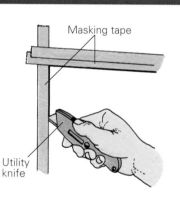

Masking tape

Utility knife

1 Tape around the area to be cut, mark the outline on the tape, and deeply score the tape and the underlying plaster with a utility knife.

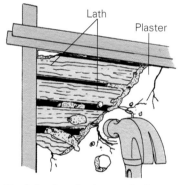

Lath

Plaster

2 Gently break up the plaster with a hammer, a little at a time.

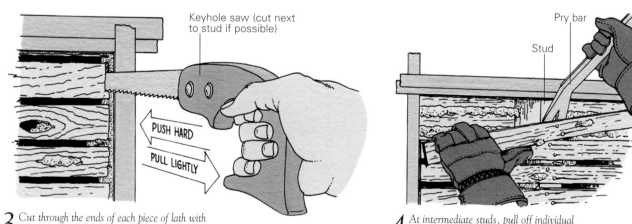

Keyhole saw (cut next to stud if possible)

PUSH HARD

PULL LIGHTLY

3 Cut through the ends of each piece of lath with a sharp keyhole saw. If the lath is wire mesh, snip it out with diagonal cutters.

Pry bar

Stud

4 At intermediate studs, pull off individual pieces of lath with a pry bar or claw hammer. Clean up the hole with a small handsaw.

in a wall is to install a new outlet on either side of the opening and run wires above the header or through the basement.

PLUMBING

Reroute plumbing pipes in much the same way as electrical wires. However, be certain that you are dealing with water pipes and not gas pipes. If you are not sure, call a plumber or the gas company. If they're gas lines, hire a plumber to move them.

If you are dealing with a water pipe, shut off the main supply valve. Cut the pipe and use elbow fittings to route it around the header or through the basement. Wherever wires or pipes are within 1¼ inches of a stud, protect them with a metal plate.

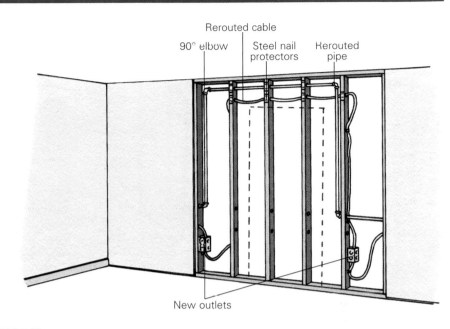

Rerouted cable
90° elbow
Steel nail protectors
Rerouted pipe
New outlets

OPENING UP BEARING WALLS

To create an opening for a door or window in a bearing wall, you must temporarily support the ceiling until you have replaced any cut studs with a header.

Build a temporary stud wall with one bottom and one top plate, about 4 feet longer than the opening and 1¾ inches short of the ceiling height. Raise the support wall into place about 4 feet back from the wall you're remodeling and drive shims between the top plate and cap plate under every joist to snug the wall into place. The cap plate will not mar the ceiling if it doesn't slip; if ceiling damage is a concern, allow a little extra room for cushioning material between the cap plate and ceiling.

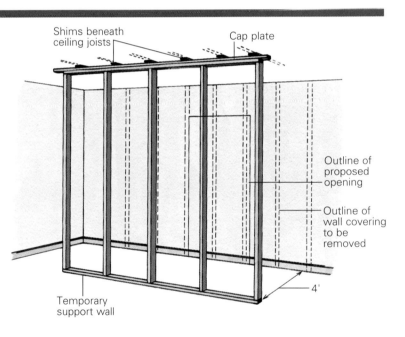

Shims beneath ceiling joists
Cap plate
Outline of proposed opening
Outline of wall covering to be removed
Temporary support wall
4'

SHORING BALLOON-FRAME WALLS

Remove the wallboard or plaster and lath from the rough opening area. Nail a 2×8 (a waler) to the exposed studs, tight against the ceiling and completely across the proposed opening. Attach the waler to each stud with ⅜×4-inch lag screws. Support the waler ends with 2×4s cut to fit snugly. Use metal splice plates for extra security.

Cut the old studs and install the header. When you install the new trimmer studs, remove the fire blocks between the existing studs and extend the trimmers all the way to the sill.

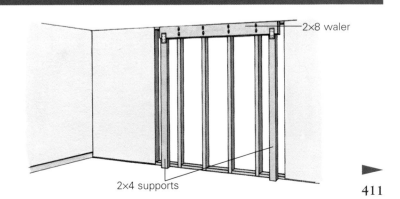

2×8 waler
2×4 supports

411

FRAMING A WINDOW OPENING

Mark the rough opening of the window on the inside wall, and remove the wallboard or plaster and lath back to the first studs outside the marks.

To size the header, consult the Header Span Table on page 331.

Choose one of the exposed studs to be the king stud. Then mark the stud cut lines for the header and the sill. Measure down from the header mark for the sill, allowing for sill material, as well as the rough opening of the window. Cut away the studs and install the header, new trimmer studs, and the sill.

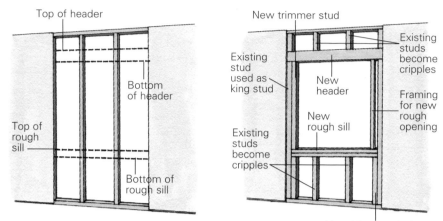

FRAMING A DOOR OPENING

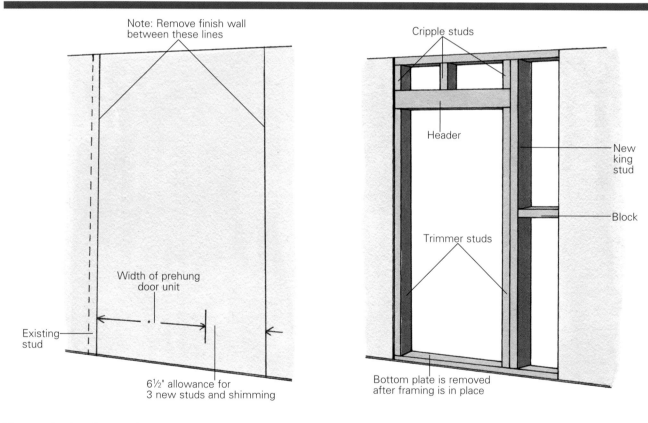

To give the door hinges the strongest support, locate the hinge side of the door against an existing stud.

When you've located the hinge-side stud, snap a chalk line along its inner edge. From the line, measure and mark the width of the door rough opening.

Find the first stud beyond this point, and remove the finish wall between it and the hinge stud, using a circular saw with a nail-cutting carbide blade. Wear goggles because there will be a lot of both sawdust and plaster dust.

Making sure the hinge stud is plumb (if it is not, you can shim the trimmer), nail an 82-inch trimmer stud to it. At the width of the rough opening, fasten new king and trimmer studs on the opposite side. Stabilize the king and trimmer at their midpoints with a horizontal block, and install the header and cripple studs. Saw through the bottom plate with a reciprocating saw and remove it.

There are several methods for building an interior wall in an existing room, depending on how much space you have to work with and whether the new wall will be a bearing wall. Always begin by stripping away the finished surface where the new wall will intersect an existing wall so that you can nail the new wall to an exposed stud or horizontal blocking.

Build your partition wall the same way you build walls in new construction except that the ceiling makes it impossible to tilt a full-sized wall into place.

BEARING WALLS

If the new wall is a bearing wall, it should have a double top plate. First, measure and cut a 2×4 cap plate, top plate, and bottom plate to equal lengths. Then stack them on top of each other with their ends flush and mark them for stud spacings. Next, cut away just enough of the ceiling for a channel in which to set the new cap plate. Set the cap plate in the channel and nail it to each joist with two 16d nails.

Set the bottom plate on the floor directly beneath the cap plate. Align it with a plumb bob so stud marks will be plumb. Set the top plate on the bottom plate (to account for its thickness when nailed later at the top of the wall) and measure the length for individual studs (don't assume they are all the same length).

Cut each stud to length. Number each one to keep them sorted out. Then set the top plate and bottom plate far enough apart on the floor to nail the studs between them. Face-nail through the plates into the studs, using two 16d nails at each end. When the wall is assembled, raise it and slide it into place beneath the cap plate. Nail the bottom plate to the floor and the top plate to the cap plate, making sure the wall is plumb.

NONBEARING WALLS

Remove baseboards and ceiling moldings where the new wall will intersect an existing wall, or saw and chisel a channel for it. Then remove the wallboard or plaster and lath so that the new wall can be attached directly to the framing. If the new wall intersects at an existing stud, you can nail it directly (sister a new stud to the one in the wall for extra strength). Otherwise, nail horizontal blocking or a new double stud in between to provide an attachment for nailing. To attach a nonbearing wall, it is not necessary to strip away ceiling material unless you are replacing the ceiling.

There are three methods for building a nonbearing wall:

■ In the first method, cut the top plate and bottom plate to length, and stack them on the floor where the wall will go. Mark the plates for stud locations and measure between the plates and the ceiling for each stud. Cut the studs to length and nail them only to the top plate. With a helper, tilt the partial wall up and slide the bottom plate beneath the dangling studs. Nail or screw the top plate to the ceiling, then nail the bottom plate to the floor. Finally, toenail the studs to the bottom plate, making sure each stud is plumb.

■ Alternatively: Cut the studs ¼ inch short and assemble the entire wall on the floor. Tilt it into place. You will find that the studs are short enough for the wall to clear the ceiling. After the wall is in place, shim the space between the top plate and ceiling, and nail top and bottom plates in place.

■ A final method: Nail or screw the top plate and the bottom plate in place. Then measure, cut, and toenail the individual studs. This method is useful when there is insufficient space to assemble the wall on the floor.

ERECTING A NONBEARING STUD WALL

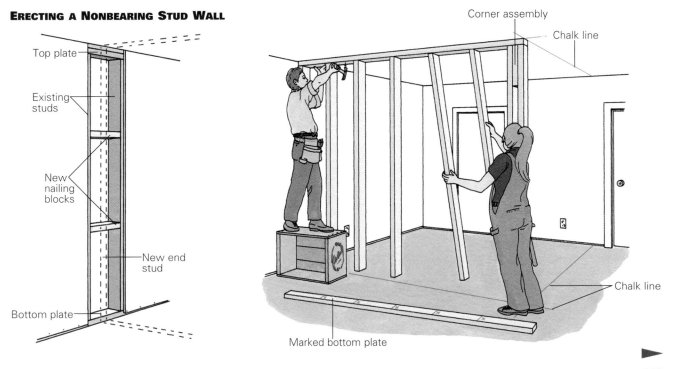

Top plate

Existing studs

New nailing blocks

New end stud

Bottom plate

Corner assembly

Chalk line

Chalk line

Marked bottom plate

REMOVING A NONBEARING WALL

First make sure the wall is not a bearing wall. If you're not able to be absolutely certain, call in the building code inspector or a contractor to verify your analysis.

Whether it is bearing or nonbearing, however, you will have to reroute wiring and plumbing, as well as determine if any gas pipes in the wall must be moved by a licensed plumber or gas installer.

REMOVING TRIM AND FINISH

Once you've determined that the wall is nonbearing, shut off the power to its circuits and dismantle it. Cover the floor with heavy plastic to protect it.

Remove the trim first, saving any pieces that you can reuse. If the trim is difficult to remove, try punching the finish nails through the trim with a nailset in order to minimize splitting.

Next, remove the wall surface. If it is lath and plaster, you're facing a messy job. Plaster dust drifts everywhere, so seal off the work area with plastic sheeting and tape. Lightly misting the plaster with water will reduce the amount of dust.

Knock down the plaster with a hammer and pull the lath away from the studs with a pry bar and claw hammer. Watch out for the nails in the lath, and wear goggles, a dust mask, and protective clothing.

After clearing away all the finish wall material, remove any wires or pipes and reroute them.

REMOVING FRAMING

If the studs are toenailed into the sole plate, you should be able to save them by pulling out the nails with a cat's paw. If they are not toenailed, remove them with a reciprocating saw and metal-cutting blade. Saw at the bottom in order to save the longest lengths possible. Once the bottom is cut, knock the stud to one side and pull it away from its top fasteners.

After removing all of the studs, saw through the bottom plate at both ends.

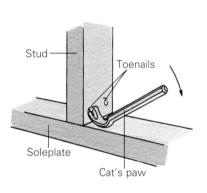

Stud

Toenails

Soleplate

Cat's paw

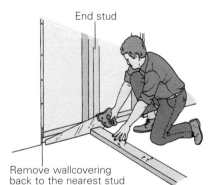

End stud

Remove wallcovering back to the nearest stud

If you don't want the floor to be scratched, use a backsaw, handsaw, or reciprocating saw (turn the blade upside down) and work carefully. After you have cut the bottom plate, cut the top plates in the same way.

Soleplate

Wrecking bar

Pry up the sole plate and remove it, then remove the top plate and cap plate in the same way. If you leave the cap plate in place, cut off the exposed nails with a hacksaw or reciprocating saw. Fill any cavities with material to match the surrounding area, or cover them with plywood flush with the adjacent surfaces.

REPLACING A BEARING WALL WITH A BEAM

First, remove the old trim. If you plan to reuse it, remove it carefully to avoid splitting the ends. Then remove the wallboard or plaster as you would for a nonbearing wall, and reroute any electrical or plumbing lines.

CLEAR SPANS FOR DOUGLAS FIR-LARCH, HEM-FIR, AND SOUTHERN PINE BEAMS

Beam Size	Building Width, ft.		
	20	28	36
BEAM SUPPORTING ONE FLOOR			
2-2×4	3' 5"	2' 10"	2' 6"
2-2×6	4' 11"	4' 2"	3' 8"
2-2×8	6' 3"	5' 4"	4' 8"
2-2×10	7' 8"	6' 6"	5' 9"
2-2×12	8' 11"	7' 6"	6' 7"
3-2×8	7' 10"	6' 8"	5' 10"
3-2×10	9' 7"	8' 1"	7' 2"
3-2×12	11' 1"	9' 5"	8' 3"
4-2×8	9' 0"	7' 8"	6' 9"
4-2×10	11' 1"	9' 4"	8' 3"
4-2×12	12' 10"	10' 10"	9' 7"
BEAM SUPPORTING ONE FLOOR AND ONE CEILING			
2-2×4	2' 3"	1' 11"	1' 9"
2-2×6	3' 4"	2' 10"	2' 6"
2-2×8	4' 3"	3' 7"	3' 3"
2-2×10	5' 2"	4' 5"	3' 11"
2-2×12	6' 0"	5' 2"	4' 7"
3-2×8	5' 4"	4' 6"	4' 0"
3-2×10	6' 6"	5' 6"	4' 11"
3-2×12	7' 6"	6' 5"	5' 8"
4-2×8	6' 1"	5' 3"	4' 8"
4-2×10	7' 6"	6' 5"	5' 8"
4-2×12	8' 8"	7' 5"	6' 7"

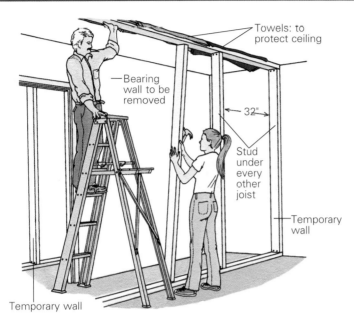

Towels: to protect ceiling

Bearing wall to be removed

32"

Stud under every other joist

Temporary wall

Temporary wall

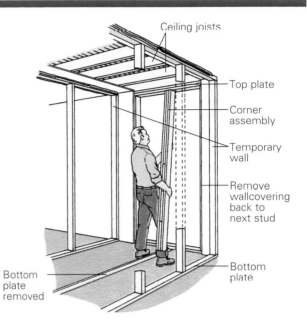

Ceiling joists

Top plate

Corner assembly

Temporary wall

Remove wallcovering back to next stud

Bottom plate

Bottom plate removed

Next, to hold up the overhead joists, erect temporary shoring (see Opening up Bearing Walls, page 409) as close to the wall as you can and still have room to work. The shoring should run the length of the wall. If the joists are lapped or butted over the wall (they usually are), set shoring on both sides. If the floor beneath feels at all springy, shore it from below, as well.

With shoring in place, remove the wall framing. If you are installing a beam, leave the cap plate of the old wall in place.

Find the required beam size from the tables (opposite). The first table is for beams which support just one floor. The second table is for beams which support a floor, a wall above, and a ceiling above that. Then follow the steps below to install the beam.

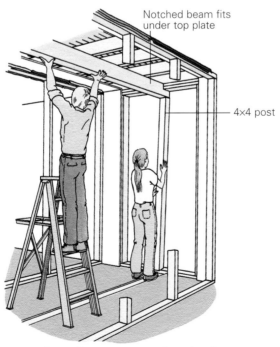

Notched beam fits under top plate

4×4 post

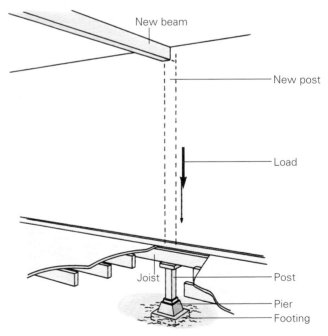

New beam

New post

Load

Joist

Post

Pier

Footing

1. Cut away the wallcovering at each end and remove the corner assembly of the old walls.
2. Install posts inside the end walls to support the beam.
3. Notch the ends of the beam at the top to fit around the top plates of the end walls.
4. Install the beam. A good fit over the new support posts

and under the top plates of the end walls will probably require tapping the beam into place with a small sledge hammer. If the fit is too tight, remove the beam and shave away the notch.

Support posts should have support all the way to the old foundation or to new footings.

A CASE OF MULTIPLE IDENTITIES

ALSO SEE...
Countertops:
Pages 70–73
Faucets & Valves:
Pages 126–129
Plumbing:
Pages 256–263
Vanities:
Pages 384–385

Washbasins—also called sinks, lavatories, and vanities—can be mounted on the wall, on a pedestal, or in a vanity cabinet.

On a wall-mounted sink, the plumbing lines will show, but access is convenient. With a pedestal-type washbasin, the plumbing is hidden. Both types can be made of vitreous china, enameled cast iron, or enameled steel.

In vanity models, the countertop and basin can be molded in one unit, or the basin can drop into—or be mounted underneath—a countertop made of tile, marble, or laminated plastic.

Whatever style you choose, the plumbing is likely to be the same.

In most cases, you will be able to connect the new basin without modifying existing supply and drain stub-outs.

If you are prepared to relocate the plumbing, you will be able to include a larger or different type of washbasin. If you wish to install two basins in a vanity that currently has only one, you can usually install the two new washbasins from the existing stub-outs.

TYPES OF WASHBASINS

Washbasins come in a surprising variety of types and shapes. There are freestanding sinks on pedestals, sinks that hang from the wall, sinks that set in a hole in a countertop, and sinks that are molded into the countertop.

Molded: This style is made almost exclusively in cultured marble, with the sink molded as part of the countertop. Fittings for drain, overflow, and supply are predrilled. Advantages include handsome appearance and trouble-free installation. The single disadvantage is the limited range of countertop sizes.

MATERIALS FOR WASHBASINS

Material	Advantages	Disadvantages
Vitreous china	Easy to clean Scratch and chip resistant Acid and stain resistant Large assortment of colors	Heavy
Enameled cast iron	Easy to clean Scratch and chip resistant Large assortment of colors Tougher than china	Heavy Expensive
Enameled pressed steel	Easy to clean Lightweight Low cost Large assortment of colors	Prone to chipping Prone to rust
Cultured marble	Easy to clean Warm to touch Easy to install	Scratches (can be buffed) Stains
Hand-painted china, pottery	Unique shapes Very decorative	Very expensive Prone to chipping

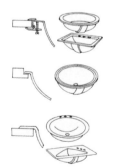

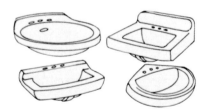

Inset: A *self-rimming* sink is set into a cutout in a custom countertop and is suspended by its rim. The rim seals to the countertop with plumber's putty or white adhesive caulk. *Flush-mount* sinks hang from a separate metal rim. *Recessed* sinks are used with tile countertops. The sink sets on a plywood countertop base, and the tile is applied flush with the sink.

Wall-Mounted: Where space is tight and vanity drawers are not required, the wall-mounted sink provides a simple and inexpensive solution. The sink slips down over a metal bracket, which is firmly screwed to the wall studs, leaving clear floor area beneath. Disadvantages are the lack of vanity storage space and the aesthetic impact of the visible drain and supply plumbing.

Pedestal: To some homeowners, the pedestal is old-fashioned; to others, its style is ultramodern. Both are right: Pedestals were stylish early in this century, neatly hiding drain and supply lines. Modern consumers find that a pedestal increases the sense of space in a small bathroom. A pedestal provides no storage, but all of the plumbing is concealed, giving it a very clean look.

INSTALLING A NEW BASIN

THE SUPPLY

First, make sure the arrangement of basin holes will fit your installation with a minimum number of modifications (or none at all). Most basins have three holes to accommodate hot water, cold water, and a drain assembly. Depending on the type of faucet, the outer holes are spaced 4 inches or 8 inches on-center.

Put plumber's putty around the base of the faucet before you set it in place. Turn the basin upside down. Under the basin, thread the washers and retaining nuts onto the faucet stems. Be careful not to crack or chip the basin when you tighten the fasteners. Connect the water supply tubes.

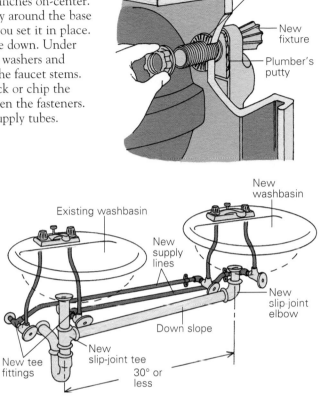

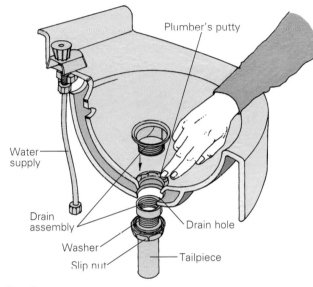

THE DRAIN

To install the drain and tailpiece, apply a bead of plumber's putty to the rim of the drain hole. Insert the drain into the hole from the top of the basin and screw the tailpiece onto it from below. If necessary, jam a block of wood into the drain fitting to hold it steady while you tighten. If you are installing a pop-up drain assembly, the tailpiece will be a tee. Tighten it so the side outlet aims straight back.

SETTING THE SINK IN PLACE

If you are installing a self-rimming or recessed basin, run another bead of putty around the rim of the cutout. Set the basin into the cutout; its weight will hold it in place. If you are installing a flush-mount sink, support it from beneath and slide six to 12 mounting clips under the rim so they are evenly spaced, then tighten them.

UNDER-SINK HOOKUP

Hook up the plumbing under the sink. Place nuts and washers or ferrules on the supply tubes and bend the tubes gently so you can to insert them straight into the outlets on top of the angle stops. Flexible, braided stainless steel or plastic supply tubes make this job easier. Tighten the nuts onto the stops.

Install the linkage mechanism for the pop-up assembly, adjusting the height of the clevis (the V-shaped clamp) on the control rod so that the drain plug will rise far enough when you push down the plunger.

Attach the P-trap by inserting its outlet end into the stub-out (after first sliding an escutcheon over the stub-out). Slide both washers and nuts onto the drainpipe. Don't tighten the nuts yet. Slide a nut and washer onto the tailpiece and install the P-trap. When all the pieces align, tighten them as far as you can by hand, then use a wrench to make another quarter turn.

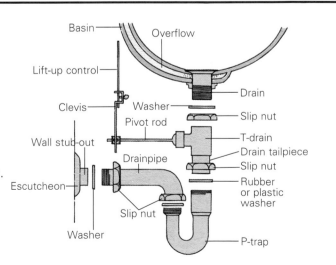

WASHING MACHINES

WASHING MACHINE BASICS

Replacing a washing machine requires few skills. Installing one in a new location requires only the most basic wiring and plumbing techniques. The most difficult task is usually finding a convenient location.

When choosing the location, weigh the benefits of convenience against the annoyance of noise and clutter. The ideal is a separate utility room close to the bedroom, but you may find space in a bathroom, hallway, or the kitchen, as long as a drain line and vent are close at hand.

Allow a space approximately 5½ feet wide for a full-sized washer and dryer pair. Use stacked units between 24 to 30 inches wide in small spaces.

BUYING NEW APPLIANCES

Start planning your new washer purchase long before you need it so you will have time to read consumer magazine ratings and shop for the best price. Be careful of all the bells and whistles on the fancy models; make sure you really need them.

Consider the energy consumption and reliability along with the initial cost. You may find that payback energy savings is worth the higher initial cost—several times over. Also check to see if the purchase price includes delivery and installation. Often, stores will throw in free delivery if that is what it takes to make the sale.

Finally, make sure the new unit will fit the available space and that it will pass through all doorways to the laundry room.

FEATURES TO LOOK FOR

Cycles: Nearly all washers have regular, permanent press, and soak or pre-wash cycles. Some also offer a heavy soil cycle that lengthens the wash cycle.

The simplest washers have a continuous dial labeled "heavy soil-regular-delicate." This feature simply adjusts the length of the wash time to the severity of the job. You still have to select the wash and rinse temperatures and the wash and spin speeds.

Wash and Spin Speed: This control lets you slow the wash speed down for delicate fabrics, which might be damaged by too violent agitation, and the spin speed for permanent press fabrics when you don't want wrinkles that form during rapid spinning.

Temperature: Most washers offer hot, warm, and cold washing, and warm and cold rinsing.

Water Level: There is no reason to use a full load of water for a half load of laundry. This control allows you to set the water level to high, medium, or low.

ENERGY SAVING

How you use hot water in your clothes washer has a tremendous effect on its energy consumption:

■ For normal washes, use warm water for wash and cold for rinse. If your water is soft and the clothes not very dirty, see if a cold/cold setting will work as well.

■ Pretreat stains and greasy spots to avoid using a hot wash.

■ Save up your laundry until you can do full-size loads. Full loads use less water per pound of laundry than small loads.

CODE REQUIREMENTS: WASHING MACHINES

Drain: The discharge from a clothes washer must have an air break to prevent back-siphoning of waste water. This break may be accomplished by discharging either into a laundry tub or into a vertical standpipe.

Electrical: Unlike an electric clothes dryer, a clothes washer does not need a separate circuit. Conventionally, a washer and a gas dryer use the same 110-volt, 20-amp circuit.

SUDS SAVER

Watch out for the suds! Detergent manufacturers are packing more power into their products every year. Without knowing it, you are probably using two to four times the amount of detergent you need, making rinsing that much more difficult. Cut the amount in half and see if your clothes get just as clean.

UPSTAIRS LAUNDRY

Although the washer and dryer often end up in the basement, there may be better locations, such as upstairs where most of the dirty laundry is generated. If you are going to locate your washer upstairs, however, install an overflow drip pan under the washer. A single overflow could damage the ceiling below, requiring either repainting or expensive replacement.

TROUBLESHOOTING

First, make sure the hose bibbs (faucets) are turned on all the way. Also, remove the hoses from the back of the machine to see if the inlet filter screens are clogged. If they are not, unplug the machine and locate the solenoid valve—the electric valve where the hoses connect to the machine. With the electricity off, label the wires and terminals and then pull the wires off the terminals. Using a volt-ohmmeter, measure the resistance between the upper pair of terminals, then the lower pair. If a resistance is less than 10 or more than 1,000 ohms, the solenoid valve is defective.

If the solenoid tests OK, check the water temperature switch. It usually has three terminals: one ground, one for the wire to the cold water solenoid, and one for the wire to the hot-water solenoid. Attach one probe of your voltmeter to the ground terminal. With the unit plugged in (but not running), turn the switch to "cold," and touch the second probe of the

INSTALLING A WASHING MACHINE

Plumbing for a clothes washer includes a 2-inch-diameter drain line and hot and cold supply lines. The 2-inch standpipe for the drain should be 33 to 36 inches tall and have a trap 8 to 16 inches above the floor. (Or, you can discharge the washer into a laundry tub). The drainpipe should be vented within 5 feet of the trap so—unless you want to run a new vent loop—you must locate the washer close to an existing vent.

The supply stops should be 33 to 42 inches above the floor, and 8 to 18 inches apart. Local codes also may require air chambers or shock absorbers on the stops to prevent water hammer.

Prefabricated laundry boxes are available that include the hose bibbs and drain inlet in one tidy package that you nail between two studs. Some boxes even include electrical receptacles. Just run the wiring and water lines to this box and after it is in place, have them inspected, then cover with wallboard.

To hook up the washer, clamp the drain hose onto the outlet at the bottom of the machine and insert the J-bend into the standpipe or over the rim of the tub. Then screw the hot and cold water hoses onto the washer inlets and onto the hose bibbs. Each hose should include a fine-mesh screen filter where it attaches to the hose bibb. The screen prevents sand from ruining the washer's electric valves.

To complete the installation, plug the washer cord into a grounded 120-volt laundry receptacle. If your dryer is gas, the washer and dryer can share the same duplex laundry outlet.

meter to the cold water terminal. The meter should read 110 volts AC. Do the same for the hot water side. This time the meter should read 0 volts. If not, replace the temperature switch.

The timer is the only other switch that might be causing the problem. This is hard to test; call a professional.

WATER WON'T SHUT OFF

First, pull the power cord. If water continues to run into the machine, the problem is the mixing valve where the

hoses are connected. Replace it.

If water stops flowing when you pull the cord, the problem may be the timer. Plug in the machine and advance the timer knob. If the water stops, the timer is bad and should be replaced. If not, the problem is most likely the water level switch. Call a professional.

WATER WON'T DRAIN

Unplug the machine and check the drain hose to see if it is clogged. Be

careful; it will be full of water. If the hose is not clogged, plug the machine back in and turn the timer to "spin." If the machine still does not drain, turn it off and bail out all the water. Refill it, turn it on, and turn the timer to "spin." If it still does not drain, the problem is the water pump. Call a professional.

WATER HEATERS

REPLACE OR UPGRADE?

ALSO SEE...
Electrical Systems:
Pages 110–115
Insulation:
Pages 186–193
Plumbing:
Pages 256–263
Solar Water Heaters:
Pages 322–323
Wire:
Pages 442–445

It is always easier to replace an old heater with an exact replacement, but there may be reasons for switching.

■ Your teenagers have come of age, increasing the demand for hot water.

■ You're relocating the water heater due to extensive remodeling.

■ Your old heater may be in violation of the code. For instance, a gas heater in a garage usually is required to be installed on a platform 18 inches above the floor. See the various Code Requirements list, *below.*

■ You may wish to install a more efficient water heater to save on your energy bills.

In warm, sunny climates a solar system is a good choice for lowering your hot water costs. Another warm-climate energy saver is a heat-pump water heater. It operates by electricity, but uses only half as much as conventional electric heaters.

An option for any climate is a tankless water heater—very popular in Europe and Japan. Instead of heating water and storing it in a tank, it only heats water as it is needed. Gas models can produce hot water as quickly as you need it; electric models are limited in flow rate.

All of these alternatives are more expensive than ordinary gas and electric heaters, but may pay for themselves within just a few years. Have the dealers prepare written estimates of your savings and years to payback.

HOW WATER HEATERS WORK

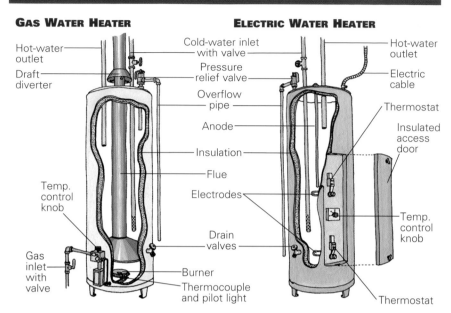

GAS WATER HEATER — Hot-water outlet, Draft diverter, Temp. control knob, Gas inlet with valve

ELECTRIC WATER HEATER — Cold-water inlet with valve, Pressure relief valve, Overflow pipe, Anode, Insulation, Flue, Electrodes, Drain valves, Burner, Thermocouple and pilot light, Hot-water outlet, Electric cable, Thermostat, Insulated access door, Temp. control knob, Thermostat

WATER HEATER VALVES

TEMPERATURE/PRESSURE RELIEF VALVE

Most building codes require a temperature/pressure relief valve (TPRV) on a water heater to prevent the tank from overheating. The valve must connect to a drainpipe that terminates no more than 8 inches above the ground.

You can reuse the old valve as long as it works. To check, pull up or push down on the handle, depending on the style. If it works, water will gush out.

DRAIN VALVE

The drain valve is located at the base of the water heater, and has a male threaded hose connection. Drain off a gallon or so every few months to remove sediment. The hose connection is convenient when you want to empty the tank and you don't have a nearby floor drain.

CODE REQUIREMENTS: WATER HEATERS

Prohibited Locations: Except for direct-vent heaters, water heaters which depend on the combustion of fuel (gas and oil heaters) shall not be located in sleeping rooms, bathrooms, clothes closets, or in confined spaces opening into bathrooms or bedrooms.

Garage Location: All appliances (including water heaters) located in a garage must be protected from impact by automobiles and must have their igniters and switches at least 18 inches above the floor.
Wiring: All electric water heaters must be on a dedicated circuit.

Relief Valves: Equipment for heating or storing hot water must be protected by:
■ a separate pressure-relief valve and a separate temperature-relief valve, or
■ a combination pressure- and temperature-relief valve.

420

INSTALLING A NEW WATER HEATER

BUYING THE HEATER

When choosing a water heater, look on the name plate for the following specifications:

- Capacity (usually listed as 30, 40, or 50 gallons)
- BTUH input rating (gas only)
- Volts, amps, and/or watts (for electric water heaters only)
- Recovery rate (gallons per hour)
- Dimensions (especially height)

What you won't find on the name plate is the warranty period. As a rule of thumb, but with amazing consistency, a water heater will last just a year or two beyond its warranty. As a consumer, consider the duration of the warranty to be the reliable service life of the heater.

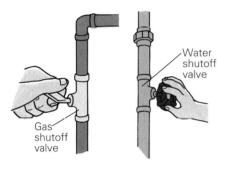

1 Turn off the electricity (electric heaters) or gas (gas heaters). Shut off water supply.

2 Drain the water from the tank (a garden hose is convenient, provided you have a place to discharge it).

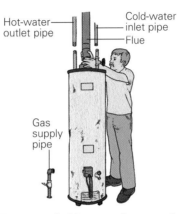

3 Disconnect all of the pipes and wires attached to the old heater. On a gas unit, disconnect the draft-diverter collar and flue pipe. Remove the old heater.

4 Set the new heater in place. Connect the flue pipe and draft-diverter collar, if gas. Connect the water lines, using flexible tubes if necessary. Connect the gas supply or the electric cable.

5 Turn on a hot water faucet upstairs. Fill the water tank until water flows from the open faucet, then restore power. Apply soapy water to any gas connections to check for gas leaks and get them stopped before lighting the gas.

TROUBLESHOOTING WATER HEATERS

Symptom	Problem	Solution
Pipes leaking	Loose or corroded fitting	Tighten the pipe fittings. If this slows the leak but doesn't stop it, replace fitting.
Wet supply pipe	Condensation of humid air	Insulate the cold water pipe with foam-jacket insulation from the main shutoff valve to the heater. (Also insulate at least the first 5 feet of the hot water pipe.)
Water too hot	Thermostat set too high	Adjust the thermostat; if adjustment makes no difference, replace the thermostat.
Water too cool	Thermostat set too low	Adjust the thermostat; if adjustment makes no difference, replace the thermostat.
No hot water (electric)	Circuit breaker tripped	Reset circuit breaker. If it trips again, call electrician or plumber.
	Thermostat broken	Turn thermostat up. If there is at least 110 volts coming into the thermostat, but no voltage to the heating element, replace the thermostat.
	Element burned out	Turn off power, remove wires to element, and measure for continuity across the element terminals. If none, replace the element.
No hot water (gas)	Pilot light out	Relight pilot light.
	Gas supply off	Check all valves from main through heater.
	Temperature control broken	Call for gas service.
Not enough hot water (gas)	Burner ports clogged	Clear burner ports with the end of a paper clip.
Gas smell (gas)	Gas leak	Turn off the main gas supply valve and open windows until smell disappears. Coat gas pipes with soapy water and turn on gas. Bubbles indicate a leak.

SOURCES OF WATER

ALSO SEE...
Electrical Systems:
Pages 110–115
Insulation:
Pages 186–193
Plumbing:
Pages 256–263
Solar Water Heaters:
Pages 322–323
Wire:
Pages 442–445

The water you drink is from one of two sources:
■ Surface water, such as a lake, pond, river, or reservoir.
■ Ground water, brought to the surface by a well.

SURFACE WATER

Surface water is exposed to contaminants, such as animal waste, insecticides, pesticides, industrial wastes and other organic materials, so it usually contains pollutants that require purification. It doesn't, however, have enough mineral content to require softening.

GROUND WATER

The source of ground water is rain that soaks into the ground, and the longer and deeper the water has been underground, the less likely it is to be polluted. On the other hand, a long stay gives it plenty of time to dissolve minerals and become "hard."

WATER TESTS

If you are on "city water" you can obtain test results from your water district. If you have your own well, however, you are responsible for having your water tested. There are generally two levels:
1. Most companies that sell water conditioners and filters will test your water for free or for a nominal amount. These tests basically cover the problems their equipment will treat: hardness, acidity, red and brown stains (iron), cloudiness (solids), and odors.
2. Water testing laboratories can perform a more complete analysis, including tests for coliform bacteria. If you have never had a complete test of your water, you should. If you can't find a laboratory to do the analysis, call your state health department.

WHAT CAN BE TREATED?

The chart below shows typical water problems and their treatments. No matter what the problem, companies which specialize in water treatment can solve it.

It makes no sense, however, to treat the water you put on your lawn or garden, and you really don't care what the water in your toilet or tub tastes like. Most of the treatments either eventually clog a filter or use up a replaceable chemical. Therefore, never treat more water than you have to. Taste filters are generally located at the point of use—the kitchen sink, for example. Mineral-removing equipment is usually located at the point of entry of your water supply, with a bypass just for hose bibbs.

WATER TREATMENTS

Problem or Symptom	Water Softener	Limestone Neutralizer	Sediment Filter	Chlorine Feeder	Carbon Filter	Reverse Osmosis	Distiller	Chemical Filter
Soap residue hard to rinse	■							
Scale buildup in pipes, water heater	■							
Metallic taste (iron, manganese, copper)	■			■		■	■	
Color (red, brown, or black sediment)	■			■	■			
Corrosion (green or red-brown stains)		■						
Turbidity (cloudy water)			■					
Bad smell (rotten eggs or other)					■			
Bacteria				■				
Salty water, brackish						■	■	
Trichloroethylene, trihalomethane								■

HARD WATER

WHAT IS HARD WATER?

Hard water is the most common problem of all. Water is "hard" when it contains more than 1 grain (1/7,000 of a pound) per gallon of dissolved calcium, manganese, and magnesium. What harm are these minerals? For some uses, such as watering your lawn, they don't cause problems. But for any use involving soap or detergent—bathing, washing dishes and clothes, shaving—hard-water minerals react with soap to form a scum that is difficult to remove from dishes, appliances, and skin and hair.

When hard water is heated the problem gets worse. Heated minerals crystallize into "scale," which may plug pipes and create sediment in hot water heaters, eventually requiring repair or replacement.

WATER SOFTENERS

The most common type of water softener is an ion exchange unit. It uses common salt (sodium chloride) to recharge resin beads that exchange minerals for sodium. As the hard water passes around the beads, the mineral ions exchange with sodium ions (ion exchange).

When the resin has no sodium ions left, it can soften no more water. It is then recharged by back-flushing with a salt brine, held in reserve in a separate tank. The sodium ions force the mineral ions off the resin beads; then the excess sodium is rinsed away, and the resin is ready to go again. The softening equipment automatically backflushes, either on a timer schedule, after a measured amount of water usage, or after an electric sensor detects the need.

IRON

If you have reddish-brown stains in your sinks and toilet bowls, you have iron in your water. Iron can be present in water in four forms: soluble (clear-water), oxidized (red-water), colloidal, and bacterial (organic-bound). The first two are simple to treat.

Clear-Water Iron: Water from deep wells often contains dissolved iron that has not had a chance to oxidize. When drawn from the tap it is clear, but it quickly reacts with oxygen in the air and turns red. This form of iron is, fortunately, removed by common household water softeners.

Red-Water Iron: Surface water often appears to be tinted red from the presence of iron oxide. The iron oxide particles can be filtered.

Colloidal and Bacteria: Both of these forms can be treated by first chlorinating, then filtering.

SMELLS

MUSTY SMELL

Organic materials in the water can produce minor musty odors. Remove these smells with point-of-use carbon filters that attach directly to faucets. Although effective, these types of filters also trap organic materials and

can become a breeding place for bacteria. Therefore, it is a good idea to replace the cartridges frequently.

ROTTEN-EGG SMELL

This is the smell of hydrogen sulfide, produced by either the decomposition

of underground organic materials, or by sulfates reacting with the magnesium anode in a water heater (evidenced by the smell being only in the hot water).

The solution in the first case is a carbon filter; in the second to replace the anode from the water heater.

EQUIPMENT

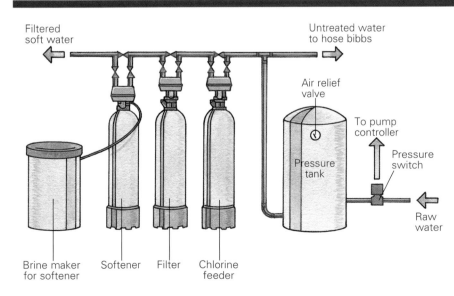

Filtered
soft water

Untreated water
to hose bibbs

Air relief
valve

To pump
controller

Pressure
switch

Pressure
tank

Raw
water

Brine maker
for softener

Softener

Filter

Chlorine
feeder

The illustration shows a typical multi-problem water treatment setup. The equipment and the problems treated include:

Unit	Problem Treated
Chlorine feeder	Bacteria, colloidal and bacterial iron
Filter	Cloudiness, red-water iron
Softener	Hardness, soluble iron

Equipment such as this can be either rented and serviced by a water treatment company, or purchased and maintained by the homeowner.

Weather Stripping

WEATHER-STRIP MATERIALS

In any building, air infiltration can be traced to two types of cracks—fixed and moveable.

■ Fixed cracks may open and close slightly with changes in humidity, but their movement is slight. Examples include joints between dissimilar building materials and joints between vertical and horizontal finish. Such cracks can be permanently sealed with flexible caulk.

■ Moveable cracks, such as those around window sash and doors, are sealed with weather stripping.

Weather stripping is simple to install and one of the most cost-effective home improvements you can make. Besides reducing the cost of heating and cooling, weather stripping keeps out dirt, noise, and moisture. It also absorbs some of the shock when you close a window or door, keeps windows and doors from rattling in high winds, and cuts down on drafts.

You don't need a professional to tell you whether a window or door needs weather stripping. A candle that flickers when held to the joint also indicates a draft.

Install weather stripping on all offending doors and windows. And don't forget doors leading to enclosed but unheated spaces, such as the garage, porch, basement, or attic. Their leakage may not be as dramatic, but it is well worth stopping.

Weather stripping is available in many forms. Of all the characteristics to consider, effectiveness should be number one, followed closely by longevity.

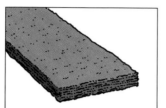

Felt: Least effective. Lasts a year. Attaches with glue or staples. The door or window presses against it. Keep it dry; don't paint it.

Reinforced Felt: An aluminum band holds and preserves the felt. Same characteristics as plain felt, but lasts a little longer.

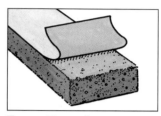

Foam Tape: Low to medium effectiveness. Lasts up to two years. Usually a urethane or vinyl strip. A temporary, but quick fix.

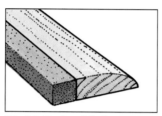

Rigid Strip: Medium effectiveness. Lasts one to two years. A wood or metal strip with a foam edge. Best for door jambs; it does not withstand friction. Install with brads.

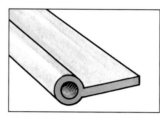

Tubular Gasket: Medium effectiveness. Lasts two to five years. Withstands friction. Window or door compresses it to form a seal. Some types stick on. Others are fastened with brads.

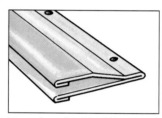

Tension Strip: Most effective if installed right. Plastic lasts one to two years; metal lasts 10 years or more. Vinyl strips with adhesive backs come in colors. Fasten with brads.

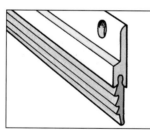

Door Sweep: Least effective. Lasts two to five years. Some automatically lift to clear carpet. All can be easily adjusted.

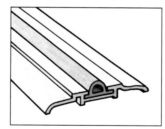

Gasket Threshold: Very effective. Lasts one to two years. Vinyl insert is replaceable. The door requires no new attachments.

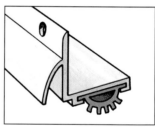

Door Shoe: Very effective. Lasts three to five years. Vinyl insert replaceable. Door must be removed to install.

WEATHER STRIPS COMPARED

Type	Effectiveness	Life	Application
Felt	Low	1 year	Apply with staples
Metal-edged felt	Low	1–2 years	Apply with brads
Foam tape	Medium	1 year	Usually self-adhesive
Rigid strip	Medium	1–2 years	Apply with brads
Tubular gasket	Medium	2–5 years	Apply with brads
Tension strip (plastic)	Medium-high	2 years	Usually self-adhesive
Tension strip (metal)	High	5–10 years	Apply with brads

WEATHER STRIPPING DOORS

There are three common ways to weather strip a door:
- Compressing a material (such as a strip of foam) between the door and the door stop.
- Compressing a thin tubular material (such as a tubular gasket) which sticks out from the stop.
- Squeezing a springy material (such as tension strips) between the door edge and the casing.

Before installing any weather strip, make sure the door is stable so the cracks won't expand, rendering the strip ineffective. For example, tighten or replace the hinge screws on a loose door; if the door hangs unevenly, square it up by adjusting the hinges.

Tack up weather-stripping material loosely, then close the door to see if there is a conflict before fastening the weather stripping in place. Tubular gasket-type weather stripping is the exception—it should be installed with the door closed. Push the material

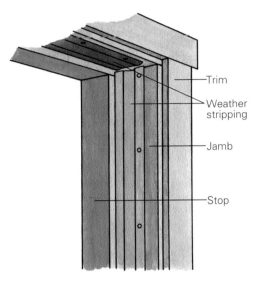
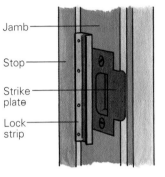

firmly against the door to seal all gaps, and fasten with tacks or small brads.

When installing any foam-pad weather stripping, choose a thickness or density that will compress enough

to allow the door to close snugly.

If you use tension strips, the open end of the "V" shape profile should always face the outdoors.

INSTALLING THRESHOLDS

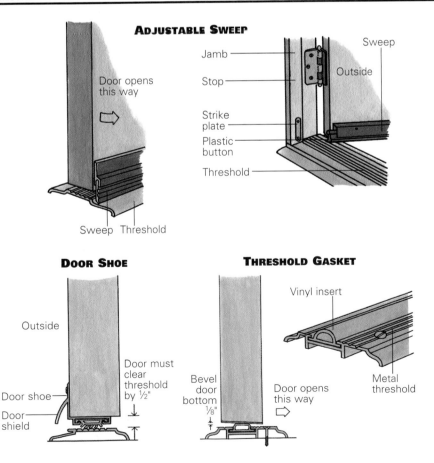

ADJUSTABLE SWEEP

Jamb
Stop
Strike plate
Plastic button
Threshold
Sweep
Outside

Door opens this way

Sweep Threshold

DOOR SHOE

Outside
Door shoe
Door shield

Door must clear threshold by ½"

THRESHOLD GASKET

Bevel door bottom ⅛"
Door opens this way
Vinyl insert
Metal threshold

The widest crack around a door (and, therefore, the one that lets in the most air) is usually at the bottom, or threshold. There are three types of threshold weather stripping:
- Door sweep
- Gasket
- Door shoe

To install a door sweep, screw it to the door near the bottom edge. Then adjust it up or down until it just grazes the threshold. Some models have retractable sweeps that raise automatically when the door opens.

Gasket thresholds generally require trimming the door. Close the door and mark the top edge of the gasket. Scribe the cutting line, then make a ⅛-inch bevel cut. Screw the threshold into the floor so the door aligns over the center of the gasket.

To install a door shoe, close the door and scribe a line ½ inch above the threshold. Remove and trim the door. Cut the shoe to length and screw it to the bottom of the door.

▶

WEATHER STRIPPING WINDOWS

TESTING FOR AIR LEAKS

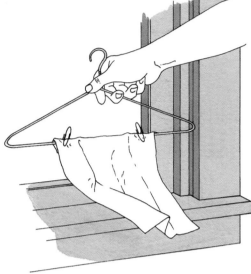

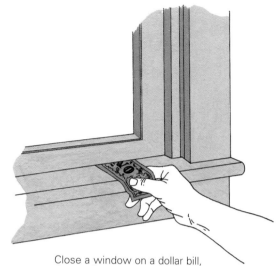

Close a window on a dollar bill,
then pull to test weather stripping

Hold clipped tissue near windows
and doors to check for drafts

WOOD SLIDING WINDOWS

Seal wood sliding windows exactly
as if they were double-hung windows
installed on their sides. Attach a
tension strip to the top channel. If
only one side of the window opens,
caulk the edges of the fixed panel,
then attach the tension strips to the
casing channels or to the sides of the
window panels, whichever looks better.
Where the two panels overlap, attach
a tension strip between them. Or
attach a tubular gasket to the edge
of the outside panel so it presses
against the inside panel when the
window is closed.

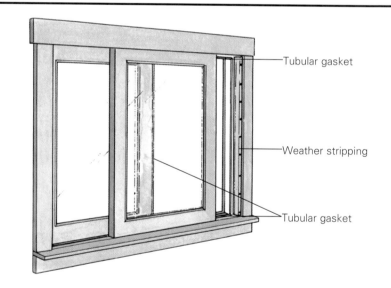

Tubular gasket

Weather stripping

Tubular gasket

CASEMENT WINDOWS

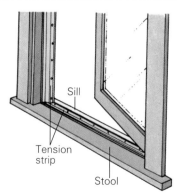

Sill

Tension
strip

Stool

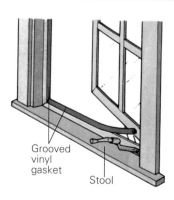

Grooved
vinyl
gasket

Stool

Wood: Attach a tension strip to the
frame in a place where the window will
cover it when closed. Face the opening
of the V toward the stop.

A tubular gasket attached to the
face of the stop would create a snug fit,
but would be very visible.

Metal: A vinyl gasket, made for
casement windows, has a groove down
the middle that fits over the edge of
the metal window frame. If necessary,
attach it with a rubber or vinyl
cement. Don't use the gasket on the
hinge side. Instead, use an adhesive
tubular gasket.

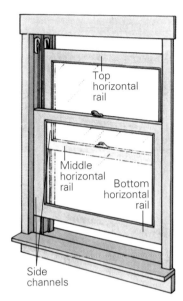

Top
horizontal
rail

Middle
horizontal
rail

Bottom
horizontal
rail

Side
channels

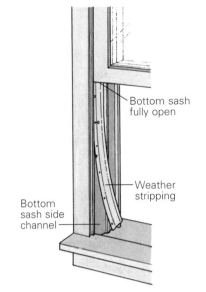

Bottom sash
fully open

Weather
stripping

Bottom
sash side
channel

Top
sash side
channel

Weather
stripping

Sash
cord

Top sash
fully open

1 Measure strips to fit both side channels and the horizontal rails at the top, middle, and bottom. One strip is sufficient where the top and bottom sashes overlap.

2 Open the bottom sash completely. Attach a strip in each channel, the V opening outward, so it extends 2 inches above the bottom of the sash. Attach the bottom strip to either the sill or the bottom edge of the sash.

3 Lower both sashes and place strips in the side channels of the top sash. The strips should extend 2 inches below the bottom edge of the top sash when it is closed. Don't cover the pulleys.

4 With the top sash still open, attach a strip to the top channel or to the top of the sash. You must cut the strip flush with the edges of the sash, so the corners won't interfere. Do the same on the bottom of the lower sash.

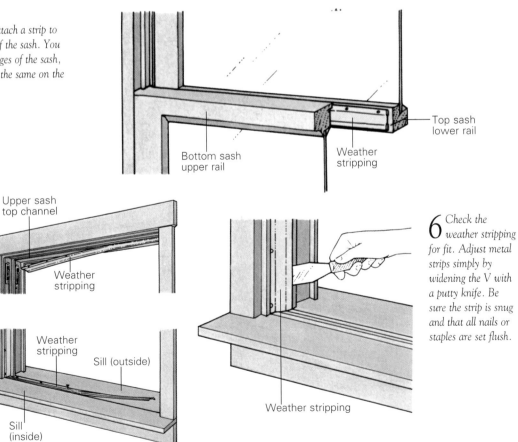

Bottom sash
upper rail

Weather
stripping

Top sash
lower rail

5 Attach the last strip between the rails of both sashes where they overlap. It will be visible from the inside of the house when the window is open if you attach the strip to the bottom rail of the top sash. It will be visible from the outside when the window is open if you attach it to the top rail of the bottom sash. Install the open end of the "V" shape to the outside in either case.

Upper sash
top channel

Weather
stripping

Weather
stripping

Sill (outside)

Sill
(inside)

Weather stripping

6 Check the weather stripping for fit. Adjust metal strips simply by widening the V with a putty knife. Be sure the strip is snug and that all nails or staples are set flush.

Window Treatments

HARD-WORKING PROTECTION AND BEAUTY

ALSO SEE...
Adhesives:
Pages 8–9
Cooling:
Pages 66–69
Insulation:
Pages 186–193
Joinery:
Pages 194–199
Windows:
Pages 432–441

We often think of the window coverings as part of a room's decor, but they also have practical functions. They provide privacy and control the amount of glare and sunlight that a room receives. Some window treatments have thermal insulating properties that help reduce heat gain in the summer and prevent heat loss in the winter. When choosing window coverings, consider thermal characteristics in addition to cost, appearance, and ease of operation.

Blinds, shades, and draperies are the most common window coverings. Shutters, screens, films, and special coatings are additional options. Most window treatments are found at home-improvement centers. Specialty stores, such as furniture stores, drapery makers, and interior design services, also offer window coverings.

BLINDS

Blinds come in many styles—classic venetian blinds, miniblinds, microblinds, roll-up blinds, and pleated blinds. They perform two functions admirably—privacy and light control. Open blinds admit bright light but without harsh glare. However, blinds do little to decrease winter heat loss. They neither increase a window's R-value, nor tighten the window against air leakage.

Blinds are slightly more effective in summer. Although their insulating value is negligible, they can reflect some heat if they are light in color. If you want dark-colored blinds, maximize their heat-reduction value by ordering duplex blinds—they feature a reflective color on the outside.

The blades of vertical blinds can be pulled aside like draperies. They can be made to any length and work especially well on sliding glass doors.

Clean blinds by dusting or vacuuming. Some vacuum cleaners have special attachments designed specifically for cleaning blinds. If blinds don't have tapes, clean the blades by dipping them in a bathtub filled with water and ammonia.

REPAIRING BLINDS

Replace worn tapes and cords by untying the cord at the bottom, sliding out all the slats, threading new tape, and returning the slats. Attach a new lift cord to the old one and pull it through the mechanism into position.

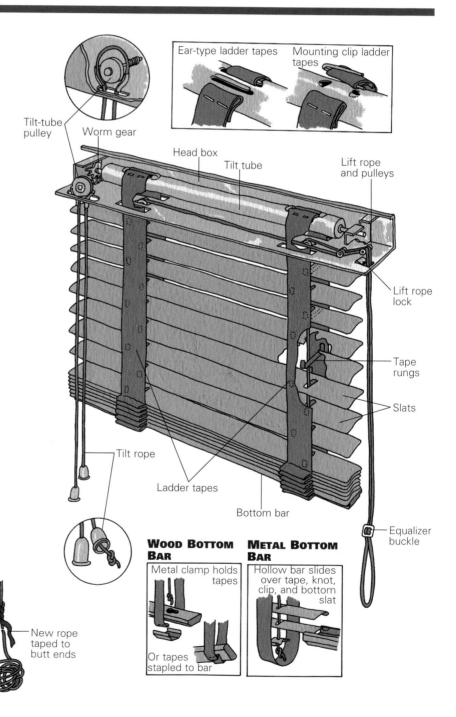

Ear-type ladder tapes

Mounting clip ladder tapes

Tilt-tube pulley

Worm gear

Head box

Tilt tube

Lift rope and pulleys

Lift rope lock

Tape rungs

Slats

Tilt rope

Ladder tapes

Bottom bar

Equalizer buckle

Cut

New rope taped to butt ends

WOOD BOTTOM BAR
Metal clamp holds tapes

Or tapes stapled to bar

METAL BOTTOM BAR
Hollow bar slides over tape, knot, clip, and bottom slat

SHADES

Roller shades provide privacy and light control. When rolled up, they are compact enough to be hidden behind curtains, drapes, or a valance.

Insulating fabrics turn these shades into energy savers. Some use quilted fabrics with a core of fiberglass to maximize heat retention in the winter. Others use aluminized polyester, which works like a one-way mirror, reflecting light and heat to enhance summer cooling. Still others achieve high R-value with multiple layers.

Insulating shades lose much of their effectiveness if the edges do not fit closely to the window jamb. Use self-sticking fasteners or a permanent track mounted in the window jambs to prevent air flow around the shades.

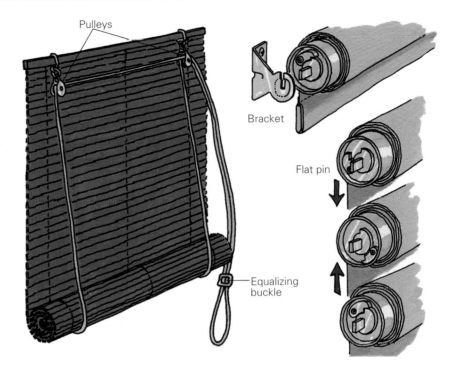

Pulleys

Bracket

Flat pin

Equalizing buckle

DRAPES AND CURTAINS

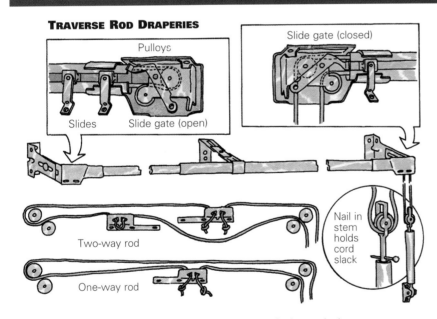

TRAVERSE ROD DRAPERIES

Pulleys

Slides   Slide gate (open)

Slide gate (closed)

Nail in stem holds cord slack

Two-way rod

One-way rod

opening and over the catch hook. Both slides should now move together.

If a loose cord on the tension pulley on the floor causes trouble, the cord needs to be tightened. Pull the stem of the pulley up 2 or more inches and hold it with either its built-in latch or by inserting a nail through the hole in the stem. Pull the rope out on the right side of the control slide gate and take up the slack in the cord with a knot. Snip off the excess cord and remove the nail or latch to restore the tension.

Draperies and curtains are decorative focal points, so you will naturally find them in a wide range of styles, colors, and fabrics. They vary widely in their ability to control sunlight or insulate against heat gain and loss, however. The choice of rods is simpler—there are two basic styles: fixed and traverse.

Traverse rods can develop problems with the slides and pulleys. To restring the cord, study the drawings of one-way and two-way rods. The one-way is straightforward; the two-way requires a loop through a second slide control.

If only one side of your draperies moves, the cord has probably come off the catch hook on a slide control and needs to be readjusted and attached. To readjust the cords, pull them to open the curtains and bring the slide control to the edge of the rod. Holding the cord so it won't move, push the other slide control to the other end of the rod. Loop the cord through the

Window Treatment Winter R-Values	
Treatment	**R-value**
None, SG* glass	0.9
None, SG acrylic	1.0
None, DG** glass	1.9
SG, plus inside storm	2.0
LowE, DG glass	3.9
Heat Mirror, DG glass	4.3
DG with quilted shade	4.4
DG with foam shutter	5–7

*SG: Single-glazed   ** DG: Double-glazed

INTERIOR STORM WINDOWS

If you hate the appearance of exterior storm windows, don't have the money for new energy-efficient replacement windows, yet can't stand the cold drafts blowing in around your old windows, consider interior storm windows.

They are a compromise between new windows and installing clear plastic wrap. A typical interior storm window kit consists of a clear acrylic panel and trim pieces, all of which you cut to fit the interior casings of your window.

Since interior storms can't be opened, you'll need to remove them during the summer months for ventilation. Most have side trim which snaps open, making removal and reinstallation easy.

INSTALLATION

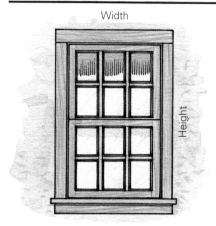

Width

Height

1 *Measure your window. Most kits assume you will be installing the panel directly to the casings. If that is the case, measure the width of the head casing and the height from the top of the head casing to the sill. From these dimensions, subtract an allowance for the storm's side trim.*

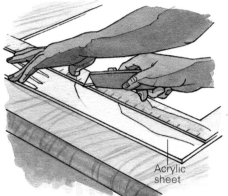

Acrylic sheet

2 *Mark and cut the acrylic panel. Using a straightedge and a sharp utility knife, score the panel firmly, then snap it along the score over the edge of a table.*

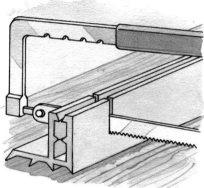

3 *Cut the two side trim pieces, then the head trim piece. Make the cuts with either a hack saw or a miter saw.*

Self-adhesive backing

4 *Assemble the panel, side trim, and top trim, then measure the distance between the trim at the bottom of the panel. Cut the sill trim piece to this length, and add to the assembly.*

5 *If the trim has a self-adhesive backing, remove it and carefully center the storm window on the window sill. Rotate the assembly up and press the trim against the side and head casings.*

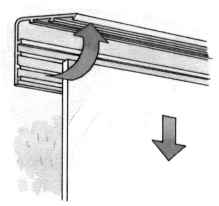

6 *To remove the panel, simply snap open the side and head trims. If the panel is acrylic, it will scratch very easily. Clean the panel with dishwashing detergent and paper towels, rubbing very gently. If the panel becomes cloudy from scratches, it can be polished clear again with auto-body rubbing compound and a lamb's wool buffing disk on a power drill.*

INSULATING INTERIOR SHUTTERS

How would you like to transform your cold north-facing windows into insulated walls next January? You can if you install insulating interior shutters. These shutters are:

- High in R-value
- Tight against drafts
- An effective vapor barrier
- Attractive from the inside
- Self-storing when open
- Rugged
- Durable
- Inexpensive

The shutters shown here can be made in an hour with simple hand tools. Make it a family weekend project with children picking the fabrics for their own rooms.

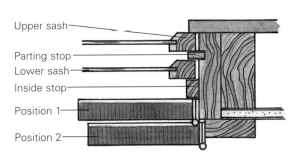

Upper sash
Parting stop
Lower sash
Inside stop
Position 1
Position 2

MATERIALS

- Thermoply®—⅛-inch thick, 4×8 foot sheets of paperboard with foil facings that is used as structural sheathing in many areas:
- Decorative fabric or vinyl wall covering of your choice.
- 1×2 or 1×3 dry pine.

- ½-inch staples.
- Construction adhesive.
- ¾×2 butt hinges.
- ½- to ¾-inch wide self-adhesive foam weather strip.
- Pair of cabinet knobs.

ASSEMBLY

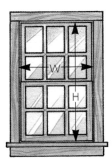

1 Measure the height and width between either the casings or jambs. Subtract ⅜ inch from both, then divide the width by two for your final dimensions.

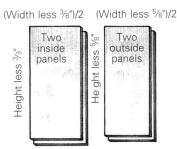

(Width less ⅜")/2   (Width less ⅝")/2

Height less ⅜"   Two inside panels

Height less ⅝"   Two outside panels

2 Cut two Thermoply panels to your final dimensions and two additional panels ¼ inch smaller in both dimensions.

1×2 strips

3 From 1×2 pine, cut two sets of frames to the same dimensions to form the frames. Butt and staple the joints together.

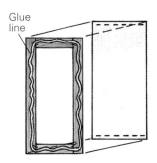

Glue line

4 Glue the thermoply panels onto the frames. Align the edges and fasten with ½-inch staples.

2"

5 Stretch fabric or wall covering around both frames. Staple it, leaving 1 inch of frame uncovered. Glue the smaller panel to the wood.

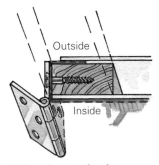

Outside

Inside

6 Screw loose-pin butt hinges to the shutter edges. Do not mortise the hinges into the frames.

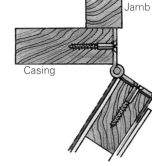

Jamb

Casing

7 Fasten the hinges to either the jamb or the edge of the casing.

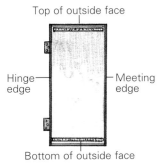

Top of outside face

Hinge edge   Meeting edge

Bottom of outside face

8 Apply weather stripping to the shutter's vertical and inside bottom edges. Install a wood strip on the sill to seal the bottom edge.

WINDOWS

WINDOW BASICS

Windows are a major component of any house. They are the primary source of all-important light and fresh air, yet they must seal tightly against cold and rain, and prevent heat from escaping during winter months.

Superior performance and durability are expected of any window that comes from a reliable manufacturer. Most home-improvement centers offer top-quality, brand-name windows that fulfill all expectations.

To a great extent, the frame determines the exterior appearance of a window. Windows with aluminum, bronze, or painted frames have a sleek, bold appearance. Wood and vinyl-clad window frames create a more conservative, substantial effect.

Inside, casings contribute to the architectural and decorative style of the room. They may be ornate moldings, slim strips of wood, or wide lumber.

The number of panes, as well as the size of the panes, will also affect the style. And, of course, given an unlimited budget, the sky is the limit in creating dramatic window walls.

Installing or replacing a window used to be a complex project requiring advanced carpentry knowledge and skills. Today's prehung window units make window installation a snap. Generally, all you have to do is frame the opening, level the window within the frame, and fasten the nailing flanges to the sheathing.

CODE REQUIREMENTS: WINDOWS

Windows Close to the Floor: Any window with an area of greater than 9 square feet—with the bottom edge less than 18 inches above the floor and top edge reaching more than 36 inches above the floor—must be of tempered glass or some other safety glass.

Exception: louvered windows and jalousies at least ³⁄₁₆ inch thick and no more than 48 inches long with smooth edges

Skylights: A skylight is any transparent or translucent glazing installed at a slope of 15 or more degrees from vertical. Glazings for skylights must be one of the following:

- laminated glass
- tempered glass
- heat-strengthened glass
- wired glass
- rigid plastic

Infiltration: The air infiltration rate of manufactured windows must not exceed 0.50 cfm per linear foot of crack when tested to ASTM E283 at a pressure differential (across the window) of 1.56 psf.

Testing and Certification: Manufactured windows must be tested and certified to comply with the following specifications:

Aluminum—AAMA 101
Wood—ANSI/NWWDA I.S.2
PVC—ASTM D409

FRAME MATERIALS

When you purchase windows, you will be confronted with a host of material choices. Of course, the glazing will be glass, but the frame may be:

- all wood
- solid vinyl (PVC)
- aluminum-clad wood exterior with wood interior
- vinyl-clad wood exterior with wood interior
- solid vinyl exterior with wood interior

Here are some things to keep in mind when making your choice:

- A wood exterior will require painting about every four years.
- The wood used in windows is generally a select grade and, whether painted or stained, can add warmth to any room.
- Solid vinyl, although less expensive and less attractive, generally performs as well and lasts as long as any other type.
- Make sure any window with aluminum in the frame has an effective thermal break to avoid winter condensation.

WINDOW DIMENSIONS

Just how large is a 3×5 window? Manufacturers specify four sets of dimensions for their products:

Unit Dimension is the size as it would appear on an architectural drawing of the house; that is, it includes the casings when they are supplied as part of the unit, but not when they are added later by the builder.

Rough Opening is the recommended size of the opening in the framing—generally about ½ inch larger than the width and height of the jambs. Knowing the rough opening ensures you'll get a window of the correct size.

Sash Size is the exact size of the sash; there can be more than one size sash in a window unit.

Glass Size is the size of the glazing in the sash. This is useful in calculating heat loss and solar gain.

FIXED WINDOWS COST LESS

Just because it's a window doesn't mean it has to open. If all you want is a lot of light and minimal heat loss at the lowest possible price, install fixed new or replacement glazings. Because millions are sold every year, the price per square foot is a third of windows that open. They come in three standard sizes: 28×76, 34×76, and 46×76. All are available as standard double-glazed (DG), DG with Low E, and DG with heat mirror.

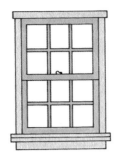

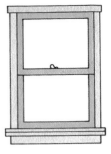

FIXED-PANE

These windows don't open, and they don't offer ventilation and easy cleaning, but their sealed edges prevent air infiltration. Window manufacturers offer framed, fixed-pane windows in a wide range of sizes to match their openable models. You also can get unframed units in any size from local glass suppliers.

Unless the windows are intended for a garage or barn or other unheated building, they should be dual-glazed for energy conservation. The best "factory-sealed" units use two separate sealants that adhere the panes to an interior metal frame. A chemical inside the frame absorbs moisture.

DOUBLE-HUNG

These are the classic windows if you are concerned with architectural style, but they provide less ventilation than casements because they open only half way, and they don't scoop the breeze. Double-hung windows with spring-loaded jambs are extremely tight barriers against air infiltration.

SINGLE-HUNG

These look like double-hung windows, but only the bottom sash opens. They are cheaper than double-hung windows.

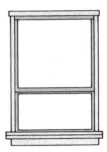

AWNING

The awning window and its upside-down cousin, the hopper window, swing like a casement window, but they are hinged on the top or bottom instead of on the side. Some swing inward, others outward. To keep the rain out, the awning window (top hinge) should swing out; the hopper (bottom hinge) should swing in.

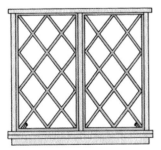

SLIDING

A "slider" is generally the least expensive in a manufacturer's line. It's similar to a double-hung window lying on its side—only half of the window opens at a time. The inner sash disassembles for easy cleaning.

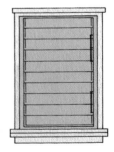

CASEMENT

The casement window resembles a small glass door. Most swing outward and feature interior screens, but you can special-order models that open inward. You also can specify the hinge side so that the window can be swung open to catch the prevailing breezes in your area.

Casement window pairs provide the best ventilation of all because either side can be opened to scoop the wind, no matter what direction it is blowing.

Older models swung on hinges; newer models pivot, which makes the entire exterior surface accessible from indoors for cleaning.

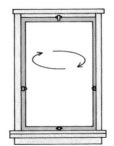

ROTATING

Either side can face inside or outside, so cleaning is simple. If it has a reflective coatings, you can pivot the glass to reflect heat inward or outward as the season demands. Some windows rotate 360 degrees, others partially.

JALOUSIE

Glass louvers form the panes of a jalousie window. Jalousie windows allow ventilation, but they have too many joints to seal well. They also present a security risk. Many codes no longer allow jalousie windows.

▶

REMOVING A WOOD WINDOW

Don't try to salvage any part of an old window, especially if it is a double-hung unit with counterweights. Replace the entire unit and fill the hollow sash weight channels–they allow significant heat loss. Or use their space to install a larger new window.

To order the new window, you need the exact measurements of the rough opening: the distance from side to side between studs and from top to bottom between the header and rough sill. Because the opening may not be square, take several measurements. Order the largest window that will fit squarely in the opening, or have a window custom-built to fit. Reframe the opening if you're putting in a larger window.

Do not remove the old window until the new one is on hand. The procedure for removing a wooden double-hung window also applies to removing most other wooden windows. If the window is 2×3 feet or smaller, remove it as one unit. If it is larger, take out the sash before removing the jambs and sill.

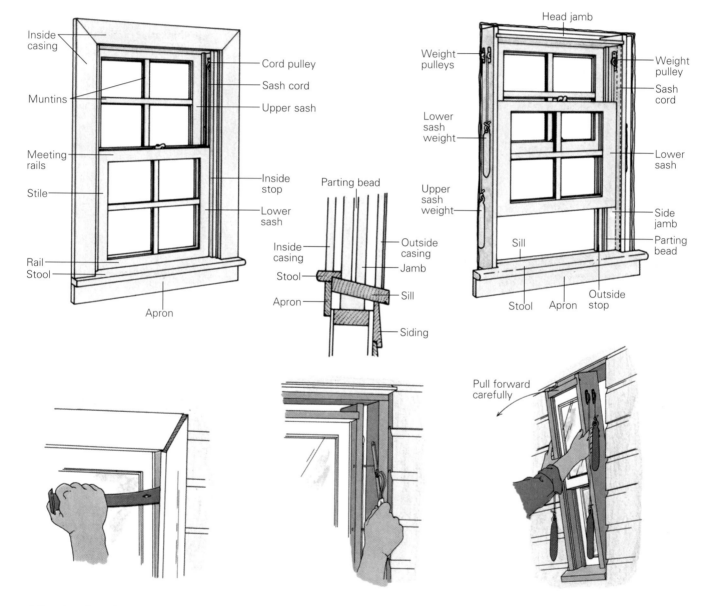

1 *Start from the inside. Remove the interior casings and stool to uncover the studs, header, and rough sill. Measure the rough opening and order the new window. When it is time to remove the existing window, cut the sash cords and remove the sash weights. If the window is small, you can leave them in, if it is easier.*

2 *If you plan to reuse the old window (in a camp or outbuilding, for example), cut all the nails that attach the jambs to the studs, then pry the casings away from the exterior wall. The entire window will come with them and be ready for reuse. If you are not reusing the unit, pry off the exterior casing before cutting the nails.*

3 *Use a reciprocating saw (or a hacksaw blade held in locking pliers) to cut the nails holding the jambs to the trimmer studs. Without the nails, the window should swing out when you pull on it. If you are working from a ladder, you might want to remove both the sashes and the sash weights in order to lighten the load.*

REMOVING A METAL WINDOW

Metal windows are held by nails or screws driven through flanges into wall framing or sheathing. Exterior siding covers the flanges, so you will have to remove siding before you can remove the window.

Start by removing the exterior window trim. Be careful not to split the trim so you can reuse it. Most flanges are 1½ inches wide; snap chalk lines around the window at a distance of 1¾ inches from the edge of the

window. Set the blade of a circular saw ⅛ inch deeper than the thickness of the siding. Using a carbide-tipped blade, cut along all four lines. Remove the nails or screws from the flange and remove the window.

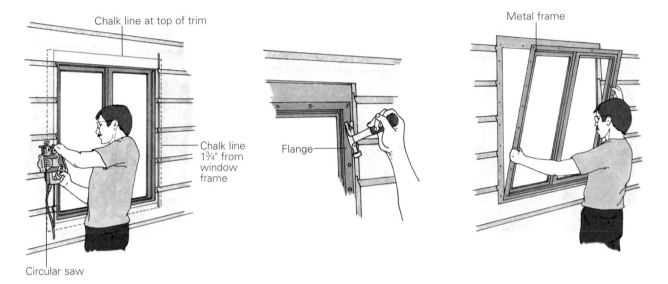

Chalk line at top of trim

Chalk line 1¾" from window frame

Circular saw

Flange

Metal frame

INSTALLING A REPLACEMENT WINDOW

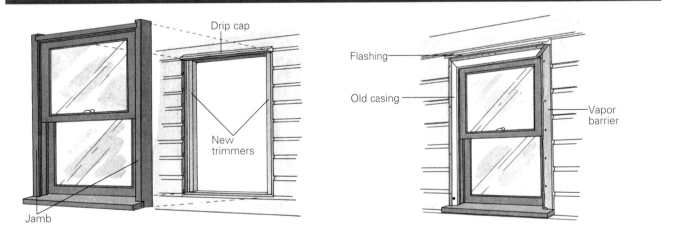

Drip cap

New trimmers

Jamb

Flashing

Old casing

Vapor barrier

Measure the rough opening to confirm that there will be ¼- to ½-inch clearance all around your replacement window. If the opening is too large, nail 1× or 2× stock to the studs to make it smaller.

If there is no building paper around the opening, loosen the siding boards and tuck a doubled layer of 15-pound felt under them as far as you can. Trim the paper flush with the opening or wrap it around the studs.

If the new window comes without preformed flashing or a drip cap, cut a piece of aluminum flashing to fit across the top of the window, and tuck it 3 or 4 inches under the siding. Bend it outward so it covers the drip cap or the top casing of the new window. Set the window in the opening, center it, and fasten it. Nail the siding boards back in place.

Some windows come with thick casings called brick molding. If your

window has brick molding, cut the siding to fit. Seal the edges with caulk.

If your house has grooved-board siding, trim it on both sides of the opening until you can install 1×1 or 1×2 edging strips around the window opening. The edging prevents drafts and insects from entering the grooves. Add insulation between the window and studs and cover it with a plastic vapor barrier.

▶

INSTALLING FIXED PATIO DOOR REPLACEMENT PANELS

FRAMING FOR A NEW WINDOW

In a window wall, or a space with large expanses of glass, it is unnecessary for all the windows to be openable. You can save money by constructing your own fixed windows made from replacement patio door glazings.

These glazings, manufactured regionally and sold by the millions, are available in three standard sizes: 28×76, 34×76, and 46×76. All are made of tempered glass and are available as regular double-glazed and LowE double-glazed.

Most manufacturers warrant their units against failure of the seal (and resulting condensation) for 10 years, provided the units are installed as recommended, and at a tilt from vertical of less than 20 degrees.

The illustrations show two installation techniques: direct to the frame, and in milled jambs.

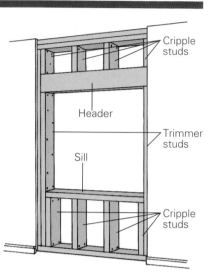

INSTALLING IN MILLED JAMBS (WHERE A FINISHED APPEARANCE IS IMPORTANT)

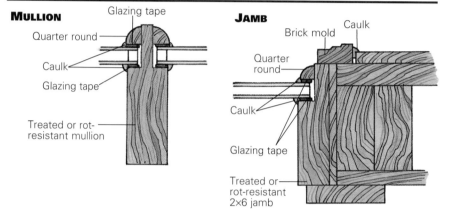

MULLION
Glazing tape
Quarter round
Caulk
Glazing tape
Treated or rot-resistant mullion

JAMB
Brick mold
Caulk
Quarter round
Caulk
Glazing tape
Treated or rot-resistant 2×6 jamb

INSTALLING DIRECT TO THE FRAME (SUITABLE FOR GREENHOUSES AND SUNSPACES)

MULLION
#14×2½" hex screw
Weather-seal washer
UGS clamping bar
EPDM gasket
¾" wood support
Treated or rot-resistant 2×4 framing

JAMB
Brick mold
Glazing tape
Caulk
Glazing tape
Treated or rot-resistant 2×6 framing

Using the dimensions provided by the window manufacturer, mark the width and height of the rough opening on the interior wall. Next, remove enough wallboard or plaster to expose the existing framing that needs to be removed or altered. If more than one stud needs to be removed, provide temporary shoring for the ceiling (see Opening Up Bearing Walls, page 409). Cut and remove the studs. Install the header, king studs, and trimmer studs as a unit, if possible. Install a rough sill and fill in cripple studs above and below the opening where needed. Using a reciprocating saw—with the studs framing the rough opening as a guide—cut out the exterior sheathing and siding.

PRINCIPLES TO FOLLOW WHEN USING EITHER INSTALLATION TECHNIQUE

The important principles with both methods are:

Don't stress the glazing. All of the weight of the glass must rest on two neoprene rubber "setting blocks" (from the glass supplier) placed at the quarter points (one quarter of the way in from each bottom corner).

Don't let the glass touch wood. In addition

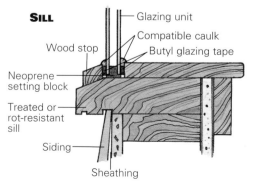

SILL
Glazing unit
Compatible caulk
Butyl glazing tape
Wood stop
Neoprene setting block
Treated or rot-resistant sill
Siding
Sheathing

to the neoprene setting blocks, the edges of the glass are bedded, on both sides, in butyl-rubber glazing tape—available as a paper-backed tape in a roll.

Provide drainage. The sill and stop at the bottom must slope away to prevent standing water. In addition, provide ⅛-inch weep holes from both sides of the setting blocks to outside the wood sill.

Seal all edges. Guard against moisture with clear silicone caulk.

The construction of most windows is similar. The glass fits in a frame called the sash. Some windows have one sash, others have two. The sash, in turn, is held in a frame composed of head jamb, side jambs, and a sill. The entire assembly rests in the "rough opening" defined by the framing in the wall.

Windows today are "prehung"—completely assembled beforehand. It's possible to install the sill, jambs, and sash separately, but consider doing so only if you are trying to recycle some old window sashes.

IN NEW CONSTRUCTION

Whether wooden or metal, windows are installed after the sheathing and before the siding. Make sure the dimensions of your framed opening are the same as the window's "rough opening," not its nominal size.

Trim the sheathing flush with the framing. Always measure both diagonals of the rough opening to verify that the opening is square. Variations of up to ¼ inch are acceptable, but if the window is out of square by more than that, adjust the framing. The most critical member is the rough sill, which should be level.

You'll need to flash the window with a special heavy-duty building paper reinforced with synthetic fibers. A layer of asphalt or other waterproof material coats one side. Window flashing comes in rolls 6 inches wide that you apply before installing the window and before applying the siding paper. If you don't have window flashing, use a 12-inch strip of 15-pound felt folded in half.

Most prehung wooden windows include the exterior casing—often called brick mold. Some units do not include the casings; you must add them after installing the siding. To do so, extend the exterior edge of the jamb beyond the framing or sheathing until it is flush with the siding. The casings bridge the gap between jamb and siding.

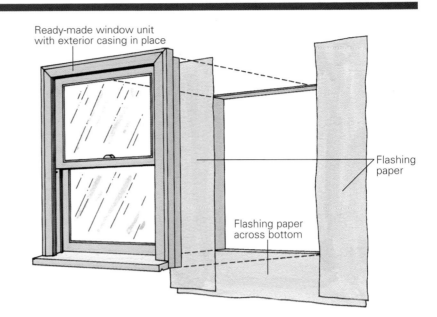

Ready-made window unit with exterior casing in place

Flashing paper

Flashing paper across bottom

1 *Prepare the window by priming surfaces that will be concealed once the window is in position. Staple paper flashing across the bottom of the rough opening and along both sides, so the side pieces overlap the bottom and all inside edges are flush with the opening. Do not apply flashing over the top until after the window is in position.*

Caulk the back of the window casings. With a helper to assist in positioning, set the window into the opening, resting it on the rough sill. While one person holds the window in place, the other levels it with shims. The new window should now be the same height as the other windows.

Once the frame is level, drill pilot holes in the casing, then drive 12d hot-dipped galvanized (HDG) casing or siding nails through the holes and into the studs to hold the unit in place.

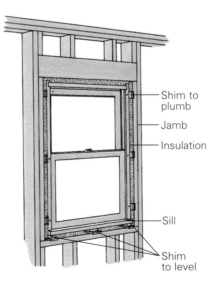

Shim to plumb

Jamb

Insulation

Sill

Shim to level

2 *From inside the building, place shims between the side jambs and the studs. Unless the unit is attached with nailing flanges, drive nails through the jambs and shims into the studs, toenailing from the edge of the jambs rather than through the face. Make sure the sill is shimmed and blocked securely. Pack insulation or foam backer rod between the jambs and rough-opening framing.*

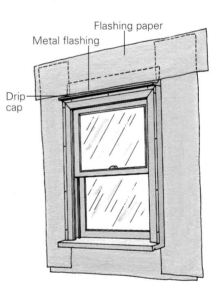

Flashing paper

Metal flashing

Drip cap

3 *From outside, finish nailing the casings. Position the nails at least every 12 inches. Install a drip cap and metal flashing above the head casing. Staple the final piece of paper flashing so that it overlaps the side pieces and covers the vertical flange of the metal flashing. You are now ready to piece in the siding.*

▶

RETROFITTING WINDOWS

There are three ways to improve the efficiency of existing windows with simple techniques and inexpensive materials. In combination, they can increase the R-value to nearly that of high-quality, double-glazed windows, as well as reduce the transmission of outside noise.

WINDOW FILMS

LowE plastic films that increase a window's R-value come in varying degrees of clarity and reflectivity. Applying the films is not difficult, but practice first on the smaller windows. Don't apply the film in temperatures below 40° F, above 90°, or when the window is in direct sunlight. Tinting film clouds while it cures, but it will clear in a few weeks. If you change your mind, remove the film by wetting it with a solution of water and ammonia and scraping it with a razor blade.

Here's how to install window film:

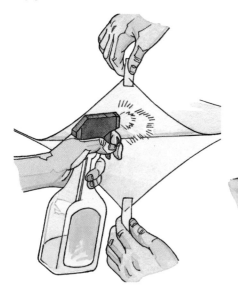

Lint-free cloth

Scraper

1 Clean the window thoroughly with a razor-blade scraper, and dry it with a lint-free cloth or paper towel.

2 Cut the plastic film approximately 1 inch larger than the window pane.

3 Wet the window according to the film manufacturer's instructions.

4 Separate the backing and film at a corner. Be careful not to crease the film. Slowly pull the backing away from the film while a helper wets the adhesive side. Warning: if the film sticks to itself, you will have to cut a new piece.

5 Place the film on the window, avoiding creases and wrinkles. Overlap the film on the sash. Spray the film with water, then smooth it with a squeegee. Wipe the squeegee across the top, down the center, then along each side.

6 If you see a bubble in the film (it will be obvious), spray it with water and slowly work it out with the squeegee.

7 Trim the excess film, leaving a 1/16-inch gap at the perimeter.

COMBINATION STORM WINDOWS

Storm windows not only increase the window's R-value by 1.0 (thereby doubling the R-value of a single-glazed window), but they significantly reduce air infiltration. Combination storms are add-on windows installed outside existing windows. Less expensive models fit over the exterior casing and are quite obvious. More expensive models fit within the casings and are not so obvious. All models have sliding screens and storm panels so you no longer have to find storage for—and install—screens and fixed storm windows twice a year.

Combination storm windows are made of aluminum—either anodized or painted—and require no maintenance. They work only on sliding, single-hung, or double-hung windows, and color selection is limited.

Before you order inset storm windows (windows that fit inside the exterior casings), check the existing window frames for square. If the frame is badly out of square, order the unit about 1/4 inch larger than the window in each direction, then trim the flange to fit. Don't distort the frame of the storm window to make it fit.

To install:

1. Measure the existing window along the outside edge of the exterior stops.
2. Drill attachment holes in the storm window flange, spacing them according to manufacturer recommendations.
3. Test-fit the storm window and make any needed adjustments.
4. Caulk along the exterior stops.
5. Position the storm window and attach it with screws.

INTERIOR INSULATING WINDOWS

These are attached to existing interior windows with magnetic or Velcro strips. Like exterior storm windows, they are easy to use, provide considerable resistance to air infiltration, and reduce sound transmission. They also minimize condensation and won't break like glass. Unlike exterior combination storm windows, however, these have to be removed if you want to open the window. Like old-fashioned exterior storm windows, you will be removing them every spring and reinstalling them every fall.

To install an interior storm with magnetic backing:

1. Nail wood 1× stops to the top and sides of the window jamb.
2. Test-fit the steel strapping. Remove the backing from the double-stick tape and press it into position.
3. Measure the insulating-window material carefully and cut the panel to size following the manufacturer's instructions.
4. Apply the magnetic strip to the perimeter of the panel.

Steel strip

Magnetic strip

Glazing

REPAIRING WINDOWS

Average-quality windows of today lose only half as much heating and cooling energy as the best windows of 20 years ago. But replacement windows are very expensive. Should you spend the money to replace them? Or should you spend your limited resources on other energy-conservation projects and do what you can to restore your existing windows to working order?

That is a complex question, involving the severity of your climate, the price you pay for fuel, and the condition of your windows. Your state energy office, or your local utility, may provide a free analysis to help answer that question. If you decide to keep the old windows, however, here are the solutions to the most common age-related, double-hung window problems:

LOOSENING STUCK DOUBLE-HUNG WINDOWS

1 If the sash is painted shut, first cut the seal with a utility knife. Then drive the blade of a wide putty knife between the sash and stops all around the inside and outside.

2 Drive a wedge, hatchet, or prybar between the sash and sill on the outside to force the sash up. Work slowly and gently, working back and forth between the corners.

3 Scrape paint or hardened dirt from the window channels.

4 If the sash moves but binds inside the channel, you need to widen the channel. Cut a block of wood that is slightly wider than the channel and tap it into the channel to force the stops apart.

5 When the sash moves but doesn't slide easily, lubricate the channels with candle wax, paraffin (canning wax), or silicone lubricant.

REPLACE DOUBLE-HUNG SASH WEIGHTS WITH SPRING BALANCES

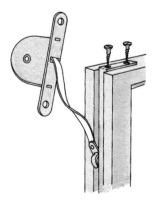

1 Remove window stop, bottom sash, parting strip, and top sash. Then remove the access panels, the sash weights, the cords, and finally the old pulleys.

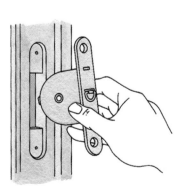

2 Screw the replacement spring balances into the old pulley recesses, and the metal sash adapters to the sashes.

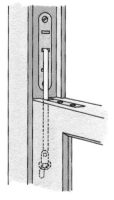

3 With the sashes out of the frame, hook the tapes of the sash balances to the adapters on both sides and replace the sashes.

440

REPLACING A BROKEN SASH CORD

Broken sash cords are easily replaced. If you live in a cold climate, however, you should take the extra steps of filling the sash-weight channel with insulation and installing replacement spring balances, *opposite*. Here is how to replace a cord (The technique applies to both lower and upper sashes.):

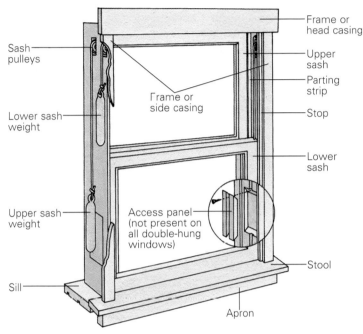

- Sash pulleys
- Frame or side casing
- Lower sash weight
- Upper sash weight
- Access panel (not present on all double-hung windows)
- Sill
- Apron
- Frame or head casing
- Upper sash
- Parting strip
- Stop
- Lower sash
- Stool

1 On the side with the broken cord, pry off the stop that retains the sash. Work the lower sash out of the frame, release the knotted cord from the window groove, and slowly let the sash weight pull the cord toward the pulley until the weight stops.

2 Remove the access panel at the bottom of the window and remove the sash weight.

3 Fish new cord down through the pulley and retrieve the end through the access hole. Using the same type of knot (study the old one before removing it) tie the end to the weight. If the "cord" is chain, use wire to attach the end of the chain to the weight. Then place the weight back in the cavity and replace the access panel.

4 Attach the free end of the cord to the sash. Set the sash into the window in a closed position, pull on the cord until the sash weight

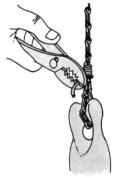

is at the top, and cut the cord. Remove the sash and attach the cord (again using the same type of knot).

Set the sash back into the opening and replace the stop. Make sure the window works smoothly.

ADJUSTING DOUBLE-HUNG TUBE BALANCES

The tube balance contains a spring that balances the weight of the sash. If a sash will not stay in place, the spring probably needs to be adjusted:

1. Lower the sash so that the tube is exposed.

2. Holding the tube firmly (to prevent it from unwinding), loosen the screw at the top of the tube.

3. Pull the tube away from the window frame and:

■ to increase the lift, twist the tube clockwise two turns;

■ to decrease the lift, twist the tube counterclockwise two turns.

4. Reattach the tube, and repeat steps 1–3 for the balance on the opposite side.

WIRE

THE LINK BETWEEN CURRENT EVENTS

ALSO SEE...
Electrical Boxes:
Pages 106–109
Electrical Systems:
Pages 110–115
Receptacles:
Pages 272–273
Switches:
Pages 352–355

Wires are conduits for electrical current. They range in size from small lamp cords to high-voltage lines running across the country. All wires resist the flow of electrons, so if the wire is too small, it will overheat. For this reason the National Electrical Code (NEC) specifies the type and size of wire which can be used when wiring appliances and circuits.

Residential wiring uses copper wire. In the 1970s, many houses were wired completely with aluminum due to the high cost of copper. Unfortunately aluminum oxidizes, causing resistance, and expands as it heats, causing connections to work loose. The loose connections can then arc, igniting nearby combustibles. Special materials are available for making proper connections with aluminum wiring, but most codes now require all residential wiring to be copper only.

CODE REQUIREMENTS: CABLES

Nonmetallic (NM) Cable:
- Stapled 1¼ inch minimum from face along stud.
- Holes in vertical framing recessed 1¼ inches minimum or protected by steel plate.
- Holes in horizontal framing recessed 2 inches minimum or protected by steel bushing.
- Metal framing holes bushed.
- Box holes bushed or otherwise protected from chafe.
- Cable support 4'6" maximum on center.
- Cable support 12 inches maximum from box with clamp.
- Cable support 8 inches maximum from box with no clamp.

Armored (BX) Cable:
- Stapled 1¼ inch minimum from face along stud.
- Holes in vertical framing recessed 1¼ inches minimum or protected by steel plate.
- Holes in horizontal framing recessed 2 inches minimum.
- Box holes bushed or otherwise protected from chafe.
- Cable support 4'6" maximum on center (not required between ceiling fixtures not spaced more than 6 feet).
- Cable support 12 inches maximum from box (24 inches maximum where flexibility is required).

COLOR CODE FOR INSULATED WIRE

Color	Purpose
Black	Hot; connects to darkest terminal of switch or receptacle.
White	Neutral; connects to silver terminal of receptacle.
Red	Hot; second hot wire when there are two, such as in a 240-volt circuit.
Bare or green	Grounding wire; connects to green screw on device and to metal box, case, or chassis.

WIRE SIZE

Wire sizes are determined by the American Wire Gauge (AWG) system. The larger the number, the smaller the wire. A No. 18 wire is very small and a No. 2 wire is very large. Note in the table that wires are numbered evenly up to No. 2, and that sizes larger than No. 1 are designated 1/0 ("one ought" or 0), 2/0 ("two ought" or "double zero"), and so on. Most house wiring is done with No. 12 wire, but No. 14 is used in some areas for 15-amp lighting circuits. Larger sizes are used for 240-volt appliances and for the main conductors into the service entrance.

COPPER WIRE SIZE, CAPACITY, AND TYPICAL USE

Wire Size	Diameter, inches	Resistance Ohms/100'	Max. Current/Voltage Drop/100'			Typical Use
			T&TW	THW	SE	
18	.040	.628	7A/4.4V	7A/4.4V	–	Lamp cord, low-voltage circuits
16	.051	.395	10A/4.0V	10A/4.0V	–	Low-voltage circuits
14	.064	.248	15A/3.7V	15A/3.7V	–	Lighting circuits
12	.081	.156	20A/3.1V	20A/3.1V	–	Small appliance/lighting circuits
10	.102	.098	30A/2.9V	30A/2.9V	–	Water heater, clothes dryer
8	.128	.062	40A/2.5V	45A/2.8V	–	Feeder for subpanel
6	.184	.039	55A/2.1V	65A/2.5V	–	Electric range and oven
4	.232	.024	70A/1.7V	85A/2.0V	100A/2.4V	Feeder for subpanel
2	.292	.015	95A/1.4V	115A/1.7V	125A/1.9V	Service entrance, 125 Amp service
1	.332	.012	–	130A/1.6V	150A/1.8V	Service entrance, 150 Amp service
2/0	.419	.008	–	175A/1.4V	200A/1.6V	Service entrance, 200 Amp service

A wire is an individual conductor of electrical current. Wires are either solid or made up of many, tightly wound strands. Each wire is wrapped in an insulating jacket made of rubber, plastic, or similar nonconducting material. An exception is a ground wire, which may either be wrapped in a green insulating jacket or be bare.

A cable is a cluster of two or more wires—each with its own insulation—wrapped together in plastic or metallic sheathing. Some types of cable include a bare ground wire within the sheathing.

The most common types of residential wire and cable are:

Type T Wire: Used for general indoor wiring, the thermoplastic (T) insulation protects against heat-induced short circuits up to 140° F.

Type TW Wire: This wire has a heavy covering that resists the elements. Use it for outdoor wiring (but not direct burial) and for wiring in damp places such as basements. It protects against heat-induced short circuits up to 140° F.

Type THW Wire: Type THW wire is similar to Type TW, but is rated to protect against heat-induced short circuits up to 167° F.

NM Cable: This plastic-sheathed cable is the one most commonly used in residential installations. It is also widely known by the trade name Romex®. It consists of two or more individually insulated Type T wires and a bare copper grounding wire. Each wire is separated from the others by paper spacers and bundled inside a covering of jute and sheathed in plastic. Don't use NM cable where it will be exposed to dampness.

NMC Cable: This cable is made specifically for damp areas, such as basements and laundry rooms. It often has a glass wrapping on each wire. The wires are embedded in a solid plastic sheath to keep out moisture. If NMC cable is not available in your area, use UF cable.

UF Cable: This cable is so durable it is the type recommended when underground burial is required. The wires are embedded directly in tough plastic that keeps out all water. It is the best choice for outdoor wiring or wiring in a barn or garage where there is a lot of moisture. SE is another type of cable that can be buried.

Armored Cable: Known by the trade name BX, this cable has heavy paper and spiral galvanized metal sheathing. The metal sheathing also acts as a ground. Don't use BX in damp areas. Some local codes require armored cable in places where wiring will be exposed to potential abrasion, such as in crawl spaces or along the insides of garage walls.

WIRE AND CABLE LABELS

In case you have wondered what all those letters on the insulation of wire and cable mean:

Letter	Stands For
WIRE:	
H	Heat resistant
R	Rubber
T	Thermoplastic
W	Water resistant
CABLE:	
AC	Armored (metal) cable
C	Corrosion resistant
F	Feeder
NM	Nonmetallic
U	Underground
SE	Service entrance

STRIPPING WIRE AND CABLE

NONMETALLIC CABLE

The plastic sheathing of nonmetallic cable should be stripped away at the end either before or after it is fed into a box. You should have 8 to 12 inches of unsheathed wire inside the box.

To removed the sheathing, slide a special tool called a "cable stripper" onto the cable. Squeeze the stripper, and pull it to the end of the cable. This slits the sheathing, which you can then pull back and cut off with a utility knife. If you don't have a cable stripper, slit the sheathing down its middle with the tip of a utility knife blade. Be careful not to cut too deeply so you don't cut the insulation on each wire. Spread the cut sheathing apart with your fingers, strip it back to the desired length, and remove it with the utility knife.

ARMORED CABLE

Cut the flexible metal sheathing of armored cable with a hacksaw. Saw the sheathing at an angle, taking care not to cut into the wire insulation inside. When you have barely broken through the metal armor, stop sawing and twist the sheathing apart.

STRIPPING WIRE

It is possible to strip the insulation from the end of a wire with a utility knife, but if you plan to do much wiring, invest in a multipurpose tool or a wire stripper.

To remove insulation using a utility knife, place the wire on a flat surface. Put the blade of the utility knife on the wire, then gently press until the blade just cuts the insulation. Roll the wire beneath the blade to cut all the way around the wire. Pull the cut insulation off with your fingers.

The multipurpose tool has a separate groove for each size of wire, usually up to No. 10, as well as crimping jaws for attaching terminals and lugs. The wire stripper has only one cutting groove, but it can be adjusted to any size.

Determine the length of insulation to be removed, then place the wire in the proper-sized groove and rotate the tool back and forth. When you have cut through the insulation, pull it straight off. Be very careful about cutting into the copper. Even an incidental nick is a weak point that may break if the wire is subjected to vibration.

▶

WIRE
continued

SPLICING WIRES

Among the several types of connectors for splicing wires, the wire nut is the most commonly used. You can wire an entire house using nothing but wire nuts of varying size for all of the connections. Before starting a large

wiring project, purchase boxes of 100 or 250 of each size of wire nut.

To make a wire-nut splice, strip each wire back ¾ inch and hold them together with their tips even. Put the nut onto the stripped ends and twist

the nut clockwise as hard as you can twist by hand. Don't use a pliers or you'll break the wire or the wire nut. When you are done, test the splice by tugging on each wire. If a wire comes loose, start over again.

WIRE-NUT SPLICE

CRIMP CONNECTOR SPLICE

Crimp

CLAMP CONNECTOR

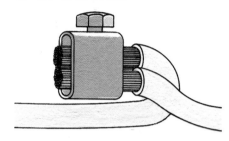

CLAMSHELL CONNECTOR

SPLIT-BOLT CONNECTOR

Metal insert with points

Lid

PLANNING NEW CIRCUITS

FIXTURES AND OUTLETS

Use a floor plan or blueprint to layout the location of light fixtures and outlets. Let your personal preferences guide your selection of locations, but be sure to follow the requirements set forth by your local building codes.

Group the fixtures and outlets into logical circuits. If you are adding only one or two outlets, you can wire them into an existing circuit. If you are doing extensive wiring, however, assign a circuit to each permanent appliance, such as a refrigerator or clothes washer. Then group the outlets required for small appliances in the

kitchen, dining room, breakfast nook, and laundry. Finally, group the general-purpose wall receptacles.

The National Electrical Code refrains from specifying the number of outlets allowed on a single circuit, but common practice is to install up to 6 receptacles on a 20-amp small appliance circuit, up to 13 outlets on a 20-amp general-purpose circuit, and up to 10 fixtures on a 15-amp lighting circuit.

PLANNING THE RUNS

After you have grouped all of the fixtures and outlets into circuits, walk

around the room and mark the locations of the boxes on the studs and joists. Then plan how best to run the cable in order to connect the boxes and divide the load among the circuits.

Don't scrimp on circuits! Circuit breakers and cable are inexpensive. If you run out of space in your service panel, just replace a few full-size breakers with half-size breakers.

Before you start running cable, it is a good idea to go over your plan with a local code official. It would ruin your day to find later that your local code is more restrictive than the NEC, requiring you to rip out your work.

A TYPICAL CIRCUIT

DRAWING THE PLAN

This plan shows a general-purpose circuit for a one-room addition. It uses the three most common symbols found in electrical plans. Notice that long arrows show the sequence of outlets from the source and that a dotted line connects each light fixture to its switch. The switches operating a light fixture from two locations are marked S3 to indicate that they are three-way switches.

Note: The current for the new room can be extended from this existing outlet, or a new circuit can be run from the service panel.

¥ Light
S Switch
‡ Outlet

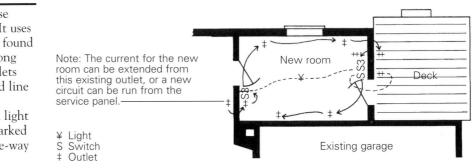

New room

Deck

Existing garage

RUNNING THE CABLE

In the framing illustration below, nonmetallic cable is run through joists and studs and along the sides of studs. The holes are ¾ inch in diameter, drilled with either a ⅜-inch drill and spade bit or a heavy-duty ½-inch drill with an auger bit. Holes through vertical framing must be at least 1¼ inches from the face of the member unless protected by a metal plate fastened to the face of the member.

When running cable under a floor, staple it alongside the joists. Instead of crossing joists, drill holes through the center, preferably near the walls supporting the joists rather than in the center of the span. If there is any chance of a nearby nail penetrating the cable, cover it with a nailing plate.

If you do run cable across the tops of joists, such as in an empty attic, it must be protected from foot traffic by ¾-inch guard strips on both sides.

Circuit loop from switch to ceiling box for light fixture

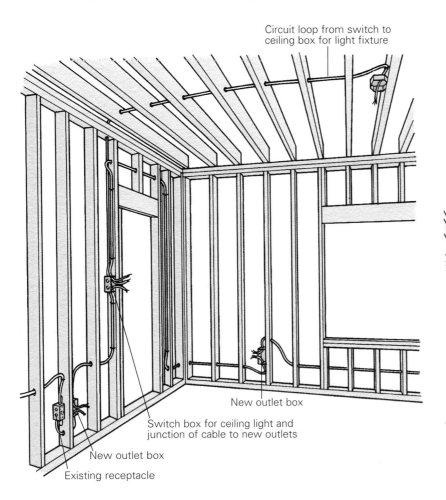

New outlet box

Switch box for ceiling light and junction of cable to new outlets

New outlet box

Existing receptacle

Protect cable with metal plate

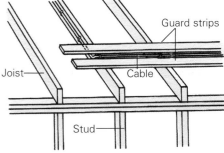

Joist

Cable

Stud

Guard strips

Joist

Cable

Stud

OOD

CUTTING THROUGH THE FOREST OF CONFUSION

ALSO SEE...
Most entries

Wood is beautiful, strong, lightweight, easy to work with, and, as if that were not enough, it also smells good. Wood is natural, renewable, and readily available in an astonishing variety of species, grades, sizes, cuts, finishes, and products. This diversity can make shopping for lumber a bewildering experience, but if you become familiar with a few basic principles, you will find what you need in one quick shopping trip.

One of the first considerations is the type of product you need, such as dimensioned lumber, milled products, or manufactured wood. When buying lumber, you need to specify dimension and length, as well as species and grade. The dimension of a board is the cross-sectional size, although the actual measurements are usually less than the stated, or "nominal" size (see Standard Lumber Sizes, page 448). Specifying rough or surfaced lumber also affects the dimension. Length, however, is more exact. Dressed (planed) lumber

is usually about ½ inch longer than nominal, while rough lumber is a few inches longer.

CODE REQUIREMENTS: LUMBER

The code specifies that all framing lumber used as studs, headers, joists and rafters be inspected and graded by an accepted grading agency, and that lumber be limited in application to the spans specified by the code according to the grade of the lumber.

HOW LUMBER IS SAWN

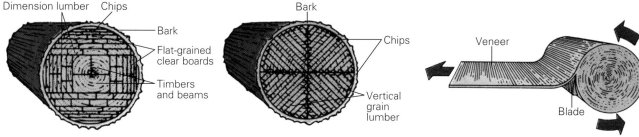

PLAIN-SAWED LUMBER

Plain sawing is the fastest and least wasteful way to saw a log. Most construction-grade lumber is produced in this manner. Plain sawing produces flat-grain lumber with a pattern, resembling marble. The grain imparts strength, but plain sawed lumber is prone to cupping and warping.

QUARTER-SAWED LUMBER

Quarter-sawed boards have vertical grain, which shows as parallel lines along the face of the board. Vertical grain is desirable for fine finish work and is more durable than plain sawed lumber when exposed to weather. More of a quarter sawed log ends as sawdust. As a result, this lumber is substantially more expensive.

VENEER

Veneer is a continuous layer of wood sliced off a rotating log. Its widest use is in plywood and paneling, but thin veneers of fine woods are also available for cabinetmaking. The grain pattern of a veneer resembles plain sawed lumber; vertical grain veneers made from thin sheets of quarter sawed lumber are also available.

MOISTURE AND SHRINKAGE

When you buy lumber you usually are concerned with size, strength, and appearance, but in some installations you also should be concerned with moisture content. That's the weight of water, as a percentage of the weight of the lumber when completely dry.

Framing lumber should have a moisture content of 19 percent or less. Lumber for finish work should have a moisture content of 8 to 11 percent, a low level achieved by drying in a kiln. A freshly cut tree can have a moisture content of 100 or 200 percent, double or even triple the weight of the tree were it completely dry.

Moisture content is an important factor because wood, unless perfectly sealed, gives off and takes up moisture in response to its environment. In a dry climate, choose lumber that has a low moisture content. Otherwise, the wood will shrink as it dries, and the result will be shrinking, cupping, bowing, and other kinds of warping. Even a small change in moisture can cause a board to bend or crack.

When wood is concealed from view, such defects are not generally a serious problem. However, use kiln-dried lumber for trim, finish work, and critical structural members, such as trimmer studs next to a door.

Because wood shrinks across the grain, a wide piece of lumber will shrink more than a narrow one. This is especially troublesome in headers over doors and windows. If new headers are too green, they will cause the wallboard nailed to them to buckle and split.

For most framing projects, use lumber with the standard 19 percent moisture content. Once lumber has been dried to this level, it will recover from rain in just a few days. To be safe, however, order lumber several weeks in advance and stack it with scrap lumber ("stickers") between rows of boards. Weight the pile to minimize warping during the process.

LUMBER DEFECTS

Trees are imperfect. Thus, when you're looking for framing lumber, you're bound to find a few warped and blemished pieces. Knowing the nature of lumber defects (see illustrations, right) and which strengths are important in given applications, makes it possible to find uses for all but the worst specimens. For example, you can make use of marginal lumber as blocking, or match doubled members of opposite curvature to produce a straight pair.

Finish lumber, however, must be straight and free of splits or defects. Inspect each piece of finish lumber before it is unloaded at your job site, and do not accept pieces that are totally unusable. If possible, select your own lumber at the yard.

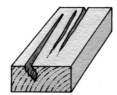

Check is caused by more rapid drying and shrinking of the wood surface than its interior. It is unsightly, but doesn't effect strength very much.

Splits pass clear through the wood and are sometimes due to rough handling. They diminish the bending strength significantly.

Shake is the separation of rings. Lumber with visible shakes should not be used in bending applications since the zone of weakness probably extends the length of the member.

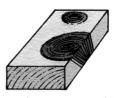

Knots are the overgrown, high-density "roots" of limbs. They are very tough, but not well connected to the surrounding wood. The rules for joists and rafters with knots are:
- Tight knots allowed in the top third.
- Missing knots are acceptable in the middle third.
- No knots larger than an inch in the bottom third.

Knotholes are, obviously, the space where knots used to be. The effect on strength is the same as for knots, except for the top-⅓ rule for joists and rafters.

Wane results from sawyer error. There simply wasn't enough tree to complete the board. Wane has little effect on strength; its chief drawback is lack of a full-width nailing surface for sheathing joints.

Warp is the general term for all the ways a board can be geometrically distorted: *cup, bow, twist,* and *crook*. These defects do not affect strength.

AMERICAN PLYWOOD ASSOCIATION GRADES

The following grades for plywood are listed in descending order of quality:

N: Smooth surface; natural finish veneer. Made of select grade wood. Free of open defects.

A: Smooth, paintable veneer with not more than 18 neatly-made repairs. Natural finish can be used if you are not too demanding.

B: Solid surface with circular repair plugs, shims, and tight knots to 1 inch. Some minor splits are permitted. Repairs may be made with wood or synthetic filler.

C Plugged: Splits cannot be more than ⅛ inch wide, and other open defects (such as knotholes) cannot exceed ¼ by ½ inch. Some repair and broken grain permitted.

C: Tight knots up to 1½ inch and knotholes to 1 inch are allowed. Repairs, discoloration, limited splits, sanding defects, and stitching (piecing) are permissible if they do not impair the strength.

D: Knots and knotholes up to 3 inches wide are allowed. Splits and stitching are permitted.

LUMBER GRADES

Each lumber species, or species group, is subject to grading rules established by association of manufactures. The rules evaluate many factors: strength, the number, size, and placement of knots, the amount of sapwood, the grain pattern, and surface appearance. The rules vary between species, so don't assume that a grading term means the same thing in regard to different species.

Although there are many associations and many grading standards, the standards within one association are usually consistent. Not all lumber producers belong to an association, however, so obtain a copy of grading criteria from your lumber dealer and inspect the lumber yourself.

Your local building code probably specifies the grades of lumber you are permitted to use for framing. Failure to understand the grading terminology in a matter of code compliance could result in an expensive mistake. For instance, "construction grade" in one system may refer to an unacceptable quality of lumber in another system, and one that your code would not accept.

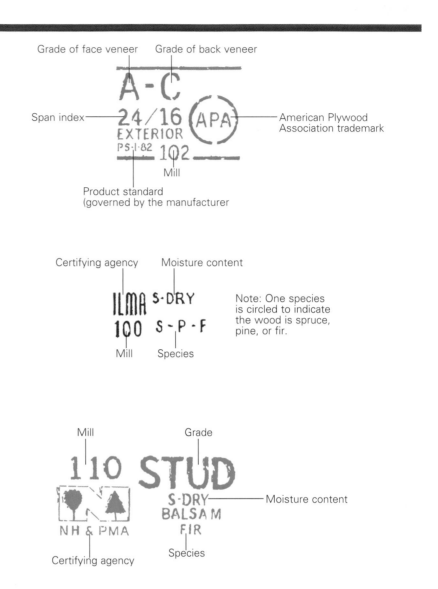

	Grade of face veneer	Grade of back veneer

A-C
24/16 (APA)
EXTERIOR
PS-1-82 102

Span index — ... Product standard (governed by the manufacturer) — Mill — American Plywood Association trademark

Certifying agency — Moisture content

ILMA S-DRY
100 S-P-F

Mill — Species

Note: One species is circled to indicate the wood is spruce, pine, or fir.

Mill — Grade

110 STUD
S-DRY — Moisture content
BALSAM
FIR

NH & PMA — Certifying agency — Species

STANDARD LUMBER SIZES

Product	Nominal Dimensions, inches		Dressed Dimensions Surfaced, inches	
	Thickness	Width	Dry	Green
Dimension lumber	2	2	$1\frac{1}{2}$	$1\frac{9}{16}$
	3	3	$2\frac{1}{2}$	$2\frac{9}{16}$
	4	4	$3\frac{1}{2}$	$3\frac{9}{16}$
		5	$4\frac{1}{2}$	$4\frac{5}{8}$
		6	$5\frac{1}{2}$	$5\frac{5}{8}$
		8	$7\frac{1}{4}$	$7\frac{1}{2}$
		10	$9\frac{1}{4}$	$9\frac{1}{2}$
		12	$11\frac{1}{4}$	$11\frac{1}{2}$
		>12	less $\frac{3}{4}$	less $\frac{1}{2}$

Most lumber species are subject to decay and insect attack and don't last long in contact with the ground or other damp locations. However, lumber can be treated by injecting preservatives under pressure, causing the preservatives to be locked permanently in the wood. Pressure-treated lumber is far superior to wood that has been merely sprayed or dipped in a chemical preservative. In many cases treated lumber will outlast naturally durable species like redwood, cedar, or cypress.

The primary chemicals used for pressure-treating lumber are the waterborne salts: chromated copper arsenate (CCA), ammoniacal copper arsenate (ACA), and ammoniacal copper zinc arsenate. Other preservatives are pentachlorophenol and creosote, but they are very toxic and the lumber cannot easily be be painted or stained.

Pressure-treated lumber is slightly green or beige in color and does not darken if left to weather. When buying it, specify whether it is for ground contact (LP-22) or aboveground (LP-2) use.

You should take precautions when working with pressure-treated lumber.

Here are the precautions the EPA requires manufacturers to supply with their products.

USE PRECAUTIONS

Wood pressure-treated with waterborne arsenical preservatives may be used inside residences as long as all sawdust and construction debris are cleaned up and disposed of after construction.

■ Do not use treated wood under circumstances where the preservative may become a component of food or animal feed. Examples of such use would be in structures or containers for storing silage or food.

■ Do not use treated wood for cutting boards or countertops.

■ Only treated wood that is visibly clean and free of surface residue should be used for patios, decks, and walkways.

■ Do not use treated wood for construction of those portions of beehives which may come into contact with the honey.

■ Treated wood should not be used where it may come into contact with public drinking water, except for uses involving incidental contact such as docks and bridges.

HANDLING PRECAUTIONS

■ Dispose of treated wood by ordinary trash collection or burial. Treated wood should not be burned in open fires or in stoves, fireplaces, or residential boilers because toxic chemicals may be produced as part of the smoke and ashes. Treated wood from commercial or industrial use (e.g. construction sites) may be burned only in commercial or industrial incinerators or boilers in accordance with state and federal regulations.

■ Avoid frequent or prolonged inhalation of sawdust from treated wood. When sawing and machining treated wood, wear a dust mask. Whenever possible, these operations should be performed outdoors to avoid indoor accumulations of airborne sawdust from treated wood.

■ When power-sawing and machining, wear goggles to protect eyes from flying particles.

■ After working with the wood, and before eating, drinking, and use of tobacco products, wash exposed areas thoroughly.

■ If preservatives or sawdust accumulate on clothes, launder before reuse. Wash work clothes separately from other household clothing.

STANDARD LUMBER SIZES

Product	Nominal Dimensions, inches		Dressed Dry Dimensions, inches	
	Thickness	Width	Thickness	Width
Finish Lumber and Boards	$3/8$	2	$5/16$	$1\frac{1}{2}$
	$1/2$	3	$7/16$	$2\frac{1}{2}$
	$5/8$	4	$9/16$	$3\frac{1}{2}$
	$3/4$	5	$5/8$	$4\frac{1}{2}$
	1	6	$3/4$	$5\frac{1}{2}$
	$1\frac{1}{4}$	7	1	$6\frac{1}{2}$
	$1\frac{1}{2}$	8	$1\frac{1}{4}$	$7\frac{1}{4}$
	$1\frac{3}{4}$	>8	$1\frac{3}{8}$	less $3/4$
	2		$1\frac{1}{2}$	
	$2\frac{1}{2}$		2	
	3		$2\frac{1}{2}$	
	$3\frac{1}{2}$		3	
	4		$3\frac{1}{2}$	

▶

WOOD

continued

STACKING LUMBER

If you store lumber for any length of time before using it, stick it and stack it. Stickers are the thrown-away edges with bark; lumberyards will sometimes give them to you for free. Use at least three stickers per layer, and set the stickers close enough so the boards do not sag. Pick a dry, well-drained area and stack the pile off the ground. If you stack green lumber this way, it will be fully seasoned in about six months.

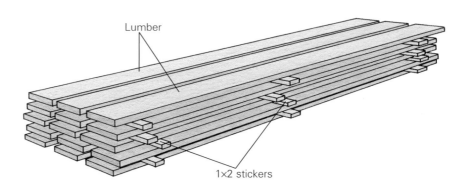

Lumber

1×2 stickers

MANUFACTURED WOOD PRODUCTS

Manufactured wood products include plywood, particleboard, and hardboard. Less familiar products include oriented strand board (OSB), laminated beams, and waferboard. All have become more common as the supply of large trees dwindles.

Manufactured wood products are widely used for furniture, subflooring, sheathing, joists, underlayment, siding, shingles, even framing. Strength, durability, and consistency of quality are often equal to or greater than the equivalent unaltered wood product.

The glues used to bond the wood fibers in these products include urea-formaldehyde and phenol-formaldehyde. These resins give off

gasses for a long period of time. If you are sensitive to ureaformaldehyde (used in particleboard and some medium-density fiberboard) choose products bonded with phenol-formaldehyde, and test your reaction to it before building an addition or a new home. When buying particleboard or MDF, check for the mark "HUD 24 CFR PART 3280," indicating compliance with federal standards for emissions of formaldehyde gas.

SHEET PRODUCTS

Plywood is made of laminated layers, the face layers consisting of veneers. It is widely used and comes in a range of strength and appearance grades.

Oriented Strand Board (OSB) panels are made of compressed strand-like particles, arranged in layers at right angles to each other and bonded with phenol-formaldehyde. OSB is used for subflooring and for wall and roof sheathing. It is comparable to plywood in ability to hold screws and nails.

Composites consist of veneer faces laminated to OSB with phenol-formaldehyde. They are available in framing timber sizes, as well as standard 4×8-foot panels.

Waferboard is made of wood chips and flakes randomly compressed and bonded with phenolformaldehyde. It can be used for paneling, as well as wall and roof sheathing. Its ability to hold nails and screws is not as great as OSB or plywood.

Particleboard consists of wood chips and sawdust bonded with urea-formaldehyde. It is used as underlayment for counter laminates and vinyl floors, the core of furniture and cabinet veneers, and the core of doors. It is extremely heavy, and its nail and screw holding power is poor; you must either use specialized fasteners or attach it to solid wood.

Hardboard is made of wood fibers compressed and bonded with phenol-formaldehyde or linseed oil. Used in furniture, drawers, siding, panels, pegboard, and doors, it comes tempered (smoothed) and untempered (rough). The tempered variety is moisture resistant and is commonly used for siding.

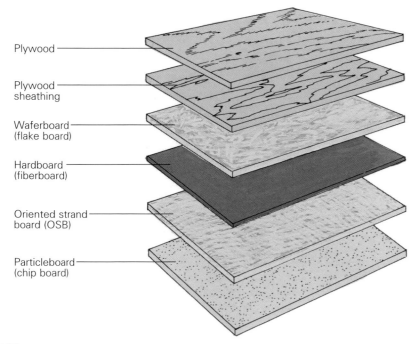

Plywood

Plywood sheathing

Waferboard (flake board)

Hardboard (fiberboard)

Oriented strand board (OSB)

Particleboard (chip board)

The long fibers in natural wood are anywhere from two to four times stronger than the design values allowed by the code. The discrepancy is due to the fact that codes take into account the strength-reducing natural "defects" found in sawn lumber: knots, splits, shake, and rot. Engineered lumber–wood that has been taken apart (sawn, veneered, or shredded) and reassembled with glue–eliminates the effects of defects. As a result, engineered lumber is actually stronger than all but the most perfect specimens of natural lumber. It can also be manufactured in larger sizes than are available from single trees. Not all products have reached home centers yet, but here are the ones you can special order from lumber yards:

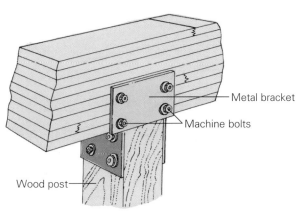

Metal bracket

Machine bolts

Wood post

Laminated Beams: You may be familiar with these large beams—called glulams—used to support roofs of churches and other large open buildings. They consist of uniformly dimensioned lumber glued together in either a straight or curved form. The beams are stronger than sawn timbers of the same size, can be much longer—up to 80 feet—and do not shrink or warp easily. Even straight glulams have a slight curve built into them, so be sure to install them with the edge marked "top" facing upward. Use metal framing aids designed specifically for them. Notching or drilling through a glulam may weaken it significantly, so consult the manufacturer's specifications before you attempt to do so.

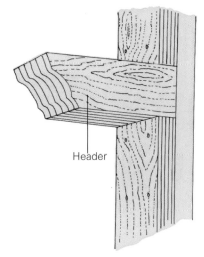

Header

Laminated-Veneer Lumber: Referred to as LVL, this material is manufactured in layers of natural veneer, similar to plywood, and comes in standard lumber sizes. It is used most frequently for beams, headers, and other structural components. Unlike plywood, all the veneers in LVL are parallel, with the grain running in the same direction. It tends to be stronger, more stable, and available in longer lengths than most sawn lumber.

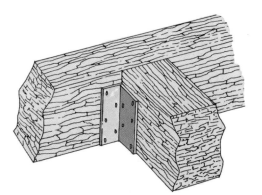

Parallel Strand Lumber: Similar to OSB, but with most of the fibers and strands in the product oriented in the same direction, PSL comes in standard lumber sizes and is used for most framing applications. Its uniform appearance makes it suitable for exposed beams.

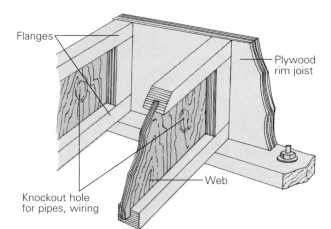

Flanges

Plywood rim joist

Knockout hole for pipes, wiring

Web

I-Joists: These are a composite of plywood or OSB and natural lumber. The joists resemble I beams, and bear weight as though they were solid wood. As long as they are kept from twisting and are installed correctly, they result in flat, quiet floors that are very stable and strong. They also allow considerable flexibility in routing ducts and pipes through the webbings. It is critical that these products be installed strictly according to the manufacturer's detailed instructions.

▶

APA PERFORMANCE-RATED PANELS

Grade Designation, Description, and Uses	Thicknesses	Typical APA Grade Stamp
APA Rated Sheathing Exposure: Suitable for permanent exterior use or for protected applications that may be exposed to prolonged weather during construction Specially designed for subflooring and wall and roof sheathing. Also for a broad range of other construction and industrial applications. Can be manufactured as plywood, as a composite, or as OSB.	$5/16$, $3/8$, $7/16$, $15/32$, $1/2$, $19/32$, $5/8$, $23/32$, $3/4$	APA THE ENGINEERED WOOD ASSOCIATION / RATED SHEATHING / 24/16 7/16 INCH / SIZED FOR SPACING / EXPOSURE 1 / 000 / PRP-108 HUD-UM-40C
APA Structural I Rated Sheathing Exposure: Suitable for permanent exterior use or for protected applications that may be exposed to prolonged weather during construction Unsanded grade for use where shear and cross-panel strength properties are of maximum importance, such as panelized roofs and diaphragms. Can be manufactured as plywood, as a composite, or as OSB.	$5/16$, $3/8$, $7/16$, $15/32$, $1/2$, $19/32$, $5/8$, $23/32$, $3/4$	APA THE ENGINEERED WOOD ASSOCIATION / RATED SHEATHING / STRUCTURAL 1 / 32/16 15/32 INCH / SIZED FOR SPACING / EXPOSURE 1 / 000 / PS 1-95 CD PRP-108
APA Rated Sturd-I-Floor Exposure: Suitable for permanent exterior use or for protected applications that may be exposed to prolonged weather during construction Specially designed as combination subfloor-underlayment. Provides smooth surface for application of carpet and pad and possesses high concentrated and impact load resistance. Can be manufactured as plywood, as a composite, or as OSB. Available square edge or tongue-and-groove.	$19/32$, $5/8$, $23/32$, $3/4$, 1, $1 1/8$	APA THE ENGINEERED WOOD ASSOCIATION / RATED STURD-I-FLOOR / 20 OC 19/32 INCH / SIZED FOR SPACING / T&G NET WIDTH 47-1/2 / EXPOSURE 1 / 000 / PRP-108 HUD-UM-40C
APA Rated Siding Exposure: Exterior For exterior siding, fencing, etc. Can be manufactured as plywood, as a composite or as an overlaid OSB. Both panel and lap siding available. Special surface treatment such as V-groove, channel groove, deep groove (such as APA Texture 1-11), brushed, rough sawn and overlaid (MDO) with smooth- or texture-embossed face. Span R (stud spacing for siding qualified for APA Sturd-I-Wall applications) and face grade classification (for veneer-faced siding) indicated in trademark.	$11/32$, $3/8$, $7/16$, $15/32$, $1/2$, $19/32$, $5/8$	APA THE ENGINEERED WOOD ASSOCIATION / RATED SIDING / 24 OC 19/32 INCH / SIZED FOR SPACING / EXPOSURE 1 / 000 / PRP-108 HUD-UM-40C
APA A-C Exposure: Exterior For use where appearance of only one side is important in exterior or interior applications, such as soffits, fences, farm buildings, etc.	$1/4$, $11/32$, $3/8$, $7/16$, $15/32$, $1/2$, $19/32$, $5/8$, $23/32$, $3/4$	APA THE ENGINEERED WOOD ASSOCIATION / A-C GROUP 1 / EXTERIOR / 000 / PS 1-95
APA A-D Exposure: Suitable for interior use and for protected applications that may be exposed briefly to weather during construction For use where appearance of only one side is important in interior applications, such as paneling, built-ins, shelving, partitions, flow racks, etc.	$1/4$, $11/32$, $3/8$, $15/32$, $1/2$, $19/32$, $5/8$, $23/32$, $3/4$	APA THE ENGINEERED WOOD ASSOCIATION / A-D GROUP 1 / EXPOSURE 1 / 000 / PS 1-95
APA B-C Exposure: Exterior Utility panel for farm service and work buildings, boxcar and truck linings, containers, tanks, agricultural equipment, as a base for exterior coatings and other exterior uses or applications subject to high or continuous moisture.	$1/4$, $11/32$, $3/8$, $15/32$, $1/2$, $19/32$, $5/8$, $23/32$, $3/4$	APA THE ENGINEERED WOOD ASSOCIATION / B-C GROUP 1 / EXTERIOR / 000 / PS 1-95

APA PERFORMANCE-RATED PANELS

Grade Designation, Description, and Uses	Thicknesses	Typical APA Grade Stamp
APA B-D Exposure: Suitable for interior use and for protected applications that may be exposed briefly to weather during construction Utility panel for backing, sides of built-ins, industry shelving, slip sheets, separator boards, bins and other interior or protected applications.	¼, ¹¹⁄₃₂, ³⁄₈, ¹⁵⁄₃₂, ½, ¹⁹⁄₃₂, ⁵⁄₈, ²³⁄₃₂, ¾	APA THE ENGINEERED WOOD ASSOCIATION B-D GROUP 2 EXPOSURE 1 000 PS 1-95
APA Underlayment Exposure: Suitable for interior use and for protected applications that may be exposed briefly to weather during construction For application over structural subfloor. Provides smooth surface for application of carpet and pad and possesses high concentrated and impact load resistance. For areas to be covered with resilient flooring, specify panels with "sanded face."	¼, ¹¹⁄₃₂, ³⁄₈, ¹⁵⁄₃₂, ½, ¹⁹⁄₃₂, ⁵⁄₈, ²³⁄₃₂, ¾	APA THE ENGINEERED WOOD ASSOCIATION UNDERLAYMENT GROUP 1 EXPOSURE 1 000 PS 1-95
APA C-C Plugged Exposure: Exterior For use as an underlayment over structural subfloor, refrigerated or controlled atmosphere storage rooms, open soffits, and other similar applications where continuous or severe moisture may be present. Provides smooth surface for application of carpet and pad and possesses high concentrated and impact load resistance. For areas to be covered with resilient flooring, specify panels with "sanded face."	¹¹⁄₃₂, ³⁄₈, ¹⁵⁄₃₂, ½, ¹⁹⁄₃₂, ⁵⁄₈, ²³⁄₃₂, ¾	APA THE ENGINEERED WOOD ASSOCIATION C-C PLUGGED GROUP 2 EXTERIOR 000 PS 1-95
APA C-D Plugged Exposure: Suitable for interior use and for protected applications that may be exposed briefly to weather during construction For open soffits, built-ins, and other interior or protected applications. Not a substitute for Underlayment or APA Rated Sturd-I-Floor as it lacks their puncture resistance.	³⁄₈, ¹⁵⁄₃₂, ½, ¹⁹⁄₃₂, ⁵⁄₈, ²³⁄₃₂, ¾	APA THE ENGINEERED WOOD ASSOCIATION C-D PLUGGED GROUP 2 EXPOSURE 1 000 PS 1-95
APA A-A Exposure: Interior or Exterior Use where appearance of both sides is important for interior applications such as built-ins, cabinets, furniture, partitions; and exterior applications such as fences, signs, boats, shipping containers, tanks, ducts, etc. Smooth surfaces suitable for painting.	¼, ¹¹⁄₃₂, ³⁄₈, ¹⁵⁄₃₂, ½, ¹⁹⁄₃₂, ⁵⁄₈, ²³⁄₃₂, ¾	A-A · G-1 · EXPOSURE 1-APA · 000 · PS1-95
APA A-B Exposure: Interior or Exterior For use where appearance of one side is less important but where two solid surfaces are necessary.	¼, ¹¹⁄₃₂, ³⁄₈, ¹⁵⁄₃₂, ½, ¹⁹⁄₃₂, ⁵⁄₈, ²³⁄₃₂, ¾	A-B · G-1 · EXPOSURE 1-APA · 000 · PS1-95
APA B-B Exposure: Interior or Exterior Utility panels with two solid sides.	¼, ¹¹⁄₃₂, ³⁄₈, ¹⁵⁄₃₂, ½, ¹⁹⁄₃₂, ⁵⁄₈, ²³⁄₃₂, ¾	B-B · G-2 · EXPOSURE 1-APA · 000 · PS1-95

WOOD-BURNING STOVES

WOOD STOVE LOCATION

ALSO SEE...
Chimneys & Stovepipes:
Pages 54–55
Energy:
Pages 116–117
Safety:
Pages 290–291

A wood-burning stove distributes heat more efficiently than a fireplace so it heats more of the house for longer periods and with less fuel. Wood-burning stoves also cost less installed than a masonry fireplace and are safer and more durable than many prefabricated metal fireplaces.

If you already have a fireplace, you can probably modify it to accept the flue pipe of a modern wood-burning stove. If your chimney is older, however, you may have to line it in order to handle the heat and creosote that a wood stove produces.

Some rooms are better sites for a wood-burning stove than others. The ideal room is central and opens to the other rooms of the house. In general, the more open and accessible the rooms are to stove heat, the better the convection throughout the entire house.

If you have a two-story house, put the stove in the lower level, but not too close to the stairwell because all the heat will rise without heating the first floor. Floor vents improve the circulation of heat upstairs and allow you to control the temperature, but check first with your building codes to see if such vents are allowed.

If your house is new and features airtight construction, you'll probably need to supply your stove with outside air. Most building codes now require that a vent be placed in the floor near the stove or behind it to allow outside air to be ducted directly to the stove.

Safety should be a primary consideration in your choice of location. Avoid rooms where small children play without close supervision. Obviously, the stove must be located near a chimney to avoid long horizontal runs of stovepipe. Observe all stove and stovepipe clearance regulations specified by your local building codes, and have a fire inspector check your installation before lighting your first fire.

HOW WOOD STOVES WORK

AIRTIGHT STOVES

When referring to a wood stove, the term "airtight" means that the amount and location of combustion air can be tightly controlled. Before the invention of airtight stoves, air leaked through the joints between the castings and around the lids and doors to such an extent that the fire would often continue to burn even after the stove was shut tight.

Airtight stoves are more efficiently designed and offer better control of the rate of combustion and production of heat. Unfortunately, their greater efficiency and slow production of heat result in low flue-gas temperatures which, in turn, result in the condensation of creosote (unburned liquid volatiles from the wood) in the chimney.

As a result of the high rate of smoke (visible unburned particulates) discharged from airtight stoves, the EPA mandated cleaner burning designs. Now every new stove sold in the United States must pass an emissions test.

CLEAN-BURNING STOVES

The latest generation of clean-burning wood stoves use two devices to achieve high efficiency:

■ Secondary combustion chambers, which circulate the smoke (unburned particulates) through the flame a second time for a more complete burn.
■ Catalytic combustors, which promote burning at lower temperatures.

These stoves are more expensive than the less-efficient models, but their increased fuel efficiencies pay back the added investment. You should monitor the performance of the catalytic combustor and replace the element every three to five years.

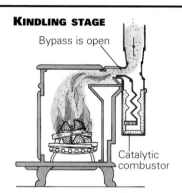

KINDLING STAGE
Bypass is open
Catalytic combustor

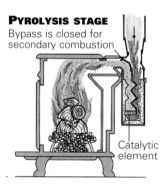

PYROLYSIS STAGE
Bypass is closed for secondary combustion
Catalytic element

CODE REQUIREMENTS: WOOD STOVES

See the tables below and opposite for common code requirements pertaining to minimum clearances for wood stoves.

REQUIRED CLEARANCES FOR WOOD STOVES WHEN ADJACENT SURFACES ARE UNPROTECTED

Combustible Surface	Radiant[1] Stove	Circulating[2] Stove	Cookstove, Firepot Lined	Unlined	Stove-pipe	UL-Listed Stove
Ceiling	36"	36"	30"	30"	18"	Follow
Front	36"	24"	–	–	18"	Directions
Side	36"	12"	Fire side 24"	Other side 24"	18"	
Rear	36"	12"	24"	36"	18"	

1 Radiant stoves are single-walled.
2 Circulating stoves have outer cabinets with convection between walls.

INSTALLATION

Installing a new stove will take from a few hours to a couple of days, depending on the location and the size of the stove. If you lack the skills or the time, but have the money, have your new stove professionally installed.

You can install a stove yourself, as long as you comply with all local code requirements, safe installation practices, and manufacturer's instructions. Be sure the chimney is in sound condition, and be aware that not all older chimneys are lined— a liner is a requirement for new stove installation. Hire a professional chimney sweep to inspect the chimney.

If you install the stove in front of an existing fireplace, connect the stovepipe to the chimney, either through the throat of the fireplace or into a hole cut above the mantel. If the chimney is unlined, you can run a stainless steel flue up the entire chimney. Pack noncombustible insulating material around the flue after it is installed. Block up the remaining fireplace opening with a metal plate or other noncombustible material.

Whether installed in front of a fireplace or not, your installation must conform to codes for distance to combustible materials and the nature of noncombustible barriers. Instructions included with a new stove will list the minimum clearances for that stove. If the stove is not new, follow the guidelines in the tables, opposite and below.

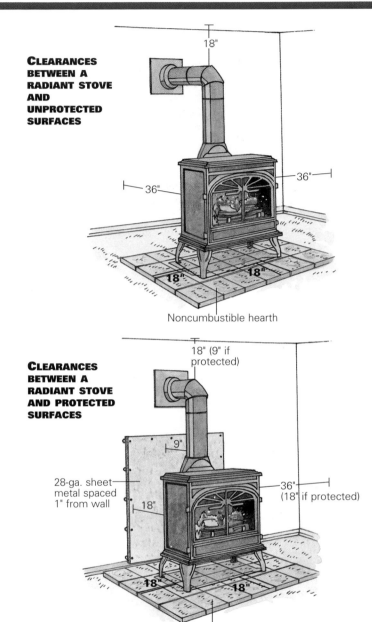

CLEARANCES BETWEEN A RADIANT STOVE AND UNPROTECTED SURFACES

18"
36"
36"
18"
18"

Noncombustible hearth

CLEARANCES BETWEEN A RADIANT STOVE AND PROTECTED SURFACES

18" (9" if protected)
9"
28-ga. sheet metal spaced 1" from wall
18"
36" (18" if protected)
18"
18"

Noncumbustible hearth

REQUIRED CLEARANCES FOR WOOD STOVES WHEN ADJACENT SURFACES ARE PROTECTED

Combustible Surfaces Covered With	Where No Protection Required, Clearance is:								
	36 inches			18 inches			12 inches		
	Above	Side	Rear	Above	Side	Rear	Above	Side	Rear
28-ga. sheet metal spaced 1" from wall and floor	18"	12"	12"	9"	6"	6"	6"	4"	4"
22-ga. sheet metal on 1" mineral batts reinforced with wire or equivalent spaced 1" from wall & floor	18"	12"	12"	4"	3"	3"	2"	2"	2"

CORD WOOD

A standard cord of wood is a stack 4 feet wide, 4 feet high, and 8 feet long, so its volume is 128 cubic feet. Due to the irregular shape of wood, the standard cord also contains 80 cubic feet of solid wood and 48 cubic feet of air.

When buying wood, beware of "face cords" which are 4 feet high and 8 feet long, but can be of any depth. A face cord 2 feet deep actually contains only half a standard cord.

THE WARMTH OF WOOD

ALSO SEE...
Adhesives:
Pages 8–9
Fasteners:
Pages 122–125
Floors:
Pages 140–141
Paints & Stains:
Pages 232–241
Resilient Flooring:
Pages 274–279

The warmth, beauty, and durability of wood make it one of the most popular flooring materials. Wood adds a feeling of quality and permanence to any room, can last the lifetime of a house, insulates, and is comfortable to walk on. If kept clean and protected, it will never even have to be refinished, but will only look better as it takes on the patina of age.

Wood is, however, subject to moisture damage from leaks or high humidity. Take precautions when installing it over an enclosed crawl space or below grade, and fix plumbing leaks immediately. A few types of prefinished hardwood flooring are made to withstand some moisture in areas such as kitchens. Ask your dealer for recommendations if you'll be installing flooring in those areas.

SELECTING WOOD FLOORING

Wood flooring is available in both hardwood and softwood and, in some cases, comes prefinished. Most flooring is hardwood: red oak, white oak, teak, walnut, maple, pecan, or hickory. Softwoods, such as pine, Douglas fir, and redwood, can also be used as flooring materials, but they don't wear as well as the hardwoods. Southern yellow pine, technically a softwood, is actually so dense and hard that it wears nearly as well as oak.

Flooring is milled in three basic formats: strip (tongue-and-groove or square edged), plank, and block.

■ Tongue-and-groove strip flooring comes in widths of up to 3¼ inches. It is usually ¾ inch thick and features tongue-and-groove edges and ends. It installs with nails driven at an angle through the tongue side. This "blind nailing" technique hides the nail head.

Square-edged flooring, typically ⁵⁄₁₆ to ¾ inches thick, is used where specialty woods or unusual widths are desired. Without tongue-and-groove edges, however, square-edged flooring expands and shrinks over time, resulting in uneven edges. Square-edged flooring must be screwed or nailed directly through the tops of the boards, a process called "face nailing."

■ Plank flooring comes in widths of up to 9 inches. It is ¾ inch thick and has tongue-and-groove edges. Sometimes the ends are held down with pegs or with screws that are countersunk and covered with plugs.

■ Wood flooring also comes in blocks of various sizes, usually square, that are arranged into parquet tiles.

ESTIMATING HARDWOOD STRIP FLOORING (BOARD FEET, ASSUMING 5% WASTE)

Area, sq. ft.	Flooring Size, Inches						
	¾×1½	¾×2¼	¾×3¼	½×1½	½×2	⅜×1½	¾×2
5	8	7	6	7	7	7	7
10	16	14	13	14	13	14	13
20	31	28	26	28	26	28	26
30	47	42	39	42	39	42	39
40	62	55	52	55	52	55	52
50	78	69	65	69	65	69	65
60	93	83	77	83	78	83	78
70	109	97	90	97	91	97	91
80	124	111	103	111	104	111	104
90	140	125	116	125	117	125	117
100	155	138	129	138	130	138	130

NAILING SCHEDULE FOR HARDWOOD FLOORING

Size, inches	Fastener	Spacing
TONGUE-AND-GROOVE FLOORING, BLIND-NAILED		
½×1½	1½" machine-driven fastener; 5d screw, cut steel, or wire casing nail.	10"
⅜×1½	1¼" machine-driven fastener; 4d bright wire casing nail.	8"
¾	2" machine-driven fastener; 7d or 8d screw or cut nail.	8"
¾×2¼	2" machine-driven fastener; 7d or 8d screw or cut nail.	8"
¾×3¼	2" machine-driven fastener; 7d or 8d screw or cut nail.	8"
¾×3–8 plank	2" machine-driven fastener; 7d or 8d screw or cut nail.	8"
SQUARE-EDGE FLOORING, FACE-NAILED		
⁵⁄₁₆×1⅓	1" 15-gauge fully barbed flooring brad.	5" alternating sides
⁵⁄₁₆×1½	1" 15-gauge fully barbed flooring brad.	2 every 7"
⁵⁄₁₆×2	1" 15-gauge fully barbed flooring brad.	2 every 7"

Installing unfinished, strip flooring requires a great deal of labor, including messy sanding and finishing. The typical homeowner, however, can install prefinished hardwood flooring quickly and easily. A drawback is that most prefinished hardwood flooring carries a warranty period of only 10 to 15 years and is too thin to be sanded and refinished more than once.

Most prefinished wood flooring is made of laminated hardwood veneer over hardboard, which is more stable than solid wood and can be directly fastened to almost any subfloor that is level, dry, and tight. The floor can be glued to concrete, vinyl, or plywood.

There are two installation systems: fastening the floor to the subfloor, and floating the floor on a pad.

FASTENED FLOOR

1. Remove the baseboard to allow an expansion gap.
2. Remove all carpeting and repair any damage to the floor.
3. Cut the door trim at the base so the new flooring will slip beneath it.
4. Move the flooring into the room. Lay out test patterns to see how the flooring material fits in doorways and irregular areas.
5. Figure out your layout. Make a plan on paper if necessary.

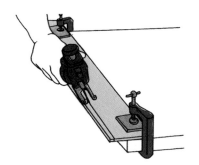

6. Cut the pieces to length as needed. A backsaw and miter box will work, but a power miter saw ("chop saw") is best. Cut pieces to width with a table saw or jig saw. Protect the finished surface when you clamp pieces to be cut.

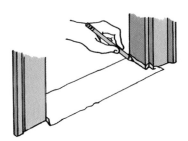

7. Make a paper template for doorways and irregularly shaped areas.

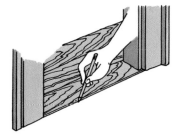

8. Mark the outlines of cut pieces on the floor.
9. Apply adhesive with a notched trowel up to the guideline, following the manufacturer's instructions.

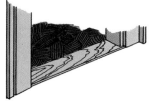

10. Install the planks. Glue should not ooze up through the cracks; if it does, you are using too much glue, or you have moved the plank too much.
11. Walk on the surface or use a roller to get a tight bond.
12. Continue to add flooring run by run. Spread only as much adhesive as you can easily cover in the time before it cures. Use a respirator and provide ventilation if the adhesive manufacturer advises you to.
13. Cut off the excess at the end of each run and use it to start the next run. Allow ⅜ inch for expansion and contraction at the walls.
14. After the flooring is laid, cover the gaps at the walls with the old baseboard or new quarter round.

FLOATING FLOOR

A floating-floor installation requires a ⅛-inch foam pad under the floor and only a little carpenter's wood glue between the pieces. The tongue-and-groove fittings are cut precisely, so the pieces must be tapped together to ensure a tight fit.
1. Remove the quarter-round shoe molding to allow an expansion gap.
2. Remove carpeting and repair any damage to the floor below.
3. Cut the door trim at the base so the new flooring will slip beneath it.
4. Roll the pad into position and trim it as needed.
5. Lay the planks, leaving a ⅜-inch gap at the walls. Cut off any excess and use it to start the next run.
6. As you lay each plank, glue it to the one already laid. Use a thin bead of carpenter's wood glue inside the bottom of the groove.

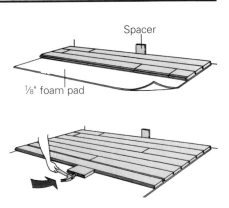

7. Tap the planks together with a scrap piece of flooring to protect the tongue-and-groove edges.
8. After the flooring is laid, cover the gaps at the walls with baseboard. Replace the quarter-round shoe molding.

INSTALLING TONGUE-AND-GROOVE FLOORING

PREPARATION

Hardwood strip flooring can bridge minor gaps, so all you have to do to prepare the subfloor is make sure there are no projections, such as nails. Carefully pry off the shoe molding and baseboards, avoiding splitting them so you can later reinstall them. Write an identifying mark on the back of each piece so you can return it to the same location. Measure doors to see if they will provide clearance over the new flooring. Plan for a gap of at least ⅜ inch below each door. If a space is tight, remove the door and trim the bottom to fit. To avoid complicated flooring cuts later on, saw off the bottoms of all door casings and door stops—but not door jambs. Saw them off just high enough for the flooring material to slide under snugly.

If you are installing wood flooring in a kitchen, the new floor will "lower" the countertop by the thickness of the flooring material. Check that any undercounter appliance, such as a dishwasher, will have clearance.

THE FLOORING

Wood flooring has a low initial moisture content and is subject to expansion if it gets wet. Avoid deliveries during rain or snow. Store the wood in the room in which you plan to install it, or at least inside the house. The room should be dry and heated to 65 or 70° F.

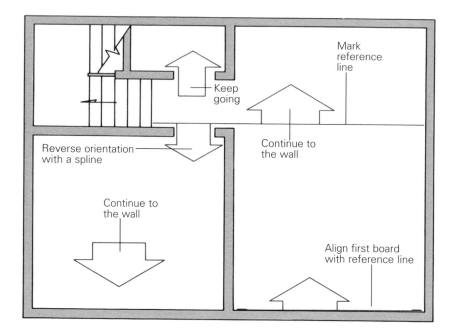

Stack the material log-cabin style or scatter it around the room, then let it acclimate for three to five days.

PLANNING THE LAYOUT

If you are flooring just one room, start along one wall and work your way across the floor, with the tongue edge exposed so you can blind nail the individual hardwood strips.

If the flooring continues into other rooms, or even a closet or hallway, plan the layout so that you can cover as much area as possible by working with the tongues in one direction. At some point you will need to change the orientation of the tongues—when you get too close to a wall to swing a hammer, when you run flooring into an alcove, or when a hall leads into another wood with the opposite orientation. To change orientation, use a spline—a strip of wood that fits snugly into the groove. Splines convert grooved edges to tongued edges (see the illustration on page 460).

THE STARTER COURSE

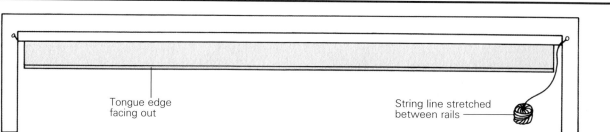

To establish a straight line for the first course of flooring, stretch a mason's line between opposite sides of the room. Align the first row of flooring with the line. If the wall is not square with the rest of the room (which you can determine by measuring the diagonals of the room) adjust the starter line so that imperfections are split evenly between the starter side of the room and the opposite, or ending, side.

Lay the first board against the line so that the left end is ½ inch from the side wall. (Floor installers refer to left and right with their backs to the starting wall.) Line up the groove edge along the string line. Beginning at the left end, carefully face-nail the board with 8d finishing nails at every joist and halfway between them. Because face nailing can split the board easily, predrill for each nail.

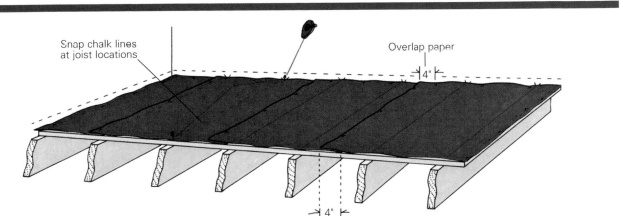

Snap chalk lines
at joist locations

Overlap paper

4"

4"

ESTABLISHING NAILING LINES

Strip flooring is usually laid perpendicular to joists, with the blind-nailing centered over them. In some cases the flooring may look better if it runs parallel to the joists. You can install it this way if the subfloor is at least ¾ inch thick.

Determine the joist locations by looking for the nailing pattern on the subfloor. Mark the joist positions on the end walls so you can still see them

even if you cover the subfloor with a layer of building paper.

On floors above unheated spaces, lay 15-pound asphalt-saturated building paper laid perpendicular to the direction of the new flooring. Overlap the paper edges 4 inches, and trim the paper around the wall so that it stays flat. Staple or tack the building paper in place. Then snap chalk lines between the joist marks on the walls.

To establish a guideline along the starting wall, measure out ¾ inch at each end of the wall and drive a small nail into the floor. Stretch a string line tautly between these two nails. The ¾-inch space will allow the wood to expand without buckling the boards and the gap will be covered by the baseboard.

RACKING THE ENDS

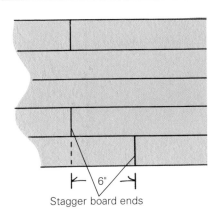

6"

Stagger board ends

45°

Predrilled
pilot hole

Face nail
starter board

Blind-nail
successive courses

¾"

To ensure a random joint pattern in the floor, loosely arrange six or seven courses at a time, mixing long and short lengths. This process is called racking the floor. Be sure that all joints are staggered at least 6 inches. Begin each course with the cutoff piece from the end of the previous course. Rack the boards loosely enough to have room to operate the flooring nailer.

If you are installing flooring of various widths, such as 3-inch, 5-inch, and 8-inch plank flooring, separate the boards into piles of the same width before racking them. This will give

you an idea of how many boards are available in each size so that you can maintain the same pattern without running out of a particular width.

Complete the starter course by face-nailing several additional boards. This ensures that the layout will not be jolted out of position when subsequent rows of the flooring are blind-nailed to the subfloor. It also provides enough room to swing a hammer effectively for blind nailing.

Cut the last board ½ inch short of the side wall. If the leftover piece is at least 2 feet long, use it to start

the following course. Save any shorter pieces to make test templates for cutouts. Blind-nail the tongue edge of these boards by hand. Drive the nails at a 45-degree angle, being careful not to damage the edge or tongue of the board. Use a nailset to set the nail heads into the tongue corners.

Blind-nail the following two courses by hand. Nail at each joist, at the midpoints between joists, and 2 inches from the end of each board.

INSTALLING TONGUE-AND-GROOVE FLOORING *continued*

├ 2" ┤

USING A FLOORING NAILER

Use a flooring nailer—available at rental stores—to install the rest of the strips. This easy-to-operate tool is especially designed for blind nailing flooring strips. It permits you to work standing up, so that you can move easily and quickly

along each row of flooring. When you hit the plunger with the mallet, it drives a specially designed flooring nail through the tongue and into the subfloor. Starting about 2 inches from the wall, stand so that your toes can hold down the board being nailed. Use a firm, easy swing, working from one end to the other.

THE LAST COURSE

When you reach the end wall, there will not be room to operate the nailer. Hand-nail the last few courses. If you cannot fit a full-width board at the edge, rip a board to fit, cutting off the tongue edge.

To snug the last board into place, wedge a prybar between the board and the wall, protecting the wall with a wood block. When the board is in position, face-nail it, predrilling a hole for each nail so that the board will not split.

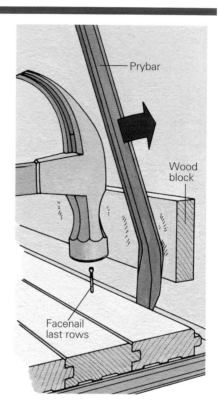

Prybar

Wood block

Facenail last rows

INSTALLING A SPLINE

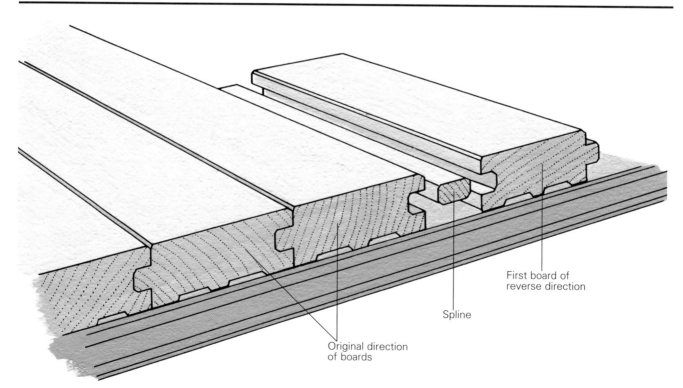

First board of reverse direction

Spline

Original direction of boards

In certain stages of installation, such as doorways and closets, you may need to change the orientation of the tongues and grooves. When you need to reverse the direction of the tongue edge, glue a spline into the groove of the previous strip and then install the reversed flooring courses. Lay the first board so that the groove interlocks with the spline. Tap it into place, using a scrap of wood to protect the tongue from being damaged by the hammer.

Square-edge flooring typically is less expensive than tongue-and-groove flooring because there is less milling waste. However, all nail holes are on the exposed face and must be filled.

PREPARING THE FLOOR

Lay down 15-pound felt, then establish a guideline along the starting wall as described for tongue-and-groove flooring (see pages 458–460)—allowing a ½-inch to ¾-inch gap along the wall. If you want a border around the perimeter of the room, stretch string lines along the two side walls and back wall, squaring them to the starter line by measuring diagonally.

LAYING THE STARTER COURSE

Begin the installation along the longest wall. Choose a long, straight strip of flooring and lay it inside the starter string line. Predrill nail holes about ½ inch from each end of the board to prevent splitting, and face-nail the board with two flooring brads every 7 inches, predrilling if necessary.

INSTALLING THE BORDER

If you are installing a border, install the course along the opposite wall next, followed by the two side walls, so that they fit tightly between the starting and ending wall courses.

To begin each side course, cut the end of the first board square with a miter saw. Align it along the string line so that the squared end fits snugly against the first course. Predrill holes and nail with two brads every 7 inches. Finish both side courses in the same way. Complete the border by alternating the courses, as shown in the illustration.

NAILING THE STRIPS

Straighten bowed boards by driving a chisel into the subfloor and using it as a lever. Protect the edge of the board with a scrap of wood. Work your way down the board (at the 7-inch intervals), maintaining constant pressure. If you ease off on the pressure, the board may split as you nail it. After completing the border, install the rest of the flooring.

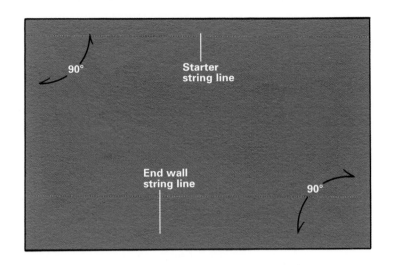

Starter string line

End wall string line

90°

90°

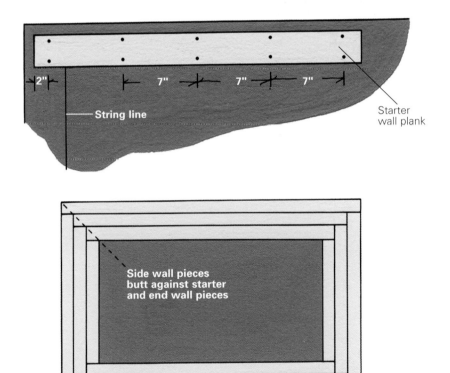

2"   7"   7"   7"

String line

Starter wall plank

Side wall pieces butt against starter and end wall pieces

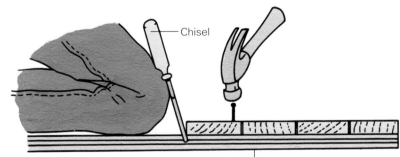

Chisel

Subfloor

DRESSING UP A FLOOR

To "dress up" a wood floor, inlay contrasting wood strips, or install plugs. Both methods are simple and will add interesting contrast to the flooring surface.

ROUTED STRIPS

With a router, you can inlay strips of contrasting wood, such as walnut or hickory. You can also use matching wood on edge to give a different grain pattern. For further emphasis, you can stain the strips darker or lighter than the floor.

Rout straight grooves of exactly the same width and depth as the inlay strips. Guide the router with a straightedge held to the floor with 4d finishing nails. Apply wood glue to the groove and press the inlay pieces into place, immediately wiping up any adhesive that squeezes out.

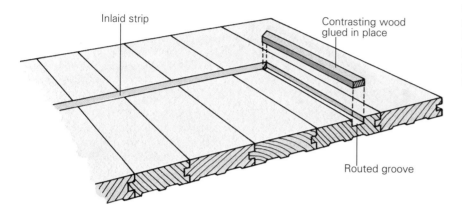

Inlaid strip

Contrasting wood glued in place

Routed groove

PLUGGING

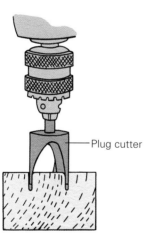

Plug cutter

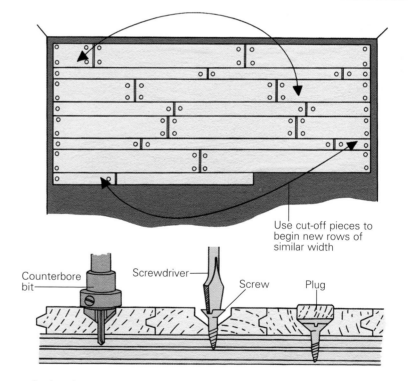

Use cut-off pieces to begin new rows of similar width

Counterbore bit

Screwdriver

Screw

Plug

Plugging (or "pegging") plank floors creates a charming, rustic look. In some cases the plugs conceal screws that hold down the extra-wide boards. In others they are merely decorative, simulating the pegged floors of bygone days. Many manufacturers offer easy-to-install wooden plugs to go with their plank flooring.

Plugged flooring is installed the same way as regular tongue-and-groove flooring, but preplugged flooring comes with an additional problem. Since you must cut boards to fit each time you end a course, the boards along the right wall will have no plugs at one end. If you use the cut-off pieces to start new courses, they, too, will have no plugs at one end. If you want the

floor to look right, you must drill and plug the cut ends yourself.

If you do install your own plugs, use one at each end for 3½-inch-wide boards, two for 6-inch boards, and three for 8-inch boards. If you are fastening the boards with screws, drill pilot holes, then counterbore them for the size plug you are using. Use No. 9 or No. 12 wood screws. Precut plugs

are available at flooring suppliers and home centers. You can also make your own plugs with a plug-cutting bit and electric drill. Glue the plug and tap it into the hole. If the flooring is prefinished, the plug should be flush with the top. Otherwise, you can chisel off the top of the plug and then smooth it flush at the same time as you sand the rest of the floor.

FINISHING WOOD FLOORS

Finishing a floor, whether new or old, involves sanding it smooth, applying sealer or stain, and covering it with a durable finish.

Before refinishing an older floor, check to see if it really needs sanding. It may be merely dulled by several layers of old wax and grime. Rub a small area with steel wool dipped in denatured alcohol, then wipe it dry with a clean rag to remove any wax. If damp-mopping the bare wood and applying paste wax brings the floor back to life, clean the entire floor the same way.

RENTING SANDING EQUIPMENT

Most tool-rental companies provide the equipment needed for sanding floors: a drum sander for the main part of the floor and a floor edger for corners and edges. Both machines are very powerful, very heavy, and require strength to operate. Have the rental agent show you how to use them; not all machines are alike. Make sure you know how to change the sandpaper, lower the drum, and empty the dust bags. You will need at least three grades of sandpaper in both sheets and disks. Take home twice as many as you think you need—you won't be charged for paper that you return unused.

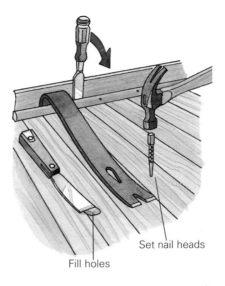

Set nail heads

Fill holes

PREPARING FOR SANDING

Before sanding, make sure the flooring is thick enough to stand losing up to ⅛ inch in thickness. Check the flooring thickness at a floor register or by removing an inconspicuous board. Then remove all furnishings, including curtains. Cover built-in furnishings and doorways with plastic sheeting. Remove the baseboards, fill deep holes, and set all nail heads at least ⅛ inch below the top surface. Make sure you have a dust mask and shoes with clean soles (not black rubber). If it is warm enough, open all of the windows in the room to flush out the dust-filled air. Wear ear protectors—most sanders are extremely noisy.

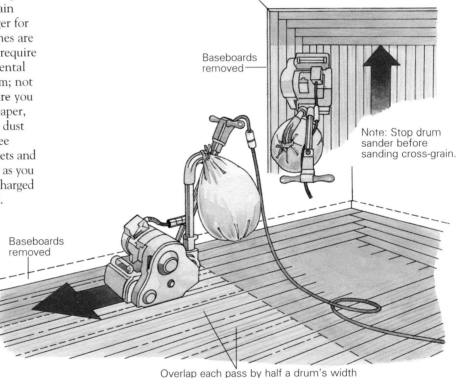

Baseboards removed

Note: Stop drum sander before sanding cross-grain.

Baseboards removed

Overlap each pass by half a drum's width

USING A DRUM SANDER

Make sure you know how to operate a drum sander—used improperly, it will gouge the floor. Start with a coarse sandpaper to remove an old finish, and a medium grade for initial sanding of a new floor. Sand in the direction of the strips. Because the drum constantly rotates, don't let it touch the floor unless it is moving forward.

Start along the right side of the room, a few inches from the side wall and behind an imaginary centerline.

Sand toward the wall. Then, with the drum still engaged, pull the sander back over the imaginary centerline and—overlapping the previous pass by half the width of the drum—sand toward the wall again.

When you have finished the first half of the floor, turn around and sand on the other side of the imaginary centerline in the same manner. Sand any border separately—with the grain—after you finish the center area.

Sand the entire floor once with the coarse paper. The floor will be coarse and fuzzy, so the next step is to smooth the wood by sanding it with the medium grit. Replace the sandpaper when it begins to lose its effectiveness. When this second sanding is complete, fill any remaining open cracks or nail holes with a wood filler, using a broad putty knife. When the wood filler is completely dry, sand the floor one last time with the fine-grit sandpaper.

FINISHING WOOD FLOORS *continued*

SANDING THE EDGES

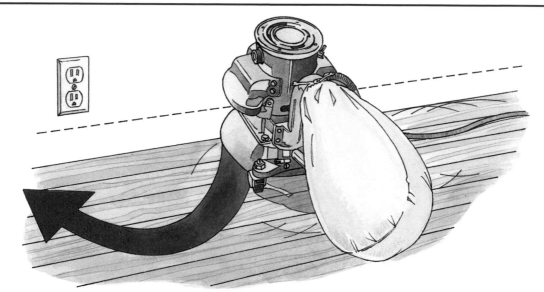

The drum sander cannot reach every part of the floor, so you need an edger to sand along walls and in tight spaces such as closets. The edger is a rotary sander and uses sandpaper disks. Its surface turns at a faster speed than the drum sander's, so it is even more prone to gouging. Begin in closets or other out-of-sight spaces until you get the feel of the machine.

Avoid gouging by using a scalloping motion of small semicircles, rather than a straight back-and-forth motion. Avoid leaning the sander to the right or left, which forces the disk to gouge across the grain. In corners where the wood strips join at right angles, turn the edger to go with the grain, and go back and forth around the turn several times. Use the same grade of paper that you use for drum sanding, filling cracks and nail holes before using the fine-grit sandpaper.

Because the disk is round and corners are square, you will be left with unsanded triangles in every inside corner. Use a small pad sander in these corners and any other spots that are inaccessible to the larger sanding machines.

SANDING PARQUET FLOORS

Using coarse paper, sand across the floor diagonally with the drum sander. Next, sand across the floor on the other diagonal with medium grit. Finish with a fine grit, sanding parallel to the walls. Go over the floor with each grit twice, first walking with the drum sander and then pulling it back with you. Overlap each pass by half the width of the drum.

Use the edger in the same way as for strip floors. A parquet floor has many joints and cracks, so it may need more filler than a strip floor. Buy a 1-gallon can if your floor has excessive cracks and open seams.

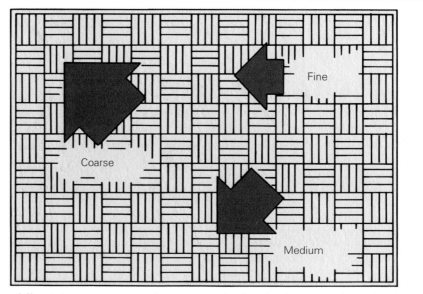

APPLYING SEALER OR STAIN

Seal the floor the same day you finish sanding to prevent it from absorbing moisture from the air. Excess sealer will not penetrate into the wood, but unless removed it will leave dark splotches on the surface. For best results, apply sealer with a sheepskin applicator, carefully wiping away any residue after 10 or 15 minutes.

Buff the room with No. 2 fine steel wool after the sealer dries, then vacuum and dust with a tack cloth.

Apply a finish wax or plastic (such as polyurethane) floor finish next. Apply at least two coats, and wait at least 24 hours after the final coat dries before moving furniture in.

FLOOR REPAIRS

DAMAGED BOARDS

If a strip or plank has been damaged so much that a little sanding or filling is not good enough, you will have to replace it. Before cutting into it, look for nails, and use a nail set to drive them as far through the board as possible.

1 Using a square, mark the section to be removed.

2 Drill holes through the board along the marks.

3 Strip out the damaged board.

4 Square up the drilled edge with a sharp chisel.

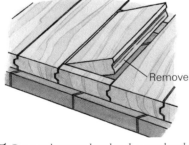

Remove

5 Cut a replacement board to the same length. Remove the bottom side of the groove.

6 Apply construction adhesive to the back side of the replacement board, tap it into place, nail it, and finish it to match the rest of the floor.

SPLIT BOARDS

Repair split flooring immediately or the crack will lengthen.

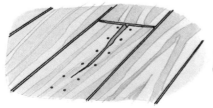

1 If you can, force carpenter's glue into the crack, then drill pilot holes and drive nails at an angle beside the crack and slightly beyond its end.

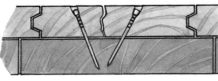

2 Countersink the nail heads and fill the holes and crack with stained plastic wood or a putty that matches the finish of the flooring.

WARPED BOARDS

1 Using paint remover, remove any wax or finish, then keep the warped boards under damp rags for 48 hours.

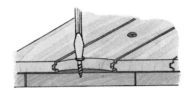

2 Screw the warped board to the subfloor with countersunk screws. Keeping the flooring damp, tighten the screws a little each day until the board is level again.

3 Let the flooring dry, then fill the screw holes and refinish the board to match the original floor.

ADJACENT WARPED BOARDS

1 Cut away the tongue in the warped section. Remove wax and finish, then keep under damp rags for 48 hours.

2 Screw the boards to the subfloor with countersunk screws. Tighten screws a half turn or so each day.

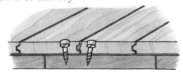

3 When flat, refinish the floor.

465

WOOD SHINGLE ROOFING

LONG-LASTING BEAUTY

ALSO SEE...
Asphalt Shingle Roofing:
Pages 10–13
Flashing:
Pages 136–139
Roofs:
Pages 282–289
Shake Roofing:
Pages 298–299

Wood shingles, like shakes, are long lasting and easy to apply, but they are lighter and more uniform in thickness. Shingles come in lengths of 16, 18, and 24 inches and are sold in bundles. Four bundles nominally cover a square (100 square feet) but, as you can see from the table, *right*, coverage depends on both length and exposure. The minimum allowable roof slope for shingles is 3-in-12. Only Grade 1 shingles are used for roofing.

Shingles and shakes have two drawbacks: combustibility and discoloration from fungi. Both can be minimized with chemical treatments, which should be applied commercially before installation. Codes in some areas with extreme fire hazard may still not allow wood roofs, even after they have been treated.

PREPARING THE DECK

Wood shingles can last a long time, but only when air can circulate both beneath and above them so that they are able to dry out completely. To provide air circulation, install them over spaced sheathing with a well-ventilated attic beneath.

Sheathing is usually 1×4s, spaced the same distance as the shingle exposure. In the example shown, the exposure is 5 inches, so the gap between 1×4 boards (actually 3½ inches wide) is 1½ inches.

Sheathing along the eaves may be solid for the sake of appearance, and should be solid for 18 inches next to a ridge to allow for changes in nail spacings.

Install 18-gauge, galvanized-steel, ribbed valley flashing before shingling a valley. Instead of drip edges, allow the shingles to project a full inch at the eaves and ⅜ inch at the rakes.

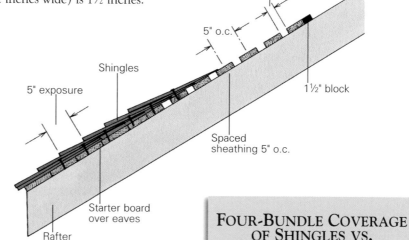

1½" between boards

5" o.c.

5" exposure

Shingles

1½" block

Spaced sheathing 5" o.c.

Starter board over eaves

Rafter

PREPARING AN OLD ROOF

OVER OLD WOOD SHINGLES

If the old roof is laid with wood shingles that are in reasonably good shape, it is possible to apply new shingles directly over them. Nail down or replace any warped shingles. Remove shingles along the eaves, rakes, and ridges to make room for 1×6 edging boards. Cut a clean line by setting a circular saw to just the right depth; cut only the shingles and not the sheathing. Use a carbide-tip blade since you may be cutting an occasional nail. Nail bevel siding to the ridge, and install new flashing in the valleys.

OVER ASPHALT ROOFING

If the roof is covered with composition shingles or roll roofing, nail the spaced sheathing directly over it. First remove any ridge and hip shingles, and replace them with a strip of 30-pound felt. Trim back the shingles with tin snips where they overhang eaves and rakes. Nail 1×6s along these edges and 1×4s for the rest of the spaced sheathing. At valleys, nail 1×4s down on each side and run the regularly spaced sheathing up to them, leaving a ½-inch gap. Then install 18-gauge, galvanized-steel, ribbed valley flashing.

FOUR-BUNDLE COVERAGE OF SHINGLES VS. EXPOSURE IN SQUARE FEET

Exposure, inches	Shingle Length		
	16	18	24
3½	70	–	–
4	80	72	–
4½	90	81	–
5	100	90	–
5½	110	100	–
6	120	109	80
7	140	127	93
8	160	145	106
9	–	163	120
10	–	–	133

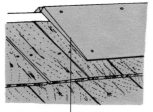

Bevel siding at ridge

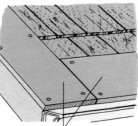

1×6 edging board

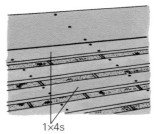

1×4s

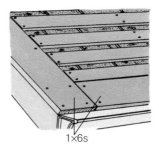

1×6s

APPLICATION

THE FIRST COURSE

Do not use a felt underlayment with shingles. Instead, nail them directly over spaced sheathing. To start, nail a shingle at each end of the eave so that it overhangs the eave 1 inch and the rake ⅜ inch. Drive a nail into the butt of each shingle, and stretch a line between them to use as a guide for the rest of the starter course. Leave a ⅛- to ¼-inch gap between shingles. Double the first course of shingles, staggering the gaps by at least 1½ inches. Then start the regular courses at the recommended exposure.

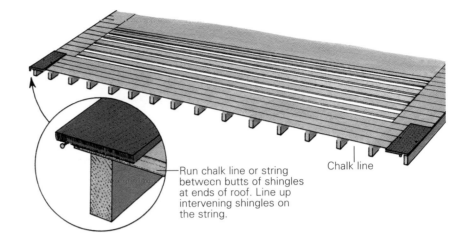

Run chalk line or string between butts of shingles at ends of roof. Line up intervening shingles on the string.

Chalk line

NAILING

Use hot-dipped galvanized (HDG) box nails, figuring that you will need about 2 pounds per square. Use 3d nails for 16- and 18-inch shingles and 4d nails for 24-inch shingles. Use 6d nails for reroofing as well as for nailing hip and ridge shingles.

You can nail with a regular 16-oz. claw hammer, but a roofer's hammer has the right heft for so much nailing and it includes handy measuring gauges. To find the right placement for each nail, measure up from the butt of the shingle a distance equal to the exposure, plus 1 or 2 inches. To measure this distance easily, mark the handle of your hammer with tape.

Nail snugly, but not so hard that the nail head breaks the wood fibers. If a shingle is crooked, don't try to realign it after driving two nails; it is better to pull it out and add it to your shim-shingle pile.

Stagger gaps between shingles at least 1½ inches between courses. The gaps should not line up over gaps in the courses below.

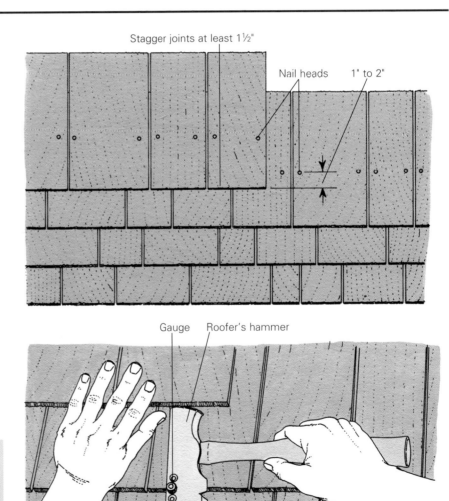

Stagger joints at least 1½"

Nail heads

1" to 2"

Gauge   Roofer's hammer

ROOF SHINGLE EXPOSURE

Shingle Grade	Length, inches	Max. Exposure at Roof Slope 3/12	≥4/12
No. 1	16	3¾	5
Blue	18	4¼	5½
Label	24	5½	7½

467

WORKBENCHES

THE PROJECT THAT MAKES OTHER JOBS EASIER

ALSO SEE...
Fasteners:
Pages 122–125
Tools:
Pages 374–383
Wood Floors:
Pages 456–465

If you are serious about having a workshop, one of the first things you'll need is a workbench. A workbench has a firm, durable surface that puts work pieces right where you need them. Build one for:

■ woodworking, including a woodworking vise.
■ metalworking, including a swivel-base bench vise.

■ electrical projects, including a small clamp-on vise.
■ portable use, placing it on casters and including a power strip.

Of course you can buy workbenches already made, but the low-cost benches often look like they were made from lumber rejects, and the decent ones cost an arm and a leg.

Why not make your own? If you are doing enough carpentry to justify owning a bench, then you certainly have the skills required to assemble one. What's more, you can have

one that fits your space and your needs exactly, all for the price of the shoddy one at the store.

A pair of sawhorses is another must for any workshop or building project. Again, you can buy a set consisting of metal brackets into which you insert 2×4 legs and a cross piece. Or, for even less money, you can make a pair of professional-looking, stacking horses.

Here are plans for two sizes of classic workbenches and sawhorses that will be your most reliable aids through many workshop projects to come.

WORKBENCH BUILDING

THE DESIGN

This is the classic workbench, meant to be placed against a garage, basement, or workshop wall, with a tool rack above, a power strip either along the backboard or under the front lip, and a mounted vice at one corner.

Adjust the length to fit your space. Most workbenches you buy are 6 feet long, but either 4 feet or 8 feet is a more economical use of materials.

Adjust the height to the height of your table saw or to a level at which your work will feel comfortable.

This table (below) has a work surface 27½ inches deep, because it consists of five 2×6s (actual 1½×5½). You can make it any depth you wish, but 27½ inches is ideal.

ASSEMBLY

1. Lay out the four 2×6 top rails and nail each butt joint with a pair of 16d common nails.
2. Lay out the five kiln-dried 2×6 top planks with no gaps. Predrill the planks, then screw them down to the top-rail frame using 3- to 4-inch wallboard screws. If you wish to mount an anvil-type vise, make sure the top extends 3 inches beyond the top rail along the front.
3. If the bench spans more than 6 feet, fasten a 2×6 support at midlength.
4. Turn the top assembly upside down and screw 2×4 legs into the corners using 3-inch wallboard screws through the rails.

5. Carefully turn the bench right-side up. Screw the two 2×4 bottom rails to the legs to support the shelf.
6. Screw the ¾-inch plywood bottom shelf on top of the bottom rails.
7. Screw the ¾-inch plywood back to the 2×6 rear top rail. If the back is 12 inches high, it will extend about 5 inches above the work surface—high enough for a rear power outlet strip.
8. Attach the ¼-inch tempered hardboard top to the planks with carpenters glue dabbed along the edges, so it can be removed and replaced easily when it becomes worn from use.

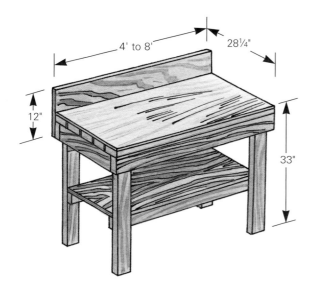

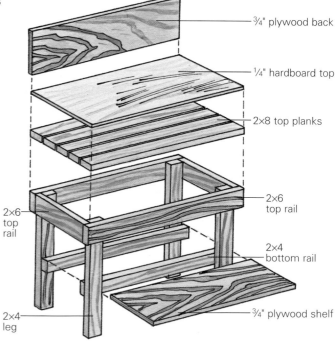

¾" plywood back

¼" hardboard top

2×8 top planks

2×6 top rail

2×4 bottom rail

¾" plywood shelf

2×6 top rail

2×4 leg

PORTABLE WORKCENTER

THE DESIGN

This rolling work center is designed to be moved to suit the job. Since it is square, it is convenient for working from all sides. The bottom shelf is a convenient place to store hand power tools. One or more power strips—mounted to the recessed top rails—keep power cords conveniently out of the way. A vise—either woodworking or swivel—adds to its utility.

Feel free to adjust the height to your needs. If you will be using it to assemble tall items, or items where you need to apply downward pressure, make it less than 33 inches high.

ASSEMBLY

Assembly is similar to the other workbench except that the ¾-inch plywood top screws down to the top rail

with 2- to 3-inch wallboard screws. If you expect to do a lot of heavy pounding on the top, glue and screw a second ¾-inch plywood sheet to the first before applying the hardboard. This provides a much more solid worktop surface.

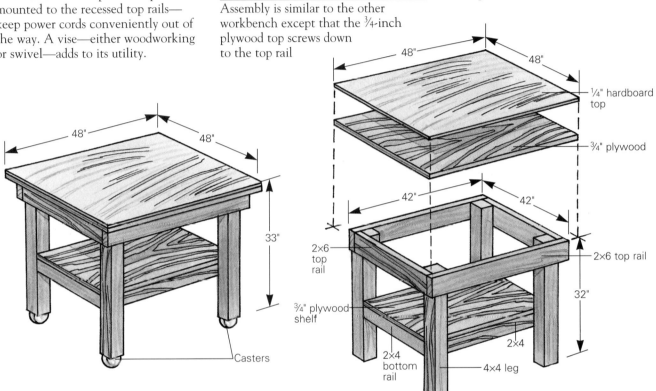

SAWHORSES

THE DESIGN

These sawhorses are lightweight, feature flared legs for stability, and can be stacked. Although not required, adding glue keeps the assembly stable.

ASSEMBLY

1. Cut one of the legs to a length that will make using the sawhorse comfortable—21 inches is good.

2. Using the first leg as a template, cut three more identical legs (for the first horse, plus four legs for each additional horse).
3. Cut two top rails for each horse, each 28½ inches long.
4. Glue and screw a pair of legs to each of the top rails. Do one side first, then use it as a model for the other side.

5. Glue and screw the ¾-inch plywood top braces and 1×4 bottom braces to the legs.
6. Finally, predrill and screw (not glue) the 2×8 top to the top rails, using 3-inch wallboard screws.

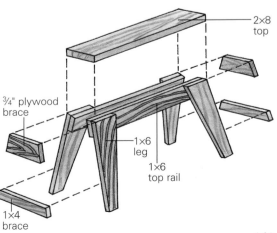

ZONING, CODES, AND PERMITS

IT'S THE LAW

ALSO SEE... Most entries include code requirements.

Before you start any improvement project, it is essential that you investigate local zoning laws, building codes, and the permit process.

To learn about these legal restrictions in your area, call or visit your local building department. If you want general information, the building department will probably refer you to whatever model codes it uses. Some departments distribute printed booklets that include additional requirements or exceptions; others have complete summaries that you can buy.

If you have a specific project in mind, take as many drawings or photos as possible to the building department to determine the feasibility of your plans. Department personnel may be unable or unwilling to advise you on the specifics of how to do something, but they can tell you if your plans comply with the code. Because laws vary from county to county, don't assume anything until you have inquired.

ZONING ORDINANCES

Zoning regulations generally affect exterior construction, not interior remodeling. The purpose of zoning is to protect the quality and safety of a neighborhood. In some areas, for example, codes allow only certain architectural styles.

Ordinances also prevent the unsuitable use of property within a specific zone. If your neighborhood is zoned for single-family houses, for example, the code protects you from a business wanting to build a factory or a fast-food restaurant next door to you.

Zoning regulations also define setbacks. A setback is the distance a building must be from a property line. These distances vary from front to back and from side to side. For example, the front setback may be 25 or 30 feet; on the side, the setback may be only 5 to 10 feet. You may be required to prove the precise location of a property line. Note that a fence or other boundary may not be an accurate indication of the actual property line.

There may be other special zoning requirements in your area; find out before you invest too much time or money in planning. For example, your zone may limit building height. If your site slopes, you need to know what the law considers to be grade level.

Zoning regulations can affect your home-improvement plans in a number of ways. For example:
- A regulation may require a larger setback on a second-story addition than on the existing first floor.
- Depending on the size of your lot, another regulation might mean the only place you may build is the rear of the house.

- You may be required to provide off-street, enclosed parking for your car; if so, you will have to scrap plans to convert your garage to living space.
- The ordinance may interpret an addition that provides living space for your parents as a conversion to a two-family dwelling.

The definition of second dwelling causes many problems. Some definitions would allow several families to live in the same house. Other definitions go so far as to categorize a home as two dwellings if it contains two ovens.

If you find that your plans conflict with the zoning regulations, consider applying for a variance—an exception to the law. The building department can tell you how to apply for a variance hearing, if one is necessary. Once you present your case and your neighbors have been contacted for their opinions, the decision is up to the local appeals board.

In addition to the variety of zoning regulations, there may be other restrictions. For example:
- An easement gives someone, such as a utility company or local municipality, the right to cross your property.
- Your deed may contain a restrictive covenant—a clause that limits or restricts use.
- If you own a condominium or belong to a homeowners' association, a set of conditions, covenants, and restrictions (CC&Rs) will most certainly apply to your property.

Eliminate surprises before they cost you money and headaches by examining your deed and checking with the building department.

BUILDING CODES

Local governments adopt—and sometimes modify—building codes in order to establish minimum standards of construction. They are designed to protect you and future owners of your property from safety hazards and faulty work. In addition, building codes can serve as valuable reference tools that cite technical information and proven construction methods.

Unfortunately, unlike the National Electric Code, there is no single, universal building code. The building code that comes closest to universal acceptance is the Council of American Building Officials' (CABO) One- and Two-Family Dwelling Code. This is the reference for most of this book's "Code Requirements" sidebars.

The only electrical code in effect in the country is the National Electrical Code (NEC), which is actually a section of the National Fire Code. Finally, most states have adopted energy codes (sometimes voluntary) that specify insulation, heating, cooling, and glazing requirements.

CODE COMPLIANCE

When you improve an older home, the codes usually apply only to new work. The building department generally does not expect you to bring your entire house up to modern standards —unless, of course, the building inspector finds something that is a definite hazard.

Some existing conditions, such as plumbing, electrical wiring, and stairs, may be governed by modern codes, but most features of your home are governed only by the applicable code

PERMITS

Improvement projects that change the structure, size, safety, or use of living space require building permits. Normal maintenance, such as painting, wallpapering, roofing, electrical and plumbing repairs, or window and door replacement, do not require a permit.

To obtain a permit, you generally need to submit scale drawings: a site or plot plan, a foundation plan, a floor plan, elevations, sections, and sometimes details of components. If your project is small, a sketch and a brief description of your intentions will probably suffice. For larger projects, you may also have to submit engineering reports, soil reports, a certificate of worker's compensation insurance, even energy calculations.

Obtaining a permit takes anywhere from a few minutes to several weeks. A permit may require that work commence within a certain period, usually within 120 days. Some permits do not specify a completion date, but others do. A typical time limit is nine months to a year. If your project is not completed on time, you may be required to apply for another permit.

A permit confers several advantages:
■ It validates work done on your home that affects resale value.
■ It decreases the possibility that an insurance company would cite your work as the possible cause of damage or fire from suspicious origins.
■ It requires thorough planning and estimating before you start.

Other departments may issue separate permits:
■ The planning board will check for zoning compliance.
■ The health department regulates septic systems and wells.
■ The public works department checks easements and may require a survey.
■ The fire department may be in charge of smoke detectors, chimneys, and wood stove installations.
■ Environmental review boards, flood control commissions, and architectural review boards may have jurisdiction.

Your building department can tell you how to obtain copies of the appropriate codes. If you plan to do much building, invest in copies. You may not need the complete code; condensed versions, often found in bookstores, may prove sufficient for the simple things you plan to do. If you have questions or disputes, however, ask your code official.

The building code influences your project by specifying:
■ The type of materials you may use. Can you use plastic pipe for your water supply? What size wallboard do you need for the garage?
■ Whether you may do the work yourself. Most codes allow unlicensed homeowners—but not friends and relatives—to work on their own home, but ask before you start.
■ Structural requirements and installation techniques. For example, the code will tell you how large the joists must be, or how the posts must be attached to beams.

at the time of construction. If the improvement involves more than a specified percentage of your total property value, however, you will have to bring the entire structure up to code.

If you are making extensive plumbing and wiring changes in an older home, it makes sense to modernize and bring your systems up to code even if it is not required. Spending a little more now may save a lot of grief later.

INSPECTIONS

Your permit will include a schedule of inspections. Naturally, the inspector will want to check an element of the job before it gets covered up. Obvious examples are wiring and plumbing runs that are concealed in the walls. The table, right, lists elements that your building, plumbing, and electrical inspectors may want to inspect.

Even when a structure is built according to plans already approved by the building department, the on-site inspector will determine whether the construction meets code. If the work does not meet the code's standards, you must correct the work and schedule a follow-up inspection.

Most inspectors are willing to answer questions about the code or about their inspection of your work. If you display a cooperative attitude, they may even show you how to do the work. Legally, they can only pass judgement on what has been done—but they are also your neighbors. If, after talking to the code official, you are still not sure of how to satisfy the code, have a professional builder who knows the local codes take a look.

REQUIRED INSPECTIONS

Job Element	Inspection
Site	setbacks, slope/grade, septic permit
Foundation	trench, forms, anchor bolts
Under floor	floor framing, utility lines
Framing	lumber grade joints, bracing
Sheathing	seams, nailing
Plumbing	pipe sizes, slopes, vents, traps, materials, pressure test
Electrical	every aspect
Roofing	materials, flashing, fire rating
Energy	R-values, Area/R of glass
Interior walls	wallboard nailing
Flues/fireplaces	clearances, materials
Gas line	fittings, test certificate
Final inspection	electrical fixtures, plumbing fixtures, stairs & railings, heating system, smoke detector

INDEX

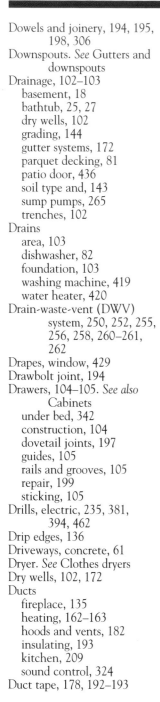

INDEX
continued

METRIC CONVERSIONS

U.S. Units to Metric Equivalents			Metric Units to U.S. Equivalents		
To Convert From	Multiply By	To Get	To Convert From	Multiply By	To Get
Inches	25.4	Millimeters	Millimeters	0.0394	Inches
Inches	2.54	Centimeters	Centimeters	0.3937	Inches
Feet	30.48	Centimeters	Centimeters	0.0328	Feet
Feet	0.3048	Meters	Meters	3.2808	Feet
Yards	0.9144	Meters	Meters	1.0936	Yards
Square inches	6.4516	Square centimeters	Square centimeters	0.1550	Square inches
Square feet	0.0929	Square meters	Square meters	10.764	Square feet
Square yards	0.8361	Square meters	Square meters	1.1960	Square yards
Acres	0.4047	Hectares	Hectares	2.4711	Acres
Cubic inches	16.387	Cubic centimeters	Cubic centimeters	0.0610	Cubic inches
Cubic feet	0.0283	Cubic meters	Cubic meters	35.315	Cubic feet
Cubic feet	28.316	Liters	Liters	0.0353	Cubic feet
Cubic yards	0.7646	Cubic meters	Cubic meters	1.308	Cubic yards
Cubic yards	764.55	Liters	Liters	0.0013	Cubic yards

To convert from degrees Fahrenheit (F) to degrees Celsius (C), first subtract 32, then multiply by ⁵⁄₉.

To convert from degrees Celsius to degrees Fahrenheit, multiply by ⁹⁄₅, then add 32.